KU-202-665

Dyslexia
A Practitioner's Handbook
Third Edition

Gavin Reid

Moray House School of Education
University of Edinburgh

SHREWSBURY COLLEGE
LONDON RD LRC

WILEY

Copyright © 2003 John Wiley & Sons Ltd, The Atrium, Southern Gate, Chichester,
West Sussex PO19 8SQ, England

Telephone (+44) 1243 779777

Email (for orders and customer service enquiries): cs-books@wiley.co.uk
Visit our Home Page on www.wileyeurope.com or www.wiley.com

All Rights Reserved. No part of this publication may be reproduced, stored in a retrieval
system or transmitted in any form or by any means, electronic, mechanical, photocopying,
recording, scanning or otherwise, except under the terms of the Copyright, Designs and
Patents Act 1988 or under the terms of a licence issued by the Copyright Licensing Agency
Ltd, 90 Tottenham Court Road, London W1T 4LP, UK, without the permission in writing of
the Publisher. Requests to the Publisher should be addressed to the Permissions Department,
John Wiley & Sons Ltd, The Atrium, Southern Gate, Chichester, West Sussex PO19 8SQ
England, or emailed to permreq@wiley.co.uk, or faxed to (+44) 1243 770620.

This publication is designed to provide accurate and authoritative information in regard to
the subject matter covered. It is sold on the understanding that the Publisher is not engaged
in rendering professional services. If professional advice or other expert assistance is
required, the services of a competent professional should be sought.

Other Wiley Editorial Offices

John Wiley & Sons Inc., 111 River Street, Hoboken, NJ 07030, USA

Jossey-Bass, 989 Market Street, San Francisco, CA 94103-1741, USA

Wiley-VCH Verlag GmbH, Boschstr. 12, D-69469 Weinheim, Germany

John Wiley & Sons Australia Ltd, 33 Park Road, Milton, Queensland 4064, Australia

John Wiley & Sons (Asia) Pte Ltd, 2 Clementi Loop #02-01, Jin Xing Distripark, Singapore 129809

John Wiley & Sons Canada Ltd, 22 Worcester Road, Etobicoke, Ontario, Canada M9W 1L1

Wiley also publishes its books in a variety of electronic formats. Some content that appears in print may
not be available in electronic books.

Library of Congress Cataloging-in-Publication Data

Reid, Gavin, 1950–
   Dyslexia : a practitioner's handbook / Gavin Reid.– 3rd ed.
    p. cm.
   Includes bibliographical references (p.) and index.
   ISBN 0-470-84851-0 (Cloth)—ISBN 0-470-84852-9 (Paper : alk. paper)
   1. Dyslexic children—Education—Handbooks, manuals, etc. 2. Dyslexic
  children—Ability testing—Handbooks, manuals, etc. 3. Curriculum
  planning—Handbooks, manuals, etc. I. Title.
  LC4708 .R45 2003
  371.91′44—dc21   2002155458

British Library Cataloguing in Publication Data

A catalogue record for this book is available from the British Library

ISBN 0-470-84851-0 (hardback)
ISBN 0-470-84852-9 (paperback)

Project management by Originator, Gt Yarmouth, Norfolk (typeset in 10/12pt Times)
Printed and bound in Great Britain by Antony Rowe Ltd, Chippenham, Wiltshire
This book is printed on acid-free paper responsibly manufactured from sustainable forestry
in which at least two trees are planted for each one used for paper production.

Contents

About the Author

Dr Gavin Reid is a senior lecturer in Educational Studies at the Moray House School of Education, University of Edinburgh. He is an experienced teacher, educational psychologist, university lecturer and researcher. He has made over 400 conference and seminar presentations throughout the UK and in many other countries including Norway, Denmark, Germany, USA (Washington, DC, New Orleans, San Francisco, Boston, New York, Atlanta), New Zealand (Auckland, Wellington, Rotorua, Palmerston North, Dunedin, Hawkes Bay, Nelson, Hamilton and Christchurch), Hong Kong, Poland, Republic of Ireland, Slovakia, Croatia, Czech Republic, Austria, Cyprus and Hungary. He has written and edited key course books for teacher training in the field of dyslexia and literacy. *Dyslexia: A Practitioner's Handbook* (2nd edn, John Wiley & Sons, 1998) has been used as a course text in many university and college courses on dyslexia worldwide. He has also written and edited other books, book chapters and articles on dyslexia and learning styles as well as co-developing screening tests to identify literacy and other specific difficulties.

Gavin Reid obtained a B.Ed. (honours) degree in History and an M.Ed. in Psychology from the University of Aberdeen, an M.App.Sci. in Educational Psychology and a Ph.D. in Psychology from the University of Glasgow and an M.A. in Education and an Advanced Diploma in Special Needs in Education from the Open University. He also has a Post Graduate Certificate in Counselling and an AMBDA from the British Dyslexia Association. He has taught in secondary schools in Aberdeen and was an educational psychologist in Aberdeenshire and Fife, Scotland before joining the staff at Moray House in 1991. His current research interests include assessment, metacognition and working with parents and adults.

Gavin Reid developed the first masters course in Dyslexia in the UK in 1992. The course was also written in an open learning format and has subsequently been revised in association with the Open University. The product of this partnership is the Post Graduate Certificate in Difficulties in Literacy Development, which was presented for the first time by both the Open University and the University of Edinburgh in October 2002. This award is also recognised by the BDA at AMBDA level.

Gavin Reid is a consultant to a number of national and international projects in dyslexia and has been involved in evaluation of provision for students with dyslexia in Scotland, England and Wales, and is a director and consultant to the Red Rose School for students with specific learning difficulties in St Anne's-on-Sea, Lancashire, England. He has held and currently holds appointments as external examiner to universities in Scotland, England and Australia. He is a member of the British Dyslexia Association Teacher Training Accreditation Board and has been involved as a consultant to other parent groups and charitable bodies in the UK, Europe and New Zealand.

Other Books by Gavin Reid

Dyslexia: A Practitioner's Handbook (2nd edn), Gavin Reid (1998), John Wiley & Sons, Chichester, UK.

Dyslexia in Adults: Education and Employment, Gavin Reid and Jane Kirk (2001), John Wiley & Sons, Chichester, UK.

Dyslexia and Literacy, Theory and Practice, edited by Gavin Reid and Janice Wearmouth (2002), John Wiley & Sons, Chichester, UK.

Learning Styles: A Guide for Teachers and Parents, Gavin Reid and Barbara Given (1998), Red Rose Publications, St Anne's-on-Sea, UK.

Dimensions of Dyslexia, Vol. 1: *Assessment, Teaching and the Curriculum*, edited by Gavin Reid (1996), Moray House Publications, Edinburgh.

Dimensions of Dyslexia, Vol. 2: *Literacy, Language and Learning*, edited by Gavin Reid (1996), Moray House Publications, Edinburgh.

Listening and Literacy Index—A Group Test to Identify Specific Learning Difficulties, Charles Weedon and Gavin Reid (2001), Hodder & Stoughton.

Multilingualism, Literacy and Dyslexia—A Challenge for Educators, edited by Lindsay Peer and Gavin Reid (2000), David Fulton Publishers, London.

Dyslexia: Successful Inclusion in the Secondary School, edited by Lindsay Peer and Gavin Reid (2001), David Fulton Publishers, London.

Meeting Difficulties in Literacy Development, Research, Policy and Practice, Janice Wearmouth, Janet Soler and Gavin Reid (2003), RoutledgeFalmer, London.

Contextualising Difficulties in Literacy Development—Exploring Politics, Culture, Ethnicity and Ethics, edited by Janet Soler, Janice Wearmouth and Gavin Reid (2002), RoutledgeFalmer, London.

Addressing Difficulties in Literacy Development. Responses at Family, School, Pupil and Teacher Levels, edited by Janice Wearmouth, Janet Soler and Gavin Reid (2002), RoutledgeFalmer, London.

Introduction to Dyslexia, Lindsay Peer and Gavin Reid (2003), David Fulton, London.

Special Needs Assessment Profile, Charles Weedon and Gavin Reid (2003), Hodder & Stoughton, London.

Preface

In 1998, when writing the preface for the second edition of the *Practitioner's Handbook*, I suggested that a revised edition was necessary at that time because of the increased activity in research and practice in dyslexia. If that was the case in 1998 it certainly is the case today. The Fifth British Dyslexia Association International Conference drew its largest audience to date in April 2001 with delegates from over 38 countries and the International Dyslexia Association Conference held each year in the USA now regularly draws around 3000 delegates. This burgeoning interest in the field is also reflected in the two major conferences devoted to multi-lingualism and dyslexia held in the UK and the USA in 1999 and 2002, respectively. Additionally, the European-wide interest in dyslexia, assisted by organizations such as the European Dyslexia Association (EDA), is constantly increasing with a considerable amount coming from central and eastern Europe. Therefore, the inception of the first European-wide dyslexia awareness week in 2002 and the first EDA All European Conference on Dyslexia in Budapest in 2004 comes as no surprise. In addition to those events mentioned above there have been successful local, national and other international events in dyslexia run by education authorities, voluntary organisations, such as parents' organisations, and professional societies. All have contributed to the developments in teacher training, assessment and teaching materials, and interest in research. This has resulted in an increased awareness and enhanced professionalism of those involved in the area of dyslexia.

These developments have certainly been evident in the UK at local as well as national level. Many education authorities have produced policy and documentation on dyslexia. Additionally, working party enquiries into dyslexia and psychological assessment, and assessment and support in further and higher education for students with dyslexia have taken place. There has also been government-led task group investigations into practice in dyslexia both in Northern Ireland and the Republic of Ireland in 2001 and 2002. The chapter on international perspectives (Chapter 15) highlights other examples of government initiatives throughout Europe, New Zealand and the USA. These are only a few of the many initiatives worldwide (which would in themselves occupy the best part of a book) in dyslexia.

At the Fifth International BDA conference the chairperson Professor Rod Nicolson called for further collaboration among all professionals and parents working in the field and the need for multidisciplinary co-operation, he suggested, was paramount. This is in fact particularly important given the breadth of perspectives now incorporated into the different areas that relate to dyslexia.

This book offers insights, information and analysis of these areas. There are a number of key themes that connect to dyslexia and have been incorporated into this book. The theme relating to the learning process is evident throughout. We, as educators, have a responsibility to facilitate the development of life skills to equip dyslexic children, for learning throughout life. The process of learning and how the difficulties experienced by children with dyslexia affect them need to be examined in a positive, constructive manner. The barriers that impede learning may in fact lie outwith the child, so it is crucial to examine the learning environment and the learning task, how the task is designed and presented, as well as the expectations and outcomes of the task.

There are chapters on learning and metacognition in this book and parts containing several chapters on literacy, assessment, teaching and inclusion. Each of these areas is highly relevant to teaching and learning, and particularly for children with dyslexia. The part devoted to inclusion (Part IV) represents a key theme that needs to be considered when developing practice and provision for children with dyslexia. Indeed, literacy, learning and inclusion are three key themes that can provide a context for dyslexia. For too long now dyslexia has been seen as a special need that may or may not be recognised, depending on the definition and specific local arrangements and systems for support. This has resulted in considerable fluctuation and variation in support and some exasperation on the part of teachers and parents. It is crucial therefore that consistency is applied. In order for this to occur it is necessary to incorporate a range of dimensions and to adopt a holistic view of the difficulties associated with dyslexia, including the task and the curriculum as well as the cognitive aspects of learning. Ideally it is important to strive for a balance—a balance between accurate and informative assessment, and constructive and positive teaching. There is a need for consultation and collaboration, and for differentiation and inclusion. There is a need to facilitate the educational development and personal growth of all children with dyslexia, and to strive to ensure that the rhetoric of equality becomes a reality at school, college, the workplace and in the wider society.

It is hoped that this book will be used to provide information to teachers: as a course text for professional training in the area of dyslexia for those seeking extended training; as a guide to administrators on the nature and effect of dyslexia, and how these factors can be dealt with within the school system; and as a source of support and encouragement to parents. Above all, it is hoped that reality will be a more equitable and successful future for all those children and adults with dyslexia. It is my wish that this book, by providing information, comment, analysis and suggestions, can in some way help toward that reality.

GAVIN REID
September 2002

Chapter 1

Introduction

THE CONTEXT

This book, as the title suggests, is about dyslexia, but it is more than that. It is about teaching and learning, about social and educational acceptance, about awareness, inclusion and teacher training, about curriculum access for all students with dyslexia and the management and enhancement of potential in further education and the workplace. It may seem a tall order to incorporate these dimensions into a handbook on dyslexia, but the key point and theme of this book is that dyslexia should not be viewed in isolation. For too long now this has been the case, and there has been a preoccupation among many to ensure that the specific difficulties experienced by people with dyslexia are prioritised in a teaching programme. While this to a certain extent is necessary, it is important to ensure that the wider aspects of teaching and learning are not overlooked. It is too easy to take a narrow approach when faced with a student with any type of specific difficulty. Although it is important to tackle the difficulty, and there are many examples in this book on how that can be done in relation to dyslexia, it is also important to incorporate a broader curriculum-oriented and inclusive approach. This is particularly important since there is a general acceptance that dyslexia can be seen within a continuum and may overlap with other specific difficulties. This implies that not all children with dyslexia will exhibit the same difficulties to the same degree and this further underlines the need to view dyslexia from both an individual and a curriculum perspective.

There are many definitions of dyslexia currently used by professionals and education authorities and although these definitions may share some similarities it can be confusing to parents and teachers to observe and understand the variety of definitions to describe dyslexia. Indeed, the British Psychological Society (BPS, 1999a) working party report on dyslexia indicated 10 hypotheses that can be associated with dyslexia. These together with definitions are discussed in this chapter.

Pumfrey (1996) suggested that the concept of dyslexia has a 'widespread and increasing currency.' This is still the case, but the concept of dyslexia needs to be realigned to contextualise it into current trends and priorities in education such as inclusion, literacy and the enhancement of learning skills. These factors therefore are discussed in various chapters of this book, and these provide an overarching rationale for the book and for an understanding of the concept of dyslexia in relation to current education thinking and progression.

DESCRIPTIVE DEFINITIONS

As indicated above there are a number of definitions currently used to describe dyslexia. These include the one used by the British Dyslexia Association (BDA), which is essentially a descriptive definition suggesting that dyslexia is 'a combination of abilities and difficulties that affect the learning process in one or more of reading, spelling and writing. Accompanying weaknesses may be identified in areas of speed of processing, short-term memory, sequencing, auditory and/or visual perception, spoken language and motor skills. It is particularly related to mastering and using written language, which may include alphabetic, numeric and musical notation' (Peer, 2001). This is a comprehensive description of the difficulties associated with dyslexia and can be a useful guide. At the same time, as was suggested in the BPS report on dyslexia and assessment (BPS, 1999a), definitions need to be operationalized for the context in which they will be applied. Why have a definition at all? What is the purpose of a definition? A definition can provide a clear statement of the 'typical' characteristics of dyslexia, and this can be a useful starting point for teachers and education authorities.

Historically, definitions have been used to label rather than inform. It has been necessary to acquire the label in order to secure the recognition and support needed. Although in most school systems there is a desire to accommodate the specific needs of all children irrespective of the label assigned to them, it is still necessary and advantageous in certain situations, such as examinations, to possess the label. Yet a definition should be more than a label or even an extended label. It is interesting that the BPS in the working party report (BPS, 1999a) opted for a working definition of dyslexia. Whether one agrees or not with the actual working definition used in the report is irrelevant. The important point is that service providers, speech therapists, psychologists, education authorities, course organisers may each have the need for their own working definition, which they can operationalise to fit into their own working practices. A definition should be informative and not merely an extended label.

DISCREPANCY-BASED DEFINITIONS

In addition to descriptive definitions, discrepancy definitions are also widely used. These definitions are based on the unexpected discrepancy between ability and performance, and although this has been incorporated into some policy documents it is still the subject of considerable criticism (Stanovich, 1996). It has been argued that this type of criteria fails to acknowledge the controversy regarding the concept of IQ and the use of an IQ test to diagnose what is essentially a reading difficulty. Furthermore, it has been argued (Stanovich, 1996, 1998) that there is no evidence for qualitative differences in reading errors between children from high- and low-IQ groups, and IQ should not be used as a measure of ability for this purpose. It has been argued that listening comprehension may be a more suitable measure of ability (Bedford-Feull et al., 1995; Stanovich, 1996). However, this view has been countered (Ashton, 1997, 2001) and the discrepancy definition is still used by education authorities in relation to allocating resources and determining cut-off points for provision (Pumfrey, 1995, 2001, 2002; Ashton, 1997, 2001). Yet, as Pumfrey (2002) points out, 'establishing a resource allocation model that is explicit, open, fair and theoretically defensible requires considerable professional knowledge ... making the model accord with the law requires additional sensitivity' (p. 256). The controversies and uncertainties regarding definitions and the responses to definitions in terms of identification, assessment and support motivated the BPS to convene a working party on this issue.

WORKING AND OPERATIONAL DEFINITIONS

The subsequent working party report *Dyslexia, Literacy and Psychological Assessment* (BPS, 1999a) opted for a working definition of dyslexia because the working party felt that a working definition did not require any causal explanation. The working definition they opted for was as follows: 'Dyslexia is evident when accurate and fluent word reading and/or spelling develops very incompletely or with great difficulty' (BPS, 1999a, p. 18). This definition should, however, be seen within the context of the report, which is based on the well-established causal modelling framework (Morton and Frith, 1995; Frith, 2002) and provides a theoretical framework for educational psychologists in relation to assessment of dyslexia. The authors of the BPS report accept that it requires to be operationalised for different educational contexts. Descriptive and discrepancy definitions have been described above; however, the key to any of these is how they are applied in practice and the specific criteria that are used.

An example of an operational definition can be seen in the East Renfrewshire Education Authority policy documentation on dyslexia. The definition used by this education authority is similar to that provided by the BDA (Peer, 2001), but develops it by using operational criteria based on identification in the early stages, including a stepped process of identification and assessment and a range of support in terms of strategies and provision (East Renfrewshire Council, 1999). Essentially, the rationale behind this process is preventative. Crombie (2002a, b) suggests that dyslexia should be reconceptualised in terms not of definitions but of preventative and descriptive criteria and a multidisciplinary working framework for intervention. This implies that dyslexic or not, the support will be there at an early stage with ongoing consultancy with relevant professionals and ongoing monitoring by teachers and the education authority. Similarly, Fawcett and Nicolson (1996, 1997) and Singleton (1996a) sought to develop early screening tests that would provide a valid indicator of dyslexia and instigate the necessary resources and approaches to minimise the effects of dyslexia in later school years. While this is commendable it is still dependent on diagnostic accuracy and the value of the label terms of early intervention. In fact, Nicolson (2001) suggested that the 'value of the label "dyslexia" is that it has no intrinsic meaning' (p. 5). Early identification should not have a preoccupation with labels—they are not synonomous, and as Crombie suggests early identification should reflect and pursue descriptive and classroom-based evidence of how the child is learning. Of course, early screening tests may well help to gather this evidence, but this should only be part of the process, which needs to be continuous and not based on a snapshot judgement.

DEFINITIONS: KEY ASPECTS

A working/operational definition of dyslexia therefore needs to recognise the following:

- *Processing style*—this can highlight the differences between individuals including those with a dyslexic profile. It is important to recognise these processing differences in the development of teaching and curricular approaches.
- *Problem-solving skills*—it is important that students with dyslexia are not limited on account of their severe difficulties in literacy. It is crucial that access to problem-solving activities are prioritised as well as literacy. Dyslexia should not limit the learning potential of the individual; indeed, there is evidence that in some areas of the curriculum, such as those that require visual, creative and problem-solving activities, students with dyslexia may be at an advantage.
- *Difficulties in phonological processing*—it needs to be acknowledged that many students with dyslexia will experience difficulties in phonological processing and that this will have implications for how reading is taught. This needs to be considered in an operational definition. The implication is that a range of teaching procedures for literacy needs to be considered and that it needs to be appreciated that one approach will not suit all students with dyslexia.
- *Discrepancies in performances* in different areas of the curriculum. This can be readily noted and acknowledged. It is important that students with dyslexia are able to capitalise on their skills as this can have a transfer effect to other areas and additionally provide a very necessary boost to self-esteem.
- *Observable behaviours*—these are the characteristics that are often detailed in descriptive definitions of dyslexia. Again, it is important to acknowledge the strengths as well as the difficulties associated with dyslexia. But a detail of these characteristics should also relate to the learning context and these can be useful for both teachers and parents.
- *Implications for specific contexts*—essentially, dyslexia is contextual; this means that information needs to be gathered about the student in different learning contexts. These can include the classroom, different subjects, home and the workplace—depending on the type of information required.

Based on this therefore a suitable definition may be:

> *dyslexia is a processing difference experienced by people of all ages, often characterised by difficulties in literacy, it can affect other cognitive areas such as memory, speed of processing, time management, co-ordination and directional aspects. There*

may be visual and phonological difficulties and there is usually some discrepancy in performances in different areas of learning. It is important that the individual differences and learning styles are acknowledged since these will affect outcomes of assessment and learning. It is also important to consider the learning and work context as the nature of the difficulties associated with dyslexia may be more pronounced in some learning situations (Reid, 2002).

Reason (2002) suggests that the term 'dyslexia' has often been avoided because its 'predominant focus on within child causative factors has tended to detract attention away from instructional circumstances' (p. 188). Following the Warnock report in the UK (DES, 1978) there were reservations about the use of the term 'dyslexia' and the report advocated the term 'specific learning difficulties'. In the USA the term 'learning disabilities' was used. However, since then many developments have taken place in research, policy and practice, and the effect of this has been that the term 'dyslexia' as Reason (2002) suggests is now 'well embedded in popular language' (p. 188). Although there are still variations and controversies on how various groups perceive the concept of dyslexia, the use of the term is preferable to the confusing array of modifications to the term that can be noted in policy documents—many of these confuse rather than clarify. The key point is not so much the term, but how the term is understood, defined and implemented in practice.

It is feasible therefore to suggest that, while a definition can help to provide some guidance to teachers and researchers, the range of definitions in use may result in some confusion. Reid Lyon (1995) suggests that the negative consequences of inadequate definitions are serious as this can result in lack of information on the precise nature of reading difficulties and consequently lead to inadequate training for teachers.

In relation to research, Reid Lyon asserts that the lack of an appropriate definition has resulted in a reliance on exclusionary criteria and lack of a clear selection criteria for the sample being studied. He suggests that a definition must be governed by a theoretical view supported by substantial research and clinical evidence. This should be based on 'constructs' that can be measured directly and consistently, and should provide clear indications of how to identify whether a person is dyslexic.

Reid Lyon believes that the working definition that was initiated by the Orton Dyslexia Society Research Committee, in conjunction with the National Center for Learning Disabilities and the National Institute of Child Health and Human Development, takes account of these factors. It is seen as an example of a research-based definition.

Dyslexia is one of several distinct learning disabilities. It is a specific language-based disorder of constitutional origin characterised by difficulties in single-word decoding, usually reflecting insufficient phonological processing. These difficulties in single-word decoding are often unexpected in relation to age and other cognitive and academic abilities; they are not the result of generalised developmental disability or sensory impairment. Dyslexia is manifest by variable difficulty with different forms of language, often including, in addition to problems with reading, a conspicuous problem with acquiring proficiency in writing and spelling (Orton Dyslexia Society Research Committee, 1994).

This definition differs from some of the others in use in the UK because of its emphasis on 'single-word decoding'. Many of the UK definitions although similar do appear to take a broader perspective.

Similarly, in the Republic of Ireland the definition of dyslexia is broad in conceptualisation and essentially views dyslexia in descriptive terms within a continuum. The definition developed by a government task force on dyslexia is:

> *Dyslexia is manifested in a continuum of specific learning difficulties related to the acquisition of basic skills in reading, spelling, and/or writing, such difficulties being unexpected in relation to an individual's other abilities and educational experiences. Dyslexia can be described at the neurological, cognitive and behavioural levels. It is typically characterised by inefficient information processing, including difficulties in phonological processing, working memory, rapid naming, and automaticity of basic skills. Difficulties in organisation, sequencing and motor skills may also be present* (Task Force on Dyslexia, 2001, p. 28).

One of the reasons that dyslexia has been the subject of government investigations, such as the task force report referenced above, and working party investigations of groups of professionals, such as psychologists, is because there is now a significant body of scientific research substantiating the various neurological and cognitive components of dyslexia.

Yet, there is still considerable controversy regarding dyslexia. Differences exist between professionals and researchers, and the debate continues. Indeed, Fawcett (2002) suggests that one of the major tensions in dyslexia research has in fact been the range of potentially conflicting viewpoints. These viewpoints have emerged from 'researchers and practitioners; parents and teachers; teachers and educational psychologists; schools and local education authorities; local education authorities and governments—all have different agendas, and much of the time this forces them into opposition.' It is interesting to note that the working party of the BPS that was convened to provide guidance on assessment for psychologists was not able to settle the controversy although it did make a number of recommendations.

CAUSAL MODELLING FRAMEWORK

Hypothesis

Using the causal modelling framework that is described below, the report (BPS, 1999a) presented 10 different theoretical accounts of dyslexia. These can be seen as alternative or complementary hypotheses to help explain some of the characteristics and influences relating to dyslexia.

The hypotheses suggested in the report that can be associated with dyslexia include: phonological deficit hypothesis, temporal processing hypothesis, skill automatisation hypothesis, working memory hypothesis, visual processing hypothesis, syndrome hypothesis, intelligence and cognitive profiles hypothesis, subtype hypothesis, learning opportunities hypothesis and emotional factors hypothesis. These hypotheses refer to different or overlapping theoretical approaches. It is suggested that the phonological deficit hypothesis provides the main focus because of the 'broad empirical support that it commands' (p. 44) and because of the impact of phonology on the other hypotheses, particularly temporal processing hypothesis, skill automatisation and the syndrome hypothesis. This view is supported by Snowling (2000) who suggests that although dyslexia can manifest itself in many ways there may be a single cause—a phonological deficit—and she asserts this is the 'proximal cause of dyslexia' (p. 138).

CAUSAL MODELLING FRAMEWORK: EXPLANATION

Frith (2002) suggests that the definition and explanation of dyslexia has long been problematic and that a causal modelling framework involving three levels of description—behavioural, cognitive and biological—can help to clarify some of the issues relating to the concept of dyslexia.

Frith (2002) suggests that dyslexia is a neuro-developmental disorder with a 'biological origin and behavioural signs which extend far beyond problems with written language' (p. 45). The three levels suggested by Frith can provide a useful guide as different professionals will have different priorities and interests—therefore, the teacher and psychologist will be interested in the behavioural and cognitive dimensions while the neuropsychologist will be interested in the neurological and biological factors. The important point is that at all three levels interactions with cultural influences occur. Frith suggests that these influences have a major impact on the characteristics of dyslexia displayed by the individual. For our purposes, therefore, it is important to consider a fourth element—environmental aspects—and to appreciate how this can affect children and adults with dyslexia. Essentially, dyslexia is contextual and therefore the nature and extent of the difficulties can vary depending on the context and the task. This means that it is feasible that adaptations to the learning and work environment, and to how the task is presented and assessed can make a significant difference to the outcome and the learning experience for the individual.

The causal modelling framework (Morton and Frith, 1995) provides a guide for researchers and practitioners and a reminder that each of these elements overlap and affect the development of the other.

BIOLOGICAL LEVEL

Genetic Factors

A considerable amount of research activity has focused on the genetic basis of dyslexia. Gilger et al. (1991) estimate that the risk of a son being dyslexic if he has a dyslexic father is about 40%. Much of this work has been focused on the heritability of reading subskills and particularly the phonological component. Castles et al. (1999) found a strong heritability element among 'phonological dyslexics', and Olson et al. (1994) also found a strong heritability component both for phonological decoding and orthographic skills.

Gene markers for dyslexia have been found in Chromosome 15 (Smith et al., 1983) and more recently in Chromosome 6 (Fisher et al., 1999a, b). These studies indicate the presence of a possible site for 'dyslexic genes' in Chromosome 6, and significantly they may be in the same region as the genes implicated in autoimmune diseases that have been reported to show a high level of association with dyslexia (Snowling, 2000). In a longitudinal study Gallagher et al. (2000) found at Age 6 more than half the at-risk group scored below average compared with a control group on literacy tasks. Genetic factors are associated with dyslexia (Leppanen et al., 1999), and this may lead to earlier identification. Although, as Reason (2002) suggests, educational psychologists are not in a position to carry out any formal neuro-diagnostic procedures or genetic analyses, they may hypothesise about the influence of specific factors within these domains. They may also observe signs, such as hereditary patterns, that they suspect may be indicative of hypothesised neurological or genetic factors. Similarly, teachers can note the tendency of members of the same family to share some of the characteristics of dyslexia.

Neurological Factors

Technology such as positron emission tomography (PET) and magnetic resonance imaging (MRI) are increasingly being used to observe the active processes within the brain as well as their structure. As a result studies have shown that (e.g., in phonological and short-term memory tasks) people with dyslexia would likely display less activation across the left hemisphere than one might find in people who do not have a dyslexic profile.

Brunswick et al. (1999) reported that the PET scans of young dyslexic adults while reading aloud and during word and non-word recognition tasks showed less activation than controls in the left posterior temporal cortex. These findings suggest that there may be processing differences indicating some deficits in left hemisphere processing among children and adults with dyslexia.

Paulesu et al. (1996, 2001) suggest that current theories of dyslexia favour a neuro-cognitive explanation. They suggest that at a neurological level people with dyslexia may have microscopic cortical abnormalities in the form of cortical ectopias and dyslamination of cortical layers.

They also suggest that there is considerable agreement that a causal link between brain abnormality and reading difficulties involves phonological processing deficits although the cause of these deficits is less clear. This also implies that these factors can be noted universally irrespective of the language used in the country although they do suggest that in languages with transparent or shallow orthography, such as Italian, learning to read is easier than in languages with deep orthography such as English and French, where they suggest the mapping between letters, speech sounds and whole word sounds is often ambiguous. This point is developed by Smythe

(2002), who argues that the differences in languages and structure can affect the incidence and the nature of the difficulties associated with dyslexia in different languages. Paulesu et al. (1996, 2001) also suggest that auditory or visual deficits are associated with dyslexia and these can be implicated with dysfunction of the magnocellular system of the brain. This view is supported by Stein et al. (2001), Everatt (2002) and Eden et al. (1996), who describe the 'magnocellular deficit hypothesis' in relation to dyslexia as a consequence of an abnormality in the neural pathways of the visual system. This pathway is divided into two areas, the parvocellular (P) and magnocellular (M) systems. These are differentially sensitive to different types of stimuli; the parvocellular system seems to respond to slowly changing (low temporal frequency) information and to colour, whereas the magno-cellular system is more sensitive to gross (lower spatial frequency), rapidly changing (high temporal frequency) or moving information. Stein et al. (2001) suggest that the dyslexic person records poor performances on tasks assessing the functioning of the magnocellular pathway. This therefore will have implications for reading and par-ticularly the visual processing factors associated with reading.

In relation to dyslexia and visual difficulties Stein (1994) and Stein et al. (2001; Stein, 2002) have also highlighted convergence difficulties and binocular instability as factors that could affect the stability of the visual stimuli when reading. Wilkins (1995) has shown how some dyslexic children and adults may benefit from coloured overlays due to difficulties in some visual processes. Everatt (2002) in a comprehen-sive review of visual aspects relating to dyslexia suggests that the visual representa-tion processes, the magnocellular system, factors associated with visual sensitivity and coloured filters, and eye movement co-ordination can each account for the visual difficulties experienced by people with dyslexia.

Everatt suggests that the diversity of the visual deficits that can be identified needs to be clarified as it may be that the visual-based difficulties derive from the same underlying cause. It should also be noted that not all those diagnosed as dyslexic present visual deficits, and indeed some people who are not dyslexic present evidence of visual deficits.

Furthermore, Stein's (2002) view on the role of the magnocellular system appears to implicate aspects of various complementary theories such as cerebellar immaturity (Fawcett and Nicolson, 2001) and deficits in essential fatty acids (Richardson, 2002).

Hemispheric Symmetry

According to Geschwind and Galaburda (1985) the difficulties in processing infor-mation shown by people with dyslexia are due to structural differences between the hemispheres, and this likely develops in the prenatal period. This view has received considerable support from subsequent studies. Knight and Hynd (2002) are of the opinion that the principle findings to emerge from these studies suggest that mis-placed cells may be present in some areas of the brain, particularly the outer layer of cortex, which is usually cell-free. According to Galaburda and Rosen (2001) these misplaced cells can be found predominantly in the left hemisphere in areas associated with language. They also note differences in the primary visual and auditory cortex, where differences in neurons and patterns of cellular symmetry can also be noted. This, they suggest, could provide a neural explanation for some of the visual, auditory, sensory and perceptual difficulties that some researchers, such as Fitch et al. (1997), Zeffiro and Eden (2000), propose are associated with dyslexia.

Reading is a complex activity that involves the interaction of multiple sensory systems and brain networks. Research findings such as those mentioned above can have implications for how the individual accesses print. The implications of this for teaching and learning to read have been the focus of the model proposed by Bakker (1979, 1990). Bakker (1990) and Robertson and Bakker (2002) called this model the 'balance model' of reading. It has been replicated in different countries (Robertson, 2000). Bakker identified different types of readers—'perceptual' and 'linguistic'— each with a different hemispheric preference and each of these preferences has implications for teaching. The 'perceptual' reader has a right hemisphere processing style and may have good comprehension, but poor reading accuracy. On the other hand, the 'linguistic' reader utilises the left hemisphere and reads accurately, but in some cases may be over-reliant on the left hemisphere and may not show the comprehension level of the 'perceptual' reader.

Wood (2000) suggests that reading is concerned with translating stimuli across all modalities and that fluency is the key factor in reading acquisition. He cites the role of the visual cortex in reading, which, he asserts, is multimodal as it will accept input from both auditory and visual modalities. The brain, he argues, is high in visual– spatial skills, and this also aids the understanding of information with high phonetic complexity. Since reading is essentially mapping across modalities according to Wood, then alternative languages such as music and visual graphics are helpful. In short, Wood suggests that our brains are better equipped for reading and more adaptable than we have given them credit for.

Motor Factors

Motor integration programmes have also been developed from research programmes (Dobie, 1996; Blythe, P., personal communication; Blythe and Goddard, 2000; McPhilips et al., 2000; Reynolds et al., 2002). Nicolson and Fawcett (1999) have shown how cerebellar immaturity may be implicated with dyslexia viewed from a broader framework and may be involved in acquiring language dexterity as well as movement and balance. Factors such as postural stability, beads-threading and naming speed are therefore represented in the *Dyslexia Early Screening Test* (Fawcett and Nicolson, 1997). There have been many studies reporting on fine motor and gross motor difficulties experienced by dyslexic children (Augur, 1992; Denckla, 1985; Flory, 2000; McCormick, 2000). Some of these relate to dyspraxia, but it is likely that some of the approaches advocated for dyspraxic children can benefit dyslexic children who may have some motor difficulties. Similarly to dys- graphia, Stracher (2000) suggests that writing problems manifest themselves in three stages that include motor factors relating to legibility, spelling difficulties and organising writing and syntactic structures. This pattern can also be seen in some dyslexic children.

COGNITIVE AND PROCESSING DIMENSIONS

While the teacher may be limited in dealing with the deficits discussed above in relation to the neurological/biological factors associated with dyslexia much can be done to improve the processing skills of dyslexic students, and particularly their phonological skills. Reason (2002), however, suggests that it is important that cognitive skills or deficits/delays are separated from observed behaviours (i.e., the characteristics of dyslexia), because these cognitive aspects can only be inferred. Nevertheless, cognitive factors such as memory and speed of processing difficulties can be noted by the class teacher in relation to the student's strategies and learning progress, and can have an impact on lesson plans and curricular progress. Some of the cognitive factors that can be influential in relation to dyslexia are shown below.

Phonological Processing

Hagtvet (1997) and Lundberg (2002) in Norwegian studies showed that a phonological deficit at Age 6 was the strongest predictor of reading difficulties. Other studies have shown speech rate to be a strong predictor of dyslexic difficulties, and this is reflected in the development of the Phonological Abilities Test (Muter et al., 1997; Hatcher and Snowling, 2002).

Wolf (1996; Wolf and O'Brien 2001) highlights the 'double deficit' hypothesis indicating that dyslexic people can have difficulties with both phonological processing and naming speed. It is interesting that speed of processing and semantic fluency are included in some of the popular tests for dyslexic children. Badian (1997) shows evidence for a triple deficit hypothesis implying that orthographic factors involving visual skills should also be considered.

Metacognition

The role of metacognition in learning is of great importance as this relates to the learner's awareness of thinking and learning and can have considerable implications for how we understand the needs of children with dyslexia (Burden, 2002; Reid, 2001b). Tunmer and Chapman (1996) have shown how dyslexic children have poor metacognitive awareness and how this leads them to adopt inappropriate learning behaviours in reading and spelling. It is important therefore to examine the processes that the child used in order to obtain a response. It may be that these processes or steps taken to complete the task were inefficient and ineffective. Chinn (2002) highlights this in relation to mathematics and Wray (2002) in relation to creative writing.

Automaticity

Similarly, difficulties in automaticity (Fawcett and Nicolson, 1992; Nicolson and Fawcett, 2000; Fawcett, 2002) implies that dyslexic children may not readily consolidate new learning and therefore find it difficult to change inappropriate learning habits. Fawcett and Nicolson (1994), in fact, propose the twin hypothesis that dyslexic children incur both dyslexic automatisation deficit and conscious compensation hypothesis. This means not only do they have difficulty in acquiring automaticity but in many cases they are able to mask this deficit by working harder. Deficits, however, will still be noted in situations where compensation is not possible.

BEHAVIOURAL LEVEL

Observations on performances in reading and spelling activities can be described at the behavioural level. These are the directly observed behaviours—the noted characteristics of dyslexia, such as words spelt incorrectly or words read inaccurately. It is important to consider that such observations will be influenced by a range of environmental factors, including the classroom environment and social and cultural aspects. Essentially the behavioural level relates to educational factors, and some of these will be discussed below.

Phonological Awareness and Multisensory Programmes

In educational settings there has been considerable activity in the study of phonological awareness in relation to dyslexia. This is reflected in the development of assessment and teaching materials such as the Phonological Abilities Test (Muter et al., 1997), the Phonological Assessment Battery (Fredrickson et al., 1997), the Dyslexia Screening Tests (Fawcett and Nicolson, 1996) and the Listening and Literacy Index (Weedon and Reid, 2001). Additionally, there are many phonological teaching approaches such as Sound Linkage (Hatcher, 1994), the Phonological Awareness Training Programme (Wilson, 1993), the Hickey Multisensory Teaching System (Combley, 2001) and the Multisensory Teaching System for Reading (Johnston et al., 1999).

Wise et al. (1999) conducted a large-scale study using different forms of 'remediation' and found that the actual type of phonological awareness training was less important than the need to embed that training within a well-structured and balanced approach to reading. Adams (1990a, b) argues that combining phonological and 'whole language' approaches to reading should not be seen as incompatible. Indeed, it is now well accepted that poor readers rely on context more than good readers (Nation and Snowling, 1998). Language experience is therefore as vital to the dyslexic child as is a structured phonological awareness programme. This is particularly important in the secondary education sector where it may be inappropriate to provide a phonological-based programme for a dyslexic student. Here the priority may be on language experience, print exposure and comprehension activities.

It is also important to note the current interest and research in the area of multilingualism and dyslexia (Peer and Reid, 2000; Cline and Shamsi, 2000), which indicates the need to obtain accurate measures of screening, identification and curriculum materials to ensure that the needs of multilingual dyslexic children are met within mainstream provision.

Right Hemisphere Processing

West (1997) has utilised Galaburda's research to show that dyslexic people who are right hemisphere processors can actually be at an advantage in some situations. This emphasises the positive side of dyslexia. Additionally, West suggests that the transmission of knowledge and understanding is increasingly becoming visual and that those with well-developed visual skills can be at an advantage in acquiring the visual language of knowledge. Furthermore, the work on multiple intelligences (Gardner, 1983, 1999) highlight how the strengths of students with dyslexia can be utilised within the classroom and mainstream learning environment.

Environmental Factors

The environment is influential at all stages of the Morton and Frith (1995) model. The model is interactive, which means that all components of the model—neurological, cognitive and behavioural—interact with and influence each other (Box 1.1). This process is however very much mediated by the environment. The environment certainly implies social and cultural factors that the individual brings to the learning situation, but it means more than that. The environment includes the learning context in the classroom, the school and the education authority. This affects learners and staff. It is important therefore to consider the individual learning styles and preferences of the learner as well as the policy of the school, the authority and the training of staff. These factors can help to provide a supportive environment that will have a profound influence on the outcome of the learning experience for students with dyslexia.

Learning styles and environmental preferences of students will be the focus of Chapter 9. It is important however that these factors are set in context as no strategy, programme or approach can stand in isolation—each has to be part of a bigger package, preferably a whole school package, that involves not only the whole child but also the family, other professionals and the cultural aspects of the community.

The field of dyslexia can claim to have made considerable progress in the last decade. As Nicolson (2001), states, with a prevalence of around 4% in most countries, dyslexia has a universal currency. There has also been significant advances in the theoretical understanding of dyslexia, and the causal modelling framework described in this chapter helps to clarify the overlapping and complementary aspects of the theory and how these factors can relate to practice. One of the significant factors has been the broadening of the conceptual understanding of dyslexia without in any way minimising the nature and function of the label. Dyslexia is rightly viewed within a continuum and can overlap with other specific difficulties as they may share similar neurological, biological and cognitive mechanisms. Nicolson (2001), however, asserts that the new theoretical developments raise more questions than they answer, but this should be viewed 'as a strength rather than a weakness, reflecting the opening up of fruitful new research avenues' (p. 22). Nicolson (2001) also suggests that the 'stage is set for undertaking ambitious, multi-disciplinary, multi-perspective projects aimed at redefining the field of dyslexia and learning difficulties as the field of learning abilities' (p. 33).

NEUROLOGICAL/BIOLOGICAL FACTORS

- genetic factors
- cortical abnormalities
- magnocellular deficit hypothesis
- the role of the cerebellum
- dietary factors
- inhibition of primitive reflexes
- left hemisphere under stimulation
- convergence difficulties and binocular instability
- visual sensitivity and coloured filters and eye movement co-ordination
- hemispheric symmetry

COGNITIVE FACTORS

- phonological processing
- naming speed
- working memory
- metacognitive factors
- automaticity

BEHAVIOURAL FACTORS

- pattern of errors in reading and spelling
- writing difficulties
- time management difficulties
- more time to complete work
- inaccuracies in copying
- avoidance of writing
- discrepancies in performances in curricular activities

ENVIRONMENTAL/CONTEXTUAL FACTORS

- learning environment
- learning styles
- education policy
- staff training
- social and cultural factors

Box 1.1   Factors associated with dimensions of the causal modelling framework.

One of the major tensions in dyslexia research, however, as Fawcett (2002) points out, has been the range of potentially conflicting viewpoints that have to be accommodated. These viewpoints might include researchers and practitioners, parents and teachers, teachers and educational psychologists, schools and local education authorities, local education authorities and governments. Fawcett suggests that many of these groups have different agendas, and much of the time this forces them into opposition. She describes the key priorities for action and suggests that the emerging consensus on causal theories should be acknowledged and addressed, the issue of co-morbidity explored, factors associated with multilingualism, and the transparency and regularity in different languages examined, as well as the nature and extent of early identification and intervention. Fawcett suggests the term 'medical model' is often used to describe abnormal development, and she asserts it is important, when using this term, to distinguish between cause, symptom and treatment. Practitioners according to Fawcett are primarily concerned with treatment, educational psychologists with symptoms and theorists with the discovery of the underlying cause(s). She explains, 'it is clear, that despite these different perspectives, a full understanding demands the investigation and integration of these three aspects. For example, in order to develop an applied test for early diagnosis of dyslexia, it is necessary to build on theoretical insights into the predictors of dyslexia which lie outside reading. Otherwise, we have no option but to return to the system where we wait for children to fail to learn to read, with all the associated trauma and negative impacts on self-esteem, which can damage children for life' (p. 13).

In relation to future considerations and priorities Fawcett (2002) maintains that there is a need to maintain 'discrepancy definitions' of dyslexia as we have not yet clearly established whether there are different causes for dyslexia as opposed to more generalised learning disabilities. It would therefore be inappropriate to abandon discrepancy definitions. She also maintains that there is a need for positive indices of dyslexia that may include an analysis of learning ability. Refined identification procedures of course need to be accompanied by enlightened and appropriate teaching and educational policy and provision. There are some good examples of dyslexia-friendly teaching (MacKay, 2001) and classroom, teaching and curriculum-focused approaches, all of which help to meet the needs of children and young people with dyslexia (Tod and Fairman, 2001; Came and, Cooke, 2002). These are discussed in some detail in Part III on teaching approaches.

It is important to acknowledge the progress and the opportunities that now exist for children and adults with dyslexia. There has been considerable progress in teacher training, education provision, the development of assessment tools and resources and in teaching and learning approaches. There have also been heartening success stories from many adults who were undiagnosed at school, but have now succeeded in a particular field of work and have begun to understand the implications of dyslexia for life and work (Bruce, 1999; Stewart, 2002). Their stories and experiences have inspired others and brought a realisation that each individual with dyslexia can succeed. There are abundant examples of positive intervention with adults with dyslexia; some of these are discussed in Chapter 12. It is also heartening that some of these resources to deal with dyslexia are allocated to young people at 'risk'. This is important because the 'cycle of failure' that can sometimes be associated with dyslexia can lead vulnerable young people into crime and offending

(Morgan, 1996; Reid and Kirk, 2001). It is heartening therefore to witness the positive work of organisations such as DYSPEL (see p. 370), which have initiated a number of projects with the probation service to prevent vulnerable young people with dyslexia from becoming engulfed in a recurrent cycle of offending behaviour. The legislation in the UK, such as the 1998 Disability Act, and the disability legislation in the USA (Reid and Kirk, 2001) has been of considerable assistance. Also government reports, such as the Moser Report (Moser, 2000) on adult literacy and employment service initiatives like the Adult Dyslexia for Education, Practice and Training Report (ADEPT) (Reid et al., 1999), have begun to highlight the needs of adults with dyslexia, especially the unemployed, particularly in relation to assessment and training.

At school and further education level considerable progress has been made. The Dyslexia-friendly Schools Campaign in England and Wales, the early intervention initiatives in Scotland and the task force reports in Northern Ireland and the Republic of Ireland and the inception of a European Dyslexia Awareness Week have set European-wide standards for addressing and dealing with dyslexia in the context of education, employment and inclusion. In countries throughout the world, Europe, the USA, Canada, Australia and New Zealand there has been evidence of strong lobbying campaigns by groups, professionals and parents, with a close professional and personal interest in dyslexia. Some of these are described in Chapter 14.

The purpose of this book is therefore to analyse, discuss and report on these and other practical initiatives in order to support the practitioner, teacher, psychologist, language specialist and occupational therapist, who together with parents have to combine experiences and expertise to pave the way for a successful and fulfilling future for all young people with dyslexia.

Part I

Literacy

Chapter 2

The Acquisition of Literacy: Reading

POLITICAL AND SOCIAL BACKGROUND

Reading is the extraction of meaning from print—literacy is much wider, this involves the appreciation of the literate culture, the conventions of society and the purposes and the responsibility placed on the use of literacy by society. Reading, therefore, as part of the literacy picture is of considerable importance, but it is vital to recognise that this involves much more than reading accuracy. Literacy, and particularly reading, is increasingly becoming a major preoccupation and concern of governments throughout the world. In England and Wales in 1996 the Department for Education and Employment (DfEE) established the National Literacy Project, which aimed to monitor and evaluate the teaching of literacy. This established clear expectations for the desired level of literacy to be attained by children at various ages and directed that the teaching of literacy should be in the main undertaken through whole class teaching and management. In 1997 and 1998 literacy targets were set for schools by central government and local education authorities, which meant that all primary schools were expected to teach an hour of literacy daily (the literacy hour) to all pupils. In 2001 the New Zealand government reported on the findings of the Education and Science Committee on the inquiry into teaching of reading in New Zealand. The report conceded that 'for most of the past decade ... schools have received little assistance from the ministry in achieving national literacy goals. We are pleased this is now changing.' The report, however, did acknowledge that current literacy strategies are effective for most of the students in New Zealand, but 'there is compelling evidence that these strategies do not work for certain groups of poor performers, which may together number up to 20 per cent of students.' The key point about this is it indicates a government concern with reading standards, how the government can influence, support and evaluate these standards and achieve national goals in literacy. This implies that the government is not only interested in standards but also how these standards are achieved. The teaching of reading and the support necessary to develop quality teaching programmes and materials are

seen as a concern of the New Zealand government in the same way as the introduction of the National Literacy strategy in England and Wales indicates a greater
government involvement with the teaching in the class as well as the outcomes of
education. Government is now concerned with how reading is taught.

According to Eames (2002), literacy educators have faced a number of challenges
relating to defining literacy and attempting to incorporate the prevailing views and
fashions over what is literacy into effective teaching approaches with measurable
outcomes. This has been particularly challenging because often disparate views have
been suggested about what constitutes literacy and how literacy should be taught.
According to Eames (2002) the responses to these challenges have often resulted in a
polarisation of the teaching community about the benefits of some approaches over
others. Au and Raphael (2000) suggest that as definitions of literacy have changed so
have the curriculum, instruction, and assessments associated with them. They cite the
example of Michigan state in the 1980s, when, following a redefinition of reading
from fluent print decoding to an interactive process emphasising comprehension,
major changes followed in English language arts' standards that tested higher
levels of comprehension and writing in response to text. The dilemmas and the
challenges associated with reading appear to surround the need to provide a balanced literacy curriculum where 'children are exposed both to direct instruction in
reading skills together with the experiences that encourage social collaboration and
constructive problem solving associated with an integrated language arts approach'
(Morrow et al., 1999, p. 474). This highlights the challenge to teachers and management who need to define literacy and evaluate the effects of different approaches.
This also explains government influence and concern over literacy standards in the
community. Essentially, literacy should reflect the pluralistic contexts in which
children live (Eames, 2002). This, therefore, has implications for teaching methodologies, resources and measures of assessment, all of which can support the different
views, the conflicts and the challenges to which educators need to respond. This
emphasises the need for a broad definition of literacy that can reflect and embrace
the cultural and linguistic diversities we increasingly meet in the classroom among
readers of all abilities including children with dyslexia.

Similarly the Programme for International Assessment (PISA) (2000), which is
described below, assessed students' achievements in literacy across three domains—
reading literacy, mathematical literacy and scientific literacy. This also emphasises
the range of purposes that rely on literacy and this has implications for dyslexic
students and for literacy access.

INTERNATIONAL COMPARISONS

There has been increasing interest in international assessment and international
comparisons. Shiel (2002) reports on this increasing interest in international assessments of literacy and suggests that many countries wish to participate in this exercise
because the results provide policy-makers with information that can be used to
monitor standards or implement reforms. For example, in 1991 the International
Association for the Evaluation of Educational Achievement (IEA) and the Reading
Literacy Study (RLS) assessed the achievement of 9- and 14-year-olds in 32 countries

(27 at the lower age level and 31 at the higher age level). Participating countries at both age levels included Finland, Canada, Ireland and the USA. Although England did not participate in the original study, the IEA test was administered by the National Foundation for Educational Research in England and Wales to a representative sample of English and Welsh 9-year-olds in 1996, so the performance of English/Welsh students can be compared with that of 9-year-olds in other countries in 1991 (see Brooks et al., 1996a).

In the IEA/RLS, reading literacy was defined as 'the ability to understand and use those written language forms required by society and/or valued by the individual' (Elley, 1992, p. 3). The national samples of students who participated in the assessment were presented with three types of texts: narrative texts (continuous texts in which the writer's aim is to tell a story, whether fact or fiction); expository texts (continuous prose designed to describe, explain or convey factual information); and document texts (structured texts presented in the form of charts, tables, maps and sets of directions). The vast majority of comprehension questions based on these texts were of the multiple-choice variety; the remainder were of the short-answer type. Test questions tapped five levels of text-processing that were assumed to be in roughly hierarchical order: literal response (verbatim match), paraphrase, main idea, inference, and locate and process information. As with other international studies, care was taken to ensure that both passages and questions represented the reading curricula in participating countries and that strict guidelines were adhered to in translating test materials, to ensure comparability of outcomes across countries.

The outcomes of the IEA/RLS were reported in a variety of ways, including mean (average) overall reading literacy scores by country as well as mean country scores for understanding of narrative, expository and documents texts. Finland achieved the highest mean score at Ages 9 and 14. In a ranking of countries at Age 9, Ireland and England/Wales were ranked 12th and 21st, respectively, out of 28 countries. However, because of measurement error, their respective mean scores were found not to be statistically significantly different from one another (Brooks et al., 1996a). At Age 14, Ireland was ranked 20th of 31 countries, suggesting a decline in achievement between 9- and 14-year-olds. However, Ireland's mean score at Age 14 was not significantly different from the mean scores of nine other countries, or from the international country average (Elley, 1992).

Differences were observed in the performance of students on the three text types used in the study. Nine-year olds in both Ireland and England/Wales did best on narrative texts, next best on expository texts and poorest on documents. This has implications for the question 'what is reading' since it covers not only different facets of literacy but can also be utilised for different functions. This is important because of governments' preoccupation with literacy standards and the implications of the apparent results of assessment of these standards for groups such as dyslexic children.

In the PISA 2000 study (Shiel et al., 2001) 28 OECD countries and 4 non-OECD countries (Brazil, Latvia, Liechtenstein and the Russian Federation) participated and only one country, Finland, achieved a significantly higher mean. The USA ranked 15th for combined reading literacy with a mean slightly above the average while Canada ranked 2nd with a score significantly higher than the mean, but Canadian students scored the highest in the subscale that measured the ability to 'reflect on and evaluate texts'. It is interesting to note that in the rankings of mathematical and scientific literacy measures, Japan and the Republic of Korea achieved the top two ratings—Japan for mathematical literacy and Korea for scientific literacy. This emphasises the different literacy priorities of different countries and underlines the functional use of literacy as a social, cultural and economic medium.

There are usually a number of reasons that one country should fare better than others in literacy attainment measures, and as mentioned above these can include social and environmental as well as educational reasons. It is important therefore that dyslexia should also be seen in that wider social and environmental context and not confined to the educational domain. This is implied in the definition of reading literacy in the PISA study. In this study reading literacy is defined as 'understanding, using and reflecting on written texts, in order to achieve one's goals, to develop one's knowledge and potential, and to participate in society' (OECD, 2000b, p. 20).

CRITICAL LITERACY

The points made above in relation to what one means by literacy and the use literacy can be put to is encapsulated in the term 'critical literacy'. Hall (1998) terms critical literacy as coming to understand what are one's own literacy practices and one's responses to texts at an individual, personal and social level. According to Eames (2002) critical literacy can be placed at the highest stage of the literacy hierarchy, the overarching concept transforming multiple literacy concepts and contexts. She suggests that critical literacy involves constructing meaning from text and that such meanings are achieved during interaction of reader and text, during discussion of text and when listening and responding to others. This has important implications for children with dyslexia and particularly young adults who may not have efficient decoding skills, but nevertheless should not be deprived of the spin-off social and cognitive benefits of literacy seen in this way.

According to Hunt (2002), however, 'critical literacy' challenges assumptions that texts can ever convey 'objective meanings' or that literacy is an ideologically neutral tool. It asserts that both readers and writers approach texts in ways that are conditioned by such factors as purpose, power relations, gender and historical period. These factors are expressed through a variety of rhetorical devices (such as vocabulary and grammatical structure choices) and by the writer's selection of which voices and positions to express and which to omit. He suggests that this can be seen in some forms of newspaper reporting and advertising that select information that favours one view at the expense of another. The implication for teachers of this according to Hunt is that they need to do more than simply train pupils to become skilled decoders. He suggests that decoding is an essential part of the reading process, but it is only one aspect of a set of sociocultural practices that also encompasses working out what the text means, knowing how to use the text in context and how the text has been constructed to produce specific effects on the reader. This implies that to become independent readers children with dyslexia need to be aware of these dimensions, questioning the choices and assumptions that underlie the writer's words.

Taking these points into consideration the goal of literacy teaching is therefore the empowerment of the reader. Critical literacy teachers, according to Hunt, approach this goal in various ways and need to encourage multiple interpretations rather than a quest for definitive meaning.

Hunt cites the following framework (from Luke et al., 2001, p. 16) of questions that can structure critical investigations:

- What is the topic?
- How is it being presented?
- What themes and discourses are being used? Who is writing to whom? Whose voices and positions are being expressed?
- Whose voices and positions are not being expressed?
- What is the text trying to do for you?
- What other ways are there of writing about the topic?
- What wasn't said about the topic?
- Why?

WHAT IS READING?

What is reading? This question, despite its apparent simplicity, can provide some insight into how reading is perceived by the learner and some answers as to why, for a significant number, the acquisition of reading skills is an arduous and sometimes deflating process. Eames reports on the revised English Language Curriculum (NCCA, 1999), which proposes that reading involves both learning to read and reading to learn. This counters the application of a narrow understanding of the concept of literacy as 'learning to read' that has been a feature of many learning support programmes for pupils with dyslexia in many countries.

Learning to read requires a number of skills, of which many are considered pre-reading skills and some develop as a result of reading itself. Being deprived of fluency in reading can therefore further affect the development of many of the reading subskills.

Some specific factors that are important in the acquisition of literacy include word attack skills (such as letter recognition, segmentation, blending, phonemic awareness, analogy strategies and grapheme–phoneme correspondence) and word recognition skills (such as recognition of word patterns and the use of visual memory skills). Other factors (such as environmental considerations, development of the concepts of print, development of language concepts and how the whole concept of reading is viewed by the learner) are also important.

Ehri (2002) suggests that, initially, to become skilled readers children need to acquire knowledge of the alphabetic system and that this process presents some difficulty to struggling readers. It is important therefore that teachers understand the processes involved in reading. Ehri suggests that learning to read involves two basic processes. One process involves learning to decipher the print (i.e., learning to transform letter sequences into familiar words). The other involves comprehending the meaning of the print. When children attain reading skill, they learn to perform both these processes in a way that allows their attention to focus on the meaning of the text while the mechanics of reading, including deciphering, operate unobtrusively and out of awareness.

Ehri suggests that children acquire listening comprehension skills in the course of learning to speak. She also argues that decoding print is not a natural process in the same way as speech. The brain is specialized for processing spoken language, but not written language (Liberman, 1992). In order for reading and writing skills to develop, therefore, Ehri suggests that written language must penetrate and gain a foothold in the mechanisms used by the brain to process speech.

These factors underline the view that reading is an interactive and reciprocal process. In other words the more skills the child has access to the more competent he or she will become not only in reading as an activity but also in the development of reading subskills. The flip side of this also applies—that is, those children who lack competence in the reading subskills will not have ready access to reading and are consequently deprived of an opportunity of developing these skills. This is described as the Matthew effect (Stanovich, 1986). This interactive and reciprocal nature of the reading process is also illustrated through the model suggested by Adams (1990b) (see Figure 2.1). This model of the reading system highlights the interactions between context, meaning, orthography (print) and phonology (speech).

The orthographic processor is responsible for sequencing the letters in a word, the phonological processor for matching those letters to the letter sound, the meaning processor relates to the reader's knowledge of word meaning and the context processor provides an overview of the meaning of the text. These processors work together and receive feedback from each other.

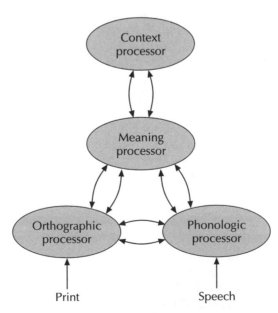

Figure 2.1 Modelling the reading system: four processors (reproduced by permission of Heinemann, part of Harcourt Education Ltd; from Adams, 1990b).

Ehri (2002) suggests children can use four different methods to read words as they process text. These are:

- Decoding words—this involves transforming letters into sounds and blending the sounds to form recognisable words.
- Analogising to known words—using this method readers may read a new word by recognising how its spelling is similar to a word they already know as a sight word; for example, reading *beak* by analogy to *peak*. Goswami (1990) showed that beginning readers can use their knowledge of rhyming words to read words by analogy, especially if the rhyming clue words are in view. However, Ehri suggests that having some decoding skills appear to be required for beginners to analogise using sight words in memory (Ehri and Robbins, 1992).
- Predicting words from graphophonemic and context cues—readers might predict the identity of an unfamiliar word by using context cues such as pictures or the preceding text (Goodman, 1976), beginning letters (Tunmer and Chapman, 1998) or their knowledge about language—the syntactic context.
- By memory (by 'sight')—reading words by sight requires children to access information stored in memory from previous experiences of reading the words (Ehri, 1992). This means that they must have previously read the word.

Ehri suggests the first three ways are strategies that can be applied to read unfamiliar words. The final way, by sight, is used to read words that have been read before and retained in memory. In each case the processes differ. As readers attain skill they learn to read words in all four ways.

CHILDREN'S PERCEPTION OF READING

One of the important factors in the reading process relates to children's perception of reading. How therefore do children perceive reading? It is an interesting exercise to ask a class of children this question. This question was put to a sample of children aged between 7 and 10 years (Reid, 1993d), and the responses illustrate the different perceptions and beliefs children hold of reading. Some of the responses include learning words, learning new words, looking at words and saying them, learning about things, finding out about things, stories, words and sentences.

The main distinction that can be drawn from the responses related to aspects of the *task* of reading rather than the *function*. Those who focused on the 'task' highlighted aspects such as the decoding of words and the learning of these words. A typical response from the 'task' group was 'reading is when you look at words and you say them in your mind.' The 'function' group recognised reading as an activity from which they derived pleasure and the purpose of reading was to obtain meaning from text.

Why do children perceive reading in such vastly different ways? Does the answer to this question lie in the method and strategy used to teach children reading? Or perhaps the answer to this is related more to the child's skills and abilities and how easy and accessible learning to read is for the child. Clearly, persistent reading failure will affect the child's perception of reading to one of a task, and the real meaning of literacy will be lost. Whichever way one might be inclined to argue, there is something fundamentally amiss if the child perceives reading as an arduous and laborious exercise—a product of classroom routine, relentless practice and slow progress. If this is the child's perception of reading, then surely the real meaning of reading is lost and books then become a confusing contradiction between the pain and pleasure of acquiring knowledge.

Children with dyslexia seldom have a perception of reading that reveals the pleasure of books and the real meaning of print. They often perceive reading as a dreaded exercise, calling for skills in precision and accuracy—an exercise that appears to stretch their natural and accessible competencies.

This presents a challenge for teachers, that is, to teach the basic fundamental structure and framework for the understanding of print, but at the same time to provide an enriched and meaningful language experience to facilitate and encourage access to books. This can help the child gain some real appreciation of the message and pleasure of books.

READING SKILLS

The skills used in reading are little different from many of the skills used in other aspects of learning.

For example, linguistic, visual and auditory skills are all essential for access to reading. These skills are also used in other learning activities such as speech, listening, creative and visual work. These skills develop independently of reading because they are used in learning activities other than reading. This does not necessarily imply that coaching in reading subskills promotes proficiency in the practice of reading. Rather, the view could be held that it is the actual practice of reading that fosters reading skills, and therefore reading practice is essential to develop skills as a reader (Smith, 1988; Clay, 1985).

Adams (1990b), however, suggests that activities designed to develop young children's awareness of words, syllables and phonemes significantly increase their later success in learning to read and write. The impact of phonemic training or reading acquisition, Adams suggests, is especially strong when phonemes are taught together with the letters by which they are represented. This suggests an important role for the teacher in the fostering of reading skills.

Adams (1990b) further suggests an important role for the three aspects of language, visual and auditory factors. For example, she suggests independent writing activities can help foster an appreciation of text and its comprehension. She also suggests that phonic instruction can help with both the sounds of words and the spellings of words; and reading aloud to children, according to Adams, is perhaps the single most important activity for building the knowledge and skills eventually required for reading.

An examination of these three factors—linguistic, visual and auditory—reveals some areas of difficulty encountered by dyslexic children when learning to read (see Boxes 2.1–2.3).

Reading is messages expressed in language and children have to transpose their understanding or oral language into an understanding of the written language. This presents difficulties for some children because:

- the flow of oral language does not always make the break between words clear
- of difficulty in breaking messages into words
- of difficulty in breaking messages into their sequences of sounds
- of problems in retaining those sounds in memory
- of difficulty in articulating sounds
- of difficulty in recognising sounds in written form

Box 2.1   Language factors.

Some of the most important visual factors include:

- recognition of visual cues
- left to right orientation
- recognition of word patterns
- recognition of letter and letter shapes

Box 2.2   Visual factors.

These include:

- recognition of letter sounds
- recognition of sounds and letter groups or patterns
- sequencing of sounds
- corresponding sounds to visual stimuli
- discriminating sounds from other sounds
- discriminating sounds within words

Box 2.3   Auditory factors.

Many of the visual (Box 2.2) and auditory (Box 2.3) aspects of reading do not develop spontaneously in children with specific learning difficulties. These skills need to be taught, and usually in a sensitive and structured manner. Some of the skills, therefore, that are required in reading include automatic rapid word and letter recognition, phonological and visual skills, knowledge of the concepts of print, vocabulary knowledge, general knowledge, ability to use context as an aid to word recognition, and comprehension and analogy skills.

How one decides to prioritise the teaching of these skills within a programme depends to a great extent on the strengths and difficulties of the child. This interaction of skills underlines the multifaceted nature of reading and the long-standing notion that no one method, medium, approach or even philosophy holds the key to the process of learning to read (DES, 1975).

Hunt (2002), however, suggests that there are dangers in using findings about what skilled readers do in order to draw direct implications about teaching practices for non-readers. He quotes an example from the work of Goodman (1976) that used the evidence from miscue analyses conducted on competent readers to argue that effective and efficient reading is driven more by cognition than graphophonemic processes. He speculated that the fluent reader 'samples the print', using just enough visual information to confirm hypotheses derived from context. This top-down model of reading persuaded many to adopt the strategy, which became known as the 'psycholinguistic guessing game' (Goodman, 1976). Thus, inexperienced readers confronted with an unfamiliar word were discouraged from sounding the word out and, instead, persuaded to guess what would make sense in the context. However, it has now been suggested that readers actually fixate on each word, and, in fact, good readers do not need to use context because they have efficient decoding skills. In fact, the reliance on context is more characteristic of poor readers who use guesswork to compensate for inefficient word recognition (Stanovich and Stanovich, 1995). According to Hunt (2002) these developments in knowledge about skilled reading behaviour have been used as arguments against teaching children to focus on the meaning of what they read until the alphabetic principle is firmly in place and children are able to recognise a number of regular words in isolation (McGuinness, 1998).

Clearly, there are dangers in exclusively depending on either the grapheme–phoneme approach and the use of whole text experience—both are necessary. According to Hunt the teaching implications of emphasising context through the use of natural language books, discussion of stories and their links to real life, and encouragement of active comprehension strategies provides learners and teachers with a vision of literacy much richer than that offered in code-based reading schemes. Nevertheless, as Hunt reminds us, the evidence that has accumulated about the importance of word recognition should act as a useful counterpoise to any holistic vision of the reading process reminding learners and teachers that text level discussion needs to be accompanied by the teaching of graphophonemic skills.

Luke et al. (2001) describes today's young readers as surfers on an ocean of signs: 'post-modern childhood involves the navigation of an endless sea of texts.' Whether or not children can recognise the actual words of these texts rapidly and automatically, they will be affected by the social and commercial pressures that they exert. Hunt (2002) suggests therefore that when developing a reading programme for children with dyslexia, word recognition teaching approaches should be accompanied by a critical literacy approach to enable texts that shape children's lives have a more direct impact. Hunt actually suggests that the types of text that critical literacy involves could provide supportive, motivating contexts for these learners to begin to acquire access to the lexicon.

READING DEVELOPMENT

There are clearly a number of important subskills that contribute to the reading process. These skills do not all appear at once, but are developing skills relating to a number of factors. Harrison (1994) cites some research evidence suggesting a child's background such as intelligence, prior learning and home background contribute approximately 85% to what is achieved in school, the other 15% to schooling includes teacher input and teaching methods. From this it follows that the reading skills acquired at an early stage are extremely important—these are skills in language, comprehension and vocabulary. These provide an impetus for the development of reading skills related to print awareness.

Adams (1990b) discusses the importance of the visual aspects of print and how this relates to the different types of print young children come across—the sources range from instructions for toys to comic books. She asserts that this visual awareness of print does not develop in isolation, but becomes a component of the developing child's environment. This leads to the child developing concepts of print such as left and right, words, sentences, the back of the book and the front. It is important, therefore, to ensure that the child has a grasp of these basic concepts of print, a point highlighted by Clay (1985) in the Reading Recovery Programme.

Furthermore, Tunmer et al. (1988) found that the performances of children on tests designed to measure concepts about print have been found to predict future reading achievement. Adams (1990a) suggests that basic knowledge about print is essentially the foundation upon which the orthographic and phonological skills are built.

It is suggested that recognising the visual identities of letters is an important stage in reading development and this skill takes time and practice and necessitates a degree of visual attention (Adams, 1990b). Adams suggests that the cause of poor readers displaying errors in letter orientation may reflect insufficient knowledge of letter shapes.

It seems, therefore, that the reading process is underpinned by the visual recognition of individual letters and then transposing these letters into their phonological correspondences.

READING DEVELOPMENT AND DYSLEXIA

There is a considerable body of evidence to show that dyslexic children have difficulties that primarily affect the phonological domain of language processing. Hatcher and Snowling (2002) suggest an extremely influential hypothesis that in recent years has indicated that the difficulties associated with dyslexia and reading can be traced to problems at the level of phonological representations. Snowling and Hulme (1994) suggested that children create phonological representations by mapping the speech they hear on to the speech they produce, and vice versa. Gradually over development, the specification of spoken words built up through this process becomes more and more detailed as the child's proficiency with speech increases. This would imply that phonological representations have a key role to play in the development of reading as well as speech.

Dyslexic children may well have some difficulties in the visual stage, but almost certainly will have difficulty in translating the letters to their phonic equivalents. From the 26 letters in the alphabet, hundreds of correspondences can be made.

Hatcher and Snowling (2002) report that the most consistently reported phonological difficulties found in dyslexia are limitations of verbal short-term memory. These can be noted in difficulties in following instructions, memorising lists, carrying numbers and in keeping up with dictation. They report that the evidence from brain-imaging studies indicates that the brain regions that are usually highly active in normal readers during short-term memory tasks show lower levels of functional activation even in highly literate dyslexic readers (Paulesu et al., 1996).

There is also evidence that dyslexic children's reading development can be affected by long-term memory factors. This can account for many difficulties such as problems memorising the days of the week or the months of the year, mastering multiplication tables and learning a foreign language. Hatcher and Snowling (2002) suggest that this long-term learning problem can be related to the retrieval of phonological information from long-term memory and can account for the word-finding difficulties often experienced by children with dyslexia.

They suggest, however, that the persistent difficulties with phonological awareness associated with dyslexia are not universal, but appear to be specific to children learning to read in irregular or 'deep' orthographies, such as English.

The task of learning to read in an alphabetic system requires the child to associate letters with their sounds, and then appreciate how sounds can be blended together to make words. At a basic level, therefore, learning to read requires the child to establish a set of connections between the letters (graphemes) of printed words and the speech sounds (phonemes) of spoken words. This relationship between 'orthography' and 'phonology' needs to be made at a 'fine-grained level'—the phoneme level—to ensure that new words that have not been seen before can be decoded, otherwise the dyslexic child will be faced with a considerable challenge at each new word, as she or he will not have the bank of phonological knowledge to decode new words.

Hatcher and Snowling (2002) argue that the relationships between orthography and phonology are important both in the early stages of learning to read and in the development of automatic reading skills that subsequently account for reading fluency. They suggest that in English these relationships also provide a scaffold for learning multi-letter (e.g., -ough, -igh), morphemic (-tion, -cian) and inconsistent (-ea) spelling sound correspondences. They hypothesise that, although dyslexic children can learn to read words they have been taught, they code the correspondences between the letters of these words and their pronunciations at a 'coarse-grained level'—chunks rather than phonemes. A consequence is that dyslexic children have difficulty generalising this knowledge, and therefore one of the most robust signs of dyslexia is poor non-word reading (Rack et al., 1992). It can be observed that some dyslexic children can circumvent decoding difficulties to some extent by relying or over-relying on the semantic and syntactic context (Nation and Snowling, 1998). But this is usually not totally successful, especially in the early years as the child will not have accumulated sufficient language knowledge to use this strategy successfully.

Even if this strategy is utilised, Hatcher and Snowling (2002) show that reading often remains slow and that use of global reading strategies may not be conducive to spelling, which usually remains poor across the lifespan.

Essentially, learning to read is an interactive process to which children bring all their language skills and knowledge of phonological processing, and a deficit in phonological representation is the most likely source of most of the reading (and spelling) difficulties experienced by dyslexic children.

It is widely accepted (Hatcher and Snowling, 2002) that all children do not learn to read in the same way. Children have different combinations of cognitive skills and have individual styles of processing information. For example, one child may have severe phonological deficits, but good visual memory skills, while another child may have weak phonological skills and slow speed of processing. Aditionally, children will very likely have experienced different methods of being taught how to read.

Teaching programmes on reading should therefore recognise this and the difficulties that will confront dyslexic children if these correspondences are taught in isolation. It is important that a teaching programme integrates the visual, phonic and the context aspects of reading simultaneously at all stages in reading from early development through to competence.

One such programme that achieves this is that developed by Reason and Boote (1994), which identifies three strands: meaning, phonics and fluency at four stages—early development, beginning to read, becoming competent and achieving competence. The three strands are taught simultaneously at all these stages through related activities.

Frith (1985) identifies the following developmental stages in the acquisition of reading skills.

Logographic Stage

The child makes use of visual recognition of overall word patterns—thus, he or she is able to recognise words as units. This may not necessarily mean the child can reproduce these words accurately (this would be an alphabetic skill), and as a result the child can easily misspell words they are able to read.

Alphabetic Stage

The child tackles the sound/symbol correspondence, and one can identify if children possess this one-to-one correspondence between the letter and the sound. Ehri suggests that the alphabetic stage can be divided into four phases that capture the changes that occur in the development of sight word reading: pre-alphabetic, partial alphabetic, full alphabetic and consolidated alphabetic (Ehri, 1995, 1999; Ehri and McCormick, 1998). Each phase is labelled to reflect the predominant type of connection that links the written forms of sight words to their pronunciations and meanings in memory. Therefore, during the pre-alphabetic phase beginners remember how to read sight words by forming connections between selected visual attributes of words and their pronunciations or meanings. This phase is called pre-alphabetic because letter–sound relations are not involved in the connections.

When pre-alphabetic readers read print in their environment, such as stop signs and fast food restaurant signs, they do this according to Ehri by remembering visual cues accompanying the print rather than the written words themselves.

The next phase is the partial alphabetic phase. Here beginners remember how to read sight words by forming partial alphabetic connections between only some of the letters in written words and sounds detected in their pronunciations. Because first and final letters are especially salient, these are often the cues that are remembered. To remember sight words in this way, partial alphabetic readers need to know some letter–sound correspondences and have some phonemic segmentation.

During the next phase, the full alphabetic phase, beginners remember how to read sight words by forming complete graphophonemic connections. This is possible because readers know how the major graphemes symbolise phonemes in the conventional spelling system (Venezky, 1970, 1999). In applying this knowledge to form connections for sight words, spellings become fully bonded to pronunciations in memory (Ehri, 1992; Perfetti, 1992).

The final phase according to Ehri is the full alphabetic phase when readers are able to decode words by transforming graphemes into phonemes, and they are able to retain sight words in memory by connecting graphemes to phonemes. These processes acquaint them with the pronunciations of syllabic and subsyllabic spelling patterns that recur in different words. The letters in these patterns become consolidated into larger spelling–sound units that can be used to decode words and to retain sight words in memory.

Orthographic Stage

The child possesses and comprehends knowledge of the letter–sound relationship as well as structure and meaning. Thus, as well as being aware of rules the child can use cues and context.

It has been argued that children with specific learning difficulties can find the alphabetic stage difficult because the sound–symbol correspondence rests to a great extent on skills in phonics. Before children, therefore, acquire a competent understanding of the relationship between letter units (graphemes) and sound units (phonemes) they need a degree of phonological awareness (Frith, 1980; Snowling, 1987).

Frith (1985) puts forward the view that writing and the desire to write helps to enhance the alphabetic stage of reading because spelling is linked more directly to the alphabetic principle and letter–sound relationships. This view is also supported by the work of Bradley and Bryant (1991), who found that beginner readers in the process of acquiring the skills of the alphabetic stage use visual strategies for reading, but phonological strategies for spelling. In their study children read correctly words that were visually distinctive such as 'school' and 'light', but failed to read simpler words like 'bun' and 'sit'. Yet these children tended to spell correctly words they had failed to read such as 'bun' and 'sit' and spell incorrectly words they had read by focusing on the visual patterns (school, light).

The alphabetic reader according to Snowling (1987) may also find difficulty reading words that have inconsistent orthographic patterns, but that are pronounced in the same way. Similarly, irregular words are *mis*pronounced (e.g., 'island' would be pronounced 'is-land').

This developmental aspect of reading serves to illustrate the importance of the procedure of error analysis and identifying the type and pattern of errors made by children with difficulties in reading.

Snowling (2000), however, suggests some limitations of the staged models of reading. She suggests that the mechanisms involved in the transitions between stages are unclear. She also suggests that the stage model of reading implies an ordered sequence of stages or phases, yet it is acknowledged that the course of reading development is not the same for all children and, indeed, the actual reading strategies used by children may be influenced to a great extent by the 'teaching regime to which they are exposed' (p. 66). Additionally in some situations some children omit one of the stages. Snowling (2000) cites the example of the German language where children quickly reach a high level of competence in the alphabetic stage, and therefore a logographic stage is not easily observed (Wimmer, 1996). Similarly, Snowling cites a number of studies that claim that dyslexic readers can reach the orthographic phase without passing through the alphabetic phase.

READING MODELS AND METHODS

There are two principal models of the reading process. These have come to be known as 'bottom-up' (i.e., data-driven) and 'top-down' (concept-driven) models (Box 2.4).

The 'bottom-up' model suggests that, first, we look at the stimulus (i.e., the components of the letters) and then move to the meaning.

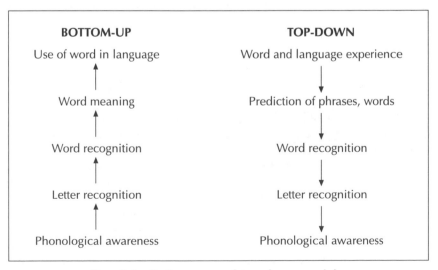

Box 2.4   Bottom-up and top-down models.

This emphasises the need to translate:

- written symbols to sound;
- sound to meaning.

'Bottom-up' theorists argue that the brain attends to every bit of available information, thus we read letter-by-letter so quickly that it becomes automatic.

The 'top-down' model is concept-driven. The reader attempts to absorb the meaning of the text from the cues that are available. These cues can include:

- the context of the passage being read—this relates to the syntactic context (i.e., the structure of the sentence) and semantic context (i.e., the anticipated meaning of the passage);
- the graphic information available (i.e., what the word looks like)—the reader anticipates the word or sentence from these descriptive cues.

Goodman's (1976) model, known as the psycholinguistic guessing game, strongly advocated a top-down approach to reading. This model asserts that good readers make efficient use of hypothesis formation and prediction in reading and thus make good use of the contextual cues available to the reader. Additionally, the efficiency in prediction of text means that good readers, according to Goodman, will have less need to rely on graphic cues and therefore do not have to process every visual characteristic of text.

Goodman's model of the reading process has however been subject to powerful criticism. The main exponents of this criticism are Tunmer (1994), Stanovich (1988), Adams (1990b) and Liberman and Liberman (1992). Essentially, the counter-arguments to Goodman's model suggest that the central tenet of the model that good readers are dependent on context for word recognition is inaccurate. It is suggested, in fact, that it is poor readers who are dependent on context, good readers do not need to rely on context as they possess efficient word recognition skills, can recognise words effortlessly and can utilise maximum cognitive capacity for comprehension. The effort required for poor readers to recognise words reduces their cognitive capacity for comprehension.

Additionally, there is now considerable evidence (Adams, 1990b) that good readers actually fixate nearly every word as they read. This process is achieved rapidly in efficient readers; therefore, less cognitive effort is required than, for example, with poor readers. So, even when the word is highly predictable, good readers actually visually process every word.

Lovegrove (1993) highlights the importance of visual factors in poor readers. He comments on the two visual subsystems—the transient and the sustained systems. The transient system, which is sensitive to contrast and more suited to identifying the general form of objects, has a fast transmission time and deals with peripheral vision. The sustained system is sensitive to black and white, detailed stimuli and is slow to change. It has a slow transmission time and deals with the central vision.

The key feature in relation to these systems is that both inhibit each other—which means that they do not operate simultaneously. Lovegrove's studies show that poor readers have a weak transient system and a normal sustained one. This results in interference between the two systems and has implications for the processing of visual stimuli in reading, since reading involves the synchronisation of both transient and sustained systems. This may therefore have implications for masking parts of a page that are not being focused on at that time. It certainly has implications for allowing sufficient processing time for poor readers; additionally, eye movement studies reveal that the eyes fixate on practically every word in a text, sometimes more than once (Ehri, 2002).

Although there may be flaws in the detail of Goodman's model many of the messages contained within it require consideration, such as the view that skilled readers have the ability and the opportunity to make efficient use of context. Additionally, Goodman's (1976) emphasis on reading for meaning should not be lost, but requires to be balanced with other reading skills within a teaching programme.

THE INTERACTIVE COMPENSATORY MODEL

Both 'top-down' and 'bottom-up' models have limitations in terms of an understanding of the reading process because clearly readers draw on both these processes when reading. The Interactive Compensatory Model attempts to explain how these dual processes work. This model acknowledges that reading involves recognising words based on information provided simultaneously from both the text and the reader, and as proposed by Stanovich (1988) focuses on the following assumptions:

- readers use information simultaneously from different levels and do not necessarily begin at either the graphic (bottom-up) or the contextual (top-down) level;
- during their development of reading skills, readers may rely more heavily on some levels of processing than on others (e.g., they may use context to greater or lesser extents);
- the reader's weaknesses are compensated for by his or her strengths.

Stanovich casts doubt on the view that good readers use the top-down model more than poor readers. Indeed, as indicated above good readers pay more attention to graphic detail and poor readers rely more on context. Thus, higher level processing of text does not necessarily need the completion of all lower levels of processing. Stanovich's model, therefore, takes account of the fact that many poor readers have developed strategies for compensating for their information processing difficulties.

Models of reading therefore need to take into account the following.

Print

- logographic stage;
- alphabetic stage;
- orthographic stage.

Language

- communicative aspects of print;
- structure of language;
- meaning.

Context

- prediction;
- life experiences;
- knowledge;
- pleasure and purpose.

Most models of reading are derivations from the 'top-down' or 'bottom-up' processes.

CONNECTIONIST MODELS

The dual route model (Coltheart, 1978) has for many years predominated in relation to the development of reading. It assumes that readers have two strategies at their disposal—a direct/visual strategy that is used for reading familiar words and an indirect route that involves the use of phonological strategies, which are used for reading unfamiliar words that are not within the child's sight vocabulary. There is now a number of alternatives to this view. These alternatives can be referred to as connectionist approaches or parallel distributed processing (PDP) models. These models offer a framework that can be applied to a range of cognitive processing activities, such as language acquisition and memory as well as reading (McClelland, 1988). The connectionist model applied to the reading process suggests that children learn to read through the reciprocal association between knowledge of letter strings and phonemes and the development of the ability to map letters and strings of letters to the phonemes that make up the sound units in language. This model would suggest that children access all their cognitive capacities at their disposal to do this. Ehri (1995a), in fact, suggests that children develop a single orthographic system over time rather than utilise a dual route model. The connectionist approach also implies that regular words will be accessed easier than irregular words as the former will conform to a pattern that the child will learn over time and exposure to print. The English language unlike some other languages such as German, Spanish and Italian contains a considerable amount of irregular patterns that contradict a pattern that the child may have learnt. For this reason regular words are more easily learnt than irregular words, and, additionally, because knowledge of irregular patterns places cognitive demands on memory and familiarity with phonological representations these therefore can be quite challenging for dyslexic children. One of the difficulties with models such as the connectionist model is that they may explain the processes involved in reading, but they do not inform about the conscious reading strategies readers may adopt. Nevertheless, this model does place some importance on over-learning as it implies that the connections become stronger with associations, and the more associations that are made then the stronger the connections will be. According to Snowling (2000) these connections form a knowledge base that can be drawn upon when the child is faced with a new word. Snowling (2000) discusses adaptations of these models and one in particular that is attractive is the adaptation by Plaut et al. (1996) that provides a role for semantic representation as well as phonological representation in the development of connections within the reading process.

BALANCE MODEL OF READING

Robertson and Bakker (2002) acknowledge in the balance model of reading that the reading process can be complex. In order to achieve fluency in reading the beginning reader, first, has to understand the perceptual features of text, and this has to become an automatic activity that the child can do without consciously thinking about it.

Second, the child eventually becomes more familiar with syntactical rules, and this is accompanied by an increase in the number of known words that the child can read automatically. This means that the child will be able to process large parts of a sentence as one chunk rather than reading individual letters and syllables. According to Robertson and Bakker the balance model of reading implies that reading is guided by syntactical rules and linguistic experience and is predominantly mediated by the left cerebral hemisphere. This means that reading develops through mediation initially of the right hemisphere when the child automatises the perceptual features of the letter and then through the left hemisphere as the syntactic and lexical features of reading develop.

Bakker (1979, 1990) suggested when he first introduced the balance model that it was possible that some children may not be able to shift from right to left in the hemispheric mediation of reading. This means that these children remain beginning readers in that they will lack the reading fluency that accompanies advancement in reading and they will continue to read slowly and in a fragmented fashion. Bakker classified these children as P-type dyslexic children (P for *perceptual*), as it was hypothesised that they very likely stick to the perceptual features of text. Similarly, it was also thought possible that some other children shift to left hemispheric processing of text too early. These children read fast, but as they tend to overlook the perceptual features they make many errors. Bakker classified these children as L-type (*linguistic*) dyslexic readers in view of their efforts to use linguistic strategies.

The implication of this for teaching has been the subject of a great deal of research, and techniques such as hemisphere-specific stimulation (HSS) have been applied. Such programmes provide for the flashing of words in the right (for P-types) or left (for L-types) visual field, in order to stimulate the left and right cerebral hemisphere. Words are spoken to the right ear of P-dyslexics (left hemisphere stimulation) while the other ear is listening to non-vocal music, and to the left ear of L-dyslexics (right hemisphere stimulation) while the other ear is listening to non-vocal music.

Hemisphere-alluding stimulation (HAS) is a technique that provides the reader with phonetically and syntactically demanding text for P-types in order to stimulate left hemispheric processing, and the reading of perceptually demanding text in order to stimulate right hemispheric processing. This model has been applied in a number of research studies and in practice in many countries (Robertson, 2000; Robertson and Bakker, 2002).

NATURE OF READING

It should be recognised, however, that reading is a holistic activity. This means that in order to engage successfully in the reading process the learner must utilise a range of cognitive and learning skills. Thus, reading depends on:

- the use of skills associated with the verbal and auditory domain, such as language knowledge and language use;
- the perceptual and spatial domain in relation to letter and word recognition;
- segmentation of words and sentences;
- contextual factors that may relate to the reader's previous knowledge and cognitive development.

The reader not only reads for meaning and for accuracy but also for 'thought'. This means that aspects including personality, experience and imagination are all related to the holistic learning activity of reading.

For the teacher the implication of this is that the learner needs to be considered as an individual in relation to reading. It is important to ensure that the general context is appropriate and suited to the individual's style and interests. Interest level, organisation of learning and careful balance between group and individual attention are important factors in the development and integration of skills necessary for reading.

The most popular methods used by teachers in the teaching of reading include the following:

- phonic;
- look and say;
- language experience.

PHONIC MODEL

The phonic method highlights the importance of phonology and the sounds of letters and letter combinations (Figure 2.2).

There are a number of structured phonic programmes in existence that teach children to distinguish the 44 phonemes or sound units of English, by using a variety of strategies. These strategies may include colour-coding and marks to indicate short or long sounds.

Although phonic programmes are structured, and structure is beneficial for children with specific learning difficulties, there are also difficulties associated with such programmes. The most important of these include the possibility that:

- they may increase the burden on children's short- and long-term memories by increasing what the child needs to remember;
- there are still words that need to be taught as sight vocabulary because they do not fall into the 'sound blending' category, such as 'one' and 'many'.

Phonics Checklist

Consonants

	Initial	Final
s		
m		
r		
t		
b		
f		
n		
p		
d		
h		
c /k/		
g /g/		
j		
l		
k		
v		
w		
z		
c /s/		
g /j/		
qu		
y		

	Final Only
ck	
x	
ss	
ll	
tt	
ff	
bb	
dd	
pp	

Short Vowels

CVC words

a	
e	
i	
o	
u	

Blends

	Initial
bl	
cl	
fl	
pl	
br	
dr	
gr	
tr	
cr	
fr	
pr	
gl	
sl	
sn	
sp	
st	
sw	
sc	
sk	

	Final
ft	
lp	
mp	
nd	
nk	
nt	
pt	
sk	
sp	
st	

Consonant Digraphs

sh	
ch	
th	
wh	
ph	

Long Vowels

CVCe words

a	
e	
i	
o	
u	

y as a Vowel

/e/ (bunny)	
/i/ (by)	

Vowels followed by r

ar	
or	
er	
ir	
ur	

Silent Letters

Initial		Final	
kn		-tch	
wr		-dge	
gh		-gh	
sc		-lk	
gn			

Vowel Digraphs

ai (paid)	
ay (pay)	
oa (boat)	
ee (tree)	
oe (toe)	
oi (join)	
oy (joy)	
ew (chew)	
ou (cloud)	
ou (soup)	
au (haul)	
aw (saw)	
ea (preach)	
ea (deaf)	

Vowel digraphs, cont.

ow (crow)	
ow (cow)	
oo (boot)	
oo (hook)	
ie (pie)	
ie (thief)	
ey (they)	
ey (valley)	
ei (ceiling)	
ui (build)	
ui (fruit)	

Prefixes

dis	
un	
re	
im	
in	
mis	
pre	

Suffixes

-ful	
-ly	
-less	
-ness	
-able	
-ible	
-ion	
-ment	
-er	
-or	
-en	

Vowels in Spelling Patterns

ind (bind)	
ild (wild)	
igh (high)	
old (cold)	
olt (colt)	
ost (host)	
ost (cost)	

Figure 2.2 Phonic checklist (reproduced by permission of Educators Publishing Service (31 Smith Place, Cambridge, MA (800) 225-5750, www.epsbooks.com); from Chall and Popp, (1996).

Phonic methods can help children who have an obvious difficulty in mastering and remembering sound blends and vowel digraphs and have difficulty in synthesising them to make a word. At the same time they present additional learning that may be seen to be meaningless and out of context. Some difficulty may be identified in merging the two components (i.e., knowledge of sound and knowledge of language) to facilitate a meaningful reading experience.

Chall and Popp (1996) emphasise the need to teach phonics and argue that if taught well it is highly meaningful—through phonics children can get close to the sound of a word and through that to the meaning of the word. They suggest a systematic phonics approach from pre-school with related activities set within a total reading programme.

Frith (1995) emphasises the nature of the phonological 'core variable' in literacy learning and particularly how it is associated with dyslexia. The Theoretical Causal Model (Frith, 1995) highlights the distinctiveness of phonological competence by focusing on three levels for assessing phonological difficulties: biological observations about brain functioning, at the cognitional level in relation to the hypothetical constructs of intellectual ability and phonological processing ability, and at the behavioural level in relation to performance in assessments such as phonological awareness tests, naming speed tests, and non-word, reading and spelling tests.

Support for the phonological core variable model as an explanation of the difficulties associated with dyslexia has led to illuminative research activity and the development of phonological skills training programmes (Reason and Frederickson, 1996; Hatcher et al., 1994; Iversen and Tunmer, 1993; Wilson and Frederickson, 1995).

LOOK-AND-SAY MODEL

Look-and-say methods emphasise exposure to print on the grounds that children will become familiar with words and build up a sight vocabulary with increased exposure. The emphasis is therefore on meaningful units of language rather than sounds of speech (Figure 2.3). This type of method therefore requires attractive books that can become progressively more demanding. The use of flashcards and pictures can be used in the initial stages. The method, however, assumes a good memory for shapes of letters and words as well as the ability to master many of the irregularities of spelling and sound–symbol correspondence. This, of course, may be difficult for children with dyslexic difficulties, particularly since their memory may be weak and can rapidly become overloaded. Some elements of the phonic approaches can accompany most look-and-say methods.

Indeed, Chall and Popp (1996) suggest that a good phonics programme needs to pay attention to sight recognition and that fluent reading depends on both automatic sight recognition and the application of phonic knowledge.

LANGUAGE EXPERIENCE MODEL

Language experience methods focus on the use of language, both oral and written, as an aid to learning to read through various modes of language enrichment. This helps the reader develop important language concepts and schemata, which in turn help to bring meaning to print. Although the child may have a decoding problem the experience gained in language can help to compensate for this and bring some

041456

THE PHONEMES OF THE ENGLISH LANGUAGE

Vowels (20)		Consonants (24)	
Symbol	Sound (or value)	Symbol	Sound (or value)
aɪ	try - write	b	back - rubber
aʊ	noun - now	d	day - rudder
ɑ	father	dʒ	judge - George - raj
ɒ	wash - odd	ð	this - other
æ	cat - trap	f	few - puff
eɪ	day - steak - face	g	got - bigger
əʊ	go - goat	h	hot
ɛ	get	j	yet
ɛə	fair - square	k	car - key - clock - trekked - quay
ɜ	her - stir - word - nurse	l	lip
i	he - see	m	much - hammer
ɪ	ship	n	now - runner
ɪə	hear - here	ŋ	sing
o	force	p	pen - pepper
ɔ	north - war	r	round - sorry
ɔɪ	noise - toy	s	see - missed
u	lunar - pool	ʃ	ship - mission
ʊ	foot - put	t	ten
ʊə	pure	tʃ	church - latch
ʌ	bud - blood - love	θ	three - heath
		v	very
		w	will
		z	zeal
		ʒ	decision - treasure

(Total = 44)

Figure 2.3   The phonemes of the English language (reproduced by permission of Whurr Publications; from Doyle, 1996).

meaning to the text. This model engages the child in the process of going from thought to speech and then to encoding in print and from print to reading.

Ehri (1999), however, suggests that there are three essential interrelated ingredients in the knowledge base for teachers that helps to inform them in making decisions on reading instruction. These are (1) knowledge about the reading process, (2) knowledge about teaching methods and how these facilitate the reading process and (3) knowledge about observational procedures to identify the processes readers are facilitating and the processes they have difficulty with. Therefore, knowledge of the reading process is important, but it is equally important to relate this knowledge to classroom practices and particularly to observing how children relate to the reading process in the class. Clay (1985) has devoted a considerable part of the assessment component of the reading recovery programme to analysing children's reading behaviours.

PRE-READING ACTIVITIES

There is considerable evidence to suggest that pre-reading activities can help facilitate the reading process. Such activities as well as developing pre-reading skills help to develop essential skills in comprehension and the development of schema. This latter aspect is particularly important as this can provide the reader with a general understanding of the text and help to relate this to previous learning. Mommers (1987), in fact, argues that conceptual development is the most powerful predictor of success in reading.

Reading is interactive, as it combines the reader's background experience and previous knowledge with the 'new' text to be read. This interaction provides the reader with meaning and interpretation. Reading, therefore, is an interaction of previous knowledge involving the use of semantic and syntactic cues and accuracy in the decoding of print. It is important that in teaching reading all these aspects are considered. It is likely the child with specific learning difficulties will find this interactive process difficult as his efforts and cognitive capacities are directed to either mechanically decoding the print or obtaining the meaning from print—the simultaneous interaction of these processes is not easily accomplished.

Two key elements of reading, therefore, are the understanding of print and the message (purpose) of the print (Box 2.5). They both have to be carefully considered in the selection and development of reading programmes and strategies for children with specific learning difficulties.

THE READING DEBATE

The teaching of reading has been subject to historical debate. Theories and methods have been reviewed and revised, often following the revelation of dismal and dis-

UNDERSTANDING OF PRINT	PURPOSE OF PRINT
• Alphabet skills	• Semantic understanding
• Organisation of letters and words	• Vocabulary skills
• Visual features of letters and words	• Use of inferences
• Phonological skills	• Comprehension skills
• Word rules	• Prediction skills
• Understanding of syntax	• Concept and schema-building

Box 2.5   Reading skills.

appointing attainment scores in national surveys. The Head Start Programme in the USA and the resultant DISTAR approach (Direct Instruction System of Teaching Arithmetic and Reading) to the teaching of reading emanated from such concerns and alarm over low standards of literacy.

The issue of reading standards is still a national concern and a national debate. Turner (1991) cites the concern over reading standards as a phenomenon that can be largely explained by the trend from phonic instruction to that of whole language, language experience and 'real' books. This argument gains some credence from the widely accepted view that beginning readers need to possess at least a basic knowledge of phonological skills before they can effectively benefit from enrichment through literacy and associated language activities. Soler (2002) suggests that much of the debate that resulted in the literacy wars, which received considerable coverage in the literature on reading from the 1970s on, was a consequence of the increase in scientific procedures to measure progress and the increasing interest in international comparisons in literacy levels.

Wray (1991), however, challenges this view by arguing that the evidence for suggesting that a decline in reading standards is due to the move toward a whole-language approach is not strong. He suggests that the whole-language movement is not practised widely enough to account for such a decline in reading standards. He further suggests that the criteria for assessing reading attainment needs to be questioned since they raise the fundamental point, 'What is reading?'

At the same time it might be argued, 'What is whole-language?' Bergeron (1990) attempted to obtain a consensual definition of whole-language from the literature and found whole-language was defined as an approach, a philosophy, an orientation, a theory, a theoretical orientation, a programme, a curriculum, a perspective on education and an attitude of mind. It is difficult either to promote or to criticise a movement when it is so loosely defined.

To attempt to find the positive aspects of this loose interpretation called 'whole-language' one can look for some common factors in Bergeron's responses. Adams (1990b) argues that some commonalities include:

- construction of meaning from text;
- developing and explaining the functional dimensions of text;
- pupil-centred classrooms;
- integration of language arts.

These points can be complementary to any education system and might be described as the flip side of the whole-language movement. The other side, promoted by Smith (1971, 1973) and Goodman (1976), suggests that skilful readers do not process individual letters, spelling–sound translations are irrelevant for reading and it is therefore not necessary to teach spellings and sounds.

Smith (1971) therefore argues that phonics teaching should not be emphasised because the child has to learn phonic rules by himself and can only do this through experience in reading. Thus, phonics teaching, according to Smith, can lead to too deliberate decoding and as a result the meaning of the text will be lost. He argues that decoding is a classroom-induced behaviour, not a natural one, and that skilled and even beginning readers only use it to a limited extent.

There are considerable arguments against this (Adams, 1990a; Turner, 1991) centring on the need for children to read words before they can obtain meaning from a text. Adams (1990a), in fact, argues that automaticity develops from actually reading words and not by ignoring or guessing them.

This view is supported by researchers and educationalists in other countries. Adamik-Jászò (1995) describes the Hungarian experience as based on reading programmes focusing on the oral language development of the child. This indicates that phonemic awareness is an essential prerequisite of reading instruction. Studies by Johnston et al. (1995) comparing the book experience approach in New Zealand with a systematic phonics approach in Scotland showed that children in the phonics programme were significantly better at reading non-words and had significantly superior reading comprehension.

Similarly, in the USA Ehri (1995a) suggests that for sight word reading to develop, learners must acquire and apply knowledge of the alphabetic system. She asserts that a weakness in the whole-language approach is the absence of systematic phonics instruction at the early stages. Attention is not paid to the need for young children to master the alphabetic system through learning letter shapes and names, sounds and letter correspondences, and blending sounds into words. Many children do not acquire these skills merely through exposure to print.

The situation, however, is not without counter-argument, which emphasises the need to engage the beginning reader with a balanced reading programme. For example, Stainthorp (1995) reports on a study that suggests that top-down, context-driven strategies can modify performance in reading. She accepts, however, that the beneficial effects of context are partly dependent upon children having developed some decoding skills and the skills required for decoding should not be left to chance. This view is reiterated by Turner (1995), who suggests that children learn to read by being taught, although he suggests that the component skills of reading are initially learned independently.

Smith (1993), however, illustrates how reading in fact relies on a combination of word-centred and meaning-centred approaches, and therefore assessment of reading clearly requires to account for these two aspects in order fully to assess reading and evaluate reading programmes. Smith, in fact, contends that the important point is that a reading approach should be clear and have a 'firm sense of purpose'. Teachers should be aware of the approach they are using and why they are using it.

Bryant (1994) contends that both forms of linguistic knowledge, constituent sounds and language experience, play an important part in children's acquisition and development of reading and writing skills. He reports on a longitudinal study in which children's scores in phonological tasks predicted the progress they made in learning about letter–sound associations, and that scores in semantic and syntactic tasks were good predictors of children's ability to use context and decipher difficult words within a meaningful context. Bryant concludes that each form of linguistic knowledge makes an independent and specific contribution to the reading process, particularly since the children's scores in the phonological task did not predict the children's success in the use of context and, similarly, scores in the semantic and syntactic tasks were not significant in predicting phonological skills.

Clearly, a balanced approach is necessary when looking at the teaching of reading. Both the phonic method and the whole-language movement have many commendable aspects—both should be utilised in relation to the needs of the individual reader.

Welch and Freebody (2002) suggest that psychology, human development and educational measurement have been the disciplines that have traditionally informed our understanding of how to teach reading, and this has assumed that the teaching of reading is politically neutral and objectively quantifiable. However, according to Wearmouth et al. (2003) this view has been countered. They suggest drawing on the work of Welch (1991) on cross-disciplinary studies that draws upon history, politics, linguistics and economics. These studies counter this traditional view of the teaching and evaluation of literacy and link them to differing dominant visions of what literacy is for and how we must teach it. The implication is that reading and literacy practices not only meet cultural and social needs but also actually shape how cultures develop.

Welch and Freebody (2002) suggest that there are some general aspects to reading debates across national and international contexts. These include concern about literacy standards and particularly declining standards (slide hypothesis), and the increase in demands for literacy competencies for effective civil, social and cultural functioning in our society have perhaps created the misleading impression of a decline in literacy standards.

It should however be noted that children with dyslexic difficulties usually have considerable difficulty in phonological awareness and, resultantly, in acquiring alphabetic and phonic knowledge. This, therefore, needs to be considered in the development of a balanced programme for dyslexic children.

READING STRATEGIES

Ehri (2002) suggests that teachers need to monitor beginning readers' progress in acquiring letter knowledge and phonemic awareness to make sure that it is occurring for each child. This is particularly important in the early stages because there is considerable variability among children in the rate of development of reading skills. Ehri suggests even at this early stage that extra teaching time is required for children who enter school without letter knowledge and phonemic awareness or for those children who experience some difficulty acquiring these skills. She suggests teaching the major grapheme–phoneme correspondences, vowel correspondences, how to segment pronunciations into the full array of phonemes and how to match these up to graphemes in the spellings of words to fully analyse words.

There are many activities that can be utilised to support a structured phonics programme. Among the most appropriate of these is the use of games and structured activities to reinforce a particular teaching point. Many of these games and activities can be developed by the teacher, although there are some excellent examples available commercially. An example of an onset and rime game is shown in Figure 2.4.

There is now some evidence of groups of teachers utilising their own resources and developing specific phonological programmes for their own particular context. One successful example of this is the Phonological Awareness Programme for Primary One Classes (Hunter et al., 1996). This is a six-week programme that

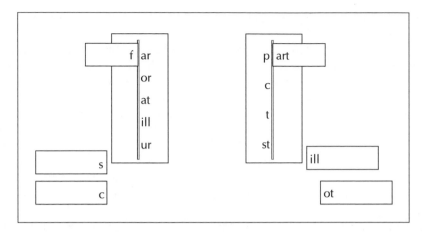

Figure 2.4 Word slides (for any number of players). Make slides from cardboard as in the illustrations. Let the pupils experiment with different onsets and rimes (reproduced by permission of Stass Publications from Gorrie and Parkinson, 1995).

focuses on syllable segmentation, rhyming skills, alliteration and resources. An example of Week 1 is shown in Box 2.6.

Other strategies that can be used are those that rely on the use of context. Readers can utilise two principal types of context:

- *syntactic context*—the grammatical structure of sentences and clues from prefixes, punctuation, word endings and word order;
- *semantic context*—the meaning of words and the meaningful relations between words.

Syntactic context helps the reader predict the written word. If the child is reading only key words he or she will not be able to draw on syntactic context for meaning.

Snowling (2000, 2002) refers to the triangle model of reading (Seidenberg and McClelland, 1989) and the connectionist model (Plaut et al., 1996), which highlight the connections between orthography and phonology, and the connections between these aspects and semantics stemming from the context (Figure 2.5).

Snowling (2002) suggests that the semantic pathway of dyslexic readers operates normally and although dyslexic children tend not to be fluent readers they can show extensive use of comprehension-monitoring strategies and self-correction to ensure they have understood what they have read. The study by Nation and Snowling (1998), which compared the ability of dyslexic readers and poor comprehenders, showed that in the context condition the dyslexic children fared best, which highlighted the view that dyslexic children benefited more from context than both a younger control group matched for reading age and poor comprehenders. Nation and Snowling therefore suggest that dyslexic readers who have decoding difficulties may be able to compensate by relying on contextual cues to support the decoding process.

Semantic or contextual context relates to the meaning of words and how they

SYLLABLE SEGMENTATION

CIRCLE GAME—It is important to begin at this level to develop listening and organisational skills. The children sit in a circle and the group leader starts the game by clapping once. Each child in turn claps his or her hands once, progressing round the circle. As the children become more confident the clapping patterns can become more complex.

CLAPPING NAMES—Each child is encouraged to clap the number of syllables in his or her name. Compare the number of syllables in each child's name. Ensure the children can clap and say the syllables together. If they have all coped with this the leader will clap a child's name without saying whose it is. The children try to identify whose name was clapped and stand up if their name matches the pattern.

RHYMING SKILLS

NURSERY RHYMES—Each child will be given the opportunity to recite a familiar nursery rhyme chosen from a picture. The leader will already have chosen one of the rhymes and written it out with the rhyming words missing. Each of the words should be written on a separate piece of card. The leader then recites the rhyme asking the children to fill in the missing word. Allow the children to draw a picture for the rhyme.

RECOGNISING RHYME—Two objects will be placed on the table and the children have to decide whether they rhyme or not.

(Suggested objects: cat–hat, snake–cake, egg–peg, bear–chair, pie–tie, box–socks, doll–ball, map–cap)

ALLITERATION

FEELY BAG—In the bag will be pairs of objects that start with the same sound. Each child will take an object out of the bag and say what it is. The group will then decide what sound it starts with. As each child pulls out subsequent objects he or she will have to decide if it makes a pair with the one he or she already has. The child with most pairs is the winner.

(Suggested objects for ten pairs: ball–bell, pen–pear, car–cat, game–goose, doll–dice, tape–teddy, fan–fish, sock–soup, money–marble, net–nine)

RESOURCES

Nursery rhymes and pictures. A rhyme written with the rhyming words omitted and cards with these words. Paper and pens. Pairs of objects for recognising rhyme. Feely bag and objects.

Box 2.6 Week 1 of the Phonological Awareness Programme for Primary One Classes (reproduced by permission of PADG, Bonnington Primary School, from Hunter et al., 1996).

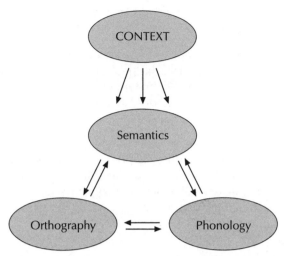

Figure 2.5   The triangle model of reading (reproduced by permission of BPS; from Snowling, 2002).

convey messages. This acts as a powerful aid to reading, and many readers with poor decoding skills can rely, perhaps too much, on the use of semantic context. Using inferences and even accurate guessing can be a powerful aid to dealing with the written word. It is important, therefore, that learners develop skills in using inferences and identifying the main theme and points in a particular story.

Context, therefore, as a reading strategy can be important and is evident in the following ways:

- within the sentence—before and after the word being read;
- within the text—before and after the sentence being read;
- within the reader—entire store of knowledge and experience.

To utilise fully the benefits of contextual reading it is also important for the reader to have a stock of sight words in order that the context can be accurately obtained. For example, it has been argued by the proponents of the language experience approach that, instead of helping children build up a stock of sight words in order to read, perhaps teaching should be directed to help children read in order to build up a stock of sight words. This would mean that sight words can be built up gradually within the context of reading itself.

It is interesting to note that the 220 words on the Dolch list—that is, the most commonly used words—make up around 75% of the words in primary reading materials (Chall and Popp, 1996).

A classic dilemma is exemplified here between encouraging, indeed insisting on, reading accuracy of all the words and accepting the accurate reading of keywords that should be sufficient through the use of semantic cues for comprehension acquisition. The reading of every word, although it may help the reader obtain the full use of the benefits of syntactic cues, can restrict the reader's use of prediction and inferences because attention and concentration are absorbed in accurate decoding.

Although accuracy may help aid comprehension, an understanding of the text is possible without full accuracy. Therefore, if the child has difficulty with accuracy, it is important that efficient use of semantic context is encouraged; although, in the pursuit of this, accuracy should not be totally ignored, but carefully considered alongside the need for efficient use of the semantic cues available.

Contextual strategies can be summarised thus:

- words are easier to identify in context than in isolation;
- beginning readers can often identify words in context that they cannot identify in isolation;
- to identify words we use preceding syntactic and semantic cues to predict what might be coming next;
- graphophonemic cues can help to identify words;
- the syntactic and semantic context can help to confirm or correct these identifications.

THE LITERACY EXPERIENCE

In an evaluation of instructional support programmes in the USA, Walmsley and Allington (1995) conclude that:

> *Poor readers have historically experienced a curriculum quite different from that experienced by better readers ... Low-achieving readers are more likely to be asked to read aloud than silently, to have their attention focused on word recognition rather than comprehension, to spend more time working alone on low level worksheets than on reading authentic texts, and to experience more fragmentation in their instructional activities.*

Au and Raphael (2000) make a strong case for supporting the literacy development of a diverse range of students with both age-appropriate and reading-level-appropriate materials. They suggest that 'teaching reading carries with it two obligations. On the one hand, we must make sure that all students are taught at an instructional level, within their zone of proximal development so that they make appropriate progress each year. On the other hand regardless of reading level, we must engage students of every age in critical thinking using age-appropriate materials' (p. 152). This has implications for dyslexic children and for motivation and positive attitudes toward the nature of literacy. Eames (2002) reports on successes despite dyslexic pupils' difficulties with written language—the children in the study reported motivation in reading about their own interests, which included car magazines, sport, history and warfare.

There is now a considered opinion that literacy can be an agent of change, and the thrust of this chapter has indicated that literacy is much broader than reading alone. Literacy has been presented in terms of a socially constructed phenomenon embedded within the cultural context (Eames, 2002; Wray, 2002; Vygotsky, 1978; Bruner, 1986). It therefore stands to reason that the teaching of literacy should consider both the diversity of the children being taught and the cultural and social implications of literacy. Moreover, the cognitive and critical thinking aspects of literacy should also be considered.

The experience of language and of learning is vital for a critical appreciation of literacy, and it is therefore vital that groups such as dyslexic children should not be overlooked as they need to obtain the broader perspectives offered by literacy to appreciate different societies and cultures. Ideally, this should be received through reading and careful provision of age-appropriate reading material. But, if this is not feasible the social, cultural and cognitive implications of literacy should be achieved through some other medium—discussion, film or through listening. Similarly, assessment needs to reflect and capture this broad view of literacy and measure appropriate outcomes. Eames (2002) suggests that these factors give rise to a number of key implications for practice. These include:

- the notion of a broad definition of literacy that stresses higher order functions and critical thinking;
- the recognition that literacy is not simply a single ability or process, but rather the symbiotic interaction of abilities and learning processes;
- the need for well-thought-out teaching programmes that reflect a broad definition of literacy and that are responsive to dyslexic children's interests and preferred learning styles;
- teaching materials and literature should reflect philosophies of teaching and need to be both age- and reading-level appropriate.

A balanced view, therefore, of the teaching of literacy needs to include constructivist approaches to learning and literacy where the teacher is the key agent. Teaching programmes should therefore emphasise a range of interactive and reflective teaching methods that engage the learner in metacognitive processes to promote critical thinking and the social and cultural factors that enrich the learning and the life of readers.

NATIONAL LITERACY STRATEGY

Framework for Teaching and the 'Literacy Hour'

The *Framework for Teaching* (DfEE, 1998) followed on from the release of the National Literacy strategy which was launched in August 1997. The Framework came into operation under a quasi-statutory status in all state primary schools in England in September 1998. This document set out the teaching objectives in literacy for pupils from reception to Year 6. It was this document that set out the format of a Literacy Hour as a daily period of time throughout the school that would be dedicated to 'literacy teaching time for all pupils' (DfEE, 1998, p. 8). The Hour was intended to cover both reading and writing and was to take the form of an introduction of 30 minutes, 20 minutes of independent work and a 10-minute plenary (see DfEE, 1998, p. 9), which has been reproduced in Box 2.7.

Whole class (15 minutes approximately): KS1 and KS2—shared text work (a balance of reading and writing).

Whole class (15 minutes approximately): KS1—focused word work; KS2—a balance over the term of focused word work or sentence work.

Group and independent work (20 minutes): KS1—independent reading, writing or word work, while the teacher works with at least two ability groups each day on guided text work (reading or writing).

Whole class (10 minutes approximately): KS1 and KS2 reviewing, reflecting, consolidating teaching points and presenting work covered in the lesson.

Box 2.7   What is the Literacy Hour? (from DfEE, 1998, p. 9).

SUMMARY

Although it is generally accepted that dyslexia is more than a reading difficulty (Fawcett, 2002), there is still little doubt that literacy is a crucial element of dyslexia and indeed in success at school. The school curriculum is dominated by the need to acquire literacy skills, and without these skills children can be placed at a marked disadvantage throughout school. Additionally, it has been shown that literacy can have significan socio-cultural as well as cognitive implications (Wearmouth et al., 2003). The acquisition of literacy, therefore, is necessary for the development of learning and life skills.

   The importance of literacy is highlighted by Welch and Freebody (2002), who argue that, 'literacy education is at the centre of debates about society and instruction, in and out of school . . . and is a site from which to view the shifting fortunes of contesting interests; public and private . . . host communities and ethnic minorities and increasingly school, work-place and market-place. Further these contests often target the issue of standards of literacy, rather than, say, the methods or the materials of literacy education' (p. 62). It is precisely this situation that can disadvantage the child with dyslexia. Governments' demands for higher overall levels of literacy achievement, while on the surface commendable, can be sought at the expense of failing to acknowledge the specific methods needed for children with specific literacy difficulties. As this chapter has shown there is more to literacy development than an increase in reading age. Eames (2002) pinpoints this when she reports that governments are essentially responding to the rising demands for literacy and not to the declining absolute standards of literacy. She argues that, 'the educational community needs to be aware that these higher demands may be unrealistic at certain developmental stages . . . (we need to) be reasonable in our expectations of pupils literacy performances and not overdriven by market forces' (pp. 336–337). It is important therefore to ensure that children with dyslexia who may require specific teaching approaches are not casualties of such market forces. The implications of this is that literacy is more than a single ability or process and should be viewed from a broader perspective. The perspective should include critical thinking skills, metacognitive processes as well as the family and socio-cultural needs. Teaching programmes for literacy therefore need to reflect this broader conceptualisation and need to consider the individual pupil's cognitive, social and cultural needs as well as the need to achieve higher attainment levels as might be measured by conventional tests. But the importance of the cognitive, social and cultural factors that can be associated with literacy development should not be lost in the increasing desire, particularly among politicians and policy-makers, for quantitative data on literacy levels.

This chapter therefore has looked at some principles in the acquisition of literacy by focusing on reading and has examined a variety of approaches by discussing some of the problems children with dyslexia may display in relation to reading. Since the concept of dyslexia is essentially a multifaceted one with neurological, psychological and educational perspectives, it follows that the teaching of reading should be flexible and should consider the child's learning difficulties and preferences, in the educational context. Clearly, no one approach can be singled out and a combination of methods involving the teaching of sight words, phonics and context is preferable. At the same time, one must also look at what the child brings to the situation and have some knowledge of the child's background knowledge and preferred learning styles and strategies. All of these aspects are important to facilitate the acquisition of literacy.

Chapter 3

The Acquisition of Literacy: Spelling and Writing

SPELLING

WHY IS SPELLING DIFFICULT?

Many children with dyslexia find spelling more difficult than reading, and this can often persist well into adulthood. To find the reason for this we need to look at the theoretical background to spelling and from that identify the reasons why children with dyslexia can find spelling quite challenging. There is little doubt that the spoken language system, how aware the child is of language and the components of language influence the development of spelling. There is also considerable evidence that children with dyslexia have difficulty with the language system, particularly phonological awareness, and the relationship between sound and symbol. Furthermore, Snowling (2000) suggests that there is less likelihood that children with dyslexia can utilise compensatory strategies with spelling as successfully as they can with reading. This would indicate that the teaching of spelling, particularly the language aspects of sounds, and the components of words are extremely important to successful spelling.

Snowling (2000) also suggests that the evidence on the development of spelling through exposure to written language in reading shows that this in itself is not enough for efficient spelling. Factors such as phonological awareness, knowledge of syntax and the syntactic function of words as well as meaning all have a role to play in the development of spelling skills. It is not surprising, therefore, that children with dyslexia consistently have difficulty with spelling, particularly as they often learn to read through the use of contextual strategies rather than phonological systems and because they cannot utilise context as successfully in spelling as in reading. This can cause some difficulty as they have to rely on their knowledge of phonic rules, letter strings and word rules. Additionally, they have to be aware of the initial sounds of the word from memory, and this can also cause some difficulty.

Spelling, therefore, can be a difficult processing operation for many—it is more difficult to use context, it requires the need to be familiar with phonological representations and the correspondence between phoneme and grapheme. Spelling places demands on the memory and because it is a written activity it can also place demands on mental operations involved in the kinaesthetic factors associated with integrating writing with a mental activity such as spelling. Many of these factors are challenging for dyslexic children, and it is not unusual for children with dyslexia to be more advanced in reading than in spelling.

SYSTEMS INVOLVED IN SPELLING

Phonological Systems

Bradley and Bryant (1991) indicated that there is a strong relationship between children's phonological awareness at Age 4 and their spelling (and reading) achievement at Age 8. Snowling (1994) highlighted the nature of dyslexic children's spelling errors and showed that there was a significant difference in the nature of the spelling errors in dyslexic children compared with a control group. The dyslexic children showed more 'phonetically unacceptable' errors than the control group. In other words the errors of the dyslexic group may not have been recognisable as the word because of a lack of phonetic similarity. This implies that the dyslexic children in this group did not have developed phonological representation, but were using letter-naming strategies to spell phonologically regular words.

Spelling and Speech

Snowling et al. (1992) analysed in detail the spelling errors of a dyslexic child in relation to the connections between spelling and speech and found difficulties were experienced with distinguishing between the voiced/voiceless sounds such as 'b' and 'p' and 'g' and 'k' in his spelling. Snowling (2000), therefore, suggests that the absence of a sound pattern of spoken words results in a lack of a framework on which to hang information needed for accurate spelling.

Visual Systems

Seymour and McGregor (1984) showed how visual difficulties can contribute to the spelling pattern of dyslexic children, particularly visual sequences. This has been confirmed by Romani et al. (1999), who found that it is possible even for spellers who have a good 'holistic' reading strategy, and therefore a good memory for visual configurations, to have a poor visual sequential memory. This means that these children would have difficulty learning letter sequences, and this can account for spelling errors.

Ehri (2002) suggests that it may be important to enhance children's interest in the spellings of new words and in discovering how letters connect to sounds systematically. Children are taught to count the phonemes in words, then to look at spellings and match up graphemes to phonemes by placing letters in Elkonin boxes that provide one space for each letter that symbolizes a separate sound. Also, teaching children to spell words by analysing and remembering how letters represent sounds in the words helps children fully analyse the graphophonemic relations needed to store words in memory.

Ehri (2002) suggests there is normally a close correlation between reading and spelling and that often the first step in adding a new sight word to memory is successfully decoding the word or reading it by analogy to a known word. She therefore argues that children need to be taught these two strategies for reading unfamiliar words. These particular strategies, Ehri believes, are easier to acquire once children reach the full alphabetic phase and once they begin to accumulate a growing number of sight words whose spellings have been fully connected to pronunciations and meanings in memory.

SPELLING SKILLS

There are many skills involved in spelling and many of these skills are those that can be difficult for the dyslexic child to acquire. It is possible to examine these skills by referring to Box 3.1, which describes the stages of spelling.

It can be noted from Box 3.1 that Stage 1 in learning to spell one of the initial prerequisites is *recognising rhymes and rhyming words*. This is usually quite challenging for dyslexic children and further emphasises the need for early intervention using an effective phonics programme with over-learning and practice at development rhyming skills. Achievement in spelling and phonics is closely associated in the early years. Chall and Popp (1996) suggest that children who are good in phonics are usually good in spelling, and those who are good in phonics and spelling are usually good in word recognition, oral reading accuracy and silent reading comprehension. This further illustrates the cumulative and associative effect of different strands of literacy acquisition. This also underlines why spelling is important of the acquisition of literacy and in the learning process.

The next skill in the model shown above is *blending spoken words into sounds*. This again emphasises the need for children to experiment with writing at an early stage as this provides practice in sounding out words as they write them and blending the sounds into words. The following skill according to the model above is *making representations of the phonic structures in writing the beginning of words*. This can be done visually as well as auditorily and again underlines the importance of multi-sensory principles, particularly in the early stages. All the skills in this initial stage of learning to spell—which all involve some competence in the early acquisition of phonological skills—are challenging for dyslexic children. Of course, what presents a greater threat is that the dyslexic difficulties at this stage may not have been identified and the child may already have feelings of failure and often a reluctance to write.

Similarly, Stage 2 of the model in Box 3.1 highlights the phonological factors associated with spelling. In this stage and the next stage children recognise the individual sounds and regular word patterns, which would involve knowledge of

STAGE 1

- Recognises rhymes and rhyming words
- Blends spoken sounds into words
- Makes some representations of phonic structures in writing the beginnings of words

STAGE 2

Can write:

- single letter sounds
- words such as *at, in, hat, sun, dog, lid, net*
- some common harder words (e.g., *have, went, likes*)

Can analyse words into costituent sounds (e.g., ch-ur-ch, re-mem-ber)

STAGE 3

Can write words with:

- consonant digraphs (eg., ch, sh, th)
- consonant blends (sl-, fr-, sk, -st, -nd, etc.)
- vowel digraphs (ea, au, ow, etc.)
- Magic e (came, mine, etc.)

Spells most common words

STAGE 4

Spells most words accurately

Knows when to use a dictionary

Box 3.1   Stages in learning to spell (reproduced by permission of Taylor & Francis; from Reason and Boote, 1994).

consonant and vowel digraphs and consonant blends. These stages relate to the spelling of common and, for the most part, regular words. Children with dyslexic difficulties do find this challenging because of the difficulty with the sound–symbol correspondence. But additionally, they find irregular words particularly challenging as these have often to be learnt visually and may not conform to the rules they are attempting to learn for conventional spellings.

This transition stage as it is often named—the stage when children move from the reliance on phonemes to a recognition of the importance of graphemic patterns—can also be challenging for dyslexic children. At this stage the spelling errors of children are often through the misuse of phonic equivalents—for example, they may put 'gait' for 'gate' because they have attempted to learn the vowel sound 'ai'. According to Marsh et al. (1980) the transitional stages of spelling can be fairly lengthy—they compared the spelling pattern of children of different ages and found that there seemed to be a ceiling for a dependency on phonological strategies at an early age—but the strategy of using analogy seemed to come later after Age 7. According to Smith et al. (1998), at the transitional stage the teacher should prioritise work on silent letters, suffixes and prefixes, and activities to encourage visual skills such as looking for small words within longer words and variations of the 'look, say, cover, write and check' method, which is discussed below.

One of the difficulties with spelling in the English language is the irregularity of many of the words. This means that children need to be aware of the phonology of the language (i.e., how the letters and sounds link together) and the orthography (i.e., the pattern of the letter strings). Because the orthography is irregular, spelling can present a difficulty to many children. Children have to understand very early on that for some words sounding out is successful, but for others they need to remember the pattern of the letter strings because the words are phonologically irregular.

SPELLING DEVELOPMENT

One of the influential studies on the development of spelling was the study conducted by Treiman (1993). This suggests that children at the very outset rely heavily on phonology. Treiman also suggests that children are aware of orthographic conventions even at an early stage. They seem to be aware of any two letters that are always grouped together; for example, 'ed' at the end of a word. This view conflicts with the stage model of spelling that suggests that the orthographic rules are not acquired until a later stage.

The developmental stages of spelling according to Smith (1994) are shown in Figure 3.1.

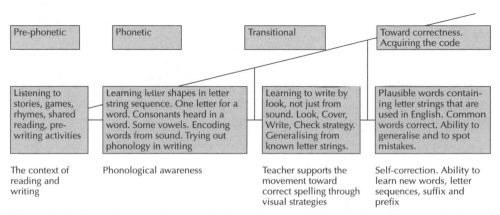

Figure 3.1   Developmental stages in learning to spell (reproduced by permission of the United Kingdom Reading Association; from Smith, 1994).

As can be seen in Figure 3.1 dyslexic children will certainly have difficulty not only with the phonetic stages but also with the transitional stage, and this requires considerable teacher support and awareness. Usually, this transitional stage would occur around the second year in school, and it would be at this stage that those children with dyslexic difficulties, whether recognised or not, will begin to be aware of their own difficulties with spelling and may begin to show a reluctance to write.

Liberman and Shankweiler (1985) have shown that a clear difference exists in the performance in phonological tasks between good and poor spellers. This implies that successful spelling is related to children's awareness of the underlying phonological structure of words. This is supported by Rohl and Tunmer (1988), who found that good spellers were better at phonemic segmentation tasks than older children matched for spelling age.

Furthermore, Bradley and Bryant (1991) showed that measures of rhyme judgement and letter knowledge in pre-school children were a good predictor of subsequent performance in spelling. Thus, children who can recognise words that sound and look alike would tend to have a good memory for spelling patterns. Indeed, Bradley and Huxford (1994) show that sound categorisation in particular plays an important role in developing memory patterns for spelling.

SPELLING POLICY

It is important that schools have policies in spelling, and ideally this policy should be seen as a whole school one—that is, not just a policy for poor spellers, but an overarching policy for all that has the mechanisms to meet the needs of all, including those with severe spelling difficulties such as the children with dyslexia. Such a policy should include some basic aims and overall rationale for the policy. In the case of spelling this is not too difficult to justify. It is indicated in the National Literacy Strategy (England and Wales) that pupils must understand the spelling system and that spelling does have a high profile in literacy or any literacy strategy—the debate, in fact, relates to how high a profile it should have and how spelling should be taught. As well as indicating the aims and rationale of a spelling policy one must also highlight the processes involved in assessment, teaching and monitoring.

SPELLING STRATEGIES

Word Lists

The use of word lists can be a successful strategy for many with some form of spelling difficulties. Word lists can be a general list composed from words commonly used by children at certain ages. Word lists can also be in the form of specific lists that focus on the child's own particular spelling difficulties. One of the difficulties

I	and	the	a	to	my	was	is
it	went	in	there	he	on	said	they
one	she	day	we	home	with	dad	so
of	me	like	had	were	at	go	going

Figure 3.2 Common words for Year 2 pupils (reproduced from Smith et al., 1998; copyright © NASEN Publications).

with using this strategy with dyslexic children is that often the spelling pattern of dyslexic children is inconsistent, therefore words not included in a list because they have been able to spell them may still be spelt wrong in some situations, such as in examinations where it may be necessary to write at speed. Smith (1995) developed a list by analysing 6000 words of creative writing from children of different age groups to identify the words commonly used. Figure 3.2 shows the common words for Year 2 pupils.

The words in Figure 3.2 according to Smith's study represented 30% of the words used by Year 2 pupils.

It may also be useful to construct a specific word list of subject-specific words and those that have similar sounds, or look similar. These can be confusing for dyslexic learners; for example 'cerebrum' and 'cerebellum'. Taking an instance in biology Howlett (2001) suggests it is useful to compile an alphabetically arranged biology spelling book for each year group. She suggests that such a spelling checklist can include other useful information such as definitions—'respiration', 'ecosystem', 'osmosis' and 'immunisation'. Additionally, the spelling book can also contain a table showing singular and plural endings such as 'vertebra' and 'vertebrae' and irregular ending such as 'stoma' and 'stomata'—these can be problematic for dyslexic children. It is usually easier for children to learn words in context, so it would be useful to have a sentence next to the word to provide a clue to its meaning as well as its spelling properties. In relation to the spelling properties, the parts of the word that are usually misspelt by the student can also be highlighted.

The benefit of this type of strategy is that it can be individualised for each child. There are many different customised and commercial strategies that can be used to help with spelling, but ideally one needs to utilise a range of approaches and strategies, as the same approach may not be effective for all. The general principles, however, of good teaching—that is, multi-sensory strategies such as visual, auditory, kinaesthetic and tactile—should not be overlooked as these help with over-learning and automaticity. The most effective way to achieve automaticity is through using the word that is being learnt in as many different forms as possible, in different subjects and different contexts.

Other spelling strategies are given in the following subsections.

Early Literacy Learning

This involves the teaching of phonological awareness at an early stage—just as in reading early phonological awareness programmes can be very cost-effective and can prevent the onset of serious spelling difficulties. This can also include work on onset and rime, vowel and consonant recognition as well as rhyming games, matching pictures, and sound and visual discrimination.

Visual Strategies

There are a number of visual strategies that can be used in spelling. In fact, Peters (1970) suggests that spelling is essentially a visual–motor activity. Some of the predominantly visual approaches are described below.

Look, Cover, Write, Check

This is a well-established strategy for spelling, and was the outcome of longitudinal research conducted by Peters (1985). Smith (1994) describes the stages in the following manner:

- *Look*—this involves active engagement of the writer looking closely at the word with the intention of reproducing it. Smith suggests that finger-tracing the word at this stage, which utilises kinaesthetic memory, can result in a stronger memory trace and enhance the chances of the child with specific difficulties remembering the visual features of the word. Bradley (1994) suggests in her 'simultaneous oral spelling' strategy that saying the letters at this initial stage can also help to reinforce the memory trace for the word. It is also important that the look stage is not skipped or rushed through before the child has had an opportunity to develop visual strategies to help memorise the visual features. Such strategies can include making visual analogies of the word by recognising the visual features and similarities of the letters and the word to other words, or acknowledging the distinctive features. For example, in the word 'window' there are a number of visual aspects that could help with memory, such as the first and last letter being the same and the distinctiveness of the letter 'w'. At this stage it is also possible to draw attention to words within words such as the word 'tent' in 'attention' and 'ask' in 'basket'.
- *Cover*—this involves visual memory and takes practice. Some children can adapt to this better than others. This type of activity lends itself very well to a game, and this can be motivating for children. Visual memory can of course be practised with a range of visual games and games and activities involving visual discrimination. For example, Crossbow Educational produce a wide range of games, such as 'Rummyword', 'Breakdown' and 'Funfish', all of which can help provide practice in visual activities that can have a spin-off for spelling. Additionally, mnemonics as well as game-type activities can be used as an aid for visual memory.
- *Write*—this is an important stage as it provides the kinaesthetic practice. Many practitioners suggest that at this stage cursive handwriting should be encouraged.

In fact, Peters (1985) suggests that there is a link between clear cursive writing and good spelling.

• *Check*—this provides the learner with some responsibility for his or her own spelling. It is important to reduce dependency on the teacher as soon as possible and to promote the activity of self-correction.

While 'look, cover, write, check' as a strategy can be very successful for many children it does place demands on memory and particularly visual memory. It is important therefore to ensure that it is suitable for the individual child and that other strategies are also considered.

Simultaneous Oral Spelling

Bradley (1989b, 1990) has shown that rhyming is a particularly useful form of categorisation for developing spelling skills and that practice in sound categorisation through nursery rhymes and rhyming word games in early language play helps spelling (Box 3.2). Many children have problems remembering 'chunks', such as 'igh' in 'sight' and 'fight'. If children cannot do this, then every word will be unique. Irregular words can also be learnt using multi-sensory techniques.

It has been shown in this chapter that phonological aspects are important in the development of reading and spelling skills. This seems to have considerable importance, particularly for dyslexic children who do not automatically relate the sounds

---

• Have the word written correctly, or made with the letters.

• Say the word.

• Write the word, spelling out each letter as it is written, using cursive script.

• The child needs to see each letter, hear its name and receive kinaesthetic feedback through the movement of the arm and throat muscles.

• Check to see if the word is correct.

• Cover up the word and repeat the process. Continue to practise the word in this way, three times a day, for one week. By this time the word should be committed to memory. However, only one word will have been learned.

• This final step involves the categorisation of the word with other words that sound and look alike. So, if the word that has been learned is 'round' the student is then shown that she or he can also spell 'ground', 'pound', 'found', 'mound', 'sound', 'around', 'bound', 'grounded', 'pounding', etc. That is, she or he has learned six, eight or more words for the effort of one.

Box 3.2 Bradley's procedure for Simultaneous Oral Spelling (reproduced by permission of Lynette Bradley, pers. commun.).

to the visual images of print. Exercises in phonological awareness are therefore of great importance, not just to assist with reading but also to help with spelling, by allowing children to learn and understand sound patterns and to recognise how these are transposed into print

Language experience approaches

Smith (1994) suggests that there is a great deal of scope for encouraging expressive writing using an adult helper to facilitate the development of language experience and spelling. She suggests that writing for communication and spelling need to be kept separate otherwise the expressive output of the writing may become inhibited through constantly checking and correcting the spelling. She suggests when children are identifying spelling errors they should first identify the mistakes and then proceed to underline them or use some other 'code'. Topping (2001), in fact, suggests actually drawing a line through the misspelling as it helps to visually reinforce the wrong spelling. Smith suggests after finding out the correct spelling the child should then proceed through the 'look, cover, write, check' process. She also suggests support for the inexperienced writer can include scribed writing, group scribed writing, an initial scribed start, collaborative writing with a more experienced writer, use of a word processor and spellchecker and using redrafting of class work as homework, rather than writing completely new material at home. Many of these strategies would be useful for children with dyslexia particularly if the writing process is seen as separate from the need for accurate spelling.

Although children do make progress with practice, this can only really effectively occur in spelling if the child has the opportunity to correct and note the correct spelling before proceeding with further work, otherwise the spelling error pattern is reinforced. It therefore requires a degree of judgement by the teacher to help the child self-correct, indicate spelling errors not noted by the child and to motivate the child to write freely irrespective of the errors. All are important and each needs to be carefully handled.

Cued Spelling

The Cued Spelling technique shares the same principles as paired reading and other peer-tutoring developments (Croft and Topping, 1992). The technique comprises 10 steps for learning and spelling, 4 points to remember and 2 reviews (see Figure 3.3). The points to remember help to consolidate the learning and the two reviews involve a daily and a weekly review. In the daily review the speller writes all the words for the day and checks them—the wrong words are then noted and the learner goes through the 10 steps again for these words.

The speller adopts the same procedure for the weekly review and identifies the wrong words. Discussion would then take place on the best approach for the learner to tackle the wrongly spelt words.

If the learner writes a word inaccurately he or she is encouraged to delete the word from memory by erasing it or boldly scoring it out. This can be particularly useful if

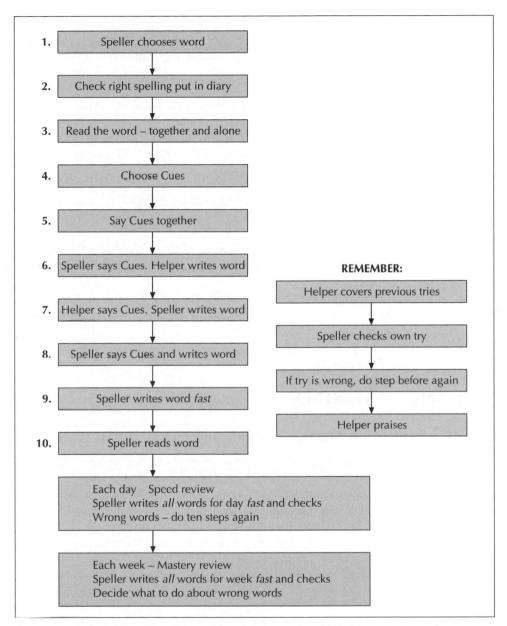

Figure 3.3 Cued Spelling: the 10 steps (reproduced by permission of Topping, 1992d, 2000, 2001; copyright © Kirklees Metropolitan Council).

the learner has a strong visual memory and the image of the incorrect word may remain and be recalled at some future point.

The cued spelling technique is highly interactive, but aims to encourage 'self-managed' learning. The technique attempts to eliminate the fear of failure through the use of prompt correction procedures. As in paired reading, modelling and praise are integral to the application of Cued Spelling. According to Topping and Watt (1992) 7-year-old children have been successfully trained in its use in about one hour, substantial progress can be made on norm-referenced spelling tests and improvements have been found in error rate and qualitative indicators in continuous free writing.

A number of studies support Topping and Watt's assertion regarding the merits of the technique (Emerson, 1988; Scoble, 1989; Harrison, 1989). Scoble (1988) describes how the technique is also used with adult literacy and provides some examples of the application of Cued Spelling in the home with spouses, parents and friends as tutors.

Oxley and Topping (1990) report on a peer-tutoring project using Cued Spelling in which eight 7- and 8-year-old pupils were tutored by eight 9-year-olds. The self-concept as a speller of both tutees and tutors showed a significant positive shift compared with a control group.

France et al. (1993) demonstrate the effectiveness of Cued Spelling, particularly in the short term, although they accept that further research on its longer term effects is still required.

The Cued Spelling technique is relatively simple to apply and the pack includes a demonstration video.

SPELLING MATERIALS

The *ACE Spelling Dictionary* (Moseley and Nicol, 1995)

This dictionary is specifically aimed at dyslexic children and can provide them with an easy and independent means of finding words at speed. Initially, students have to be taught how to use the dictionary, but there are many examples where teachers have indicated that this can be done in around three lessons (Turner, 1991). Additionally, there are activities that accompany the dictionary—ACE Spelling Activities. These consist of photocopiable worksheets with spelling activities based on the use of syllables, discriminating between different parts of speech and other activities linked to the *ACE Spelling Dictionary*. It also includes advice on the use of common word lists.

Catchwords

This set of books can be useful for observing the progression from the semi-phonetic to phonetic to the transition stage in spelling. The first book provides examples of rhyming activities, and subsequent books in the series highlight word-building and common letter patterns. The series also contains suggestions on developing a whole school spelling policy, a comprehensive word bank and guidance for involving parents.

Photocopiable Resources

There are a number of photocopiable resources for spelling usually in ring-bound files, which can be easily accessed by the teacher:

- *Exercise Your spelling* (Hodder & Stoughton).
- *Early Steps to Literacy* (Kickstart Publications).
- *Folens Spelling File* (Folens).
- *High Frequency Spelling Fun* (Timesavers).
- *Limericks, Laughs and Vowel Digraphs* (Crossbow Educational).
- *Rime Time* (Crossbow Educational).
- *Sound Beginnings* (LDA).
- *Spell It Out* (Hilda King Educational Services).
- *Spelling Rules OK* (Chalkface Publications).
- *Thrass Spelling Book* (Collins Educational).
- *Wordsnakes* (Crossbow Educational).
- *Crackerspell* (Jordanhill Publications).

All these photocopiable activities would be useful for children with dyslexia as they can be used and developed in a multi-sensory way, and because they are photocopiable they can be used repetitively interspersed with other activities, therefore promoting over-learning.

WRITING

RELATIONSHIP BETWEEN WRITING AND SPELLING

There is a wealth of research that indicates that there is a strong relationship between spelling and writing (Read, 1971; Chomsky, 1986; Moseley, 1989). In fact, Moseley (1989) suggests that lack of confidence in spelling can have a considerable detrimental effect on children's written expression. This also encourages children to sound out the words as they write them and this helps them become aware that the letters represent sounds. According to Chall and Popp (1996) the practice of writing and sounding is an excellent preparation for learning conventional spelling and phonics. Additionally, they suggest that early writing also illustrates the important principle that learning is cumulative—which means that the children need to know the alphabet letters in order to use them in writing. This in turn helps to provide children with the opportunity to practise using these letters in writing, together with the sounds of the letters.

The Importance of Writing

Both the skills involved in writing correctly formed letters and the expressive skills needed for extended and creative writing are often used as a measure of accomplishment and level of academic competence in children and young people. These skills may not be easily accessed by dyslexic children and can often place the young person with dyslexia at a disadvantage. Yet dyslexic learners can be quite creative and can have the potential to write some exceptionally creative pieces of work. This, however, is not straightforward as creative writing is not an isolated activity. Creative writing involves many other skills, particularly skills associated with sequencing, focusing on a story line, grammar, spelling and directing the responses to meet the needs of the task that has been set—in other words ensuring the written piece is both relevant and coherent.

EXPRESSIVE WRITING: THE PROCESS

There are many stages involved in the writing process. Eames (2002) suggests that children come to writing with a range of prior experiences and preconceived ideas, and many, particularly dyslexic children, view writing as hard work despite the potential to write creatively and still see it as a challenge and a chore. It almost goes without saying that it is important for pupils to associate writing with enjoyment and success.

Strategies

There are many strategies that can be utilised to make writing more meaningful and fulfilling for the dyslexic child:

- the use of themes related to the particular interest of the dyslexic child;
- examining the purpose of writing and introducing different reasons for developing a piece of writing;
- using writing to experience poetry, drama and script-writing;
- linking the writing task to the interests of the child; and
- introducing the writing task in a manner consistent with the student's learning style.

WRITING AND METACOGNITION

Eames (2002) studied the writing pattern of dyslexic children and indicated that the sample of dyslexic children studied made little use of metacognitive strategies. She reports that in mainstream classes the boys frequently displayed lack of interest, opted out and used diversion tactics. Yet, in one-to-one review/revision exercises with these pupils about their written drafts, there was increased evidence that they knew a lot about writing. They were able to comment on the application of self-correction strategies, were able to evaluate their own writing and make suggestions for improvement. Eames suggests that the important aspect related to this example is that the pupils have the ability to monitor their own work and develop their writing style, but need some initial impetus from the teacher in order to activate these skills.

The more pupils monitor their own work and utilise metacognitive strategies the more likely they are to take responsibility for their own learning. This is important and vital for children with dyslexia, who need to reflect on their own learning and be aware of how they carried out a particular piece of work and how they could utilise similar strategies in a different piece of work.

Eames (2002) suggests that this has considerable implications for teachers and for teacher education. She suggests that teachers need to:

- talk to pupils before designing and implementing programmes of work to establish pupils' interests and preferred learning styles and learning environment;
- know how to facilitate writers on the journey from initial to final draft;
- understand that the writing task will not be completed in one sitting;
- facilitate interim sessions, mid-process, where writers have an opportunity to reflect on what they have written, to discuss it, to share it and to self-monitor their work in progress; and
- engage in these practices habitually until they become part of pupils' normal practice.

Writing is a vehicle for expression, and this can influence thought and the development of concepts. Children learn through the exercise of writing, and it is therefore important that this opportunity for cognitive and metacognitive development should not be minimised for children with dyslexia. Often they may avoid writing, but writing like any other learning task can be made dyslexia-friendly.

HANDWRITING

Sometimes children are reluctant to write because they actually have a handwriting difficulty. Certainly, the use of computers and specialised computer software can help to overcome any demotivation that might arise from handwriting difficulties. Keyboard skills should in fact be learnt at as young an age as possible, especially for those with handwriting difficulties.

Nevertheless, there is a considerable amount of materials on handwriting that can help in the development of a programme for children with difficulties in forming letters. If children have extreme difficulty with pencil grip and letter formation they may have dyspraxic or dysgraphic difficulties—these are briefly described in Chapter 14 in the section on specific learning difficulties. Many handwriting programmes have been customised and developed by teachers and these can be very successful (Kiely, 1996). Alston (1993, 1996) has developed a number of programmes and some key principles in the teaching of handwriting:

- the use of a structured handwriting programme that should be used each day, even for a short time—the important point is that it should be used consistently on a daily basis;

- the use of multi-sensory methods and practice in pre-writing skills such as beads-threading, shape and pattern-copying, tracing, colouring and writing letters in sand;
- encouraging children to verbalise the nature and direction of strokes while tracing and drawing individual letters;
- allowing extra time to complete work;
- encouraging children to repeat back key points as well as to talk through tasks, as their own voice will help to direct their motor movements and serve as a useful memory aid.

One programme that is now well established is THRASS (The Teaching of Hand-writing, Reading and Spelling System), which can provide a structured handwriting programme. THRASS uses multi-sensory principles and contains pupil workbooks, as well as supplementary activities including a dedicated website with motivational activities.

Comment

It might be argued that spelling and handwriting are not as high a priority for the child with dyslexia as reading or creative writing. The difficulties associated with spelling and handwriting can be to a great extent compensated and overcome with the use of technology. While there may be an element of justification in this it is nevertheless the case that both spelling and handwriting difficulties can have an effect on self-concept and motivation, and if these difficulties are addressed at an early stage then the possibility of dealing with them effectively without relying on technology is all the greater. This should obviously be attempted in the early stages. Technology, however, can still be seen as supportive. If spelling and handwriting are still problematic as the child progresses through a school, then technology may well assume a more important role. Like any learning task that is challenging, it is crucial to seek out approaches that are fun and motivational at the appropriate level for the child and can provide opportunities for the child to observe some degree of success. This is the most meaningful and motivational factor in most learning tasks and certainly applies to spelling and writing.

Part II

Assessment

Chapter 4

Assessment: Criteria and Considerations

OVERVIEW OF CRITERIA

This chapter will provide an overview of some of the criteria that need to be considered for identification and assessment of dyslexia. The following two chapters will provide more detailed analysis of specific examples of assessment practices and processes that can be used in the identification and assessment of dyslexia. The Appendix to this book also contains comment on some further assessment tests and materials. Assessment for dyslexia, however, involves much more than selecting and administering a test. It is a dynamic process rather than a static one, and one that needs to consider a number of factors that can provide an indication of the presence of dyslexia. The assessment process should also provide an indication of the implications of the dyslexic profile for the individual, the school or college, the parents and the family, and for subject and career choice. There are therefore wide-ranging implications that can arise from an assessment for dyslexia. It is important to discuss these implications with the parents and, if appropriate, with the child. Much of the information that is needed for an assessment cannot be gathered from the administration of a basic checklist, nor indeed from a snapshot assessment using a standardised test. Assessment is a dynamic process, and ideally this process should involve a range of strategies and be conducted in the learning context and over a period of time. The use of background information can help to provide a fuller picture, but ideally the person or team conducting the assessment should have information about the curriculum and the teaching and learning context.

Some of the factors and criteria that need to be considered for an assessment include the following:

- the reasons for the assessment;
- the nature of the assessment;
- what the assessment may reveal;

- age and stage of the child;
- the learning pattern and cognitive style of the child;
- cognitive factors associated with learning and dyslexia;
- previous history;
- information from parents;
- assessment of the curriculum;
- information on attainments;
- metacognitive factors; and
- how the assessment can link with intervention and the curriculum.

Some of this information may well vary depending on the child, the school and, indeed, the country as different countries seem to operate different principles in relation to the purposes and processes of an assessment for dyslexia. It is essential, nevertheless, that assessment should be seen from different perspectives, and although information-processing/cognitive aspects may well have an important role in relation to dyslexia it is also important that other factors should be included in the assessment process.

Information-processing is a cognitive activity. This means that factors such as how information is presented (input), how the information is memorised and learnt (cognition), and how it is displayed by the learner (output), which of course can be in a written mode, are each part of the cognitive processes associated with learning. These processes are involved in learning new material and recalling and utilising material already learnt.

The factors within these components of information-processing are important in relation to dyslexia. Often children with dyslexia have difficulty in actually receiving the information—input—particularly if it is provided verbally. This can have implications for the use of standardised tests, which are often administered verbally, and the child has to process the information using the auditory modality. Similarly, there is much evidence that children with dyslexia can have difficulties in relation to cognition. Cognition essentially involves how children think and process information in order to understand it, to relate it to previous knowledge and to store it in long-term memory. Since these cognitive factors can represent difficulties often associated with dyslexia there is a tendency to focus an assessment principally on these cognitive factors. This happens particularly if there is a snapshot assessment and it is conducted outwith the child's normal learning environment. The other factor associated with dyslexia and information-processing is the output of information. It is interesting to note that often children with dyslexia do not reveal their full ability in tests because responding to test items involves immediate responses, many of which are in written form and all of which have to be delivered without any help from the examiner. Yet, children with dyslexia more often than not respond well to cues and 'information steps' to help them engage in the line of thinking that will elicit the correct response. But, in standard tests this type of help is not permitted because the norms and conventions of tests are the same for all children; this fact ignores the nature of the difficulties experienced by dyslexic children. It is therefore reasonable to suggest that a one-off, snapshot, cognitive-type assessment will not provide a full picture. It may however provide sufficient information for an experienced and trained teacher, psychologist or other professional to put forward a strong hypothesis relating to the child's processing and attainment pattern, and the connections between this and the presence of dyslexia.

It is important, therefore, to reinforce at this point the view expressed above that identification and assessment of dyslexia is a process. This process should be conducted over time and should include curriculum aspects, learning factors and observations made within the teaching and classroom environment as well as information from parents.

AIMS AND RATIONALE

There are a number of reasons that an assessment should be undertaken. It may be to identify a baseline for the child in order to identify the appropriate level of text and learning materials, or to diagnose a difficulty, to review progress and to help identify suitable teaching and learning materials. Additionally, in some countries there are statutory obligations to conduct assessments at certain age bands. This is touched on in Chapter 14 under international perspectives.

Box 4.1 highlights some of the specific aims that may be considered when conducting an assessment for dyslexia.

In some cases the assessment may confirm what the teacher already suspects, as children's strengths and weaknesses and levels of attainments may be known to the class teacher. The teacher is in daily contact with the child, and this ongoing contact provides valuable insights into the child's strengths and weaknesses.

The assessment should, however, also uncover some explanations for children's difficulties and look for particular patterns, such as errors that may be due to visual, auditory, motor, memory or some other cognitive difficulties. These may be identified as a specific pattern. The unearthing of a pattern of difficulties can help the

---

- Identification of the learner's strengths and weaknesses

- Indication of the learner's current level of performance in attainments

- An explanation for lack of progress

- Identification of aspects of the learner's performance in reading, writing and spelling, which may typify a 'pattern of errors'

- Identification of specific areas of competence

- Identification of student's learning style

- Understanding of the student's learning strategies

- An indication of specific aspects of the curriculum and curriculum activities that may interest and motivate the learner

Box 4.1 Aims of assessment.

teacher decide on the nature of the child's difficulty and so can assist in the planning of appropriate programmes of work.

Assessment, however, should aim not only to assess the child but also to assess the curriculum, to analyse which factors motivate the child and help to promote development in thinking and progress in attainments. This is what is meant by the comment made earlier that assessment is dynamic; that is, it should involve more than a description of the child's cognitive abilities and attainments, and provide a full picture to incorporate aspects about the learning situation and the learner as well. Similarly, it is important to identify the child's learning style, looking at how the learner relates to the classroom environment, the task, the other children in the class and the curriculum in general. This will be dealt with in more detail in Chapter 9 on learning styles.

It is important, therefore, to be aware of the aims of the assessment and the process that the assessment should follow. These can be used as a framework for the assessment and adapted depending on the purpose of the assessment. To develop both aims and a framework a number of key questions need to be addressed. These can be categorised in the following—what, why, how and the effect of assessment.

What?

What is one looking for when conducting an assessment?

In relation to dyslexia one may be looking for a specific pattern of cognitive difficulties, such as difficulties in organisation, sequencing, speed of processing, memory and motor difficulties. A pattern of difficulties in attainments in literacy may also be focused on, such as difficulties in phonological awareness, word recognition, spelling rules, visual errors in spelling, letter and word confusion with similar sounding words and omissions of words, parts of words and individual letters and sounds.

At the same time the focus for the assessment can also be on the curriculum, and one may be looking for an explanation as to why a particular child is having difficulty in a specific area of the curriculum and perhaps not another. For example, why may the child be experiencing difficulty in English, but not History or Geography or Science? These are questions that would need to be investigated, and this investigation is as important as individual cognitive and other child-focused assessments. For example, Dargie (2001) suggests that in order to read effectively in History, learners must be able to decode, contextualise and analyse a range of types of text such as diaries, letters, recorded oral testimony, press journalism, posters, leaflets, official documentation such as Acts of Parliament and government reports. Each textual genre, according to Dargie, can be challenging and may be couched in a specific language format that will not exactly aid comprehension. Moreover, History courses often additionally require learners to be comfortable with this variety of textual types across a range of chronological and cultural contexts. This is an example, therefore, why it is important to look at the actual demands of the curriculum as well as the abilities of the learner.

The assessment should also identify particular strategies or resources that can help to access the curriculum for a particular child, and for that reason it is important to focus part of the assessment on the actual curriculum. This in fact can be achieved through curriculum-focused teaching approaches that may have strands and targets build in to the teaching process. One such example of this is the 5-14 curriculum programme in Scotland (Crombie and Reid, 1994).

Why?

Why should an assessment be carried out and what purpose does this serve?

Although there may be a number of different reasons that an assessment is required there are usually some common factors. The assessment may be used for diagnostic purposes in order to provide information that may account for the child's difficulties in learning. At the same time the assessment may be used as a predictive tool in order to obtain some information that can help the teacher predict how the child will cope with particular aspects of the curriculum. Used in this way, however, the information from the assessment may in fact be misused since it may lead to unnecessary curricular restrictions being placed on the child. This, indeed, is one of the misuses of IQ tests since the case may arise where a child assessed as having a low IQ is disadvantaged in terms of curricular access and expectation, and, of course, this should be avoided at all costs.

The assessment may be used in a 'normative' way by comparing the child with his peers. Again some caution should be applied, although it may be useful to obtain some kind of data in relation to how the child is progressing in relation to others in the same chronological age range.

If the child has already been assessed, then further assessment can contribute to monitoring and review. This is an important element of any assessment since it assists in measuring the effects of teaching. Assessment should be linked to teaching. There can be a prescriptive element to assessment in that it may offer some suggestions for teaching approaches or programmes.

If there is a suspicion that the child may have dyslexic difficulties and the assessment is being conducted to discover if this is indeed the case, then feeding back this information, particularly to the parents, is essential. If the difficulties are to be effectively tackled then it is important that the school, parents and the child should be working collaboratively. This is particularly important as research undertaken by Heaton (1996) indicates the relief parents often experience following the many months of uncertainty prior to a formal assessment. Heaton provides a number of accounts of parents' reactions to receiving feedback that their child was dyslexic. One such account sums up quite well the concern and relief usually harboured by parents: 'What the psychologist said made a lot of sense to me. I suppose it's obvious, but I didn't think about it. His ego's bound to be fragile and that's why he is so difficult to handle. When she (the psychologist) explained all the other things about dyslexia, I began to understand what was going on better' (Heaton, 1996, p. 16). Biggar and Barr (1996) agree with this statement and suggest that mixed messages and anxieties between parents and the school can be extremely damaging for the child's self-concept.

How?

The issue of how an assessment should be conducted is an important one. It is necessary to access a range of assessment strategies and not simply opt for one particular type of assessment or test. Indeed, although there are a number of tests—'dyslexia tests'—there is actually no single test for dyslexia. In fact, Turner (1997) suggests that the best contemporary psychological assessments may draw on 20–30 individual test results. Essentially, assessment to identify dyslexia involves a process, not a test. The following two chapters will discuss how tests may be applied within the assessment process. It is important to ensure that a test, and the manner in which the results are used, is valid. Clearly, how one tackles the assessment depends to a great extent on the purpose of the assessment. For example, standardised tests, although these may be limited in terms of diagnostic information, can provide useful information with which to measure progress.

It is useful to have a battery of strategies prepared, or an assessment framework that can accommodate and be adapted to the school context. Such a framework is provided in some detail in the Report of the Task Force on Dyslexia (2001). In the report there is a Phased Process of Assessment that suggests details of procedures, tests and strategies that can be used by the teacher from Phase 1 (ages 3–5), Phase 2 (ages 5–7), Phase 3 (ages 7–12), Phase 4 (age 12 onwards). In each of the phases indicators of dyslexia are provided as well as guidance to the teacher on which aspects should be considered, what the tests should be attempting to identify as well as the possible outcomes of reviews. This aspect of the document without doubt represents a clear framework for the identification of dyslexia. An example of one of the phases is shown in Box 4.2.

It is essential to link assessment, teaching and the curriculum. Assessment, therefore, should not be conducted in isolation, but within the context of the curriculum, the child's progress within the classroom and particular learning preferences. It is, therefore, important to look at the process of learning—the strategies used by the child—in addition to the product; that is, the actual outcomes or the attainment level.

Many forms of assessment that look at attainments can be described as static, in that they test what the child can do without assistance. Assessment, however, can also be provided with an additional dynamic dimension, thus allowing the assessment process to be used more flexibly. It has been argued (Campione and Brown, 1989) that when conducting an assessment the teacher should *not* be asking, '*what can the child do?*' but '*what do I need to do to help the child successfully complete the assessment?*' The help that is necessary to facilitate the correct response from the child should be noted. Thus, the teacher is focusing on the process of the assessment not the product or the outcome of the assessment.

Effect

A consideration throughout the assessment process is the effect of the assessment—the assessment outcome for the child, the family and the school. It is important to ensure that the assessment provides information that can be readily linked to a

Many of these indicators may also be noted in students with other possible learning difficulties:

- Is slow to learn the connection between letters and sounds (alphabetic principle)

- Has difficulty separating words into sounds, and blending sounds to form words (phonemic awareness)

- Has difficulty decoding single words (reading single words in isolation)

- Has difficulty repeating multi-syllabic words (e.g., *emeny* for *enemy*; *pasghetti* for *spaghetti*)

- Has poor word-attack skills, expecially for new words

- Confuses small or 'easy' words: *at/to*; *said/and*; *does/goes*)

- May make constant reading and spelling errors including:

    —letter reversals (e.g., *d* for *b* as in *dog* for *bog*)

    —letter inversions (e.g., *m* for *w*)

    —letter transpositions (e.g., *felt* and *left*)

    —word reversals (e.g., *tip* for *pit*)

    —word substitutions (e.g., *house* for *home*)

- Reads slowly with little expression or fluency (oral reading is slow and laborious)

- Has more difficulty with function words (e.g., *is*, *to*, *of*) than with content words (e.g., *cloud*, *run*, *yellow*)

- May be slow to learn new skills, relying heavily on memorising without understanding

- Reading comprehension is below expectation due to poor accuracy, fluency and speed

- Reading comprehension is better than single-word reading

- Listening comprehension is better than reading comprehension

- Has trouble learning facts

- Has difficulty planning or organising

- Uses awkward pencil grip

- Has slow and poor quality handwriting

- Has trouble learning to tell the time on an analogue clock or watch

- Has poor fine-motor co-ordination

Box 4.2 Indicators of a possible learning difficulty arising from dyslexia (ages 5–7+) (reproduced from Task Force on Dyslexia, 2001; copyright © Government Publications, Government of Ireland).

teaching programme or that can be used to help the child cope more effectively with the curriculum.

It is also important to bear in mind that a formal assessment, by necessity, provides a "spotlight" on a particular child, and the child, understandably quickly becomes aware of this. The assessment, therefore, should be implemented judiciously in order that the child is not exposed to any feelings of failure additional to those already resulting from his or her particular difficulties. The assessment should uncover data that will help in the development of a teaching programme.

CONSIDERATIONS

Self-concept

The identification and assessment of dyslexia is of crucial importance since a full assessment will facilitate the planning of appropriate intervention that will help to prevent the child from becoming engulfed by a feeling of learned helplessness. Preventing, or at least minimising, such failure removes the threat that intransigent learning difficulties will become so deeply embedded that they not only penetrate the affective domain and in particular the child's self-concept but also result in inappropriate reading styles embedded within the child's learning pattern.

Clearly, therefore, assessment should consider the child's self-concept. Every effort should be made to ensure that the difficulties displayed by the child and the underlying problems do not detract from the development of skills in learning and in access to the curriculum. At the same time feedback to the child needs to be handled very carefully.

Hales (2001) discusses the hidden effects of dyslexia and suggests that while much research has gone into developing methods of addressing the obvious effects of dyslexia in relation to reading, writing and spelling much less has been done with the less visible aspects such as anxiety, loss of confidence and low self-esteem. Hales argues that there is a tendency to address the 'mechanics' of the difficulty because these are more obvious and more directly problematic in day-to-day life. The supposition is that if the practical problems of reading and spelling could be solved then dyslexic people would be in a better position to tackle the way they felt. Yet, Hales argues this is a false premise and that a number of research studies show that a high level of anxiety and frustration is a consistent factor in relation to dyslexia.

He suggests that the difficulties of dyslexia cannot be addressed in isolation from other factors and that there is a reciprocal relationship between learning and living and in particular how each affect the person's self-concept.

Hales suggests that the effect on dyslexic children participating in school produces an almost immediate drop in self-confidence and that their self-confidence begins to fall almost from the start of formal education and does not return to even approximately its original level until schooldays are nearly over. Reid and Kirk (2001) discuss the cycle of 'disaffection, defiance and depression' and provide evidence from a number of studies to suggest that people with dyslexia, and in particular teenagers, are particularly vulnerable and that the whole aspect of self-esteem needs to be carefully considered and managed. This point is also supported by Hales, who suggests the vulnerable period of transfer from primary to secondary is one that needs careful attention.

Hales (2001) describes various strategies that the dyslexic young person can adopt. These include denial, which can be deliberate or indeed unconscious according to Hales. Children with dyslexia do not want to be different, and this may lead to denial and counterproductive feelings. The result of this is usually a lowering of self-esteem as the person knows they are not facing the reality of the situation.

Another strategy or reaction according to Hales is the denial of responsibility — this can lead to pointing the blame at others or indeed not adjusting to the demands of school and perhaps society. On the other hand, some dyslexic children react by overcompensating by trying to be 'perfect' and become heavily involved in extra-curricular areas and often achieve acceptance and popularity in this way. This, however, may not be possible and some children can become the 'class clown'. This can of course result in difficulties with authority. Eventually, this can become a 'learned behaviour' and an automatic reaction to a situation of stress. This may lead to the cycle of defiance and deviance described by Reid and Kirk (2001) and the lasting situation of the effect of the 'scars of dyslexia' described by Osmond (1994). According to Hales the situation can arise when the 'group' rejects the individual and the person realises that he or she is no longer the leader—or even a member of the group. This realisation can also lead to lowering of self-esteem.

This may help to explain why dyslexic children and young people have difficulty in dealing with many of the pressures often associated with learning and the classroom, such as the 'pressure to keep up' and being told to read aloud in front of their peers. This can result in feelings of inadequacy (Riddick, 1995a, b; 2002). Chapman and Turner (1997) found that pupils aged 5–7, who were having problems with reading, were also developing a 'negative self-concept' where reading was concerned. They suggested that this had a negative influence on the individuals' 'actual attainment' and progress within the academic setting.

PARENTS

Advice from parents in particular is helpful to decide how best to provide feedback to the child, but irrespective of its form feedback is essential. Riddock (1996) shows how some children have reacted to finding out they are dyslexic. One child suggested, 'I did not want to tell anyone, because I think they will tell everyone else and then everybody might tease me' (p. 147). Interestingly, the mother of the same child confirmed this view when she said, 'she doesn't like going in school time (to see the special teacher). She does not want anyone to find out. In fact, she tells them she is going swimming, she really does not want other children to know. It is the same in class, she doesn't want any obvious help in class' (p. 147).

What role, therefore, can parents play in an assessment. Parents usually know their child very well and can note, for example, the differences in the learning pattern and skills between different children in the same family. They may note that one child, for example, may take longer to master the alphabet, may be more reluctant to read than others, may be more forgetful, maybe even a bit more clumsy. Many of these things can be quite normal and merely highlight the normal individual differences between children—even children in the same family.

But if parents are concerned it is usually for a reason and every professional and individual needs to treat that concern seriously.

Parents may be concerned if they know someone with dyslexia, or have read about dyslexia, and see some similarities between these observations and descriptions to their observations of their own child.

Box 4.3 lists some factors that may prompt concern, but again it is important to note that this list is not exclusive and much depends on the individual child's stage of development. This is particularly important in younger children as many of the signs of dyslexia can in fact be an early phase of the normal developmental process of a particular skill and normal developmental stages of learning.

You can note from the list in Box 4.3 that there are factors both parents and teachers may recognise in a child—that is why it is important for each to work together. Communication between home and school is vitally important in both the identification and the support of the young child with dyslexia.

PUPILS' PERSPECTIVES

Wearmouth and Reid (2002) suggest that one of the major challenges facing teachers of pupils with dyslexia is the need to fully appreciate and understand the perspectives and the experiences of the pupil. Ideally, this should be tackled in a positive and meaningful way. They suggest that pupils should have more scope for self-advocacy. This, of course, can be uncomfortable and difficult for the teacher to manage. Wearmouth and Reid suggest that self-advocacy in this way can run counter to more traditional models of teaching and learning. Many of these traditional models, in fact, place an emphasis on conformity and 'fitting in' to the established pattern of the school and education system. Pupils' views are not always sought, but in the case of dyslexic children it can be highly desirable to obtain such views. Self-advocacy, therefore, should not be seen as a threat to classroom control and class discipline, but as a positive and welcome aspect relating to the emotional and social well-being of the child.

It is also important that the child has some awareness of dyslexia, what it is, and how it may affect learning and subject and career choice. Ideally, dyslexia should place no limitations at all on the child, particularly if the school system is an inclusive one. It is, therefore, beneficial and perhaps essential that time is taken to explain to the dyslexic child exactly how he or she can cope with dyslexia and any difficulties that may arise from this. The child may be concerned with any stigma, real or imaginary, that may arise from the label dyslexia. There may well be a need to educate not only some members of staff about what dyslexia is but also some of the child's peer group. Friendship and acceptance by a child's peer group is of high importance to the child, and this should be acknowledged in the assessment and preparation of any individual programme that is developed following the assessment.

INCLUSION

Peacey (2001) suggests that children with special educational needs do not always require different teaching approaches, but what is crucial is that the school and the teacher utilise the best possible teaching approaches based on what has been seen and known to work. Peacey suggests that the key aspect of inclusion is a vision of 'teamwork within school communities, teamwork within local authorities, and other systems of management and, indeed, teamwork supported by government ministers' (p. 25). The success of an inclusionary system, however, demands more than teamwork and Peacey stresses strongly that the learning environment is vitally important. The quality of the environment, the way that everybody feels about the place in which they work, has real importance.

An assessment, therefore, needs to consider the learning environment and, in particular aspects of the school, the school climate as well as the need for teamwork. These are key factors in the fully inclusive school. This view is also supported by Wearmouth (2001), who suggests that the learning environment can potentially create barriers to or facilitate literacy development, and one of the complex challenges for those planning programmes to address dyslexic pupils' learning needs is to focus on this aspect. In relation to the assessment process Wearmouth suggests that this challenge can be met by focusing on the characteristics of the individual pupil, the perspectives of the parents and the school, and the planning of programmes that take account of all these perspectives, which can then be embedded into the whole-school curriculum within an inclusive school.

INCLUSION AND BILINGUAL LEARNERS

Landon (2001) suggests that for bilingual learners the problem may lie with the system as well as the lack of sensitive instruments to diagnose dyslexia in this population. He suggests that inclusion of bilingual learners requires recognition and positive accommodations in relation to both language and culture. He suggests that if schools fail to appreciate this it will likely lead to poor standards of literacy development. If this is the case, Landon argues, the school need look no further to explain the literacy difficulties that bilingual learners have—by definition, they simply are unable to meet the standards. This would imply that any concern as to whether a child is dyslexic is immaterial. The language and the cultural needs of bilingual learners need to be met within the education system, and this needs to be considered within an assessment. Indeed, the Task Force on Dyslexia (2001) noted that there were no Irish (the language) norms for many of the test instruments in general use and no recently developed, standardised norm-referenced tests of reading in Irish. The report recommended that the Department of Education and Science should seek to remedy this and that the cultural appropriateness of testing and

PRE-SCHOOL

Concern may be raised in a pre-school child if some of the following are present:

- forgetfulness
- speech difficulty
- reversal of letters
- difficulty remembering letters of the alphabet
- difficulty remembering the sequence of letters of the alphabet
- if there is a history of dyslexia in the family
- co-ordination difficulties (e.g., bumping into tables and chairs)
- tasks that require fine-motor skills such as tying shoelaces
- slow at reacting to some tasks
- reluctance to concentrate on a task for a reasonable period of time
- confusing words which sound similar

SCHOOL AGE

- reluctance to go to school
- signs of not enjoying school
- reluctance to read
- difficulty learning words and letters
- difficulty and phonics (sounds)
- poor memory
- co-ordination difficulties
- losing items
- difficulty forming letters
- difficulty copying
- difficulty colouring
- poor organisation of materials

AFTER AROUND TWO YEARS AT SCHOOL

- hesitant at reading
- poor word-attack skills
- poor knowledge of the sounds and words

continued

- difficulty recognising where in words particular sounds come from
- spelling difficulty
- substitution of words when reading (e.g., *bus* for *car*)

UPPER PRIMARY

- as above but also:
- behaviour difficulties
- frustration
- may show abilities in other subjects apart from reading

SECONDARY

- as above
- takes a long time over homework
- misreads words
- wants others to tell him or her information
- poor general knowledge
- takes longer than others in most written tasks

Box 4.3   Factors that may prompt concern.

teaching materials in English should be considered before using these for students with learning difficulties. The report also recommended that guidelines should be provided to all Gaeltacht schools on the appropriate language, through which additional support should be given, in those cases in which the language of the home is different from the language of the school.

LINKING ASSESSMENT WITH THE PLANNING OF INTERVENTION

It is vital that the approaches and strategies selected provide the data and information to facilitate an effective teaching programme, preferably within the context of the classroom and the curriculum. Careful preparation and planning are necessary before embarking on assessment, and the questions relating to what, why, how and effect must be addressed at this planning stage and reviewed throughout the assessment.

In many countries 'individual educational programmes' are drawn up following an assessment. These are important, and it must be emphasised that although dyslexic children share common aspects they are still essentially individuals. Each assessment needs to be discussed and intervention planned to meet the needs of that individual, bearing in mind the actual learning environment and the curriculum experienced by that child.

Tod and Fairman (2001) suggest that many of the features of effective, individual educational programmes reflect aspects that are considered as important for inclusion.

- a focus on pupil outcomes;
- provision for diverse needs embedded in whole-school practice;
- the need for formative reflection and analysis rather than merely summative reporting;
- student and parent involvement;
- the use of a variety of instructions;
- rigorous evaluation of the effectiveness of additional or otherwise extra support;
- sharing of responsibility for special educational needs' support with other adults;
- peer involvement; and
- collaborative multi-agency planning.

CO-MORBIDITY

Co-morbidity is a term often used to describe the overlap that may exist between different specific learning difficulties. It has been suggested (Richardson, 2002) that this term is not a useful one and that descriptive features of the different conditions would be more appropriate. This concurs with developmental work (Weedon and Reid, 2002) that has identified 16 specific learning difficulties with specific features. These data have contributed to the development of an assessment tool called SNAP (Special Needs Assessment Portfolio). This has not only highlighted the distinctive features of different specific learning difficulties but also the overlap between them. It is important to consider this overlap, which will be discussed in some detail in Chapter 14, as it is becoming an important factor in assessment and practice.

PERFORMANCES

An assessment needs to consider the student's performances in the classroom situation. Although valuable data can be gathered from cognitive assessment, this should be accompanied with information on how the individual performs in relation to the different components of curriculum. Curriculum-orientated assessment can be diagnostic and preventative. It does not necessarily focus on the child's deficits, but on the strengths; and, if noted, these strengths can form the basis of a subsequent teaching programme. Crombie (2002) suggests what she describes as a 'solution-based' approach to assessment. This implies that pupils' performances within the curriculum should be the measuring tool for assessing for dyslexia, not psychometric tests. Therefore, pupils who perform measurably better when reading and writing criteria are removed from the task can be described as dyslexic. This suggestion, which focuses on performance and the curriculum, holds much promise in terms of developing education authority policy and early identification. According to Crombie, using this premise, 'dyslexia' is not a name for the deficit, but a name for how the deficits manifest themselves in different individuals.

CRITERIA: SUMMARY

Assessment for dyslexia should consider three aspects—difficulties, discrepancies and differences. The central *difficulty* is usually related to the decoding or the encoding of print, and this may be the result of different contributory factors. For example, some difficulties may include phonological processing, visual-processing difficulties, memory factors, organisational and sequencing difficulties, motor and co-ordination difficulties, language problems or perceptual difficulties of an auditory or visual nature.

Discrepancies become apparent when we make comparisons between decoding and reading/listening comprehension, between oral and written responses and between performances within the different subject areas of the curriculum.

It is also important to acknowledge the *differences* between individual learners. This particularly applies to dyslexic children. An assessment, therefore, should also consider learning and cognitive styles as well as the learning and teaching environment. An appreciation of this can help to effectively link assessment and teaching. This also helps to take the child's preferences for learning into account, which, in fact, should be a principal aim in an assessment.

A wide range of assessment strategies can be used to help recognise the difficulties, discrepancies and differences displayed by learners. Some of these are described and discussed in this and the next chapter as well as in the Appendix.

Looking at both the process and the criteria for assessing for dyslexia, I would suggest the five factors in Box 4.4 should be considered. These criteria can be used as a guide as well as a framework for developing in the context of the school, the curriculum or the school system.

The five aspects (Box 4.4) will be discussed in detail in the following chapter, but it is important to note here that they can form some basis for criteria for conducting an assessment. The *purpose* of the assessment must be the first question asked, as this is crucial to the method selected and the type of outcome expected from the assessment. Similarly, the *profiles* give an indication of the child's strengths and weaknesses, and it is important that this should include an indication of cognitive functioning as well as attainments. This is particularly important as there is much evidence regarding the cognitive/information-processing aspects related to dyslexia. Although the information from the profiles can be used comparatively to note discrepancies in the performances of cognitive and attainment tasks, this is not the only use this information can be put to. It should be used diagnostically to help provide some information about the learner's strategies and the nature of the difficulties and, indeed, the type of tasks that may present difficulty and some possible reasons for this difficulty. For example, in a cognitive, working memory task

Purpose	What is the context for the assessment? Why is the assessment being carried out?
Profiles	Obtain information on the child's strengths and weaknesses Attainment profile Cognitive profile
Performances	How is learning carried out? The process Level of attainment Learning behaviours
Provision	The context The curriculum The classroom The community
Parents	Background information Concerns Effective home/school links

Box 4.4   The assessment criteria to consider.

involving digits that are reversed, one should be interested in how the learners achieved the correct or incorrect response. What strategies did the learners use and what could have helped them extend their performance. This is highlighted in Box 4.5. This type of information can be considerably important in relation to assessing the factors that provide the learner with difficulties. Is it the auditory nature of the task, does the task place too much burden on the short-term memory capacities of the learner and how can this be related to the classroom situation?

In Box 4.5 three children got the correct response and two did not. But the important aspect is their responses to the question: How did you do that? Each provided a different response, and this response elicits probably more useful information than the fact that they were able to correctly or, indeed, incorrectly respond. Child 1 would clearly benefit from information being introduced visually while Child 2 seems to be auditory and Child 3 kinaesthetic. Each of these children would benefit from information being introduced in their preferred learning mode.

Whatever the motivation for undertaking an assessment it is important to have clear aims and objectives, and these should be related to the parents well before the assessment commences. An assessment, of course, can consist of a blend of formal and informal measures, both of which provide crucial information.

It is also important to perceive assessment from the curriculum and learning perspectives as opposed to within-child factors. In fact, Wearmouth et al. (2002) discuss barriers to literacy, and these need to be investigated to assess why the child is not acquiring literacy skills. In developing criteria for an assessment it is important therefore to incorporate all those aspects that relate to the curriculum and to attempt to identify the barriers to learning and literacy that might be experienced by the

---

CHILD 1

Assessor	Repeat these digits backwards—25918
Child	81952
Assessor	How did you do that?
Child	As you said them I imagined the numbers as pictures in my head

CHILD 2

Assessor	Repeat these digits backwards—25918
Child	81952
Assessor	How did you do that?
Child	I listened to the sound of your voice and thought of that when I had to repeat them

CHILD 3

Assessor	Repeat these digits backwards—25918
Child	81952
Assessor	How did you do that?
Child	I traced the numbers with my fingers on the table and when I had to recall them I retraced them in the table. I had an image of the numbers, but I had to physically trace them with my fingers to recall them

CHILD 4

Assessor	Repeat these digits backwards—25918
Child	81259
Assessor	How did you do that?
Child	I listened to your voice, but I think I got the numbers jumbled a bit

CHILD 5

Assessor	Repeat these digits backwards—25918
Child	81259
Assessor	How did you do that?
Child	It was easy—I just pictured them in my mind

Box 4.5   Working memory.

learner with dyslexia. These barriers can be identified by observing and discussing with the child, and the parents, the difficulties encountered by the learner and how these are currently being tackled. Just as there is no 'magic' formula for overcoming the difficulties associated with dyslexia, there is no 'magic' tool for *identifying* these difficulties. Certainly the range of tests that are discussed in the next chapter can be of considerable assistance, and many of these tests have strong predictive validity. Essentially, however, identifying dyslexia involves more than administering a test—it involves a process, and that process needs to include the learning environment, the curriculum and the student's learning opportunities, as well as the cognitive factors associated with dyslexia. That is why it is crucial to identify and develop a rationale for assessment and, specifically, the 'next step' after the assessment. It is important that assessment is linked to intervention, and by identifying 'barriers to learning' the link between assessment and intervention can be strengthened. For that reason it is also important that the teacher adopts a leading role in the assessment. Historically, in the UK and in most other countries, assessment for dyslexia has been the responsibility of a specialist teacher or an educational psychologist. This is understandable as the specialist teacher has an appreciation of how dyslexia can affect the progress of the student in the classroom situation and the educational psyshologist can provide refined quantiative and qualitative insights relating to the cognitive abilities and difficulties experienced by the student. Ideally, both the information that can be obtained from cognitive measures and that which can be obtained from classroom and curriculum assessment are needed. It is interesting to note that one of the recommendations of the BPS Working Party Report on Dyslexia (BPS, 1999) was that 'educational psychologists work more closely with schools to develop effective school-based assessment, intervention and monitoring and, within that context, also carry out detailed psychological assessment and programme planning . . .' (p. 69). It is therefore clear that no one individual, nor one test, holds the key to identifying dyslexia, but that this can best be achieved with reference to a range of strategies and the involvement of a number of key personnel. The following two chapters, therefore, will look in detail at these barriers to literacy and learning, by focusing on how existing tests can be used and how a range of assessment strategies can be utilised.

Chapter 5

Assessment: Practice

RATIONALE

Although there are a number of tests that include the term 'dyslexia' in the title there is, in fact, no dyslexia test—the identification of dyslexia is a process and that process includes more than the administration of a solitary test. These tests, however, will be discussed in this chapter, and further examples can be found in the Appendix. This chapter will look at the specific practices of assessment, and the following chapter will discuss the processes involved in an assessment. This process includes the gathering of data from a wide range of sources because it is necessary to investigate the influence of factors other than those relating to the individual.

It can be suggested that dyslexia is contextual, which means that the extent of dyslexic difficulties will be more obvious in some environments and contexts than in others. It is important, therefore, to observe and gather information on the learning environment and the learning or work context, as these factors may be influential in assessing the performance of the person with dyslexia. Environmental, classroom, curricular or workplace considerations may in fact be sufficient to minimise the effects of dyslexia, but in order to ascertain the role of these factors, part of the assessment has to be conducted in that environment—classroom or workplace. An assessment, therefore, is not only about the individual but about the learning opportunities, the environment, the individual's learning preferences, and the biological and cognitive factors associated with dyslexia as well.

This chapter will discuss the range of assessment strategies and then describe the environmental and learning factors that can be influential in the outcome of an assessment for dyslexia.

TESTS AND STRATEGIES

The previous chapter looked at the criteria and factors one should consider in an assessment. These factors are influential in the selection of a test or an assessment strategy. Usually, one follows a process of stages. This should commence with a preliminary screening and then a more detailed screening that should incorporate the classroom environment and other factors, such as home factors, language and cultural aspects and the nature of the tasks that are challenging for the child. The factors will not diagnose dyslexia, but can provide some indicators that the child may have some of the characteristics associated with dyslexia. This can justify the need for further diagnostic assessment and to investigate in detail curriculum, contextual and environmental factors as well as factors associated with learning styles.

It is necessary, therefore, to use a broad range of assessment strategies in order to ensure that adequate attention is given not only to the student's learning and cognitive profile but also to the process of learning itself and the context within which learning takes place.

An outline of some of the tests and strategies that can be used is shown in Box 5.1.

STANDARDISED/PSYCHOMETRIC

This form of assessment consists of standardised or norm-referenced tests that provide some form of score or measure, which is compared with the average scores of a standardised sample. From this type of test one can obtain, for example, a reading age or IQ score. As well as providing an indication of the pupil's progress in relation to his peers, these tests can also provide information that can be used diagnostically. Important factors in standardised tests relate to test construction and, particularly, aspects relating to validity and reliability. Standardised tests must have high validity and reliability, and this is usually indicated in the test manual. This means that the tests are well constructed and, therefore, the teacher can use the data from the test with some confidence. There are, however, some potential pitfalls in the use of standardised tests, and they are described in this section. However, if a standardised test is to be used, for whatever purpose, it is important to check that it has been constructed soundly and has high content validity and high reliability.

STANDARDISATION

If one is attempting to standardise a test that can be used nationally across different populations of children or, indeed, selecting a standardised test for use, it is important to note a number of important points:

- The sample: It is important that the sample is a representative one. Factors that should be considered include urban/rural locations, cultural background, age and sex, first language, and size and selection of sample. It is important, therefore, for users of tests of any type to check the standardisation procedures that were used in the construction of the test. It is also important to check the nature of the piloting that was carried out before the standardisation data were gathered.
- Reliability: This refers to the reliability in obtaining the same responses from the test if repeated under similar conditions. Reliability can be called 'replicability' or

STANDARDISED

- Wechsler Intelligence Scale (WISC III) (Wechsler, 1992a)
- Wechsler Objective Language Dimensions (WOLD) (Wechsler, 1996)
- Wechsler Objective Number Dimensions (WOND) (Wechsler, 1996)
- Wechsler Objective Reading Dimensions (WORD) (Wechsler, 1996)
- Wechsler Individual Achievement Test UK (WIAT) (Wechsler, 1992b)
- Wechsler Individual Achievement Test UK (WIAT) (Quicktest) (Wechsler 1996)
- Wide Range Achievement Test (WRAT3™) (Wilkinson, 1993)
- British Ability Scales (BAS) (Elliot et al., 1996)
- New McMillan Reading Analysis (NMRA)*/New Reading Analysis (NRA) (Vincent and De La Mare, 1987)
- Neale Analysis of Reading Ability (Neale, 1989)
- Aston Index (Newton and Thomson, 1982)

DIAGNOSTIC

- As above
- Miscue Analysis (Arnold, 1992)
- Bury Infant Check (Pearson and Quinn, 1986)
- Reading Assessment for Teachers (RAT Pack) (Cooper et al., 1991)
- Listening and Literacy Index (LLI) (Weedon and Reid, 2001)*
- Assessing Metacognitive Needs (Ayres, 1996)
- Early Literacy Test (Gillham, 2000)*
- Edinburgh Reading Tests*/Moray House Tests (University of Edinburgh, 2002)*
- Diagnostic Reading Record (Arnold, 1992)
- Slingerland Screening Tests for Identifying Children with Special Learning Difficulties (Slingerland, 1985)
- Spadafore Diagnostic Reading Test (Spadafore, 1983)
- Literacy Probe 7–9 (Bentley and Reid, 2001)

DIAGNOSTIC SPELLING TEST

- Boder Test of Reading and Spelling Patterns (Boder and Jarrico, 1982)
- Graded Word Spelling Test (Vernon, 1977)

* These tests are also standardised.

continued

- Adult Assessment (Klein, 1993)

- Unscrambling Spelling (Klein and Miller, 1990)

- Spelling in Context (Peters and Smith, 1993)

- Spelling teaching programmes often include diagnostic spelling activities (see Smith et al., 1998)

NUMERACY

- Informal Assessment of Numeracy Skills (Chinn, 2000)

- Numeracy Progress Tests (Vincent and Crumpler, 2001)

SCREENING

- Lucid Cognitive Profiling System (CoPS) (Lucid Software)

- Lucid Assessment System for Schools (Secondary) (LASS), ages 11–15 (Horne et al., 1999)

- Lucid Assessment System for Schools (Junior) (LASS), for primary-aged children (Singleton and Horne, 2001)

- Lucid Adults Dyslexia Screening (LADS), adult 16+ (Lucid Software)

- Pre-school Screening Tests (PREST) (Fawcett et al., 2001)

- Dyslexia Screening Test (Fawcett and Nicolson, 1996)

- Dyslexia Early Screening Test (Fawcett and Nicolson, 1997)

- Dyslexia Adult Screening Test (Fawcett and Nicolson, 1998)

- Quest Reading and Number Screening Tests

- Bangor Dyslexia Test

- Group Screening Tests (Philips and Leonard, Ann Arbor)

- Checklists

PHONOLOGICAL

- Phonological Assessment Battery (PhAB, 1996)

- Sound Linkage (Hatcher, 1994)

- Phonological Awareness Procedures (Gorrie and Parkinson, 1995)

- Lindamood Auditory Conceptualisation Test (LAC Test) (Lindamood and Lindamood, 1979)

- Phonological Abilities Test (Muter et al., 1997)

continued

COMPONENTS APPROACH

- Decoding/Listening comprehension
- Non-word Reading (Snowling)

OBSERVATIONAL

- Observational Survey/Running Record (Clay, 1993)
- Observational Framework (Reid, 1996)

METACOGNITIVE

- Assisted Assessment (Campione and Brown, 1989)
- Pass Model (Das et al., 1994)
- Portfolio Assessment (Ayres, 1996)
- Multiple Intelligences Approaches (Lazear, 1994, 1999)

Box 5.1   Assessment tests and strategies.

'stability' (Weedon and Reid, 2001). It essentially refers to the extent to which a pupil would get the same score in a test if he or she had done the test on a different day. It can be measured by determining how far the score on one question can be predicted from the same pupil's score on other questions in the test. In the standardisation for the Listening and Literacy Index (LLI) (Weedon and Reid, 2001), a reliability of one meant that exactly the same score would have been obtained on another occasion. A reliability of zero meant that one did not know what the score would have been on another occasion. The reliability can be calculated using the Kuder–Richardson formula 20 (KR20).

- Validity: This refers to the design of the test and whether the test actually measures what it was designed to measure, such as IQ, decoding, verbal comprehension, spelling. This is not the same as reliability. A test may well be reliable and give consistent results over time, and this would mean something: very likely that the test is a good measure of something, but not necessarily the item it is intended to measure. Sometimes, the term 'content' or 'face validity' is used to describe validity. This refers to the extent to which the questions in the test conform to expert opinion of what good questions for that test should be. This may refer to the language used and the age appropriateness of the test material and whether cultural and social factors have been considered in the development of the test items.

- Confidence interval: This refers to whether the pupil, if he or she took the test repeatedly, would obtain around the same score. In the construction of the LLI (described later in this chapter) this means that there would be about a two-thirds chance that the pupil's average score, if the test were given repeatedly, would be the actual score attained plus or minus the confidence interval.

- Homogeneity: This means that if the different items in the test actually measure the same skill or attainment then it should be expected that, over a group of pupils, test items should show high levels of intercorrelation. At the same time if items are accessing different skills or attainments they would likely show lower levels of intercorrelation.

PSYCHOMETRIC

The term 'psychometric' refers to measurement and the use of standardised instruments to measure some ability or attainment. It is understandable, given the different aspects described above that are essential in the development of a standardised test, that such tests need to be treated with some caution. Sometimes, tests such as these can be misinterpreted and misused.

Psychometric or standardised tests attempt to establish what would be the norm for children of a specific age. Such norm-referenced tests typically produce measures in terms of ranks (e.g., standardised reading scores), but they may fall short of highlighting appropriate intervention strategies because the scores do not provide any information on the child, apart from a score. It says little or nothing of the child's strategies for providing a response, nor of the process of thought that was utilised by the child to obtain a response.

An example of a psychometric and widely used standardised test is the Wechsler Intelligence Scales (WISC). Although the concept of IQ is a controversial one, this is still a good example of a standardised test because it has been well constructed and standardised.

Wechsler Intelligence Scale

One such standardised test in widespread use for the assessment of children who may have dyslexia is in fact the Wechsler Intelligence Scale for Children. This test was originally devised as an assessment tool for psychologists and psychometricians. It provides both an IQ and subtest profile. It was revised and restandardised in 1974 and a new version with more modern and appropriate test materials was produced in 1992 (WISC III) and a new adult version was published in 1999—the Wechsler Adult Intelligence Scale (WAIS-III).

Wechsler Adult Intelligence Scale

The subtests of the WAIS-III are grouped according to indexes:

- *Verbal comprehension*
  —vocabulary
  —similarities
  —information
- *Performance organisation*
  —picture completion
  —block design
  —matrix reasoning

- *Working memory*
  —arithmetic
  —digit span
  —letter–number sequencing
- *Processing speed*
  —digit symbol-coding
  —symbol search

Like the children's version, WAIS-III is also divided into verbal and performance IQ scores. Additionally, WAIS-III is also co-normed with the Wechsler Test Memory Scale. This can be useful in the assessment of adults with dyslexia.

Wechsler Intelligence Scale for Children

The WISC-III consists of six verbal subtests—information, similarities, arithmetic, vocabulary, comprehension and digit span—and seven performance (non-verbal) tests—picture completion, coding, picture arrangement, block design, object assembly, symbol search and mazes. In addition to verbal and performance IQ scores, the tests can yield index scores relating to verbal comprehension, perceptual organisation, freedom from distractibility and perceptual speed. These can provide very useful information in a diagnosis of the child's strengths and weaknesses.

Cooper (1995) suggests that the WISC series of test are probably the best validated and most widely accepted measures of children's intellectual functioning in the world. However its use is not without controversy. The use of ability measures such as the WISC according to Siegal (1989, 1992) rests on all or some of the following assumptions:

- that tests of ability or IQ are valid and reliable measures, so that there is some virtue in examining discrepancies between ability and achievement;
- particular subtests are valid instruments in the assessment of specific cognitive subskills;
- distinctive patterns may emerge that can be reliably correlated with specific learning difficulties;
- that IQ and reading share a causal dependency, with IQ factors influencing reading ability.

Siegal, however, argues that the evidence in relation to these points is inconsistent. She argues that IQ tests do not necessarily measure intelligence, but in fact measure factual knowledge, expressive language ability, short-term memory and other skills related to learning. The implication of this for children with dyslexia is that, because of the nature of their difficulty, their scores in relation to factual knowledge, expressive language and short-term memory will provide an artificially depressed IQ score. This view is in fact supported by Miles (1996), who suggests that the concept of global IQ for dyslexic children is a misleading one because it will not provide a valid reflection of their real abilities.

This assertion clearly undermines the view that the subtests and even subtest patterns can reveal useful information in the assessment of specific learning difficulties. Yet, factor analytic studies of the WISC-R (Lawson and Inglis, 1984, 1985) show that verbal skills can be isolated as a discrete factor. Interestingly, the subtests that had a high loading value for the factors Arithmetic, Coding, Information and Digit Span (ACID) are those subtests that present problems for children with dyslexia. This is consistent with the ACID profile that identified the same set of subtests and provides some evidence for a distinctive, dyslexic, cognitive profile (Thomson, 1984). Miles (1996) also suggests that the WISC can reveal patterns of strengths and weaknesses that can be useful in a diagnosis of dyslexia. The acid profile however has been subject to criticism (see p. 133).

Wechsler Dimensions

In addition to the WISC there are a number of other related assessments that focus on particular dimensions of learning. These include the Wechsler Objective Reading Dimensions (WORD), Language Dimensions (WOLD) and Number Dimensions (WOND). The combined subscales of the WORD, WOLD and WOND produce the measures obtained from the Wechsler Individual Achievement Test (WIAT):

- WORD assesses reading and spelling abilities from the ages of 6 years up to 16 years 11 months. It consists of three subtests and basic reading, spelling and reading comprehension.
- WOLD focuses on language attainment, and the subtests are listening comprehension, oral expression and written expression.
- WOND provides assessment in numerical attainment, and the subtests are called mathematics reasoning and numerical operations.
- WIAT provides a screening of potential achievement difficulties by using the subscale scores from the dimensions tests described above.

British Ability Scales

The British Ability Scales (BAS II) (Elliott et al., 1996) may be used as an alternative to the WISC.

The BAS II is divided into two batteries: the Early Years Battery, which consists of cognitive scales, and the School Age Battery, which comprises both cognitive and achievement scales. The BAS can provide a comprehensive cognitive profile that can be used to assess the relative strengths and weaknesses of the profile of children with dyslexia.

Comment

The use of an intelligence test to identify children who have essentially a reading difficulty has however accumulated some controversy. There is strong evidence to dispute the assertion that IQ and reading ability share a causal dependency. Stanovich (1992) argues that the key to reading disability is related to the problem of phonological processing. This notion has indeed widespread support (Frith,

1995). Stanovich further argues that phonological processes are independent of intelligence and are not measured or directly taken account of in IQ tests.

The difficulty known as hyperlexia (Aaron, 1989; Healy, 1982, 1991) can be used as evidence to dispute any valid association between IQ and reading attainment. Hyperlexia has been described as affecting those children with good decoding skills, but poor comprehension, indicating a low general IQ.

Siegal (1989) cites the existence of a hyperlexic group as further evidence of the need to disassociate IQ and reading attainment. It has been argued that listening comprehension correlates more highly with reading ability than IQ. The evidence from studies of hyperlexia (Healy, 1992) therefore suggests that children with low IQ scores can be good mechanical readers. This clearly indicates that a causal relationship between IQ and reading ability is a doubtful one.

It is important, therefore, that both the WISC and the BAS are used diagnostically, particularly in the assessment of children with dyslexia. In addition to obtaining a score one can observe how the child/adult responds to specific test items, which ones appear to motivate him or her more than others and how sustained his or her attention is throughout the assessment. It is important that administration of these tests is not a means to an end—but if they are selected to be used it should be accepted that they only constitute part of the assessment process. The importance of this part can place a demand on a number of factors, but this chapter and the preceding chapter has strongly indicated the role of teachers in the assessment process and this role of trained and experienced teachers cannot be underestimated.

There are a number of other tests that are directed toward identifying abilities as opposed to actual attainments. One such test is the Aston Index. This test has been well used by teachers since it was first developed in 1982.

The Aston Index

The Aston Index was developed by Aston University in Birmingham. It consists of a series of tests that claim to be able to:

- identify children with potential language-associated problems early in their education (it can therefore be used as a screening device);
- be used to analyse and diagnose reading and language difficulties displayed by children who are experiencing difficulties in coping with basic attainments.

The Aston Index produces a pupil profile based on a number of tests. The tests are divided into:

- 'General Underlying Ability' and attainment;
- 'Performance Items'.

The 'General Underlying Ability' section consists of tests on:

- picture recognition;
- vocabulary;

- the Goodenough draw-a-man test;
- copying geometric designs;
- grapheme/phoneme correspondence;
- the Schonell reading test;
- spelling test.

The 'Performance Items' consist of tests on:

- visual discrimination;
- child laterality;
- copying name;
- free-writing;
- visual sequential memory (pictures);
- auditory sequential memory;
- sound-blending;
- visual sequential memory (symbolic);
- sound discrimination;
- graphomotor test.

The tests within the Aston Index help the teacher diagnose the nature of the problem that may be preventing the child from achieving a satisfactory level in basic attainments. The Aston Index, however, has been the subject of criticism in relation to weaknesses in both construction and standardisation. There is also some doubt as to the potential of the test to discriminate between various groups of children experiencing specific learning difficulties (Pumfrey and Reason, 1991).

The Aston Portfolio Assessment Checklist is essentially a development from the Index and consists of assessment cards, checklists and teaching cards that help the teacher identify specific difficulties associated with attainments and suggest possible methods of dealing with this difficulty.

PHONOLOGICAL ASSESSMENT

Since there is significant research that supports the 'phonological representation hypothesis' in relation to the nature of the difficulties experienced by children with dyslexia, it is important that some form of phonological assessment is carried out. There are a number of commercially available phonological tests and others that are integrated into teaching programmes as well. Examples of both these types are discussed here.

Essentially, phonological assessment focuses on the question arising from what dyslexia is as opposed to what it is not. This is supported by the work of many researchers in this area who are critical of the use of discrepancy or exclusionary definitions of dyslexia (Stanovich, 1991; Frith, 1995; Gallagher and Frederickson, 1995; Reason and Frederickson, 1996; BPS, 1999a; Hatcher and Snowling, 2002). Additionally, early intervention studies have shown that phonological skills-training facilitates the acquisition of reading skills (Blachman et al., 1994; Lundberg, 2002), and that even within a comprehensive literacy programme phonological skills-training has enhanced the progress of children with reading difficulties (Hatcher et al., 1994). As Lundberg (2002) indicates, many factors can contribute to the poor phonological structure of words, such as genetic factors, early hearing impairment and lack of stimulation. Of significant importance, however, is the view that the poor phonological structure of words not only impairs the beginning stages of reading but also the development of vocabulary and syntactic ability due 'to the fact that various subcomponents of the language system influence each other reciprocally' (Lundberg, 2002, p. 10). In view of this convincing evidence of a relationship between phono-logical processing and reading skills it is of some importance that a detailed phonological assessment should be conducted.

Hatcher and Snowling (2002) suggest that the status of a child's representation of spoken words determines the ease or difficulty with which they learn to read and that it is important to assess the quality of the phonological representations, to discover whether they are well developed or 'fuzzy'.

Hatcher and Snowling acknowledge that it is a major difficulty in attributing the problems of dyslexic people to the level of phonological representations as such representations cannot be assessed directly because it is difficult to describe the precise nature of the phonological representation of the sounds.

It is necessary, therefore, to attempt to identify the various aspects that make up phonological representations. They suggest that some of the easier phonological tasks can be completed by children before they have started reading, while others are only attainable by children once they have started the process of learning to read and these test different underlying abilities. It is, therefore, important to have an understanding of the phonological level of the tasks in order to present them appropriately and interpret them correctly.

Adams (1990b) reviewed various phonological tasks and was able to identify at least five levels of difficulty:

- knowledge of nursery rhymes, which involves only an ear for the sounds of words;
- awareness of rhyme and alliteration, which requires both sensitivity to the sounds and an ability to focus on certain sounds;
- blending of phonemes and splitting of syllables to identify phonemes—this demands an awareness that words can be subdivided into smaller sounds;
- phoneme segmentation requires a thorough understanding that words can be analysed into a series of phonemes;
- phoneme manipulation requires a child not only to understand and produce phonemes but also to be able to manipulate them by addition, deletion or transposition.

It is important that assessment of phonological representations should identify the specific aspects of the different types of phonological tasks that contribute to the reading process.

Hatcher and Snowling (2002) suggest that rhyme recognition and detection tests, rhyme oddity tasks that present the child with a set of three or four spoken words and requires the child to identify which is the one that does not belong to a group, and alliteration tasks that assess the ability to isolate initial sounds in words are all phonological awareness tasks.

Phonological production tasks are those that include rhyme production, syllable-blending, phoneme-blending and phoneme segmentation, which assess a child's ability to segment words into separate sounds, while phonological manipulation can be identified by adding, deleting or transposing sounds. A phoneme deletion task assesses the child's ability to isolate a single phoneme, remove it from a word and thereby produce a new word. A spoonerisms test is also useful as it assesses a child's ability to segment words and to synthesise the segments to produce a new word. For example, exchanging the beginning sounds of the words 'bold–coat' would become 'cold–boat'.

Hatcher and Snowling (2002) also suggest that naming speed and fluency tests are useful as they assess the speed of phonological production. If an item is weakly represented, it may be irretrievable, retrieved incorrectly or remain on the tip of the tongue. Short-term memory tasks are also sensitive to the accessibility of phonological representations.

In order to read, children need to be able to combine the ability to segment words into sounds with their knowledge of letter names and sounds. Hatcher and Snowling therefore argue that it is fundamental that letter knowledge is assessed and monitored. A number of commercially produced assessment batteries are now available to do this. They include a range of phonological awareness and phonological processing tests, and some are described below and in the Appendix.

The Phonological Assessment Test (PAT) (Muter et al., 1997)

This is a standardised test that can be used with children between the ages of 4 and 7 years. It is useful as a screening measure for identifying children at risk of reading difficulties. It can also be used diagnostically with older children experiencing reading difficulties, in order to assess the nature and extent of their phonological weaknesses. The subtests in PAT are:

- rhyme detection;
- rhyme production;
- word completion;
- syllables and phonemes;
- phoneme deletion—beginning and end sounds;
- speech rate;
- letter knowledge.

The Phonological Assessment Battery (PhAB) (Frederickson et al., 1997)

This battery is based on the Theoretical Causal Model (Frith, 1995), which provides convincing support for a phonological 'core variable' in literacy difficulties and highlights the view that phonological competence is distinct from general cognitive ability. The battery consists of six measures:

- alliteration test—assesses children's abilities to segment sounds into single syllable words;
- rhyme test—assesses the ability to identify the rhyme in single syllable words;
- spoonerism test—tests whether the child can analyse single syllable words into segments and then synthesize the segments to provide new words or word combinations;
- non-word reading test—assesses the decoding of letter strings without drawing on previous knowledge;
- naming speed test—assesses the speed of phonological production;
- fluency test—tests the accessibility and retrieval of phonological information from long-term memory.

Each of these subtests seem to be ideally suited to assess dyslexic difficulties. There is good evidence that dyslexic children have difficulty with rhyme and alliteration, and some researchers have indicated that naming speed is in itself a significant feature of dyslexic difficulties (Wolf, 1991, 1996, 2001; Nicolson and Fawcett, 1994; Nicolson, 2001). This battery offers some advantages over other tests that aim to assess dyslexic difficulties. Both the content of the battery and the clear theoretical rationale that underpins it are impressive. Furthermore, Gomez and Reason (2002) have shown that the PhAB can be used with Malaysian children. The study conducted with 69 Malaysian children aged 7–8 years showed that the children's performance on the PhAB was at least comparable to UK norms, and it was concluded that this battery of tests was 'viable as a starting point for further development' (Gomez and Reason, 2002, p. 31).

Sound Linkage

The Sound Linkage Test of Phonological Awareness (Hatcher, 1994), which precedes the teaching programme of the same name, includes tests of rhyme, sound-blending, phoneme deletion and transposition. These items can be used as a criterion-referenced test, although it is also standardised to the end of Year 3. It can be used for identifying young children at risk of reading failure and those children whose reading delay may be attributable to limited phonological skills.

As indicated earlier in this book the purpose of assessment is very important, and if the purpose is to directly link the assessment with teaching then this is an appropriate test because it provides an opportunity for the analysis of a child's strengths and weaknesses in relation to phonological skills and, therefore, should inform future teaching and learning (Hatcher and Snowling, 2002).

Sound Linkage is, therefore, essentially a teaching approach introduced by the test. The test aims to measure the extent to which young children can manipulate sounds within words. Additionally, as it is linked to the teaching programme it is possible to measure progress at various intervals. The test consists of:

- syllable-blending;
- phoneme-blending;
- rhyme;

- phoneme segmentation;
- phoneme deletion;
- phoneme transposition.

Phonological Awareness Procedures

This programme (Gorrie and Parkinson, 1995) essentially has three components: assessment, games and resources. The assessment section provides a very detailed analysis of the child's phonological awareness. The assessment covers the following areas:

- polysyllabic word/non-word repetition and recognition;
- syllable segmentation, deletion of prefixes and suffixes, and deletion of syllables;
- intra-syllable segmentation such as detection of onset and rime at rhyme judgement and production;
- phoneme segmentation such as blending, detection and deletion of initial and final phonemes.

These procedures provide a straightforward method to help the teacher obtain useful information in relation to the child's phonological awareness.

Lindamood Auditory Conceptualisation Test (LAC Test)

This highly acclaimed procedure (Clark, 1988) was developed to measure phonological awareness (Lindamood and Lindamood, 1979). The test consists of a procedure in which coloured blocks are used by students to represent sounds heard in words.

The Lindamoods found strong correlations between students' performances in this test with word recognition, reading comprehension and spelling.

SCREENING

The screening of children at virtually any stage in education is an issue that has aroused considerable debate and controversy. Three main questions can be raised in relation to screening:

- What is the most desirable age (or ages) for children to be screened?
- Which skills, abilities and attainments in performances should children be screened for?
- How should the results of any screening procedures be used?

Additionally, the benefits of screening need to be weighed against the costs in terms of staff and resources that are necessary to implement effective screening procedures. This raises the issue as to whether screening should be for all children, or only for those who do not appear to be making satisfactory progress. Crombie (2002b) has developed a curriculum and multidisciplinary approach to screening to identify children in the nursery and early years who are at risk of dyslexia, throughout one education authority. She suggests that some generic principles should be taken into account when considering how to identify the learning needs of dyslexic pupils at an early stage. She argues that teachers are often hesitant to label a child dyslexic, but suggests that good communication with parents and an understanding of dyslexia will enable teachers to discuss with parents the reasons for their reluctance to label. Again, the message of early identification is the same whether the purpose is to label or not—that is, to identify appropriate intervention strategies for struggling readers.

Crombie's nursery screening procedure is intended for use during the pre-school years. The purpose of this procedure, according to Crombie, is that the screening should also flag up any children who show signs of specific problems. This may indicate that such children are slightly slower to develop certain specific skills or are less mature than the rest of the group. When considering children's profiles, account needs to be taken of children who may be up to a year younger than the rest of the pre-school year group. At this stage some apparent problems may only be due to immaturity, so it is important not to read too much into this information at this stage. The key aspect is that specific intervention rather than a label is the prime objective of these screening procedures.

Crombie's screening focuses on five main areas of learning:

- *Emotional, personal and social development*. This looks at home background and culture as these factors are likely to have a strong influence on emotional, personal and social development.
- *Communication and language*. Children who have poor phonological skills at this stage and a lack of awareness of rhyme and rhythm may have later difficulties in learning to read and write. It is important to acknowledge this as the pre-school year is generally a period of rapid growth in language, with increasing awareness of sounds and words. Difficulty in listening to stories at this stage can also be identified, and this may indicate later attention problems. Memory is also important in language and communication skills, and children who are unable to remember more than two items of information, for instance, may appear as disobedient when, in fact, they are unable to remember what it is they were told to do. Information can also be gathered on whether they are able to remember the sequence of events in a story or may be unable to repeat the syllables that make up a polysyllabic word. Speech too can be informally observed to ensure that the child has sufficient control of the tongue and lips to reproduce sounds in the desired way. This can be assessed when the child is telling or retelling a story. Polysyllabic words and nonsense words can be repeated as part of a game. The teacher can also note any problems with pronunciation.
- *Knowledge and understanding of the world*. From this the child's interest and motivation to learn can be recognised. One can note the extent to which the child needs adult direction to explore and investigate an appreciation of the learning environment. The skills the pupil uses in some activities, such as categorisation, naming, ordering and sequencing, can be noted. One can also note the extent of integration of the senses and the extent to which the child can take advantage of multi-sensory learning—hearing, seeing, touching, saying, acting out, singing and the sense of smell, where this is appropriate. Crombie (2002b)

suggests that more able children will be observed through their problem-solving abilities and their strategies for coping with unusual or different situations. From this one can assess the level of concept development.

- *Expressive and aesthetic development.* An awareness of rhythm will facilitate language-learning and will help in music. Provide opportunities for children who are weak in tapping out a rhythm or keeping reasonable time to music to gain expertise in these areas. Activity-singing games and simple dance sequences will identify those children whose short-term memory is likely to inhibit their learning. They will also identify those children who seem likely to be able to develop a high level of expertise in these areas.
- *Physical development and movement.* Movement can be assessed by the teacher as part of the routine observations made within the classroom situation. Co-ordination skills can be assessed at this early stage through observation in physical activities and in writing. Balance has been found to be an important ability for learning: children who are poor at balance tasks while doing something else are likely to encounter other learning problems. This can be done by asking the child to balance on one foot while at the same time reciting a rhyme.

Crombie's 'Nursery Screening' assesses characteristics associated with the individual learner in the learning environment. This is important as it provides not only pointers to those children who may be at risk of literacy failure but also promotes multidisciplinary collaboration between professions and with parents. This type of screening, because it utilises the context of the learning environment, can be seen as a preventative approach and one that provides a link between assessment and teaching.

Some other commercially available screening strategies are described below.

Bangor Dyslexia Test

This is a commercially available, short screening test developed from work conducted at Bangor University (Miles, 1983a). The test is now used in many different countries. It is divided into the following sections:

- left–right (body parts);
- repeating polysyllabic words;
- subtraction;
- tables;
- months forward/reversed;
- digits forward/reversed;
- b–d confusion;
- familiar incidence.

It is important to note that this test is only intended as a screening device to find out whether the subject's difficulties are or are not typically dyslexic and may therefore offer a contribution toward an understanding of the subject's difficulties. It should not therefore be seen as a definitive diagnosis.

Dyslexia Screening Test (DST)

The authors of this test (Fawcett and Nicolson, 1996) claim it was developed due to both the wider theoretical understanding of dyslexia, particularly since the publication of the earlier Bangor Dyslexia Test, and the changes in the British educational system, particularly relating to the formal procedures for assessing whether children have special educational needs. It may also have a use, according to the authors, of assessing whether some children should have concessionary extra time in examinations.

The DST can be used for children between 6.6 and 16.5 years of age. There are also two other tests developed by the same authors for younger children: the Dyslexia Early Screening Test (Nicolson and Fawcett, 1996) and the Pre-School Screening Test (PREST) (Fawcett et al., 2001). PREST can screen children aged between 3 years 6 months and 4 years 5 months. It consists of PREST 1—rapid naming, beads-threading and paper-cutting, digits and letters, repetition, shape-copying and spatial memory. PREST 1 is intended to screen all children, and PREST 2 those children with an 'at risk' score in PREST 1. The subtests in PREST 2 are balance, phonological discrimination, digit span, rhyming, sound order and form-matching.

There is also an adult version— the Dyslexia Adult Screening Test (Fawcett and Nicolson, 1998). The norms for the DST were the result of extensive testing involving over 1000 children. The test consists of the following attainment tests:

- one minute spent on reading;
- two minutes spent on spelling;
- one minute spent on writing;

and the following diagnostic tests:

- rapid naming;
- beads-threading;
- postural stability;
- phonemic segmentation;
- backward digits span;
- nonsense passage-reading;
- verbal and semantic fluency.

These tests are consistent with the current theoretical standing of dyslexia, particularly in relation to the phonological representation hypothesis, the research on the cerebellum (Fawcett and Nicolson, 2001) and the rapid naming hypotheses (Wolf, 1996; Wolf and O'Brien, 2001). The wide range of factors considered in this test does enhance the value of the DST as a screening device.

Cognitive Profiling System (CoPS) This computerised screening programme represents an exciting breakthrough in this area (Singleton, 1996a, b). The programme constitutes a user-friendly package, complete with facilities for student registration, graphic report and printout of results. The CoPS suite has undergone extensive piloting and has also been converted to several languages. CoPS is now used in over 3500 primary schools in the UK and elsewhere in the world (Singleton, 2002). There is also the CoPS baseline assessment (Singleton et al., 1998).

In 1999 Lucid published the Lucid Assessment System for Schools-Secondary (LASS) (Horne et al., 1999), and in 2001 this was followed up by LASS Junior for primary schools. These programmes are now used in over 1000 primary and secondary schools in the UK. The Lucid Adult Dyslexia Screening Test is also available (see Chapter 12).

The Lucid/CoPS range of tests benefit from the advantages associated with computer programmes such as greater provision in presenting assessment tasks and greater accuracy in measuring responses. The programme can be administered with only the minimum of training and generally provides a greater degree of objectivity than some other forms of screening. These school-based tests have the potential, therefore, to fulfil an important function, particularly in curriculum-planning for children with dyslexia difficulties.

Quest—Screening, Diagnostic and Support Kit (2nd edn, Robertson et al., 1995)

Quest consists of group screening tests and individual diagnostic tests. The responses from the diagnostic test together with the associated workbooks can help in the planning of learning support programmes for pupils with difficulties in language and mathematics.

The screening is related to Key Stage 1 of the National Curriculum in England and Wales and Key Stage 1 of Standards of Attainment in the National Curriculum in Northern Ireland as well as Level A of the 5–14 curriculum in Scotland.

Essentially, the materials aim to identify those pupils at the beginning of the third year of schooling who may require support in learning. The materials, reading and number-screening tests, and reading and number diagnostic tests are accompanied by a series of workbooks: reading Quest, looking Quest, writing Quest and number Quest and a teacher's Quest manual.

These materials represent a comprehensive list that can identify children's difficulties early and offer a good example of materials that effectively link assessment and teaching. Examples of the test descriptions in the Quest Diagnostic Reading Test are shown below:

- pre-reading;
- auditory discrimination;
- auditory sequential memory;
- visual discrimination;
- visual sequencing;
- visuo-motor co-ordination.

Word search skills in the Quest Diagnostic Reading Test include:

- sight vocabulary;
- letter recognition (sounds);
- simple blends;

- beginnings and endings;
- digraphs, silent 'e' rule and silent letters;
- word-building;
- reading comprehension.

Listening and Literacy Index (Weedon and Reid, 2001)

This assessment comprises group tests for profiling literacy development and identifying specific learning difficulties. It contains linked, standardised tests of listening, reading and spelling and is designed for use by the classroom teacher with whole-class groups. The tests have been standardised with a large UK sample and the handbook contains norms, guidelines for scoring and teaching follow-up. There are four subtests:

- listening, which assesses the child's ability to understand spoken language about everyday situations;
- regular spelling, which assesses phonological processing and memory;
- sight word spelling, which assesses visual-processing and memory; and
- reading comprehension, which assesses the ability to read silently, for meaning.

The results of this test can display comparisons between these factors, and this may provide an early indicator of the presence or at least the risk of specific learning difficulties. For example, in the comparison between listening and the other scores it may be noted that a child who can listen well and with understanding, but whose spelling is poor and whose silent reading is laborious, may have a specific difficulty of a dyslexic type. If sight word spelling is better than regular spelling there may be an auditory difficulty, and where the two tasks that need sustained attention (listening and reading comprehension) are relatively weak there may be an attentional difficulty (Weedon and Reid, 2001).

Checklists

There are many variations of checklists for identifying dyslexia. This in itself highlights the need to treat checklists with considerable caution. Checklists are not, in any form, a definitive diagnosis of dyslexia and are therefore of fairly limited value, except perhaps for a preliminary screening to justify a more detailed assessment. Some checklists can however provide a range of information that may produce a picture of the child's strengths and weaknesses. However, even these are still very limited and no substitution for a comprehensive assessment looking at the classroom environment, the curriculum, and the learner's strengths and weaknesses.

However, checklists can be used as a way of recording details that are often comprehensive, and this can make them quite useful. This can include medical details or information about attendance, general ability, language, fine-motor difficulties, general co-ordination, motivation, learning style, social adjustment, parents' support and about attainments. It is important, however, that a checklist is not used in isolation, but is a component in the identification and support process. This is important as checklists can then be used to monitor progress.

ATTAINMENT TESTS

There are a number of standardised attainments tests that can be used to help identify dyslexia, and in addition to providing measures of attainment these tests can also provide diagnostic information. Some examples of these are discussed below.

Neale Analysis of Reading Ability

The revised edition of the Neale Analysis of Reading Ability (Neale, 1989) consists of a set of graded passages for testing reading rate, accuracy and comprehension of oral reading, and can be used as an attainment test and a diagnostic test. A demonstration cassette is also included that provides useful extracts from test sessions. The test material has an appealing format: a brightly coloured book with pictures accompanying each of the graded passages.

There is also a Diagnostic Tutor Form with extended passages for further error analysis and supplementary diagnostic tests focusing on discrimination of initial and final sounds, names and sounds of the alphabet, graded spelling, and auditory discrimination and blending, which can provide very useful information to help the teacher both diagnose and prepare teaching programmes.

Wordchains (Miller Guron, 1999)

This word-reading test is for people of all ages. Developed by Louise Miller Guron of Gothenberg University, wordchains comprise a timed word-reading test that can be used to screen for specific learning difficulties and can be used diagnostically to assist in the identification of children with poor reading skills. It can be used by teachers in primary schools, secondary schools and further education colleges—it can also be used as a whole-class resource and for individual screening. Wordchains comprise two parts:

- Letterchains, which screen for visual–motor dysfunction and consist of clusters of letters presented in the form of 90 chains of 3 or 4 clusters over a 90-second period.
- Wordchains, which consist of 400 nouns, verbs and adjectives appropriate for the beginning reader. These are presented in the form of chains in 3 or 4 clusters. The aim is to make as many clusters as possible in 3 minutes.

The scores for these tests can be converted to year group equivalents and a word recognition age can be obtained.

Early Literacy Test (Gillham, 2000)

This test is designed for use in pre-school as well as in infant classes and provides a standardised, diagnostic assessment to identify the bottom 25% at each age level before reading problems become severe. The Early Literacy Test profiles three key aspects of early literacy: book and story concepts, word recognition and knowledge of sounds and letters. The user handbook also contains follow-up teaching activities.

The Boder Test of Reading and Spelling Patterns (Boder and Jarrico, 1982)

This test is intended to fulfil the need for a practical, direct, diagnostic screening procedure that can differentiate developmental dyslexia from non-specific reading disorders. It attempts to classify dyslexic readers into one of three subtypes on the basis of their reading–spelling patterns. The unique feature of the test is that it jointly analyses reading and spelling as interdependent functions. The key features of the test include:

- reading and spelling tests with equal numbers of phonetic and non-phonetic words;
- a reading test based on sight vocabulary and phonic attack skills;
- an individualised written spelling test based on the results of the oral reading test.

The author claims that it is beneficial to examine two basic components of the reading–spelling process: the Gestalt and the analytic function. These correspond to the two standard methods of initial reading instruction: the whole-word (look–say) method that utilises visual/Gestalt skills and the phonics method that relies on the student's ability to analyse words into their phonic components.

Furthermore, the authors argue that the strengths and deficits of the Gestalt and analytic functions of dyslexic children are displayed within three characteristic reading–spelling patterns:

- The dysphonetic group. This type of reader has difficulty integrating written words with their sounds. Thus, he or she will display poor phonic word analysis and decoding skills. Typical misspellings are phonetically inaccurate, and mis-readings are word substitutions that can be semantic (e.g., 'bus' for 'car' and 'tree' for 'wood') or might be Gestalt substitutions (e.g., 'bell' for 'ball'). This category—the dysphonetic—is likely to be the largest among the dyslexic readers.
- The dyseidetic group. This group displays weaknesses in visual perception and memory for letters and whole-word configurations. They may have no difficulty in developing phonic skills, but will have a weakness in the visual/Gestalt area. Their typical misspellings are phonetically accurate and can be decoded (e.g., 'wok' for 'walk'), and their misreadings are good phonetic attempts at non-phonetic words (i.e., 'talc' for 'talk'). Visuospatial reversals can also be seen in this group (e.g., 'dab' for 'bad' and 'for' instead of 'of').

- Mixed dysphonetic and dyseidetic patterns. This group has difficulty in both the development of sight vocabulary and phonic skills.

Clearly, if learners from the dysphonetic group are identified, then their strengths will be on the visual side rather than phonic analysis skills. The implications of this for teaching may be a preference for a visual whole-word approach to help build a sight vocabulary before tackling the difficulty with phonics, which will be very evident.

Dyseidetic readers are unable to perceive whole words as a visual entity. Although it is important to build up a sight vocabulary with this type of learner, reading skills can be more readily attained through a phonics programme.

For children who have difficulty with both visual and auditory stimuli, learning can be provided through the third channel: tactile–kinaesthetic. Both phonic programmes and whole-word techniques can be supplemented with an emphasis on the tactile–kinaesthetic.

Teaching Reading through Spelling

This programme produced by teachers at the Reading Centre at Kingston upon Thames, called Teaching Reading through Spelling, contains a very useful booklet on diagnosis of specific learning difficulties (Cowdery et al., 1987).

The programme provides a very comprehensive diagnosis and assessment, but both the time and the expertise required for such comprehensive assessment is likely to be outwith the scope of the class teacher. Some of the strategies, however, particularly in relation to informal testing and diagnosis can be readily utilised by the class teacher.

The assessment objectives outlined by the authors include compiling a case profile, obtaining sample data of the problems, obtaining criterion-referenced and diagnostic information and obtaining age-related data. The objectives are achieved by means of interviews with parents and the child, observation, informal testing and diagnosis, and standardised testing and diagnosis.

Each of the stages has a specific function. For example, the interview conducted in a 'relaxed and supportive manner' attempts to provide an initial estimate of the child's abilities and parent's perception of the problem. Observation can take account of aspects such as directional confusion, co-ordination, movement, attention span, eye movements and general level of activity.

Informal testing involves noting conversational and listening skills and then noting errors, omissions and difficulties in conversation. Mispronunciation of words and asking for questions to be repeated or clarified can also be noted. In addition to conversational and listening skills, sequencing skills such as reciting the days of the week and the months of the year can be recorded as well as aspects of dominance—eye, ear, hand and foot—and directional aspects such as knowledge of left and right, below and above, and ability to mix laterality, such as being able to touch the left ear with the right hand.

Further information may be derived from observation of classroom activities by noting competencies in using different types of materials such as scissors, paints and paste, and observations can be made in physical education by noting general move-ment skills and motor co-ordination. The diagnostic programme provides some useful activities that the teacher can use with the child in order to obtain further data, including threading a needle, dealing cards, throwing and catching a ball, kicking a ball, screwing a lid on a jar, tying a shoelace and doing up buttons.

The programme also provides pointers to the assessment of language skills by noting the child's word-finding difficulties, vocabulary range, expressive difficulties, receptive language skills, phonological difficulties (such as the confusion of sounds), grammatical errors and articulation difficulties.

Slingerland

The Slingerland Assessment (Slingerland, 1976) is a diagnostic assessment that can provide data relating to both the child's skills in learning and preferences in learning style in relation to language and literacy.

The test has three components, each applicable to a different stage: Test A is directed at infants, Test B to middle primary and Test C to upper primary. The tests can be administered to a group or individually. There are nine subtests in the assessment, and the tests can be administered over several sessions. There are also pre-reading screening procedures (Slingerland, 1985) that can highlight auditory, visual and kinesthetic difficulties. These difficulties can be due to short attention span, faulty perception and recall of visual or auditory symbols, and fine-motor difficulties. As in other Slingerland tests this screening pack also attempts to high-light for classroom teachers the 'strengths and weaknesses of the learning modalities of their pupils'. As well as a pupil assessment booklet, the test also contains a teacher observation sheet. This observation sheet focuses on attention span, behaviour and social relations, general maturity and indications of mental growth, language factors, co-ordination in terms of gross movement and fine-motor control and general information in relation to activity of modality preferences.

In the screening procedures test each of the subtests performs a different function, but can be used to cross-check on data to confirm diagnostic opinions. For example, in Test A, Subtest 1 focuses on the visual–kinaesthetic area. It involves copying from the blackboard and can help to identify children with perceptual motor difficulties and visual scanning. Because it is a visual copying task, it can also provide data on the linking of the child's visual–kinaesthetic skills.

Subtest 2 performs a similar task, except the information that is to be copied is closer and comparisons between the results of this test and the previous one can be drawn.

Subtest 3 looks at visual perception, visual discrimination and memory. It involves displaying a card with a written word to the child, then distracting him before asking him to identify the word from a number of words on the test sheet.

Subtest 5 is similar, except that the child has to reproduce the word in writing, thus associating visual memory with the kinaesthetic channel.

The other subtests focus on auditory memory, which involves listening to the word, then selecting it from the test sheet. It also involves visual discrimination and linking the auditory and visual channels through listening and looking activities to identify words.

The Slingerland Test has no norms. Its use, therefore, is diagnostic and the insight provided by the test into the student's strengths, weaknesses, modality preferences and modality integration can help the teacher identify appropriate teaching materials for the student.

CURRICULUM ASSESSMENT

While standardised assessment can yield some important information that can be used diagnostically, it is vital that the assessment should also include an analysis of the task/curriculum that the child is working on. It is important to note how the child tackles specific tasks, the type of tasks that prove difficult and how aspects of the task can be adapted to enable the learner to succeed. This form of assessment can be very instrumental in the development of individual educational programmes. Holloway (2000) focusing on secondary age students with dyslexia suggests curriculum assessment procedures, which she has termed 'realistic assessment procedures' (RAP), whose aim is to assess language-based learning needs in the curriculum context. This procedure includes the following:

- cloze procedure—this involves the student completing sentences and passages where words have been deleted. This helps to encourage skimming and scanning as well as reading for meaning.
- Silent reading fluency—this is a timed two-minute reading exercise. At the end of that time the reader has to mark how far he or she has read—Holloway suggests that if the reader has read less than 100 words a minute it is likely that the reader is using a mechanical approach. The reader also has to write a sentence about the passage that has just been read.
- Individual assessment through reading aloud—while this may be difficult and stressful for students with dyslexia it can provide useful information on the student's reading behaviour, such as finger-pointing at words, mispronunciation and fluency.
- Timed free-writing/free-writing assessment—this involves a five-minute exercise that can reveal a number of aspects about the student's performance, such as the quality of the actual content of the piece, the writing style, spelling errors, use of sentences and paragraphs, and if there is a mismatch between the student's oral and written performance. This can also be used to assess the spelling needs of the student.
- Spelling test—the response to this can be analysed diagnostically, and inconsistencies in the spelling pattern and the type of spelling errors (visual/phonological) can be identified. For example, some of the error types suggested by Holloway include: contraction errors such as 'volve' for 'involve'; kinaesthetic errors that relate to poorly formed letters such as 'mdrket' for 'market'; sequencing errors such as getting the order of words mixed; transposition errors that are frequently noted in dyslexic children when parts of words are in the wrong order, such as 'canibet' for 'cabinet'; and phonological errors such as 'brot' for 'brought'.

Holloway also suggests curriculum assessment to include note-taking and dictation skills that would be particularly challenging for most students with dyslexia, and, therefore, this would have to be administered judiciously. This example is typical of a structured, curriculum-based assessment for literacy skills focusing on literacy performances. The key point is that the assessment is based on the student's own performances in a natural environment using work activities that are meaningful to the student at that time. Furthermore, it also offers a structured framework based on curriculum assessment. It is important that diagnostic information is obtained on the student's performances, and this must be done in as natural a way as possible.

Examples of assessment for dyslexia based on progress within the school curriculum can be seen in the policy guidelines on dyslexia and dyspraxia (Durham County Council, 2002), which provide descriptors of dyslexia in relation to curriculum targets. This is done within the key stages of the English National Curriculum. Descriptors, indicating some of the difficulties that may be encountered, are provided for ranges within the national curriculum at different 'key stages'. For example, the Key Stage 1/2 descriptors include: unevenness in targets, within national curriculum attainment targets which means that a pupil may be at Level 3 for speaking and listening, but at Level 1 for reading and writing; specific difficulties such as unexpected problems in learning to tell the time, general organisation and timekeeping; and marked and unexpected difficulties remembering information in a sequential order. At Key Stage 3/4 descriptors include word-finding, memory and labelling difficulties, and insufficient range of reading skills to cope with the wider variety of reading text types and technical vocabulary encountered in the secondary curriculum. As indicated earlier it is important to access a wide range of information in order to come to informed and diagnostic opinions relating to the presence and extent of any dyslexic difficulties that the student may be encountering. This is also recommended in the guidelines issued by Durham County Council. The guidelines include information from carers/parents and other professionals including health professionals. Assessments, the document suggests, should include baseline assessment, national curriculum attainment targets, checklists, standardised tests, diagnostic assessment measures and ongoing curriculum assessment.

MISCUE ANALYSIS DURING ORAL READING

The system known as miscue analysis can also offer a structure to investigate reading behaviours in a natural manner using curriculum-related text. This strategy is based on the 'top-down' approach to reading that has developed from the work of Goodman (1976). Goodman argued that the reader initially has to make predictions as to the most likely meaning of the text. Such predictions were based on how the reader perceived the graphic, syntactic and semantic information contained in the text. The reader, therefore, according to Goodman, engages in hypothesis-testing to either confirm or disprove the prediction—this he named the 'psycholinguistic guessing game'.

It was therefore assumed that miscues occur systematically and occur irrespective of whether reading is silent or aloud and that the degree of sense the child makes of the material reflects his use of prior knowledge.

The marking system that is usually adopted in miscue analysis is indicated below:

- *Omissions.* These may occur in relation to reading speed (e.g., when the child's normal silent reading speed is used when reading orally). As the child progresses in reading ability and reading speed increases, omissions may still be noted as they tend to increase as reading speed increases.
- *Additions.* These may reflect superficial reading with perhaps an over-dependence on context clues.
- *Substitutions.* These can be visual or semantic substitutions. In younger readers substitutions would tend to be visual, and in older readers contextual. In the latter case they may reflect an over-dependence on context clues.
- *Repetitions.* These may indicate poor directional attack and perhaps some anticipatory uncertainty on the part of the reader about a word to be read.
- *Reversals.* These may reflect the lack of left–right orientation. Reversals may also indicate some visual difficulty and perhaps a lack of reading for meaning.
- *Hesitations.* These can occur when the reader is unsure of the text and perhaps lacking in confidence in reading. For the same reason that repetitions may occur, the reader may also be anticipating a different word later in the sentence.

Self-corrections

These would occur when the reader becomes more aware of meaning and less dependent on simple word recognition.

It is important to observe whether the miscue produces syntactically or semantically acceptable text and whether the child is able to self-correct.

It is, therefore, possible to obtain useful data on the child's reading pattern by observing the reading errors and noting the significance of these oral errors.

There are some specifically designed assessment materials to use with the miscue analysis strategy. Arnold (1984) has developed a series of graded passages that have been specially prepared with miscue analysis in mind. The graded passages range from reading levels for 6-year-olds up to 12-year-olds. They vary in length and are written in autobiographical, narrative and informational styles.

Arnold (1992) has also produced a diagnostic reading record. This also contains case studies that highlight assessment through the use of miscue analysis. In addition it includes a teacher's handbook and pupil profile sheets and focuses on observations of reading behaviour and an examination of oral reading through discussion in order to obtain the child's level of understanding of the passage.

Curriculum Assessment in Context

Dargie (2001) provides examples of how dyslexic learners can be assessed in a range of skills within the context of the History curriculum. An instance of this is the examination of primary sources of historical information and assessment of how the dyslexic learner deals with tasks associated with this. One example is for students to contrast the facts about Macbeth known to modern historians with the key elements of the fictional representation offered by Shakespeare (Dargie, 1995).

Dargie (2001) also suggests that examples of writing by dyslexic pupils on historical matters frequently exhibit aspects of the following organisational symptoms:

- difficulty in appreciating the relative importance and relevance of information/ ideas;
- difficulty in sorting and arranging historical information into an appropriate textual format; and
- difficulty in distinguishing between general and particular pieces of evidence and in judging their relative importance.

Additionally, students with dyslexia usually possess a relatively restricted vocabulary, and this is also a factor that can restrict evaluative comment on historical evidence.

Dargie suggests that internal school-based assessment in History should take account of the cognitive and emotional difficulties that the dyslexic pupil can face when being tested. He cites the example of one model that was designed to provide pupils with a range of assessment activities in order to structure the amount of reading and writing required of pupils in a suitably progressive way. The test consisted of six short tasks that focused upon the previous month's work on the topic of early peoples. As this was the first History test experienced by these Term 1 pupils (new arrivals in the secondary school), bolstering the self-esteem of less confident learners was a key principle underlying the design of the test. Learners who had been previously identified by primary teachers as experiencing difficulties in reading, writing and information-processing were provided with a differentiated degree of support in three of the activities.

The first section of the test consisted of four relatively simple tasks that required little writing and that were intended to remind pupils of the work covered throughout the unit:

- Completing a simple cloze passage with an answer box provided.
- Matching a table of names to pictures of specific artefacts used by early people.
- Listing things from the prehistoric period found by archaeologists in the school's local area. The test papers contained a memory trigger in the form of a local map used by the teacher in the lesson on this aspect of the topic.
- Completing five sentence stems such as 'We know the Skara Brae people in Orkney were shepherds because ...' This fourth exercise required pupils to apply recalled subject knowledge to complete the sentence appropriately. However, three of the five sentence conclusions had been clued up by triggers in the first exercise to provide assistance for pupils with memory difficulties. Line indicators were used in the test paper to encourage pupils to write as fully as possible. This fourth task also acted as a bridge from the deliberately simple initial tasks requiring a short response to the second section of the test, which consisted of two extended writing activities in which dyslexic learners were assisted by a

five-stem writing frame. This form of assessment is also metacognitive as it provides an opportunity for scaffolding to other more complex tasks and concepts and helps pupils to be aware of how they achieved certain tasks. Importantly, however, this example provides a link between assessment and practice within a meaningful context.

In Biology, Howlett (2001) suggests the following list can present difficulties and can therefore be used as a means of helping to identify the nature of the difficulties experienced by dyslexic students in this subject:

- remembering and recalling 'names' accurately, for text and diagrams;
- spelling of technical words;
- learning of many factual details;
- assimilating abstract concepts;
- drawing and labelling of diagrams;
- practical work—remembering and following instructions accurately and fully, and recording observations/data accurately, in orderly manner and fast enough;
- having confidence to ask about anything not understood or to come up with original questions and comments.

EXAMINATIONS AND ASSESSMENT

These examples highlight the potential and the desirability of assessing within the subject and curriculum context. This will be discussed further in Chapter 11 on secondary school dimensions. Naturally, one has to consider the function of examinations, and it is usually a concern for parents, student and teachers. Tod and Fairman (2001) highlight some key aspects of curriculum assessment and curriculum planning and, particularly, its importance for dyslexic children. Table 5.1 is an example of this that focuses on the secondary student in relation to national examinations.

Table 5.1 shows quite clearly how some aspects that can usually be taken for granted with students who have no obvious difficulty cannot with students with dyslexia. Aspects such as understanding the syllabus structure are important for dyslexic students as it provides them with some framework that can help to structure their study and understanding of the subject. As well as this they may have difficulty in understanding how marks are allocated for different parts of a question as well as the metacognitive factors associated with exactly what the examiner is looking for. Students with dyslexia may also have a limited vocabulary in written work and have awkward use of grammar, and some terms and phrases may be used inappropriately. Needless to say this can result in low motivation unless some of the supports indicated in Table 5.1 are put in place.

Table 5.1 Planning (reproduced by permission of David Fulton; from Tod and Fairman, 2001).

What	Why	How	
		Group	Individual
Need to understand the syllabus structure	To allow energy to be expended efficiently and facilitate time planning	Give students a visual summary of the syllabus. Ask them to highlight areas of key importance. Check match between student and teacher perceptions	Ask individual student how he or she thinks each section fits into the whole. Mediate understanding as to rationale for syllabus design and ordering. Peruse revision guide
Explicit analysis of the marking scheme	To capitalise on areas needed to boost grade attainment. Prioritise areas for action	Look at marking schemes produced by exam boards	Ask student to identify from his work what he often omits (e.g., diagrams and quotes)
Metacognition and understanding what the examiner is looking for	Facilitate a match between what is required and what students produce	Look at perfect answers. Identify strengths. Self-assess work in peer support groups	Ask individual to identify where he or she could make improvements based on 'model answer exemplars'. Action plan to improve performance
Improve understanding of vocabulary as used in subject areas	It is possible to misinterpret questions and lose marks	Give subject vocabulary list, with definitions	Reinforce, help learn or reduce size of list
Clarify use of language	Impacts on marks	List key examples. Show examiner's reports	Highlight problem areas. Prioritise for extra practice under exam conditions
Motivation	To complete work	Extrapolate a grid of grades	Explain how 'additional' effort on coursework elements can compensate for exam performance and influence overall grade

METACOGNITIVE ASSESSMENT

Metacognition refers to the child's self-knowledge of learning. It examines the quality of the learning process: the structure and organisation of the learner's knowledge base, of mental models (schemata) and efficiency of student self-monitoring. Metacognitive knowledge therefore involves both content and process knowledge.

Most traditional forms of assessment look only at the content base, and what the child can and cannot do becomes the product of the assessment. Glaser et al. (1987) recommended developing tests that examine the process of learning and how the child's knowlege base changes with learning.

It is important that a preoccupation with identifying the nature of the dyslexic difficulties should not prevent an assessment of the child's learning processes, as this has considerable linkage with appropriate teaching and how materials should be presented.

There are a number of ways of assessing the metacognitive strategies of dyslexic children. Some of these are described below.

Assisted Assessment

Campione and Brown (1989), dissatisfied with the limited information that can be obtained from normative procedures, have developed a soundly researched model for assisted or dynamic assessment, focusing on the task and the process of learning. They have also linked this form of assessment with the intervention model known as Reciprocal Teaching (Palincsar and Klenk, 1992).

The focus of Campione and Brown's work relates to aspects of learning and transfer; the information obtained provides an indication of the nature and amount of help needed by the child, rather than the child's level of attainment or improvement. This can be revealed through 'prompts', memory tasks and help with developing learning strategies.

Campione and Brown argue that there should be a link between assessment and instruction. They argue that traditional tests are intended to be predictive and prescriptive, *but* fail on both counts. Their argument rests on the assertions that children can be too readily mis-classified and that traditional tests do not really provide a clear indication of what is really required for instruction.

Campione and Brown (1989) argue that the context of assessment is important and divide assessment into two aspects.

Static Tests

In these the child works unaided on sets of items and is given but a single chance to demonstrate his or her proficiency. Thus:

- no aid is provided;
- social interaction between the tester and the child is minimised;
- objective scoring systems can be readily implemented;
- norms can be available.

Although such tests may fulfil a purpose they have considerable shortcomings:

- they say nothing about the processes involved in the acquisition of the responses;
- some children may get the right answer for the wrong reason;
- students may be mis-classified because they have not yet acquired the competence, but are in the process of acquiring it.

Dynamic Tests

Dynamic-type tests emphasise the individual's potential for change. Such tests do not attempt to assess how much improvement has taken place, but rather how much help children need to reach a specified criterion and how much *help* they will need to transfer this to novel situations. Such tests are therefore metacognitive in that they can provide information on how the child is learning. By noting the cues necessary to facilitate the correct response from the child, the teacher can obtain some information on how the child thinks and learns. Such information can be relayed back to the child to illustrate how he or she managed to obtain the correct response. Thus, assessment is *a learning experience, not a testing one*.

There are a number of different forms of dynamic assessment models, such as Feuerstein's Learning Potential Assessment Device (LPAD), which is inextricably linked to the Intervention Model—Instrumental Enrichment (Feuerstein et al., 1980) is an intervention programme that aims to develop an individual's thinking skills and overall cognitive ability. The programme consists of 14 sets of cognitive activities that can be utilised in a classroom situation as part of the curriculum activities or as an individual programme (Burden, 2002). The LPAD battery includes both verbal and non-verbal tasks, analogical reasoning, numerical reasoning, memory strategies and conceptual categorisations; it also utilises Raven's Progressive Matrices (Raven, 1992, 1993), which is a measure of non-verbal reasoning, as one of the measures. Extensive training is required to develop proficiency in the administration of the LPAD, although it has been described as the 'most comprehensive and theoretically grounded expression of dynamic assessment' (Lidz, 1991).

Elliott (1996) maintains that dynamic assessment offers considerable promise by providing valuable information about children's true potential and can be used to help develop educational intervention programmes. He also argues, however, that, because dynamic assessment research is in its infancy and it represents more of a general concept than a specific technique, it does not readily fit into 'Western models of professional thinking'. This thinking, according to Elliott, is characterised by the perseverance with familiar techniques because of time demands and the increasing number of formal assessments professionals need to undertake to assist in decision-making regarding placements and resources. It is, however, unfortunate if the need for quantitative data overburdens professionals at the expense of developing and disseminating qualitative strategies, which can provide a real insight into students' learning skills and development.

PASS Model

Das et al. (1994) offer a model that highlights planning skills as an indicator of metacognition. This is called the PASS model (Planning, Attention, Simultaneous and Successive processes) and focuses on *how* information is processed, not *what* is processed. This model conceptualises the brain as being concerned with three major, interconnected systems that relate to strategies:

• attention—maintains alertness, motivation and arousal;

- information—receives, processes and stores information using simultaneous and successive information-processing;
- planning—regulatory use of strategies and approaches to tasks.

With this model, skills in successive and simultaneous processing can also be detected. The dyslexic child may have difficulty with successive processing where items are processed linearly and logically in sequential fashion. Simultaneous processing, however, involves dealing with information holistically and integrating and synthesising information into a meaningful whole.

The third dimension of the PASS model, planning, represents an important aspect of metacognition. This relates closely to strategy development in problem-solving. Ayres (1994) argues that planning is accompanied by a number of functions that relate to metacognition, such as the ability to form plans of action, to regulate behaviour so that it conforms to the planned outcome and to evaluate performance. Few existing tests actively measure planning—although the Mazes subtest of the WISC III (Wechsler Intelligence Scale) relates to this in some way through visual planning and digit span backwards involves planning processes as the child endeavours to convert the digits backwards.

Das et al. (1994) in fact argue that 'planning' discriminates good from poor readers of comparable IQ. Poor planners perceive a page in a disorganised manner, choose incorrect targets, often impulsively, make more errors and fail to change their strategy if it is inefficient.

Multiple Intelligences Approaches

Lazear (1994, 1999), by utilising Gardner's theory of multiple intelligences (Gardner, 1985), has contributed greatly to a new assessment paradigm consisting of multiple intelligences approaches. Though the author quite rightly argues that a multiple intelligences assessment should grow out of a multiple intelligences curriculum, some significant insights can be gained for assessment in general by utilising the approach advocated by Lazear.

The multiple intelligences model is discussed in Chapter 8, 'Metacognition and Study Skills'. This model suggests that assessment should be comprehensive and consider a number of different elements. Lazear contends that assessment should be used to enhance students' learning and, particularly, to experience their ability to transfer learning to other areas and, indeed, beyond formal schooling. Lazear further contends that, because there are no standard students, instruction of testing should be individualised and varied. Lazear's model lends itself to curriculum-based assessment. Assessment, therefore, should be occurring simultaneously with learning and should be an inbuilt factor within the curriculum. Curriculum-based assessment, particularly using a multiple intelligence approach, ensures that the assessment process is relevant to the actual curricular work with which the student is involved. This helps to clearly identify teaching and learning aims, it establishes criteria for success and tasks can be matched to pupils' previous experiences of particular abilities (Weedon and Reid, 1998).

A COMPONENTS APPROACH

The limitations of discrepancy models of assessment such as intellectual/attainment discrepancies have led to the development of alternative criteria and procedures to assist in the differential diagnosis of reading difficulties.

One such approach, known as the 'components approach' (Aaron, 1989, 1994; Aaron and Joshi, 1992), examines the components of the reading process. The main aims of the components approach to assessment are:

- to distinguish the dyslexic child from the 'slow learner' child who displays reading difficulties;
- to distinguish the dyslexic child from the child who has a comprehension deficit in reading;
- to adapt the assessment for classroom use, to make it available for the teacher and psychologist;
- to allow for a complete diagnostic procedure that would be comprehensive enough to include quantitative as well as qualitative information that is relevant to the reading process.

The main strands of the components approach are:

- the identification of the factors that determine performance;
- a description of the components of reading;
- an evaluation of the child's functioning in relation to these components.

Aaron (1989) describes four main components of reading:

- verbal comprehension;
- phonological awareness;
- decoding speed; and
- listening comprehension.

It can be argued that decoding and comprehension are the two most important components of reading, representing visual and auditory processing skills together with meaningful comprehension. (This simultaneous processing involving decoding and comprehension may require hemispheric integration and justify the claim that reading is a holistic activity.)

In normal readers, decoding and comprehension are consistent and complementary. Thus, as a child reads (decodes the print) meaning is simultaneously expressed. It can be suggested that:

- *comprehension* is a controlled process (i.e., is attention-demanding) with limited capacity;
- *decoding* is an automatised process (i.e. is not attention-demanding) and does not require reader's conscious control.

It is known that for dyslexic children decoding does not readily become automatised (Fawcett, 1989) and therefore requires:

- attention-demanding operations;
- conscious control from the reader.

These are also factors in comprehension, and hence it is argued that dyslexic readers, when decoding, draw on some of the capacities that should be focusing on comprehension and thereby weaken their potential for comprehension while reading. This suggestion is supported by work on visual imagery in reading (Bell, 1991a), which claims that the decoding process weakens the dyslexic child's gestalt (right hemisphere) and consequently comprehension.

Aaron (1989) suggests that differences in reading achievement are due to factors associated with either decoding or comprehension or a combination of both. To differentiate between these two abilities, it is necessary to assess them independently. Thus, reading comprehension has to be assessed without involving the decoding of print.

Some researchers suggest that reading comprehension and listening comprehension share the same cognitive mechanisms and that the two forms of comprehension are related. Palmer et al. (1985) obtain a highly significant correlation between these two forms of comprehension and state that 'reading comprehension can be predicted almost perfectly by a listening measure—therefore a test of listening comprehension can be used as a measure of reading comprehension.' It is suggested, however, that although the correlation may still be significant it may be lower than some studies have shown (Bedford-Feull et al., 1995).

Certainly, in the early reading stages there seems to be a close relationship between decoding and reading comprehension, so one can use a decoding assessment procedure in the early years. One must, however, attempt to use a task that is closely related to decoding, but not influenced by environmental or contextual factors.

A components approach to assessment that can be readily carried out by the teacher can include the following:

- decoding test (non-word-reading test);
- word-reading test;
- phonological awareness test;
- listening comprehension test;
- reading comprehension test.

Aaron (1989) has indicated three different categories of reading disorders: dyslexic readers, hyperlexic readers and non-specific-reading disabled readers. Dyslexic readers have poor decoding, but relatively good comprehension, while non-specific-reading disabled readers would show poor comprehension and poor decoding skills. The hyperlexic reader would have good decoding skills, but poor comprehension.

An interesting difference can be noted between hyperlexic readers and dyslexic readers. Hyperlexic readers are those who can decode and are therefore good at reading mechanically, while dyslexic readers are poor at decoding and read inaccurately, but can perform better in reading comprehension tasks.

This emphasises that the key components of the reading process that are to be assessed are:

- decoding;
- listening/reading comprehension.

The components approach is a diagnostic procedure that does not rely solely on norm-referenced, standardised tests, but can be applied with locally developed assessment materials from which programmes can be developed in the context of the curriculum and the classroom activities.

Aaron and Joshi (1992) contend that a measure of listening comprehension is more appropriate in diagnosing reading difficulties than, for example, an IQ measure. Listening comprehension tests do not possess the same drawbacks as IQ measures (Siegal, 1989), and the diagnostic findings can link directly to teaching procedures. The components approach, therefore, gains support from the view that reading comprehension and listening comprehension are highly correlated and that reading is made up of two components: comprehension and decoding.

It is suggested (Gough and Tunmer, 1986) that the reading difficulty of a student who has good listening comprehension but lower reading comprehension can be attributed to poor word recognition skills. A formal diagnostic procedure involving decoding and listening comprehension would therefore seem to be an appropriate one.

OBSERVATIONAL ASSESSMENT

The essence of this chapter is that while there are a number of assessment tools dedicated to identifying dyslexia these should be used in conjunction with other curriculum-based forms of assessment. One method of accumulating this type of data is through observation. This form of assessment can also yield informative data that can inform teaching. Observational assessment is contextualised and can be used flexibly to ensure that the data obtained is the type of information required. It is important, however, that the observer recognises the drawbacks of observational assessment in that often it only provides a snapshot of the child unless it is implemented in different contexts over time. Nevertheless, this type of assessment can be particularly useful for children with dyslexic difficulties as some standardised tests may not provide the kind of diagnostic information that is needed in order to develop a teaching programme. There are a number of different forms of observational assessment. These can provide important data and offer some pointers as to appropriate teaching strategies as well.

An observation schedule or framework should be constructed before an assessment. A number of benefits of observation schedules can be identified; for example, they can be flexible, adaptable to different situations and can be used within the context of the learning situation. Hopefully, a 'natural' response will then be recorded free from the influence of 'test contamination' factors.

Throughout the observation it is important to record not only what the student does or can do, but how the response is achieved—the cues required, the level and extent of the assistance needed at the stages the student needs to go through to solve a problem or obtain a response.

With increased importance being placed on early identification and metacognitive aspects of learning, procedures such as observational criteria can have an important role to play in the assessment process.

Observational Framework

In this framework one is looking at a broad range of areas that can relate to some of the difficulties experienced by children with specific learning difficulties or dyslexia.

It is important to gather information that relates to the child, the learning situation and context. The aim is not just to find out how or why the child is having difficulty, but to gain some insight and understanding into the strategies and processes of learning for that child.

A framework for observational assessment for specific learning difficulties can therefore include the areas listed below.

Attention

- What is the length of attention span?
- Under what conditions is attention enhanced?
- What are the factors contributing to distractibility?
- What is the level of attention or distractibility under different learning conditions?

Organisation

- What are the organisational preferences?
- What degree of structure is required?
- How good is the organisation of work, desk, self?
- What are the reactions to imposed organisation?

Sequencing

- Is there the ability to follow sequences without aid?
- Is there a general difficulty with sequencing (e.g., with work, carrying out instructions, words when reading, individual letters in written work)?

Interaction

- What degree of interaction is there with peers, adults?
- What is the preferred interaction: one-to-one, small groups or whole class?
- How is the interaction sustained?

Language

- Is language expressive?
- Is the meaning accurately conveyed?
- Is language spontaneous or prompted?
- Is there appropriate use of natural breaks in speech?
- Is there expressive language in different contexts (e.g., one-to-one, small group or class group)?
- Are there errors, omissions and difficulties in conversation and responses (e.g., mispronunciations, questions have to be repeated or clarified)?

Comprehension

- How does the child comprehend information?
- What type of cues most readily facilitate comprehension?
- Are schemas used?
- What type of instructions are most easily understood: written, oral or visual?
- How readily can knowledge be transferred to other areas?

Reading

- What are the reading preferences: aloud, silent?
- What type of errors crop up?

Visual

- Is there the ability to discriminate between letters that look the same?
- Is there inability to appreciate that the same letter may look different (e.g., 'G' or 'g'?
- Does omission or transposition of parts of a word occur (this could indicate a visual segmentation difficulty)?

Auditory

- Are there difficulties in auditory discrimination?
- Is there inability to hear consonant sounds in initial, medial or final position?
- Is there auditory sequencing?
- Is there auditory blending?
- Is there an auditory segmentation?

Motivation/Initiative

- What is the interest level of the child?
- How is motivation increased, what kind of prompting and cueing is necessary?
- To what extent does the child take responsibility for his or her own learning?
- What kind of help is required?

Self-concept

- What tasks are more likely to be tackled with confidence?
- When is confidence low?
- What is the level of self-concept and confidence in different contexts?

Relaxation

- Is the child relaxed when learning?
- Is there evidence of tension or relaxation?

Learning preferences

The following learning preferences need to be ascertained:

- auditory;
- visual;
- oral;
- kinaesthetic;
- tactile;
- global;
- analytic.

It is important, therefore, to note in observational assessment the preferred mode of learning. Many children will of course show preferences and skills in a number of modes of learning. Multi-sensory teaching, therefore, is crucial in order to accommodate as many modes as possible.

Learning context

When assessing the nature and degree of the difficulty experienced by the child, it is important to take into account the learning context. This context, depending on the learner's preferred style, can either exacerbate the difficulty or minimise the problem (Reid, 1992, 1994a; Given and Reid, 1999). The contextual factors below should therefore be considered:

- classroom;
- role of teacher;
- task;
- materials and resources.

Observation and assessment therefore need to adopt a holistic perspective:

- observing components within a framework for learning;
- observing some factors within that framework associated with specific learning difficulties or dyslexia;
- observing preferred styles of learning;
- acknowledging the importance of the learning context.

Systematic Observation

Structured systematic observation can yield some important information in relation to the student's strengths, difficulties and actual performances in the classroom context. Perhaps the most sophisticated of the systematic observation strategies are those devised for the Reading Recovery Programme. Clay (1993) provides a detailed analysis of systematic observation. This analysis is called the 'running record' and the observation tasks are designed to help the teacher focus on precisely what happens when the child is reading. Although the Clay observation tasks were designed to develop a running record for use with the Reading Recovery Programme some of the general principles can be utilised for use with dyslexic children. Clay suggests that, to observe systematically, one must:

- observe precisely what children are saying and doing;
- use tasks that are closely related to the learning tasks of the classroom;
- observe what children have been able to learn;
- identify from this the reading behaviour they should now be taught;
- focus the child's general reading behaviour to training on reading tasks rather than on specific subskills such as visual perception or auditory discrimination.

In order to achieve the above Clay has developed a 'diagnostic survey' (the Running Record), which looks at directional movement, motor co-ordination, reading fluency, error behaviour, oral language skills, letter identification skills, concepts about print and writing skills.

This latter aspect is particularly important as writing skills may provide some indication of any reading problems (e.g., a poor writing vocabulary may indicate the child is taking very little notice of visual differences in print). The weakness in visual discrimination may be because the hand and eye are not complementing each other, and this is an important aspect of early writing. Additionally, other factors in writing such as language level and message quality are also important to note. In writing, children are required to pay attention to details of letters, letter sequences, sound sequences and the links between messages in oral language and messages in printed language.

Other useful aspects of Clay's model involve the 'concepts of print test', which addresses vital aspects relating to the child's knowledge of print and familiarity with books. Questions about whether the child can distinguish the front from the back of the book, left from right, recognise errors in print, distinguish between capital and lower case and locate first and last letters are all addressed. This provides crucial information at this early stage of reading—information that certainly should be gathered for children who are at risk of failing in literacy.

Clay's observation approach also focuses on strategies for decoding. The teacher should therefore record the different strategies the child uses in relation to location and movement, language, how the child deals with difficulties (e.g., seeking help, searching for further cues and the extent of self-correction). Self-correction according to Clay is an important aspect of reading progress and needs to be accurately recorded.

SUMMARY

A range of approaches have been described in this chapter. To recap, these include standardised, diagnostic, phonological assessment, curriculum, components of reading assessment, metacognitive, screening and observational approaches. Clearly, no one approach can provide both sufficient data to identify and assess dyslexia and provide a sufficient and effective linkage with teaching. Different factors need to be taken into account and all assessment procedures discussed in this chapter have considerable merits. The factors that determine what approach or approaches should be used relate to the reasons for the assessment and the purposes for which the information is to be put. It is, however, important to bear in mind that different children may well display different profiles and still be identified as dyslexic. Ideally, the assessment should link with teaching, and if this is a successful outcome of the assessment then it will have been put to a valid and worthwhile use.

Chapter 6

Assessment: Process

The previous chapter provided descriptions and comments about many of the assessment practices that can be used in the identification of dyslexia. This chapter will describe and comment on these approaches in relation to possible frameworks or processes that can be utilised and adapted to accommodate the identification of dyslexia in different educational contexts and systems.

One of the key issues in the assessment process is that of early identification. How such identification should take place and when it can most effectively and most sensitively be conducted are matters of some debate. This is clearly an important aspect of the assessment process, and it is important that schools have procedures in place to meet the needs of early identification. Other aspects also need to be considered, such as whole-school policy, role of other professionals, linkage with teaching, role of parents, and professional development and training. These will also be discussed below.

EARLY IDENTIFICATION

- When should this take place, how should it be conducted and by whom?
- What criteria should be used at this early stage for a diagnosis?

If teachers ask the first of these questions (when should this take place?), then I would suggest they have misunderstood the whole concept of early identification. Certainly, as the term implies, 'early identification' means some form of intervention to note any signs of difficulties that children may have, which may (or may not) lead to dyslexia or some other specific learning difficulty. To ask when this should take place is to recognise that these 'signs' can be identified in an almost one-off assessment in the nursery or early stages. While this may well be the case (a list of criteria and strategies relating to this are shown in Table 6.1), this may also be misleading. To speak of early identification is almost to suggest that there is some within-child deficit that can be apparent almost before the child has had an opportunity to sample the learning opportunities in nursery or school. This, of course, runs counter to the

Table 6.1   Assessment process in the nursery school.

Assessment	Procedure	Outcome
Speech and language development	Parental discussion and observation	
Motor development	As above	
Letter knowledge	Screening	
Problem-solving skills	Observation/Screening	
Interest and motivation	Consultation with colleagues and parents	
Attention and concentration	Observation	
Social skills	Observation	

* The blank column is for noting results of assessments.

whole concept of inclusion where the onus is not on the child to 'change', but on educational factors such as the learning environment and the curriculum to accommodate the needs of the child. The term 'early identification' would therefore be more accurate if it were extended to 'early identification of learning needs'.

Many systems currently used to identify these learning needs at an early stage utilise a combination of both the needs model and the child deficit model. It is possible to merge these two in a complementary manner. Looking at Table 6.1 one can see there is a column 'outcome' that is incomplete, but would of course be completed after the information is gathered.

It is important to attempt to envisage what the possible outcome will be before the intervention, if this type of intervention model is being used. Outcome should relate to curriculum development and should recognise potential and actual barriers that may prevent the child from progressing. This emphasises the difference in curriculum access rather than the deficit in the child. An example of a document that does include 'outcome' as an integral part of the identification procedures for dyslexia is the *Report of Task Force on Dyslexia* for the Republic of Ireland (Task Force on Dyslexia, 2001). This document highlights the phrase 'Continuum of Identification and Provision.' An example of the part that applies to the nursery and early stages is shown in Table 6.2.

Table 6.2 is an example of a policy-led identification and support model. This model provides some general and specific guidelines, but its success or otherwise in relation to practice depends to a great extent on resources.

SIDNEY

Bentote (2001) reported on an example of an early screening that has been implemented and followed up with intervention as part of a cohesive package within an education authority in England. The assessment and intervention is called SIDNEY (Screening and Intervention for Dyslexia, Notably in the Early Years) and is a major project funded by Hampshire County Council. It involves screening pupils in the

Table 6.2   Continuum of Identification and Provision (nursery and early stages) (Government of the Republic of Ireland Task Force on Dyslexia, 2001).

Phase	Procedure	Main persons involved	Outcomes
1. Initial identification of a learning difference (ages 3–5, preschool/junior infants)	Informal assessment by caregiver/teacher; input from parents; identification of a marked learning difference	Child, principal teacher, caregiver, class teacher, parents/ guardians	Response to learning differences within child's own class by noticing and adjusting; some differentiation of instruction; recording child's response to adjustments
2. Identification of a possible learning difficulty arising from dyslexia (ages 5–7+, infants in their first class)	Formal and informal assessment; diagnostic assessment to determine seriousness and persistence of students's learning difficulties; review of progress through regular assessment	Student, principal teacher, class teacher, learning support teacher; parents/ guardians, educational psychologist (for guidance and advice if needed)	Identification of students who are at risk of developing learning difficulties arising from dyslexia; provision of individual or small-group differentiated response by class or learning support teachers; development and implementation of individual learning programme and monitoring outcomes, as per the learning support guidelines

third term of their reception year to identify if they are at risk of developing future literacy difficulties, including dyslexia. Three methods of screening were used: CoPS (Cognitive Profiling System), DST (Dyslexia Screening Test) and teacher screening. Those pupils identified are placed on an intervention programme that runs during their first term of Year 1.

During the full day's training, schools are instructed in the characteristics of young dyslexic children and are then shown how to carry out the screening and how to run the intervention programme. Over a three-year period, 360 infant and primary schools in Hampshire have received training in the screening, and they are now implementing the SIDNEY intervention programme. This is a good example of an assessment process that utilises commercially available procedures that has been developed and customised for the context within an education authority.

Other possible types of identification models are described and commented on below.

MODELS OF IDENTIFICATION

Pumfrey (1990) suggests that the concept of diagnosis and treatment is based on a medical model and is not therefore appropriate to the education context. Teachers, Pumfrey asserts, ought to be wary of moving down the classification escalator, which he describes as moving from individual differences to deviations, difficulties, disabilities, deficits and eventually to defects.

Yet, while this 'classification escalator' is clearly something that ought to be avoided and something that underlines the inherent dangers of hasty diagnosis or perceiving lack of attainments as a within-child difficulty that requires diagnosis and perhaps a label, it is still beneficial to implement some form of early identification procedures, despite these risks. It has been well argued that the intricacies of the reading process result in significant numbers of children adopting ineffective reading strategies, which need to be identified and modified by the teacher lest the error behaviour becomes too entrenched, thus placing a restriction on further progress (Clay, 1993; Pumfrey, 1990; Tunmer and Chapman, 1996). To ensure, however, that a medical diagnosis–treatment model is not perceived as the principal assessment strategy, it is important that assessment is undertaken by the class teacher, using a range of strategies, and that this assessment is linked to teaching and the curriculum. This type of model has some advantages over formal assessment by specialist teachers, but if difficulties do persist there is a definite role for utilising the expertise of specialist teachers. Some of the models currently in use are described below. It is often the case that countries/education authorities use a combination of the key elements in the models below, but some identifiable overriding principles can be noted from, on the one hand, a child deficit/medical perspective to, on the other hand, a full curriculum-directed approach that focuses on curriculum access rather than specific deficits.

EXPERT/INTERVENTION—ATTAINMENT DISCREPANCY MODEL

This model is essentially a child deficit model and usually focuses on concerns that may arise from parents and teachers relating to lack of expected progress in attainments. This model usually operates through the intervention of another professional such as an educational psychologist or speech and language therapist. This often happens when some concern is expressed, and usually the diagnosis is based on cognitive and clinical evidence as well as background information and case history. While this model can be used as a basis for resource allocation it is not without critics. One of the main points of contention stems from the lack of agreement of 'experts' as to exactly which criteria, and to what extent, various factors can contribute to a dyslexia diagnosis. For example, Turner (1997) suggests that a 'dyslexia index' can be observed from various calculations using at least six core or ability tests, four diagnostic tests and three achievement tests. The result is a comprehensive accumulation of data on the child and his or her academic achievement. Turner suggests that a dyslexia index comprising six levels can be detected from this information. This index would range from 'no dyslexia signs' at 0.0 standard deviation to 'very severe dyslexia' at above 2.0 standard deviation. Turner provides comprehensive and convincing examples to support the value of such an index, and its major achievement lies in the attempt by Turner to quantify what has been described as 'a variable syndrome' (Pumfrey, 1995). In view of this variability it is perhaps desirable to obtain some measurable data to quantify the degree of severity, or the presence of dyslexia. Pumfrey (2001, 2002) applauds the explicit rationale and methodology of the Dyslexia Index and suggests that this constitutes a challenging contribution to professional practice in assessment. At the same time, of course, it rests on the diagnostic assumptions made by these tests, and that they are sufficiently robust and sufficiently wide-ranging to incorporate all the variables that can contribute to the presence of dyslexia. This point is also noted by Pumfrey (2001) when he suggests that 'whether his seven point scale of dyslexia severity will be seen as fair depends on the validity of the assumptions on which the diagnostic procedures are based' (p. 151).

Similarly, cognitive criteria that have a long-established history for use in the identification of dyslexia are often termed the ACID profile, because of their use of the Arithmetic, Coding, Information and Digit span profile from the Wechsler Intelligence Scale (WISC). Indeed, these criteria were used in the Hillingdon judgement (Garland, 1997) when it was suggested in the report that 'individuals with a pattern of dyslexic difficulties typically do rather badly on ACID compared with the remainder' (p. 3). Yet, Frederickson (1999) draws together evidence from several studies (Ward et al., 1995; Watkins et al., 1997; Prifitera and Dersch, 1993) to suggest that the 'statements on the ACID profile contained in the Hillingdon judgement are not supported by the research evidence ... (and that) educational psychologists cannot legitimately be criticised if they do not use an ACID profile to identify children with special learning difficulties, but can be criticised if they place strong reliance on its use for this purpose' (p. 7). The evidence that supports Frederickson's assertion is based on the view from the research studies noted above. These studies suggest that although the incidence of the presence of an ACID profile in children with special learning difficulties may have been greater, it did not reach any level of statistical significance. Ward et al. (1995) suggest that this low incidence renders it 'clinically meaningless'. This point can also be seen as an implication of the BPS working party report (BPS, 1999a), which noted that in relation to approaches to assessment and models of responses some of the responses indicated 'what is distinctive about Educational Psychologist assessment as opposed to specialist teacher assessment?' (p. 91). Another response indicated that 'it would be helpful to have an assessment model which can be used by teachers in consultation with E.P.s' (p. 92). Similar conclusions can be made about the SCAD profile—this profile refers to a calculation of the sum of the picture completion, picture arrangement, block design and object assembly minus the sum of the scaled scores for symbol search, coding, arithmetic and digit span of the WISC. If the result of this calculation leads to a score greater than 9 then this represents a statistically significant difference. While the SCAD profile may have been found to be higher in a population with special learning difficulties than in a random sample, Frederickson (1999) suggests that the differences are significant enough to make them useful in a diagnosis. This view is supported by Kaufman (1992), who suggests that any differences noted as a result of using a SCAD formula would not necessarily distinguish children with learning disabilities from other exceptional children.

It is not too surprising, therefore, in view of these comments that one of the conclusions to the working report published by the BPS on dyslexia and psychological Assessment indicated that 'assessment of and intervention in relation to dyslexia/specific learning difficulties is seen largely to be the responsibility of mainstream schools with educational psychologists supporting schools in identifying and meeting needs' (p. 93). These statements and certainly the conclusion to this report seem to cast some doubt over the expert/intervention model expressed above and, indeed, places the responsibility in the hands of the school and, in particular, trained and experienced school staff. Clearly, this has implications for training and resourcing. Such training has been the focus of a number of university and other courses, and to date the British Dyslexia Association has accredited over 30 courses at a level that would permit successful course participants to undertake informed assessment of dyslexia in some way.

STAGE/PROCESS MODEL

This model is long established and can often be seen as a 'policy' for the practice of identification and intervention. It presupposes that the child should reach certain 'benchmarks' by a certain age or stage. This is essentially a child deficit model, but uses curriculum features to assist in the diagnosis. This, in fact, is alluded to in the Code of Practice (DfES, 1994, 2001). Under the 1994 Code of Practice, Stage 3 provision included guidelines to schools on recognising and teaching pupils with dyslexia and assessment by educational psychologists for input to individual education programmes (IEPs) through the school's SENCO (Special Education Needs Co-ordinator). Stage 5 provision followed a statutory demand for out-of-county placements in special units and specialist day and residential schools. It is interesting to note comparisons with the 2001 Code of Practice, which although still a stage model does appear to be more rooted within the school and the curriculum. This is apparent from descriptions such as 'school action' and 'school action plus' replacing the stages of the 1994 Code of Practice. Rightly, the code states that 'assessment should not be regarded as a single event but rather as a continuing process' (para 5.11 of the SEN Code of Practice 2001). The Code of Practice is a stage process model because it does have distinct stages. 'Initial concern' is the stage when the class teacher registers concern because the child is not learning as effectively as he or she could—this knowledge clearly results from the teacher observing the child in the class situation over a period of time. The next stage 'school action' occurs when the child makes little or no progress, even when teaching approaches are targeted at dealing with the child's identified weaknesses. At this stage the school SENCO will make further assessments and consult with colleagues, parents and other relevant professionals, although the class teacher will remain responsible for working with the pupil on a daily basis and for planning and implementing an IEP.

The next stage would be 'school action plus', which is when the school accesses additional specialists who might in fact have a whole-school role as well as being able to provide advice on individual pupils. 'School action plus' occurs when the child makes little or no progress over a long period and is working at a level well below his or her age.

Within the stage process model and within the Code of Practice it is possible to engage in methods of assessment that can be associated with some of the assessment strategies from other models described in this chapter. For example, Came and Cooke (2002) provide a 'Problem to Solution Approach' (Figure 6.1) which is under-pinned by essentially teacher self-questioning about the child and the learning and teaching plan. This process also has a built-in monitoring and evaluation com-ponent. The four stages of this approach developed by Came and Cooke are 'clarify-ing', 'evidence', 'planning' and 'action'. This can reveal useful information not only about the child but, importantly, about the development and implementation of the teaching programme as well.

POLICY-LED MODEL

This model attempts to put some form of structure and consistency into the identi-fication process. It can incorporate elements of the three models above, but its distinguishing feature is that it forms a documented policy that can be monitored by parents, teachers and administrators. Sometimes this model can be seen in terms of guidelines, and often it has resource implications. This means that the success or otherwise of the implementation of this model rests to a great extent on resources to ensure that training and assessment and teaching materials are available. There are many examples of this in the UK. One mentioned in Chapter 4 on assessment criteria described the policy document *Dyslexia, Policy on Specific Learning Difficulties* (East Renfrewshire Council, 1999). This is one of many examples, but they usually follow a similar format; for example, the East Renfrewshire document has sections on incidence and terminology, identification and assessment process, support, early intervention, technology, staff development, psychological services, parents and further reading. This particular document also has very clear and helpful appendices on stepped approaches to meeting the needs of children who may be dyslexic as well as checklists at various school stages and appropriate strategies. There is also an accompanying document on supporting bilingual pupils. This is a good example of a policy document that has a clear framework and one that can be understood by teachers and parents.

CURRICULUM-FOCUSED MODEL

This model essentially operates in the classroom, and the key person is the class teacher. Irrespective of a diagnosis the teacher tackles the child's learning from a problem-solving perspective using curriculum access as the target and often

What if I am concerned about a pupil?
Target Setting - A Problem to Solution Approach

1. Clarify the concern **(I_____)**	**2. Get your evidence** **(A_____)**
What is the real source of my concern? How will I define it? Is it something to do with me, school, child, family, others? Who has actually got the problem?	What is the extent of the problem? What patterns can I identify? What evidence is available? Have I got a balanced view of the issue? What else might I need but haven't got?
3. Plan **(Pr_____)**	**4.Action** **(M_____)**
What ways are open to me to improve the situation? What planning strategies could I use? Am I moving towards a solution? What are the significant outcomes? Where is the child's voice in this process?	How will the plan be converted into action? How will I know I am doing what is intended? How will I know if it is working? How will the results of the review be fed back into the plan? *Is it working?*

Name _____   **Class** _____

1. Clarifying	**2. Evidence**
3. Planning	**4. Action**

Figure 6.1   A problem to solution approach (reproduced by permission of Learning Works; from Brough et al., 2002).

differentiation as the means. Many teaching approaches based on behavioural principles also follow the principles of this model. This model is consistent with the practice as well as the principles of inclusion and requires clear curriculum objectives to pinpoint the pupil's progress. The 5–14 Programme in Scotland offers an example of a curriculum-focused approach that, like the National Literacy Strategy in England and Wales, blends curriculum needs with specific skills that pupils need to attain. In both these cases, however, further child-focused assessment may be necessary in order to identify reasons for any noted lack of progress.

BARRIERS TO LEARNING

It is useful, therefore, to view early identification and, indeed, the assessment process in terms of overcoming barriers to learning rather than through a child-deficit focus. In reality, however, both information on the child and the curriculum are needed. Essentially, however, the overcoming barriers to learning approach requires that all children undertake the same curriculum, irrespective of the perceived abilities and difficulties. An example of this can be the way in which curriculum objectives are identified and assessing the extent to which the child has met them and what action may be needed to help him or her meet the objectives more fully. This action can take the form of some assistance for the child, but equally it can be in terms of reassessing the objectives or refining them in some way to make them more accessible.

An example of using a curriculum/attainment objectives method that focuses on the monitoring of attainments is shown in Box 6.1.

The key aspect in Box 6.1 is that this is a monitoring process based on actual curriculum attainments. Clearly, there are some important issues that arise from this. The process can be extended to include details of the nature of the work within the curriculum that the child is finding challenging; for example, which letters does the child know and not know and which books can the child read fluently and why should this be the case? Such an approach needs to view the child's class work in a comprehensive and detailed manner, otherwise it can become merely another type of checklist. Additionally, a degree of precision is needed to assist the teacher to see whether the child is achieving the targets. In order to do this, a sample of work is necessary and should be taken from the actual work of the class. An example of this is shown in the previous chapter in relation to History. The importance of this type of perspective is that the emphasis is on the barriers that prevent the child from meeting these targets rather than identifying what the child cannot do. This is essentially a whole-staff and therefore a whole-school responsibility as it is important that attitudes relating to progress and curriculum access are consistent throughout the school. Children who do have some difficulties and find aspects of the curriculum challenging are usually very sensitive and can detect a change of attitude with a change of teacher. It is important, therefore, that there is a consistent view throughout the school on the notion of dyslexia and the role of teachers and the curriculum in making effective learning a reality for all children including those with dyslexia through the medium of the curriculum.

- Chooses to spend time looking at books
- Reads to other children
- Knows how to hold books and turn pages appropriately
- Knows the conventions of the layout of English language texts
- Knows the difference between letters and words
- Understands the relationship between print and illustrations
- Uses a range of strategies to read familiar text
- Recognises own name and signs and labels in the environment
- Identifies words that start or end with the same or different sounds
- Shows understanding of the structure of text by retelling or predicting content
- Identifies the letters of the alphabet in upper and lower case

ATTAINMENT STATEMENT

- The child has achieved few of these features and will require further assessment and continuing, planned support
- The child has achieved up to half of these features and will require planned support for continued progress
- The child has achieved more than half of these features and is making good progress and will require continuing encouragement and support.
- The child has achieved all or almost all these features and will require further challenging opportunities

Box 6.1   Reading objectives (adapted from South Lanarkshire Council, 2002).

WHOLE-SCHOOL INVOLVEMENT

It is the view of many involved in this area that dyslexia identification and how to teach dyslexic children are the responsibility of specialists, and such specialists should therefore be identified within schools and undertake the responsibility of identifying and meeting the needs of children with dyslexia. This, however, should not be the case. Ideally, responsibility should be on a whole-school basis and all teachers should have some knowledge of dyslexia; in particular, the literacy and learning needs of children with dyslexia.

One of the key questions relating to this is how can whole-school involvement be successfully and effectively implemented? Some of the factors below can be used as a guide to this as each will have some role in the development and implementing of whole-school policies on dyslexia.

Multi-professional Assessment

- How can the different professions co-ordinate their roles in relation to assessment and intervention?
- What are the roles of the speech therapist, educational psychologist, school medical officer, specialist teacher and class teacher?

Linkage with Teaching

- How can identification and assessment be most effectively related to teaching and the curriculum, in particular?
- How appropriate is assessment outwith the context of the curriculum?

Role of Parents

- How can the school most effectively communicate with parents?
- Why is it important that parents' contributions to the assessment process are not overlooked?

Professional Development

- The importance of training in relation to assessment must be emphasised. Training should not only be provided for a small number of specialists, who are subsequently over-stretched because of the demands being placed on them. Training needs to be provided for all professionals involved in assessment, particularly the class teacher.

Assessment has been described as 'hypotheses generation followed by intervention' (Pumfrey, 1990), but before hypotheses can be generated in even a vague way a high degree of awareness and training is necessary. This makes it possible for assessment procedures and models of identification to be encapsulated into the context of the curriculum and the classroom. It is also important that such models and training should be included in the training of other professionals, such as speech therapists and educational psychologists.

The focus for this model is the school, not necessarily the child (Figure 6.2).

The model in Box 6.2 may enable the philosophies concerning individual needs and whole-school approaches to interact effectively, minimise role conflicts and misconceptions between professionals and provide appropriate and effective support for children with specific learning difficulties, teachers, parents and other professionals.

This model can be viewed as one that is interactive and involves the whole school, because it emphasises the need for staff training, awareness of the curriculum and teaching implications, and regular consultancy. Key aspects include initial early warning signs, assessment and consultancy, and monitoring and review. These are described below from the perspective of the class teacher.

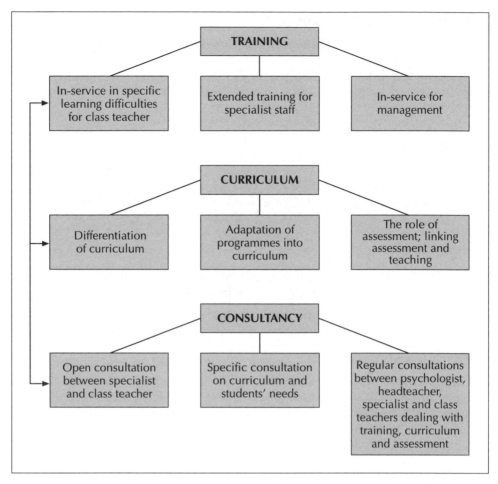

Figure 6.2   The whole-school interactive model.

Initial Early Warning Signs

The class teacher may identify co-ordination difficulties, difficulties with pencil grip, immature use of language, sequencing or organisational difficulties *prior* to the teaching of reading skills. These difficulties can be highlighted through classroom observation, discussions with parents and diagnostic assessment.

Assessment/Consultancy with Management Team

The discussion of difficulties and possible materials and resources that can be used, is an important aspect, and time should be specifically allocated for this. Close monitoring of progress is needed when reading skills are taught, looking out for:

- difficulties with *phonological awareness* (e.g., awareness of rhyme, syllabification, natural breaks in speech and written language);

- *auditory discrimination* in recognising and repeating sounds;
- *visual difficulties*, such as failure to recognise letters, comparison between visually similar letters, missing lines when reading confusing picture cues;
- *sequencing difficulties*, such as confusing the order of letters, words or digits;
- *organisational difficulties*, such as directional confusion, laterality problems and sequencing difficulties;
- *memory*—inability to follow instructions, particularly when more than one item is to be remembered;
- *motor difficulties*—for example, poor pencil grip, awkward gait, poor co-ordination, difficulty doing two simple tasks simultaneously.

Monitoring/Review meeting

This meeting would probably be with the school management and nursery staff to discuss the necessity of a fuller assessment and how this should proceed. Some suggestions about revision of the teaching methods, to support the teacher, need to be made at this stage. Discussions with parents are also important here. Such suggested revisions to teaching should then be carried out, during which time the teacher records progress and difficulties.

School management would then call a meeting with parents to review and discuss progress and determine any further action if necessary; for instance, the involvement of other professionals, such as educational psychologists and speech therapists.

AN ASSESSMENT FRAMEWORK

In order to establish some form of assessment process within the school it is useful to develop an assessment framework that includes the kinds of procedures, tests and strategies that can be utilised within the particular school context in which the teacher is working.

An example of one possible framework is shown below. The framework was originally devised in response to the needs of mainstream and specialist teachers for some reassurance and control in the identification and assessment of specific learning difficulties or dyslexia (Kettles et al., 1996). A revised framework is shown in Box 6.2.

OBSERVATIONAL ASSESSMENT—A FRAMEWORK

The following framework (Box 6.3) is *not* a checklist, but a guide to the type of factors that should be observed in identifying learning strategies, strengths and weaknesses. When completed, this framework should provide an overview of the child's learning skills within the context of the classroom.

The framework in Box 6.3 can be accommodated within the school process. An example of such a process is shown in Box 6.4 (adapted from Jackson and Reid, 1997, 2002).

FACTORS TO BE CONSIDERED

CURRICULUM INFORMATION

- Observational assessment
- Background factors
- Sensory assessment
  —Family history
  —Educational background
  —Other relevant information

ATTAINMENTS

- Word recognition test
- Spelling test
- Free-writing
- Reading/Listening comprehension test
- Reading fluency test
- Writing skills

DIAGNOSTIC INFORMATION

- Non-word-reading test
- Phonological assessment
- Miscue analysis
- Pencil grip
- Use of language

COGNITIVE INFORMATION

- Short-term memory
- Understanding of concepts
- Processing speed

PERFORMANCES

- Discrepancies in different subject areas
- Structure and detail in written work
- Discrepancies in attainments

LEARNING STYLE

- Learning environment
- Metacognitive processing

Box 6.2   An assessment framework.

INTERACTION   *COMMENTS*

Pupil/Teacher interaction

Interaction with peers?

Attention/Concentration

FOCUS ON TASK

Major sources of distraction

Concentration span in different tasks

ORGANISATIONAL ASPECTS

Sequence of activities

Organisational strategies

Materials and desk in order

Teacher direction

MOTOR FACTORS

Handwriting skills

Body posture

Colouring

Tracing

Copying

LEARNING STYLE

Reliance on concrete aids

Memory strategies

Listening/Auditory skills

Oral skills

Visual approaches

Learning sequentially

Learning globally

EMOTIONAL FACTORS

Self-esteem

Confidence Motivation

Signs of tension

Box 6.3   An observational framework.

PRE-SCHOOL—DEVELOPMENTAL HISTORY

Criteria	*Assessment strategy*
Speech and language	Parental discussion
Co-ordination	Observation Dyslexia early screening test
Problem-solving skills	Screening
Cognitive skills	CoPS
Interest in activities	Consultation with nursery/ kindergarten staff
Attention/concentration	Observation
Social skills	Observation

PRIMARY 1–4

Criteria	*Assessment strategy*
Phonological difficulties	Phonological Assessment Battery (PhAB) Phonological Abilities Test (PAT) Listening and Literacy Index (LLI) DST
Sequencing problems	Observation
Laterality	Observation

Auditory sequential memory/
  visual discrimination
	CoPS 1; Bury
	  Infant Check; Aston
	  Index

Reading/Listening comprehension	Non-word-reading tests/listening comprehension passage
Oral and written work	Comparison of performances; observation

PRIMARY 5–7

Criteria	*Assessment strategy*
Organisational strategies	Metacognitive assessment; observation
Writing/Copying	Assessment on task Visual/Kinaesthetic assessment

Persistent phonological difficulties	Integrated phonological assessment/
	  teaching programme (e.g., sound
	  linkage)

continued

Memory	Aston Index, digit span, DST Mind-mapping strategies
Concepts/Schema	Problem-solving assessment Thinking skills Psychological Portfolio (Frederickson) Study skills
Persistent spelling difficulties	Diagnostic spelling test Unscrambling spelling (spelling strategies)
Self-esteem	Behavioural objectives (i.e., target words, goal, objectives Portofolio (Frederickson) Masterly learning Learning styles

SECONDARY SCHOOL	
Criteria	*Assessment strategy*
Adjustment difficulties	Shadow in different subjects/observation
Persistent reading and spelling difficulties	Miscue analysis Learning styles
Preparation for examination	Study skills Visualisation approaches Mind Mapping® Organisational strategies Learning styles

Box 6.4 Criteria and strategies—school process.

SUMMARY

In Scotland there is a degree of flexibility in relation to how the assessment process to identify dyslexia is devised and implemented. There are different examples from different areas. The example from East Renfrewshire is described in this part of the book on assessment, as indeed are examples from Northern Ireland and the Republic of Ireland (see also Chapter 14). There are other examples such as the policy guidelines in Fife (Fife Education Authority, 1996) and in Edinburgh, which involve issuing a support pack and handbook to pre-school, primary and secondary sectors (Brice, 2001; Edinburgh City Council, 2002).

In England the situation is less flexible, but more uniform, due to the Code of Practice that operates there DfES, 2001). In 2001 a revised Code of Practice was issued by the Secretary of State for Education. This provides guidance to education authorities and school boards relating to their duties to make special provision for pupils. The code provides specific requirements for local education authorities (LEAs) regarding assessment as well as provision. The four 'cornerstones' that form the legal obligations for education authorities are: the need to identify any child who may have a special need; the duty to assess, particularly if there is some doubt whether the child has needs greater than those that his or her school can meet; and the duty to issue a statement that would determine the special educational provision that the child needs. This entitles the child to detailed provision that matches the identified needs. The fourth cornerstone of the code is the duty to arrange the special education provision. There is an entitlement for the child to have exactly what is set out in the statement and even if LEAs do not have the facilities to meet that entitlement themselves they must ensure that they can identify appropriate provision through other means. The Code of Practice is based to a great extent on the identification of need, and this need can be met and monitored through individual education plans (IEPs). These plans need to detail: the short-term targets set for, or by, the child; the teaching strategies to be used; the provision to be put in place; when the plan will be reviewed; the criteria for evaluating the plan and the outcomes that are recorded when the IEP is reviewed (Wearmouth et al., 2003).

This chapter has sought to contextualise the previous chapters on assessment criteria and practice. The actual detail of the examples of the process described here is not so important as the principles that it seeks to establish. These principles include the need to have some form of school-based process for assessment and for staff to be provided with support, awareness and training to feel competent to implement those procedures. The range of assessment strategies that can be used to identify dyslexia can result in confusion and uncertainty on the part of the teacher. It is, therefore, of some importance that assessment is not left to one specialist, but should be an integral and continuous component of school practice and policy.

Part III

Teaching and Learning

Chapter 7

Teaching Approaches

FACTORS TO CONSIDER

This chapter will comment on some of the most popular and appropriate teaching approaches for use with children with dyslexia. Teaching approaches can be divided into four broad areas: individualised approaches, support approaches, assisted learning and whole-school approaches. In determining the most appropriate programmes and strategies for children with dyslexia, a number of factors must be considered; the most important of which are:

- *The context.* What are the nature of the learning and teaching provision and the age and stage of the individual?
- *The assessment.* In what way does the assessment inform teaching? Can the individual's strengths and difficulties be readily identified from the results of the assessment?
- *The curriculum.* How can the teaching programme be related to the curriculum? Are any gains made by the programme readily transferable to other aspects of the curriculum.
- *The learner.* What are the individual factors that can help the learner make appropriate gains from the programme? Is the programme suitable for the individual's learning style?

It is important, therefore, to view teaching programmes in relation to the individual and not in relation to the syndrome—dyslexia. Some programmes may be highly evaluated by practitioners and have an established reputation as a successful multi-sensory programme, but this does not necessarily mean that the programme will be effective with all dyslexic children. Each child has to be viewed individually, but if an established programme is to be used then it is wise to check out the views of colleagues who have used this particular programme. Many national and international organisations associated with dyslexia now have an Internet-based forum where practitioners can exchange ideas.

The Context

The context relates to the classroom, the type of provision and the teaching situation. The issue of one-to-one tuition, withdrawal and within-class support for children with dyslexia is an ongoing issue of debate—there are many pros and cons to each type of provision. This underlines the importance of recognising that not all dyslexic children will require the same type of provision and support to the same extent.

In many schools, specialist teachers work co-operatively with class teachers, and in this situation intervention may be of a different nature to that where specialist teachers withdraw children for individual tuition and, indeed, where specific provision is provided outwith the mainstream school. Each of these systems can be effective. It is important, therefore, that the teacher uses the context to its maximum benefit through the provision of materials and teaching and learning programmes that can be effectively adapted to different teaching situations and contexts.

Assessment and the Curriculum

One of the objectives, perhaps the principal objective, of an assessment is to provide some guidance to help in the development of teaching programmes. It is important, therefore, to find out which teaching programmes and strategies have already been used and how successful they have been. It is also important to attempt to find out why particular approaches have or, indeed, have not been successful. This will help to determine which teaching approaches should be implemented for that student.

It is important to examine the assessment findings in a holistic manner by looking at all aspects of the assessment, such as strengths, weaknesses, self-concept, interest, motivation, the learning preferences of the student, and to link these factors to an appropriate teaching programme.

The Learner

It is important to adopt a holistic perspective, looking not only at the learner's strengths and weaknesses, but the preferred learning style. Under what conditions would the child be most likely to learn? Which approaches may be preferred by the learner? In what way would these approaches help to maintain the learner's interest and motivation as well as enhancing self-esteem? These questions and issues must be considered before deciding on appropriate intervention and teaching programmes. Although children with dyslexia have some common core difficulties they do not represent an identical discrete entity with identical profiles. Therefore, intervention and teaching programmes will be tailored to the profile of needs of the individual learner, and this will vary depending on the preferred learning style and cognitive profile of each dyslexic child. The knowledge of the learner that can be most readily recorded by the class teacher is, therefore, of extreme importance. This knowledge will help to successfully match the needs and learning style of the child with the teaching and the requirements of the curriculum.

Programmes and Strategies

It is important to link programmes and strategies together because, while there are a considerable number of well-evaluated and effective commercially produced programmes for dyslexia, it is very seldom that the programme can be used by untrained teachers. Even if a programme has clear instructions, there is some skill attached to implementing such programmes. Therefore, the teacher needs to be aware of strategies that can be used to reinforce the programme and to evaluate the effectiveness of the learning that can take place through the use of the programme.

Considerations—Automaticity, Over-learning and Challenges

There is a considerable body of evidence that intervention strategies for teaching reading and spelling skills to dyslexic children should be both multi-sensory and phonic and that this type of teaching can benefit most children in any class at most stages (Crombie, 2002c). Additionally, it is a well-established view that dyslexic children require considerable over-learning to achieve automaticity. Automaticity is important for the learning of any skill, but it is particularly important for children with dyslexia as there is evidence (Fawcett, 1989, 2002; Fawcett and Nicolson, 2001) that dyslexic children have a dyslexia automatisation deficit—the 'DAD hypothesis' (Nicolson and Fawcett, 1994). This means that children with dyslexia will require additional time to develop automaticity in any skill, but particularly in literacy, and this factor needs to be considered in a teaching programme.

As well as the additional time factors needed to acquire automaticity, it is also important to develop a carefully planned structure for a teaching programme that takes automaticity into account. Crombie (2002c) suggests that 'structure' requires much more than detailing the teaching order of the points that children must learn, but should also involve the learning experiences provided to the student. For example, Crombie suggests that if a child requires to spell a word, but is unaware of the order of the sounds being heard, jumbling of letters will be likely to occur unless visual memory can compensate for this weakness. Teaching the child to repeat words to herself or himself, while listening to the order of the sounds, is according to Crombie time well spent. This is particularly important as, often, children with dyslexic difficulties do not automatically pick up the order of sounds. This means that the interaction between teacher and student is important and some children need to be taught before they can learn a particular skill or sequence.

Automaticity can also be acquired through over-learning, but it is important that this is not seen as rote repetition of the material to be learned. Over-learning provides a good opportunity to utilise a range of materials and a variety of techniques. There are a considerable number of games and 'fun type' activities available that can help to vary the learning experiences and promote automaticity. For example, games where children have to find picture cards beginning or ending with specific sounds or where children have to think of as many words as possible ending in that particular letter sound can be fun and can also help to develop automaticity. There are also games available (see resources in the Appendix) such as homophone games that are designed to improve spelling and recognition of key-words, and a vowel discrimination game that helps to increase auditory awareness and improve word attack skills. Many types of word games and activities also include memory games, sequencing activities, mnemonics, free-writing games and rhyme songs.

These game activities can be used by the class teacher as they do not require any specialist training. It is important, however, that class teachers have some awareness of dyslexia so that these activities can be used appropriately in a teaching programme. Crombie (2002c), in fact, argues that one of the main challenges facing teachers is the need to find varied approaches to learning that will motivate children and will provide the key elements that the child requires as well. If the child does not respond to a structured programme, the teaching programme should then be re-evaluated. This would help to decide whether it is the most appropriate programme to use. It is also important to consider other factors as the child may not be responding because she or he may only need a longer period to achieve the objective of the programme. It is important that objectives should not be seen only in short-term attainment gains—in fact, it is often the case that children with dyslexia require sustained and persistent support. Sometimes this support can be, in fact, more of the same. This is why it is important to vary the learning experiences, otherwise the child can become bored and demotivated.

According to Crombie, therefore, teachers need to have or be able to access a range of knowledge about technology, hardware and software that is available to support individual needs, as well as having a knowledge of how the appropriate materials can be accessed. This is a challenge because structured, multi-sensory, phonic work may well benefit many children at the early stages, but the provision of support within the classroom becomes more difficult for the teacher as the child becomes older, and this can be a particular challenge to teachers at the secondary stage.

PRINCIPLES

Townend (2000) suggests that the principles of a specialist teaching programme for children with dyslexia should include:

- Structure—the progression should be logical and in small steps and, importantly, the links between the steps should be explicit.
- A multi-sensory element—this should be active and interactive as well as incorporating elements of all the modalities—visual, auditory, kinaesthetic and tactile.
- Reinforcement—skills that are learnt need to be practised, learnt and preserved in long-term memory. This can be achieved through reinforcement and is, in fact, necessary for automatic access of the word or skill that has been learnt.
- Skill teaching—teaching is not only about providing information, but about accessing useful and transferable skills as well—for example, phonological awareness skills can be later transferred and utilised in writing skills.
- Metacognitive aspects—this should be seen as an integral component of all programmes and helps with bridging and transferring knowledge, understanding and skills. Essentially, it involves thinking about thinking and the learners self-questioning how a particular response was arrived at.

FACTORS

According to Townend (2000) an effective teaching programme for dyslexic children should include, apart from phonological aspects, other factors such as the promotion of attention and listening, the development of spoken language, development of fine-motor skills and handwriting, sequencing and directionality, and the development of short- and long-term memory skills. It has been well documented that the principles of a teaching programme for dyslexic children include multi-sensory, structured, cumulative and sequential aspects (Reid, 1996). Additionally, it is likely the programme will also have a phonic emphasis although a number of dyslexic children may present with more pronounced visual difficulties, rather than those of a phonic nature (Everatt, 2002). It is important, as indicated earlier, that each dyslexic child should be viewed as an individual, and therefore any programme formula should not be too prescriptive.

Walker (2000), however, discusses an evaluation study using the structured, cumulative, multi-sensory teaching formula (Rack and Walker, 1994) and shows that the students who were taught in this way for one to two hours a week for just over two years doubled their rate of progress in spelling and did even better in reading. According to Walker (2000) this emphasises some key factors in developing a programme: such as the view that the student with dyslexia may need more input and a different structure of teaching from other children; the teacher should be aware of the factors associated with the acquisition of literacy and the particular difficulties in literacy that can be noted in dyslexic children; the principles of multi-sensory teaching; the importance of selecting clear and coherent teaching aims and an awarenesss of the important role played by pre-reading strategies and proof-reading as a post-writing strategy in the teaching of students with dyslexia.

It is important, therefore, that the principles of constructing a teaching programme for dyslexic children and the factors that should be recognised in implementing such as programme are acknowledged. It is also important, however, that programmes should not be used too prescriptively and that commercially produced programmes fit into the aims of the school. The teacher should be ready to discard or adapt a particular programme for a child if it does not seem to be making real headway. This point is emphasised by Lannen (2002a, b), head teacher of a day school for children with dyslexia and other specific learning difficulties. Lannen indicates that any programme needs to fit into the overall context of the classroom environment. She suggests that the role of the school ethos and the holistic nature of the intervention required for children with dyslexia cannot be underestimated.

PROGRAMMES IN PRACTICE: FRAMEWORK

It is important, therefore, that factors other than the components of the actual programme need to be considered. Some of the various types of programmes and strategies that can be used are outlined below.

Individualised Programmes

These are usually programmes that are highly structured. They can be seen as essentially free-standing and can form a central element of the overall strategy for teaching children with dyslexia.

Support approaches and strategies

These may utilise the same principles as some of the individual programmes, but can be used more selectively by the teacher, thus making it possible to integrate them more easily within the normal activities of the curriculum.

Assisted learning techniques

These strategies utilise many different methods, but a central, essential component is the aspect of learning from others. These programmes could therefore involve either peer or adult support and interaction and utilise some of the principles of modelling.

Whole-school Approaches

These approaches recognise that dyslexia is a whole-school concern, and not just the responsibility of individual teachers. Such approaches require an established and accessible policy framework for consultancy, whole-school screening and monitoring of children's progress. Early identification is a further key aspect of a whole-school approach.

It is important to consider the rationale for using particular programmes and strategies. Within the areas described here of individualised learning, support approaches and strategies, assisted learning and whole-school approaches, there are many effective means of dealing with the dyslexic-type difficulty that are at the teacher's disposal. Therefore, the criteria for selection—the context, the assessment, the curriculum and the learner—must be carefully considered. These factors are as influential in the selection of teaching approaches as the actual programme or strategy itself (Box 7.1).

INDIVIDUALISED PROGRAMMES

Most individualised programmes incorporate some or all of the following principles and approaches:

- multi-sensory;
- over-learning and automaticity;
- highly structured and usually phonically based;
- sequential and cumulative.

INDIVIDUALISED APPROACHES	SUPPORT APPROACHES AND STRATEGIES
Alphabetic Phonics	Aston Portfolio
Alpha to Omega	Simultaneous Oral Spelling
Bangor Dyslexia Teaching System	Counselling approaches
DATAPAC	**Phonic Codecracker/Crackerspell
DISTAR	Specialised software programmes
Hickey Language Course	Neuro-motor programmes
*Letterland	*Special Needs Manual*
	(Reason and Boote, 1994)
Reading Recovery Programme	Study skills
*Spelling Made Easy	Quest materials
Slingerland	Visual acuity activities
Orton–Gillingham Method	Word games
Sound Linkage	Computer programmes
Skill Teach	Davis programme
Multi-sensory Teaching System	DDAT
for Reading	
Toe by Toe	Educational kinesiology
THRASS	Units of Sound
ASSISTED LEARNING PROGRAMMES	WHOLE-SCHOOL APPROACHES
Apprenticeship Approach	Counselling strategies
Paired reading	Literacy projects
Peer-tutoring	Study skills programmes
Reciprocal teaching	Thinking skills
Cued-spelling	Counsultancy

*These can also be used as the main teaching programme for the whole class.
**This can also be used as an individualised programme.

Box 7.1   Teaching approaches.

Multi-sensory methods utilise all available senses simultaneously. This can be summed up in the phrase 'hear it, say it, see it and write it'. These methods have been used for many years and have been further refined by Hornsby and Shear (1980) and Augur and Briggs (1992) in phonic structured programmes that incorporate multi-sensory techniques.

Over-learning is deemed necessary for children with dyslexic difficulties. The short- and long-term memory difficulties experienced by dyslexic children mean that considerable reinforcement and repetition is necessary.

The structured approaches evident in programmes of work for dyslexic children usually provide a linear progression, thus enabling the learner to complete and master a particular skill in the reading or learning process before advancing to a subsequent skill. This implies that learning occurs in a linear developmental manner. Although there is evidence from learning theory to suggest this may be the case, there is still some doubt in the case of reading that mastery of the component subskills results in skilled reading.

In reading, a number of cognitive skills such as memory and visual, auditory and oral skills interact (Ellis, 1990). This interaction is the key feature; so, it is important that the skills are taught together and purposefully with the practice of reading as the focus.

Sequential approaches are usually appropriate for children with dyslexia because it may be necessary for them to master subskills before moving to more advanced materials. Hence a sequential and cumulative approach may not only provide a structure to their learning but help to make learning more meaningful and effective as well.

Many of the individual programmes, however, have been evaluated fairly positively. For example, Hornsby and Miles (1980) conducted a series of investigations examining 'dyslexia-centred teaching' programmes with the aim of evaluating how effective these programmes were in alleviating dyslexia. This study and a follow-up study (Hornsby and Farmer, 1990) indicate that the programmes did result in an improvement in terms of pupils' reading and spelling ages. Additionally, other programme providers have published reports on the effectiveness of particular programmes as well as the publication of independent evaluations. For example, Johnson et al. (1999) reported on the Multisensory Teaching Scheme for Reading, Moss (2000) on Units of Sound and other programmes such as the Bangor Dyslexia Teaching System and teaching Reading through Spelling (Turner, 2002a).

PROGRAMMES IN PRACTICE—SOME EXAMPLES

Below is a description of some of the individualised programmes that may be utilised for children with dyslexia. There are many such programmes, often they have a slightly different focus, with different types of materials and strategies. A more comprehensive list of these can be found in the Appendix.

Letterland

Letterland, developed by Lyn Wendon, consists of many different elements. The materials are extremely useful for teaching reading, spelling and writing, and for developing and sustaining motivation. The programmes are internationally renowned, as well over 50 per cent of all primary schools in England and Ireland rely on this programme (Letterland International, 1997).

Letterland encompasses a number of teaching elements based on recognised and essential components of the teaching of reading. The major elements are: language, with an emphasis on listening, speaking and communicating; phonic skills; whole-word recognition skills; sentence awareness; comprehension; reading and spelling connections; and preliminary skills in creative writing. The materials consist of teachers' guides, wall-charts, code cards, flashcards, wordbooks, cassettes and songbooks, photocopiable material, workbooks, games and resources, software, videos, and materials specifically designed for use at home.

The programme may also be seen as a preventative approach, since it is appropriate for early intervention and may also facilitate the reinforcement of important developmental concepts in learning, such as object constancy.

The Letterland system essentially grew out of close observations of failing readers, and the materials reinforce the importance of a reading-for-meaning orientation to print. The system encourages motivation and exploration of written language and results in schools. Wendon (1993) suggests that Letterland can account for a measurable decrease in the number of children in schools requiring extra help with reading and spelling.

Letterland focuses on letters and sounds, and by using pictograms encourages children to appreciate letter stages and sounds, thereby reinforcing both shape and sound of letters and words. Integrated within this, however, are the programmes and exercises on whole-word recognition, reading for meaning, spelling and creative writing. Spelling is not presented as a series of rules, but instead through a story approach, focusing on the Letterland characters.

Progress through the Letterland programme is by a series of steps. These steps can provide the teacher with choice and flexibility, and the programme can be implemented to the whole class, in small groups or individually.

There are a number of aspects about Letterland that make it useful for some children with specific learning difficulties. These include the use of pictograms—which can be particularly beneficial to the learner with difficulties in phonological awareness and auditory skills. The use of the story approach to reading and spelling that encourages the processing of information using long-term memory is particularly beneficial to dyslexic children whose short-term memory is generally weak. The range of activities incorporating different approaches allows the learner to develop imagination and creativity in the use of letters and words. Other useful aspects include the focus on the context aspects of reading and the use of syntactic and semantic cues.

Alpha to Omega

Alpha to Omega is a phonetic, linguistic approach to the teaching of reading and can be used as a programme or as resource material. It is highly structured and follows a logical pattern of steps that promote the acquisition of phonological and language skills.

There is an emphasis on learning the 44 phonemes from which all English words are composed. These consist of the 17 vowel sounds and the 27 consonant sounds. There is also an emphasis on the acquisition of language structure, focusing on content words (nouns, verbs, adjectives) and finite words (prepositions and participles). There is, therefore, an emphasis on using words in the context of a sentence. The programme provides a highly structured format for the teaching of sentences and for grammatical structure.

There are also three accompanying and very useful activity packs designed for different stages. These packs provide appropriate back-up exercises to reinforce the teaching programme. There is also an extremely useful programme of learning games—before Alpha—that can be used with children under five. These games are in a series of structured stages, are multi-sensory and aim to foster language development and other pre-reading skills such as visual and auditory perception and discrimination, fine-motor control, spatial relationships and knowledge of colour, number and directions.

Orton–Gillingham

Programmes based on this approach have become a central focus for multi-sensory teaching. The programmes offer a structured, phonic-based approach that incorporates the total language experience and focuses on the letter sounds and the blending of these sounds into syllables and words. The approach rests heavily on the interaction of visual, auditory and kinaesthetic aspects of language.

Orton–Gillingham lessons, according to Henry (1996), always incorporate card drills, spelling and reading and usually include activities such as:

- Card drills—this involves the use of commercial or teacher-made cards containing the common letter patterns to strengthen the visual modality: phonemes (sounds) for auditory and kinaesthetic reinforcement and syllables and whole words to help develop blending skills.
- Word lists and phrases.
- Oral reading selection—this involves the teacher first reading the passage, then the student.
- Spelling of phonetic and non-phonetic words.
- Handwriting—with attention being placed on pencil grip, writing posture and letter formation. This would also include tracing, copying and practice and making cursive connections such as *br*, *bl*.
- Composition—encouragement to develop writing of sentences, paragraphs and short stories.

According to Clark (1988) the introduction of letters is a carefully sequenced procedure and is carried out in the following way:

- to begin with, 10 letters are taught—2 vowels (a, i) and eight consonants (f, l, b, j, h, m, p, t);
- each of the letters is introduced with a keyword;
- the difference between vowels and consonants is taught together with the position of the mouth in the pronunciation of the sounds (different coloured cards are used for vowels and consonants).

Once the child has mastered the letter name and sound, the programme then advances to introduction of blending the letters and sounds. This begins with simple three-letter words and the child repeats the sounds until the word is spoken without pauses between the constituent sounds.

The visual–kinaesthetic and auditory–kinaesthetic associations are formed by the pupil tracing, saying, copying and writing each word. Reading of text begins after the pupil has mastered the consonant–vowel–consonant words to a higher automatic level (i.e., when the pupil can recognise and use these words).

The initial reading material is taken from the programme and contains words the pupil has learnt from the teacher's manual.

The programme gives considerable attention to the learning of dictionary skills as well as development of written language from pictographs to ideographs and eventually to the alphabet.

The programme does appear to be more suited to a one-to-one situation, and it would be difficult to integrate the programme within the school curriculum. As in many of the programmes derived from the Orton–Gillingham approach, the key principles of over-learning, automaticity and multi-sensory approaches are very apparent, and these principles *can* be utilised within the classroom curriculum. In the USA, Morgan Dynamic Phonics (www.dynamicphonics.com) have produced a series of phonic programmes that focus on user-friendly approaches using the principles of Orton–Gillingham, which includes the use of humour and interaction. Ott (1997) suggests that the following programmes are based on the Orton–Gillingham method:

- *Alpha to Omega* (Hornsby and Shear, 1980);
- *The Bangor Dyslexia Teaching System* (Miles, 1989);
- *The Hickey Multisensory Language Course* (Augur and Briggs, 1992);
- *Dyslexia: A Teaching Handbook* (Thomson and Watkins, 1990);
- *Units of Sound* (Bramley, 1996).

The Hickey Multisensory Language Course

The Hickey Multisensory Language Course (Augur and Briggs, 1992; revised by Combley, 2001) recognises the importance of the need to learn sequentially the letters of the alphabet. The dyslexic child, however, will usually have some difficulty in learning and remembering the names and sequence of the alphabetic letters as well as understanding that the letters represent speech sounds that make up words.

The programme is based on multi-sensory principles and the alphabet is introduced using wooden or plastic letters; the child can look at the letter, pick it up, feel it with eyes open or closed and say its sound. Therefore, the visual, auditory and tactile–kinaesthetic channels of learning are all being utilised with a common goal.

The programme also suggests some activities to help the child become familiar with the alphabet:

- learning the letters sequentially;
- positioning of each letter of the alphabet;
- naming and recognising the shape of the letters.

These programmes involve games and the use of dictionaries to help the child become familiar with the order of the letters and the direction to go (e.g., he needs to know that 'I' comes before 'K'), the letters in the first half of the alphabet

SHREWSBURY COLLEGE
LONDON RD LRC

and those letters in the second half. The alphabet can be further divided into sections, thus making it easier for the child to remember the section of the alphabet in which a letter appears, for example:

A B C D

E F G H I J K L M

N O P Q R

S T U V W X Y Z

The Hickey language course includes: activities related to sorting and matching the capital, lower case, printed and written forms of the letters; practising sequencing skills with cut-out letters and shapes; and practising positioning of each letter in the alphabet in relation to the other letters (this involves finding missing letters and going backwards and forwards in the alphabet).

The course also indicates the importance of recognising where the accent falls in a word, since this clearly affects the spelling and rhythm. Rhyming games can be developed to encourage the use of accent by placing it on different letters of the alphabet. This helps to train children's hearing to recognise when a letter has an accent or is stressed in a word.

The course includes reading and spelling packs that focus on securing a relationship between sounds and symbols. This process begins with single letters and progresses to consonant blends, vowel continuations and then to complex letter groupings.

The reading packs consist of a set of cards; on one side, the lower case letter is displayed in bold with an upper case (capital) letter shown in the bottom right-hand corner in order to establish the link between the two letters. The reverse side of the card indicates a keyword that contains the sound of the letter with the actual sound combination in brackets. Rather than providing a visual image of the keyword, a space is left for the child to draw the image. This helps to make the image more meaningful to the child and also utilises and reinforces visual and kinaesthetic skills.

The spelling pack is similar in structure to the reading pack. On the front of the card the sound made by the letter is displayed in brackets, while the back contains both the sound and the actual letter(s). Sounds for which there is a choice of spellings will in time show all the possible ways in which the sound can be made. Cue words are also given on the back as a prompt, in case the child forgets one of the choices.

Spelling is seen as being of prime importance by the authors of the programme since they view it as an 'all round perceptual experience'. The multi-sensory method used involves the following process:

- the child repeats the sound heard;
- feels the shape the sound makes in the mouth;
- makes the sound and listens;
- writes the letter(s).

This process involves over-learning and multi-sensory strategies.

The third edition of *The Hickey Multisensory Language Course* was revised by Combley (2001) and now incorporates aspects of the National Literacy strategy and the requirements of the Literacy Hour.

Bangor Dyslexia Teaching System

The *Bangor Dyslexia Teaching System* (Miles, 1989) is a structured, sequential teaching programme developed for teachers and speech and language therapists involved in supporting children with dyslexia.

A useful aspect of this programme is the division between primary and secondary pupils. Although it is acknowledged that some secondary pupils are still 'beginning' readers and need to go through the same initial stages of acquiring literacy as 'beginning readers' in the primary school, the programme makes some special provision and adaptations for secondary students. This helps to make the secondary material more age appropriate.

The basic philosophy of the programme is not unlike that of other structured, phonic programmes for dyslexic children. It focuses on phonological difficulties and the problems dyslexic children have in mastering the alphabetic code. The programme attempts to provide children with some competence, at the earliest stage possible, in recognising and categorising speech sounds. Miles (1989) argues that it is not possible for children to benefit from 'top down' language experience approaches to reading if they have not mastered the basic principles of literacy. Some of these principles, which the programme for primary aged children focuses on, include: the teaching of basic letter sounds and the structure of words, long vowels, common word patterns, irregular words, alphabet and dictionary skills, grammatical rules and silent letters.

The programme attempts to acknowledge that dyslexic children may have difficulties with both visual and auditory processing. The issue of auditory processing, particularly relating to the acquisition of phonic skills, is well documented (Frith, 1985; Stanovich, 1991; Rack, 1994; Snowling, 2000; Lundberg, 2002). Additionally, studies by Stein et al. (1994, 2001) helped to raise the debate on visual aspects of reading and the difficulties some dyslexic children may have in picking out visual letter patterns.

The programme shares the same principles as that utilised by other similar programmes for dyslexic children. It is highly structured and the teacher has to proceed systematically through the programme. The aspect of over-learning is acknowledged to be important, and therefore revision of material already learnt occupies an important place in the implementation of the programme.

One of the difficulties inherent in following the principle of over-learning is the aspect of boredom, which may result from repetitive revision of material already learnt. This programme acknowledges that pitfall and suggests ways of overcoming it through the use of games and other adapted materials.

The multi-sensory teaching element is also crucial in this programme. Some of the exercises attempt to engage all the available senses simultaneously, thus acknowledging the accepted view that dyslexic children benefit from multi-sensory learning.

The programme also utilises the particular benefits of mnemonics for dyslexic children as well as the notion of reading and spelling as an integrated activity. Some emphasis is also placed on encouraging dyslexic children to use oral language to plan their work. It is felt that such verbalisations help children clarify their thoughts and planning before embarking on a course of action. There is also a useful appendix containing guidance on handwriting, alphabet and dictionary skills.

The secondary component of the programme provides useful advice on dealing with the problem of teaching basic literacy to older students. Miles (1989) suggests that the material for older pupils should include words of more than one syllable, even though the student is at the early stages of literacy. Some effort is made to ensure that the student is familiar with polysyllabic words in order that the potential for creative writing is not unduly restricted. At the secondary stage the aspect of reading for meaning is of great importance in order to ensure sustained motivation. The Bangor Dyslexia Teaching System acknowledges this and suggests a range of techniques that can help to support the student through the decoding difficulty in order that maximum meaning and pleasure can be derived from the text. Such suggestions include: supplying difficult words; introducing the story and the book's background and characters; pointing out clues such as capital letters and titles; encouraging fluency by reading from one full stop to the next; omitting words that are difficult, thus encouraging the use of context to obtain meaning; practice; and reading rhymes and limericks that aid sound and syllable awareness.

The programme for secondary students, although less structured than that for primary students, includes sections on syllabification and stress, plurals, short and long vowel patterns, silent letters, prefixes and suffixes.

The Bangor Dyslexia Teaching System clearly attempts to teach the dyslexic child the basic rules of literacy and the English language. Although the programme can stand on its own, it would be advisable for the teacher to attempt to integrate and relate the programme within the child's class work. This can be possible by selecting those aspects of the programme that are most useful and would be particularly appropriate for secondary students, whose learning priorities, Miles acknowledges, the teacher would need to take into account.

Tackling Dyslexia (Cooke, 2002)

Cooke (2002) has developed a different version of the above and incorporates new approaches to teaching phonics. She also indicates that the nature of the task is important, and the programme she has developed takes this into account as well as literacy and numeracy skills. Cooke's programme also considers the role of parents, estimating the reading level of books, computer technology and factors relating to the National Literacy strategy and the Literacy Hour in England and Wales.

Alphabetic Phonics

The key principles found in the majority of individualised programmes for dyslexic children—multi-sensory techniques, automaticity and over-learning—are all found in the Alphabetic Phonics programme. Additionally, the programme recognises the importance of discovery learning. Opportunities for discovery learning are found throughout this highly structured programme.

The programme, which stems from the Orton–Gillingham multi-sensory approach, was developed in Dallas, TX, by Aylett Cox. She has described Alphabetic Phonics as a structured system of teaching students the coding patterns of the English language (Cox, 1985).

Cox asserts that such a phonic-based programme is necessary because around 85 per cent of the 30 000 most commonly used English words can be considered phonetically regular and therefore predictable. Thus, learning phonetic rules can allow the child to access the majority of commonly used words.

Alphabetic Phonics provides training in the development of automaticity through the use of flash cards and over-learning through repetitive practice in reading and spelling until 95 per cent mastery is achieved.

The programme also incorporates opportunities to develop creativity in expression and in the sequencing of ideas.

The programme is highly structured with daily lessons of around one hour. Lessons incorporate a variety of tasks that help to keep the child's attention directed at the activities and prevents tedium or boredom. In this programme, reading comprehension instruction does not begin until the student has reached a minimal level of accuracy in relation to decoding skills. Cox, however, does recognise that children will learn and retain new vocabulary more effectively and efficiently through experiential learning and that this is particularly applicable to dyslexic children.

Although a number of studies have claimed impressive results using the Alphabetic Phonics Programme (Ray, 1986; Frankiewicz, 1985), it has been asserted that the research methodology used and the lack of effective control groups somewhat diminish the impressive results of these studies (Clark, 1988). Additionally, in order to teach the programme effectively, it has been maintained that 480 hours of teacher training is required, based on knowledge of the structure of the English language, knowledge of phonetic rules and patterns in spelling, and integration of these activities into a structured, hierarchical curriculum. An accompanying text (Cox, 1992) *Foundations for Literacy* does however provide an easy-to-follow lesson guide for the teacher.

In the programme Cox suggests a number of linkages between multi-sensory activities and the letter, such as association of cursive shape, speech sound, graphic symbol and kinaesthetic memory. The principles and practices of this programme, such as structure, multi-sensory technique, emphasis on automaticity, emphasis on building comprehension skills, experiential learning and listening skills, and in particular recognition of letter sounds, can have desirable outcomes. These can readily be adapted and implemented into teaching programmes devised for different needs and contexts.

The Slingerland Programme

The Slingerland Programme is an adaptation of the Orton–Gillingham Programme. Essentially, the programme was developed as a screening approach to help minimise the difficulties experienced by children in language and literacy. The Slingerland

Screening Tests accompany the programme and are usually administered in the early stages of education.

The programme shares similar features with other programmes. Multi-sensory teaching permeates the programme, which begins by introducing letters of the alphabet. The programme follows the format below.

Writing

This is the first step and usually the following order is adopted:

- tracing;
- copying;
- writing in the air;
- simultaneously writing from memory and saying the letter.

Letter Sounds

This involves naming the letter then the keyword associated with the letter and then the letter sound.

Blending

This is introduced with oral activities and may involve repetitive use and blends with kinaesthetic support to reinforce the material being learnt.

Decoding

In decoding, students begin with three letters—consonant-vowel-consonant (e.g., words such as 'bay' and 'way'). They are required to:

- pronounce the initial consonant;
- then the vowel;
- then blend the two;
- and pronounce the final consonant;
- and say the whole word.

Vowel digraphs and vowel–consonant digraphs are taught as units, although Slingerland maintains that consonant blends are usually learnt more easily.

Reading for Meaning

Once decoding has been sufficiently mastered a whole-word approach is encouraged in the reading of text. Initially, students undergo a 'preparation for reading' lesson when some time is spent producing, recognising and reading words and the students become familiar with the image of the word. There is also some emphasis on teacher modelling by reading aloud. To foster reading comprehension skills, the teacher cues in appropriate clues into the questioning technique (e.g., which seven words tell us where the house was?—'it was built on a high hill'). The Slingerland Programme is highly specific and highly structured and contains some useful strategies and ideas.

Research into the effectiveness of the Slingerland Programme indicates that it can produce significant gains in a number of language aspects, such as listening comprehension, punctuation, grammar, syntax, spelling and study skills. Gains have also been noted in vocabulary and the use of inference in reading (Wolf, 1985; McCulloch, 1985).

DISTAR

DISTAR (Direct Instruction System of Teaching Arithmetic and Reading) was originally designed for socially disadvantaged children in the USA as part of the Project Follow Through scheme launched by the US government in 1968. The programme is orientated to achievement in basic attainments and tasks and skills to enhance effective learning.

Some of the features of DISTAR include: the transfer of learning from specific examples to general concepts; continual, positive reinforcement to enhance motivation and success; and the monitoring of progress through the use of criterion-referenced assessment. In addition to reading skills, the current DISTAR programme covers language, spelling and arithmetic (Engelmann and Bruner, 1983).

The reading programme, which commences at pre-school level, incorporates both decoding and comprehension lessons. The programme includes elements of pre-reading skills, pronunciation of letter sounds, different types of sounds, oral blending activities, rhyming activities, sound associations and sequencing skills. The individual lessons utilise a variety of teaching methods including games. These games aim to develop various strategies to help in the retention of letter sounds.

The programme is interspersed with activities to monitor progress in relation to reading accuracy, speed and comprehension.

Evaluation studies display impressive progress in attainments among students undertaking the DISTAR programme—results that appear to continue through to secondary education (Meyer, 1984). Some criticism, however, has been raised that the teacher's manual is too prescriptive and places too much restriction on teachers (Becker, 1977). The focus of the programme on transferring skills from the specific to the underlying general task concepts is, indeed, commendable and can make the DISTAR materials a useful resource.

Reading Recovery

Reading Recovery is an early reading and writing intervention programme, developed by Marie Clay (1985, 1992), that focuses on children who after one year at school have lagged significantly behind their peers in reading and writing. Marie Clay originally introduced the programme in New Zealand, but it has now been shown that the programme can be successfully transferred to other countries and contexts (Pinnell et al., 1988a, b, 1991; Wright, 1992; Cazden, 1999).

The programme aims to boost the reading attainments of the selected children over a relatively short period, around 12 to 20 weeks, with specially trained teachers carrying out the programme, seeing children on an individual basis for 30 minutes daily. The programme centres around the individual child's strengths and weaknesses as assessed by the actual reading programme. It is not, therefore, structured around a set of principles and practices to which the child has to be accommodated, but rather the programme adapts itself to the child's specific requirements and needs. It utilises both bottom-up and top-down reading approaches and, therefore, encourages the use of decoding strategies through the use of phonics and awareness of meaning through an awareness of the context and language of the text.

The programme aims to produce 'independent readers whose reading improves whenever they read' (Clay, 1985). There is an emphasis, therefore, on strategies that the reader can apply to other texts and situations, and there is evidence that gains made in the Reading Recovery programme will be maintained over time.

For some children the Reading Recovery programme may need to be supplemented by additional sessions, which could include:

- rereading familiar books;
- taking a running record;
- reinforcing letter identification;
- writing a story, thus learning sounds in words;
- comprehension of story;
- introducing a new book.

It is also important that the child is helped to develop a self-improving system. This would encourage the child to:

- be aware of his own learning;
- take control and responsibility for his own learning.

The goal of teaching reading is to assist the child to produce effective strategies for working on text, and according to Clay this can be done through focusing on the practices of self-correcting and self-monitoring. The main components of the programme include:

- learning about direction;
- locating and focusing on aspects of print;
- spatial layout of books;
- writing stories;
- learning sounds in words;
- comprehension;
- reading books;
- using print as a cue;
- sound and letter sequence;
- word analysis;
- fluency.

A typical Reading Recovery lesson would include the analysis of the child's decoding strategies, the encouragement of fluent reading through the provision of opportunities to link sounds and letters, the reading of familiar texts and the introduction of new books.

Identification

Since the programme provides an intensive input to those children lagging in reading, it is vitally important that the identification procedures are sound in order to ensure that the children who receive the benefits of this programme are those who would not otherwise make satisfactory progress. The lowest achieving children in a class group, after a year at school at around six years of age, are admitted into the programme. Clay believes that by the end of the first year at primary school it is possible to identify children who are failing. She suggests that this can be achieved through systematic observation of children's learning behaviour, together with a diagnostic survey.

The systematic observation takes the form of noting precisely what children are saying and doing in relation to reading, so the focus is on reading tasks rather than specific subskills such as visual perception or auditory dissemination. In order to identify the child's reading behaviour Marie Clay has developed a diagnostic survey that involves taking a 'Running Record' of precisely how the child is performing in relation to reading. This type of analysis of children's errors in reading can provide clues in relation to children's strengths and weaknesses in reading.

The diagnostic survey includes directional movement (which looks at general directional concepts, including motor co-ordination, impulsivity and hesitancy), error behaviour (focusing on oral language skills, speed of responding and the use of semantic and syntactic context), the use of visual and memory cues, the rate of self-correction, and the child's preferred mode of identifying letters (alphabetic, sound or cueing from words). The survey also includes details of the child's writing skills. This is particularly important since it may provide some indication of any reading problems as well as language level and message quality.

Evaluation of Reading Recovery

Much of the research evidence that examines the effectiveness of this programme is impressive. The participating children appear to display gains that allow them to reach average levels of performance in reading within a relatively short period (Wright, 1992). There are, however, a number of studies that are critical of the programme.

Meek (1985) argues that the programme is rather restrictive in that it does not allow for children's reading preferences in relation to choice of material, and Adams (1990b) observes that the phonics element in Reading Recovery is not systematic and does not emphasise structures such as 'word families'. The programme, according to Topping and Wolfendale (1985), does not make adequate allowance for the effective role that parents can play in enhancing literacy skills, and Glynn et al. (1989) argue that many of the gains made by children who have participated in the Reading Recovery Programme have disappeared after a year. Johnston (1992) feels that programmes such as Reading Recovery are only necessary because of the trend from phonics-focused programmes, and she concludes that 'rather than wait until children fail in a non-phonics programme, it would be very much better for them either to be taught routines in a reading programme which emphasises phonics as well as reading for memory, or for the class teacher to have such a scheme available for those who are making very slow progress.'

Dombey (1992), arguing on behalf of the National Association for the Teaching of English, puts forward some doubts about the efficacy of Reading Recovery because it focuses on one particular age group—six-year-olds—and because it requires intensive training of a few specialists with little opportunity for dissemination of the skills of these specialists so that the effects of the programme do not fully percolate into mainstream classes.

Dombey further argues that it could be more cost-effective to study the existing provision for the teaching of reading and to identify ways in which this could be improved; for example, by ensuring that all teachers of young children have the time needed to teach reading thoroughly and by providing those teachers with adequate training in the teaching of reading for all children.

The introduction of the Reading Recovery programme in Surrey has shown that the programme can be readily adapted to the UK classroom context. Wright and Prance (1992) provide an illustrative case study of one six-year-old girl, the lowest progress reader in the class group. At the start of the programme this girl displayed 75–97 per cent accuracy in reading three one-line caption books and was able to write accurately 13 of the 37 words on a dictation passage. By the end of the programme the girl had progressed to 98 per cent accuracy on more demanding readers and scored full marks on the dictation passage. In addition, the girl displayed considerable gains in the full battery of reading tests administered at the end of the programme. Wright and Prance also acknowledged some qualitative improvements in the girl's reading behaviour; for example, she began to recognise similar patterns between words. This is a good example of the application of word knowledge that could be transferred to other contexts—a difficulty, in fact, that seems to pervade children with dyslexia and prevents effective transfer of word knowledge to other contexts. The general monitoring of her own work appeared to improve, something which was highlighted by the increase in her self-correction rate and in the use of the strategy of scanning the print before summarising to read aloud.

Longitudinal studies in Ohio and New Zealand showed that the gains made by children after three to six months of the programme were maintained: the former Reading Recovery pupils were still functioning within the average band at Age 9 (Clay, 1985; Delford et al., 1987).

A further evaluation conducted by Wright (1992) showed that in Surrey, the gains made by children participating in the Reading Recovery programme were impressive. Ninety-six of those participating reached average levels of attainment in literacy after around 17 weeks of the programme.

The study did reveal marked differences between schools, which reflected the difficulty some teachers had in seeing the pupils every day.

Only 3 of the 82 children taken into the programme did not achieve average levels for their classes after 20 weeks. This appears as an impressive statistic when it is considered that at the start of the programme the participating children were only able to read their names or a short sentence, displayed poor recognition of letter names or sounds and could write only 5 words unaided in 10 minutes. The results are broadly similar to those gains achieved in the New Zealand and Ohio studies (Clay, 1985; Pinnell et al., 1988a, b), and Wright therefore concludes that the Reading Recovery programme was successfully imported to the Surrey context. Indeed, the Surrey children made greater gains than the New Zealand children in all areas except sight vocabulary, although the former did remain in the programme on average several weeks longer than the New Zealand children. Clearly, further research needs to be carried out to assess whether the gains made are maintained in the same manner as those made by the New Zealand children.

Cazden (1999) comments on the demonstrated success of reading recovery, but suggests that despite this it continues to be controversial. This is because some children who have not progressed sufficiently after a time on reading recovery continue with the programme, and this can mean that they do not fully participate in the language teaching in the class. This has been a particular criticism of those proponents of the 'whole language' movement. Clay and Cazden (1990), however, argue that 'Reading Recovery' is neither 'whole language' nor 'phonics', but takes what they describe as 'instructional detours'. These instructional detours are the part of the programme that focuses on the reading skills the child requires in order to make sense of 'whole language'. The phonics element of reading recovery is conceptually different from the usual implications of phonics teaching because reading recovery sees phonological awareness as an outcome of reading and writing, rather than as a prerequisite. Cazden (1999) suggests that it is this mix between the invisible pedagogy of whole language and the visible pedagogy of systemic phonics that has contributed to the success of reading recovery. It is this mix, she suggests, which is consistent with Bernstein's classification of invisible and visible pedagogy (Atkinson et al., 1994), that should be seen as an example of programme effectiveness in literacy education. This she suggests has also succeeded in weakening the relationship, suggested by Bernstein, between social class and literacy education.

Teaching Reading through Spelling

This programme produced by staff at the Kingston Reading Centre (Cowdery et al., 1984–88) provides a very detailed and comprehensive analysis of the diagnosis of specific learning difficulties and programmes of remediation.

It is based on the original Orton–Gillingham programme and follows the same basic principles as those adopted by other specific programmes recommended by the British Dyslexia Association (BDA). The programme is, therefore, phonically based, structured and cumulative. These principles ensure that the programme has a coherent organisation and a progression through alphabetic knowledge to sounds, leading to sound–symbol correspondence. The programme also develops multisensory strategies in teaching and learning. Repetition is also built into this programme as the authors acknowledge the value of automaticity for dyslexic children.

The Teaching Reading through Spelling programme is essentially a psycholinguistic approach because, although it recognises the importance of phonic knowledge, particularly for dyslexic children who may not obtain full benefit from 'look and say' approaches, it also emphasises articulation and speech training. Linguistic competence, performance and linguistic concepts are, therefore, guiding principles of this programme.

The authors of the programme appreciate that spelling, being a recall skill (as opposed to reading, which is a recognition skill), can present more serious difficulties for the child, and, therefore, the programme attempts to develop an understanding of the spelling system as an aid to developing the processing skills necessary for reading.

The programme is structured in units aimed at different activities. For example, there are units on the foundations of the programme, the early stages, later stages, spelling, activity for infants and beginners, and a handwriting copy book.

Section 1 of the foundation programme begins with alphabet work and includes the use of a variety of strategies to help the child become familiar with and retain the letters of the alphabet. Games such as alphabet bingo, alphabet dominoes, mazes and crosswords introduce some variety and enjoyment in this section of the programme.

The early stages programme proceeds through sound–symbol relationship (auditory), sound–symbol relationship (visual), short vowels, voiced and unvoiced consonants, initial and final consonant blends, syllables, syllable division for reading and spelling, grammatical rules and suggested lesson plans for teaching letters and sounds.

The later stages programme develops the work of the early stages and, in addition, looks at word families and elaborates on the use of the reading and spelling pack.

The Teaching Reading through Spelling programme is very detailed and thorough in its approach to phonic and linguistic aspects of teaching reading and spelling. Such a structured approach may easily lend itself to monotony and dullness, particularly since it incorporates the essential aspects of over-learning and automaticity. The programme authors, however, have attempted to overcome this by introducing a variety of stimulating games and strategies that help to provide enjoyment to children, as well as reinforcing the central aspects of the programme. In general, the programme provides a good, clear structure and can be readily utilised by the class teacher.

Toe by Toe, Multisensory Manual for Teachers and Parents—Cowling and Cowling

Toe by Toe is a multi-sensory teaching method highly recommended for teachers and parents, with clear and precise instructions that can be used by a teacher who is new, a classroom assistant, a parent. The programme has a multi-sensory element, a phonic element that places some demands on the student's memory through the planning and the timing of each of the lessons in the book. It can be readily used by parents and the instructions are very clear. The same author has also published a programme called Stride Ahead—An Aid to Comprehension, which can be a useful follow-up to Toe by Toe. Essentially, Stride Ahead has been written for children who can read, but may have difficulty in understanding what they are reading.

Comment

The range of individualised programmes for children with dyslexia is impressive, and this section has provided summaries of some of the main approaches.

Some of the principles of the programmes and the methods advocated by their authors, such as 'multi-sensory', 'structured' and 'cumulative' approaches, can provide useful pointers in the development of support materials for dyslexic children. Ideally, for a programme to be of maximum benefit to teachers, it should not only be easily understood and implemented but also flexible and adaptable to different contexts and types of dyslexic difficulties. The next section, 'Support Approaches and Strategies', emphasises the benefits of such flexibility and adaptability.

SUPPORT APPROACHES AND STRATEGIES

Conceptually, most of the individualised programmes have much in common, emphasising aspects such as structure, multi-sensory aspects, over-learning and automaticity. Support materials, however, do not necessarily provide an individual programme, but rather can be used by the teacher to help the child develop some competencies to allow access to the full range of curriculum activities. Some of these support materials and approaches are discussed below.

Ann Arbor Publications

Ann Arbor Publications provide a considerable amount of resources, most of which focus directly on literacy skills. For example, in relation to written expression the resource Teaching Written Expression may be useful. This programme offers a theoretical framework and a practical step-by-step guide to developing sentences, constructing paragraphs, editing and developing a 'sense of audience'.

Interactive Literacy Games

Crossbow Education specialise in games for children with dyslexia and produce activities on literacy, numeracy and study skills. These include 'Spingoes', a spinner bingo that comprises a total of 120 games using onset and rime; 'Funics', a practical handbook of activities to help children to recognise and use rhyming words, blend and segment syllables, identify initial phonemes and link sounds to symbols. 'Funics' is produced by Maggie Ford and Anne Tottman and available from Crossbow Education. Crossbow also produce literacy games including: Alphabet Lotto, which focuses on early phonics; 'Bing-Bang-Bong' and 'CVC Spring', which help develop competence in short vowel sounds; and 'Deebees', which is a stick-and-circle board game to deal with b–d confusion.

They also have board games called: 'Magic-E Spirit and Hotwords', a five-board set for teaching and reinforcing 'h' sounds such as 'wh', 'sh', 'ch', 'th', 'ph', 'gh' and silent 'h'; 'Oh No', a times table photocopiable game book; and 'Tens n' Units', which consists of spinning board games, designed to help children of all ages practise the basics of place value in addition and subtraction.

Multi-Sensory Learning

Multi-Sensory Learning produce homophone games that are designed to improve spelling and recognition of 120 keywords. The pack includes: lotto scorers and coloured counters; a vowel discrimination game, which helps to increase auditory awareness and improve word-attack skills; domino word chunks; and a dyslexia games manual that has 50 pages of games and activities suitable for all ages in photocopiable format. The manual includes word games, memory games, sequencing activities, mnemonics, free-writing suggestions and rhyme songs.

Language Experience

It is also important that top-down approaches to reading are considered, in order that dyslexic children receive enriched language experience. This can be achieved through discussion and activities such as paired reading described above. It is important that even if the child cannot access the print content of some books, the language, concepts and narratives should be discussed. This helps to make literacy motivating and emphasises the view that literacy is more than just reading. Literacy embraces many of the social conventions in society and is a powerful tool for social awareness, essential for young people when they leave school. Literacy also has a powerful cognitive component and can help to develop thinking skills in young children as long as reading is seen as much more than accuracy. That is one of the reasons why the experience of extended language and language concepts are important even though the child may not have that level of reading accuracy.

THRASS

The Teaching of Handwriting, Reading and Spelling System (THRASS) can be useful as a support approach and an individualised programme. THRASS has many different aspects that can be accessed by children and parents. Details of these can be found in the comprehensive THRASS web page: www.thrass.com

Reading Fluency

The Hi-Lo readers from LDA, Cambridge and other similar books such as those from Barrington Stoke Ltd (10 Belford Terrace, Edinburgh EH4 3DQ) can be beneficial in relation to motivation. These books, particularly those from Barrington Stoke, have been written with the reluctant reader in mind, and they can help children with dyslexia with reading fluency and help to develop reading comprehension and reading speed.

TextHelp

The programme known as TextHelp is particularly useful for assisting with essay-writing. TextHelp has a read-back facility and a spellchecker that includes a dyslexic spell check option that searches for common dyslexic errors. Additionally, TextHelp has a word prediction feature that can predict a word from the context of the sentence, giving up to 10 options from a drop-down menu. Often, dyslexic students have a word-finding difficulty, and this feature can therefore be very useful. This software also has a 'word wizard' who provides the user: with a definition of any word; options regarding homophones; an outline of a phonic map; and a talking help file.

Inspiration

Inspiration is a software programme to help the student develop ideas and organise thinking. Through the use of diagrams it helps the student comprehend concepts and information. Essentially, the use of diagrams can help to make creating and modifying concept maps and ideas easier. The user can also prioritise and rearrange ideas, helping with essay-writing. Inspiration can therefore be used for brainstorming, organising, pre-writing, concept mapping, planning and outlining. There are 35 inbuilt templates, and these can be used for a range of subjects including English, History and Science. Dyslexic people often think in pictures, rather than words. This technique can be used for note-taking, for remembering information and organising ideas for written work. The Inspiration programme converts this image into a linear outline.

Multisensory Teaching System for Reading (MTSR)

This is a well-evaluated programme, designed to promote phonological awareness, ensure over-learning and to give time for review and attainment mastery. It is based on cumulative, structured, sequential, multi-sensory delivery with frequent small steps. The authors (Johnson et al., 1999) conducted a research study into the use of the programme and found, as well as the above, that it also encourages independent learning and improves self-esteem.

Phonological Awareness Approaches

There is strong evidence to suggest that phonological factors are of considerable importance in reading (Ellis and Large, 1981; Stanovich, 1991; Rack, 1994; Wilson and Frederickson, 1995). Children with decoding problems appear to be considerably hampered in reading because they are unable to generalise from one word to another. This means that every word they read is unique, indicating that there is a difficulty in learning and applying phonological rules in reading. It therefore emphasises the importance of teaching sounds–phonemes and ensuring that the child has an awareness of the sound–letter correspondence. Learning words by sight can enable some children to reach a certain standard in reading, but prevents them from adequately tackling new words and extending their vocabulary.

If children have a phonological awareness difficulty they are more likely to guess the word from the first letter cue and not the first *sound* (i.e., the word 'KITE' will be tackled from the starting point of the letter 'K' and not the sound 'ki' so the dyslexic reader may well read something like 'KEPT'). It is important therefore that beginning readers receive some structured training in the grapheme–phoneme correspondence; this is particularly necessary for dyslexic children who would not automatically, or readily, appreciate the importance of phonic rules in reading. Descriptions of some structured programmes are given below.

Sound Linkage

Sound Linkage (Hatcher, 1994) is an integrated phonological programme for overcoming reading difficulties. In addition to a section on assessment it contains 10 sections on teaching, each dealing with a specific aspect of phonological processing. For example, sect. 3 deals with phoneme-blending, sect. 5 deals with identification and discrimination of phonemes, and other sections deal with phoneme segmentation, deletion, substitution and phoneme transposition.

Although Sound Linkage can be used as an individual structured programme, each section contains a series of activities that can be used to support mainstream curriculum work with dyslexic children. The activities are clearly presented and no complex instructions are necessary. Many of the activities are however not new, and many teachers will be aware of the importance of them. To have all these activities in a methodical package, linked to assessment, with a clear overall rationale is an appealing feature of the programme.

Sect. 10 of the programme, which contains phonological linkage activities, and the programme's appendix 1 can be related to the child's work in the classroom. Indeed, there is no reason that all the activities cannot in some way be transferred to curriculum activities.

The section on phoneme transposition would be difficult for younger children, particularly the activities related to spoonerism (e.g., 'mouse' 'cat' becomes 'cause' 'mat'). Walton and Brooks (1995), however, suggest that spoonerisms are attractive items in an assessment programme for phonological awareness because they offer an alternative that is more appropriate for older children than rhyming and alliteration and one that is not too contaminated by any difficulties the child may have with reading and writing. Brooks (1990), however, suggested the use of semi-spoonerisms as he found full spoonerisms too difficult in a programme for 11- to 14-year-olds. Hatcher (1994) attempts to overcome this in Sound Linkage by describing activities that can introduce the child to the use of spoonerisms. One such activity involves pictures of a cow, dog, horse and fish, each cut into two parts (i.e., head and body). The teacher then explains that as well as changing heads we could change the first sounds of the name and get two funny words. Sound linkage is a comprehensive programme of activities, linking assessment and teaching, can be a useful addition to the support materials available to enhance the phonological skills of dyslexic children.

Phonological Awareness Procedure

The useful and easily accessible series of activities to promote phonological awareness (Gorrie and Parkinson, 1995) also begins with an assessment section. Following this the remainder of the programme is in the form of game activities designed to develop specific areas of phonological development. For example, there are game activities on syllable segmentation, rhyme judgement, rhyme production, alliteration, onset and rime, and phoneme segmentation games. These games provide an excellent resource for the teacher and are suitable for children at different stages of phonological development.

Phonic Code Cracker

Phonic Code Cracker is a set of materials subdivided into 12 units, each unit covering a different aspect of teaching literacy; for example, Unit 3 deals with initial and final consonant blends, Unit 5 deals with common word endings and Unit 9 deals with common silent letters.

Phonic Code Cracker (Russell, 1993, revised 2000) is a very comprehensive and teacher-friendly set of materials. The scheme has been devised to provide intensive phonic practice for children who have been having difficulty acquiring basic literacy skills. It has been successfully used with children with specific reading difficulties in mainstream primary and secondary schools.

Essentially, the scheme consists of support material and can be successfully used in combination with other schemes. Precision teaching methods are used, but no timescale is recommended as the author acknowledges that each child will have a different rate of learning. Assessment of the pupil's progress is measured through the use of pupil record skills. There are also fluency tests, time targets, accompanying computer software and—very important for building self-esteem—a mastery certificate that the child can retain as a record of his or her achievement.

Quest—Screening, Diagnostic and Support Kit (2nd edn, 1995)

This kit is described in Chapter 5, 'Assessment: Practice', since it is a screening and diagnostic test. However, it is a test that provides excellent guidance to link the assessment with teaching. A learning support programme can be developed and implemented from the results of the diagnostic tests, using the relevant Quest workbooks.

Helping Children with Reading and Spelling

Reason and Boote (1994), in their special needs manual *Helping Children with Reading and Spelling*, provide the teacher with a comprehensive teaching kit including a structured framework for teaching reading, spelling and handwriting, along with activities that can be readily utilised by the class teacher and case studies complete with teaching plans.

The model of literacy learning, which underpins this book, provides a superb illustration of the importance of both bottom-up and top-down approaches to reading. The main themes in the literacy learning model cover meaning, phonics and fluency. This is described in an integrative manner that emphasises a holistic view of literacy learning. This interconnecting approach shows the importance of meaning, phonics and fluency at all stages of reading development from the earliest to one where basic competence has been mastered.

As well as a step-by-step teaching approach, the book contains a number of activities on aiding the development of phonics, spelling and writing; the last section of the book illustrates how these ideas can be applied to the classroom. It is important upon selecting a teaching programme that every effort is made to link the activities contained within the programmes to the child's curriculum in the mainstream setting. Reason and Boote in this manual accomplish exactly that and provide a plethora of ideas and constructive guidance for the class teacher. There is also an additional case study chapter showing the practical application of a 13-week programme on working with a group of Year 2 children.

Aston Portfolio

The Aston Portfolio consists of teaching strategies that provide some framework and direction for the teacher. The Portfolio can be used in conjunction with the Aston Index, an assessment kit that highlights areas of strengths and difficulties (see Chapter 5). Once such information has been obtained, the teacher can then locate the appropriate teaching technique card in the Portfolio box. Each card provides specific remediation exercises and areas on which the teacher should focus.

The teaching technique cards in the Portfolio include: reading–visual skills; reading–auditory skills; spelling; handwriting; comprehension and written expression. The reading–visual skills section, for example, contains cards relating to teaching, sequence, discrimination, reversals, memory, sight vocabulary and word structure. It also contains lists of materials that can be used by the teacher to help the child develop visual reading skills. The Portfolio box also contains a handwriting checklist.

Although the Aston Portfolio can be useful in helping to direct the teacher to appropriate teaching areas and can also be used selectively by the teacher, it does possess some drawbacks. Clearly, the size of the cards, by necessity, restrict the amount of information that can be provided; therefore, the information is presented more as a collation of helpful 'tips' than as a structured programme of teaching. Yet, the cards do have a tendency to be prescriptive and, because of the nature of the Portfolio, overlook the individuality of children. Perhaps a closer link between the Index and the Portfolio could have helped to overcome this.

Although the handbook indicates that the teaching technique cards can be used to help to construct an individual programme for the child, this may in fact be rather difficult without extensive reference to other appropriate resources and strategies. If the teacher is to use the Portfolio, it can only be to provide some 'ignition' to help identify other appropriate resources.

High-interest Books—History

The BBC Education Scotland Series, published by Wayland (now Hodder-Wayland), on History books for primary-aged children written by Richard Dargie provides an excellent and stimulating source for reluctant readers. The books are on popular topics such as the Vikings and the Romans and include colourful illustrations. They are written in clear text with added features such as date time lines and glossaries, both of which are useful for children with dyslexia.

Start to Finish Books

The Start to Finish Books series can be beneficial as the series, designed to boost reading and comprehension skills, provides a reader profile, a computer book, audiocassette and paperback book. Designed to engage children in reading real literature the series can help with fluency and motivation. Some of the topics included in the series are: History, famous people, sports, original mysteries and retellings of classic literature. Don Johnston also produces some excellent software for children with literacy difficulties. This includes Write:OutLoud3, a programme that supports each step of the writing process including:

- generating ideas—helps with brainstorming and researching topics;
- expressing ideas—this allows children to hear their words as they write;
- editing work—using a spellchecker that is designed to check for phonetic misspellings;
- revising for meaning—helps with word-finding and improves written expression.

Differentiated texts

An example of this is the series of differentiated texts by Hodder Wayland, a series of books with two books on each of the themes covered. These texts cover History topics (such as World War 2), Geography topics (such as floods and the world's continents) and other diverse topics from energy to cultural festivals. The differentiated texts differ in that they have a reduced text length, more open page layout, bullet points to help with accessing information, clear type face and captions in different print from the main text. There are separate glossaries and indices for the differentiated and non-differentiated texts.

Counselling Approaches

Some studies (Hales, 1990b, 1995; Biggar and Barr, 1993; Miles and Varma, 1995) support the view that teachers need to appreciate the emotional needs of children with specific learning difficulties. In a number of studies, Hales showed that even very young children are adversely affected by the realisation of their difficulty with literacy. Indeed, Hales also provided evidence for the persistence of personality traits of inadequacy among dyslexic people. His study of a group of adult male dyslexics showed they had a preference to be 'people who were unconventional, individualist and more likely to be rejected in group activities.'

Hales therefore suggests that considerable scope exists for personal counselling of the dyslexic individual. This would allow people with dyslexia the opportunity of talking through their fears, and some attempts could be made to help to match 'self-image' with reality since, often, dyslexic children have a self-image that presents a distorted and unrealistic picture of themselves. Although Hales points out that, while there is no specific personality disorder that affects dyslexic children independently of other factors, there is still a strong case for considering closely the individual and personal aspects of children and adults with dyslexia. Indeed, he argues that it may be important to consider counselling and social support of the 'dyslexic person' before dealing with the 'dyslexic difficulty'. He further emphasises (Hales, 1995) that effective provision for dyslexic employees in the work situation cannot only reduce potential stress in the workplace but also facilitate the performance of a large number of competent and experienced individuals to work up to their full potential.

This view is reinforced by Newby et al. (1995), who provide first-person accounts of the effects on the individual of being dyslexic. For example, Newby asserts that 'our depths of feelings usually derive from childhood experiences. At school such negative comments led me to truant frequently' (p. 105). Another dyslexic person in the same chapter suggests, 'I personally believe today that the overwhelming levels of anxiety created by the daily ignominies and embarrassments of being a dyslexic person ... fuelled my abusing myself with prescribed medication and alcohol' (p. 116).

These views are reinforced by Biggar and Barr (1993, 1996), who reported how children with specific learning difficulties seemed acutely aware of their failure to develop literacy skills in a similar fashion to their peers, and how they would attempt to deal with this by concealing or denying their difficulty. The research conducted by Biggar and Barr indicated that factors such as inappropriate attributions, disagreement between adults, and teasing and verbal abuse hindered emotional development. They suggested the following strategies to help facilitate the emotional development of the child:

- ensure that the child's difficulties are accurately described in order to remove doubts, anxieties or prejudices;
- ensure agreement between the significant adults in the child's life, such as parents and teachers;
- ensure the child has a voice, is understood and has a trusting relationship with those adults.

This research places some emphasis on the adult and teacher to attempt to appreciate how it may *feel* for the child to have this type of difficulty.

There is also considerable evidence that shows the positive correlation between self-esteem and scholastic achievement (Burns, 1986; Bar-Tal, 1984). Clearly, therefore, it is particularly important to recognise the value of counselling, sensitivity and success for children with specific learning difficulties.

Furthermore, research has shown (Lawrence, 1985) that counselling, in addition to specific teaching programmes, can not only enhance the self-esteem of children but also enhance their reading attainments to a level in excess of children who received only the teaching programme. In his study, the teaching programme used was DISTAR and counselling continued for 20 weeks, once a week, and was conducted by non-professionals.

Lawrence suggests certain curriculum subjects have the potential to be particularly enhancing in terms of self-esteem. These include music, art, drama and creative writing. Clearly, therefore, this offers scope for the teacher to optimise the confidence of children with specific learning difficulties since art and drama have less of a reliance on literacy. Music and creative writing may well be skills that are well developed among children with specific learning difficulties, but the degree of literacy difficulties that they possess may well prevent them from gaining full access and full success from those areas. This, however, should not be the case! Supporting and encouraging the creative writing and musical ability of children with specific learning difficulties is of great importance, just as is, for example, the development of phonological awareness.

The case for a dual approach to the teaching of reading, incorporating counselling, seems in the case of children with specific learning difficulties very strong. Lawrence draws the distinction between the teacher's view of children with severe reading difficulties as 'potentially improving readers' and that of the children who may continue to see *themselves* as 'permanently retarded readers'. It seems therefore that some children have internalised their reading failure, so that irrespective of the benefits of an approach or programme success will be either superficial or minimal.

Counselling itself, therefore, can perform a dual role—it can be utilised as a mode of interaction with children to create the correct therapeutic environment and state of mind to aid the fostering of skills in learning, in order to maximise the child's potential; it can also be seen as integral to the implementation of a teaching programme and conducted simultaneously with teaching. This may be seen as a counselling approach, and may be conducted more informally than planned and progressive individual counselling.

There are some excellent self-esteem programmes available that can also be successfully utilised for dyslexic children. These include the Mosley (1996) 'circle time' activities and the White (1991) 'self-esteem' activities, which will be discussed in Chapter 8, 'Learning—Metacognition and Study Skills'.

Visual Aspects

It may be useful for the teacher to consider the influence of visual aspects in the development of literacy skills. Although the research appears to lean toward phonological and linguistic areas as the principal difficulty relating to dyslexia (Stanovich et al., 1997; Snowling and Nation, 1997; Snowling, 2000; Hatcher and Snowling, 2002), there is a body of opinion that highlights the visual areas and recommends strategies to help deal with such difficulties (Lovegrove, 1996; Stein, 1991, 1994; Wilkins, 1995; Irlen, 1983, 1989).

Research has been conducted on eye dominance and binocular control (Stein and Fowler, 1993; Stein, 2001; Everatt, 2002) and eye-tracking has also been the subject of some research (Blau and Loveless, 1982). Pavlidis (1990a) suggests that children with dyslexia have less efficient control over eye movements.

Research evidence relating to the visual magnocellular system, which consists of large cells used for depth perception, indicates that these cells appear to be more disorganised and smaller among dyslexics (Galaburda, 1993a). This would mean that stimuli would need to be delivered more slowly in order to be accurately processed.

Stein and Fowler (1993) and Stein (1994, 2001) argue that a number of children with dyslexia have binocular instability and suggest that this can be remedied through short-term use of monocular occlusion.

Bishop (1989) argues that practice in reading can develop binocular stability, but Stein and Fowler (1993) suggest this is *not* the case and that short-term use of monocular occlusion will result in binocular stability and should thus help promote significant gains in reading.

Furthermore, Cornelissen et al. (1994) found that children who experienced visual confusion of text during reading, because of unstable binocular control, were less likely to incorporate visual memories for letter strings into their spelling strategies, relying instead on sound–letter conversion rules, thus spelling words phonologically. This supports the view, therefore, that unstable binocular control not only affects how children read but also how they spell.

Stein and Walsh (1997) have linked control of eye movement with the magnocellular pathway deficit hypothesis. They suggest that movements of the eyes may be controlled primarily by areas of the brain that receive input from the magnocellular pathway. Stein and Walsh (1997) also suggest that impaired magnocellular pathway functioning might destabilise binocular fixation, as it has a dominant role in the control of eye movements.

Irlen (1991) has made claims for a scotopic sensitivity syndrome that can affect the child in terms of light sensitivity, the ability to see print clearly without distortions, the ability to perceive groups of words at the same time and the ability to sustain focus for a period of time.

Irlen recommends the use of coloured perspex overlays or tinted lens treatment to help overcome these difficulties. The research to support this is, however, fairly patchy. Rosner and Rosner (1987) reviewed the majority of studies of the tinted lens treatment and found significant problems in experimental design, and Moseley (1990) found that any significant effect of coloured overlays was due to the reduction in light rather than due to any specific colour. Studies, however, by Richardson (1988) and Wilkins (1990, 1993) have shown some significant improvement in children using overlays and lenses, particularly in visual activity and muscle balance, and subsequent reading attainments.

Kyd et al. (1992) used the Irlen overlays for children with specific learning difficulties and found significant improvements in reading rate. They are currently involved in follow-up studies examining the effect of the overlays on reading comprehension and accuracy. The results of this study are consistent with the findings from a project in Norfolk (Wright, 1993), which also provides impressive data for reading rate progress. In fact, Wright (2001, pers. commun.) supports the use of coloured overlays for a range of specific learning difficulties. Wilkins (1993, 1995), following extensive research, has developed a set of materials called Intuitive Overlays that can be used both in assessment and learning situations.

Furthermore, Wilkins et al. (1996) have developed a Rate of Reading test designed to assess the effects of coloured overlays. It is claimed this test has some advantages over conventional tests in that it actually tests the linguistic and semantic aspects of reading at least as much as the visual. Additionally, with conventional tests performance is limited by a reader's vocabulary. The Rate of Reading test therefore seeks to minimise the linguistic and semantic aspects of reading and maximises the visual difficulties.

The same 15 common words are used in each line in a different random order. The words were selected from the 110 most frequent words in a count of words in children's reading books. The text is printed in small typeface at an optimal level for visual distortion. The test is scored by noting the total number of words in the passage read correctly and calculating the average number correctly read per minute.

Wilkins et al. (1996) found the test both reliable and valid, and it successfully predicted the individuals who, when offered a coloured overlay, continued to use it. They also show that the use of the overlays had an effect on reading speed and did so immediately. The authors also report on a study in which 93 children in primary school and 59 in the first year intake of a secondary school reported an improvement in perception of text with a particular colour, and the 22 per cent of the sample who continued to use them for 10 months demonstrated a mean improvement of 14 per cent in reading speed with their overlay. This improvement was not seen in children who had failed to persist in using the overlay.

Mailley (1997), however, suggests that the present system of vision-testing in school and the community does not address the diversity of the difficulty. She suggests (Mailley, 2001) that a comprehensive visual screening procedure is necessary to identify those children at risk and that schools and colleges should consider how to manage this procedure.

The Use of Visual Skills

It has been argued (Bell, 1991a) that, although programmes directed at enhancing alphabetic and phonological skills are essential, one has to be wary of the 'cognitive cost' of such programmes—a cost that is reflected in a weakening of the gestalt, right hemispheric skills. The gestalt hemisphere is usually associated with visual imagery, creativity and comprehension.

The stress and effort that is necessary for children with dyslexia to fully engage their cognitive resources and to develop phonological skills is so great, according to Bell, that a weakening of the gestalt hemisphere results as resources are diverted from the right hemispheric functions to concentrate on the left hemispheric skills of decoding and phonological processing. Not only does this result in a restriction in the use of visual imagery but also in a stifling of the development of skills in comprehension and perhaps in creativity.

Bell (1991b) has developed a programme 'Visualizing and Verbalizing for Language Comprehension and Thinking'. This programme provides a comprehensive procedure for the use of visualising to promote and enhance reading and comprehension. The stages outlined by Bell include picture imagery, word imagery, single sentence, multiple sentence, whole paragraph and whole page.

Additionally, the programme provides an understanding of the functions of the gestalt hemisphere and useful strategies for classroom teaching.

Motor Aspects

There are a number of programmes and activities that can be used for children with dyslexia. Some of these are discussed in Chapter 14 in the section 'Specific Learning Difficulties and Alternative Therapies'. Nevertheless, there are a number of user-friendly activities that have been developed by practitioners. McIntyre (2000, 2001) has developed handbooks of approaches on motor development, particularly for children from the early years to 11. Portwood (1999, 2001) has produced excellent guides for parents and teachers on dyspraxia that contain a number of practical suggestions. Furthermore, she has also produced a text on understanding developmental dyspraxia (Portwood, 2000), which can be a useful source for staff development in this area. Russell (1988) developed a set of graded activities for children with motor difficulties that is very teacher-friendly and contains clearly illustrated activities. The programme consists of 14 sections including gross-motor, balancing, catching, throwing, kicking and jumping, directional orientation, visual–motor co-ordination and handwriting activities. These activities, though essentially directed at children with motor problems, can be extremely useful for a number of dyslexic children.

Nash-Wortham and Hunt (1993) have produced an extremely comprehensive book that contains pointers on different areas of motor difficulty, such as timing and rhythm, sequencing and laterality. These are followed by a series of exercises for each of the six pointers described. Additionally, there has been considerable interest in the whole area of motor development and how it relates to other cognitive factors (Blyth, 1992, 2001, pers. commun.; Goddard Blythe, 2001; McPhilips et al., 2000) in relation: to programmes relating to inhibition of primitive reflexes (Dennison and Hargrove, 1986; McCarroll, 1999; Fox, 1999; Longdon, 2001; Taylor, 2002); to Educational Kinesiology (Brain Gym®) (Fox, 1999; Reynolds et al., in press); and to the series of exercises influenced by the research conducted by Fawcett and Nicolson (1994) on the cerebellum—the Dyslexia, Dyspraxia, Attention Disorder Treatment (DDAT). Some of these are discussed in more detail in Chapter 13 of this book.

Although the rationale for these programmes vary in both the research supporting the programmes and the theoretical roots that have influenced them, they do serve to reinforce the concept of the link between motor development and learning in general.

ASSISTED LEARNING

Assisted learning approaches are essentially teaching approaches that require considerable interaction between the learner and others. This interaction may take the form of some kind of participant modelling. There may be an element of repetition and even simplicity in these approaches, but, based on the principles of modelling and of facilitating the learning process, they can be successfully utilised with reading, writing and spelling.

Paired-reading, peer-tutoring, cued-spelling and the apprenticeship approach to reading are examples of this kind of approach. Metacognitive approaches can also come under this category, as such approaches can be based on interaction between teacher and student, and this interaction can help the student acquire concepts and knowledge of the learning process. Metacognitive approaches will however be dealt with in some detail in the following chapter. As an example of assisted learning paired-reading will be described and discussed below.

Paired-Reading

Paired-reading was originally devised to meet the need for a reading approach that could be both applied generally and utilised by non-professionals with a minimum of training (Morgan, 1976).

Studies have shown (Neville, 1975; Wilkinson, 1980; Bell, 1991a) that releasing children from the burden of decoding can facilitate or enhance comprehension.

This is highlighted in a study examining the decoding processes of slow readers (Curtis, 1980), which found that the cognitive applications to decoding reduced the amount of attention available for other reading processes. This resulted in deficits in comprehension of text. Emphasis, therefore, can be placed on the use of context rather than the skill of decoding, but the question remains whether poor readers are able to utilise context as successfully as proficient readers.

Clark (1988) observed an inefficient use of context among dyslexic children, although she noted that dyslexic children utilised a wide variation of strategies and preferences in an attempt to use context to aid comprehension.

Lees (1986), however, in an examination of the data from four different studies, concluded that poor readers had similar capabilities to good readers in the utilisation of context to aid word recognition. Evans (1984b) reported on two studies using paired-reading for dyslexic children, both of which showed significant gains in reading comprehension and vocabulary.

Topping and Lindsey (1992), therefore, argue that the evidence suggests that poor readers have an over-dependence on decoding strategies at the expense of developing skills in comprehension, using contextual cues. This is a practice reinforced by many teaching programmes that over-emphasise analytical decoding approaches, resulting in sequential decoding processes that can inhibit full use of comprehension skills. This is indeed consistent with the literature on learning styles (Carbo, 1987), which suggests that young children tend to have a preference for processing information globally rather than analytically. Yet, one must be cautious of fostering global processing methods such as the whole-word method at the expense of analytical methods such as phonics, since the teaching approaches that combine both these approaches are arguably more effective (Vellutino and Scanlon, 1986; Reason et al., 1988).

Paired-reading may be particularly useful for children with specific learning diffi-culties since it provides both visual and auditory input simultaneously. It is a simple technique that focuses on the following:

- parent and child reading together;
- programme to be carried out consistently;

Figure 7.1   Paired-reading.

- child selects reading material;
- as few distractions as possible;
- use of praise as reinforcement;
- discussion of the story and pictures (see Figure 7.1).

The two principal stages of paired-reading are reading together and reading alone:

- *Reading together* is when the parent/teacher and child read all the words aloud, with the adult adjusting the speed so that the pair are reading in harmony. The adult does not allow the child to become stuck at a word and if this happens will simply say the word to the child. This process, together with discussion, can help the child obtain meaning from the text and therefore enjoy the experience of language and of reading.
- *Reading alone* occurs when the child becomes more confident at reading aloud. The adult can either read more softly, thus allowing the child to take the lead, or remain quiet. This can be done gradually to allow the child's confidence to build up (Topping, 1996). When the child stumbles at this stage, the adult immediately offers the word and then continues reading with the child again, until he or she gains enough confidence to read unaided.

Topping and Lindsey (1992) report on a number of other programmes, mostly from North America, that show similarities to paired-reading. One such programme is the Neurological Impress Method (NIM). This method involves the student and the instructor reading aloud together in unison. The instructor sits a little behind the student and speaks directly into the right ear of the learner. No corrections are made during or after the reading session. The method is intended for use by professionals.

There are few evaluation studies of this particular technique, but an interesting comment can be made on the strategy of speaking directly into the right ear. Presumably the purpose of this is to engage the left language hemisphere, yet a study looking at sensory deprivation and particularly auditory perception (Johanson, 1992) suggests that children with reading problems have a better left ear than right in relation to auditory discrimination.

Evaluation of Paired-reading as a Strategy

Topping (2002) has extended the strategy of paired-reading to include paired-spelling (see Chapter 3) and paired-thinking. The evaluations of these, like paired-reading, are promising (Topping and Lindsey, 1992; Topping, 2002).

Paired-reading may well help children with dyslexia develop a desire to read. Clearly, an adult model or indeed a peer in the case of peer-tutoring (Topping, 2001; Topping and Bryce, 2002) can act as a good reinforcer.

Other factors have also been attributed to the success of paired-reading. These include pacing the text, which helps to regulate the child's reading flow and may help to overcome the segmentation and syllabification problems outlined by many researchers (Bradley, 1990; Snowling, 1993a, b). The fact that it is multi-sensory, particularly utilising the combination of visual and auditory modalities, may also be significant. It may also help to provide weaker readers with a global strategy through the practice of non-interruption of the reading flow. The value of paired-reading in enhancing self-image should also not be ignored. The importance of this for children with reading problems (Lawrence, 1985, 1987) is well documented in the literature. Some other advantages of paired-reading are:

- failure is not an evident factor because if the child 'sticks' at a word the adult says the word almost immediately;
- the experience of gaining enjoyment from the language of the text helps reading become pleasurable and increases the desire to read;
- children are provided with an example of how to pronounce difficult words and can simultaneously relate the auditory sound of the word with the visual appearance of that word;
- children can derive understanding from the text because words are given expression and meaning by the adult and discussion about the text follows at periodic intervals.

Thus, paired-reading can be useful as:

- a strategy to develop motivation and confidence in reading;
- an aid to the development of fluency and expression in reading;
- a technique that could also enhance comprehension on the part of the reader.

Paired-reading, however, is seen as complementary to other strategies, such as structured language teaching and phonics skills, and does not attempt to replicate or replace this dimension of learning to read. However, it utilises the participation of parents, and this is clearly a great advantage both for the child and the school.

Topping (1993) and Topping and Hogan (1999) suggest paired-reading can reduce the anxieties of reading for dyslexic children, reduce their all-consuming fear of failure, and encourage motivation and reading practice.

The approach is essentially one that can effectively combine the psycholinguistic aspects of the use of context with the phonic skills associated with word attack. This, coupled with parent or peer support and appraisal, may well account for its success.

Comment

Assisted learning implies that learning, quite rightly, is an interactive process and the role of peers and adults is of great importance. This form of learning in many ways minimises the adverse effects of failure, because if the child cannot respond to a particular text or situation then assistance is provided. The important point is, however, that assistance is not necessarily provided because the child is not succeeding, but because it is built into the reading or learning strategy. The learner, therefore, is not necessarily obtaining the sense of failing, but rather of working co-operatively with another person.

SUMMARY

This chapter on teaching has sought to describe the vast range of different types of teaching approaches that can be used with children with dyslexia. It is fair to say that no one single approach holds the key to completely dealing with dyslexic difficulties and many of the programmes and strategies described in this chapter can be used together and can be complementary to other teaching and curriculum approaches. Irrespective of the type of provision that is being provided for dyslexic children, it is important that at all times every opportunity is taken to help access the full curriculum. This can present real difficulties for some dyslexic children, but this challenge can be met through careful planning, utilising the skills of teachers and being aware of the abundance of approaches and strategies available.

One of the most important considerations when selecting an appropriate teaching approach(s) for students with dyslexia relates to issues concerning the context and the curriculum. Teaching approaches, such as those discussed here, should not be seen in isolation and need to be linked to the curriculum and the pupil's current work in the classroom. Specialised teaching approaches therefore should be part of an overall programme that includes differentiation as a means of curriculum access. There are many examples of differentiated texts (see pp. 247–249), and these, together with pre-planning and curriculum development with the dyslexic learner in mind, can provide a comprehensive and effective form of intervention. One of the key points about differentiation as a means of curriculum access is that it is seen as a way of supporting all students, thus minimising any stigma that might be felt by the student who is receiving a different type of programme from others in the class (DfES, 2001). It is important, however, to ensure that differentiation is not merely a reduction in the content coverage to release more time for literacy development. Effective differentiation should incorporate principles and practices, such as those advocated by Visser (1993), that see differentiation as a process whereby teachers meet students' needs for curriculum progression by selecting appropriate teaching methods that match an individual child's learning strategies, within a group situation. As Philips (1999) points out, differentiation must build on past achievement, present challenges to enable further achievement and provide opportunities for success. Wearmouth el al. (2003) note that differentiation is linked to text readability. Considerations therefore, such as the interest level of text, sentence length, complexity, word familiarity and step-by-step explanations of difficult concepts, can all be considered in a differentiated approach, as well as the visual aspects of presentation and the individual pupil's learning style. Although it is tempting, in terms of time-saving, to rely on a packaged programme, the benefits from this may not be readily transferred to other areas of the child's class work. For that reason it is crucial that any approach is seen as being part of an overall programme that should be closely matched to curriculum objectives. According to Tod (2002) individual education programmes can provide a means of achieving this. Tod, however, acknowledges there needs to be some clarity about the educational purpose of an IEP both for the individual pupil and as part of whole-school planning and provision. She suggests that IEPs cannot be divorced from the context in which they have been developed and that 'targeted, focused, additional, phonological support offered via the IEP needs to be housed within a rich interactive effective literacy curriculum' (Tod, 2002, p. 264).

Some of these points will be developed in the following chapters on metacognition, study skills and learning styles. This emphasises the importance of other factors such as the learner, learning environment, and the teaching and learning process. These will indicate how some of these programmes and approaches can be utilised and be effectively integrated within the school curriculum.

Chapter 8

Learning—Metacognition and Study Skills

Effective learning involves a number of interactive cognitive activities and processes. The learner can control these activities and processes to make learning efficient and effective. The skills therefore associated with learning need to be developed from an early age, yet often these skills are not given the attention they warrant within the school curriculum. Study skills, for example, that essentially provide the learner with an opportunity to practise and experiment in learning in order to find the most efficient method for each individual are often not given full prominence in the curriculum, until at least secondary age. Yet, study skills can help to develop not only retention of information but also comprehension and concepts. It is vitally important therefore that learning skills are addressed at an early stage in education.

LEARNING SKILLS AND DYSLEXIA

The development of skills in learning are particularly appropriate for children with dyslexia as often they may have difficulty in identifying key points and developing efficient learning strategies. Indeed, it has been noted (Tunmer and Chapman, 1996) that children with dyslexia can have poor metacognitive awareness, which means that they may select inappropriate strategies for reading (very likely on account of their difficulties in phonological awareness) and have difficulty in unlearning once a method has been utilised over time. This can be noted, for example, in spelling when a word is habitually misspelt even after the correct spelling has been shown to the child. Additionally, children and indeed adults with dyslexia can often take inefficient routes when solving problems. They may use, for example, many different steps to get to the same end as someone who can achieve the answer using a more direct process. In some mathematical problems children with dyslexia may take twice the amount of steps to get the correct response as other children (Chinn, 2002). This means that they may lose track of the actual problem, and certainly the additional time needed to solve problems in this tangential manner can be disadvantageous.

Leather and McLoughlin (2001) suggested that people with dyslexia appear to have some difficulty developing metacognitive skills for some tasks—especially those dealing with information-processing. They suggest that people with dyslexia have difficulty identifying demands and selecting the most appropriate strategy because of an overload of information, which can account for learning tasks being misdirected, which in turn leads to wrong strategy selection.

It has been noted, however (West, 1997), that this tangential problem-solving process may well enhance creativity. Nevertheless, this emphasises the importance of developing effective learning skills and strategies at an early age. This can be achieved through study skills and through developing concepts and schema, using strategies such as scaffolding and comprehension-building exercises. There is a significant role, therefore, for study skills, metacognition, learning to learn and learning styles in relation to dyslexia. These aspects will be discussed in this and the following chapter.

THE PROCESS OF LEARNING

What does one mean when using the term 'process of learning'? There are three principal elements to learning: the input, the cognition and the output (Figure 8.1).

The input can be absorbed in various forms (e.g., by hearing or speaking; seeing events, print or illustrations; writing or experiencing through whole-body activities). Cognition occurs when the material is undergoing some form of change as the learner attempts to make sense of it. The output indicates the level of understanding that the learner has achieved with the new material. Consideration needs to be given

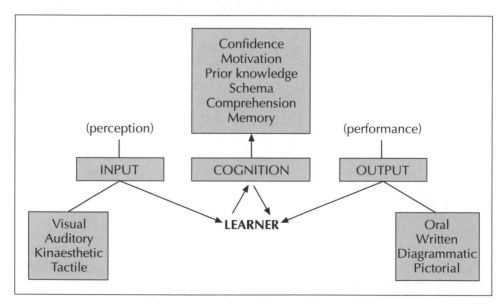

Figure 8.1   The process of learning.

to the learner and the learning style at all stages of these processes. This is particularly important for dyslexic learners as they can display particular difficulty in the input and output stages, and this can influence the 'cognition' process, thus preventing the learner from obtaining a full understanding of the learning task.

In order that the dyslexic child can effectively access the curriculum it is important that these three dimensions are matched to the learner—a mismatch would obviously result in increased stress being placed on the learner with an accompanying degree of demotivation and possible task failure. There is no one single recipe for success. All the modes of input of information are important in learning, although very young children are inclined to respond best to input of a tactile or kinaesthetic nature, and not necessarily of a visual or auditory nature (indeed, very few students prefer learning by listening). It is necessary, therefore, to consider each child individually in relation to the components of the learning process; individual preferences may be evident and these will influence the success or otherwise of both teaching and learning.

Burden (2002) suggests that learning difficulties may arise at the input phase of information-processing because the learner may have an impulsive learning style or may suffer from a blurred or sweeping perception of incoming stimuli. This means that at the initial, vital stage of learning there is a breakdown in the learning process, which can therefore affect attention and make effective learning at this important input stage less efficient. Burden also suggests that during the elaboration or cognitive phase, the learner may be unable to discriminate between relevant and irrelevant cues in defining a problem. This has been noted both among students in school and in tertiary education (Reid and Kirk, 2001) and can result in inappropriate responses to a problem or excessive elaboration, much of which is unnecessary. This excessive elaboration is often a compensatory mechanism because the student has not been able to grasp or access the key points. Burden further emphasises the potential difficulties at the output stage of the learning cycle. He suggests that people with dyslexia may have difficulty being aware of the needs of the audience or the purpose of the activity. This can also be seen in writing where they may well be redundant pages of information.

Vygotsky (1962, 1978) differentiated between the 'cognitive' (i.e., learning how to do things) and the 'metacognitive' (i.e., a gradual conscious control over knowledge and learning), and being able to use that knowledge to help with further learning. Both cognitive and metacognitive aspects are important in Vygotsky's model, and both have been applied to many areas of assessment and learning. In particular, the cognitive aspects of learning and how it relates to the theory of social constructivism has been given some prominence. This essentially means that one needs to look at not only cognitive, within-child factors but also how the child's understanding of langauge and learning is mediated by the learning context and the classroom environment. Burden (2002) suggests that the cultural and social context within which learning takes place is crucial in mediating how a child learns. This implies that learning involves more than just presentation of information but embraces factors relating to the whole child and particularly the child's previous cultural and learning experiences as well. Previous experiences and learning can make new learning meaningful, and it is important to establish these before or as new learning is being presented. This process has been named as reciprocal teaching (Palincsar and

Brown, 1984), where the interaction between learner and teacher can establish a scaffold to help the child bridge between his or her existing knowledge and experiences, and the new learning. Essentially, this is achieved through effective question-and-answer interaction between teacher and child, which should build on the child's response in order to extend his or her thinking.

ZONE OF PROXIMAL DEVELOPMENT

The procedure described above—reciprocal teaching—is essentially the same as what Vygotsky describes as the Zone of Proximal Development (ZPD) and acknowledges as an important aspect of learning. This refers to the interaction between the teacher and the child and how much of the learning can be independently accessed by the child and how much requires the teacher to mediate in order for the child to access full understanding and develop further related concepts.

Burden (2002) describes the ZPD as the zone where learning can be scaffolded by others, and then when independent cognitive activity takes place the scaffolding is gradually removed at appropriate moments. This can be seen as active rather than passive learning as it is a dynamic process, and the child can actually determine the nature and extent of the learning experience. This has considerable implications for children and adults with dyslexia as they benefit from active learning, and the scaffolding experience can also help to clarify and establish concepts before the child moves on to further learning. This processes can be metacognitive because it involves learners' thinking about their own thinking processes.

MODELS AND STRATEGIES

Metacognition, which essentially means thinking about thinking, has an important role in how children learn, and this can be vital to help dyslexic children clarify concepts, ideas and situations and therefore make reading more meaningful. This also helps in the transfer of learning from one situation to another. Flavell (1979) greatly influenced the field of metacognition and its applications to the classroom, and since then metacognition has been given considerable prominence in schools and in assessment and curriculum activities.

There have been a number of models implemented in relation to metacognition. One that is well established and relevant to the learning of dyslexic children is that proposed by Brown et al. (1986). This model contains four main variables relevant to learning:

- *text*—the material to be learnt;
- *task*—the purpose of reading;
- *strategies*—how the learner understands and remembers information;
- *characteristics of the learner*—prior experience, background knowledge, interests and motivation.

Rowe (1988) identifies three aspects of importance to metacognitive learning:

- Children's knowledge of their metacognitive activity, which can be achieved through thinking aloud as they perform particular tasks.
- The encouragement of conscious awareness of cognitive activity such as self-questioning. Have I done this before? How did I do it? Is this the best way to tackle this problem?
- The encouragement of control over learning. To develop particular strategies for dealing with a task, whether it be reading, spelling or creative writing.

Wray (1994) reports on a study by Ekwall and Ekwall (1989) that defines differences between good and poor readers. The researchers suggest that the main difference relates to comprehension-monitoring behaviour. For example, good readers generate questions while they read, are able to transfer what they read into mental images, reread if necessary and actively comprehend while they read.

Poor readers, on the other hand, lack a clear purpose of reading, view reading as essentially a decoding task and seldom reread or actively comprehend while they read. Tregaskes and Daines (1989) report on some metacognitive strategies such as visual imagery, obtaining the main ideas from text, developing concepts through strategies such as mind maps or webbing and self-questioning, which attempts to relate previous knowledge with the new material to be learned. It is important that dyslexic students are encouraged to use these metacognitive strategies, otherwise they may become too entrenched in the actual process of reading rather than in the meaning and purpose of the activity.

Wray (1994) suggests that teachers should teach metacognitive strategies directly and always within the context of meaningful experiences (e.g., within children's project work). Cue cards that contain ideas for thinking aloud are also suggested as being useful to stimulate self-questioning during creative writing. Metacognition, therefore, should be an integral part of the learning process, and to be an effective component it should be embedded within the curriculum and within curricular activities.

METACOGNITIVE TEACHING

Reciprocal Teaching and Scaffolding

Reciprocal teaching refers to a procedure that both monitors and enhances comprehension by focusing on processes relating to questioning, clarifying, summarising and predicting (Palincsar and Brown, 1984). This is an interactive process. Brown (1993) describes the procedure for reciprocal teaching as one that is initially led by the teacher. The teacher leads the discussion by asking questions, and this generates additional questions from participants, the questions are then clarified by teacher and participants together. The discussion is then summarised by teacher or participants, following which a new 'teacher' is selected by the participants to lead the discussion on the next section of the text.

Scaffolding

The procedure described above can be referred to as scaffolding, in which a 'scaffold' or supports are built to develop the understanding of text. This may be in the form of the teacher either providing the information or generating appropriate responses through questioning and clarifying. The supports are then withdrawn gradually, when the learner has achieved the necessary understanding to continue with less support.

Cudd and Roberts (1994) observed that poor readers were not automatically making the transfer from book language to their own writing. As a result the students' writing lacked the precise vocabulary and varied syntax that was evident during reading. To overcome this difficulty Cudd and Roberts introduced a scaffolding technique to develop both sentence sense and vocabulary. They focused on sentence expansion by using vocabulary from the children's readers, and using these as sentence stems encouraged sentence expansion. Thus, the procedure used involved:

- selection of vocabulary from basal reader;
- embedding this vocabulary into sentence stems;
- selecting particular syntactic structures to introduce the stem;
- embedding the targeted vocabulary into sentence stems to produce complex sentences;
- discussing the sentence stems, including the concepts involved;
- completing a sentence using the stems;
- repeating the completed sentence providing oral reinforcement of both the vocabulary and the sentence structure;
- encouraging the illustration of some of their sentences, helping to give the sentence a specific meaning.

Cudd and Roberts (1994) have found that this sentence expansion technique provides a 'scaffold' for children to help develop their sentence structure and vocabulary. Preliminary examination of writing samples of the students has revealed growth in vocabulary choice and sentence variety. The children, including those with reading and writing difficulties, were seen to gain better control over the writing process and gained confidence from using their own ideas and personal experiences.

Transfer of Skills

Transfer of skills can best be achieved when emphasis is firmly placed on the *process* of learning and not the product. This encourages children to reflect on learning and encourages the learner to interact with other learners and with the teacher. In this way effective study skills can help to activate learning and provide the student with a structured framework for effective learning.

Nisbet and Shucksmith (1986) describe one example of such a framework that focuses on preparation, planning and reflection. Preparation looks at the goals of the current work and how these goals relate to previous work. Planning looks at the skills and information necessary in order to achieve these goals. The reflection aspect assesses the quality of the final piece of work, asking such questions as: 'What did the children learn from the exercise and to what extent could the skills gained be transferred to other areas?'

This example displays a structure from which it is possible to plan and implement a study skills programme and at the same time evaluate its effectiveness in relation to the extent of transfer of knowledge and skills to other curricular areas.

The traditional view of teaching dyslexic children is based on a number of well-founded principles (Thomson, 1988, 1989; Augur and Briggs, 1992; Reid, 1998; Ott, 1997; Johnston et al., 1999; Peer and Reid, 2003). These principles tend to suggest that dyslexic children would benefit from a teaching programme that is characterised by its multi-sensory, sequential, cumulative and structured nature. Often, this type of programme is implemented on a one-to-one basis with considerable over-learning. While this procedure may be effective for those with a low base line in literacy, it is suggested here that this can perform a mis-service to many dyslexic children by overlooking the metacognitive aspects of learning and the potential in thinking skills and learning styles.

It is argued that dyslexic children may have difficulty with the metacognitive aspects of learning (Tunmer and Chapman, 1996). This implies that they need to be shown how to learn and the connections and relationships between different learning tasks need to be highlighted. This essentially means the emphasis should not necessarily be on the content or the product of learning, but the process (i.e., how learning takes place). Metacognitive strategies can facilitate new learning by using strategies and rules from previous learning, thereby enhancing the efficiency of the task of learning.

Metacognition has an important role in learning and can help to develop thinking skills; it enhances an awareness of the learning process and the utilisation of effective strategies when learning new material. The teacher then has an instrumental role to play in assessing metacognitive awareness and supporting its development (Peer and Reid, 2001). This can be done by asking the student some fundamental questions and through observing the learning behaviour of students, as exemplified in the following section.

ASSESSING METACOGNITIVE AWARENESS

When tackling a new task does the child demonstrate self-assessment by asking questions such as:

- Have I done this before?
- How did I tackle it?
- What did I find easy?
- What was difficult?
- Why did I find it easy or difficult?
- What did I learn?
- What do I have to do to accomplish this task?

- How should I tackle it?
- Should I tackle it the same way as before?

The use of metacognitive strategies can help to develop reading comprehension and expressive writing skills such as:

- visual imagery—discussing and sketching images from a text;
- summary sentences—identify the main ideas in a text;
- webbing—the use of concept maps of the ideas from a text;
- self-interrogation—ask questions about what learners already know about a topic and what they may be expected to learn from the new passage.

Wray (1994) provides a description of some of the skills shown by good readers—these can provide a good example of metacognitive awareness in reading. Good readers according to Wray usually:

- generate questions while they read;
- monitor and resolve comprehension problems;
- utilise mental images as they read;
- reread when necessary; and
- self-correct if an error has been made when reading.

These factors can help to ensure that the reader has a clear picture of the purpose of reading and an understanding of the text about to be read. There is considerable evidence to suggest that such pre-reading discussion can enhance reading fluency and understanding.

Ulmer and Timothy (1999) developed an alternative assessment framework based on retelling as an instructional and assessment tool. This indicated that informative assessment of a child's comprehension could take place by using criteria relating to how the child retells a story. Ulmer and Timothy suggested the following criteria: textual (what the child remembered); cognitive (how the child processed the information) and affective (how the child felt about the text). Their two-year study indicated that all the teachers in the study assessed for textual information, but only 31 per cent looked for cognitive indicators and 25 per cent for affective. Yet, the teachers who did go beyond the textual found rich information. Some examples of information, but provided by the teachers indicated that, by assessing beyond the textual level, the use of the retelling method of assessment could provide evidence of the child's 'creative side', and teachers discovered that children could go 'beyond the expectations when given the opportunity'. This is a good example of how looking for alternative means of assessing can link with the child's understandings of text and promote development thinking. It can be suggested that assessment instruments are often based on restrictive criteria, examining what the child may be expected to know, often at a textual level, but may ignore other rich sources of information that can inform about the child's thinking, both cognitive and affective, and provide suggestions for teaching.

ASSESSMENT: DYNAMIC AND METACOGNITIVE

Traditional forms of assessment such as standardised assessment can provide information on the child's level of attainments, but usually they do not provide information about the process of thinking utilised by the child. Metacognitive aspects that focus on the process of learning can be extremely valuable and can identify the strategies being used by the child. They can also be a useful teaching tool through the development of concepts and ideas through teacher–student interaction.

MULTIPLE INTELLIGENCES

Ever since Howard Gardner wrote *Frames of Mind* (Gardener, 1983) the concept of intelligence and its applicability to education has been re-examined. Before then there was a commonly held view of intelligence as a unitary concept, although that was constantly being re-examined during the second half of the 20th century. Gardner suggests that when Binet attempted to measure intelligence in the early part of the 20th century there was indeed an assumption that intelligence was a single entity and an assumption that this entity could be measured by a single paper-and-pencil test (Gardner, 1999). This, of course, had considerable implications for how children were assessed and taught during the mid-20th century and was particularly influential in streaming and in deciding the most appropriate education provision for children. Gardner himself acknowledges, however, that there has been considerable movement away from this view about intelligence greatly supported by his attempts to highlight the need to 'pluralize the notion of intelligence and to demonstrate that intelligences cannot be adequately measured by short answer paper and pencil tests' (p. vii).

Gardner also acknowledges that his conceptualisation of intelligence is part of a larger effort to examine and define the concept and pluralisation of intelligence. At present the multiple intelligence concept developed originally by Gardner involves eight intelligences.

Since the publication of *Frames of Mind*, Gardner has developed his concept of multiple intelligence and now no longer sees intelligence as a set of human potentials, but rather 'in terms of the particular social and cultural context in which the individual lives.' According to Gardner this means that a significant part of an individual's intelligence exists outside his or her head, and this therefore broadens the notion of assessing intelligence by involving many different aspects of a person's skills, thoughts and preferences. The notion of multiple intelligence therefore sits well with this contextualisation view of intelligence and because of this can be more comfortably applied to educational settings. Gardner accepts that intelligences do not work in isolation, but are usually interactive and combine with other intelligences, and where one differs from another is in that combination and how that combination works for the learner. Gardner suggests that all possess these intelligences in some combination and all have the potential to use them productively. This has clear implications for the classroom and indeed for children with dyslexia as they will possess these intelligences. Although perhaps in a different combination from some others, they will still have the same potential to develop these intelligences in classroom activities. It is important, therefore, that the notion of multiple intelligence is incorporated into not only assessment (see Chapter 5) but also into the teaching and learning process in schools.

Lazear (1999) has made considerable effort to incorporate Gardner's model of intelligence into both assessment and teaching. Each of the eight intelligences (Figure 8.2) can be incorporated in this way, and if this is achieved within one's teaching and in curriculum development then children who may have weakness in some aspects of language or other processing, such as dyslexic children, will benefit. This essentially turns the concept of deficits on its head, and as Gardner points out every child has the potential for effective learning, but their learning preferences and strengths need to be accessed. The eight intelligences can be summarised as follows: verbal–linguistic involves language processing; logical–mathematical is associated with scientific and deductive reasoning; visual–spatial deals with visual stimuli and visual planning; bodily–kinaesthetic involves the ability to express emotions and ideas in action such as drama and dancing; musical–rythmic is the ability to recognise rythmic and tonal patterns; interpersonal intelligence involves social skills and working in groups; intrapersonal involves metacognitive-type activities and reflection and only recently an eighth intelligence has been added—naturalist intelligence. This relates to one's appreciation of the natural world around us, the ability to enjoy nature and to recognise different species and how we incorporate and react emotionally to natural environmental factors such as flowers, plants and animals. Each of these intelligences can be incorporated into teaching and learning and into curriculum development. It is important therefore that the skills and preferences of, for example, children with dyslexia are utilised within a multiple intelligences curriculum. Lazear (1999) has made considerable effort to highlight the potential of multiple intelligences within daily classroom activities. For example, the verbal–linguistic mode can incorporate creative writing, poetry and storytelling; the logical–mathematical mode involves logic and pattern games and problem-solving; the visual–spatial mode can involve guided imagery, drawing and design; the bodily–kinaesthetic mode involves drama, role play and sports; the musical–rythmic mode involves classroom activities that can relate to tonal patterns and music performance; the intrapersonal intelligence mode can involve classroom activities on thinking strategies, metacognition and independent projects; and naturalist intelligence can take the form of fieldwork as well as projects on conservation, evolution and the observation of nature. Multiple intelligences, as a guide to classroom practice, can be very helpful in ensuring that the curriculum, learning and teaching provide the opportunity for the child to display and extend his or her natural abilities in many areas.

Historically, there has been considerable preoccupation with the verbal–linguistic aspects of intelligence, and this has resulted in a curriculum and examination system that appears to give a preferential status to these areas. This can be disadvantageous to children with dyslexia. It is interesting to note the comment by Pringle-Morgan as long ago as 1896, when he suggested that there is a group of otherwise intelligent people who have difficulty in expressing their understanding of a situation in writing

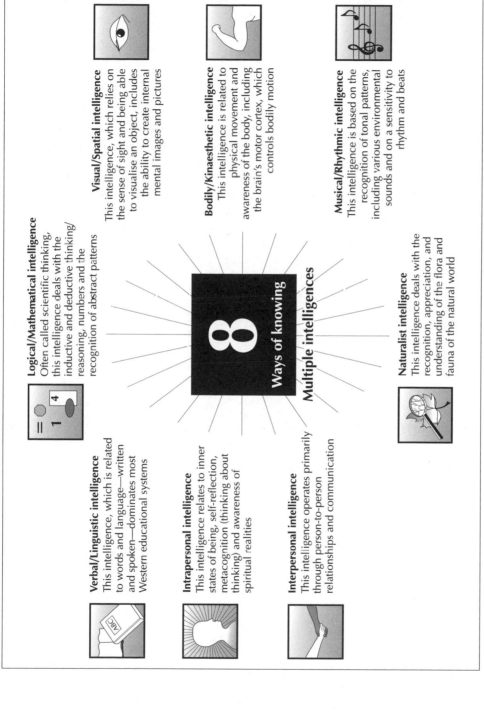

Logical/Mathematical intelligence
Often called scientific thinking, this intelligence deals with the inductive and deductive thinking/ reasoning, numbers and the recognition of abstract patterns

Visual/Spatial intelligence
This intelligence, which relies on the sense of sight and being able to visualise an object, includes the ability to create internal mental images and pictures

Bodily/Kinaesthetic intelligence
This intelligence is related to physical movement and awareness of the body, including the brain's motor cortex, which controls bodily motion

Musical/Rhythmic intelligence
This intelligence is based on the recognition of tonal patterns, including various environmental sounds and on a sensitivity to rhythm and beats

8
Ways of knowing

Multiple intelligences

Naturalist intelligence
This intelligence deals with the recognition, appreciation, and understanding of the flora and fauna of the natural world

Verbal/Linguistic intelligence
This intelligence, which is related to words and language—written and spoken—dominates most Western educational systems

Intrapersonal intelligence
This intelligence relates to inner states of being, self-reflection, metacognition (thinking about thinking) and awareness of spiritual realities

Interpersonal intelligence
This intelligence operates primarily through person-to-person relationships and communication

Figure 8.2 Eight ways of knowing (reproduced by permission of Pearson Education; from Lazear, 1999; see also Gardner, 1999).

and if this group were provided with the opportunity to present their knowledge in some other form (such as orally) they would score considerably higher in examinations. Over 100 years later the message is beginning to get through, but there have been many casualties along the road and children with dyslexia can account for some of them.

Study Skills

Study skills are an essential component of any programme that aims to access the curriculum for dyslexic children. There is some evidence that dyslexic children require particular help in this area, principally due to their organisational problems. A well-constructed study skills programme therefore is essential and can do much to enhance concept development, metacognitive awareness, transfer of learning and success in the classroom.

Such programmes will vary with the age and stage of the learner. A study skills programme for primary children would be different from that which may help students cope with examinations at secondary level. Well-developed study skills habits at the primary stage can provide a sound foundation for tackling new material in secondary school and help equip the student for examinations. Some of the principal factors in a study skills programme that will be discussed in this section include:

- communication skills;
- transfer of knowledge and skills;
- mapping and visual skills;
- memory skills.

COMMUNICATION SKILLS

'Communication skills' is a fairly general term and relates to those aspects of study skills that govern oral and written communication. Some of the factors that influence such skills include:

- organisation;
- sequencing;
- context;
- schemata development;
- confidence and motivation.

ORGANISATION

Children with specific learning difficulties or dyslexia may require help to organise their thoughts. A structure should therefore be developed to help encourage this. It may not be enough to ask children, for example, on completion of a story, 'What was the story about?' They need to be provided with a structure in order to elicit correct responses. This helps with the organisation of responses (output), which in turn can help to organise learning through comprehension (input). A structure that the teacher might use to elicit organised responses may include:

- What was the title?
- Who were the main characters?
- Describe the main characters.
- What did the main characters try to do?
- Who were the other characters in the story?
- What was the story about?
- What was the main part of the story?
- How did the story end?

In this way a structure is provided for the learner to retell the story. Moreover, the learner will be organising the information into a number of components such as 'characters', 'story', 'conclusion'. This will not only make it easier for the learner to retell orally but will help to give him or her an organisational framework that will facilitate the retention of detail as well. The learner will also be using a strategy that can be used in other contexts, which will help with the new learning and retention of new material.

SEQUENCING

Dyslexic children may have some difficulty in retelling a story or giving information orally in the correct sequence. It is important that sequencing of information should be encouraged and exercises that help facilitate this skill can be developed. Thus, in the retelling of a story, children should be provided with a framework that can take account of the sequence of events. Such a framework could include:

- How did the story start?
- What happened after that?
- What was the main part?
- How did it end?

Various exercises, such as the use of games, can be developed to help facilitate sequencing skills.

Contextual aspects are also important elements in acquiring study skills techniques. Context can be used to help the learner in both the sequencing and organisation of materials as well as in providing an aid to comprehension.

Context can either be syntactic or semantic. In study skills, semantic context can be particularly valuable as a learning and memory aid. If the learner is using or relying on semantic context, this provides some indication that the material is being read and learnt with some understanding. The context can therefore help to:

- retain information and aid recall;
- enhance comprehension;
- transfer learning to other situations.

SCHEMATA DEVELOPMENT

The development of schemata helps the learner organise and categorise information. It also ensures the utilisation of background knowledge. This can aid comprehension and recall.

When children read a story or a passage, they need to relate this to their existing framework of knowledge (i.e., their own schema). So, when coming across new knowledge, learners try to fit it into their existing framework of knowledge based on previous learning, which is the schema they possess for that topic or piece of information. It is important for the teacher to find out how developed a child's schema is on a particular topic before providing more and new information. Being aware of this will help the teacher ensure the child develops appropriate understanding of the new information. Thus, some key points about the passage could help the reader understand the information more readily and provide a framework into which the reader can slot ideas and meaning from the passage. Schemata, therefore, can help the learner:

- attend to the incoming information;
- provide a scaffolding for memory;
- make inferences from the passage that also aid comprehension and recall;
- utilise his or her previous knowledge.

There are a number of strategies that can help in the development of schemata. An example of this can be seen in an examination of a framework for a story. In such a framework two principal aspects can be discerned:

- the structure of the story;
- the details related to the components of the structure.

The *structure* of a story can be seen in the following components:

- background;
- context;
- characters;
- beginning;
- main part;
- events;
- conclusion.

The details that may relate to these components can be recalled by asking appropriate questions. Taking the background as an example, one can see how appropriate questioning can help the learner build up a schema to facilitate understanding of the rest of the story:

- What was the weather like?
- Where did the story take place?
- Describe the scene.
- What were the main colours?

BACKGROUND KNOWLEDGE

This is an important aid to comprehension. It is postulated that background knowledge in itself is insufficient to facilitate new learning, but must be skilfully interwoven with the new material that is being learnt. It is important that the learner is able to use the new information in different and unfamiliar situations. Hence, the connections between the reader's background knowledge and the new information must be highlighted in order for the learner to incorporate the new knowledge in a meaningful manner.

The ideas contained in a text, therefore, must be linked in some way to the reader's background knowledge, and they need to be presented in a coherent and sequential manner. Such coherence and sequencing of ideas at the learning stage not only allows the material to be retained and recalled but also facilitates effective comprehension. Therefore, being aware of the learner's prior knowledge of a lesson is of fundamental importance. Before embarking on new material, prior knowledge can be linked with the new ideas in order to pave the way for effective study techniques and strategies to enhance comprehension and recall.

SELF-ESTEEM

One of the most important ingredients in any intervention programme for children with dyslexia is self-esteem—without a positive self-concept children with dyslexia will soon opt out of learning. It is important therefore that all teaching should be directed to enhancing self-esteem. There are several ways of achieving this. There are some programmes that have been specifically developed to boost self-esteem, and others that can indirectly boost self-esteem through the student's achievements. Among the first type are those programmes that focus directly on self-esteem, and some of the best known are the circle time programmes (Mosley, 1996). There have been many deviations of these programmes, but essentially they involve a degree of positive feedback and place a high regard on the individual person. They also promote group work, peer support and conflict resolution (Lannen, pers. commun. and 2002). These can be particularly suitable for children with dyslexia because they are whole-class activities, and although these can be beneficial in boosting the self-esteem of children with dyslexia they have the added benefit that the dyslexic child is not given different activities.

Self-esteem can also be boosted through achievements in literacy or any other area of the curriculum. Some of the programmes based on behavioural principles can be extremely useful in this respect. One such programme is Phonic Code Cracker (Russell, 1992). This programmes provides opportunities for students to monitor their own learning and their progress. Indeed, they may get some tangible reward such as a certificate for completing a particular objective. Therefore, this type of objective or behavioural approach can be beneficial. It is important that children with dyslexia can see that they are making some progress—however small that progress may seem. A programme operating in this manner is usually developed in a step-by-step approach and is also based on mastery learning. One of the benefits of this for children with dyslexia is that it can also promote over-learning and therefore help to achieve automaticity. It is important for children with dyslexia to attain a degree of automaticity because there is a tendency to forget, for example, spelling rules if these are not used. Automaticity can be achieved by using these rules or indeed any skill in different learning contexts. So, for example, if a new word is being learnt it should be introduced into different subject areas and in different ways. Using the new word in this way will help with automaticity as well as in the development of comprehension skills. Therefore, programmes based on mastery principles or behavioural objectives can help to achieve this as they can be quite readily adapted to develop automaticity.

CONFIDENCE AND MOTIVATION

Therefore, programmes that boost self-esteem will have a beneficial effect on confidence and motivation. Such programmes will:

- Enable the student to succeed. This is important as the learner needs to have some initial success when beginning a new topic—success builds on success and early and significant success is an important factor when new material is being learnt.
- Encouraging independent thinking. This is also important as this helps to promote independent decision-making and helps the student come to conclusions without too much direction from the teacher, which can also help to develop confidence in a learner and help to motivate the learner to tackle new material.

Some of the above can be achieved through the use of thinking skills programmes such as Somerset Thinking Skills (Blagg et al., 1988) and the CORT programme, the latter devised by Edward De Bono (1986). These can not only help to achieve enhancement in thinking skills but can also help students to use these skills by helping them to structure their own studying. This can aid the development of appropriate study habits and maximise retention and transfer of information.

TRANSFER OF KNOWLEDGE AND SKILLS

A key aspect of effective study skills training is the transfer of skills to other curriculum areas. A number of studies support the view that to achieve this great importance must be given to the context in which learning takes place (Nisbet and Shucksmith, 1986). Study skills, therefore, should be integrated into day-to-day teaching in a meaningful context, and not as a separate area of the curriculum. Nisbet and Shucksmith criticise the study skills movement for being too general, too removed from context and in many cases merely consisting of a collection of 'tips' for coping with specific difficulties. To overcome these pitfalls it is necessary to teach study skills within some theoretical or thematic perspective, such as schemata theory or reciprocal teaching, in order that applicability to the wider curriculum and transfer of skills can be achieved (Brown, 1993; Burden, 2002).

VISUAL SKILLS

Children and adults with dyslexia may have orientation problems that can be evident in directional confusion (Miles and Miles, 1991). This aspect, even though it may not directly affect every aspect of the curriculum, can lead to loss of confidence, which may permeate work in other areas.

To what extent can the teacher help to promote and enhance visual and orientation skills in children with specific difficulties? According to the principles of skills transfer (Nisbet and Shucksmith, 1986) it is important that such enhancement takes place within the curriculum and is contextualised within a meaningful task. Games or specific exercises in mapping and orientation can help to build up confidence in the learner, but there is some uncertainty as to whether such exercises, in isolation, would have a significant skills enhancement effect. So, it is important to use directional and visual cues as much as possible within the context of the curriculum. It may be advantageous therefore to develop specific exercises from materials the learner is using and to focus particularly on visual cues and directional aspects.

Lazear (1999) suggests that visual–spatial skills can be developed through multiple intelligence training that is integrated into everyday class work. This can be done through exercises involving active imagination, creating patterns with colour pencils and paper, through forming mental images and describing them, developing graphic representations and using perceptual puzzles in games by spotting similarities and differences. Lazear (1999) suggests that our education system, which has an emphasis on reasoning, can diminish the importance of imagination—often, the imagination is very fertile in young children but that can be lost in the shift to the importance of logic and reason as they progress through school. Lazear emphasises the importance of awakening visual–spatial intelligence, and suggests that this can be developed in everyone. This is particularly important for children and adults with dyslexia as they can have significant abilities in the visual area (West, 1997) and need to have the opportunity to develop this strength.

Directional skills can also be developed within a class study. If, for example, the student is working on a thematic study of the Romans, exercises and questions can emphasise particular directional aspects such as:

- direction of travelling armies;
- location of walls, forts and camps;
- planning of towns, forts and camps.

These aspects are likely to be central to most studies on the Romans, but students with dyslexic difficulties would benefit from the additional focus on the directional aspects of the study. The use, and indeed the construction, of maps utilising the principles of multi-sensory learning would also be helpful.

MEMORY SKILLS

Children with dyslexia may have difficulties in remembering, retaining and recalling information. This may be due to working memory and short-term memory problems (BPS, 1999a) or naming difficulty, particularly at speed (i.e., difficulty in recalling the name or description of something without cues: Wolf and O'Brien, 2001). It is important, therefore, to encourage the use of strategies that may facilitate remembering and recall. Such strategies can include repetition and over-learning, the use of mnemonics and Mind Mapping©.

REPETITION AND OVER-LEARNING

Short-term memory difficulties can be overcome by repetition and rehearsal of materials. This form of over-learning can be achieved in a variety of ways and not necessarily through conventional, and often tedious, rote learning.

In order to maximise the effect of repetition of learning it is important that a multi-sensory mode of learning is utilised. Repetition of the material to be learned can be accomplished through oral, visual, auditory and kinaesthetic modes. The learner should be able to see, hear, say and touch the materials to be learned. This reinforces the input stimuli and helps to consolidate the information for use, meaning and transfer to other areas. There are implications here for multi-mode teaching, including the use of movement, perhaps drama, to enhance the kinaesthetic mode of learning.

MNEMONICS

Mnemonics can be auditory or visual, or both auditory and visual. Auditory mnemonics may take the form of rhyming or alliteration while visual mnemonics can be used by relating the material to be remembered to a familiar scene, such as the classroom.

MIND MAPPING©

Mind Mapping© was developed by Buzan (1993) to help children and adults develop their learning skills and utilise as much of their abilities as possible. The procedure is now widely used and can extend one's memory capacity and develop lateral thinking

(Buzan, 1993). It can be a simple or a sophisticated strategy depending on how it is developed and used by the individual. It is used to help the learner to remember a considerable amount of information and encourages students to think of, and develop, the main ideas of a passage or material to be learned. It adopts in many ways some of the principles already discussed in relation to schemata theory.

Essentially, mind maps are individual learning tools, and someone else's mind map may not be meaningful to you. It is important, therefore, that children should create their own, in order to help with both understanding of key concepts and in the retention and recall of associated facts.

Mind Mapping© can help not only to remember information but also to help organise that information, and this exercise in itself can aid understanding. Elaborate versions of mind maps can be constructed using pictorial images, symbols and different colours.

According to Buzan (1993) a Mind Map© is an expression of 'Radiant Thinking and is therefore a natural function of the human mind. It is a powerful graphic technique which provides a universal key to unlocking the potential of the brain. ... Mind Maps help you to make a distinction between your mental storage *capacity*, which your Mind Map© will help you demonstrate, and your mental storage *efficiency*, which your mind map will help you achieve' (pp. 59–60). Buzan suggests that storing data efficiently multiplies your capacity. This clearly has considerable implications for students with dyslexia as they may have considerable capacity for learning, but lack efficiency. This point is touched on by Chapman and Tunmer (1996), who suggest that people with dyslexia have poor metacognitive awareness and lack the efficient means of learning and organising information.

Buzan suggests that a Mind Map© has four essential characteristics: a central image that is the main subject; the main themes of the subject that *radiate* from the central image; associated topics to the main theme and a connected 'nodal' structure that connects the associated topics and its branches to the main theme. It is best to practice Mind Maps© with a simple topic such as 'a football game' or 'weekend activities'. For 'weekend activities' the associated topics might be sport, school work, money, friends, family, television and these can be divided into further subthemes or branches. Mind Mapping© does require practice, but once mastered it can be used for note-taking in lectures, from videos and films, planning revision and structuring and organising essays. Developing this skill therefore can prove to be extremely helpful for the student with dyslexia. Mind Mapping© is also a visual and graphic strategy, and this can favour the person with dyslexia. Mind Mapping© therefore can be seen as both a metacognitive strategy, as it helps the learner become aware of planning how to use their knowledge, and a study skill strategy, as it helps with learning efficiency as well as learning capacity.

SUMMARY

Metacognitve strategies and study skills are important, and it is essential that the development of these skills is given a high priority for children with dyslexia. The main aspects that have been discussed here are: communication skills, which can be aided by organisation, sequencing, context, schema, confidence and motivation; the transfer of these skills to other areas of the curriculum; mapping and visual skills; and strategies in remembering and retention. All these aspects are important and can be developed with and by the learner. Although the teacher can help to facilitate these strategies and skills in the learner, it is still important that any skill or strategy that is developed must be personalised by the learner. This means that different learners will adopt different ways of learning and remembering materials, but the responsibility to allow the learner to do this and to understand the principles associated with study skills rests with the teacher.

Chapter 9

Learning Styles: Assessment and Teaching

LEARNING STYLES

It is important that students are aware of their learning preferences. The acquisition of a successful learning style is an important determinant of successful learning—irrespective of the task or the material to be learned. It is, therefore, rather surprising that recognition of learning styles is not seen as perhaps as high a priority as it should in the development of curricular materials. There is a considerable emphasis on content, outcomes and literacy achievement, but often the variety of means and methods to achieve these outcomes are overlooked.

Certainly, educational thinking has moved considerably away from the content-driven curriculum with its aim of filling the student with knowledge, stemming from the presupposition that if the student had the ability the content would be retained, and, if not, the content would need to be recycled into a simpler 'watered down' form. Although educational reforms have helped to steer a course away from such a dilution of the curriculum, there is still a risk that this may still be offered to some students with dyslexia.

The reasons for this are twofold. First, the specific difficulties of dyslexic learners may be undiagnosed, or mis-diagnosed, and consequently their skills and abilities may be overlooked. This can be noted in children for whom English is a second language (Deponio et al., 2000). Second, the pressures inherent in teaching children with severe literacy problems may prevent teachers from focusing on the learning process as, perhaps understandably, they will harbour a preoccupation with improving attainments. As a result it is more likely that teachers will look for a solution to a severe literacy difficulty through curriculum and 'resources' approaches, rather than through a detailed analysis of the learning processes and learning style of the child. That is not to say that these points are overlooked entirely—they are most certainly not and may in some cases determine the teacher's decision to use a particular programme or approach.

THE CONCEPT OF LEARNING STYLE

'Learning style' is a broad term to describe those factors that influence all aspects of learning and can be summarised as:

> *Learning styles are characteristic, cognitive, affective and physiological behaviours that serve as relatively stable indicators of how learners perceive, interact with, and respond to the learning environment* (NASSP,* 1979, quoted in Keefe, 1987).

According to this definition, learning style encompasses a broad perspective incorporating cognitive style as well as the physiological–environmental factors and affective–emotional considerations of learning. It is therefore crucial that in dealing with dyslexic learners, both in assessment and in teaching, factors associated with learning style are taken into consideration.

Keefe (1987) proposes a three-dimensional view of learning styles incorporating cognitive, affective and physiological aspects. The cognitive dimension includes modality preferences, attention, automisation, memory processes and concept development; the affective dimension includes personality variables that can influence learning such as persistence and perseverance, frustration and tolerance, curiosity, locus of control, achievement motivation, risk-taking, cautiousness, competition, co-operation, reaction to reinforcement and personal interests; the physiological dimension includes sex-related behaviour, health-related behaviour, time-of-day rhythms, need for mobility and environmental elements. These dimensions and elements have been the focus of considerable research and applied learning styles models have been developed. One of the most widely used and well-researched models is the Dunn and Dunn model (Dunn et al., 1975, 1979, 1985, 1987, 1989; Dunn and Dunn, 1992, 1993). This model is one of the most popular and widely accepted models of learning styles. It has been the subject of extensive research (Dunn and Dunn, 1992; Given and Reid, 1999).

Given (1996) and Given and Reid (1999) merged several approaches to personality and learning styles into one comprehensive model for teaching and learning. The model developed by Given used Dunn and Dunn's (1993) five learning style domains—environmental, social, psychological, cognitive and physiological—for the structural framework. Within this structure Given includes personality types as first articulated by Carl Jung (1923) and later organised by David Kolb (1984) and Susan Dellinger (1989). The five major personality types Given developed (Figure 9.1) define the predominant ways individuals react to the world—by intuition, empathy, analysis, ambition or inquiry. Intuition falls in the emotional domain, empathy in the sociological domain, analysis is representative of the psychological domain, ambition (which suggests movement and action) falls in the physiological domain and enquiry (because it is conducted within an environment) represents the environmental domain.

Given calls the merged styles 'areas of influence' because each area is interdependent on and influences all other areas. When individual personality types and learn-

* National Association of Secondary School Principals.

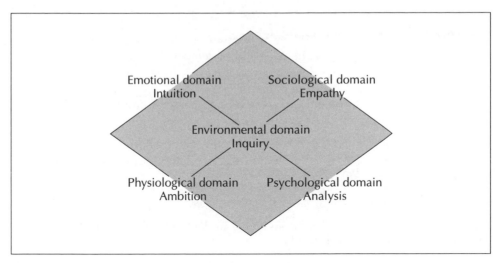

Figure 9.1 Areas of influence (reproduced from Given and Reid, 1999; copyright © Red Rose Publications).

ing styles are accepted, habit formation for lifelong learning is nurtured, such as the habits of self-determined learning, collaborative learning, intentional learning, self-managed learning and reflective learning. When they are ignored or left to chance, individuals learn in a trial-and-error, hit-and-miss fashion that tends to result in low self-esteem, intolerance and negativism, limited achievement, lethargy and depressed interest in learning. Given states that a learning environment that acknowledges individual personality and learning styles and one that fosters corresponding learning habits allows each person to reach his or her fullest potential in all five inter-connected areas.

The learning styles research suggests that consideration of learning styles within teaching programmes and the curriculum can help students 'learn how to learn' and that 'at risk' students such as those weak in analytic and discrimination skills can learn to control their learning and thus process information more efficiently and effectively.

Keefe (1991) suggests that teachers who are planning learning styles based on instruction should follow the steps in Box 9.1.

LEARNING STYLES AND DYSLEXIA

Multi-sensory strategies are used widely in the teaching of dyslexic children. The evidence suggests that the effectiveness of these strategies is based largely on the provision of at least one mode of learning with which the learner feels comfortable. Thus, if the learner has a difficulty dealing with information by way of the auditory channel, this could perhaps be compensated for through the use of the visual channel. The use of such compensatory strategies is well documented in the literature and is a feature of teaching programmes for dyslexic children. It is logical, therefore,

1 Diagnosing individual learning styles

2 Profiling class or group tendencies and preferences

3 Determining significant group strengths and weaknesses

4 Examining subject content for areas that may create problems for learners with weak skills

5 Analysing students' prior achievement scores and other products (curriculum-referenced tests, skills tests, portfolios, etc.) for patterns of weakness that may reflect cognitive skill deficiencies

6 Augmenting (remediating weak cognitive skills)

7 Assessing current instructional methods to determine whether they are adequate or require more flexibility

8 Modifying the learning environment and developing personalized learning experiences

Box 9.1   Steps in planning learning style-based instruction (from Keefe, 1991).

that consideration of the learner as an individual should be extended to a holistic appreciation of the learner's individual style. Factors such as affective and physiological characteristics will have some bearing on how the dyslexic child responds to the learning situation, and a holistic perspective should therefore be applied both in assessment and teaching of dyslexic children.

Dunn and Dunn's model identifies 5 principal domains and 21 elements, all of which affect student learning. It is hypothesised that all these elements have to be considered during the assessment process and in subsequent planning of teaching. The 5 principal domains are environmental, emotional, sociological, physiological, and psychological, and the are 21 elements are divided between those domains. The domains and the corresponding elements can be broken down in this way: environmental (sound, light, temperature, design); emotional (motivation, persistence, responsibility, structure); sociological (learning by self, pairs, peers, team, with an adult), physiological (perceptual preference, food and drink intake, time of day, mobility) and psychological (global or analytic preferences, impulsive and reflective).

Looking at the Dunn and Dunn learning styles model, one can recognise how the elements identified can influence the performances of dyslexic learners. It must be appreciated that dyslexic learners are first and foremost learners and like any other learners will be influenced by different conditions. Some dyslexic students, therefore, will prefer a 'silent' environment for concentration while others may need some auditory stimuli, perhaps even music, in order to maximise concentration and performance. Similarly, with 'light'—individual preferences such as dim light and bright light should be recognised. In fact, Overy et al. (2001) and Overy (2002) report on cognitive benefits in music training. They suggest that music training can be used as a multi-sensory medium for the development of timing skills, in which a strong emphasis can be placed on analytical listening and the development of motor skills.

In relation to emotional variables, two of the elements, responsibility and structure, should certainly be addressed. It has been well documented that dyslexic
learners benefit from imposed structure—most teaching programmes recognise this
and follow a highly structured formula. At the same time, however, taking responsibility for one's own learning can be highly motivating and can generate success—
dyslexic learners, therefore, should not be deprived of the opportunity to take
responsibility as some may possess a natural preference for responsibility and
structure.

In relation to global and analytic preferences, dyslexic students like other learners
will display differences. Carbo et al. (1986) showed how most primary-aged children
are more global than analytic, but much of the teaching, including reading programmes, has a tendency to be analytic. It is thus important that if an analytic
reading scheme such as a phonic, structured and sequential approach is used it
must be balanced by global activities such as creative work, language experience
and visual imagery.

Prashnig (1994) reported on studies on learning styles that were carried out by
universities in the USA and revealed that the learning styles of those who failed to
finish the course were significantly different from those students who remained in
school and finished it successfully. She noted, based on the Dunn and Dunn Model,
that the highly at-risk students have eight statistically different learning style elements compared with students who remain at school. The characteristics include a
strong need for: mobility at frequent intervals; variety of instructional resources;
informal seating arrangements in classrooms; soft illumination because of the tendency to be over-stimulated, especially by fluorescent light; tactile–kinaesthetic
learning tools and resource materials that introduce new and difficult information
through their perceptual preferences to make learning easier and more appealing;
late morning or afternoon for difficult subjects rather than early morning classes;
non-authoritative teachers and recognition of their high motivation despite their
inability to learn in some situations.

Deschler and Schumaker (1987) discuss the creation of a 'strategic environment'
in the classroom. This involves the teacher performing classroom tasks such as giving
directions, reviewing assignments, giving feedback, classroom organisation and
classroom management in a 'strategic' fashion. The creation of such an environment
is helped by, for example, the teacher thinking aloud when discussing problems, so
that students can understand some of the processes and strategies that a good learner
uses in solving problems.

For example, Deschler and Schumaker describe how the use of such metacognitive strategies may be achieved. They suggest the teacher may start: by analysing the
problem; then a specific cognitive strategy might be selected to deal with the
problem, perhaps referring to previous knowledge; this may then be rejected when
the teacher realises that it is inadequate to solve the problem; another strategy would
then be selected and its effectiveness would be monitored; and finally a self-coping
statement would be generated regarding the teacher's ability to deal with the
problem. This complete process would be a public one with the teacher thinking
aloud. This would enable students to cue in to the teacher's strategies and encourage,
not necessarily the replication of the teacher's strategies, but the student's own
metacognitive thinking.

This example helps to highlight the link between metacognition (learning how to learn) and (learning styles) one's learning preferences. Clearly, it begs the question of whether one should be manipulating students' learning preferences to suit an appropriate learning situation. Nevertheless, the teacher has a responsibility to help identify both preferred and appropriate learning styles, and encourage and develop these in students. This is particularly the case for dyslexic learners who may become so 'hooked' into the learning aspects that cause them to fail, such as the difficulty with decoding, that they fail to develop or utilise other avenues of learning. The decoding difficulty effectively blocks the development and awareness of their learning skills and this requires recognition and consideration by the teacher so that she or he can help the student recognise and develop a learning style and learning skill. This is particularly important as it should be recognised that it is just as appropriate to learn to read by *decoding* as it is by *recognising* words that have become familiar, as it is to learn new words through a *kinaesthetic* floor game as it is to learn through *tactile* resources.

The important point is that all children can learn to read *initially* through their learning style, which can subsequently be reinforced by the deployment of other strategies, thus allowing other skills to be developed. Competence in decoding, therefore, may be one of the *additional* skills rather than the *initial* one, since it would be difficult for dyslexic children to acquire this skill in the beginning stages of reading. In support of this viewpoint Dunn (1992) contends that the strategy of decoding appears to be the best for analytic auditory learners, linguistics is most successful with analytic visuals and whole language is most successful with global auditory and visual learners. It is important to match the method and the child's strong preferences (Sullivan, 1993).

LEARNING STYLES ASSESSMENT

Students' learning styles can be assessed using questionnaires (Dunn et al., 1975, 1979, 1985, 1987, 1989) and through observational strategies (Reid, 1992). In relation to the former, several instruments have been developed to identify individual students' learning styles (Canfield and Lafferty, 1970; Dunn et al., 1975; Gregorc, 1985; Hill, 1964; Keefe et al., 1986). Most of these measure one or two elements on a bipolar continuum. Three instruments are considered comprehensive in nature: the Learning Style Profile (Keefe et al., 1986), Cognitive Style Mapping (Hill, 1964), the Learning Style Inventory (LSI) (Dunn et al., 1975, 1979, 1985, 1987, 1989) and its Primary Version (Perrin, 1983). They are termed comprehensive because they assess multiple elements in combination with each other. The LSI (Dunn et al., 1975, 1979, 1985, 1987, 1989) is a comprehensive and widely used assessment instrument in elementary and secondary schools.

The LSI directs students to 'answer the questions as if you are describing how you concentrate when you are studying difficult academic material.' The instrument can be completed in approximately 30 to 40 minutes by elementary and secondary students. After answering all the questions on the LSI answer form (the test itself), each student's answer sheet is optically read and processed individually.

Each student then receives his or her own LSI individual printout—a graphic representation of the conditions in which each learns most efficiently.

LEARNING STYLES AND THE INFORMATION PROCESSING CYCLE

Consideration of learning styles can be useful for both assessment and teaching of dyslexic children and can provide them with an opportunity to focus on their own understandings of text and utilise their own strengths in learning to access text across the curriculum.

Learning is a process, and this applies to literacy as well as other aspects, particularly as literacy usually plays a central role in learning. It is important, therefore, to focus on the information processing cycle and to consider potential areas that can relate to learning styles within the information processing cycle.

The stages of the information processing cycle essentially relate to input, cognition and output. These are discussed in the previous chapter (Chapter 8) in relation to metacognition, but some suggestions that highlight the importance of each of these stages in relation to learning styles are shown in Box 9.2.

LEARNING STYLE APPROACHES

The above information processing cycle can highlight the importance of learning styles as a crucial factor in all stages: input, cognition and output. At present there are more than 100 instruments specially designed to identify individual learning styles. Most were developed to evaluate narrow aspects of learning such as preference for visual, auditory, tactile or kinaesthetic input (Grinder, 1991). Others are far more elaborate and focus on factors primarily associated with personality issues such as intuition, active experimentation and reflection (Gregorc, 1982, 1985; Kolb, 1984; Lawrence, 1993; McCarthy, 1987).

Many approaches attempt to identify how individuals process information in terms of its input, memory and expressive functions (Witkin and Goodenough, 1981). A few theorists emphasize the body's role in learning and promote cross-lateral movement in hopes of integrating the left and right brain hemispheric activity (Dennison and Dennison, 1989). Some perspectives of learning style approaches are briefly described below:

- Riding and Raynor (1998) combine cognitive style with learning strategies. They describe cognitive style as a constraint that includes basic aspects of an individual's psychology such as feeling (affect), doing (behaviour) and knowing (cognition), and the individual's cognitive style relates to how these factors are structured and organised.
- Kolb's (1984) LSI is a derivative of Jung's (1923) psychological types combined with Piaget's emphasis on assimilation and accommodation, Lewin's (1936)

INPUT

- Acknowledge the students preferred learning style—visual, auditory, kinaesthetic or tactile

- Information should be presented in small units

- It should be ensured that over-learning is used, and this should be varied using a range of materials

- Key points should be presented at the initial stage of learning new material

COGNITION

- Organisational strategies should be encouraged. This means that the new material to be learned should be organised into meaningful chunks or categories at each of the stages of the information processing stages

- Information should be related to previous knowledge to ensure that concepts are clear and the information can be placed into a learning framework or schema by the learner

- Some specific memory strategies such as Mind Mapping© and mnemonics can be used

OUTPUT

- Use headings and subheadings in written work to help provide a structure

- Encourage the use of summaries in order to identify the key points

Box 9.2   Some suggestions highlighting the importance of input, cognition and output.

action research model and Dewey's purposeful, experiential learning. Kolb's 12-item inventory yields 4 types of learners: divergers, assimilators, convergers and accommodators.

- The Dunn and Dunn approach utilises the LSI (Dunn et al., 1989), which contains 104 items that produce a profile of learning style preferences in five domains (environmental, emotional, sociological, physiological and psychological) and 21 elements across those domains. These domains and elements include (as already mentioned on p. 212): environmental (sound, light, temperature, design); emotional (motivation, persistence, responsibility, structure); sociological (learning by self, pairs, peers, team, with an adult), physiological (perceptual preference, food and drink intake, time of day, mobility) and psychological (global or analytic preferences, impulsive and reflective).

- Given (1996) and Given and Reid (1999) constructed a new model of learning styles derived from some key elements of other models. This model consists of emotional learning (the need to be motivated by one's own interests), social learning (the need to belong to a compatible group), cognitive learning (the need to know what age-mates know), physical learning (the need to do and be actively involved in learning) and reflective learning (the need to experiment and explore to find what circumstances work best for new learning).

LEARNING STYLES USING OBSERVATIONAL CRITERIA

In addition to using standardised instruments, learning styles may be identified to a certain extent through classroom observation. It should be noted that observation in itself may not be sufficient to fully identify learning styles, but the use of a framework for collecting observational data can yield considerable information and can complement the results from more formal assessment.

Observational assessment can be diagnostic because it is flexible and adaptable, and can be used in natural settings with interactive activities. Given and Reid (1999) have developed such a framework—the Interactive Observational Style Identification (IOSI). A summary of this is shown in Box 9.3.

There are too many manifestations of style to observe all at once. One way to begin the observation process is to select one of the learning systems and progress from there. The insights usually become greater as observation progresses.

THE LEARNING ENVIRONMENT

Frederickson and Cline (2002) suggest that there is substantial literature that supports the importance of the learning environment for accounting for performances in examinations as well as other factors such as school attendance, motivation and skills in inquiry. Burden and Fraser (1993) report that student attitude as well as achievement can be enhanced through paying careful attention to the classroom environment, particularly by ensuring that the factors that can be associated with classroom environments are present. This indicates that the learning environment is crucial, particularly in relation to learners who may have difficulties in acclimatising to different teaching styles and, indeed, in the case of children with dyslexia to auditory-based learning. Well-established theoretical models of the influence of the environmental factors in learning have been developed and many of them have advocated a systematic approach to assessment of the learning environment (Lewin, 1936; Bandura, 1977; Bronfenbrenner, 1979). Wearmouth and Reid (2002) report on the influence of Bronfenbrenner's model. They indicate how the learning environment can produce barriers to pupils' learning and that the ecosystemic perspective developed by Bronfenbrenner (1979) is useful because it identifies four levels that influence child outcomes: the *microsystem*, the immediate context of the child—school, classrooms, home, neighbourhood; the *mesosystem*, the links between two microsystems (e.g., home–school relationships); the *exosystem*, outside demands/influences in adults' lives that affect children; and the *macrosystem*,

EMOTIONAL

Motivation

- What topics, tasks and activities interest the child?

- What kind of prompting and cueing is necessary to increase motivation?

- What kind of incentives motivate the child: leadership opportunities, working with others, free time or physical activity?

Persistence

- Does the child stick to a task until completion without breaks?

- Are frequent breaks necessary when working on difficult tasks?

Responsibility

- To what extent does the child take responsibility for his or her own learning?

- Does the child attribute success or failure to self or others?

Structure

- Are the child's personal effects (desk, clothing, materials) well organised or cluttered?

- How does the child respond to someone imposing organisational structure on him or her?

SOCIAL

Interaction

- When is the child's best work accomplished: when working alone, with one another or in a small group?

- Does the child ask for approval or needs to have work checked frequently?

Communication

- Does the child give the main events and gloss over the details?

- Does the child interrupt others when they are talking?

COGNITIVE

Modality preference

- What type of instructions does the child most easily understand: written, oral or visual?

- Does the child respond more quickly and easily to questions about stories heard or read?

continued

Sequential or simultaneous learning

- Does the child begin with one step and proceed in an orderly fashion or have difficulty following sequential information?

- Is there a logical sequence to the child's explanations or do her or his thoughts bounce around from one idea to another?

Impulsive/reflective

- Are the child's responses rapid and spontaneous or delayed and reflective?

- Does the child seem to consider past events before taking action?

PHYSICAL

Mobility

- Does the child move around the class frequently or fidget when seated?

- Does the child like to stand or walk while learning something new?

Food intake

- Does the child snack or chew on a pencil when studying?

Time of day

- During which time of day is the child most alert?

- Is there a noticeable difference between morning work and afternoon work?

REFLECTION

Sound

- Does the child seek out places that are particularly quiet?

Light

- Does the child like to work in dimly lit areas or say that the light is too bright?

Temperature

- Does the child leave his or her coat on when others seem warm?

Furniture design

- When given a choice does the child sit on the floor, lie down or sit in a straight chair to read?

continued

Metacognition

- Is the child aware of his or her learning style strengths?

- Does the child demonstrate self-assessment

Prediction

- Does the child make plans and work toward goals or let things happen?

Feedback

- How does the child respond to different types of feedback?

- How much external prompting is needed before the child can access previous knowledge?

Box 9.3   The IOSI framework (from Given and Reid, 1999).

cultural beliefs/patterns or institutional policies that affect individuals' behaviour. This indicates that the environment is complex and comprehensive, and assessment must include all aspects of the systems and influences that can affect educational outcomes. This point cannot be overemphasised, particularly as there may be a tendency to focus on narrow environmental factors in relation to children with special needs. In the three-part framework outlined by Dockrell and McShane (1993) the environment is included as well as the task and the child. This interactional analysis is helpful for students with dyslexia and other learning difficulties as it can inform teaching and minimise the effects of the difficulty and enhance performance and self-esteem. It is crucial, therefore, to move away from the standpoint of individual difficulties in isolation and narrowly based assessment procedures that highlight child-centred difficulties. It is for that reason that the learning styles paradigm that includes the learning environment as well as the curriculum and teaching approaches can hold the key to helping children with dyslexia progress successfully through school.

The notion of learning styles should in fact be an influential factor in a school's daily practices, its policy and philosophy. In order for learning styles to be effectively implemented it should be seen not at the individual teacher level, but at a whole-school level, including the learning environment. Classrooms therefore need to be designed with learning styles in mind. For example, it may be necessary to redesign desks or to provide students with a choice of desk styles. One example of this is the Red Rose School in St Anne's-on-Sea, UK where classrooms have no desks, but have corrals instead which seem to help students focus on their own work. Music can also be used to generate a relaxed and creative learning environment (Lannen and Reid, 2002, 2003). These points serve to highlight one of the most important factors in relation to learning styles: the learning environment. It is important to give careful consideration to the classroom environment as environmental factors are very influential in promoting effective learning. These environmental factors include furniture, design, light, sound, colour, space and the general ambience of the class or school.

TEACHING TO LEARNING STYLES

Other considerations in relation to learning styles include the teaching approaches and the needs of the pupils as perceived by themselves. One of the most crucial factors in relation to teaching is the need to present information in a range of modalities within a multi-sensory framework: visual, auditory, kinaesthetic and tactile. But, it is also important that the student should be assessed and present his or her work in a range of modalities. Therefore, activities involving drama and art, poetry and creative writing should be highly regarded in learning and assessment. This is particularly important as it is well established that a great number of dyslexic children have skills in these areas, but are often turned off and demotivated by constant failure in the more traditional subjects assessed through traditional assessment.

It is important that teachers have an awareness of the student's learning preferences. Although some inclination of this may be identified through observation, it is often a good idea to ask the student. Children are often able to say whether they prefer music, low light, make lists or start a task with drawing. Obtaining this information can help the teacher present new information initially in the child's preferred style of learning as this will maintain motivation. Often, dyslexic children are motivated to learn until they start learning—then they are turned off by repeated failure or having to expend considerable effort for little return. It is crucial, therefore, that dyslexic children are aware of their own style of learning.

CHILDREN'S AWARENESS OF LEARNING STYLE

Knowledge of learning styles should help students become aware of their own style of learning, and this will help them develop self-sufficiency in learning. Increasingly, as young people enter college and the work place they will come across new learning, and this may be a burden for them if they are not aware of how to learn and unaware specifically of their own preferred style of learning. Lannen and Reid (2003) asked students how they achieved a certain response to a task. The task chosen was a fairly simple one of reading a passage and noting the words that had the same sounds. Here is an extract of some of the responses.

> Tom, aged 13: *'Firstly I read the passage which is okay for me because I am now a good reader. I then identified all the words with "ck" sound and underlined these words, then checked that I had not missed any. My next task was to write 8 words ending in "cket"—well I knew the first one was "rocket" which I read in the passage. I then thought of some words which rhymed with rocket such as "sprocket" and made a list with these.'*

There are a number of important points to emerge from this extract. First, Tom was aware of how to tackle this particular task. When asked how he did it he was able to respond immediately and fully, so he was aware of the process he used. This implies that he would be able to use this process with other similar tasks. Some children are not aware of the processes they use to obtain certain responses. Tom, in fact, was very aware of his own style—he acknowledged that he liked quiet when working, preferred working on a table than the floor, liked a lot of instructions before embarking on a task and preferred words to pictures. The learning style that seemed to be emerging from this discussion with Tom can be described as an analytic one. This would mean that Tom would respond well to a structure, can deal with a lot of information and organise it appropriately. When asked how he would design a rocket, since the passage was about rockets, Tom replied that he would first decide on the shape, then equipment, fuel capacity, strength and safety. This list also suggests that Tom is an auditory and analytical learner, but it is still interesting that his immediate response related to a visual aspect—design. It is very common for children with dyslexia to start tasks with visual stimuli, even if they may have as Tom has an analytic preference.

Another student interviewed, Philip (aged 14), on the other hand, had a visual and global learning style. He had some difficulty thinking and articulating his strategies in the language-based task—the same one that was presented to Tom—and because Philip had difficulty in recognising the strategies he used, he would likely have difficulty in transferring this strategy and using it with other similar tasks. In other words, Philip would see all tasks of this type as new tasks.

Interestingly, Philip provided a range of visual- and global-type responses when asked how he would design a rocket. He was interested in the design and elaborated on this to include aerodynamics and the shape of the rocket.

Similarly, Chris, aged 13, focused on all the visual and kinaesthetic aspects involved when asked to make a rocket.

The important points to be drawn from these examples are that often children are not aware of how they did something until you actually ask them. Even then they may give you a brief response, but with further questioning you can note that they did not describe all the steps they went through in the exercise. Often, to find out this information from children you need to question and requestion the process—how they actually tackled the task. When asked how to tackle the 'ck' passage task, it was interesting that Philip, who has a visual and global learning style, said he would look to find out what the other questions relating to the passage were. This illustrates a typical global preference when he needs to get the whole picture before embarking on the smaller, individual aspects of the task. So, Philip actually needed to know what all the tasks were that related to the passage before starting the first of these tasks, which was identifying the words with 'ck'.

COGNITIVE STYLE

According to Riding and Rayner (1998) cognitive style 'is seen as an individual's preferred and habitual approach to organising and representing information' (p. 8).

They suggest that cognitive style emerges from a number of psychological fields such as perception, cognition, mental imagery and personality constructs.

Given and Reid (1999) suggest that cognitive style is part of the individual's cognitive learning system and therefore a component of the process of learning (see Figure 8.1, p. 190). Nevertheless, distinct styles relating to an individual's preference for assimilating information can be noted. In fact, Riding and Cheema (1991; Rayner and Riding, 1997) found over 30 labels to describe cognitive style, and after reviewing these found they could be grouped into two principal cognitive-style dimensions: the wholist–analytic and the verbal–imagery style dimensions. The wholist–analytic style dimension relates to whether an individual tends to organise information into wholes or parts, and the verbal–imagery style dimension relates to whether an individual is inclined to represent information during thinking verbally or in mental pictures. Other labels that have been associated with cognitive style include: tolerant–intolerant; broad–narrow; cognitive simplicity–cognitive complexity; risk-taking versus cautiousness; and splitters and lumpers (Riding and Rayner, 1998). These all appear to be representative of either left or right hemisphere-dominated approaches. For example, 'splitters' would be left (analytical) hemisphere processors while 'lumpers' would very likely be right (wholist) processors. Riding and Rayner suggest that wholists are top–down processors, have a global approach to learning, can process different pieces simultaneously, are conceptually orientated, have a comprehension learning bias, but have low discrimination skills. On the other hand, analytical learners are bottom–up processors, prefer linear processing and a step-by-step approach, detail-orientated and have high discrimination skills.

Riding and Rayner (1998) also distinguish between cognitive style and learning strategies by suggesting that 'style' has very likely a physiological basis and is fairly fixed for the individual, while strategies are adaptive ways of coping with learning situations and tasks.

LEARNING STYLES: KEY POINTS

The key points, therefore, in relation to learning styles is that every effort should be made to organise the classroom environment in a manner that can be adapted to suit a range of styles. In classrooms where there is a number of dyslexic learners the environment should be global (Given and Reid, 1999), which means lighting, design and indeed the whole learning atmosphere need to be considered. It is also important that the teacher has an awareness of what is meant by learning styles and how to identify different styles in children. Although there are many different instruments that can be used, teachers observations and discussion with students while they are engaged on a task can be extremely beneficial. The different stages of the information processing cycle can be considered in relation to how children learn and how this can be used with a learning styles structure. The experience of learning may be more important to children with dyslexia than the actual finished product. At the same time, it is important that children with dyslexia become aware of their own learning style. This is the first and most important step toward achieving a degree of self-sufficiency in learning. Mortimer (2000) in fact suggests that parents also should help their child identify his or her learning style and this can help enhance understanding between parents and children. Acknowledging learning styles, therefore, can help to promote skills that extend beyond school. Knowledge of learning styles can equip students and particularly students with dyslexia for lifelong learning.

Part IV

Inclusion

Chapter 10

Inclusion:
Principles and Practices

THE CHALLENGE AND CONFLICT

'Inclusion' is a term that has a universal currency. The term can be associated with equality, fairness and the individual's right to a democratic share of the country's resources: political, educational, economic and social. These aspects are not free-standing—each relate and interact with the other. Without political awareness inclusion would be impossible to achieve, particularly in educational settings. Educational settings refer to more than school: the community, the university and the workplace are all educational settings and each has to be considered to see if it is meeting the principles of full inclusion. This is the challenge facing educators today, and within that challenge there are conflicts resulting from traditional, pedagogical perspectives, social attitudes, conventions, habits and perceptions. This chapter will look at some of these challenges and conflicts, and particularly within the context of meeting the needs of children and adults with dyslexia.

INCLUSION AND INTEGRATION

Inclusion can be seen as a logical extension of integration. Integration has been taking place in schools in the UK, Western Europe, Australia, New Zealand and the USA and many other countries gradually over the last 20 years at least. This has resulted, however, in an almost piecemeal attempt to meet the needs of children who are, in relation to the legislation of the country, seen as having a special educational need. This is usually through a statement in England and Wales, a Record of Needs in Scotland or through reference to case law in the USA, particularly with reference to Public Law 94-108.

In the UK children with special educational needs are entitled in law to have those needs identified, assessed and then met with appropriate provision guaranteed by their local education authority (LEA). While this endeavour may have commendable aims it can be divisive and inequitable. Often, for example, successful mainstreaming depends more on the support available and attitudes of the staff in schools than on the power of legislation. Additionally, it means that some children for whatever reason may miss out, perhaps fractionally, on the criteria for additional support. Pumfrey (2001) has shown how this can be the case with dyslexic children who may not meet the arbitrarily set cut-off point in terms of the criteria laid down by the local authority for additional support.

Dyson (1997) argues that the trend of integration essentially targeted the individual pupil, and as a result provision tended to remain on the periphery of the school curriculum rather than becoming an integral part of it. Those with expertise in special education have therefore been seen as a necessary accompaniment to these children rather than as an integral part of the school's processes. Another problem with the trend of integration is the disparate forms that can be witnessed throughout the country (both in the UK and the USA). Therefore, much of the success of this movement has depended on location and the willingness of professionals to accommodate to the perceived needs and wishes of different groups including those of parents.

Inclusion, however, should be seen as more all-embracing than integration. Essentially, it should be more penetrating in relation to meeting the needs of all groups in the community, and not only those who are categorised as having a special educational need. Mittler (2001), for example, suggests that inclusion needs to be seen as a process of restructuring the school as a whole. This includes access to the full curriculum as well as the need to consider appropriate assessment, recording and reporting of pupils' achievements.

THE CHALLENGE

Inclusion, therefore, involves a number of facets and issues: one's understanding of the concept of inclusion; how to achieve the objective of equality of learning opportunities; the implications for assessment, teaching and staff development; the management of learning for all students; and the equitable use of resources. This presents a challenge to educators: teachers, management, administrators and support staff. The challenge is how effectively teachers and other professionals can meet the needs of all students within an inclusive environment, but particularly those students who have an identified, or indeed unidentified, 'special need' and may require some form of intervention that is different from most other students. Given that all students offer a uniqueness and present a range of individual variations in learning and personality, the aspect of special needs is extremely challenging. Giorcelli (1995, 1999) suggests that the controversy surrounding the inclusion movement is due to a number of factors including the lack of preparedness of teachers in mainstream schools for students with high support needs and the adoption of inclusion practices without a rigorous focus on educational outcomes and, in particular, the problems that can be experienced by older students.

It is important therefore to address some of these challenges by examining the tensions and contradictions, and principles and practices of inclusion, including the nature of interventions and, particularly, how they may apply to children with dyslexia. This, along with student advocacy, will be discussed in this chapter as well as the crucial role of staff support and training.

TENSIONS AND CONTRADICTIONS

Wearmouth et al. (2002) suggest that the current UK national context is one that attempts to reconcile the principles of individuality, distinctiveness and diversity with inclusion and equal opportunities. There are inherent conflicts in this, and therefore tensions and contradictions will be evident. Wearmouth et al. (2003) suggest these tensions and contradictions permeate policy and practice throughout the whole education system in the UK. There is a drive to raise the learning and achievement standards of all pupils through whole-class and whole-group teaching, standardised assessment and the encouragement of competition between schools through a focus on league tables based on academic performance. Yet, there is a statutory obligation to acknowledge the principle of inclusion for all pupils, including those with significant difficulties in the development of literacy skills such as children with dyslexia.

The revised National Curriculum for England and Wales (QCA, 2000) contains a statutory General Statement on Inclusion about providing effective learning opportunities for all pupils. This sets out three key principles for inclusion: setting suitable learning challenges; responding to pupils' diverse learning needs; and overcoming potential barriers to learning and assessment for individuals and groups of pupils. Wearmouth (2001) indicates that these statements can provide complex challenges for those who are planning programmes to address the learning needs of children with dyslexia. She suggests that to achieve the aims of the inclusion statement it is necessary to focus on ways in which the learning environment can potentially create barriers to literacy development. It is significant that Wearmouth identifies the learning environment as a crucial factor in achieving inclusion. Many educators would immediately focus on the child's specific difficulties and specific teaching programmes designed to deal with these difficulties. It is interesting that Wearmouth chose to identify the learning environment as one of the most influential factors. She also suggests it is important to engage in multidisciplinary assessment and to plan programmes that take account of these perspectives and that these should be embedded in the whole-school curriculum. Wearmouth argues that the complexity of the issues relating to inclusion must be tackled and policy-makers need to understand the long-term nature of embedding change of this nature in relation to teacher development and the provision of resources and technology. On the one hand, while inclusion can be seen as a desirable outcome in terms of equity, it can also be seen as a threat and a potential conflict between meeting the needs of individuals within a framework that has to be established to meet the needs of all.

Diniz (2001) suggests that the notion of inclusion in education and society is 'inherently contentious in nature and problematic to resolve, and that any school wishing to attain the accolade of an inclusive school cannot underestimate the degree of conflict that it will encounter' (p. 21). This conflict according to Diniz centres round the wide range of political expectations and the conceptual ambiguities contained in the term 'inclusion'. Diniz, however, argues that the Scottish Parliament Inquiry (Scottish Parliament, 2001) into the issues of inclusive education made a significant contribution to the debate on inclusion. It defines inclusive education in terms that emphasise environmental, structural and attitudinal barriers to participation and highlights the under-representation of disabled and 'minority ethnic professionals in the system' (p. 2). Diniz argues that documents such as this that attempt to analyse exactly what is meant by inclusion and how it should be defined and implemented are essential, otherwise inclusion will be perceived as no more than an update of the integration movement. This movement witnessed the shift from segregated, special education provision to its provision for some children, who were previously in special schools, within mainstream schools. This, of course, is also an essential ingredient of inclusion, but as Diniz argues inclusion needs to be perceived by the profession as much more than this and needs to include social and ethnic groups who may be at a social, economical and educational disadvantage.

INCLUSION: MEETING NEEDS

In 2001 a revised Code of Practice for England and Wales was issued by the Secretary of State for Education, giving guidance to education authorities on their duties in making special provision for pupils. Legally, local authorities must have regard to the provisions of the Code. This means that education authorities need to uphold the fundamental principles of the code: entitlement to a broad curriculum, integration, pupil self-advocacy and parental involvement. This means that the views of parents and children need to be considered and that all children will be entitled to have their needs met in mainstream schools. The Code also provides specific requirements that have implications for LEAs regarding assessment and provision. Education authorities therefore have an obligation to assess any child who has special educational needs and to provide a statement that clearly defines the child's needs and the provision needed to meet these needs.

Wearmouth et al. (2002) report that the Northern Ireland version of the Code of Practice is more succinct than that provided for England and Wales. One of the important differences relates to the time limits within which local authorities have to assess pupils whose needs may require a statement. Time limits for the various stages of developing a statement in England and Wales are precisely laid down while in Northern Ireland, however, the majority of the process is given as guidance in the Code, which does not carry the force of law. This means that where the process is delayed parents have no recourse to the tribunal. Another important difference relates to the role of education plans. In Northern Ireland teachers in the province have the chance to consider group education plans rather than solely plans for individuals as is the case in England and Wales. The importance of the Code of Practice in England and Wales, however, is that it is enforceable by law. This means that education authorities must meet the child's educational needs and that the provision identified in the statement is actually implemented.

In Scotland the approximate equivalent to a statement is the Record of Needs.

The decision to open a Record of Needs can depend on the individual school's level of resources and the deployment of those resources. Although children with special educational needs in Scotland are legally entitled to have their special needs identified, assessed and then met with appropriate provision, guaranteed by their LEA, children only need a Record if their learning needs cannot be met within the resources generally available to their school. Although there are some instances of a Record of Needs being opened for children with dyslexia it is not commonplace. All authorities in Scotland interpret the guidance from the Scottish executive within the procedures and practices in their authority, and many have written policies to indicate this (Scottish Executive, 2002; Haddock, 2002). Essentially, with developed and appropriately funded school and authority policies on dyslexia there should be no need to rely on a Record of Needs. Scotland has opted heavily toward early intervention. A number of well-funded projects throughout Scotland have been implemented, and these have attempted to ensure that the needs of children with dyslexia are identified early. This, together with the high priority on special educational needs training (Mackay and McLarty, 1999), the flexibilty of the 5–14 curriculum (Crombie and Reid, 1994), the intention to reduce the potential overload in the 5–14 curriculum (Scottish Executive, 2003) and the impetus for early identification as a result of the early intervention programme, can mean that the structures and the practices are in place, but nevertheless local variation in the satisfaction of parents of children with dyslexia is still evident (Reilly, pers. commun.).

These legislative and government-driven initiatives should pave the way for the development of the practices that need to be associated with an inclusive school. Much of the success of this in relation to dyslexia, however, rests on the need for effective communication between parents and school staff in relation to shared concerns and attitudes over the most appropriate provision and curriculum for children with dyslexia.

PRINCIPLES AND PRACTICES OF INCLUSION

Assessment, Need and Accountability

One of the key features of educational provision in most countries involves the concept of accountability. Governments demand results, schools want results and parents expect results. How these results are measured is a matter of debate. The government's expectations may be measured differently by schools and by parents—the measure of progress can be dependent on how one views the purpose of education and the means of achieving that purpose. These two variables—purpose and means—may differ, even within an inclusive setting. Inclusion, therefore, is not the educational product, but the educational vehicle that can contain the methods, means and purposes of the educational experience for all students. That experience, however, can be dependent and even restricted by the need for accountability, as it attempts to define the educational experience as a measurable commodity. National testing, government benchmarks and league tables to identify 'high performing' and 'low performing' schools are examples of political pressures on an education system that seeks to serve 'all', but recognises that the individual differences in children mean that 'all' will not progress in the same way and at the same rate. An enlightened education system would not expect that, but the reality of market forces and accountability of the public purse may determine the nature of the educational process in schools and the educational experience of children in the classrooms. Some groups of learners may be a casualty of this drive to measure achievement. Viall (2000) argues, for example, that this practice of 'high stakes assessment' in the USA, which is intended to measure and enhance student progress, can in fact be discriminatory in relation to students with dyslexia. These 'high stakes' tests are usually standardised, as is also the case in the UK with national testing, and many of these types of tests do not accommodate to the needs of dyslexic students, nor in fact to the needs of students from different cultures. Moreover, Viall argues that this practice carries a risk of the teacher teaching to the tests and neglecting the importance of critical thinking and the metacognitive aspects of learning. One of Viall's suggestions to overcome this potentially discriminatory practice is that there should be meaningful alternative assessments that take into account the types of difficulties experienced by students with dyslexia. This is different from providing support or examination allowances in conventional examination systems to aid the student with dyslexia—alternative assessment means 'different' assessment. This would need a complete rethink of the aims and objectives of the examination system, coupled with the need to identify exactly what are the important elements to assess and how that assessment could be performed in an equitable fashion. There has been some evidence of this in examples of portfolio assessment that have the potential to examine the performances of students with dyslexia in a much fairer way than a one-off test or national examination.

EQUITY

The desire to include all students within the mainstream setting and the mainstream curriculum is not only about getting the teaching right but also about measuring and assessing progress in a fair, non-discriminatory manner. It is also about political desire, financial commitment and a community embracement of the concept and the practice of including all in a culture-fair manner in all the community's activities. As well as honouring cultural diversity, inclusion has implications for gender and those who may have more than one 'disability'. It is interesting to note that, at school level, considerably more boys than girls are diagnosed as having dyslexia, yet, in higher education, females outnumber males among those identified as dyslexic for the first time (Singleton, 1999a). The implication of this is that girls are not as readily identified as boys at school, and one can postulate that girls may not 'act out' and be more accepting of the difficulties they face in certain subjects than boys—they may become proficient at compensating for their difficulties or expect less academically from themselves. Whatever the reason the fact remains that in terms of equity and the desire for full and effective inclusion the abilities and needs of some females may be overlooked (Lloyd, 1996). Additionally, Daniels et al. (2001) express concern with boys' underachievement and the conflicts surrounding the cultural messages of masculinity that affect boys. They found that gender was influential in the identity positions children adopted, and this had an effect on overall achievement. Furthermore, they suggest that certain types of competitive practices in schools may actually inhibit boys' performances. Delamont (1999) discusses the notion of the 'feminisation' of teaching and suggests that this has meant that school cultures can actually be partially blamed for the failing of boys. Clearly, therefore, gender issues are influential within the impetus to achieve full inclusion, and since boys seem to outnumber girls in relation to identified dyslexia at school this is therefore a major concern.

Similarly with the needs of students who may have a visual or hearing impairment, with perhaps undiagnosed dyslexia. Their dyslexic needs may be overlooked because of the obvious needs that can stem from the presence of a sensory impairment. Inclusion, therefore, affects the whole community and requires not only political initiatives but social acceptance and community awareness as well.

Another example of an equity issue can be that of 'travelling children' who may in fact be incorporated into the 'learning opportunities' hypothesis (BPS, 1999a) as an explanation for dyslexic difficulties. Jordan (2001) suggests that the dropout rate is high for groups such as gypsies or travellers, and this can occur at an early age. Jordan shows that this can be as young as nine. 'Travelling children', because of the nature of the oral culture, can also experience discrimination in terms of the comments made by Viall quoted earlier in this chapter on discriminatory practices in assessment. Jordan (2001) also supports this viewpoint and claims that 'reading, writing and other attainment levels are usually much lower than their peers yet in listening and talking they often outstripped their classmates' (p. 131).

PRINCIPLES

It may be suggested that inclusion is as much about principles as about practices. The principle of equity leads to the practice of meeting the needs of all. But, often the principle can be enunciated without evidence of the accompanying practices. Principles should guide practice, and many of the statements and policies on inclusion have well-articulated principles. Many of these stem from the Salamanca Declaration (Box 10.1), which followed a conference held in June 1994 when representatives of 92 governments and 25 international organisations formed the World Conference on Special Needs Education, held in Salamanca, Spain. They adopted a new Framework for Action, the guiding principle of which is that mainstream schools should accommodate all children, regardless of their physical, intellectual, social, emotional, linguistic or other conditions. Johnson (2001) quotes aspects from the Salamanca Declaration as a precursor to the principles of inclusion.

This statement essentially sets the path for an inclusionary school and implies that syndromes such as dyslexia need to be catered for within an inclusionary ethos. Yet, one needs to be realistic and appreciate that not all children will benefit from mainstream provision without some preparation on the part of the child and the teacher. This point is made by Johnson when he quotes an extract from the DfEE guidance on inclusion:

For most children (with SEN [special educational needs]) placement in a mainstream school leads naturally on to other forms of inclusion. For those with more

- every child has a fundamental right to education and must be given the opportunity to achieve and maintain an acceptable level of learning

- every child has unique characteristics, interests, abilities and learning needs

- education systems should be designed and educational programmes implemented to take into account the wide diversity of these characteristics and needs

- those with special educational needs must have access to regular schools that should accommodate them within a child-centred pedagogy capable of meeting these needs

- regular schools with this inclusive orientation are the most effective means of combating discriminatory attitudes, creating welcoming communities, building an inclusive society and achieving education for all. Moreover, they provide an effective education to the majority of children and improve the efficiency and ultimately the cost-effectiveness of the entire education system

Box 10.1   The Salamanca Declaration (from van Steenlandt, 1998).

complex needs, the starting point should always be the question: 'Could this child benefit from education in a mainstream setting?' For some children a mainstream placement may not be right, or not right just yet (DfEEa, 1998, p. 23).

This, therefore, implies that full inclusion in a mainstream setting for some groups of children, although socially and politically desirable, may not be educationally appropriate at a given point in time. This means that, with support, all children can aspire toward an inclusionary educational environment, but there should not be an assumption that, for all, this is the best practice at every point in their school career. There are examples in practice of children who have initially failed in an inclusionary setting, but after a period of supportive and appropriate teaching in a structured, dedicated resource for dyslexia are able to return to a mainstream setting and benefit more fully socially and educationally from the facilities on offer (Lannen, 2002b; Calder, 2001). Lannen cites the experience at the Red Rose School, a dedicated short-term provision for children with specific learning difficulties in St Anne's-on-Sea. Most of the children admitted to the school have failed in the mainstream setting and have, not surprisingly, low levels of self-esteem as well as low attainments. But, with dedicated facilities and the skills of staff combining to develop a caring learning environment children progress, and many are able to be readmitted to mainstream schools. Even within this dedicated special provision it can be argued that the principles of inclusion are operating. All children within this environment have an entitlement to the full curriculum and to have their social, emotional and educational needs met. Calder (2001) describes an example of a specialised resource that attempts to respect the students needs to be part of an inclusionary educational curriculum and environment. This resource, at Denny High School near Falkirk in Scotland, is essentially a 'customised package' that aims to help students access the common curriculum. Because the package is customised to their specific needs it is possible for the students to achieve educationally. This type of provision centres on comprehensive assessment, full multi-professional and parental involvement, appropriate differentiation as well as the building of self-esteem, the encouragement of learner autonomy and the development of necessary skills for learning and life. According to Calder this formula is based on 'an eclectic mix of strategies and approaches; pragmatism; customisation of the balance of the child's needs and her/his preferences and the reconciliation of a well-established collaborative approach with some specialised interventions to suit the (student's) needs.' It is clear that the example cited by Calder is the product of considerable planning and preparation—this, including the training of staff, is essential.

At the same time, one needs to be aware of parental choice and student wishes. Wearmouth et al. (2002) suggest that a powerful argument that is often made in favour of inclusion is that every child has the right to be educated in the neighbourhood school together with peers. They suggest, however, a 'right' to be in a school does not necessarily mean that the resources will be available there to meet any particular learning need. Additionally, not every parent wishes his or her child to attend the neighbourhood school, and not every child wishes to go there. It is important, therefore, to consider the individual within the system, however well intended the system is in the desire to achieve equality.

AN INCLUSIVE SCHOOL

At school level Mittler (2000) suggests that the three principal aspects of inclusion are:

- all children attend their neighbourhood school in the regular classroom with appropriate support;
- all teachers accept the responsibility of ensuring that all pupils receive appropriate support and are given opportunities for professional development;
- schools rethink their values, restructure their organisation, curriculum and assessment arrangements to overcome barriers to learning and participation, and cater for the full range of pupils in their school and in their community.

The three key principles here are: first, that all children are included; second, that staff need to accept this premise; and, third, that this can have implications for the values/attitudes of the school and the community.

Diniz and Reed (2001) believe that schools wishing to attain the accolade of *an inclusive school* should not underestimate the degree of conflict that it will encounter. This conflict can be seen in the wide range of political expectations in addition to the competing voices within and outwith the school. The conceptual ambiguities, which can be evident in some of the specific learning difficulties according to Diniz and Reed, do not make the challenges relating to attitudes and conflicts any easier to resolve. An argument, in fact, can be levied that the practical demands relating to inclusion sharpen the debate over the conceptual ambiguities of dyslexia and the other specific learning difficulties. For example, if children with dyslexia do require special teaching that needs to be considered in the development of a policy on inclusion then one must suggest why and exactly what those special requirements would be. This, therefore, can only be healthy for the debate on dyslexia and beneficial in terms of addressing the needs of students with dyslexia and staff in mainstream schools.

Further, Diniz and Reed suggest that what is really required is a complete break from past practices as these focus on 'differences' between students, particularly in terms of categories, needs and deficits. It seems, therefore, that we are some way from implementing theories and practices that assimilate and normalise; rather, we are still focused on the concept of specialisation, but within the guise of inclusion. Diniz and Reed suggest that one of the principles of inclusion is the realisation of social equity and human rights. This, they contend, can only be achieved by insightful leadership, strategic policies, collaborative institutional cultures and equitable resource allocation. This sums up the challenge of formulating equitable policies and practices for inclusion to take account of the individual challenges presented by children who do require some additional considerations, such as dyslexic children, as well as the needs of the community of learners.

INTERVENTIONS AND DYSLEXIA

The Debate

There is an ongoing debate regarding the special type of teaching that is required for children with dyslexia. This debate is encapsulated in the paradigm presented by Norwich and Lewis (2001). In this paper they investigate the claims that differential teaching is required for children with special educational needs, including dyslexia. They claim that the 'unique differences position' (p. 313), which suggests that differentiated teaching is needed for this group, has little supportive, empirical evidence and are in fact nothing more than adaptations to common teaching approaches. Conner (1994) argues that specialist teaching approaches are little different from teaching literacy to any pupil, although arguably there seems to be more of a preference for bottom-up approaches toward phonological awareness, structure and over-learning. Reason et al. (1988) also question the differences in specialist approaches, indicating that individual differences within dyslexic students are more important in relation to utilising teaching approaches.

This point is developed in detail by Dyson (2001), who suggests that a radical rethink of categorisation-led interventions is needed. Dyson argues that what is required in order to achieve full equity—which is essentially the key aspect of inclusion—'is a move away from the individualisation of current approaches towards the development of systemic interventions embedded in mainstream schools and classrooms' (p. 99). In essence this means a shift from the practice of categorisation in order to identify interventions—moving from individual interventions, based on traditional special needs categorisations, to one of attempting to guarantee quality school provision for all, rather than case by case. Dyson's argument, which is firmly couched in equity principles as well as, he would argue, more cost- and time-effective interventions, appears to undermine the years of skill, experience, planning and development of individually based programmes that are currently used for example, for children with dyslexia. This, however, is the key question that needs to be asked: What is the evidence that these individually based programmes are more effective than a more global, systemic, curriculum-based approach?

The BPS report (1999a) suggests that bottom-up approaches to achieve 'accurate and fluent word decoding is a pre-requisite for efficient reading for interest and information' (p. 65) and that 'reading development is dependent on the teaching methods deployed, and, also, the language in which children are learning to read . . . and the efficiency and integrity of underlying phonological abilities will determine how effectively children are able to learn through independent reading' (p. 65). This implies that some principles that are common to all need to be considered at the beginning stages of reading, but that close monitoring is required to ensure that the necessary, prerequisite, phonological skills are incorporated into the learner's reading pattern. What happens next if the learner is not acquiring these skills is the point of debate. Do they require more of the same or something quite different? The answer to that lies in both the assessment and ongoing monitoring while acknowledging the individual differences between dyslexic children as well as the common principles needed for efficient reading acquisition. Norwich and Lewis (2001), however, would argue that such an approach, which emphasises the need for more bottom-up phonological approaches to literacy, is 'not qualitatively different from teaching which involves less emphasis on these approaches' (p. 326).

IMPLICATIONS

The implications are that, first, we need to justify that dyslexic children need different interventions and, second, we need to know exactly what the nature of that intervention and the implications for teaching provision should actually be. Chapter 7 highlighted an array of teaching approaches specifically designed for children with dyslexia. This would therefore imply that they do, in fact, need a different kind of intervention. Yet, there are very few studies that compare these approaches for dyslexic children with approaches normally offered to mainstream students who have no real literacy difficulties. Does the difference therefore lie in the nature of the pace of learning and the need for more time, more individual attention and more repetition, rather than production of a special programme that represents a 'dyslexia formula' for intervention.

Lewis and Norwich (1999) suggest that an analysis of their evidence:

rejects distinctive SEN teaching strategies and accepts that there are common pedagogic principles which are relevant to the unique differences between all pupils, including those designated as having SEN (p. 3).

They also suggest in relation to dyslexia that:

> *specialist approaches have much in common with teaching literacy to any pupil,*
> *though there is a tendency to bottom-up approaches (e.g. Synthetic Phonics).*
> *Other differences include the degree of structure, detail, continuous assessment,*
> *record keeping and overlearning* (p. 39).

These differences, which are accepted by Norwich and Lewis, of structure, continuous assessment and over-learning are indeed beneficial to all, but the point is that they are crucial for children with dyslexia, and many of the specialised approaches are indeed built upon these facets. Norwich and Lewis accept that:

> *pupils with specific learning difficulties also generally require more practice than*
> *other pupils and practice that is well designed. They need, like other pupils, to be*
> *actively engaged in managing their learning, though they tend to have difficulties in*
> *applying learning and performance strategies. However, evidence has shown that*
> *such pupils can be taught to use and apply such strategies* (p. 41).

Therefore, while there may be similarities in the nature of the intervention, the means and rationale for a certain type of intervention will be different. Teachers' awareness of the type of difficulties experienced by children with dyslexia is also crucial to a full understanding of how 'common pedagogic principles' can be utilised for children with dyslexia.

Whatever the answer to this, the fact remains that the educational systems in most countries are now committed in some fashion toward inclusionary policies and practices. These present special challenges to teachers because the teacher has to cater for a wide range of learning differences within a single class.

Whatever the arguments regarding the 'specialness' of the intervention for dyslexic children there is little doubt regarding the difficulties they can experience and present in acquiring literacy. The development of literacy can often be restricted by cognitive factors relating to memory, organisation and metacognition. Inclusion, therefore, although in principle aims to maintain equality and equitable distribution of teaching time and resources, in reality can be stressful for the teacher and actually become exclusionary for some students as their needs may be neglected in view of the multiple demands placed on teaching staff.

HEALTHY SCHOOLS

Peacey (2001) suggests that inclusion has a much broader base than curriculum factors and relates to the health of the school. He cites the National Healthy Schools Standard, which, as well as healthy eating, emphasises the emotional well-being of students, including those with disabilities. Pacey makes an interesting point regarding pressure and the stress that normally accompanies excessive work pressure, by challenging the assumption that stress automatically follows pressure and that pressure is therefore something to avoid. He suggests the issue is not whether we should be applying pressure, rather it is the appropriateness of the support that accompanies any perceived pressure. Of course, if the support is not forthcoming then by applying any form of pressure, such as that involved in meeting the needs of children with dyslexia, we will in fact be creating stress. Therefore, for inclusion to be successful in terms of student and teacher outcomes support needs to be available.

SUPPORT SYSTEM

The exact nature of that support, of course, is a matter of debate, but perhaps it also rests on the crucial question presented at the start of this chapter regarding the 'specialness' of teaching approaches for dyslexic children. Diniz and Reed (2001) put forward some questions that a school should ask in relation to support:

- What are the underlying assumptions that underpin the support system?
- Who gets support and who does not?
- What are the operational strategies in providing support?

These questions clearly need to be answered. The assumption that underlies the support system relates to the quest to achieve equality, but to do this some children will require more support and maybe a different form of support than others. This seems a perfectly reasonable assumption to make and should not run contrary to the principles of equity inherent in inclusionary practices. The question of how this support should be divided and distributed is much more contentious.

Pumfrey (2001) infers that definitions of dyslexia can be used, and misused, for resource allocation purposes. This does occur, but it is controversial as it assumes that particular cut-off points can be identified and that children's needs can be measured in terms of discrepancies and attainments. One of the contentious aspects of providing a 'special' approach for children identified with disabilities is that some form of segregation of need has to take place, and this is usually in the form and extent of the support offered. This can be divisive and can lead to unfair practices, disparity and inconsistencies in different areas of the country.

Diniz and Reed (2001) contend that much of the discourse on 'including' children with special educational needs, such as dyslexia, in mainstream schools erroneously rests on 'integration' assumptions. They suggest that discrimination and social exclusion are institutionally and systemically created, and necessitate a holistic transformation of education support systems if 'inclusion' is to be achieved. Such thinking they suggest is rare in dyslexia practice. The likeliest explanation for this, if this is the case, is that the dyslexia population are the beneficiaries of this educational support system, which according to Diniz and Reed lends itself to inequitable practice. It is, however, worth noting that charitable organisations such as the British Dyslexia Association (BDA), International Dyslexia Association (IDA) and Dyslexia in Scotland appear to be inundated each year with calls for help mainly from anxious parents who feel that the support that they believe is needed is not available or accessible. There are a number of perceptions and misperceptions regarding support, and these need to be clarified before inclusion can become a reality. Support should not be measured in terms of 'extra hours' of tuition, funding for resources or additional personnel—certainly, these will help, but can also be wasted and squandered if they are not focusing on the real difficulty and not leading to full inclusion. Support is as much about attitudes as about materials, recognition of the difficulty as much as resources and above all the need to utilise effective communication between all involved in the educational well-being of children. These factors should therefore govern operational strategies in the provision of support. Support should be available to all, not a few. The challenge for educators is to establish a means to ensure that support systems are in place so that any who require it will be able to access it without passing through many of the hoops that are currently in place.

Pacey (2001) contends that appropriate support in terms of materials, ideas and cultures are important as they enable people to build and grow, and this will contribute to the success of an inclusionary school. But, according to Pacey, it is also important to address issues regarding the health and well-being of the school. He suggests it is no accident that concern for the well-being of schools (i.e., both students and staff) goes hand in hand with high attainment in schools.

STAFF SUPPORT AND TRAINING

In England and Wales the National Special Educational Needs Specialist Standards (TTA, 1999) establishes a set of core standards to guide teachers. These include identification, assessment and planning, effective teaching to ensure maximum access to the curriculum, development of literacy and numeracy skills, developing ICT capabilities as well as the promotion of social and emotional behaviour. The Standards also include 63 extension standards with detailed summaries of how these core standards can be met. There is also a crucial role for the Special Educational Needs Co-ordinator's (SENCO) in schools, which can include whole-staff professional development. Much of the success of initiatives such as these 'standards' depends on the commitment and the management skills of head teachers to guide staff through the standards and ensure adequate support and professional development is available and accessible.

The Teacher Training Agency in England and Wales (TTA) does provide some exemplars of case studies of how the national SENCO standards can be implemented in schools (TTA, 2000).

In Scotland the programme Improving Our Schools: Special Educational Needs: The Programme of Action (Scottish Executive, 2000) produced a 'Programme of Action Summary' that indicated that resources available to local authorities for SEN in-service staff development and training had doubled. This report also indicated a commitment for the government in Scotland, at a national level, to work with local authorities on priorities for staff development and training.

Mittler (2001) highlights a key challenge when he suggests that one of the main challenges, particularly for staff development, is to distinguish 'between areas of knowledge and skill that are required by all specialist teachers and those that are distinctive to specific groups' (p. 144). This also begs the question of how to differentiate in practice between those needs of all students and those who have some form of special need—clearly, the overall needs should be the same in terms of projected outcomes—but the means of achieving those needs may be different. Following this point one must then ponder on the issue of what is special about meeting the needs of students who are recognised as having a special educational need. Do the implications of this rest on accurate analysis of needs through informative assessment procedures and the development of programmes of work? Many would answer yes—but, again, does not every student require informative assessment and programmes of work? Can these assessments and programmes be the same for all? In relation to dyslexia the conventional wisdom from the field would answer no—particularly in relation to identifying the cognitive and metacognitive factors associated with dyslexia and some of the other specific learning difficulties, which can have considerable implications for teaching and learning.

STUDENT ADVOCACY

The equity principles of inclusion also need to be extended to students. In many societies and education systems such advocacy is not evident or, if it is, it usually appears in a superficial way—perhaps through student consultation. But, there are very few examples of full and effective student advocacy. This is particularly important for students with dyslexia.

Muskat (1996) argues that education by its very nature should be empowering, but often it actually has the opposite effect. She suggests that the system of categorisation can run counter to advocacy, and this can occur due to inappropriate assessment and diagnosis. She suggests that classification practice must be considered within a developmental framework, as criteria that may be appropriate in the early stages of education may not be appropriate in later school stages. This point is emphasised by Crombie (2002e), who suggests that dyslexia can be redefined in the early stages by focusing on criteria-learning and multidisciplinary early intervention. This, she argues, would make the concept less stigmatic and less 'special' in later primary and secondary schools. In fact, what Crombie is advocating is a normalisation of dyslexia. This would have important effects on the self-advocacy of students and would only work if both school and the workplace accept such normalisation.

Muskat argues that student advocacy can only become a reality if others, such as teachers and parents, are advocates and feel free to express their own views and have these views considered. Arguably, the ethos of the provision and the accessibility of management are vital factors that can contribute to student self-expression and advocacy.

Dyson and Skidmore (1996) also suggest that dyslexia needs to be reconceptualised so that a shift in conceptualisation can occur from that of 'diagnosis, intervention and remediation to circumvention, coping, participation and achievement' (p. 478). They argue that this reconceptualisation can contribute to the four main strands that provision should fulfil: differentiation, building self-esteem, building learner autonomy and developing skills. It might be argued that the debates over what dyslexia is, best provision, resources and intervention can leave the student less empowered.

SELF-ADVOCACY: CHALLENGE OR THREAT

Developing self-advocacy for students in schools can be both challenging and threatening to staff. Essentially, self-advocacy is built on a foundation of enquiry and self-identification of students' rights and needs. This is a shift from the traditional role of teachers, which rests on the premise of transmitter of knowledge.

Garner and Sandow (1995) suggest that this development of the teacher's role may be uncomfortable as self-advocacy may run contrary to the traditional models of learning often seen in schools. These models usually depend on teaching and learning, which reinforce desired behaviours and inhibit undesired behaviour as perceived by the teacher. Wearmouth (2001) believes that, following on from the views of Garner and Sandow, it is possible that some teachers may view certain students as either undeserving of the right to self-advocacy or incapable of contributing rationally to decisions about their own lives. Self-advocacy, Wearmouth suggests, may be threatening because it can provide a challenge, and perhaps a verbal challenge, to teachers' authority as well as to the structure and organisation of the school.

Lannen (2002b) argues that the success of a school rests on the degree of exploration of pupil perspectives, as this helps teachers understand the motivating factors associated with a student's perception of success or failure.

Wearmouth (2001) cites the work of Gersch (2001), which reports on a project that aimed to enhance the active participation of pupils in school through encouraging self-evaluation and advocacy. The dilemmas encountered in the project are shown in Box 10.2.

The questions in Box 10.2 are of fundamental importance and indicate that the success of student advocacy rests on the assumptions that potential conflicts can be resolved and that attitude shifts will occur.

- How does one deal with other colleagues who might feel that children should be seen and not heard?

- Are some children not mature or capable enough to participate?

- How does one deal with parent–child dislike?

- What about scope needed for children to negotiate, try things and change their minds?

- How do adults distinguish what a child needs from what he or she prefers or wants?

Box 10.2   Dilemmas encountered in a project to enhance the active participation of pupils (from Gersch, 2001, quoted in Wearmouth, 2001, p. 118).

DYSLEXIA AND SELF-ADVOCACY

While self-advocacy is important for the development of independence and self-esteem in students, it is vitally important in the case of students with dyslexia. If dyslexic people are to be fully included in school and in society, they need to be able to assert their rights, identify their feelings and express their intent. These factors require practice, but often such practice is not encouraged and the scenario can occur when students with dyslexia through sheer frustration assert their rights in an inappropriate manner by acting out. There are many examples of this, and usually the result of such actions is expulsion or disaffection on the part of the students. Kirk and Reid (2003), in a study of people in a young offenders' institution, found that when some were identified as dyslexic their immediate reaction was one of anger, and they seized the opportunity to talk about a denial of their educational rights. Many adults with dyslexia have described how they moved from school to school in an attempt to have their needs met and to be able to express themselves in a non-threatening situation (*Genius, Criminals and Children*, Channel 4, 1999; Kirk and Reid, 2001).

An example of a student talking about his rights and the need for self-advocacy was recorded for a staff development programme on literacy (Open University, 2002). This interview highlights factors associated with communication, self-advocacy and self-esteem as crucial in terms of developing positive student perceptions of dyslexia.

STAFF SUPPORT

If inclusion is to be successful and achieve its aims of equality and meeting the diverse learning needs of individuals and groups of pupils as indicated in the general inclusion statement discussed earlier in this chapter (QCA, 2000), then considerable emphasis will be required in the area of staff support. Giorcelli (1999) supports this view from her experience in Australia. She noted:

> *the move towards a merged special and regular education system has changed the face of schooling and has forced all teacher preparation and development programmes to prepare teachers to accommodate students with disabilities and learning differences in regular school environments and to equip support or specialist teachers for consultation and teaming functions as well as for direct specialist teaching functions* (p. 269).

This view therefore suggests that training and supporting staff for an effective role in an inclusive school rests on building and developing existing knowledge bases and ensuring that the expertise that has been accumulated among specialists over a number of years is not lost, but forms the basis of staff development for mainstream teachers. While it is accepted that the label of specialist may run counter to the concept of inclusion, the expertise that specialist can bring to mainstream schools needs to be appreciated. This expertise, however, should not be seen as a 'how to', but rather as a 'what if'. This means that specialists are not the purveyors of knowledge, but the catalysts for attitude change, confidence-building and ongoing consultation. It seems that a balance between the effective use of specialist knowledge and the development of teacher skills to respond to student diversity is needed, without the need to retreat to extreme positions often echoed in the categorisation and anti-categorisation argument.

KEY FACTORS

Some of the key factors in relation to successful inclusion and, in particular, in relation to children with dyslexia include: a commitment by the education authority and the school to an inclusive ideal; a realisation by staff of the widely embracing features of inclusion and the equity issues inherent in these features; awareness of the particular specific needs associated with children with dyslexia and to accommodate to these through curriculum and teaching approaches; acceptance that inclusion is more than integration in that it embraces social, cultural and community equity issues as well as educational equality; regard for the cultural differences in communities and families and acknowledgement that children with dyslexia require flexible approaches in assessment and teaching; and honouring not only the child's individual rights but the individual differences as well.

Chapter 11

Secondary Education: Accessing the Curriculum

Many of the approaches suggested for children with dyslexia appear to be more appropriate for the primary than the secondary stage. Many phonics programmes, for example, are not really suitable in content for children of secondary age. This can present a difficulty and a challenge to those working in the secondary sector. Although some structured programmes have been used successfully with adolescents and indeed adults, such as Toe by Toe (Cowling and Cowling, 1998), there has also been a considerable thrust in secondary schools toward learning skills, study skills, curriculum access through examining potential difficulties in different subject areas and through differentiation. These factors are very appropriate and can help to meet the needs of students with dyslexia. This chapter will therefore look at some of the challenges facing staff in secondary schools and how these challenges may be met, with examples of some of the responses that have been established by teachers and education authorities.

RESPONSIBILITY

It is necessary for teachers, management and policy-makers to acknowledge that, in order to meet the needs of secondary age children, it is necessary to embark on whole-school approaches and a comprehensive programme of staff development. This can help subject staff realise the responsibility they have for students with dyslexia and not pass that responsibility to learning support or other specialists. For too long now the responsibility to deal with the challenges presented by students with dyslexia have rested with the specialist teacher. This type of model lends itself to the possibility that subject teachers may opt out of providing for students with dyslexia by acknowledging that it is a specialist area in which they have no expertise and that therefore it should be left to specialists.

One of the key issues, therefore, in secondary schools relates to the notion of responsibility. Peer and Reid (2002, 2003) suggest that the ethos of the school should be supportive and that all staff need to be made aware of the type of difficulties in different subject areas that may be displayed by students with dyslexia. It is important that departments tackle this through discussion with specialists, if available, and through differentiation. They also suggest that whole-school approaches to issues such as marking should be put in place—where children can receive a high mark for understanding and knowledge, rather than always being marked down due to poor presentation skills, spelling, punctuation and grammar.

FEATURES OF SECONDARY SCHOOLS

There are some factors that are inherent in secondary schools that can present the student with dyslexia with some difficulty. It will be beneficial, therefore, if subject teachers were aware of these potential difficulties so that they can anticipate them before they do become a problem for the student. What of course can compound the situation is that some students have not been identified as dyslexic, even after a few years in secondary school, but have to persist and compensate for these difficulties. On the positive side, there is now significant awareness in primary schools, and the rationale behind the Code of Practice in England and Wales (DfEE, 2002) as shown in the stages 'school action' and 'school action plus' is that schools take responsibility for identifying difficulties such as dyslexia and identify means of dealing with these difficulties within the curriculum and the system.

One of the key points relating to the debate on dyslexia (Nicolson, 1996, 2001) is that dyslexia can be seen as being more than a difficulty with reading. Yet, many teachers, particularly those in secondary schools, have a perception of dyslexia as being a difficulty with reading. There are many other factors associated with dyslexia that can disrupt learning for the student with dyslexia, including cognitive factors such as memory, speed of processing, possibly co-ordination, identification of the main points in text, and organisation and study skills. These should be part of a staff development programme. Thomson and Chinn (2001) provide an overview of some of the difficulties relating to the secondary school situation for students with dyslexia. They divide these into organisational, co-ordination, note-taking and project work. For example, some students with dyslexia may need additional help in finding their way around the school even after some time at the school. There are many ways of helping with this, but providing a colour-coded map of the school may be useful. Co-ordination difficulties if present will likely be noted in sports, although many students with dyslexia can also excel at sport; in fact, it provides an outlet for frustration and a refreshing outlet from the challenges of some academic subjects. Thomson and Chinn also suggest that difficulties in taking notes can be evident and that the pressures inherent in this type of activity can easily be avoided. Typed notes in colour with large, user-friendly fonts such as Sassoon or Comic Sans are preferable. Students with dyslexia can also have difficulty with extraction of information, and this can be a particular feature of secondary schools where much of the work is done through independent study. Thomson and Chinn therefore suggest it is not only necessary for the teacher to anticipate these potential difficulties but also to be aware of the positive aspects relating to dyslexia. For example, the secondary school teacher can note how students with dyslexia could apply more global thinking to a problem and, therefore, be able to develop unusual and creative solutions to some problems. Essentially, besides indicating the need to provide strategies for students, the secondary school curriculum can also be analysed and made more dyslexia-friendly at least in its presentation. Thomson and Chinn suggest that there is a need for additional high/low material that would allow information to be presented at a reading level commensurate with the student's decoding skills, but at an informative and inquiry level, in keeping with the student's actual abilities. This, of course, is a challenge, but there are a number of good examples of how this can be done with readers in primary schools, such as the high low series (LDA) and the series of novels published by Barrington Stoke. Indeed, Barrington Stoke have also launched a special series of high/low readers on teenage fiction, which are written with the secondary school student in mind.

Secondary schools have of course to follow the specific curriculum of the country, and this can be restrictive in subject content. Even in generic curricula, such as the National Curriculum in England and Wales and the 5–14 Programme in Scotland, there will be specific strands that are challenging for students with dyslexia. Thomson and Chinn (2001) provide examples of some of these challenges in relation to the National Curriculum and argue that it can be quite problematic for teachers to evaluate the progress of students with dyslexia, particularly in English. They quote the example of reading, which has two attainment targets, one indicating that students should be able to read fluently and accurately, and another attainment target suggesting that students should be able to read in a variety of ways (e.g., by using phonic, graphic and syntactic cues). This, of course, can be difficult, but the key point is that difficulties in acquiring the lower order skills in reading and writing should not prevent achieving success in the higher order skills of literacy.

Yet, the assumption is made throughout many examples of national curricula documents that have divided subject areas into attainment targets and strands that there is a linear progression in literacy and in the acquisition of most other skills. However valid this may be, the fact remains that it is not necessarily the case of students with dyslexia.

Crombie and Reid (1994), recognising this difficulty with the 5–14 Programme in Scotland, suggested the use of 'bridges' to help students access the target attainment—this means that additional targets and steps need to be imposed and accepted in the case of students with dyslexia. The difficulties, therefore, need to be tackled on two fronts: development of strategies to help the student cope with dyslexic difficulties and the recognition of inherent curricular difficulties that can disadvantage the student with dyslexia. Both these areas need to be tackled, and above all this can only really be achieved through teacher and management awareness of what dyslexia is and how it may affect the performances of students.

Thomson and Chinn (2001) suggest that, with some minor adjustments and recognition of the difficulties associated with dyslexia, teachers can make a considerable difference. They suggest the following: help being given discreetly to individuals; additional time being provided to complete a task; printed handouts being provided together with summaries of the work; students working together in small groups; grades and marking that show individual improvement so that it is meaningful for that individual student; marking that is constructive; and work judged for content not spelling.

While training is important, it is also important that the subject teacher should have knowledge and understanding of dyslexia and how this knowledge can be applied to their specific subject area. The strategies mentioned above need little training, only recognition of the difficulties that may be experienced by students with dyslexia.

DIFFERENTIATION AND CURRICULAR DEVELOPMENT

Differentiation and curricular development are both challenges and responses to meeting the needs of students with dyslexia in the secondary school. Kirk (2001) suggested that the subject-based curriculum of the secondary school, in which subjects are pursued in isolation, could leave pupils with a highly fragmented educational experience. It is important that these experiences are contextualised and made meaningful. Differentiation can help to make subject content meaningful, and curriculum development such as developing thematic units of work can make it less fragmented. Kirk suggests that it is important that the common features that most subjects share can be utilised to help the student develop concepts and automaticity. For example, she argues that all subjects should foster the capacity to think, to communicate, to solve problems, to engage with others, and to acquire important skills of various kinds, and that failure to recognise these features can lead to a limitation of the educational experiences for students with dyslexia.

Dargie (2001) maintains that secondary teachers need to be aware of the need to structure materials provided for students with dyslexia to meet their specific needs. He suggests that long, multi-clausal sentences and the use of metaphorical language should be avoided.

There are many examples of differentiation that have been the product of consultative collaboration within school departments (Lucas, 2002, pers. commun.; Dodds, 1996). Ideally, the needs of students with dyslexia should be met in this way and the resources and guidance on differentiation can provide a framework for the development of a differentiated approach. One of the important points to consider is that, although the language and sentence structure may be different and the overall plan of the page designed in a user-friendly fashion in a differentiated text, the underlying concepts that are to be taught should be the same. Therefore, the cognitive demands and the learning outcomes should be the same in text and tasks for all learners—differentiation only implies that the means of achieving these outcomes will be different, but not the conceptual outcomes.

DIFFERENTIATION AND ASSESSMENT

Dargie (2001) suggests that subjects such as History need to be assessed in a differentiated mode for students with dyslexia. He argues that students with dyslexia need opportunities to talk extensively in the History classroom. This can allow them to engage in 'print-free' debate and utilise their strengths in oral discussion. He suggests that talking to an issue can help pupils develop a theme in sequence, and this can be useful for students with dyslexia. Additionally, practice in discussion can also have an impact on the pupil's ability to question, infer, deduce, propose and evaluate. Differentiation, therefore, is not only about making the work and the texts more accessible for students with dyslexia but also about making the assessment more appropriate and effective. This latter aspect is often overlooked due to the restrictions imposed by national examinations on the nature of the support that can be offered in assessment.

It can be argued that traditional forms of assessment can disadvantage the dyslexic student because usually there is a discrepancy, and this may be a significant discrepancy between their understanding of a topic and how they are able to display that understanding in written form. This may be overcome through continuous and portfolio assessment in most subject areas. This view is supported by Ayres (1994, 1996), who strongly argues that portfolio assessment can also have a metacognitive function as this type of assessment encourages students to think about the processes of learning in more detail. Ayres suggests that many internal school exams are in fact no more than preparation for major public examinations, and if this is the case then they will very likely follow the same style and format as public exams, which of course implies that students have to develop compensatory strategies to help deal with the difficulties they may have in written work and in recall of information. Dodds and Lumsden (2001) point out that the deficit may not lie with the student with dyslexia, but with an assessment process that is unable to accommodate to the diversity of learners. They strongly advocate, therefore, that both teaching and assessment should be differentiated and diversified. This can be achieved through use of the multiple intelligence paradigm, which avails itself of Gardner's eight intelligences (Lazear, 1999) (see Chapter 8 of this book). This includes formal speech, journal-keeping, creative writing, poetry, verbal debate and storytelling as a means of assessing the verbal linguistic modality. While we are still a long way from a dynamic assessment paradigm that focuses on metacognitive strategies and views assessment as a teaching rather than a testing tool, such assessment is reported as being used in some classroom contexts (Ayres, 1996).

Metacognitive assessment can be informative, as it can provide information about children's actual levels of understanding and can be used to develop the most effective teaching approaches for students, which can strengthen the link between assessment and teaching.

DISSEMINATION

It is important that good practice is disseminated to all staff and to staff in different schools. Quite often, the good practice that is available is not fully acknowledged, simply because it has not been effectively disseminated. It is not unreasonable to assume that what works in one secondary school will work in another, but the knowledge and experience of one school needs to be shared with others. A good example of this is the 'good practice framework' developed by Edinburgh City Council (Brice, 2001). This framework was developed over a period of two years by a working party consisting of managers, parents, teachers, psychologists and the authority's advisory staff and is supported by an in-service training package aimed mainly at secondary subject teachers and a video made in local schools setting the context of the framework. The good practice framework helped to ensure that schools had systems in place to support students with dyslexia.

Essentially, the principal thrust was that of a whole-school approach, with flexible support and curriculum differentiation. Ideally, the framework provided opportunities for students to celebrate success. It was seen as important that all students with dyslexia should succeed, and it is the school's responsibility to ensure that some success is possible.

The key role in the framework is given to the subject teacher. Although schools often had experienced, trained learning support teachers, it was advocated that they should not take the responsibility for supporting students with dyslexia away from the subject teacher. The framework consists of guidance from the authority, school policies and curriculum issues, such as matching the curriculum to individual needs, as well as examples of good practice.

The package also includes workshop materials for use with teachers, support staff, parents and students.

SUBJECT AREAS

Although this section will examine some of the key aspects of different subject areas in relation to the secondary school, some of these aspects may also have relevance to primary teachers and students.

Mathematics

Coventry et al. (2001) examined the demands that Mathematics can present for students with dyslexia. They suggest that Mathematical thinking exists as a distinctive entity partly because it explores areas of thought beyond the easy control of words. Weedon (1992) suggests that Mathematics is about ideas and relationships that cannot easily be put into words. These abstract concepts and ideas can be difficult for students with dyslexia because as Coventry et al. suggest this requires organisation and access to knowledge, rules, techniques, skills and concepts. Often, rules that play an important part in Mathematics have to be rote-learned. Other skills that may be difficult to access for students with dyslexia are the spatial skills that are needed to help understand shape, symmetry, size and quantity, and linear skills that are needed to help understand sequence, order and the representations found in the number system. These aspects can prove demanding for dyslexic students, and in addition they still have the literacy and other difficulties associated with dyslexia such as working memory, speed of processing and automaticity. These can all have some implications for Mathematics.

Coventry et al. suggest the technical language of Mathematics may be a difficulty. A student, for example, may understand the meaning of words such as 'difference', 'evaluate', 'odd', 'mean' and 'product', but then find that they have a quite different meaning in the context of Mathematics. They suggest the following factors contribute to the demands of Mathematics for students with dyslexia: linear and sequential processing (this can be demanding because dyslexic students usually have some difficulty with order and sequencing and yet in some mathematical problems logic and sequence are crucial in order to obtain the correct response); precision is also necessary; and accuracy and detail because dyslexic people tend to be more global and random in their thinking (West, 1997; Chinn, 2001).

Long-term memory and information retrieval can be problematic for students with dyslexia. Much of this is due to the lack of organisation at the cognitive level—that is, at the initial stage of learning. If learning is not organised at this crucial initial stage then retrieval will be difficult at a later stage. Students with dyslexia may therefore have some difficulty with effective storage as well as accessing and retrieving information. It is for that reason that learning styles in Mathematics is important (Chinn, 2001). Assisting a student to utilise a preferred learning style can help effective storage, retrieval and access to information.

Working memory can also present some difficulties because working memory implies that students need to hold information in their short-term store, which could be a fraction of a second, and process that information into meaningful stimuli. This is very important in mathematics as mental operations are necessary to do this, which can be demanding for students with dyslexia, especially if information has to be held, even for a short time, in the student's head. It also emphasises the importance of writing down the 'working' and the steps of a mathematical problem clearly, so that the student can retrace his or her steps when necessary.

Mathematics can therefore present a difficulty for students with dyslexia because of the sequential processes usually necessary for calculations, the burden such calculations usually impose on short-term working memory and the language aspects associated with descriptions of mathematical problems.

There are some excellent texts in the area of Mathematics for dyslexic students. These include: *Maths and Dyslexics* by Anne Henderson (1989, 1998), which is a practical guide with illustrations indicating ways to tackle complex concepts; *Mathematics for Dyslexics* by Chinn and Ashcroft (1993), which also offers practical suggestions; and *Maths Solutions: An Introduction to Dyscalculia* by Jan Poustie, which is also practical and contains photocopiable sheets and the *Paired Maths Handbook* (Topping and Bamford, 1998).

Chinn (2001) suggests that learning style is an important factor in assisting the student deal more effectively with mathematical problems. Although Riding and Rayner (1998) suggest that 'a person's cognitive style is a relatively fixed aspect of learning performance ...', Chinn urges teachers to view learning styles, certainly from the Mathematics view, with more flexibility and states that learning styles can be modified and adapted with teaching. Chinn suggests that much of the individuality associated with learning styles can be managed in a classroom setting. He does acknowledge, however, that teachers need to recognise the differences in strategies and in presentation preferences selected by different learners. Some learners, therefore, prefer oral instruction while others need visual input, some will need concrete materials while others find them unnecessary. The Dunn and Dunn (1993) learning styles environmental model described in Chapter 9 is also applicable to the learning environment in Mathematics and indeed in all secondary subjects. Therefore, some will prefer to sit formally at a desk while others will feel more comfortable in a more relaxed position. The environment must be right for the individual; although this may present difficulties in a class of 30 students the student should still be provided with the opportunity to experiment with his or her style, as much of the work may be done at home.

Chinn (2001) describes some of the learning styles that have been associated with Mathematics. The research from Bath et al. (1986) and Chinn (2000) describes cognitive style in Mathematics by describing the characteristics of 'inchworms' and grasshoppers'. The inchworm [a caterpillar of a geometrid moth] would focus on parts and detail of a mathematical problem while the grasshopper would view the problem holistically; so, while the inchworm would be orientated toward a problem-solving approach and examine the processes needed to solve the problem, the grass-hopper would be answer-orientated and very likely use a flexible range of methods. The inchworm would prefer to use paper and pen while the grasshopper would rarely document the method used.

Marolda and Davidson (2000) also describe the characteristics of Mathematics. They describe these as Mathematics Learning Style I and Mathematics Learning Style II. The former is highly reliant on verbal skills and prefers the how to why, while the latter prefers perceptual stimuli and often reinterprets abstract situations visually or pictorially, preferring the why to how. Similarly, Sharma (1989) describes two learning personalities: the qualitative style, which is characterised by sequential processing from parts to whole and is procedurally oriented; and the quantitative method, which is characterised by visual processing from whole to parts. This type of student would generally approach problems holistically, may be good at identifying patterns and is more comfortable with mathematical concepts and ideas.

Dyscalculia

An extreme difficulty in Mathematics may be termed dyscalculia. This term is used when the student has a difficulty with number concepts, difficulties in literacy and the other difficulties associated with dyslexia that are described in Part II, 'Assessment'. There may therefore be some overlap between dyslexia and dyscalculia, but the use of the term 'dyscalculia' suggests that the student has pronounced difficulties with mathematical concepts.

Music

Difficulties Associated with Music

Ditchfield (2001) suggests that Music can present a different type of challenge to students with dyslexia from that faced in other subjects. Yet, it can be noted that some dyslexic students can be very musical and find music relaxing and a natural outlet for the difficulties experienced in literacy. The reading of music can relate to learning a new language. Students have to learn the meaning of symbols, some with only subtle differences between them, and know when and how to use them.

Visual Difficulties and Music

Ditchfield suggests that because reading music requires visual, as well as memory skills, this can put some additional burden on the visual processing system. There is evidence that some students with dyslexia may have a degree of unstable vision relating to convergence difficulties (Stein et al., 2001), other difficulties relating to visual sensitivity (Mailley, 2001) and visual processing difficulties relating to the magnocellular visual system (Everatt, 2002; Stein et al., 2001; Eden et al., 1996). These difficulties can result in visual disturbances especially when one considers the nature of music scores. Lines are positioned close together, and visual blur may occur as well as omissions and additions due to eye-tracking difficulties; indeed, in some cases the lines in a music score may close up and appear distorted.

Processing Difficulties

Ditchfield also identifies a number of potential complexities such as the need to convert the language of music, which is essentially drawn on a vertical plane, to a horizontal plane for such instruments as keyboards. The difficulties associated with working and short-term memory have already been noted elsewhere in this book, and these difficulties can also be challenging for the student reading Music. Sight-reading in Music can therefore be difficult for the student with dyslexia, as different forms of information have to be processed simultaneously. Essentially, the student has to read the score, reintepret it for his or her instrument and reproduce it in a different form in the instrument being played. There are at least three simultaneous tasks in that activity, and these will present some difficulties for the student with dyslexia and impose a burden on working memory. Additionally, these activities have to be carried out at some speed. It has already been noted that dyslexia can be associated with speed of processing difficulties, which means that the person with dyslexia may require more time to process the different aspects of the information compared with someone who is not dyslexic. Additionally, the student has to keep in time with other instruments in the orchestra and, perhaps, also watch the conductor. There are, therefore, considerable simultaneous processing activities occurring when the person with dyslexia is reading Music and playing an instrument at the same time.

Co-ordination Difficulties and Music

There is also a view that there may be an overlap between dyslexia and dyspraxia (Peer, 2001; Portwood, 2000) and that the person with dyslexia may have eye–hand co-ordination difficulties or experience other motor difficulties that can account for difficulties in processing and conducting different tasks simultaneously (Dore and Rutherford, 2001; Fawcett and Nicolson, 2001). This can result in co-ordination difficulties and affect the performance of the student.

Strategies

It is important that effort is made to provide the student with some strategies that can help overcome these difficulties in Music. Ditchfield (2001) suggests that relatively simple procedures like enlarging a normal size score and using coloured paper may help. Some dyslexic people find that it helps if scores are printed on tinted paper and if coloured overlays are used. The important point is that strategies should be individualised for each student—not all students with dyslexia will benefit from the use of colour. It is necessary therefore to adapt specific strategies to suit individual needs.

Hubicki and Miles (1991) recommend the use of coloured staves as these can help students identify and decipher particular notes and patterns. The use of computer technology will also help some students, and there are some excellent programs to help individuals learn conventional notation and other aspects of theory and practice. Ditchfield in fact suggests that it is possible to dispense with traditional methods that use ink and manuscript paper when recording musical scores. Computer technology may be used as an aid to composing and in helping students learn musical notation.

The main points regarding music and dyslexia is that, first, the student with dyslexia may have considerable natural musical ability, but not be able to read or copy music scores. Second, this can be frustrating for the student, and it is important that strategies are put in place to help the student overcome these difficulties. It is important to appreciate that students with dyslexia will have other associated difficulties in addition to reading, and this can result in time management and organisational difficulties as well as speed of processing and co-ordination factors.

Science Subjects

General Science

Hunter (2001) argues that for many students with dyslexia science subjects are areas of the curriculum where they can excel. Usually, the need for extended writing is less than in English or social subjects, and they are able to focus on content to a greater extent without finding the writing demands overpowering.

Additionally, assessment is often by multiple choice or short answers rather than lengthy essays, and this can be advantageous to the student with dyslexia. Hunter also makes the point that communication within the school is of vital importance in helping to assist the student with dyslexia in all subjects, but particularly those subjects where supports can be provided. However, it is necessary for the teacher to know which supports would be most beneficial. She argues that it is not enough to note that a student is dyslexic: the individual strengths and weaknesses need to be detailed. For example, she suggests that information should be available on whether the student can make use of a laptop or use the computer in the classroom.

Details on the student's familiarity with technology, with reading accuracy and spelling, particularly when under time pressure, should be provided to the subject teacher. It is also important to know how the student may respond to the help available. Not all students with dyslexia accept support readily, as some like to discreetly manage as best they can. It is also important for the subject teacher to recognise that self-esteem can often be affected after many years of struggling with literacy in school. As in most teaching programmes it is important to ensure that the student will achieve some success. However slight that may seem to the teacher, it can be an enormous leap for the student. Hunter also recognises that the learning environment in Science can be quite different from that found in other classrooms, such as the English classroom, and the student may need time to adjust to this: a detailed and labelled plan of the science laboratory can be helpful.

Strategies (such as the use of Mind Maps©) can be helpful as they provide a visual plan that is meaningful for the student and can make notes more meaningful as well as helping with organisation and recall. The use of technology, Hunter argues, can be of considerable benefit in conducting and reporting on experiments in Science. Often, the student with dyslexia may not complete his or her experiment in normal class time and may not be able to access the information needed outside the laboratory. However, by networking computers via an intranet, or Internet, system the student can finish work after class and utilise the supports available in the school. Notes can also be put on the internal school intranet network, so that they can be fully accessed by students with dyslexia. This can also help to encourage and establish independent learning.

It is important that students with dyslexia enjoy some success. Hunter therefore suggests that clear, logical, short, achievable targets are necessary. It is important that the student is aware of exactly what is expected from the unit of work and should also be in a position to assess whether they are on target to achieve those outcomes. Self-esteem can be enhanced in science subjects by developing students' abilities in group work and ensuring that some of the responses are provided orally. Hunter argues that if this is done the problems often experienced in recording and accessing information can be overshadowed by the successes experienced by the student in Science.

Biology

Howlett (2001) argues that, compared with other subjects, Biology involves a considerable amount of factual detail. Additionally, there are many technical words that are rarely used in everyday speech. In this subject, therefore, the students with dyslexia will come across new words and combinations of letter and sounds that may still have Latin or Greek spellings—some of these words may also look and sound similar, but yet have entirely different meanings. She also suggests that many of the words and concepts are abstract, such as 'homeostasis', 'ecosystem' and 'respiration', and that it is important that the student has a clear idea of these abstract words, has developed a visual representation of them and has an accurate schema. For example, when remembering particular parts of plants or animals most of the words will be new, but the function of the words can apply across most species of plants and animals. It is therefore important, for example, that the student has understood the concept of respiration in both plants and animals, as this can help in the understanding of the concept of breathing. It may be necessary to highlight this transfer of learning to students with dyslexia, as they may not note this without assistance. A great deal of the work in science subjects such as Biology involve practical experiments and assignments based on practical work. There are certain skills associated with practical work, such as understanding the instructions, that in fact may be quite complex: organising the experiment, ensuring all the information and components are at hand and reporting on the experiment in a clear manner.

Howlett (2001) provides a summary of the type of difficulties that dyslexic students may experience in Biology. These include remembering and recalling 'names' accurately (both in text and labelling of diagrams), spelling of technical words, learning a considerable quantity of factual information, understanding abstract concepts, remembering and following instructions accurately in practical work and recording observations accurately.

Diagrams

It is worthwhile spending some time on diagram construction and presentation. Diagrams are important for students with dyslexia, and they are also an important part of science and particularly Biology. Howlett (2001) suggests it is useful to spend a little time on the mechanics of producing diagrams, as this will have long-term benefits and be helpful in other subjects, such as Geography. She suggests that before making a detailed diagram it is preferable to make a plan that will serve as a rough draft. Other factors that should be considered include deciding how much of the page is to be used, as often the drawing may extend to a larger area than first thought, and using colour purposefully, which means only using it if it will help the student understand the diagram better. It is important therefore to have a consistent colour key. Additionally, since it is acknowledged that dyslexia can be associated with word-finding and word retrieval, it is important that labels are used clearly and accurately—the use of labels together with a diagram, if clearly presented, can help to reinforce the organisation, understanding and retrieval of information. Biology can lend itself to multi-sensory learning using the tactile and kinaesthetic modalities, and this can also introduce a degree of fun into the activities that will make them more meaningful and help in the transfer of concepts to other areas of Biology and, indeed, the curriculum (Wyatt, 2002).

Physics

It can be argued that much of the subject content of secondary school subjects is determined by examination considerations. This can make it extremely difficult for the class teacher. At the same time, there are many examples of good practice using the principles of differentiation and acknowledging the nature of the difficulties that can be experienced by students with dyslexia (Brice, 2001; Dodds and Lumsden, 2001). One example of this in relation to Physics has been described by Holmes (2001). Physics is a subject that can present some difficulties to dyslexic students because of the abstract nature of its concepts and sequential logic as well as the memorising of formula, but it is also one of the subjects in which they can do well because, like some of the other science subjects, it may involve less reading than some of the social science subjects. Holmes suggests a top-down approach that provides a whole-school awareness of dyslexia and allows subject teachers to reflect on the implications of providing for dyslexic students in their own subject. Other factors that Holmes considers include: building a bank of support materials that can become a whole-school resource and recognising the implications of secondary difficulties that can affect a student's performance in subjects such as

Physics. There is also scope for cross-curricular transfer, such as the relationship between Mathematics and Physics, which could mean that the student's difficulties in Physics are a consequence of Mathematics difficulties. This emphasises the need for a whole-school approach to dealing with the needs of students with dyslexia.

Clearly, therefore, there is a management role in ensuring that cross-curricular communication is effective, as such collaboration can reinforce the transfer of the learning strategies and skills developed in each of the subject areas.

English

It is interesting to note that, despite the general perception that students with dyslexia would find English challenging and would try and avoid that subject, when given a choice, this does not in fact appear to be the case. There is a considerable percentage of students with dyslexia who undertake English as the main topic in further and higher education courses. Although the 'grammar' aspects of English can be challenging for dyslexic students, the critical thinking associated with English literature is often stimulating. Turner (2001) suggests that many dyslexic students derive great enjoyment from studying literary works, and accessing age- and ability-appropriate literature. She suggests, however, that this still needs careful handling, since many students with dyslexia will very likely not have much background reading to refer to, and this can account for gaps in knowledge that make it extremely important for teachers to explain all concepts to them. Turner also emphasises that teaching the language of literature is important. She believes that all students in a class need to be given vocabulary support since poetry, novels and prose can be tackled with more ease when students have this background knowledge about literature.

Many literature classics are now available in video and audio, and this can help the student develop a picture of the scene and the situational context of the novel or play. Turner rightly suggests that using video or audio materials should not be considered a 'short cut'. They are, in fact, a real alternative and can be more in keeping with the student's learning style than reading the novel, when first introduced to the theme. It may be better to commence any theme with background discussion to develop ideas and concepts and then present the theme for the novel in visual or drama form, before the student actually commences to read the book. Turner suggests that strategies, such as pointing out underlying themes, encouraging the use of Mind Maps© to plan an overview and observing the connections between characters and the main ideas of the novel, are support techniques that the English teacher can use.

One of the difficulties, apart from grammar and spelling, that may be experienced by students with dyslexia is the construction and structuring of written work. They may have numerous ideas, but lack of structure can mean that some key points may be omitted or that much redundant information will be included. Additionally, the argument may be jumbled and confusing.

Clearly, the student with dyslexia may benefit from some assistance in essay-writing. Although this may come under more general study skills, strategies such as those described below can be contextualised for essay-writing and, indeed, for a specific essay.

Essay and Report-writing

Some stages that may be useful to consider in report-writing are outlined in the following subsections.

Preparation

This can involve the following examination of the question or topic, and the student can ask himself or herself the following questions:

- What does the question mean?
- What do you already know about the topic?
- What do you still have to find out?
- At this initial stage what do you think is the answer to the question?
- What kind of detail do you think you may need to support your answer?

Information

- What sort of information do you need?
- Where will you find it?
- What are the key points?
- How did you identify the key points?
- Are there any other points you may wish to consider?
- Keep a note of where you obtained information you are using—this includes references and quotes.
- Organise your notes into headings and subheadings, or use a Mind Map© strategy.

Constructing

- Write a draft essay plan identifying the purpose of each section or paragraph.
- Identify the key points that you will use in the introduction—these should be general points, but you need to write beside them the specific detailed points that will form the main part of your essay.
- Check that you have interpreted the question accurately—often there may be more than one way to interpret a question.
- From the general key points in your introduction note down the specific points and examples you will use to support your points.
- Try to ensure you have a coherently developed argument.
- The conclusion should provide a firm answer to the question, try to avoid flowery and elaborate language in your conclusion—this takes time and is often unnecessary as it may not add anything to your answer.
- Your conclusion should relate to your introduction.

Writing

- Use short sentences when constructing arguments and ensure you have used evidence to support your assertions.
- Try to ensure that each paragraph has a specific focus, is self-contained and does not repeat what you have already said.
- Proof-read for meaning first and then, very importantly, for grammar and spelling.

Reviewing

- Have you identified the key points and the appropriate subpoints that fit into these key points.
- Write them out in note form and check them against the key points in your essay.
- Have you included the implications of your key points in your essay?
- Check your presentation and then submit it.

While the above framework can be useful, it is important that it is contextualised for the subject and topic that is being studied. This means that the teacher can give examples at each of the main stages on what is meant and how it may relate to the topic.

Modern Foreign Languages

It has been suggested (Crombie and McColl, 2001) that children with dyslexic difficulties may find modern languages quite challenging. There are a number of reasons for this: the need to learn new vocabulary; the new grammatical structure to be learnt; the tendency for the teaching of foreign languages to be verbal, auditory and usually at a pace that is too fast for the student with dyslexia to assimilate.

Crombie and McColl (2001) make some suggestions that can help make modern languages more dyslexia-friendly:

- use charts and diagrams to highlight the bigger picture, add mime and gesture to words;
- add pictures to text;
- use colour to highlight gender and accents;
- label diagrams and charts;
- use games to consolidate vocabulary, make packs of pocket-size cards, use different colours for different purposes;
- combine listening and reading by providing text and tape;
- use Mind Maps© and spidergrams;
- allow the student to produce own tape;
- present in small amounts, using a variety of means, giving frequent opportunities for repetition and revision;
- provide an interest in the country concerned and show films, etc.;
- rules and other information about the language should be provided in written form for further study and future reference.

It is also important to consider the information processing cycle (i.e., input, cognition and output) (see Figure 8.1, p. 190) and to help the student develop separate strategies for each of these stages. Modern foreign languages should be accessible to all students with dyslexia. It is therefore important to consider how materials are presented. Students with dyslexia are usually predominantly visual processors, and it is important that even subjects with a heavy language and perhaps phonological emphasis are presented in a visual or indeed a kinaesthetic manner. The latter aspect relates to role play and drama-type activities that can be fairly readily incorporated into language-learning.

Social Subjects

Social subjects such as History, Geography and Modern Studies usually involve a considerable amount of reading and writing. This can be challenging for students with dyslexia, and can also be challenging for the teacher to present the subject in an accessible manner. Dargie (2001) suggests that discussion is a good reinforcing vehicle, and that this should always be used as a follow-up to the study of history texts. He provides examples of discussion and problem-solving activities on, for example, the Act of Union in 1707 and shows how this can relate to current developments in parliament and to topics and themes on devolution that have universal currency. The key point is that subjects such as History can be broadened and incorporate current events that can make it more meaningful for the student. Learners with dyslexia will understand more fully if the information is relevant and meaningful. This is the key to accessing subjects such as History for students with dyslexia. This would also mean that they would not need to read every word in a text as they would be able to utilise contextual cues. This would certainly be the case if the student had a sound background of the topic and contextual knowledge and understanding of the principal ideas and concepts relating to that historical period. This can also be achieved through group discussion as well as visually through films and videos.

In relation to Geography, Williams and Lewis (2001) emphasise the importance of differentiation. They suggest that differentiation does not mean developing worksheets with reduced or simplified content. To embark on differentiation effectively, teachers need to undertake considerable preparatory work. They need to consider factors such as readability levels, how resources will be designed, how diagrams will be labelled, the use of colour, the provision of printed materials such as notes and maps to prevent tracing and excessive note-taking as well as the provision of keywords and specialised vocabulary. Williams and Lewis also suggest that differentiation by task should be considered. This will provide the student with dyslexia with a choice of tasks from which to select. They also emphasise that the outcome of the learning experience and student assessment can also be differentiated without diluting the quality of the task or assessment procedure. This would also mean that a range of assessment strategies need to be considered in order that dyslexic students can demonstrate their knowledge and understanding of the subject.

Dodds (1996), using Modern Studies as an example, shows how worksheets can be created using visual examples to support the text and the tasks, together with the use of appropriate language that can be easily understood by the student. The higher order thinking and problem-solving skills, however, are the same for all students. It is important that accessiblity does not compromise the need to develop critical thinking in social subjects.

MULTIPLE INTELLIGENCE IN SECONDARY SCHOOLS

The multiple intelligences framework discussed in Chapter 9, 'Learning Styles', can have particular applicability for the secondary school. Subjects such as History and Geography can involve the eight intelligences quite readily. Lazear (1999) highlights how they can be used not only in individual subjects but also across the whole curriculum to ensure metacognitive transfer. One example of this can be the use of visual imagery combined with music—practice at this can help the student develop visual abilities, and, if she or he were to verbalise them, they can have a spin-off effect on language and storytelling. He also indicates how the reverse can apply when students try to impose appropriate sound into a story they have read. Similarly, bodily–kinaesthetic intelligence can be applied in all subjects: in History a dramatic account of a historical incident can help develop kinaesthetic–bodily intelligence, as can learning particular folk dances from different cultures or a different historical period. Bodily–kinaesthetic intelligence is one modality that is often overlooked in class subjects because it usually involves movement in class and perhaps some disruption. This, however, can be brought into all subjects: Science, in terms of measurement or practical activities, and English, in relation to drama and performing plays. Role-playing activities that can be used in all subjects can also capitalise on most of the eight intelligences. Not only does a multiple intelligence framework ensure that students have opportunities to develop their skills, as well as work on their weaknesses, but multiple intelligence approaches are usually multi-sensory by nature as well. This means that all modalities will be used in either learning or in assessment, and this is beneficial for students with dyslexia. The multiple intelligence framework is shown in Chapter 8, 'Learning—Metacognition and Study Skills'.

Most subjects, such as Modern Foreign Languages, English, Art and Drama, which may be challenging in terms of the amount of reading students need to complete, can lend themselves to kinaesthetic approaches by focusing on experiential learning activities. This, therefore, is the very essence of multiple intelligence—to ensure access to all components of the curriculum and ensure that all the student's modalities are being utilised. This will also help the student become familiar with his or her preferred choice of learning, and therefore go some way toward promoting self-sufficiency in learning.

PHYSICAL EDUCATION

Physical education is a subject that can have applicability to a multiple intelligence framework as well as implications for other areas of learning across the curriculum.

It is a subject that can be crucial in the metacognitive aspects of transferring learning. Some students with dyslexia can have co-ordination difficulties, and these should be known to the physical education (PE) specialist. This, however, should not deter the student from fully participating in the PE curriculum. Exercise and sport can be beneficial not only in acting as a stress reducer, but also may have a spin-off to other skills such as reading. There have been a number of different types of exercise programmes established for students with dyslexia and, although these may have a specific rationale (Dore, 2001; Longdon, 2001), they do utilise physical factors for the cognitive development of the individual. Specific exercises have also been developed as part of PE programmes involving specially tailored programmes for children with specific difficulties (Portwood, 2001; MacIntyre, 2001; Russell, 1988) and relaxation exercises such as yoga. The important point is that PE teachers should be aware of the important role they can play in dealing with the difficulties associated with dyslexia and the overlap between the benefits of an exercise programme and the development of skills such as reading.

At the same time, some students with dyslexia can in fact excel at sport and PE. This is important as it may be the only component of the curriculum in which they can achieve any success. If this is the case, then it may well have a positive spin-off to other curricular areas. The relationship therefore between physical activity and learning should not be overlooked, and this can have implications for teacher training and staff development in general.

STAFF DEVELOPMENT

In order to achieve a whole-school awareness of dyslexia and the needs of students with dyslexia, it is crucial that staff development is given a high priority. Ideally, this should be a whole-staff initiative and not one in which individual teachers can opt out. Although different subject teachers may have different needs relating to dyslexia, it is important that some of the general principles are discussed and that this is followed up with activities involving individual subject areas.

Palmer (2001) reports on developments in training and provision for secondary students with dyslexia in Somerset. The system developed in Somerset involves monitoring and evaluating schools' special educational needs provision through a process called 'A Framework for Supported Self-Review' that deals with systems and provision for special educational needs in mainstream schools. This initiative commenced in September 2000 and involves a rolling programme of specialist training for teachers, ongoing professional development, Special Educational Needs Co-ordinator (SENCO) training and a certificate course—Special Needs in Mainstream Schools. Palmer also reports on the local education authority's policy document, Specific Learning Difficulties—Policy Document: Policy into Practice. There are a number of authority and county-wide initiatives in the UK on dyslexia. Many describe the development and implementation of training programmes for specialist and mainstream teachers (Reid, 1998, 2001a).

Another example of this comprehensive desire to provide training for secondary (and primary) teachers is the Edinburgh City Council model. The importance of these training programmes is that they indicate a commitment by education authorities to provide for children and young people with dyslexia. This commitment can inspire confidence in parents as well as teachers.

CHALLENGES: KEY AREAS

Peer and Reid (2002) suggest some key areas that can present a challenge to teachers in their efforts to provide effectively for students with dyslexia in the secondary school:

- the subject content;
- subject delivery;
- assessment;
- cross-curricular aspects;
- metacognitive factors;
- learning styles/multiple intelligences; and
- initial teacher education and staff development.

Thomson (2002) reported on these developments by asserting that the difficulties experienced by students with dyslexia at secondary school were rooted in the curriculum. She suggests that the need to inform subject teachers of a range of aspects on dyslexia, such as the characteristics, the skills often possessed by students with dyslexia and the difficulties which can be associated with dyslexia, was paramount. Thomson advocates a curriculum perspective in dealing with dyslexia and views the curriculum as the vehicle for change and support. She relates this to the development of 'co-ordinated support plans' that have been developed to help ensure that all students are 'included' and that all subject teachers are aware of how to support students with dyslexia in the classroom. She further advocates that subject teachers should be aware of issues relating to dyslexia in the whole-school assessment process, in curriculum-planning and in the selection and the appropriate use of resources. As Kirk (2001) points out, however, cross-curricular staff development requires a considerable investment in time, particularly from the learning support staff, and, additionally, it may be necessary to convince senior management of the need for such initiatives.

It is important that these issues are responded to in order that the student with dyslexia can achieve some success in different subject areas. Some of the implications of these factors relating to assessment, teaching and learning are discussed elsewhere in this book, but this chapter has presented an overview of how these challenges and responses to them may help students with dyslexia to access the full curriculum. Many subject areas of the curriculum appear to be content-driven. The 'content' therefore dominates the teaching methods and the pace of learning, and this can be detrimental to the potential success of students with dyslexia. It might even be argued that subject-teaching in the secondary school is dominated by examinations, and this would also dictate the pace of learning. This means that aspects such as learning styles and the cognitive and metacognitive aspects of learning are dwarfed by the need to absorb vast quantities of information for examinations. It is crucial therefore that subject teachers have an accurate learning profile of the student as this can at least make the subject teacher aware of the individual student's particular strengths and weakness. Often, when the pace of learning is dominated by examinations the individual's specific needs can be overlooked.

Chapter 12

Inclusion: Further and Higher Education and the Workplace

ACCESS AND AWARENESS

One of the major advances to benefit people with dyslexia in recent years has been the increased access to further and higher education. All universities and colleges in the UK now have to provide for the needs of students with dyslexia. The Disability Discrimination Act (1995) has helped to prevent discriminatory practices in the workplace and in education, and support is now available for students with dyslexia (DfES, 2001). Similarly, in the USA, Canada, New Zealand and Australia there are many examples of good practices, particularly in providing support for students with dyslexia.

In the UK the *Dyslexia in Higher Education* working party report (Singleton, 1999a) provided clear guidelines on assessment and support for students with dyslexia as well as guidelines for disability staff and course tutors. Subsequently, a number of informative texts have been available aimed directly at dyslexia in adults (Reid and Kirk, 2001; Bartlett and Moody, 2000; Morgan and Klein, 2000; Heaton and Mitchell, 2001; McLoughlin et al., 2002). In addition, a number of reports have been commissioned and published—such as the Moser report in adult literacy (Moser, 2000) and the *Adult Dyslexia for Employment, Practice and Training* (ADEPT) report on best practice in assessment and support for adults with dyslexia particularly focusing on the unemployed (Reid et al., 1999). Additionally, the DfEE have funded a number of projects in England and Wales on a range of practices in assessment and support in further education and universities, and in Scotland the Scottish Higher Education Funding Council (SHEFC) have funded similar projects—one such project has resulted in the publication of a user-friendly guide for students with dyslexia that is also beneficial for tutors (Hammond and Hercules, 2000). The guide devised at the Glasgow School of Art recognises the need for information to be dyslexia-friendly and utilises good practices in presentation of information. The layout, use of contrasting colour, the index and the content all highlight good practice in presentation of information to students with dyslexia.

The term 'dyslexia' is recognised as a disability under the terms of the Disability Discrimination Act, and each educational institution has to employ a disability co-ordinator and in many instances a dyslexia adviser. While it is appreciated that many advances have been made in the recognition of students with dyslexia at college, there are still a number of issues relating to this that can provide challenges to disability and dyslexia advisers, as well as tutors and students themselves. Some of these issues will be discussed in this chapter.

In the USA, legislation such as the 'Americans with Disabilities Act' (1994) can also provide a framework and opportunities for employees with dyslexia to resolve work disputes, although Gerber (1997) suggests that the ongoing reference to case law is still a powerful influence.

Luecking (1997) suggests that one should be 'reframing the message to employers' in the USA and that direct inquiry into the needs of the employer should replace charitable appeals. He believes that each job and each individual offers a distinct pattern of needs and support, and it is crucial that the employer is aware of this. A partnership between job preparation programmes and employers is therefore para-mount. Clearly, although legislation is in place in many countries, the success of this will need to be judged in terms of the effect of its implementation and the attitude of those in positions of responsibility. There are still many instances of lack of under-standing in both colleges and the workplace on dyslexia.

This chapter will deal with some of these issues, particularly in relation to the identification of students with dyslexia, accessibility of further and higher education for dyslexic students, the support that can be provided to help ensure the successful completion of the course of study and some suggestions that may be useful for students themselves. Additionally, this chapter will also focus on the needs of people in employment as well as employers in relation to dyslexia. These may also provide pointers to the development of similar practices in other countries.

FURTHER AND HIGHER EDUCATION

Identification and Assessment

One interesting point to note is the alarmingly high percentage of students with dyslexia identified for the first time after entering university. In a UK study of over 100 institutions, 43% of the total dyslexic student population were diagnosed as dyslexic after admission to university (Singleton, 1999a). There are likely a number of reasons for this, but in the course of time this number should be reduced as more students are identified at school level. Young people with dyslexia can be quite adept at developing coping strategies to compensate for their difficulties. This may be satisfactory at school, especially as there is usually an imposed struc-ture, and even if they have not been diagnosed as dyslexic there is still very often support available to assist them. At university or college, however, the picture can be quite different. Very often students have to structure and organise their own work, and usually time limits are imposed in submitting completed work. It is this type of situation that can be daunting for the undiagnosed dyslexic person, and this usually prompts them to seek some help, perhaps for the first time in their educational career.

ASSESSMENT: THE CONTEXT

An assessment should not be carried out in isolation. The assessment needs to be contextualised for the course of study and for the needs of the student. The demands and the skills needed for different courses can vary considerably.

The demands of training in nurse-training will be quite different from those experienced in some science, engineering or teacher-training courses. Additionally, the person conducting the assessment needs to know about some of the other factors that may influence the outcome of the assessment and the student's performance in the course. Factors such as English being a second language and factors relating to the student's school and life experiences may also influence course performances. It is also important to recognise that dyslexia is about how reading difficulties affect individuals and how this can contribute to low self-esteem and other difficulties. It is for this reason that constructive feedback following an assessment is beneficial for the student. Such feedback can make a considerable difference to the self-esteem of the student, if handled sensitively.

ASSESSMENT: THE PROCESS

There are several procedures that can be used by colleges and universities to identify students. In practice, in the UK this is usually by referral to an educational psychologist who has experience at assessing dyslexia in adults. This latter point is very important because not all educational psychologists have experience at assessing for dyslexia and fewer have experience with adults. An examination of the UK Directory of Chartered Psychologists (BPS, 1999b) shows that only 27% of those providing educational psychology services indicated that they can perform dyslexia assessments on adults (Reid et al., 1999).

Many universities and colleges in the UK have implemented screening procedures before undertaking a full psychological assessment. Indeed, some of these screening procedures are quite sophisticated, and tests such as the dyslexia adult screening test (DAST) can provide much of the information needed for a diagnostic evaluation of the student's needs.

In addition to the DAST (Fawcett and Nicolson, 1997), computer screening procedures for dyslexia are also available. Computer-based assessment can be the first line in identification; although it may not give a definitive diagnosis it can be useful as an initial screening. It is feasible that students can access computer-screening from a central database within the college or university (Kirk, 2002). Additionally, checklists can be used. Smythe and Everatt (2001; pers. commun., 2002) have developed a sophisticated checklist that takes into account cognitive as well as behavioural factors associated with study and work.

Computer-screening or a checklist will provide the student with feedback that may prompt him or her to make an appointment with the dyslexia adviser to discuss further assessment. As mentioned above, this could be in the form of a psychological assessment or through the use of diagnostic screening procedures, such as the Dyslexia Adult Screening Test (DAST) (Fawcett and Nicolson, 1998), as well as attainment tests. Additionally, a structured interview with the student is extremely valuable.

FACTORS TO CONSIDER

Reid and Kirk (2001) suggest that a structured system of identification and assessment could include:

- initial screening and interview;
- cognitive assessment;
- diagnostic assessment;
- workplace and course needs assessment;
- implications for the course, student and/or workplace;
- recommendations for support;
- user-friendly report, which should have a clear summary attached.

There are a number of factors that need to be considered in an assessment and in the provision of support and feedback to the student. One of those factors involves organisational aspects, including how notes and information are organised, organisation of work diary and timetable, and an examination revision programme—these aspects can often present difficulties for students with dyslexia and can also be very time-consuming and, indeed, time-wasting. Other factors that are important include cognitive aspects such as memory and processing speed. These aspects have considerable implications for study and for examinations and would need to be considered in the support that is offered to the student. Metacognitive aspects that relate to the efficiency of learning, including transferring learning to new situations, are important for effective learning. Study skills, therefore, are important and some time needs to be spent with the student in exploring the most effective methods of studying for that particular student. Often, studying is very individual and strategies can vary depending on the student and, indeed, the nature of the course.

In general, students with dyslexia will display some difficulties in literacy. This may not be in reading accuracy, but very likely in speed of reading. Indeed, they may show a reluctance to read in general, and 'weighty' textbooks can be daunting. However, if the reading is structured this can make a considerable difference to the student's motivation to read. It should, however, be considered that the student will require additional time to complete some reading tasks.

PSYCHOLOGICAL ASSESSMENT

Usually, psychological assessment is conducted by using the Wechsler Adult Intelligence Scale (WAIS III) (Wechsler, 1999a). The subtests of the WAIS III are grouped according to indexes:

- verbal comprehension;
- vocabulary;
- similarities;
- information;
- performance organisation;
- picture completion;
- block design;
- matrix-reasoning;
- working memory;
- arithmetic;
- digit span;
- letter–number sequencing;
- processing speed;
- digit symbol-coding;
- symbol search.

Like the children's version, the WAIS III is also divided into verbal and performance IQ scores. Additionally, the WAIS III is co-normed with the Wechsler Memory Scale (WMS III) (Wechsler, 1999b), which can be useful in the assessment of adults with dyslexia.

THE WECHSLER MEMORY SCALE (WMS III)

This test is co-normed with the WAIS III described above. It can provide useful information on three main aspects of memory: immediate memory (both auditory and visual); general memory (delayed); and working memory, which involves letter number and spatial span. This can provide additional cognitive information, if required, on the memory processes.

The cognitive assessment needs to be supplemented by information on attainments. As well as the Wechsler test of adult reading, other adult reading and spelling tests are available. These include the Wide Range Achievement Test (WRAT3), which is a standardised assessment for use between the ages of 5 to 75 years and provides a reading and spelling level and a percentile score. There is an alternative form for retest purposes, and the complete battery can be administered in around 30 minutes. The norms are based on US samples and show good validity and reliability (Singleton, 1999a; McLoughlin et al., 1994).

SCREENING QUESTIONNAIRES AND CHECKLISTS

A great deal of information can be obtained from questionnaires and checklists, and there are a number of commercially available screening materials that can be suitable for initial identification.

Checklists

A checklist by definition suggests that 'one size fits all'. This, of course, is not the case with dyslexia, as it needs to be acknowledged that dyslexic people are individuals and they may not all show the same characteristics, nor to the same degree. They each have specific processing styles and these can be influenced by the environment. It has also been indicated that dyslexia is contextual, and, therefore, the degree of difficulty will depend on the study or work environment and, indeed, the nature of the task to be carried out.

A checklist could therefore be used as a guide rather than a definitive assessment tool. Smythe and Everatt (2001) have, however, developed a more sophisticated checklist, offering more detailed cognitive and processing information for dyslexia. Further and ongoing developments in this area offer considerable promise (Smythe and Everatt, pers. commun., 2002).

Kirk and Reid (2003) identified some of the difficulties associated with dyslexia in students—these can be used as a guide in the development of a checklist of study factors for students in further and higher education:

- difficulties in reading accuracy;
- speed-of-reading difficulties;
- persistent spelling errors;
- difficulties with grammatical structure;
- sequencing difficulties in words and in ideas;
- need to reread text;
- difficulties planning and organising written work;
- difficulty memorising facts;
- difficulty memorising formulae;
- taking notes in lectures;
- planning essays;
- study skills;
- transferring learning from one situation to another;
- noting inferences in texts;
- written examinations, particularly if timed;
- difficulty with technical words;
- difficulty identifying main points;
- short attention span;
- difficulty with proof-reading;
- unable to read aloud;
- poor sequencing, history, events, ordering information.

DYSLEXIA ADULT SCREENING TEST (DAST)

The Dyslexia Adult Screening Test (DAST) (Fawcett and Nicolson, 1998) is one of the established and successful screening tests for dyslexia in adults. It is user-friendly, takes around 30 minutes to administer and can provide a considerable amount of diagnostic data.

The DAST test consists of 11 subtests: rapid-naming; one-minute reading; postural stability; phonemic segmentation; two-minute spelling; backward span; nonsense passage; non-verbal reasoning; one-minute writing; verbal fluency; and semantic fluency.

The test incorporates aspects of the most recent research in dyslexia, particularly relating to the role of the cerebellum in relation to dyslexia, phonological processing and processing speed. The verbal fluency and semantic fluency tests can be useful and can relate more directly to some forms of occupations. As well as articulation these tests call for a degree of recall from long-term memory and organisational skills.

COMPUTER-SCREENING

Computer-screening can provide an easily accessible and accurate screening. Singleton (2001) suggests they provide a more precise measurement, especially when complex cognitive skills are being assessed. Although there are some disadvantages in terms of the extent of the diagnosis, particularly the impersonal aspect of computer-screening, it can have some advantages if used in conjunction with other assessment strategies. There are several computer-screening programs available and the following subsections describe two of them.

Lucid Adult Dyslexia Screening

The Lucid Adult Dyslexia Screening (LADS) (Singleton et al., 2002) is a computerised test designed to screen for dyslexia in persons of 16 years and older. It comprises four assessment modules: word recognition, word constructions, word memory and reasoning. It is suggested that the first three are dyslexia-sensitive measures. Each of the four modules takes around five minutes to complete and the tests are self-administered.

LADS is designed to be used for routine screening for dyslexia and individual screening in adults and can be used in universities and colleges as well as prison and youth offender units and employment centres. The LADS provides a categorisation of persons taking the test into 'low probability of dyslexia', 'borderline', 'moderate probability' and 'high probability'. The report provides a brief description of the results, and this method can provide a cost-effective initial screening for dyslexia.

StudyScan

StudyScan (Zdienski, 1997) is a computerised screening programme that also incorporates a shorter version called 'QuickScan'. QuickScan consists of 100 questions and takes around 15 minutes to administer. The responses to the yes/no questions provide information on whether the adult has dyslexic characteristics and provides information on their learning style as well. StudyScan was developed specifically for the student population.

ASSESSMENT: THE EFFECT

One of the objectives of conducting and assessment is to identify whether or not the student has dyslexia. This is important in terms of securing the additional allowances that students with dyslexia are entitled to, such as extra time for examinations. Additionally, however, an assessment needs to provide students with some specific strategies that may be appropriate in relation to their profile and the needs of their course.

Feedback

It is also important to spend some time after the assessment ensuring that the student is clear on the results and the implications of the assessment. It can be quite daunting for students to be assessed for a 'disability', and the results may come as a surprise to some students. Often, however, many students who are diagnosed as dyslexic for the first time at university usually, though not always, have a suspicion that they have dyslexic difficulties. Nevertheless, it is still important to provide full and informative feedback, which may well take the form of a counselling session. It is important that feedback should be clear and jargon-free. It may be necessary at this point to provide the student with encouragement; they may wish to meet other students with dyslexia perhaps in the form of a study skills group. It is important also to emphasise that dyslexia is simply a difference in how information is processed and in some situations it may be a disability, but the disability aspect does not need to take prominence. There are many encouraging accounts from students with dyslexia, who are now employed in a range of occupations and there are many examples of successes (Reid and Kirk, 2001). For example, Reid and Kirk record how one student, who still experienced anxiety over his studies, commented on the positive aspects of tutorials. Indicating that he likely over-prepared for tutorials and read too much, he found that his experiences in life and in coming to terms with his dyslexia helped him in tutorials. He felt this gave him a balanced perspective on some issues. At the same time, it is important to learn from unfortunate experiences endured by some students with dyslexia. Reid and Kirk (2001) report on one student Vanessa, who 'received a computer, but little else' (pp. 168–170). She indicated that she was not shown how to use it, and indeed the computer that she received was not the most appropriate for the course. To make matters worse, she did not actually receive the computer until the start of her second year. The message here is the need to ensure there is effective communication and follow-up after the assessment. The student needs to be in open and accessible contact with those who can provide advice and support throughout the whole period of the student's studies, not just immediately after the assessment. It is also important that dyslexia does not represent being given a computer—this can be an easy option and, while a computer can be helpful in most instances, it is important that the other needs of the student, including emotional needs, are not forgotten. Additionally, the student needs to have the opportunity to speak with a member of the computer staff who can advise on the most appropriate computer and software.

EXPERIENCE OF FURTHER AND HIGHER EDUCATION

For some students, entry into further and higher education can present a challenge to their long-standing perception of themselves (Ivanic, 1998). Many can be intimidated by 'academia', and their self-esteem can be adversely affected. It is important, therefore, that course tutors and all teaching staff are familiar with dyslexia and how dyslexia may affect a person's self-esteem. This is important when the tutor is giving feedback to students following an assignment, as often the student with dyslexia has very likely spent more time than others in the preparation of the essay and will become very discouraged if the results do not equate with this effort. For that reason it is crucial that students are aware of how they performed and how they can develop their skills for subsequent assignments.

One-to-one feedback is essential in order to highlight the strengths and the weaknesses of the written assignment. Some aspects of the written assignment that may need to be commented on are:

- spelling;
- grammar;
- organisation;
- introduction;
- relevance of argument;
- use of evidence;
- the extent to which the question has been answered;
- examples of how the arguments could be developed.

Throughout the feedback an opportunity should also be provided for dyslexic students to develop the essay and the arguments orally. This can boost their confidence for subsequent essays.

It is important for the tutor to appreciate that dyslexic students will often take longer than other students to plan and complete a written piece of work. A pre-assignment discussion to help the student talk through some of the main issues would be helpful, as would an interim discussion on progress. The student may need some precise guidance on reading, as it is important that the dyslexic student does not waste time in reading aspects of a book that are not totally relevant.

Pollak (2001a) refers to both the views and feelings of the students and the challenges facing academic institutions. He suggests that it is necessary to consider the self-image of the student with dyslexia, but that this also presents a challenge to the higher education sector to accommodate to students whose sense of identity is challenged not only by the label 'dyslexic' but also by academic writing in general.

PRE-COURSE SUPPORT

Waterfield (1996) provides some suggestions of supports that institutions can provide to help dyslexic students prior to actual commencement of the course. These include access to open days, informal information days for potential students, an 'action line' available to dyslexic applicants and an information handbook for students with disabilities such as dyslexia. In the UK there are also Access Centres and a national network of disability co-ordinators.

While these pre-entry supports can be of great benefit to the applicant with dyslexia, quite often the completion of the application form, which is usually done without support from the institution, can present some difficulties. In addition to application completion, the difficulty of course selection, which often necessitates a considerable amount of reading about course information, can also be a problem (McLoughlin et al., 1994).

THE APPLICATION FORM

The actual application form, therefore, can present a difficulty and, in particular, the less structured parts of the application. For example, the section in the form relating to 'additional information which may support the application' is usually open-ended, and dyslexic applicants may have difficulty in providing the most relevant information to support their application, unless some structure or detailed guidance is provided. If no structure or subheadings are provided, the dyslexic student should attempt to draft some subheadings before completing this section. This should also be helpful in preparing students with dyslexia for an eventual interview as it will help to organise their thoughts.

Additional Information to Support the Application

Before completing this section the dyslexic student should consider:

- What skills do you think are necessary for the course?
- In what way has your previous experiences helped you develop these skills?
- Why do you think these skills would help you in your course?
- What would you wish to achieve through your experiences gained from this course?
- In what way do you think the course would help you achieve this?

Make two lists on your page—on the left-hand side the skills/experiences you have already acquired and on the right-hand side the skills/experience you think would be helpful for the course for which you have applied. Compare the two lists. Look at what you still need and write down how you can eventually acquire these skills/experiences.

THE INTERVIEW

The actual interview itself can often be seen as an ordeal for most applicants, but perhaps more so for dyslexic applicants. Many factors are important during interviews, such as being able to identify key points in questions and respond appropriately; these may present some difficulty for dyslexic students. Gilroy (1995a) offers very clear guidance to dyslexic students applying to higher education and suggests some interview questions that may be asked of the dyslexic student applying for a university course of study:

- Why have you chosen to study this subject?
- Why have you chosen this department?
- What do you see yourself doing when you graduate?
- What do you do in your spare time?
- Can you explain to us what dyslexia is?
- How does it affect your work?
- How did you find out that you were dyslexic?
- What kind of support do you need?

SUPPORTS

Models of Supports

There are different models of supports that can be utilised at colleges and universities. Kirk and Reid (2003) refer to the individual and social models of perceiving a disability, and these perspectives often determine the type of support that is available. Essentially, support should incorporate all perspectives. This means that student skills in relation to both learning and studying need to be developed, but the responsibility should be shared by the institution and the staff. Courses, course presentation and the assessment criteria need to be dyslexia-friendly. Many students with dyslexia find written assignments, note-taking in lectures and the pace of study in some courses quite challenging. Academic writing can be a difficult skill for the student with dyslexia to acquire, although with practice and full and constructive feedback over time this skill can be acquired.

Pollak (2001a) refers to the different models of perceiving academic writing developed by Lea and Street (2000), such as the 'study skills' model, which proposes that there is a potential student deficit in the technical skill of writing; and the 'academic socialisation' model, which implies that students can be acclimatised into academic discourse. Pollak suggests these models can be related to different perspectives of support offered to students with dyslexia.

The 'study skills' model views difficulties with student learning as a kind of 'disorder' within the student that needs to be treated. Pollak argues that this view can be equated to the 'disability model' noted in many academic institutions. This notion of disability is further emphasised through the funding arrangements in the UK that usually sees learning support staff in higher education placed within a 'disability office' or unit. Additionally, support for students is usually arranged through the Disability Students Allowances Scheme, and this further emphasises the notion of disability and, indeed, can be equated to the medical–deficit-type model of dyslexia. The 'academic socialisation' model, on the other hand, according to Pollak focuses on the role of a student's learning strategies or style in the process of acculturation into academic discourse. This, Pollak suggests, parallels the discourse of dyslexia that sees it as a 'difference', rather than a deficit.

Universities and colleges that have refined their definition of 'study skills', focus more on student adjustment to learning or interpretation of the task of learning. This places responsibility for supporting students with dyslexia on course tutors, the management and those developing the programme of study and the assessment criteria.

This is similar to the paradigm identified by Reid and Kirk (2001) that highlights the individual and the social model of perceiving dyslexia. The 'individual model' focuses on the individual and the individual's difficulties, such as the inability to undertake certain tasks like note-taking, proof-reading, following instructions, meeting deadlines, using libraries, accuracy in typing and poor organisation. On the other hand, the 'social model' implies that adaptations can be made to tasks and the study environment to make the course and the institution dyslexia-friendly. This means that the dyslexic person would cope without necessarily accessing additional support, such as open learning, materials written in a dyslexia-friendly style, information provided in a variety of means, oral assessment rather than written examinations and lecture theatres, libraries and other facilities that have been made dyslexia-friendly.

Perceptions of Support

It is certainly necessary for universities and colleges to make support provision available for students, but as can be noted by the comments above this support needs to be accepted by the student and the label that is often attached to that support needs to be accepted by all—both in education and in the workplace. It is often a concern of students that, although they may get the support throughout their course, their aim is to secure employment and they often harbour concerns about how their 'disability' will affect their career opportunities. While this is a legitimate concern, it should not be a reality because all professions, even those with rigid traditional recruitment histories such as some aspects of the medical profession, are now becoming increasingly aware of dyslexia. There are now examples of examinations for medical consultants and the armed forces becoming dyslexia-friendly (Reid and Kirk, 2001).

Yet, attitudes can take a long time to change and, although some professions have moved forward, there are still examples of young people with dyslexia experiencing difficulty in the few professions where attitudes appear more inflexible. Yet, people with dyslexia can often show more empathy to others especially in the caring and teaching profession, as they themselves have experienced difficulty and usually are in the process of overcoming their difficulty. Therefore, they often relate to others more effectively.

Riddock (2001) interviewed a number of practising teachers and trainee teachers with dyslexia about their experiences of teaching, training and the specific coping strategies they have adopted in the classroom. They were all asked if (and how) their own experiences of literacy difficulties had influenced the way they teach children, and especially those with literacy difficulties. All the participants reported using a number of effective coping strategies and felt that on balance the advantages of being dyslexic outweighed the disadvantages in terms of giving them greater empathy and understanding of children's problems. The majority felt that their own very negative experiences of school had been a strong motivating factor in wanting to teach in order to give children a better educational experience than their own.

Yet, despite that, many trainee and new teachers were reluctant to admit to being dyslexic. Riddock argues that in a climate of inclusion a more enabling and open attitude to teachers with dyslexia should be adopted in order that trainee teachers do not harbour a fear that they are in some way inferior to colleagues because of their dyslexia. Riddock points out that in the USA similar concerns have been expressed about the conflict between making accommodations for student teachers with learning disabilities and the demand for teachers with high literacy and numeracy standards (Wertheim et al., 1998). She suggests it is not surprising that there is a high percentage of trainee teachers who are dyslexic not declaring their disability on application, because of fear of rejection. However, it is the policy in all institutions in the UK not to discriminate against an applicant on the basis of any disability including dyslexia. Nevertheless, Riddock's findings suggest that a substantial proportion of students feel that they need to hide their disability, perhaps also feeling that their employment prospects may be disadvantaged by revealing their dyslexia. At the same time, there are many examples of students, including trainee teachers, obtaining support and empathy both in training and in the profession (Reid and Kirk 2001).

COPING STRATEGIES

People with dyslexia, whether students or in the workplace, usually find their own way of coping with situations that can put demands on them. Many of these coping strategies are individual for that person, but it is often informative to learn from the experiences of others in similar positions. Support groups can therefore be of some benefit to the adult with dyslexia. Usually, local organisations have help lines (Reid and Kirk, 2001), and these can often provide on-the-spot advice. Jameson (1999) suggests that support groups should have a programme encapsulating four choices: a discussion group for adult dyslexic people only; an open discussion group that welcomes partners and friends; a programme of invited speakers; or a mixture of the above. She also suggests that a support group should have a development plan that encapsulates a mission statement, keeps a record of activities and obtains charitable status.

Riddock et al. (1999) suggest that dyslexic adults have relatively low self-esteem and, significantly, that this low self-esteem is not confined to academic self-esteem. This would imply that support may be needed in relation to a number of life factors and, particularly, at critical and vulnerable points of people's lives, such as when they are moving job or house. This means that literacy is only one aspect of a much bigger picture, and low self-esteem can affect performance in a range of life skills.

Often, people with dyslexia will expend more effort perhaps than is necessary for a task and, in fact, over-prepare. This was the view of a student interviewed by Reid and Kirk (2001) who suggested he over-prepared for tutorials and did not use all the materials he had prepared. Often, in fact, this is due to poor organisation—perhaps the difficulty in identifying the key points. The student may have notes of relevant information, but lacks the general headings—the key points within which to contextualise these notes. This makes retrieval difficult, especially in a tutorial situation where it can involve a free flow-type of discussion.

Riddock (2001) asked teachers about the kind of coping strategies they used in the classroom. They stressed the importance of extra preparation and advance preparation. She cites one trainee teacher remarking that 'preparation is power'. Many, however, always carried a spellchecker or dictionary with them.

She comments that, although all the trainee teachers had developed effective coping strategies, they were fearful of negative reactions from schools and would have welcomed support, such as mentoring or advice from experienced teachers with dyslexia.

INSTITUTIONAL SUPPORTS

Institutional supports should be enabling, not compensatory. This means that every effort should be made to enable students to manage their own learning and determine their own model of support. The overriding principle, therefore, is essentially facilitating, rather than compensatory.

Cottrell (1996, 1999) suggests that a number of considerations need to be made before making recommendations for support. She argues that there is a common misconception that 'dyslexia' equals 'computer' and that is all that is necessary to support dyslexic students. It is important to appreciate that there are a range of supports that are available and that these supports should be suggested in relation to the difficulties the student experiences throughout the course. Cottrell suggests that disability *is* related to context and that institutional settings may reduce the effects of dyslexia.

Kirk (2002) has developed both a programme of individual student study supports and a comprehensive programme of staff development, staff awareness and student support groups. She suggests that it is important to communicate with individual course tutors and directors of study. Communication and staff development, she suggests, can help to change attitudes regarding the notion of dyslexia as a disability. She sees her role as a dyslexia co-ordinator as a facilitator of this attitude change.

STUDY SKILLS

There are a number of factors that can contribute to the dyslexic student succeeding in further and higher education. The key areas include preparation for examinations, successfully completing essays, preparation for tutorials, being able to access re sources, effective note-taking in lectures and learning from others, such as course tutors and other course members. In addition to the above factors, dyslexic students need to be familiar with the means and processes for accessing additional support and resources, should they be required. Sutherland and Smith (1997), in a large-scale research study involving secondary schools, showed how the use of laptop computers improved the quality of written work and the general confidence of the dyslexic student. It is important, therefore, that this facility be provided and encouraged in further and higher education.

Stacey (2001) suggests the technique of mindset (Russell, 1979) can be helpful for the student with dyslexia. This is a process through which the mind is 'energised' to be receptive specifically to the new information that a student is going to study. It is essentially metacognitive and involves the reactivation of ideas and experiences, and attempts to bridge current knowledge with the new information to be learnt. This preparation can help to enhance comprehension.

Other strategies, according to Stacey, that can be useful include the use of Mind Maps©, flow charts, diagrams, pictures and identifying keywords. Certainly, being able to recognise and use keywords can help with note-taking as well as with recall. It is also important that the student is aware of the purpose of the task. Certainly, preparation for a tutorial will require a different approach from that of preparing for an essay. In both tasks the key points would be needed, but the essay would need to refer to wider literature, have a structured introduction and extend the argument into coherent paragraphs. Often, in tutorials the key points followed by a list of examples of evidence including sources can be enough, as essentially a tutorial should be seen as preparation in the development of one's thinking. It is probably preferable to enter a tutorial with the facts and being in a position to discuss these points with others—this process will help the student develop a hypothesis and should extend and justify their thinking in the subject.

ESSAY-WRITING

McLoughlin et al. (1994, 2002) highlight some of the difficulties dyslexic students can encounter in a course of study and suggest some strategies for dealing with these. Some problems include lack of confidence and feelings of inferiority, verbal and written communication problems, difficulties in time-keeping, poor memory, lack of organisational skills, coping with large volumes of reading, poor concentration and being unaware of spelling errors. Most of these aspects could also have some bearing on perhaps one of the most important aspects of a course of study—essay-writing.

Essay-writing can place considerable demands on the student, and often most of the effort seems to be used for the reading—that is, the content of the essay rather than the method (i.e., the process of writing an essay). Some, but certainly not all, universities and colleges spend time with students looking at how to write academic essays—for many students this process can be assimilated fairly readily and normally marks a logical extension of the type of essays and work they have done at school. For students with dyslexia, however, this is not the case. It is not uncommon for students with dyslexia, even in third and subsequent years, to display persistent difficulties with the structure and organisation of essays. It is, therefore, well worth the effort to spend time with a student to explain how to approach the writing of an essay.

As indicated above, students with dyslexia may have particular difficulty in identifying key points and may also lack confidence in presenting a written answer. This can contribute to an abbreviated argument that does not reflect the student's background reading, effort or abilities.

Selecting the Essay Question

There are a number of ground rules about selecting a topic. In an exam and also in a course essay it is important not to waste too much time selecting an actual question. Additionally, once a decision has been made on the actual question to be tackled, it is important to adhere to that and not change to another question midway through researching the question.

It can be useful to write down a few points on each of the questions you think you are in a position to tackle. This should just take a few minutes, but will give you experience in interpreting and understanding essay questions. This in itself is a useful skill that needs to be practised. It also allows you to make an actual decision, perhaps based on your current knowledge of the topic, your interest and your understanding of what is actually being asked.

What Is the Question Asking?

Before actually reading and researching the question you will need to identify the key areas that should be examined in your reading and, specifically, exactly what the question is asking. This will provide you with a starting point to guide you with your reading; you should keep referring back to the actual question periodically to ensure you are still on track.

What Do I Need to Read?

The reading stage is probably the stage that will be most time-consuming. It will provide you with the content for your answer, but it is important that you select your reading carefully, otherwise valuable time may be lost through irrelevant reading.

It is probably useful to identify a core text, perhaps a general one, but one that will provide you with much of the information you may need. Throughout your reading of the main texts you should write down the key points and all the issues that relate to the question. This can also provide you with the opportunity of revisiting the question.

Note-taking

This is a very individual exercise, but it is important that you organise your notes under each of the key points you have identified. It is important to remember that organisation of your information starts during the initial stages of your reading and not after you find yourself with pages and pages of scrambled notes. The actual amount of notes taken varies from individual to individual, but the key point is their relevance in terms of the question. If the notes are organised into relevant aspects relating to the question, this will help considerably when you are writing the essay.

Having a framework for your reading also helps in the selection of additional material, from perhaps research articles or specialist books. You will have a fairly good idea of what you are looking for, so time wasted on irrelevant reading will be minimized.

At this stage it is also important to make a note of all specific references you use, rather than attempt to locate them on completion of the written essay.

Writing the Essay

It is not unusual for students with dyslexia to show some reluctance to put 'pen to paper' or unnecessarily delay the writing stage. Writing the essay in draft form should in fact take place as you progress with the reading. After each stage of reading it is a good idea to write some implications or arguments that can be readily integrated into the finished essay. So, writing, at least in the initial draft, should take place at the same time as your reading. The stages involved in writing an essay are shown below.

Stages of Essay-writing

Introduction

The introduction can be the most important part of an essay and should, therefore:

- identify the key points in relation to the topic;
- very briefly provide an answer to the actual question;
- provide a plan on how the question will be answered.

The introduction should, therefore, provide a framework for your answer, and a good introduction will help considerably in providing the detail of your answer in the main part of your essay.

The Main Part

The main part of your essay should essentially follow the key points outlined in your introduction. You should, therefore, continually refer back to your introduction to ensure that your argument is relevant to the points made in the introduction and the actual essay question. The main part should consist of argument and evidence on each of the points and always in relation to the actual question. It is important to support each point you make with well-referenced evidence and to use a paragraph for each argument and point.

Conclusion

A good conclusion is an essential part of your essay. It should be a reinterpretation of your introduction, but with the addition of some of the points you make in the main part of the essay. The conclusion should also leave the reader in no doubt as to your answer to the essay question.

References

It is important to write down references throughout the reading stage of your essay. You may also wish to write down page numbers for your own benefit in case you need to refer back to the original source.

Your course tutor would very likely provide you with an acceptable referencing format, but if in any doubt you could refer to some of the standard books in your subject and use the referencing style of these books.

Coles (1995), in a particularly helpful book, describes some stages of essay-writing for students in general:

- choosing the question;
- initial planning;
- understanding what is being asked;
- the essay plan;
- reading and note-taking;
- additional material;
- organise the main stages of the argument;
- break the subject down into its main topic areas;
- organise each main section;
- add the detail;
- divide each main stage of the arguments into separate paragraphs;
- write the introduction;
- first final draft;
- write the conclusion;
- final draft;
- edit it at least twice.

This can provide a useful framework for the student with dyslexia. Drafting and editing is, of course, extremely important. There are many other study skills texts, such as Cotterill (1999), that are very informative and can provide many ideas and suggestions for essay-writing, and other study aids that will be useful for the student with dyslexia.

THE WORKPLACE

The models of support that can be adopted in the workplace also follow the same pattern and come up against the same kind of issues that are found in education settings. Employers can make adaptations to tasks, provide dyslexia-friendly equipment and make the work environment dyslexia-friendly, which will benefit all employees, or they may make 'special arrangements' for dyslexic people, which often leaves individuals with dyslexia feeling that they have been provided with favours and privileges. If special arrangements are put in place for the person with dyslexia, it is important that the individual should not be reminded of this even if they make a dyslexic-type error. Often, people with dyslexia can be quite sensitive, and some work tasks, particularly those that may require a degree of sequencing and accuracy, can be stressful.

Kirk and Reid (2003) identified a number of work factors that could be demanding for people with dyslexia in the workplace:

- difficulty following a number of instructions if given at the same time;
- following a technical manual;
- reading reports quickly;
- writing short memos;
- recalling telephone numbers;
- remembering what was said at meetings;
- filing documents;
- visual orientation;
- hand–eye co-ordination difficulties may result in poor presentation of work;
- reporting at meetings;
- diary-keeping;
- frustration, anger or embarrassment in the workplace;
- difficulty doing more than one task at the same time, such as speaking on the phone and writing messages.

Many of these can be overcome by careful and sensitive management, which would ensure the person with dyslexia is not overexposed to these situations.

Moody (1999) explains that the weaknesses of people with dyslexia that can affect efficiency at work include:

- *literacy skills*—following a technical manual, reading reports quickly and writing memos in clear English;
- *memory*—remembering telephone numbers and recalling what was said at meetings;

- *sequencing ability*—difficulty in filing documents in correct place and looking up entries in dictionaries and directories;
- *visual orientation*—may have difficulty dealing with maps;
- *hand–eye co-ordination*—can result in poor presentation of written work and figures;
- *speech*—may talk in a disorganised way, especially at meetings and on the telephone;
- *organisational skills*—may miss appointments and their work area can look disorganised;
- *emotional factors*—may display anger, embarrassment and anxieties.

FACTORS TO CONSIDER

Assessment and Feedback

The assessment and, particularly, the feedback are as important in the workplace as they are in educational settings. Payne (1997) suggests aspects such as knowledge of learning styles, understanding job descriptions, knowledge of strategies that have already been developed and views on disclosure should all be discussed with the dyslexic person at the time of the assessment and certainly be part of the feedback process. In a UK study, Reid and Kirk (2000) also revealed the need to focus on metacognitive skills by asking the individual how a task was performed.

As in Payne's US study, Reid and Kirk found that in many instances the dyslexic person had compensated for their difficulty exceptionally well, and while this is very positive for the individual concerned it does make it more difficult to diagnose. Assessment, however, should not be solely clinical and needs to be contextualised. In the UK a survey revealed that workplace assessment is the key factor in a dyslexia assessment because many of the difficulties are situational (Reid et al., 1999).

The dyslexic difficulties experienced by the individual can, in fact, become more obvious depending on the type of employment or career choice. Knowledge of dyslexia and the dyslexia assessment process can have implications for career counselling. This has implications for employment, yet only a few career counsellors have an adequate knowledge and understanding of dyslexia.

INITIATIVES

Young (2001) provides very positive comments on initiatives in the USA. He reports how the federal government has sponsored a series of grants, pilot projects and national working groups that have focused on how adults with learning disabilities can be best served in such programmes as adult literacy and job-training. These efforts, according to Young, have led to the development of an overall design for programmes such as these. Young suggests the following elements as contributory to a successful programme:

- screening—using valid screening tools;
- diagnostic testing using appropriate measurements that take into account race, class, gender—this should include recommendations on accommodations and assistive technology, accommodations in job-training programmes, adult education programmes and work;
- trained case managers, who are trained to understand what the diagnostic reports mean and have the resources needed to provide for accommodations and assistive technology;
- community links—government and community-based programmes in association with trained employers who understand learning disabilities and their impact on the individual;
- ongoing support—such as job-coaching, mentoring, literacy skill development and on-the-job personal relationship training;
- consumer empowerment throughout the whole process—Young suggests that where the consumer is informed and participates in the process, with informed consent, for screening and testing and in development of employment options, this will help in the development of skills in self-advocacy and enhance the possibilities of a successful outcome.

BDA/FORD MOTOR COMPANY

Another promising initiative in relation to the workplace was the joint initiative between the British Dyslexia Association and Ford Motor Company that culminated in a conference 'Dyslexia and Employment: Making It Work', held at the Ford Motor Product and Development Centre in Dunton, Essex, UK in October 2002. The conference, at which one of the guest speakers was Sir Jackie Stewart, was attended by a range of employers and representatives from the management, training and recruitment areas. It also marked the launch of the BDA's employability campaign. The objectives of the campaign are:

- to recognise that dyslexia often brings qualities and talents as well as challenges;
- to examine the five key principles (see below) that will guide the BDA's approach to help employers become 'dyslexia-wise'.

The five key principles identified by the BDA for the campaign were:

1   'Understand what dyslexia is'—to promote an understanding of dyslexia through a programme of awareness-raising.
2   'Ensure access to information'—to highlight the most dyslexia-friendly forms of written communication in terms of readability and presentation.
3   'Identify the issues in your workplace'—to encourage employers to assess the balance between written and non-written communication, to review key documents, such as health and safety policy and job descriptions, and to consider physical aspects of the office environment, such as lighting and desk layout.

4   'Develop specialist knowledge and support'—this principle aims to encourage employers to ensure that assessment and screening facilities can be readily accessed by staff who may need them and to seek out opportunities from government that are designed to promote staff development.

5   'Create a culture of confidence'—this principle encourages employers to provide the means whereby people with dyslexia can be open about their dyslexia, without fear of embarrassment. This principle encourages employers to appreciate the benefits that different learning and working styles can bring to a team (BDA/Ford Motor Company, 2002).

THE DYSLEXIA AND DYSPRAXIA TOOLKIT (KEY 4 LEARNING 2002)

Another interesting initiative is the above toolkit. The toolkit is more than a package of dos and don'ts, but a well-constructed and comprehensive attempt to ensure that 'change' takes place from within an organisation and is employer-led. The toolkit states that the individual cannot make change alone and that organisations and management need to understand and adapt to obtain the best from their staff. This toolkit, which has been pioneered in government departments, is now available to a range of industries. It consists of an accessible information source about dyslexia and dyspraxia (and is being extended to include ADHD, Asperger's syndrome and Autistic Spectrum disorder). It also contains descriptions of particular work-based difficulties, strategies and tactics for solutions as well as screening checklists, an overview of disability legislation and advice for different departments within an organisation, such as training, management and recruitment. The value of this type of toolkit is that it can be proactive and encourage employers to become aware of their role in providing for people with dyslexia or dyspraxia.

CONCLUDING COMMENT

There a number of key factors that affect adults with dyslexia in both education and in the workplace, many of which are very similar. The situations may differ, but the need for support, for a common understanding and for a positive and constructive attitude toward dyslexia is the same, irrespective of the setting. It is too easy to become complacent when supports have been set and funding secured—these aspects are by no means the answer, but can provide a pathway toward equality and success for all adults with dyslexia. It is important, however, to consider 'dyslexia' within the wider notion of equality, whether it be gender, race or culture, and ensure that, in fact, equality does prevail. The key factor in relation to the implications of disability legislation, workplace policies and course arrangements on dyslexia is that there should be understanding and an acknowledgement on the part of all employers, course managers and administrators that adults with dyslexia are not being *supported*, but, in fact, are being *accepted*. Only with this acceptance can real equality be achieved.

Chapter 13

Multilingualism and Dyslexia

CHALLENGES AND ISSUES

Multilingualism is an area that can present a challenge to those involved in assessment and teaching of children and adults with dyslexia. Recently, there has been much interest in this area, and many writers, researchers and teachers have put forward opinions on what can and should be done. This area presents a challenge because it has been neglected for too long. Additionally, although considerable advances were being made during the 1990s in teacher-friendly assessment and teaching materials based on current research on dyslexia, it was in many cases assumed that these materials would be suitable for all children with dyslexic difficulties, irrespective of their cultural and social background.

The British Psychological Working Party Report (BPS, 1999a) emphasises the importance of culturally relevant materials for children with dyslexia and, particularly, culture-fair assessment. Dyslexia, the report suggests, may be 'masked by limited mastery of the language of tuition' (p. 60). It is acknowledged in the report that dyslexia can occur across languages, cultures, socio-economic status, race and gender. Yet, the report notes that the tools needed to uncover the masking of dyslexic difficulties are not readily available. Furthermore, the message that this gives to teachers is that the key reason why a child is not acquiring literacy skills in the language being taught is because of the bilingual dimension, and not due to any other factor such as dyslexia.

It is interesting to take account of the views of teachers on this issue. Landon (2001) reports on a paper by Smyth (2000) who suggests that there is a dominant cultural model, which she terms the 'Master Model'. This model suggests that bilingual pupils need to become monolingual in order to succeed, and those, according to Smyth, who do not fit the master model are problematic and require learning support. This is, in fact, consistent with what Reed (2000) calls self-serving agendas, which are attitudes and practices that in fact work against the development of culture-fair assessment and teaching practices. Reed suggests that the only way to avoid the risk, for example, of restrictive assessment practices is to develop a comprehensive contextual assessment framework that explores cultural as well as language factors.

Landon (2001) reports on a number of studies (CRE, 1996; Deponio et al., 2000b) that have revealed a relatively low percentage of bilingual learners diagnosed with dyslexia compared with the incidence of dyslexia in the population as a whole and a high incidence of reading failure among children acquiring literacy through a language other than their home language (Cline and Cozens, 1999). The MacPherson Report (MacPherson of Cluny, 1999) draws attention to the unconscious norms that continue to operate within our society, which can exclude and certainly disadvantage people from ethnic groups. The Report comments on institutional racism and suggests that this can be detected in processes, attitudes and behaviours that amount to discrimination through unwitting prejudice and ignorance. This can certainly apply to the identification of dyslexia, as the knowledge of how to assess children from ethnic backgrounds is not widely available and the prevalent use of tests that are standardised on monolingual populations illustrate this.

There are, therefore, a number of key issues that need to be addressed in terms of policy and practice before teachers can feel adequately prepared to meet the diverse needs of diverse groups of children who may have 'masked' dyslexic difficulties. There is also a responsibility to prevent a child being misdiagnosed (false positive) by describing the child as having a learning difficulty when one is not present (Peer and Reid, 2000). This chapter therefore will discuss some of the issues raised above and provide some pointers and principles for teachers in order to acknowledge and appreciate the role of the dual dimensions of dyslexia and multilingualism.

IDENTIFICATION

One of the key challenges facing educators in relation to bilingualism and dyslexia is that of identification. This is a challenge because syndromes such as dyslexia do not occur for only one reason—usually, there are a number of factors that contribute to the presence of this type of literacy difficulty, and if a child is also bi/multilingual then this will be an added factor that needs to be taken into account throughout the assessment. As indicated earlier, many assessment strategies and tests do not explicitly take this into account. It has been noted that cultural and language factors in many standardised tests (Deponio et al., 2000a; Everatt et al., 2000) can mitigate against the child whose first language is not English. Many standardised assessment strategies have been developed for use with a monolingual population, and this can account for the underestimation or, indeed, the misdiagnosis of dyslexia in bilingual children. Landon (2001) addresses this by asking, 'what factors appear to lead to low rates of detection of dyslexia amongst bilingual learners and could the same factors also explain the poor standards of literacy amongst many learners of English as an Additional Language (EAL learners)?' The importance of these questions is that they actually investigate the issues and provide a good example of the types of questions teachers need to ask when assessing children who are bilingual.

To answer the questions presented by Landon one must consider the range of factors that contribute to dyslexia. It is important to acknowledge that culture-fair assessment can be of two types. It is important to develop assessment materials in the language being taught, but to make those materials culture-fair, and this may also involve a heavy visual emphasis. Additionally, it may be necessary to develop assessment materials in the first language of the child to assess whether dyslexia is present and affecting the development of skills in literacy in that first language.

Deponio et al. (2000a) suggest that children who are bilingual and dyslexic are doubly challenged. These children have to meet the demands of a curriculum that is not in their first language, as well as deal with the language and learning difficulties associated with dyslexia. They suggest this emphasises the need to identify dyslexic difficulties as opposed to difficulties occurring because of first language/second language confusions. In order for this to take place they suggest the education and learning context must acknowledge more vigorously than at present the multicultural context of school and society. Identification will not be effective if it is carried out within a context that is conceptualised in terms of a monolingual, monocultural population. Such a context will exclude bilingual children as it categorises them in terms of their linguistic and cultural differences.

CULTURAL FACTORS

Often, approaches that exist to meet their needs are considered to be separate and 'specialist' in nature, and this has the effect of excluding mainstream teachers from accepting the responsibility to meet the needs of bilingual learners alongside, and together with, the needs of monolingual learners. This, according to Deponio et al. (2000a), also excludes bilingual learners and their parents from being considered as an integral and proper part of the diverse school community.

Kelly (2002) suggests that teachers need to consult and collaborate with people who have a sound knowledge of the cultural background of the pupils in order to avoid confusing common second language errors of bilingual pupils with indicators of dyslexia. She suggests that these can sometimes overlap: as in the case of left–right confusion in Urdu, which is written from right to left; and with auditory discrimination with Punjabi speakers, who may have difficulty with 'p' and 'b'. Kelly suggests that it is important to consider information from parents as they will have a more complete picture of their child in a range of settings, including those not involving language skills. Kelly therefore suggests that teachers should be alerted if the child has a lack of interest in books, discrepancy between listening comprehension and reading skills, difficulties in acquiring automaticity, difficulties with balance, as well as persistent problems in phonological awareness despite adequate exposure to English.

In New Zealand, Mcfarlane et al. (2000) suggest, however, that there is little evidence that dyslexia is more or less prevalent among Maori than in any other ethnic group. They concede, however, that it is possible that some Maori have been wrongly labelled 'dyslexic', when they may have no or some other learning difficulty that could be better ascribed to other sources. They cite the research from Spreen (1988), which indicates that movement in and out of the 'dyslexic group' is due to a large number of variables that can potentially affect reading development: family background, behaviour variables and cognitive variables. Additionally, this view is further supported by the views of McNaughton (1995) on socialisation values that, he suggests, match home culture.

Although there are a number of screening and diagnostic tests used to assess dyslexic children, such as those described in Chapter 5, these are essentially directed at the monolingual population of dyslexic children, although there are data to suggest that the Phonological Assessment Battery (PhAB) can be applicable to other languages (Reason, 2002).

Some assessment procedures have been developed specifically for the bilingual learner (Sunderland et al., 1999). These focus on checklists, interview guidelines, diagnostic tests, and cultural and linguistic factors that may affect diagnosis. For example, they have developed an interview form for bilingual students that looks at: language history; schooling (primary and secondary); language–listening behaviours; reading (approaches used by the student); writing and spelling (planning strategies used and spelling approaches); Mathematics; memorisation difficulties; and spatial–temporal factors such as difficulties following directions, map-reading and following oral instructions. The interview schedule is extremely comprehensive and includes such aspects as visual and motor factors. Essentially, this process is a diagnostic interview and notes any considerations that should be put in place for the students, such as extra time in examinations. These procedures are extremely useful, not least because they are dedicated to assessing the bilingual learner but also because they provide follow-up guidance for teaching, which is a crucial element in all forms of assessment.

THE CONTEXT AND THE INDIVIDUAL

In addition to noting language and cognitive factors, it is important to take a student's learning context into account and to view the person as an individual. Many of the blanket approaches can yield informative screening and diagnostic data, but these need to be adapted and interpreted for each individual being assessed and any subsequent programme must take into account the person's learning style and learning context. Deponio et al. (2000a) therefore suggest some key issues in relation to assessing bi- or multilingual children:

- *Screening*—When should this take place and what is the nature of, and the criteria for, screening?
- *Diagnosis*—Can adapted, formal standardised tests be used successfully? How valid can they be with different populations of children?
- *Language*—Should we be focusing on dynamic, rather than static assessment for bilingual children. This takes into account elements of the test situation, such as language and links with teaching in scaffolding and building language concepts.
- *Learning style*—It is important to view the bilingual child as an individual learner and to take into account the particular learning styles of each individual and context. Is the learning environment conducive to the learner's cultural experiences and her or his cognitive style of learning. This can have implications for different cultures, as often there is a culture-dominant learning style. Mcfarlane

et al. (2000) discuss the learning style of the Maori people in New Zealand and suggest that Maori people view learning as a natural consequence of one's interaction with people and the environment. They have an oral tradition and the notion of the written counterpart to learning is a relatively recent phenomenon in Maori culture. Mcfarlane et al. argue that allowances must be made for different learning styles and teaching styles to ensure that the student's *mana* (integrity) is not devalued. Mcfarlane and Glynn (1998) contend that it is the right of Maori students to see their language, cultural knowledge and preferred learning styles legitimated within the classroom.

- *Learning context*—It is important to consider the educational context and the individual child's linguistic, educational and social history, when making a diagnosis (Hall, 1995). Dewsbury (1999), in discussing the First Steps Literacy Programme that was devised in Western Australia for early literacy acquisition, emphasised the importance of appreciating that 'linguistic behaviours do not necessarily represent cognitive development.' It is, therefore, important that a diagnosis should not draw conclusions about the child's cognitive abilities on the basis of performance and difficulties in literacy.
- *Personal*—It is important to take organisational difficulties and how the individual copes with everyday activities into account. Observation and interviews with parents and interviews with the individual can be useful in relation to acquiring this type of information.

CULTURE-FAIR ASSESSMENT

According to Cline (1998), this may represent the 'holy grail', but analysis of test performance within specific cultural and linguistic groups is important, as this can help to identify particular test items that consistently lead to cultural confusion or misperception. Landon (1999) suggests that the failure of a bilingual child, who is orally competent in the first language, to respond to pre-reading support in that language may be an indicator of a specific learning difficulty.

Mcfarlane et al. (2000) report on the New Zealand Literacy Taskforce (set up in March 1999), which made it clear that student achievement is influenced by personal, cultural, family and school factors. They report that the Taskforce was adamant that the expectations of the achievement of all children should be the same, regardless of the language of instruction or their ethnicity. This group also agreed that, although the goal is relevant and appropriate to children in Maori-medium education, the procedures and approaches for achieving the goal may well be different from those in English-medium education. This is a clear statement that makes no apologies for upholding the cultural and the linguistic needs of a specific group within society. Mcfarlane et al. suggest that there are many general features of learning to read and write that apply across countries, but some of these are specific to New Zealand, as the cultural context within New Zealand includes recognition of the educational and language needs of both Maori and non-Maori (deriving from obligations of the Treaty of Waitangi and such official policies as the recognition of both English and Te Reo Maori as official languages). It was interesting to note, therefore, that the Literacy Taskforce endorsed 11 principles of best practice of instruction, significant among which is the one that refers to teaching that takes account of children's linguistic and cultural backgrounds.

Mcfarlane et al. (2000) suggest that the complexity of human communication can lead to problems in accurately diagnosing actual linguistic difficulties in such groups as Maori children. In some cases, Maori children may have been assessed as experiencing literacy difficulties, yet can excel in reciting intricate and lengthy *waiata moteatea* (ancient song and verse), *whaikorero* (speech-making) and *karakia* (incantations). Additionally, they comment on the role of linguistic and cultural features of Maori communication as a factor that needs to be considered in a culture-fair assessment. Communication can operate through verbal units of sounds, syllables, words, sentences and discourses, but, they argue, non-verbal behaviours that have a cultural basis also need to be considered. Such non-verbal signals include facial expression, eye contact, proximity, tone of voice, pitch of voice, gestures, body movements and speech pace. These may have a more prominent role and communicative function in some cultural groups than others.

LANGUAGE DIFFERENCES

Smythe and Everatt (2001) suggest that any study that attempts to develop tests in different languages must first overcome translation problems. This requires experts in both languages to understand what the tests are trying to measure, rather than simply changing the wording from one language to another. For example, Smythe and Everatt suggest that a test of rhyming is unlikely to be a test of rhyming across several languages if direct word-for-word translations were implemented. Indeed, Wimmer and Goswami (1994) and Wimmer (1993) suggested that a universal model of reading was not possible and that the German language may not necessarily pass through the three stages of reading development—logographic, alphabetic and orthographic—but may omit the logographic stage of reading development.

Smythe (pers. commun., 2002) confirms this view by suggesting, following research in five countries, that it may be inappropriate to generalise research findings across languages and that any reporting should in fact always indicate the specific language context. Results, therefore, according to Smythe need to be contextualised in language and script.

Smythe and Everatt (2000) suggest a framework for testing in different languages. This framework is presented as a model that is derived from a review of research into dyslexia and the acquisition of reading, writing and spelling in different orthographies, as well as from an analysis of assessment tools available in different countries. The framework incorporates several theoretical perspectives based on subtypes of reading disability and factors associated with phonological processing skills (Fletcher et al., 1997; Wagner and Torgesen, 1987). Smythe and Everatt's model refers to the fragmentation and assembly of words, occurring on several different levels, such as the phoneme, syllable and rime–onset level. This has to be distinguished from the auditory system (which includes auditory discrimination, auditory perception, auditory sequential memory and auditory short-term memory). The model postulated by Smythe and Everatt also includes speed of processing (indicated by naming speed), as well as processes related to the visual system—such as visual discrimination, visual perception, visual sequential memory and visual short-term memory—and the semantic use of language.

Smythe and Everatt (2000) suggest that the differences in language construction and script in different languages can be a key factor in the acquisition of literacy, particularly for learners with dyslexia. They suggest that, in more regular orthographies, problems in the visual system or with short-term retention of initial sounds can lead to reading problems and that slow access of the meaning of the word may lead to poor understanding when placed in continuous text. They cite the example of a Hungarian child with reading problems who had few deficits in the area of phonological processing, yet still presented severe problems with acquiring accurate and fluent word reading. Smythe and Everatt suggest that an understanding of the language script is necessary in order to identify the reasons why the child was not acquiring literacy skills.

Focusing on the Welsh language, Forbes and Powell (2000) describe some of the language issues encountered when developing literacy assessment measures for a population, such as that in parts of Wales, who are exposed to two different languages at levels that may vary widely both within and between home and school. They suggested, therefore, that test materials for young pupils should not contain items that might discriminate against some children because of their unfamiliarity with language forms more prevalent in other parts of Wales, particularly across the North–South dialectal divide. Some of the key factors to emerge from the subsequent development and piloting of the test included the need to use a 'comic' format, a storyline that involves school, appropriate print size and inclusion of as many pictures as possible.

TEACHING

Teaching approaches should consider the child's strengths as well as noting the difficulties experienced by the child. Additionally, it is important that any Individual Educational Programme (IEP) that is developed is a result of wide-ranging deliberation between professionals and parents. Many of the teaching approaches advocated will be an adaptation of those suggested earlier in this book for monolingual dyslexic learners, and it is important that this adaptation occurs following consultation with school staff, support staff and specialist teachers. This type of programme should contain many different strands, including phonological awareness and reading through analogy. Although these approaches can be offered within a programme for the whole class, it is important that they are contextualised for the bilingual child. However, as Deponio et al. (2000a) indicate, care should be taken to note that some bilingual learners may have difficulty articulating some sounds, especially English vowels and final consonantal morphemes, and speakers of syllable-timed languages such as Cantonese, may have difficulty in hearing unstressed syllables in stress-timed English utterances. Previous experience of reading logographic, as opposed to alphabetic, script may also cause difficulties with analogical reading for a literate Chinese pupil (Goswami and Bryant, 1990). Therefore, more practice in recognising rhyme and syllable may be necessary for learners from certain language backgrounds.

THINKING SKILLS

It is important to consider the development of higher order thinking skills when teaching children with dyslexia. This equally applies to dyslexic children who are bilingual as well as those who are not. Programmes involving thinking skills are important elements in this, and there may be a tendency to overlook these types of programmes in preference for a more direct decoding–literacy acquisition-type of intervention. Dynamic assessment offers an opportunity to utilise a thinking skills paradigm, as it encourages responses relating to what the child does know and how the learner actually processes information, as well as the level and type of conceptual knowledge the learner has acquired. This approach essentially links assessment and teaching and highlights the child's learning process. Usmani (1999) suggests the bilingual, bicultural child may have a broad range of thinking skills, which may go undetected if the professional is unaware of the cultural values or fails to understand them in relation to the assessment and teaching programme.

CULTURAL VALUES

Usmani further suggests that the 'big dip' in performance noted in some bilingual children in later primary education may be explained by a failure of professionals to understand and appreciate the cultural values and the actual level of competence of the bilingual child, particularly in relation to conceptual development and competence in thinking skills. Landon (1999) comments that teachers may misinterpret bilingual children's development of good phonic skills in the early stages of literacy development in English. They may fail to note the difficulties that these children might be having with comprehension. When the difficulties later emerge, these children are grouped inappropriately with native-speakers of English who have the more conventional problems with phonic awareness, or their difficulties are assumed to derive from specific perceptual problems rather than from the cultural unfamiliarity of the text.

In order for a teaching approach with bilingual students to be fully effective, it has to be comprehensive, include parents and take community factors into account. One such approach in New Zealand was the two-year exploratory project called School Community Iwi Liaison (SCIL). The Curriculum Division of the Ministry of Education commissioned a specialist education services firm, Poutama Pounamu Education Research and Development Centre based in Tauranga, as the contractor to develop a professional development contract called 'Pause Prompt Praise' (PPP). The programme was designed to raise Maori student literacy achievement in mainstream settings. The Centre focused on improving the teaching and learning of reading and literacy as well as strengthening links between the school, the community and local Iwi groups. The participants in the SCIL project were in no doubt that adult-tutoring, as a teaching–learning strategy to help children read, really does work.

FIRST LANGUAGE FACTORS

It is also important to recognise the nature of the first language, according to Smythe (2002). He suggests that it is important to acknowledge the role of syntactic context in order to resolve any lexical ambiguity. Smythe shows how in some languages processing and lexical differences can differ and that this can effect the learning preferences of the child. For example, the Japanese language may be represented by two scripts, and Smythe reports how direct lexical access is used for concrete words, such as 'house', and phonetic coding for processing abstract words, such as 'feel', and how the two scripts—'kanji' (Chinese) and 'kana' (a syllabary)—can become dissociated with each other. This can result in the situation reported by Wydell and Butterworth (1999) where a child was dyslexic in English (first language), but not in Japanese. Similarly, Smythe reports on the research conducted by Leker and Biran (1999), which describes a person who had a reading difficulty in Hebrew, but showed no difficulties in English—this shows according to the researchers the existence of a separate, language-associated neuronal network within the right hemisphere that is important for different language reading modes, thus emphasising the importance of understanding the factors associated with the first language as well as the difficulties the child has in accessing the second language.

KEY PRINCIPLES

The key principles in the teaching of children with dyslexia, such as multi-sensory to incorporate all the modalities, cumulative and sequential to help achieve mastery and over-learning to achieve automaticity, are equally important for learners who are bilingual. Therefore, information needs to be presented to the dyslexic learner on different occasions and in different ways to help consolidation of the information or task. This also helps to strengthen short-term memory, and by using the information in different contexts long-term memory can also be strengthened.

A range of activities—both computer and game—are also useful for bilingual children. Computer games can be multi-sensory and give some responsibility to the learner. Although additional language learners may need support, it is important that they are not over-supported. Children when learning need practice at making decisions and taking responsibility for their own learning, which is why it is often best to adapt a programme so that it can be used flexibly by the teacher and the child.

METACOGNITIVE AWARENESS/SCHEMA

There is a view that children with dyslexia may have poor metacognitive awareness, particularly in relation to print and literacy (Tunmer and Chapman, 1996). When children are learning to read words they develop 'recognition', then 'understanding' and then 'transferable' skills, which means that they need to develop concepts and an understanding of the text before they can use the new word or text in other contexts—this transferring of skills is crucial to the development of metacognitive awareness. To achieve metacognitive awareness, children usually develop schemata (children's specific understanding, from their perspective, of a situation or text). To achieve schemata of a situation children need to be able to express their understanding of the situation verbally or in written form, identify the specific concepts and how these relate to the overall picture. This process requires considerable teacher direction and interaction with the student. Usually, this can be achieved by means of a reciprocal teacher, which is discussed in Chapter 8. The teacher, through a process called scaffolding, helps to build up this understanding and the conceptual and schematic development of the child.

The awareness of schemata is important to the understanding of text for all children, but this particularly applies to children with dyslexia and can also have important implications for children who have a bilingual background. Therefore, the child who for some reason activates inappropriate schemata will not fully understand the text and, in fact, may elicit the wrong meaning from a piece of text. Consideration of schemata therefore, is particularly important for learners who are dyslexic and bilingual, as often their experiences are socially, culturally and perhaps linguistically different from their monolingual peers.

One of the most effective means of developing schemata and ensuring the child has an appropriate schema is through pre-reading discussion. This sets the scene, introduces the characters, describes the situation and provides some of the keywords and concepts for the child.

Pre-reading discussion can involve the parents and can be initially in the child's first language, particularly with children whose English is not well developed. Texts relating to the cultural experiences of bilingual learners will assist in the development of schemata and the subsequent development of metacognitive awareness. This strategy of using the parents for pre-reading discussion may also help in the development of short-term memory and visualisation (Steffensen et al., 1979).

Given and Reid (1999) discuss the advantages of pursuing a global learning strategy with children who are having difficulty in learning in a conventional way. This view suggests that it is advantageous to first give an overview of a story, situation or task, so that a child can have the clear picture from the beginning. This can also lead to comprehension-monitoring before the child begins to read the text. Wray (2002) suggests that realising that one has failed to understand is only part of comprehension-monitoring as one must also know what to do when such failures occur. The discussion of concepts and schemata can provide pointers as to why the child is not comprehending the text. Additionally, comprehension-monitoring can lead to development of the skills needed for the writing process. Wray (2002) suggests that the writing process involves knowledge of person, knowledge of task and knowledge of process. The person here refers to the child herself or himself, and this knowledge needs to be built up through discussion that can incorporate personal, social and cultural factors as well as knowledge about the text being discussed.

Essentially, therefore, metacognitive strategies consist of organising learning, skimming, previewing the text, selecting a purpose for reading and scanning to fulfil the purpose, as well as self-monitoring, editing and reviewing the effectiveness of the completed task and the learning experience. The aims of these activities should be to achieve self-direction, self-monitoring and self-assessment. This means that the child is taking responsibilty for her or his own learning, and this is surely one of the principal aims of the education process.

Stamboltzis and Pumfrey (2000) acknowledge that no single method can be effective for all bilingual pupils with dyslexia. They comment on the programmes derived from Bakker's (1990) balance model that are based on the assumption that the normal developmental process of literacy acquisition (either in the first or in a subsequent language) begins with greater involvement of the right cerebral hemisphere and subsequently transfers to the left hemisphere. In the balance model of reading, Bakker (1990) suggests that the underused hemisphere needs to be stimulated and he has developed two interventions to do this—hemisphere-alluding stimulation (HAS), based on the presentation of perceptually modified text, and hemisphere-specific stimulation (HSS), which involves flashing words to the right or left visual fields, dependent on the type of dyslexia.

The theory suggests that when the demands of learning a second language are considered, it becomes apparent that many of the challenges in this are similar to those in acquiring a first language. Bakker's neuropsychological model, therefore, can be utilised for dyslexic pupils who have English as an additional language (Robertson and Bakker, 2002).

It is of course very important that a multi-sensory approach is used. Stamboltzis and Pumfrey (2000) suggest that this provides learners with the advantage of learning alphabetic patterns and words by utilising all three pathways (visual, auditory and kinaesthetic), which would benefit students of all ages. All multi-sensory teaching programmes contribute to the same purpose, namely that of remediating the phonological weaknesses of children by the systematic building up of associations between speech sounds and their representations in writing.

Stamboltzis and Pumfrey (2000) also recommend the Multisensory Structured Language (MSL) approach for teaching first language skills to dyslexic pupils. Grammar, syntax and phonology are taught through a programme that emphasises hearing, seeing, speaking and writing. Another major source of information on how to teach bilingual pupils, according to Stamboltzis and Pumfrey, comes from genre-based approaches to literacy. Genre-based ideas have implications for the selection of reading materials and the adaptation of reading instructions for the various groups of pupils. They suggest that genre theory can be useful, since it suggests that pictures, captions and labels can enhance the decoding and comprehension of text for bilingual pupils who learn to read by extensive use of visual material, and this would clearly be very helpful.

They also suggest that listening to stories can help children develop vocabulary, concepts, oral fluency and sense of story and that this can be particularly effective for bilingual pupils, in particular. All types of listening activities and role-playing provide exposure to natural, English-speaking situations, and these should be incorporated into a teaching programme.

As far as possible the teaching of reading to bilingual learners should be based on top-down strategies, otherwise described as language experience approaches. It is also important to ensure that the programme has a clear structure and that the child should be aware of that structure—this can also help the child view the programme or task in a holistic way, providing a complete picture of the activity.

ATTITUDES, RESPONSIBILITY AND MOTIVATION

It is always more effective if a child's strengths and interests are recognised and utilised during the process of teaching and learning. This would make progress more likely than for the child who finds the learning experience confusing, remote and stressful. It is therefore important that bilingual children from culturally different backgrounds from the teacher need to be fully engaged in selecting resources and learning approaches that are appropriate and meaningful. The teacher should not anticipate in advance what the child will select, as this is likely to reveal more about the teacher's stereotypes than about awareness of the pupil's interests. In one literacy project in a multilingual class (Landon, 1999), bilingual children were encouraged to make free choices from materials on offer in the classroom. The girls chose the same kinds of stories as their monolingual peer group; the boys, however, tended to select non-fiction, possibly because it was less culturally loaded than the fictional materials and because the topics were more related to conventional male interests. Landon's study therefore emphasises the need to help children develop skills in selecting materials. It is too easy for the child to rely on the teacher for this, and lack of practice can in fact reinforce this dependence on the teacher.

The outcome of any teaching programme is an important element—outcomes should be in small steps and stages. It is important for the child to recognise the progress they are making. This of course presents a challenge to teachers, as the programme has to be constructed in a manner in which progress, however small it may seem to the teacher, can be made. It is also important that this progress is recognised by the child. The teacher may well have a different expectation of the outcome of the task from the student. For bilingual learners, their different experiences of reading in different cultural contexts may require different outcomes. It is important that the teacher should make clear to the child the aims and expectations of a task. This will be more motivating for the child and help to develop the crucial element in any classroom learning—self-esteem. Self-esteem is important, as it not only helps the child feel good about herself or himself but also helps to maintain and develop motivation. Considering that the child may be entering the educational process with a gap between her or him and the peer group in reading and language aspects, this becomes a crucial element. It is crucial the child does not switch off or, indeed, perceive learning and school as stressful.

INCLUSION

Ideally, the policy of inclusion should prevent any of the difficulties, such as those described above of low self-esteem and failure at an early stage, from arising. Inclusion means that the needs of all pupils should be regarded without the need for stigmatisation or the use of labels with negative connections. Children from a bilingual background, therefore, should not need to feel that they are receiving special treatment; rather, the onus is on the teacher to develop and present teaching approaches that will meet the needs of all in the class. It goes without saying that this is rather ambitious, given the current class sizes in most countries and the increasing demands placed on teachers.

Diniz and Reed (2001) suggest that inclusion of bilingual learners at a macro level requires negotiation and restructuring of power relationships as well as the recognition and positive accommodation of differences in language and culture. Failure to include bilingual learners and their families within the school's definition of 'itself' will inevitably, according to Diniz and Reed, affect children's performance and sense of well-being and is likely to lead to poor standards of literacy development. They suggest it is possible that a school will not be able to meet its standards if it cannot recognise the barriers that its perception of itself and the practices that stem from that perception present for the child and family who have low status and cultural and linguistic differences. The school, according to Diniz and Reed, may need to dismantle existing norms and standards and commit itself to renegotiation with the whole-school community of the school's self-definition. Additionally, they suggest that there is a need for a restructuring and realignment of existing perceptions and practices.

INITIAL TEACHER EDUCATION

Haley and Porter (2000), recognising the needs of linguistically diverse students in the USA, suggest that teachers need to be trained in how language and culture influence learning. Initial teacher education programmes, they argue, play a vital role in providing teachers with an understanding of linguistic, cultural and socio-economic variables and their effects on the teaching and learning process. Additionally, training must include methods of using assessment data to plan teaching and to select, adapt and/or develop curricula to meet the needs of linguistically diverse students with dyslexia.

They argue that teacher training in the USA (and indeed elsewhere) faces a challenge in order to meet the needs of an increasing number of linguistically diverse children, some of whom have many of the characteristics of dyslexia. There are far too many teachers, they suggest, who do not share, or know about, their students' cultural or linguistic backgrounds, and too few have had the professional preparation to work well with linguistically diverse students with dyslexia. They cite the example from George Mason University, Fairfax, Virginia of the UTEEM programme (Unified Transformative Early Education Model), which is an innovative model for preparing graduate students to work with diverse young children and their families in inclusive early childhood settings. Emphasis in this programme focuses on culturally diverse children with special needs who are second language learners. This is a component that should be a part of all training programmes, especially where there is a large culturally and linguistically diverse population. Many initial teacher education courses in the UK and Europe are now also considering the needs of second language learners and becoming aware of the special cultural and learning needs of these groups.

Diniz and Reed (2001) highlight the thorny question about the educational attainment of minority ethnic pupils, where there are notions of underachievement, school exclusion, bilingualism/EAL, learning difficulties and now institutional racism. They suggest these are now regarded as integral to competing discourses on anti-racist education and/or multiculturalism and/or multilingualism, with tentative links to special education. Diniz and Reed, therefore, identify potential and, indeed, real conflict between satisfying the cultural and the educational needs of children from minority ethnic groups. They suggest that it is essential that academic discourse in this area is heightened—only then will significant shifts occur in attitude and training. They cite the research by Cline and Reason (1993), who analysed the basic parameters of 27 research reports appearing over a 15-year period and found that ethnicity was considered briefly in only 3 of the works.

Some racial groups, Diniz and Reed argue, 'are ... resolutely invisible as participants in the dyslexia discourses as they are in the pages of special educational research journals' (p. 28). They suggest that this is happening because British education provision has failed to take account of the bicultural and multilingual backgrounds of minority ethnic children and that 'institutional racism' has permeated research, policy and practices (CERES, 2000).

RESOURCES

Stamboltzis and Pumfrey (2000) provide examples of specific teaching methods for bilingual pupils with learning difficulties, such as the resource pack for teachers in multicultural classrooms. This was produced by University College, London (Cline and Frederickson, 1991). This set of learning materials aims to help teachers and educational psychologists improve their knowledge and understanding in relation to work with bilingual children, in general, and with those considered to have learning difficulties, in particular.

These materials come in a user-friendly ring folder. They comprise an introductory chapter and a 'menu' of six substantial units on:

- language and community;
- language development;
- cognitive development and learning difficulties;
- the National Curriculum in multilingual schools;
- multi-professional assessment of special educational needs; and
- additional resources.

Stamboltzis and Pumfrey (2000) recommend the programme 'Peer-tutoring—Integrating "Bilingual" Pupils into the Mainstream Classroom'. This is available from the Ethnic Minority Support Service (Curtis, 1990). This method suggests structured peer-tutoring techniques to support children with limited proficiency in English. It has been argued that the collaborative work of children in pairs has a positive outcome, if teachers are able to organise and monitor this activity carefully. Structured pair work, therefore, is suggested for children of differing ability in which a fluent English-speaking child helps a less fluent English-speaking child in a co-operative learning environment.

They also draw attention to the increasing range of resources found on the Internet, such as Multicultural Education Resources (AIMER,* Reading University, UK). This is a national database that offers students, teachers and advisers information on multicultural, anti-racist teaching materials. It includes about 3000 resources on all areas of the national curriculum (including English, Mathematics, History, Geography, Technology, Life Sciences, Music, Art, etc.), as well as English language support materials and materials in community languages.

In Europe, European Children In Crisis (ECIC, Brussels, Belgium) is a non-profit organisation that promotes concrete actions for scholastic development of children with learning difficulties whose families move around Europe. ECIC acts on behalf of these children by organising training sessions to bring parents and teachers together with experts, providing information and raising awareness of the issues involved for individual children in crisis. ECIC has produced a multimedia training pack on the effect of dyslexia across cultures. They have produced a programme Language Shock, which comprises a 30-minute video that explores the experience of learners with dyslexia having to cope with new languages and new cultures. The video is accompanied by a guide that informs learners, parents, teachers and schools where to go for help on assessment, training and resources.

THE USE OF COMPUTERS AND TECHNOLOGY

Dimitriadi (2000) suggests that technology can facilitate access to the curriculum for bilingual children. She suggests that equipment and programmes can support simultaneous input from different languages in oral, written or visual format and provide bilingual learners with the opportunity to enrich the curriculum with their diverse cultural experiences. There is little doubt that Information and Communication Technology (ICT) has transformed the educational experiences of children in schools. Technology offers the opportunity to enhance conceptualisation and expression of ideas, and Dimitriadi suggests it can be used both as a means to approach regional culture and to promote the differentiation in learning styles as a norm in the educational process (Dimitriadi, 1999). She suggests that technology can help to reinforce alphabet skills by establishing correspondence between phonemes and graphemes in one language, and making the necessary connections between the way in which apparently similar graphemes have different sounds in other languages.

* AIMER stands for Access to Information on Multicultural Education Resources.

A talking word processor provides the learners with immediate aural feedback by typing out individual graphemes.

She suggests that a voice recognition system, programmed to understand regional accents and problematic utterance, will encourage the input of speech and translate it into script. This can help with spelling, allow the opportunity to self-check and to construct simple sentences. Spellcheckers with phonically constructed word banks facilitate the writing process by generating lists of possible alternatives. Andersson (2001) has developed a computer programme in Swedish specifically for dyslexic learners to take account of their potential spelling errors and to ensure that these are recognised and that reasonable alternatives are offered. Spelling rules can also be presented in a colourful manner by using computer images or PowerPoint. It is possible, therefore, according to Dimitriadi, to include simultaneously an oral and written translation of the rule into another language. Talking word processors with pre-recorded word banks can provide immediate aural feedback to users by repeating each word or sentence typed and by prompting the learner to self-correct the sentence by seeing their spelling mistakes in the form of highlighted words. Dimitriadi (1999) discusses the versatility of talking word processors and, particularly, how they can be programmed to repeat each phoneme typed, which provides users with constant practice of exploring the relationships between graphemes and phonemes in the target language.

Dimitriadi suggests that computers can help with some of the difficulties related to the directional flow of the learner's written language structure, such as in Cantonese Chinese or in Arabic scripts where the characters follow a different course to that of European languages. She suggests a multimedia computer allows learners to record their voices, instead of typing the information, and, temporarily, they overcome the burden a new script might pose.

The Internet is considered a great source of information. Dimitriadi (1999) suggests it offers endless possibilities of finding passages in different languages and topics related to the interests and cultural experiences of the learners and using them as a reference point to improve their literacy skills.

COMMENT

There are a great number of issues that remain unresolved in relation to dyslexia and bilingualism. There are still issues over the use of tests and the need to take culture into account, as well as issues relating to the actual identification of dyslexic difficulties in children who are bilingual. The question still remains over the nature and content of intervention and, in particular, the materials to be used. It is crucial for educators, teachers and psychologists to be aware of culture factors in both assessment and intervention recommendations for children whose first language is not English. Considerable progress has been made in awareness of the needs of diverse cultural groups, both at a political and a social level. This thrust toward equality needs to be extended to educational settings and to consider the needs of specific groups of learners, such as those with dyslexia. There is some evidence that this shift has begun and that the agenda for research and practice in multilingualism and dyslexia will eventually have a high profile.

Part V

Perspectives

Chapter 14

Specific Learning Difficulties: Practice, Parents and Practitioner Research

This chapter will discuss a range of perspectives from the following areas: specific learning difficulties, including co-morbidity and alternative interventions; the role of parents; the nature, purpose and the process in conducting practitioner research. The following chapter will discuss international perspectives, highlighting the universality of issues and developments relating to dyslexia.

SPECIFIC LEARNING DIFFICULTIES

OVERLAP, CONTINUUM AND INTERVENTION

What do we mean by the term 'specific learning difficulties'? Indeed, a frequently asked question is: What is the difference between specific learning difficulties and dyslexia? Essentially, specific learning difficulties refers to a specific processing difficulty that is significantly discrepant in relation to that individual's other processing abilities. Some of these are significant enough to attract an actual label, such as dyspraxia, dysgraphia and dyscalculia. In fact, Weedon and Reid (2002) identified 15 specific learning difficulties during the development work of a screening procedure for specific learning difficulties. It was indicated during the piloting of the instrument that at least seven of these had strong correlations (Weedon and Reid, 2003).

Like dyslexia, many of the other specific learning difficulties can be seen within a continuum. The term co-morbidity is now used to describe the overlap between the different specific learning difficulties. This is an acknowledgement that specific learning difficulties can be found within a continuum and that there is likely to be some

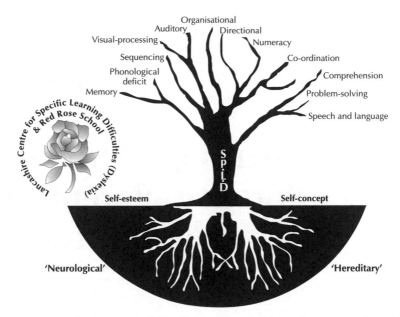

Figure 14.1 Specific learning difficulties' roots and branches (reproduced by permission of Red Rose Publications).

overlap between several of these as they tend to be factors associated with left hemisphere, language-associated functioning. Moreover, since neurological processing activities tend to be interactive rather than independent, it is likely that, for example, children with dyslexia may share some of the characteristics with children diagnosed as having a specific language impairment. This is illustrated in Figure 14.1, which was developed by a team teacher with a specialism in art, who is herself dyslexic to explain the concept of co-morbidity to a pupil. She indicated in her explanation to a pupil, who wanted to know why he and his friend both had a specific learning difficulty, but did not share the same difficulties in every subject area, that the thicker branches represented severe difficulties while the thinner ones indicated slight or no difficulty. The roots indicated the biological basis for the difficulty while self-esteem was the nourishment needed to help the roots and the tree develop. So, although there are differences in presenting difficulties, many of the treatments–interventions can be similar.

It is not unusual for dyslexia, dyspraxia and to a certain extent ADHD (attention deficit hyperactivity disorder) to share some common factors. Perhaps the syndrome that has attracted the most interest in terms of co-morbidity is ADHD, yet this syndrome itself is subject to controversy and debate about whether it has a distinct aetiology. Before discussing the value or otherwise of the term 'co-morbidity', it will be beneficial to briefly describe the specific learning difficulties that seem to be in popular use.

Clearly, dyslexia is one of these because it can be seen within a continuum in terms of its severity and the range of the difficulties associated with it. Therefore, it is not surprising that there is some overlap with other difficulties.

DYSPRAXIA

Dyspraxia is essentially a motor–co-ordination difficulty. Again, it can be seen within a continuum from mild to severe and can affect fine-motor activities, such as pencil grip, and gross-motor activities, such as movement and balance. Portwood (2001) describes dyspraxia as 'motor difficulties caused by perceptual problems, especially visual–motor and kinaesthetic–motor difficulties.'

The definition of dyspraxia provided by the Dyspraxia Trust in England is an 'impairment or immaturity in the organisation of movement which leads to associated problems with language, perception and thought' (Dyspraxia Trust, 2001).

The processing difficulties described above appear to relate to skills that are necessary for a range of learning tasks and will affect attention, memory and reading. It is not surprising, therefore, that some overlap exists between them. The same can be noted with ADHD.

ATTENTION DEFICIT DISORDERS (ADHD)

There has been considerable debate regarding the concept of attention disorders. A number of perspectives can be noted ranging from the medical, educational and social. It is, however, interesting to note that in the American Psychiatric Association's *Diagnostic and Statistical Manual of Mental Disorders* (DSM-IV; APA, 2000), ADHD is noted as the most prevalent neuro-developmental disorder of childhood. DSM-IV provides such criteria for diagnosis as factors relating to inattentiveness, hyperactivity and impulsivity—'often runs about or climbs excessively' and 'often interrupts or intrudes on others'. To qualify as ADHD these factors need to have persisted for at least six months to a degree that is maladaptive and inconsistent with developmental level. Although there has been a considerable amount of literature on ADHD, there is still controversy regarding the unitary model of ADHD as a discrete syndrome. There is also some debate on the nature of the syndrome and, particularly, its primary causes. For example, Barkley (1997) suggests that it is a unitary condition and that the primary impairment relates to behaviour inhibition, which has a cascading effect on other cognitive functions. This view is, however, countered by Rutter (1995), who suggests that a cognitive deficit specific to ADHD has still to be determined and that even if the majority have cognitive impairments the trait is not common to all children with ADHD. It is perhaps useful at this point to attempt to place the symptoms and characteristics of ADHD into some form of framework to help understand the different strands and various characteristics that can contribute to ADHD.

FRAMEWORK FOR ATTENTION DIFFICULTIES

The causal modelling framework used to describe dyslexia in Chapter 1 (Morton and Frith, 1995) can actually be applied to ADHD. Levine (1992, 1993), although he does not relate ADHD to a framework, such as the causal modelling framework, makes many of the comments shown below in the bullet lists.

Neurological Level

At the neurological level, in relation to attention difficulties, the following factors may be relevant:

- Hemispheric preferences—usually, a child with ADHD would be a right hemisphere processor.
- Saliency determination—that is, recognising what is relevant. Often, a child with ADHD would have difficulty in recognising the relevant features of conversation or written work.
- Auditory distractibility—this would imply that they would be easily distracted by noise of some sort.
- Tactile distractibility—similarly, touch could be distracting, and, often, the child with ADHD may want to touch in order to be distracted.
- Motor inhibition—often, children with ADHD may have difficulty in inhibiting a response and may react impulsively in some situations.

Cognitive Level

In relation to the cognitive dimensions, the following factors may be significant:

- Depth of processing—if the child is not attending to a stimulus then it is likely that the processing will be at a shallow as opposed to a deep level. Clearly, if this is the case then the child will not gain much from the learning experience, neither in understanding nor in pleasure—therefore, the learning experience will not be automatically reinforced.
- Information processing—just as in the case of dyslexia, the information processing cycle of input, cognition and output can be influential in identifying the types of difficulties that may be experienced by children with attention difficulties. This would therefore have implications for teaching.
- Metacognitive factors—these are important for reinforcing learning, for transferring learning and for developing concepts. It is likely the child with attention difficulties will have poor metacognitive skills, and this will also make learning less meaningful and have a negative effect on attention span.

Classroom Factors

In relation to educational or classroom factors, the following can be considered:

- Factors associated with free flight—this means that the child will have little control over the thinking process (essentially, what may be described as a right hemisphere processing style). This would mean that the individual would require some structure to help to direct their thinking processes.

- Unpredictability, inconsistency and impulsivity—this again indicates that there is little control over learning and that many actions would be impulsive.
- Pacing skills and on-task factors—these again indicate a lack of control over learning and that students with attention difficulties have a problem with pacing the progress of work and, therefore, may tire easily or finish prematurely.

IDENTIFYING AND DEFINING ATTENTION DIFFICULTIES

Examining the factors described above would lead one to believe that attention difficulties and ADHD can be confused easily and the syndrome would be difficult to identify as a discrete syndrome.

It is not surprising, therefore, that a number of definitions of ADHD are currently used and a considerable amount of literature on the subject has expounded different views and a variety of interventions. Essentially, however, identification seems to be through the use of diagnostic checklists or observations, such as the Brown Rating Scale (Brown, 1996, 2001) and the Conners scale (Conners, 1996). These are widely used, but they do demand an element of clinical judgement on the part of the assessor. The important aspect about them is not so much whether they give a diagnosis, but rather that these instruments provide a list of definable and observable characteristics that can inform a teaching programme, irrespective of the diagnosis.

It is therefore feasible to identify attention difficulties within an education setting, although in practice much of this type of diagnosis appears to be undertaken by medical professionals—even though presenting difficulties are usually more obvious in school. If a child is said to have attention difficulties, then these should be obvious in every subject and in all activities. In practice, this is rarely the case and must cast some doubt on the validity of the diagnosis.

INTERVENTION

Intervention can be: medical in the form of drugs, such as Ritalin; educational in relation to classroom adaptations, task analysis and investigation of the student's learning preferences; or even dietary in relation to examining children's reactions to certain foods. There is also a view (Lloyd and Norris, 1999) that ADHD is a social construction. There is certainly a strong commercial basis to ADHD, and this may have fuelled the impetus for acceptance of ADHD as a discrete specific difficulty. Indeed, there is a view that special educational needs, whatever they might be, can be approached from a situation-centred perspective (Frederickson and Cline, 2002). They quote Deno (1989), who argues that proponents of this view believe that special educational needs 'can only be defined in terms of the relationship between what a person can do and what a person must do to succeed in a given environment' (Frederickson and Cline, 2002, p. 40). This view indicates that learning difficulties are in fact environmental and a construction of the education system. This would

- A child with special educational needs should have their needs met.

- The special educational needs of children will normally be met in mainstream schools or settings.

- The views of the child should be sought and taken into account.

- Parents have a vital role to play in supporting their child's education.

- Children with special educational needs should be offered full access to a broad, balanced and relevant education, including the foundation stage curriculum and the national curriculum.

Box 14.1   Special educational needs Code of Practice (DfES, 2001, para 1.5).

imply that teaching and curriculum approaches hold the key to minimising the effect on the child of what may be termed a 'special educational need'. Along the same continuum of the environmentally focused approach, one can also view the interactional approach to SEN. Frederickson and Cline suggest this is the 'complex interaction between the child's strengths and weaknesses, the level of support available and the appropriateness of the education being provided' (p. 420). This can be viewed in the form of three components—the task, the child and the environment—and assessment should include all three aspects. This is implied in legislation, but in practice much of the focus is on the child and the difficulties the child brings to the learning situation, rather than the other way round. As noted in Box 14.1, the Code of Practice for England and Wales suggests fundamental principles that, if maintained and fully implemented, would ensure success for all children with special educational needs. But one factor that is overlooked is the historical perception of special educational needs and the shift in thinking from a content/achievement-driven curriculum and school system to one that primarily promotes the development of learning skills.

CO-MORBIDITY AND ADHD

It is not surprising that there is a strong view that an overlap exists between ADHD and dyslexia. Many of the cognitive attention-processing mechanisms, which children with ADHD seem to have difficulty with (such as short-term memory, sustained attention, processing speed and accuracy in copying), can also be noted in children with dyslexia.

Willcutt and Pennington (2000) noted in a large-scale study that individuals with reading disabilities were more likely than individuals without reading disabilities to meet the criteria for ADHD and that the association was stronger for inattention than for hyperactivity.

But this notion of co-morbidity has been criticised and the value of the term questioned (Kaplan et al., 2001). They suggest that the term 'co-morbidity' assumes that the aetiologies of the different specific difficulties are independent. Yet, in practice according to Kaplan et al., it is very rare to see discrete conditions existing in isolation. In a research study involving 179 children, the researchers, in order to investigate the notion of co-morbidity, used criteria to assess for seven disorders: reading disability, ADHD, developmental co-ordination disorder, oppositional defiant disorder, conduct disorder, depression and anxiety. It was found that at least 50% of the sample tested met the criteria for at least two diagnoses and the children with ADHD were at the highest risk of having a second disorder. The question presented by Kaplan et al. is whether children are actually displaying several co-morbid disorders or, in fact, are displaying manifestations of one underlying disorder. This, of course, raises questions regarding the assessment procedures and was the rationale behind the special needs assessment profile (SNAP) (Weedon and Reid, 2003). This indicates that it is likely that children will show indicators of other conditions and that the accumulation of descriptive information on presenting difficulties can be useful for the class teacher. It is important, however, that information is not based solely on clinical assessment or clinical judgement, but gathered from professionals and parents about how the child performs in different situations.

Knivsberg et al. (1999), however, suggest that it is important to identify co-morbidity before planning and implementing educational programmes. They suggest that two of the most common developmental disorders to show simultaneous occurrence are dyslexia and ADHD.

It is not the intention of this section, however, to provide detailed descriptions of the various syndromes associated with specific learning difficulties. Rather, it is the intention to investigate the evidence for co-morbidity and, particularly, to examine its usefulness as a working concept for the practitioner. It is suggested here that its usefulness lies in the descriptive data that are available from the observations, interviews and assessments conducted on the child. Its usefulness does not lie in the provision of a label, since co-morbidity assumes that a combination of processing difficulties will be present and, therefore, a label can be misleading. Its usefulness, in fact, lies in the description of presenting characteristics that may or may not lead to a label—these can be informative and beneficial in terms of intervention.

SPECIFIC LEARNING DIFFICULTIES AND ALTERNATIVE THERAPIES

One of the areas that may have far-reaching consequences and potential deals with those interventions that can be classed as 'alternative therapies'. These tend to be popular, new and often have media appeal. That is not to say they are not helpful—some of the evidence, in fact, seems to support the use of some of these alternative forms of interventions.

DIETARY

There has been considerable popular coverage on the use of food additives, and much anecdotal evidence to support the view that these may have an adverse affect on learning, particularly for children with ADHD. Richardson (2001) suggests that there is a wide spectrum of conditions in which deficiencies of highly unsaturated fatty acids appear to have some influence. Further, Richardson argues that fatty acids can have an extremely important influence on dyslexia, dyspraxia and ADHD. Richardson argues that it is not too controversial to suggest that there is a high incidence of overlap between these three syndromes. In fact, she suggests that overlap between dyslexia and ADHD can be around 30–50% and even higher in the case of dyspraxia. Richardson also argues that the truly essential fatty acids (EFA), which cannot be synthesised by the body, must be provided in the diet—these are linoleic acid (omega 6 series) and alpha-linoleic acid (omega 3 series). She suggests that the longer chain highly unsaturated fatty acids (HUFA) that the brain needs can normally be synthesised from EFAs but, this conversion process can be severely affected and limited by dietary and lifestyle factors. Some of the dietary factors, for example, which can block the converstion of EFA to HUFA include excess saturated fats, hydrogenated fats found in processed foods, deficiencies in vitamins and minerals as well as excessive consumption of coffee and alcohol, and smoking. Richardson suggests that the claims connecting hyperactivity and lack of EFA are not new. Colquhoun and Bunday (1981) noted various clinical signs of possible EFA deficiency in a survey of hyperactive children, and Richardson reports on further studies that support these early claims (Stevens et al., 1996; Richardson and Puri, 2000). Furthermore, studies on dyspraxia have highlighted the possibility of links with EFA and suggested that fatty acids supplements can be beneficial (Sordy, 1995, 1997). In relation to dyslexia and ADHD, Richardson suggests that fatty acid supplements have also shown to be successful, and supplementation has been associated with improvements in reading. She further reports on school-based trials, indicating that this intervention can be realistically applied in schools (Richardson, 2002; Portwood, 2002).

EXERCISE AND MOVEMENT

There has been long-standing interest in exercise and therapies based on movement for children with specific learning difficulties. Fitts and Posner (1967) provided an account of the learning stages in motor skill development and, particularly, the development of automaticity. Denckla and Rudel (1976) found that children with dyslexia had a deficit in rapid, automatised naming, and Denckla (1985) suggested that children with dyslexia are characterised by a 'non-specific developmental awkwardness' that is irrespective of athletic ability. In terms of intervention, Doman and Delacato (see Tannock, 1976) through a series of exercises related motor development to the development of other cognitive skills, and this aspect can also be noted in the work of Ayres (1979) and has been developed considerably by Blythe (1992; pers.

commun., 2001), Blythe and Goddard (2000), Goddard-Blythe and Hyland (1998), Dobie (1996) and McPhillips et al. (2000).

The work of Dennison (1981; Dennison and Hargrove, 1985), Dennison and Dennison (1997, 2001) in relation to the Brain Gym® and Hannaford (1995, 1997) on the importance of dominance and laterality and, particularly, the influence of dominance patterns on learning have also been influential in classrooms, especially with children with specific learning difficulties.

As indicated in Chapter 7, 'Teaching Approaches', there are a number of programmes that involve movement and claim to have beneficial cognitive and learning effects for children with a range of specific learning difficulties. These include: programmes relating to the inhibition of primitive reflexes: the programme entitled Dyslexia, Dyspraxia, Attention Disorder Treatment (DDAT) (Dore and Rutherford, 2001); and programmes utilising Educational Kinesiology (Edu.K®) (Dennison and Dennison, 1997, 2001). These will be briefly discussed here.

THE INHIBITION OF PRIMITIVE REFLEXES

Blythe (1992) found that 85% of those children who have specific learning difficulties and do not respond to various classroom intervention strategies have a cluster of aberrant reflexes. He argues that as long as these reflexes remain undetected and uncorrected the educational problems will persist. These reflexes should only be present in the very young baby and would become redundant after about six months of life. But, if these reflexes continued to be present after that time, Blythe argued, the development of the mature postural reflexes is restricted, and this will adversely affect writing, reading, spelling, copying, Mathematics, attention and concentration.

Blythe (1992) and Goddard-Blythe (1996) have developed a programme—the Developmental Exercise Programme, an assessment and intervention programme— for assessing the presence of these reflexes and a series of exercises designed to control primitive reflexes and release postural reflexes. Argument in favour of the effect of uninhibited primitive reflexes on learning has been supported by other studies (Bender, 1976; Ayres, 1979; Mitchell, 1985; Retief, 1990). McPhillips et al. (2000) suggested that foetal movements, which form the basis of the Institute for Neuro-Physiological Psychology (INPP) reflex inhibition programme (Blythe, 1992; Goddard-Blythe, 1996), may play a critical role in the maturational processes of the development of the infant's brain and that this can have implications for cognitive development and subsequent skills involved in, for example, the reading process. In fact, Goddard-Blythe and Hyland (1998) found birth complications as the single most significant factor in children who later went on to develop specific learning difficulties.

In a study in Western Australia, Taylor (2002), in view of the work of Blythe and Goddard-Blythe referred to above, examined the effects of retention of primitive reflexes in children diagnosed as ADHD. Her results supported the evidence of the importance of this area for cognitive development and learning and, in fact, suggested 'cumulative associations between high stresses, atypical brain lateralization and uninhibited reflexes on scholastic competency' (pp. 216–217).

EDUCATIONAL KINESIOLOGY

Educational Kinesiology is a combination of Applied Kinesiology and traditional learning theory, although some aspects of yoga and acupressure are also evident in the recommended programme.

Kinesiology is the study of muscles and their functions with particular attention paid to the patterns of reflex activity that link effective integration between sensory and motor responses. It has been argued (Mathews, 1993) that children often develop inappropriate patterns of responses to particular situations and that these can lock the child into inappropriate habits.

Dennison and Dennison (1997, 2001) have produced a series of exercises (Brain Gym®) from which an individual programme can be devised for each child according to the assessment. Many of these exercises include activities that involve crossing the midline, such as writing a figure eight in the air, or cross-crawling and skip-a-cross—activities that require crossing the midline of the body to help achieve hemispheric integration. The aim is to achieve some form of body balance so that information can flow freely and be processed readily. This programme known as the Brain Gym® has been widely and successfully implemented in the school setting (Fox, 1999; Longdon, 2001; Taylor, 1998). Dennison and Dennison (1989, 2000) developed a system called Brain Organisation Profile (BOP) to visually represent their theory. Taylor (2002) examined the basis and application of this profile with children with ADHD and was able to develop a useful BOP for each child in the research sample. Taylor found that children with ADHD did show more evidence of mixed laterality processing than in the control group.

DYSLEXIA, DYSPRAXIA, ATTENTION DISORDER TREATMENT (DDAT)

DDAT is the name given to the exercise-based treatment (Dore and Rutherford, 2001) that is based on the cerebellar deficit theory (Fawcett and Nicolson, 1994; Nicolson and Fawcett, 1999; Nicolson et al., 2001). This theory implies that the cerebellum has an important function in relation to dyslexia and other learning difficulties, and their hypothesis is supported by earlier work on automaticity (Nicolson and Fawcett, 1990) and more recent work on the role of the cerebellum in language (Silveri and Misciagna, 2000). The treatment programme also implicates other aspects of neurological–biological development, such as the functioning of the magnocellular system, the inhibition of primitive reflexes and fatty acid deficiencies. Dore and Rutherford suggest that the cerebellum maintains its plasticity throughout childhood, and, therefore, that it is theoretically possible to retrain the cerebellum to function more efficiently. The resultant Balance Remediation Exercise Training Programme assesses vestibular and cerebellar functioning and implements a series of exercises directly related to the individual profile of each child following a series of sophisticated tests using an electronystagmography system for assessing eye movement and a posturography balance system. Controlled studies, which have sought to provide clinical evaluation of the DDAT treatment, have been implemented and reported (Reynolds et al., 2003), although earlier reports on improvements have not been without criticism. Wilsher (2002) commented on the 'placebo effect' in this type of treatment. However, the results reported by Reynolds et al. are encouraging and indicate that after six months' treatment clients showed physiological changes with substantial improvements in vestibular function and visual-tracking, and improvements in fundamental cognitive skills. While the transfer of these improvements to reading has yet to be demonstrated, it is encouraging that physiological and cognitive changes have been noted and that the developers of the programme are utilising data from school-based as well as clinic-based programmes. This is important, for if a programme of intervention can be accommodated within a school setting then it can be seen to be more inclusive and less alternative, and this will very likely enhance its acceptance and indeed its success.

COMMENT ON ALTERNATIVE TREATMENTS

There are many views on the ethicacy of alternative programmes of treatment. These programmes are usually not harmful, and indeed those reported here appear to hold much promise. Many may appear different, but actually arise from similar causal concerns relating to the neurological–biological developmental processes and, indeed, may be complementary to each other. It is important, however, that enthusiasm for any particular treatment or intervention does not minimise the effect of good classroom teaching. There is an abundance of well-researched teaching and learning programmes, and the strategies reported in this book have been developed following years of practice and research. I recall speaking at a conference on dyslexia and being the only speaker to focus on what actually happens in the classroom. That is not to minimise the contributions from the other speakers—far from it—but rather to highlight that an essentially educational problem requires an educational solution. Certainly, the theoretical justifications of various approaches are important, as are treatments supporting the foundations of learning, such as those reported in this section; but, it is also important to strive for a comprehensive view and multidisciplinary approach to supporting children and adults with dyslexia and other learning difficulties. Without collaboration and co-operation between all the professionals involved in seeking to help people with learning difficulties confusion, concern and anxiety may well arise and reach exaggerated proportions. Interestingly, the organisation Dyslexia in Scotland (2002) found it necessary to send all its members a special fact sheet on an alternative approach, because of the questions raised by parents. This informative fact sheet did much to present the facts, which clearly was what the parent and teacher members wished, but an interesting and reflective comment was made in conclusion to the fact sheet by the authors, 'dyslexic adults we have spoken to don't want a cure they simply want an improvement in their literacy skills and their organisational skills. They do not want to lose their special gifts' (Dyslexia in Scotland, 2002, p. 4). It is important, therefore, to consider the child or the adult who has to be subjected, in whatever form, to the particular programme. Educationalists and, in particular, those involved in literacy development have for years striven to make literacy enjoyable and rewarding. This is the motivating factor for children, not the fact that reading books will improve their reading. The child is concerned with the here and now, which is why learning needs to be stimulating and motivating. This must be considered in the development of these alternative approaches. I have spoken to more than one head teacher who have commented that it may well work, but the children don't like it. For any approach to be successful the child must like it!

Silver (2001) makes illuminative comments on 'controversial therapies' and suggests that the process from initial concept to acceptance of a particular treatment approach is slow and can take years. Research needs to support a particular approach and the results need to be published in peer-reviewed journals. There is a great deal of anecdotal evidence that often convinces parents on the value of certain approaches. These usually stem from people who have benefited from the treatment or whose children have—these views are not to be discounted, although it must be acknowledged that what works for one child may not be successful for another.

There are many other alternative treatments that have not been discussed here, but are popular with parents. They include the Davis Dyslexia Correction Method, which involves orientation and symbol mastery (Davis and Braun, 1997), Sound Therapy (Johanson, 1997), which is based on frequency-specific, left hemisphere auditory stimulation with music and sounds (Auditory Discrimination Training); and many others, often too many for the parent or teacher to handle or understand. This further underlines the need for collaboration between parents and professionals—perhaps the approach that always works is one that involves 'effective communication'. This, therefore, leads on to the subject of the next section in this chapter: the role of parents.

THE ROLE OF PARENTS

The role parents can play in helping their child(ren) deal with the difficulties associated with dyslexia is of far-reaching importance. In fact, the role played by parents' associations in helping to bring attention to the needs of young people with dyslexia has also been considerable. Parents have informed successive governments and participated in policy-making forums at local and national levels that have had a significant effect on practice. While thriving organisations such as the British Dyslexia Association (BDA), International Dyslexia Association (IDA) and the European Dyslexia Association (EDA) exist and continue to have an impact on policy and practice in the UK, Europe and the USA, there are other means open to parents in order to help their child fulfil his or her potential. By far the most accessible and potentially rewarding means is through direct communication with the school. This, without doubt, needs to be the parents' first port of call, as communication at this level has the potential to quell anxieties and maximise both the skills of parents and those of teachers. Yet, in practice this may be difficult. Some parents, rightly or wrongly, are still reluctant to approach the school and may therefore find it difficult to openly consult with the school regarding any difficulties their child may be experiencing. In fact, Mittler (2001) suggests that the whole basis of home–school relationships need to be reconceptualised. Although, as he suggests, schools have undergone considerable transformation in both accountability and accessibility over the last generation, many parents, who had little direct experience of this during their own schooldays, are still more familiar with an outdated model of home–school links. Mittler talks of a 'velvet curtain between home and school ... and there is an unavoidable underlying tension that arises from the imbalance of power between them' (p. 151). Mittler therefore suggests that every school needs to have its own home–school policy that goes beyond 'fine words' (p. 153). In England and Wales the Ofsted (Office for Standards in Education) frameworks for inspection indicate that inspectors must evaluate and report on the effectiveness of the school's partnership with parents, including parental involvement with the school and the school's links with the community. The Special Educational Needs and Disability Act (DfEE, 2001) outlines steps that aim to enhance parent–school partnerships by ensuring that all local education authorities (LEAs) make arrangements for parent partnership services and by encouraging LEAs to work with voluntary associations if necessary to achieve this. Frederickson and Cline (2002) suggest that the steps indicated in this legislation could prevent many cases of dispute from going to a tribunal. Similarly, in Scotland there has been a considerable thrust toward parent partnerships, particularly in the area of dyslexia. There have been several instances of parents being involved in the development of policy documents and in dissemination (Fife Education Authority, 1996; Edinburgh City Council, 2002). There is also evidence of ministerial interest in dyslexia with government ministers and inspectors involved in conferences and seminars (Scottish Dyslexia Forum, 2002), and parents and parents' associations have been involved in government consultation papers on a range of special educational needs (Scottish Parliament, 2001; SOIED, 1999).

It is essential therefore that schools develop proactive working policies to promote home–school partnerships, particularly in relation to parents of children with dyslexia. Not only will this help to utilise the skills of parents but it will also avoid potential legal wrangles and tribunals that have been evident in the last 10 years.

PARENTAL CONCERNS

Concerns harboured by parents are usually about either the lack of diagnosis or a feeling that what their child needs is not forthcoming. Understandably, there is strong belief among parents that a label (identification of the special need) is necessary in order for their child to get appropriate help. While this may well be true in some instances, particularly if the child is significantly lagging in attainments and additional resources or a review of provision is needed, in many cases the label is not the most essential factor. The most essential factor is for the school to be aware of the child's progress in all aspects of the curriculum, to communicate this to parents and together discuss how the school (and parents) plan to deal with any lack of progress.

A comment often made by parents is that the school may not outwardly acknowledge the label 'dyslexia' or may in fact be waiting for a more formal diagnosis from an educational psychologist. This, of course, can be frustrating for parents, and while this is unfortunate it is not the 'end of the world', because the school will accept responsibility for the child's progress and will investigate, by whatever means, the child's progress and seek to find an explanation for any lack of progress. All this will be done without any recourse to a label. A label, of course, is helpful and in some situations, such as examination support, essential. In fact, Heaton (1996) found that many parents felt considerable relief when the label 'dyslexia' was provided. She quotes one parent as saying, 'I was so relieved to know that it had a name' (p. 15) and another saying, 'my family had begun to hint she might be mentally retarded because she was illiterate. I could never explain why I knew she wasn't, so the diagnosis helped me a lot' (p. 16). It is important, therefore, to consider that a label can often be accompanied by acceptance, and this can pave the way for constructive collaboration between home and school.

Fawcett (2001), in fact, suggests that anxieties can arise from the potential conflict between the views of individuals and interest groups who may have different agendas. This potential conflict can be noticed between parents and teachers, in particular, and indeed this may force parents and LEAs into opposition. It is important that this is avoided as anxieties and stresses can usually be felt by the child (Biggar and Barr, 1996). It is important, therefore, to ensure that the aims of the school in relation to any particular child are made clear to the parents and that both parents and teachers share a common agenda in relation to the child's progress and level of work.

Crombie (2002d) suggests that co-operation and collaboration between school and parents is at the heart of the dyslexia policy and practice established in East Renfrewshire. She believes that teachers were often hesitant to label a child dyslexic. She suggests, though, that good communication with parents and an understanding of dyslexia will enable teachers to discuss with parents the reasons for their reluctance to label before the child has had the chance to make a real effort to learn to read.

Mittler (2001) maintains that when parents and practitioners work together in early years' settings, the results have a positive impact on the child's development and learning. It is important, therefore, at an early stage to seek an effective partnership with parents. This, in fact, is the rationale behind the many early intervention initiatives in education (Fraser, 2002). Frederickson and Cline (2002) comment on the findings of Wolfendale (1989) that found that parent–school partnerships had made little impact.

An interesting and innovative example of parent–teacher partnership can be seen in the development of a baseline assessment procedure in Australia—the 'parent screening inventory for learning, and behaviour, difficulties' (PSILD) (Reddington and Wheeldon, 2002). The instrument was developed to cover potential areas that might predict learning and behaviour problems. Following a number of years of clinical research and revision, its usability with parents in school, its construct and content validity and its predictive validity were established. In addition to providing a parent–teacher collaborative baseline assessment tool, the PSILD was also seen to have a role in early identification by providing school entry data, as well as helping teachers implement individual strategies and structure parent–teacher interviews. Reddington and Wheeldon point out that this combination of parent-screening and teacher evaluations has actually expanded the utility of baseline assessments, as well as providing illuminative insights into the needs of individual children. The PSILD appears to fulfil a similar function to the early screening procedures developed and reported by Crombie (2002e). The key point about both the Crombie and the Australian initiative is that they value the input of the parents and see it as an integral component in the development of procedures.

PARENTAL SUPPORT

It has been outlined above that effective communication can provide a strong platform for parental support. It has also been noted that actual diagnosis and, if appropriate, a label can also be welcome and provide some reassurance and, indeed, relief on the part of the parents. It can also be noted that a label can in fact make a difference to the child (Biggar and Barr, 1996). A further example of this is the case of Philip, a day student at a school for children with specific learning difficulties in England (Open University, 2002). In the interview with Philip, he quickly pointed out that it was a relief for him to get the label 'dyslexic' because it meant, 'I was not stupid.' It can also provide children and young people with some indication of what dyslexia is and how it might affect them—positively as well as negatively. It can also make them develop skills in self-advocacy that can be extremely useful beyond school, particularly in the workplace.

Heaton (1996) provides an indication of the kinds of issues and strategies that parents need to be familiar with. For example, one of the most frequently asked questions by parents is how much homework should the child with dyslexia undertake. This anxiety can stem from the fact that it may take him or her much longer than others in the class to complete the same exercise. Heaton interviewed parents on this subject who had tried a variety of strategies to make this issue as comfortable as possible for the child. She found that parents felt it was effective in some cases to use colour-coding for different subjects. This helped to save time when the child was packing for school, and it was easier to access the homework for that subject. Heaton also reports on the issue of time spent doing homework. It was indicated that some parents felt that a compromise was necessary: if the child had spent a given amount of time on the homework it should be stopped at a prearranged time, even if the homework was not fully finished.

It is important to maintain the motivation of children with dyslexia, and pouring over arduous homework nightly may not be the most effective way to achieve this. Heaton also suggests that parents should not spend too much time thinking about the extent of their child's difficulties, as this can become an obsession and eventually become counterproductive.

There are a number of activities that parents can utilise to help their child with literacy. However, whatever the parent is doing should be communicated to the school and vice versa without exception. Some programmes, however, do lend themselves more to be used by parents in conjunction with school than some others.

Many parents interviewed in Heaton's research vouched for the beneficial effects of technology and, in particular, laptop computers. One parent said, 'the computer is the best thing we ever bought, but you need to make sure you get the right one'. This is very important, as the choice and the advances in computer technology can be confusing. The BDA has a well-established computer committee, who have provided advice to parents and professionals in this area (Corelli, 2001).

There are also some reading programmes that have been well received by parents and can be used in conjunction with schools, such as Toe by Toe (see Chapter 7). The programme called 'Paired Reading' is another good example of a joint school–home programme in literacy (Topping, 1996). He suggests that paired-reading is a very successful method that involves the parent (tutor) and the child (tutee) reading aloud at the same time. It is, however, a specific, structured technique. Both parent and child read all the words out together, with the tutor modulating the speed to match that of the child and acting as a good model of competent reading. The child must read every word, and when the child says a word incorrectly the tutor just tells the child the correct way to say the word. The child then repeats the word correctly, and the pair carry on. Saying 'no' and giving phonic and other prompts is forbidden. However, tutors do not jump in and correct the child straight away. The rule is that tutors pause and give the child four or five seconds to see if they will put it right by themselves. It is intended only for use with individually chosen, highly motivating, non-fiction or fiction books that are *above* the independent readability level of the tutee. Topping suggests, however, that the name has been a problem—the phrase 'paired-reading' has such a warm, comfortable feel to it that some people have loosely applied it to almost anything that two people do together with a book. One of the important aspects of paired-reading and, indeed, any reading activities is praise—the parent should look pleased when the child succeeds using this technique (adapted from Reid, 2002).

Topping indicates that paired-reading is suitable for children 'of all reading abilities' and can help to avoid stigmatisation.

Reid (2002) suggests there are many teaching programmes, many of which will be useful for children with dyslexia. It may be misguided for parents or for teachers to pin their hopes on any one programme.

The key issue is that programmes and teaching approaches should be considered in the light of the individual child's learning profile. The school should have a good knowledge of both the child and specific teaching approaches. Again, because there is such a wealth of materials on the market, it is important to monitor and evaluate the approach and the progress periodically. It is also important that parents share in this monitoring. Indeed, research conducted by the Scottish Dyslexia Association (now Dyslexia in Scotland, see Roxburgh, 1995), which took the form of a survey of parents' perceptions of provision for dyslexic children, revealed that around 80% of the children within the survey were first identified by their parents. This research, which is currently being updated, highlights the value of parental involvement and collaboration in relation-monitoring and providing opinions on the nature and the level of provision for their dyslexic children.

In relation to support, it is important to recognise that support should not be measured in terms of hours or days. It is difficult to quantify the optimum length of support for any individual young person with dyslexia. Consistency is important, and frequent periodic reviews should provide guidance on the effectiveness of the approaches being used and whether particular approaches should be continued. It is also important to recognise that such monitoring need not be in terms of reading and spelling ages. These are important of course, but it is also necessary to obtain information and assess performances on particular aspects of curriculum work, such as comprehension, problem-solving and other activities that embrace much more than reading and spelling accuracy.

PRACTITIONER RESEARCH

The chair of the BDA International Conference, Rod Nicolson, called for multi-disciplinary approaches to dyslexia both in research and practice. This point has been reiterated by Fawcett (2002), who, in identifying research priorities, suggested a number of research areas relating to theoretical factors and practical aspects of assessment and teaching. There has been a tendency in dyslexia research to leave the research aspects to researchers, mainly from the theoretical domain. It is encouraging that an international and peer-reviewed periodical like *Dyslexia* (published by John Wiley & Sons) has a section devoted to practice called 'innovations and insights'. It is hoped this type of initiative will not only encourage innovation but also encourage practitioners to evaluate their practice and embark on research that can be widely disseminated to guide the practice of others. Having had the opportunity as course leader of a master's course in dyslexia and external examiner to a number of universities (to examine the work of students and particularly dissertations), I find much research is characterised by thoroughness in method and insightfulness in reporting. It is certainly an advantage to be a practitioner researcher. Practitioners such as teachers usually have well-conceived research proposals, stemming from their own practice. This means that the results will be of direct relevance to them and will very likely be appreciated by colleagues and school management. The opportunities for practitioner research are certainly available, but should not be confined to the type of example above, which tends to relate to an award-bearing master's programme. Practitioner research should in fact be an integral component of teachers' roles. Other priorities of course make this untenable in practice, but with collaboration and management support this could be a reality.

Fawcett (2002) suggests that what constitutes dyslexia-friendly teaching could be an area of research. She comments:

> we need carefully controlled evaluation studies aimed at identifying the cost-effectiveness of different support methods for different groups of children with reading problems. This will allow us to check whether the standardised pace of ... [for example] ... the Literacy Hour is appropriate for dyslexic children ... we need to establish whether the same techniques are appropriate for dyslexic and non-dyslexic poor readers, as well as normal readers (Fawcett, 2002, p. 26).

RESEARCH QUESTIONS

Irrespective of whether the research exercise is part of a course of study or whether it is a school-developed initiative to inform practice, a number of fundamental questions need to be raised. These questions include the reasons for the research, what particular areas are to be investigated, when the research is to be conducted and why the research is necessary. It is also important to consider what the envisaged gain from the research might be, what the short- and long-term effect will be, and what kind of follow-up and dissemination can be implemented after the research has been conducted. These fundamental research questions can provide a framework for the research project and help to clarify the actual purpose and potential outcomes of the research at the outset.

Identifying the 'why' and 'what' aspects of the research should help to define some of the research questions. It is important, therefore, to be clear about exactly what is under investigation. It is not uncommon for some practitioner researchers to begin with too ambitious a plan and realise after commencement that it is not workable in its present form. While it is important to consider the range of factors that may affect the outcome of the research, the actual topic itself must be clearly defined and identifiable. So, for example, if the teacher wants to evaluate programmes that are available for students with dyslexia, the actual programme to be investigated must be first identified. It is probably too broad and too vague to say that multi-sensory programmes will be investigated, as they may well differ in their approach. If it was the aim of the teacher/researcher to investigate multi-sensory programmes, then it would be necessary to examine a range of these types of programmes as the first stage of the research, identify some common principles and then evaluate these principles. If the topic is broad-based as it would be in this case, then it is necessary to undertake the research in stages and these stages can be spread over a long period, depending on the time available. It should be possible, therefore, once the research topic has been decided, to indicate in one simple sentence what the research is to be about. This should therefore include 'why' and 'what' questions, why the research is being conducted (as any research exercise should arise from a perceived and identifiable need) and what exactly is being investigated.

The question of 'when' is also important. The practitioner/researcher needs to consider issues such as access to other schools and other year groups/classes. Discretion and consultation need to be applied here at an early stage of the research. Naturally, at this early stage one also needs to gain consent from all people directly and indirectly involved with the research; this would clearly be parents, other teachers and the school management. In some education authorities, the central administration also like to be aware of any research projects. This may avoid duplication, and it may also help with dissemination. It is also essential to consider the children who are to be the subject of the research; again, discretion needs to be used here, but the children should be informed and consulted in some manner about the initiative.

The question of 'how' the research is to be conducted will raise a number of issues regarding analysis. Again, it is not uncommon for people new to research to accumulate vast quantities of data, but find them unwieldy and too time-consuming to analyse. A fundamental difference in method can relate to whether the research is quantitative (measuring amounts as in questionnnaire analysis) or qualitative (examining the types of differences that can occur and why they may occur). For example, examining the principles of a multi-sensory programme can be qualitative, but measuring the gains from that programme over time with a large sample will be quantitative. Many research projects can have elements of both. The actual method, therefore, can be determined by practical factors and by the nature of the research.

SELECTION OF SAMPLE

Practical considerations may influence the choice, location and size of the research sample. Irrespective of this, it is important that the researcher is able to justify the choice of the sample and be clear of the criteria that were used. Although, in some cases the sample may be a 'convenience' sample, every effort should be made to ensure that this does not in any major way compromise the purpose and the effect of the research. Munn and Drever (1990) provide some guidelines regarding sampling, such as ensuring the clear definition of the population to be studied. Clearly, the greater the size of the sample (certainly in quantitative research) the greater the possibility that the results can be replicated.

It is also important that the group to be studied should have readily definable features: age, stage, level of attainments, reading age and spelling age, depending on the criteria for the research project. Usually, one can identify independent and dependent variables. Independent variables are those that remain constant and are not expected to change throughout the research, while dependent variables, on the other hand, are those that are expected to change in some way and the object of the research could be to record, either qualitatively or quantitatively, the extent of that change.

As for research in dyslexia or some other specific learning difficulty, it is important that the definition used is consistent and the criteria are clear; so that if a group of children with dyslexia are to be studied, then the criteria that have been used, to justify the use of the term 'dyslexia' for that group, are known and are consistently applied. This is important, as it can be seen from earlier in this chapter and in other chapters that definitions of dyslexia can differ. Some researchers tend to use measurable criteria (such as reading age or IQ, if appropriate) when defining a sample, but although the criteria are important it is more important that they are uniform and applied consistently throughout the whole sample. This would enable one to say that the sample is as far as possible a discrete one.

DEVELOPING A RESEARCH PLAN

It is important at this early stage to develop a research plan that incorporates all the points made so far, as well as the proposed method of analysis and the projected outcomes. The latter could also be in the form of a hypothesis(es). An example of a research plan is shown in Figure 14.2, investigating early identification of dyslexia.

A development plan of the research can be more detailed than the example shown in Figure 14.2, but essentially it would serve the same purpose—that is, to ensure that there have been well-thought-out steps to the research. This is important, as one should be aware of what the subsequent steps are in a research programme. At the

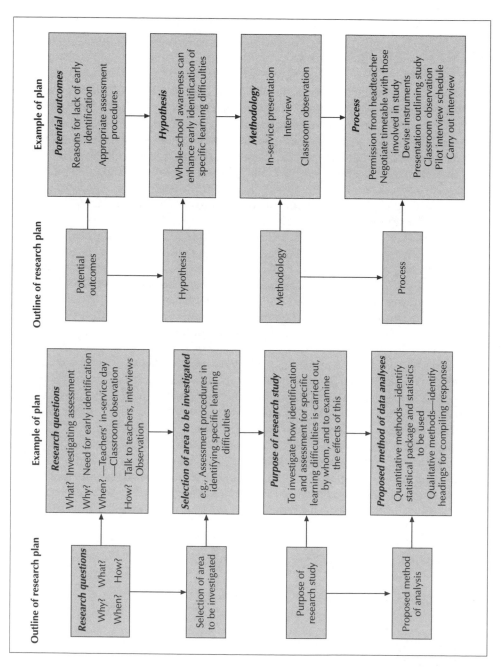

Figure 14.2 Developing a research plan.

same time, it is worth considering that the detail of the next steps may well be determined by the outcome of an initial stage in the research. This happens in 'action research' where the subsequent steps are determined by the outcome of some form of 'research action', and clearly this outcome is not known at the outset of the research. Even in other types of research, it is beneficial not to be too rigid; although the sequence of the plan of the research should be known, it can still be adapted in the light of some situation that may arise as a result of the research. So, although one needs to have a clear research plan of the stages, one has also to be aware that the content and detail of this may have to be adapted or amended in the light of how the research might progress.

METHOD

There are a number of texts aimed at undertaking small-scale research: *Doing Your Research Project* (Bell, 1993); *A Guide for First-Time Researchers in Education and Social Science* (OU, 1991); and *So You Want to Do Research* (Lewis and Munn, 1993). These publications can help in the planning and implementation of the research project by looking at aspects such as planning, recording, negotiating access, interviews and questionnaire design, interpreting and presenting the evidence, and writing the research report.

Usually, however, the data can be collected in the form of a questionnaire, interview, observation or recording the responses to a task in a small sample study.

In each of these it is crucial that the method is discussed and decided on before embarking on the research and that the most appropriate type of data collection is selected. In making this choice one needs to consider the time that can be spent on the project, as some very lengthy questionnaires can take a considerable amount of time to analyse.

INSTRUMENTS

Whatever means or instruments are selected to obtain the data, it is crucial that they are piloted and revised if necessary. For example, if it is the intention to use an interview technique, then an interview schedule must be prepared well in advance so that it can be piloted and revised if necessary, very much in the same way as a questionnaire.

The interview schedule or the questionnaire needs to be structured. This is a good exercise, as it enables the researcher to identify the key subareas that may well form separate sections in the reporting of the results and in the discussion. If four or five key headings can be identified, this also makes the recording of data much simpler.

For example, if the research project is on factors associated with early identification of dyslexia and a parent was being interviewed, there may well be sections on: family history, birth-related factors and early milestones; motivational factors; social and personality factors; parental concerns; and contact with school. Each of these factors can generate a number of questions, the responses to which can be summarised under each of the key subheadings. This can make the data more manageable for recording and reporting.

Although anonymity would be preserved in the reporting, the researcher will obviously know the person being interviewed, but can tabulate the responses in an anonymous manner rather than use a name. Similarly with interviews, unlike questionnaires these can be totally anonymous, but it is a good idea to code each of the questionnaires for research purposes just in case one needs to revisit the person to obtain a follow-up response or some clarification. The coding should only be known to the research team, and the people being interviewed or completing the questionnaire should be aware of this. It is important at all stages of the research to seek permission from those involved and to let then know how the data will be used.

SOURCES

It is important to refer to sources either from journal papers or chapters of books, as these provide the researcher with ideas, give some indication of what has been done before and provide a possible outlet for dissemination. It is necessary, however, to justify the choice of research area not only from a practical but from a theoretical standpoint also. It is essential, therefore, to refer to the current theoretical positions in general areas as well as the specific need in relation to the specific area selected. So, for example, if the research was on early identification of dyslexia, it would be necessary to discuss briefly the various theoretical positions in relation to dyslexia and this should lead to the research topic selected (i.e., early identification), indicating both the theoretical and practical justification for this selection.

The Internet can also provide sources of information, but one needs to take great care that any articles referred to have been written and published by respected authorities, preferably in peer-reviewed journals. Many journals are now available online, so it is not always necessary to have physical access to a library. Additionally, literature search engines, such as the British Education Index and the Educational Resources Information Centre (ERIC, a current index to journals in education and resources in education databases), can quickly provide references and sometimes abstracts of current work in the area selected.

REPORTING

The researcher should also be aware from the outset that the results of the research will have to be recorded and reported in some form. If the research is part of an award-bearing qualification, then the university or college will usually provide guidelines on how the reporting should be done (such as the format, the number of words and style and the use of references).

Nevertheless, it is good practice to use an established format that, broadly speaking, is followed by most universities and journals. An example of this is shown in Box 14.2.

RESEARCH REPORT

1 *Title*—This should be relevant and short. Make sure that the key areas of your research are indicated in the title.

2 *Abstract*—This is a brief summary of the research, how it was carried out, the rationale for the research, the results and the implications. In the abstract you may also want to refer to the new aspects of the research since this can help to provide a rationale for the research.

3 *Acknowledgements*—These are important as it is impossible to carry out research without goodwill and assistance from others. Their role in the research process must be acknowledged.

4 *Contents page*—This should contain clear chapter headings with the use of subheadings to outline what each chapter contains.

5 *Introduction*—This part should provide an indication of the reasons for the research, the background to the research, the hypothesis and research questions, and a literature review outlining the previous studies relevant to the area that is being researched. In the literature review, you may want to start in a general way looking at the field from a wide perspective and then focus on the narrower aspects of your research. At this stage, effort should be made to link the literature with your research questions.

6 *Method*—In this section you should outline and justify the selected method for collecting the data. This should also include how you selected the sample as well as some demographic information relating to the sample and the geographical area of the study.

7 *Results*—This section should provide the factual information relating to the actual results. This could be in the form of tables and graphs, but some commentary explaining them is necessary. You should avoid, however, discussing the implications or reasons for the results at this point. This should be left to the next section—the discussion.

8 *Discussion*—This is an extremely important part of the research report. In this section you examine and suggest the reasons that you obtained the results you did, and then discuss the implications of your results. This should relate back to your introduction, your hypothesis, your research questions and your literature review.

9 *Conclusion*—This should be a fairly brief summary of your study and, in particular, the implications of your results for further research and for practice. In this section you should ensure that the research questions have been answered.

10 *References*—You must reference all articles, books and other material actually referred to in the report. There are several different styles of references, it may be wise to check with the body to whom the report is being presented as they may have a preference. One such acceptable style is the Harvard system (the one used in the references to this book).

Box 14.2 Writing a research report.

APPLICATION, DISSEMINATION AND RE-EVALUATION

Often, once a research exercise has been completed, the process of application, evaluation and dissemination can begin. It is hoped that the research will inform practice, so that the results of the research can be applied and monitored. This can be the focus of a follow-up piece of research, as the results may also be applied by others not directly involved with the research. It is good practice to examine the implications of the results for other geographical areas and other stages. Dissemination can help to extend the value of the research to others involved in the same field. As indicated above, dissemination can be through journals and books. This is usually very useful, as these publications will normally be peer-reviewed or certainly subject to some form of editorial scrutiny. Feedback from this source can also provide helpful pointers for follow-up research.

TOPICS, ISSUES AND COMMENTS

There are many areas of potential research for the practitioner who is engaged in the field of dyslexia:

- awareness and perceptions of staff of dyslexia;
- baseline assessment and early identification;
- assessment and the processes involved in assessment;
- evaluation of commercially produced assessment materials;
- metacognitive assessment;
- learning styles and teaching styles;
- evaluation of teaching programmes;
- evaluation of learning approaches, such as Mind Mapping©, and other popular approaches relating to study skills;
- aspects of policy and provision;
- curricular aspects and differentiation;
- individual education programmes (IEPs) and target-setting;
- specific aspects of the reading, spelling and writing processes;
- self-concept and self-concept programmes;
- co-morbidity—the overlap with, for example, behavioural difficulties;
- aspects of further and higher education, such as role of staff, awareness of staff, role of support services and student perceptions;
- follow-up evaluation following a school initiative or an education authority project.

This list provides only a limited number of examples of the general areas that can be of interest to the practitioner/researcher. The topic selected should stem from both a need, identified by practice, together with theoretical justification from the literature, or from the results of a pilot or an earlier study. Irrespective of what generated the impetus for the research, it is important to be aware of research ethics and always to consider those who will be the subject of the research. As outlined earlier, permission needs to be obtained from all involved in the research.

Research is a valuable exercise, and this should be recognised by management as well as teachers. Research in dyslexia is also a dynamic field that is constantly developing in relation to theory and practice. However small the research study might be in scale, it will offer something in some way to the researcher, colleagues and perhaps the wider audience. It is this dissemination and cross-fertilisation of ideas that help to clarify and explain many of the issues in relation to dyslexia. This, therefore, is essential not only for the advancement of theory but for the justification of practice as well.

Chapter 15

International Perspectives

DYSLEXIA: A GLOBAL ISSUE

Nicolson (2001), in his introductory keynote at the BDA 5th International Conference, suggested there is a need for a consensus and for an attitude of partnership to facilitate coherent and effective policies and practices in dyslexia. Furthermore, Smythe and Everatt (2000) suggest that there can be little doubt that dyslexia is an international concern, but there are obvious differences in perspectives. For example, they cite the examples of the UK, where it is estimated that there are two million severely dyslexic individuals including 375,000 schoolchildren (BDA, 1997), and China, where no such estimates are available. They hypothesise that this may reflect the acceptance of the term 'dyslexia' and its importance/or otherwise in educational policy and provision, or in fact relate to differences in the actual incidence of dyslexia for whatever reason. Given the perceived importance of dyslexia assessment, support and policy throughout the world, Salter and Smythe (1997) suggest there is very likely a need for systematic research that identifies similarities and differences between different countries and different contexts, as this type of research helps in the development of culture- and language-appropriate diagnostic and intervention strategies. This aspect was brought a step nearer reality when Vogel and Reder (2001) co-ordinated a major research exercise involving 'distinguished researchers in the field of dyslexia/learning disabilities representing nine countries' (p. 218). Belgium, Canada, Germany, the UK, Ireland, New Zealand, the Netherlands, Sweden and the USA all participated in the International Adult Literacy Survey (IALS), which was discussed in Chapter 2. The unique aspect of the IALS was that all the assessment measures used were the same in the different countries and utilised under the same conditions. The study examined three different aspects of literacy: prose literacy, document literacy and quantitative literacy.

This type of study offered an opportunity to gather data on the prevalence of dyslexia, age and gender distribution and the educational attainment of those with dyslexia in each country. The study, which is ongoing, also brought an opportunity to deal with some of the concerns voiced above by Salter and Smythe on the need for a co-ordinated approach to identifying the prevalence of dyslexia. The study also addressed specific differences relating to the role of linguistic features in different languages, such as phonology and their morphological and orthographic aspects, as well as the approaches to teaching reading. The purpose of the study, therefore, was to interpret the IALS findings for each nation and to compare the findings cross-linguistically and cross-nationally. The results indicated that the prevalence of self-reported learning disabilities ranged from the highest 7% in New Zealand to the lowest 1% in Sweden, and the initial implications of this was studied in terms of the educational, social and economic dimensions of each country. The study supported the notion of the link between literacy and historical frameworks, peda-gogical approaches, length of schooling, legislation and teacher-training. All those factors irrespective of the country were seen to be important.

The study was reported at the BDA International Conference in 2001 (Vogel, 2001), and it was indicated that the next steps would be: to engage in cross-national dialogue regarding these findings on literacy levels; examine cross-national differ-ences in the history of learning disabilities' awareness, public policy, special educa-tion services, reading methodology and teacher-training; and examine cross-national differences regarding self-identification questions asked and understood in each country (Vogel, 2001).

Clearly, this type of study can help to provide data on different models of identification in different countries and the role of different professionals and profes-sions in assessment. In some countries, school identification takes place while in others much of the identification seems to be clinic-based. There is, therefore, considerable value in this type of co-ordinated study, and it could lead to more enlightened policy and practices in assessment and intervention in relation to dyslexia. In the meantime, many individual initiatives have been progressing in a number of countries, some of which are commented on below.

ENGLAND AND WALES

In England and Wales, the 1988 Education Reform Act introduced a prescriptive and detailed curriculum with statutory national-testing in the primary school at Age 7 and Age 11. It also initiated an inspection system that was controlled by Ofsted. Also, the National Literacy Strategy (DfEE, 1998) emerged due to the government's awareness of increasing public, including employer, concern over declining standards in basic and functional literacy. As in other countries, concern over 'literacy standards' has led policy-makers to adopt 'literacy benchmarks', leading to the nationwide introduction of pedagogical approaches, such as the Literacy Hour, that are designed to raise 'literacy'. Wearmouth et al. (2002) suggest these policies can reinforce the concept of 'basic literacy', because the policies imply that literacy consists of a set of technical skills that can be measured in a quantifiable manner.

The BDA were instrumental in initiating a government-supported, dyslexia-friendly schools campaign in 1999 and have been influential in curriculum develop-ment and in recognition of the needs of students with dyslexia both at school and in tertiary education. They have also initiated and collaborated with initiatives and programmes involving the armed forces and industry. Their views are often sought in initiatives in special education and literacy.

REPUBLIC OF IRELAND

In the Republic of Ireland, there appears to be flexibility in the literacy curriculum and therefore in the assessment measures. The Republic of Ireland (Task Force on Dyslexia, 2001) has recommended a phased assessment model specifically for identifying difficulties arising from dyslexia:

- Phase 1—Initial identification of learning differences (Ages 3–5).
- Phase 2—Identification of a possible learning difficulty arising from dyslexia (Age 5–7 onwards). This includes monitoring, observation, diagnostic assessment reviews by class teacher and learning support teacher, and consideration of intervention approaches that can also include home–school programmes.
- Phase 3—This phase reports on the formal identification of dyslexia and an analysis of needs from Ages 7–12 onwards. This includes a review of the interventions that have been implemented up to that point, including input from parents as well as teachers. This phase also considers the effects of the child's learning difficulty on his or her self-esteem as well as the effects of any other related learning difficulty.
- Phase 4—This involves the provision of multidisciplinary annual reviews from Age 12 onwards. These reviews would ensure the presence of an individual education programme. This phase also alerts the school to the possibility of unrecognised difficulties that may not become obvious until entry to post-primary education. The report therefore recommends that an early recognition system should be in place in all post-primary schools—this should include close liaison with feeder primary schools before transfer as well as information from parents on incoming students.

Clearly, the issuing of a comprehensive document such as the task force with clear recommendations relating to the key issues on assessment is highly commendable.

NORTHERN IRELAND

The Task Group on Dyslexia was set up in January 2001 to audit provision for children and young people with dyslexia, from nursery level to further education, and to identify training needs and opportunities for teachers. The Task Group consisted of representatives from the Education and Library Boards' educational psychology services, curriculum advisory and support services, special education sections and peripatetic services, together with representatives from universities and colleges. In its report (Task Group on Dyslexia, 2002) the Northern Ireland Task Group endorsed the Republic of Ireland definition (Task Force on Dyslexia, 2001):

> *dyslexia is manifested in a continuum of specific learning difficulties related to the acquisition of basic skills in reading, spelling, writing and/or number, such difficulties*

being unexpected in relation to an individual's other abilities. Dyslexia can be characterised at the neurological, cognitive and behavioural levels. It is typically described by inefficient information processing, including difficulties in phonological processing, working memory, rapid naming and automaticity of basic skills. Difficulties in organisation, sequencing, and motor skills may also be present (Task Group on Dyslexia, 2002).

Martin McGuinness, the Northern Ireland Minister for Education, in the preface to the report suggested that the report highlighted a very real concern and provided challenges for all in education:

particularly the need for training for classroom teachers in recognising where children have, or may have, dyslexia, and in putting in place the means to address their difficulties—and, most importantly, to ensure that the obstacle which their difficulties presents in accessing the rest of the curriculum is minimised. Equally, these are challenges for further and higher education, for employers and for society.

This clearly puts on record a government commitment not just to recognise dyslexia but also to implement strategies and training to effectively deal with dyslexia at all levels.

The Task Group recommended early intervention to minimise the risk of children suffering the negative experience of academic failure and associated consequences. It also suggested that these interventions include whole-school policies, within-class approaches and individual interventions, as well as the type of external support available through the various Education Library Board Services.

The report also made the very important statement that all current and future initiatives in Northern Ireland should take account of pupils with dyslexia and made a commitment to training by setting up both specialised and accredited training courses on dyslexia and awareness-raising courses for mainstream teachers.

The report referred to the causal modelling framework (Morton and Frith, 1995) as a guide to the research in dyslexia, particularly from the biological, cognitive and educational perspectives. It was strongly indicated in the report that all teachers and support staff should have a good general understanding of the nature of dyslexia and of the difficulties that a dyslexic child may have when coping in the school environment.

John Clarke, of the Northern Ireland Dyslexia Association, suggested in the report that there were a number of issues that had to be dealt with, such as the need for schools to develop expertise in the area of dyslexia and the development of more appropriate provision (e.g., units and special classes). He suggested that, overall, there was a lack of resources in the schools for dealing with the difficulties associated with dyslexia. These concerns have clearly been of a long-standing nature, but the encouraging point is that inquiries such as the one conducted by the Ministry of Education, and the significant recommendations made, go a long way to at least inspiring a degree of confidence among parents and educators—hopefully, once these recommendations have been fully implemented that confidence should be converted to competence, and this will have a long-term benefit for all children and adults with dyslexia and their families.

SCOTLAND

In Scotland concern over standards and an unbalanced curriculum in the 1980s (*A Policy for the 90's: Concern over Falling Standards*, SED, 1984, 1990) was addressed through the introduction of the innovative 5–14 Guidelines, which has become a major and essential part of the initiative to extend and monitor the standard of pupil achievement in Scotland. These Guidelines offer some flexibility to education authorities and schools and provide for a range of measures to assess outcomes. For example, the 'English Language Document 5–14' outlines four overall attainment outcomes: listening, talking, reading and writing. Within each of these outcomes, 'strands' outline the specific aspects of learning and assume progression through a series of attainment targets. So, for example, in the reading attainment outcome the strands include reading for information, reading for enjoyment, reading to reflect the writer's idea and craft, awareness of genre and reading aloud.

Clearly, therefore, the curriculum, how it is offered and the selection of the criteria used to assess standards will affect how one perceives assessment and determines the aims and rationale of assessment. The flexible approach of the 5–14 Guidelines in Scotland can be compared with the prescriptive approach of the National Literacy Strategy in England. This is emphasised in an interview with an Ofsted inspector, reported by Wearmouth et al. (2002), which states:

> when evaluating literacy inspectors must look for a thorough knowledge of the national literacy strategy framework for teaching, secure understanding of the literacy skills pupils will be taught, secure knowledge and understanding of the literacy skills pupils will need. A good understanding of how to teach phonics, good use of the national literacy objectives in planning and a balance between word, sentence and text level work.

There has been a considerable drive in early identification and early intervention in Scotland with many funded projects on literacy being held as examples of good practice. This early intervention initiative has been evaluated (Fraser, 2002), and the results indicated that considerable value has been derived from this with almost total participation across the geographical areas of Scotland and the effect has been felt in classrooms, in projects involving parents and in teacher-training.

Also, in Scotland the voluntary sector is active with a number of organisations such as Dyslexia in Scotland, the Dyslexia Institute and Scottish Dyslexia Forum involved in consultation with government, delivering courses, running seminars and conferences, and conducting specialist teaching. The Scottish Dyslexia Trust has largely been responsible for funding major initiatives in specialist teacher-training in the area of dyslexia and in the development of other initiatives throughout Scotland. One of the major achievements, in relation to the voluntary sector, was the initiative by the Scottish Dyslexia Trust to convene 'The Scottish Dyslexia Forum', which is very likely unique in Europe, and perhaps the world, as an organisation that has representation from all groups, voluntary and government, with an interest in dyslexia. The Forum has organised seminars, held consultations with government officials and is involved in a variety of issues concerning adults with specific learning difficulties.

NEW ZEALAND

The report of the Education and Science Committee (NZ Department of Education, 2001), on the inquiry into the teaching of reading in New Zealand, puts the issue in perspective and does so quite bluntly, in fact, when it reports:

> *assessment, evaluation and ongoing monitoring of students' development of reading skills are critical. We [the report authors] identified two important failings that need to be urgently addressed. The first is the lack of a complete battery of up-to-date assessment tools that teachers might use to inform their teaching programme. The second is the gap in teachers' knowledge about how to best use the tools that do exist and how to best analyse the information from those tools to modify teaching practice* (p. 19).

The NZ government's alarm at reading standards was very likely heightened by the results of the major IALS (OECD, 1996), which revealed that 42% of working New Zealanders scored below the minimum level of literacy competence, although these data should be viewed in relation to the high benchmark set for literacy competence by the IALS. Nevertheless, this very likely provided some motivation for the development of the New Zealand Adult Literacy Strategy in May 2001.

One of the major and successful initiatives in the area of special needs and literacy, including dyslexia, has been the development and the training of the group of teachers known as 'resource teachers for learning and behaviour' (RTLB). These highly skilled and trained teachers are organised in clusters to cover every geographical area of New Zealand. Each cluster is responsible for a number of schools in the area, and the RTLBs share responsibility with the schools for those children who need additional support to meet educational attainments. One of the far-reaching and unique aspects of the development of the RTLB system has been the collaboration of four of the major universities in New Zealand to jointly prepare and deliver the training for RTLBs. The resource clearly has considerable potential, and RTLBs can have a key role to play in the assessment and intervention relating to children with dyslexia.

Also, in New Zealand charities such as the Federation for SPEcific Learning Disabilities Associations (SPELD) have played an important role in supporting the system by employing specialist tutors, often in tandem with schools, to provide additional tuition to children with dyslexia. This role was recognised in the report mentioned above, and the indication was that this co-operation should in fact be made stronger and that SPELD should be engaged more within the system. Other charities, such as the Learning and Behaviour Charitable Trust New Zealand (LBCTNZ), have also provided impetus for recognition of learning difficulties, including dyslexia, and have played an advocacy role in relation to adults with learning disabilities as well as children and parents. Additionally, the online periodical *The*

School Daily (www.TheSchoolDaily.com) provides a wealth of useful and up-to-date information on education and dyslexia.

UNITED STATES OF AMERICA

In the USA, the main steps taken toward a programme of intervention for learning disabilities are: referral for psychological assessment; assessment and development of an individualised education plan; assessing for and accessing appropriate provision, taking into consideration the concept of 'least restrictive environment'; and annual follow-up assessments and meetings to discuss the student's progress in meeting the goals set.

Assessment is governed by the requirements of the Individuals with Disabilities Act (1997), which requires that assessment should be carried out through a multi-disciplinary team approach, utilising a comprehensive range of procedures, such as standardised achievement and intelligence tests, teacher checklists and behavioural observations. If a disability is identified, a further meeting (which will include parents as well as representatives from the special education services) is arranged to discuss the accommodations required and a programme of intervention is designed to meet the child's needs. In many states of the USA discrepancy criteria are used to determine whether a student has a specific learning disability and, although alternative approaches are practised because the literature on discrepancy criteria is critical of this method (Stanovich, 1996), many states still utilise discrepancy criteria (usually between intellectual ability and attainments). One example of the use of diagnostic criteria is the Louisiana Literacy Profile Inventory to Identify Reading Difficulties (Ronka, 2000), which essentially provides an assessment of needs and, at the same time, provides guidance on instruction. The Louisiana Literacy Profile Inventory focuses on the kindergarten to third grade and observes and records student progress on a literacy continuum. It recognises that children develop literacy at different rates and, although teachers record this progress, they do not adhere to a prescribed timetable of stages of literacy development, preferring to focus on a child's readiness to develop specific reading behaviours instead. At the same time, the teacher is primed to identify when a child's lack of knowledge puts him or her at risk for learning problems. The Inventory is comprehensive and focuses on oral language, book and print awareness, phonemic awareness, graphemic knowledge, analysis of oral reading, responses to text and written language and, very importantly, recognises individual variations in the development of literacy among children as well as being sensitive enough to identify the at-risk students.

As a direct result of the implementation of Public Law 94–142 in 1975, the Education Act for All Handicapped (EAH) and the Rehabilitation Act of 1973 (Section 504), the individual needs of exceptional bilingual (linguistically diverse) students have received much needed attention.

The Individuals with Disabilities Education Act (IDEA) (1997) strengthens the concept of 'least restrictive environment' for children with disabilities. In spite of these federal laws, according to Haley and Porter (2000), the majority of special education programmes as presently structured do not meet the needs of limited

English proficiency dyslexic students. IDEA does not address the training or preparedness of teachers or the language of instruction issues.

One of the major thrusts in relation to dyslexia in the USA has come from the IDA, which is an international, non-profit-making, scientific and educational organisation dedicated to the study of learning disability and dyslexia. It was founded in 1949 in the USA (formerly called the Orton Dyslexia Society). It aims to monitor government legislation, offer information and support to teachers as well as to parents and dyslexic individuals, produce publications, undertake research and organise conferences. The IDA is, in fact, influential in research, policy and practice and publishes a periodical, *Perspectives*, four times a year. It has branches in virtually every state—many of which hold annual conventions. The IDA annual conference usually attracts around 3000 delegates. IDA's address is 8600 LaSalle Road, Chester Building, Suite 382, Baltimore, MD 21286-2044 (tel.: (410) 296 0232; fax.: (410) 321 5069; email: info@interdys.org; website: http://www.interdys.org IDA).

FRANCE

The Ministry of Education report, *Concerning the Dysphasic Child and the Dyslexic Child* (Ringard, 2000), provides a comprehensive investigation into dyslexia (and dysphasia) in France. It is quite intriguing and, indeed, surprising that both dysphasia and dyslexia can be examined with a view to making recommendations for assessment, practice and training in the same report. The report acknowledges the controversies within the field of dyslexia and provides comment on a 'scientific synthesis' involving definitions and the conceptual and ideological understanding of dyslexia. Essentially, the authors of the report suggest 'two fields of definition which are clearly distinct': the first of which are the difficulties experienced with written language and disorganisation in the process of writing. The report suggests that this is 'not a simple discrepancy, but a deviancy' (p. 17). This field of definition suggests the most common type of difficulties associated with dyslexia are phonological. The report describes phonological dyslexia as a difficulty in utilising the graphophonemic relationship. The child is unable to analyse the constituent parts of a word and often relies on whole-word strategies, although even these are limited because of the poor graphophonemic relationship that makes new words difficult to decipher.

The other field of definition described in the report is the 'bad reading' explanation for dyslexia. This hypothesis suggests that there are three key deficiencies experienced by 'bad readers': decoding (i.e., poorly developed word-attack skills; poor reading and metacognitive strategies preventing full exploration and questioning of text); and cultural deficiencies in relation to the purpose of text (viewing reading as a narrow, utilitarian process, thus ignoring its symbolic, social and cultural aspects). This hypothesis, according to the report, suggests that there are very few 'true dyslexics if one applies exclusion criteria to children who have failed to read because of low intelligence, cognitive difficulties in particular tasks, poor language elaboration skills, poor social–cultural environment and poor education facilities.' The exponents of this view suggest that 'in most cases the state of non-reading is linked to the quality of the educational environment and the pedagogical and didactic intervention' (p. 21). The report therefore suggests that the figure often quoted of 10% is an overestimation (of the school population being dyslexic) and 'is not very plausible' (p. 24).

In relation to identification and assessment, the report recommends a number of principles:

- the *principle of precaution*, which suggests that too early a diagnosis may induce decisions that are detrimental to the child;
- the *principle of prevention*, which suggests that a diversified and structured language curriculum will have a preventative dimension for all children, including those children who are potentially at risk of dyslexia;
- the *principle of recognition*, which implies that there must be a deficiency, which is different from a delay;
- the *principle of the right to schooling*, which is appropriate in terms of the teaching methods; and
- the *principle of educational partnership*, which emphasises the role of the family as 'co-educator of the child'.

AUSTRIA

The leaflet *Educational Options in Austria* provides an overview of the Austrian system (available at http://www.bmbwk.gv.at). Although there are no special classes or schools for children with dyslexia in Austria, there are opportunities to take extra classes in specific subject 'integration classes' after school (ECIC, 2000). The school psychologists carry out most of the diagnostic assessments and decide whether the child has dyslexia and have produced a set of quality criteria for effective support of dyslexic children. In Austria there are also a number of active voluntary and other types of dyslexia groups, and details of these can be obtained through the EDA.

EUROPEAN DYSLEXIA ASSOCIATION (EDA)

The EDA was founded by the European Commission. It offers supports to dyslexic people, promotes links between groups, publishes news and information papers and conducts studies and organises conferences. At present it is involved in a pioneering East–West Europe project, which aims to improve teaching of children at risk of being dyslexic and to improve awareness of the need for early recognition and intervention. It also aims to highlight the need for changes in legislation of the participating countries and, at a European level, to ensure that the educational rights of dyslexic people are met.

Since its foundation in 1987 the EDA has grown significantly, and presently has over 40 member organisations in almost 30 countries. The aims of the EDA are: to assist and develop support for dyslexic people in all aspects of society; to promote co-operation between parents, teachers and other professionals; and to encourage and disseminate research relating to diagnosis, intervention and prevention. The EDA has organised a number of campaigns in member countries, including campaigns to promote the early recognition of dyslexia and one aimed to influence teacher-training establishments to include dyslexia recognition and intervention strategies as part of pre-service and in-service teacher training.

East–West Project

The planned future integration of the Central and Eastern European countries into the European Union has prompted the EDA to develop a research programme: 'East–West Europe Project', The dyslexia associations of Poland, Hungary and the Czech Republic as part of this project agreed to jointly participate in an awareness campaign in their respective countries. The aims of the project include the raising of awareness among policy-makers on the magnitude of the problems associated with dyslexia, especially the severe emotional damage that in some cases can be attributed to dyslexia. Additionally, the project aims to raise awareness of the need for early recognition of dyslexia in the pre-school years and the need for appropriate pre-service and in-service training of teachers and other professionals dealing with children with dyslexia. One of the proposed goals of the project is to highlight the need for legislative change and to encourage governments to recognise the rights of people with dyslexia to receive appropriate education in school, support in training and in employment. It is proposed that each of the East European countries involved will twin with a West European country.

The EDA has a co-ordinating role in the East–West Project and will also assist with the dissemination and the publicity associated with the project's outcomes. This type of project is highly commendable and does much, not only to promote European-wide dyslexia awareness but also to help bring all countries of Europe closer together through positive and constructive co-operation. Many other awareness campaigns have taken place in other European countries and have involved participation by government ministers as well as education policy-makers, such as that run by the Province of Tuscany in Italy (Centro Servizi Amministrativi, Lucca; Associazione Italiana Dislessia, 2002) and the North Cyprus Dyslexia Association (NCDA, 2002). Both were major two-day events to bring dyslexia awareness to universities, schools, governement departments and parents. The events culminated in a two-day international conference.

The EDA has initiated an annual European Dyslexia Week. It has also organised the First All-European Conference on Dyslexia in October 2004 in Budapest. There are dyslexia associations in most European countries including Hungary, Poland, the Czech Republic, France, Germany, Italy, Austria and Spain. Details of full membership and contacts can be obtained from the European Dyslexia Association. The EDA's address is Bodenweg 21, CH-8406 Winterthur, Switzerland (website: www.bedford.ac.uk/eda; email: Bertschinger@gmx.ch).

OTHER EUROPEAN ORGANISATIONS

There are other European organisations that have an interest in dyslexia. Details of three of them are shown below:

European Dyslexia Academy for Research and Training (E-Dart)

This organisation runs courses and conferences and publishes materials. See Further Reading and Resources for details.

Dyspel

Dyspel is a non-profit-making organisation in Luxembourg, run entirely by volunteers, many of whom have children with dyslexia or other special needs. Her Royal Highness the Grand Duchess of Luxembourg is its patron. Dyspel has a membership of 70 families from 12 nationalities with children in many different schools in the Grand Duchy. It has published and distributed a Dyspel (2002) book in French, German and English for teachers, written by professionals within Dyspel, about dyslexia and how to help children in the classroom learn more effectively. Eventually, it hopes to have a drop-in centre for parents and children with a library of resources. See Further Reading and Resources for contact details.

World Dyslexia Network Foundation

The World Dyslexia Network Foundation was set up in 1995 as a non-profit-making, online organisation looking to further co-operation and collaboration in research into dyslexia. Its website (http://web.ukonline.co.uk) provides information on dyslexia and links to major, related websites. Details of other organisations, such as the BDA and the IDA, can be found earlier in this section in the discussion on the developments in different countries. Contact details of all major organisations, including this one, can be found in Further Resources and Information.

COMMENT

It can be noted, therefore, that there is considerable worldwide activity at a number of levels in relation to dyslexia: at local parent level, at school level and at government level. This is clearly very encouraging, and the major initiatives, such as awareness campaigns, lobbying, collaboration and conferences throughout the world, have all helped. Nicolson (2001) in addressing the BDA international conference, attended by delegates from over 30 countries, called for collaboration and co-operation in the quest for multidisciplinary and multi-organisational co-operation in both research and practice in dyslexia. Clearly, the time is right, and will be for some time, to achieve this objective.

Chapter 16

Comments and Conclusion

This book has presented a comprehensive picture and a range of perspectives that can be associated with dyslexia. It can be noted, particularly from the previous chapter, that dyslexia can be both a local issue and an international concern. In some situations it can be seen as an educational priority, in others an issue of controversy, perhaps a source of frustration. Yet, for the child or the adult with dyslexia, it represents more than an issue of educational policy or an academic debate on educational philosophy and practice. For children and adults with dyslexia, it represents a personal challenge—a challenge that we in education can observe and share, but not feel. No-one other than the person with dyslexia knows how it feels—others can try, and empathy and support are always necessary and always appreciated. But, the child with dyslexia—who panics at the prospect of reading aloud, who rehearses an answer from a text to such an extent that learning is relegated to rote rehearsal, who spends many more hours than he or she should over homework and examination preparation—knows this feeling only too well. He or she is very aware of the difficulties and the challenges. Unfortunately, often this challenge represents an uphill struggle and the pleasure of learning is lost at too early an age. For many others, however, with support and developing self-knowledge, success is an option and can be a reality. Increasingly, we are moving to an age of unorthodox thinking, of visual images and of fast-moving developments in computer technology. This may herald educational practice that is genuinely rooted in enquiry thinking, independent study and flexible learning and one that acknowledges individual learning preferences. The development of multimedia resource learning can, with appropriate support, be extremely beneficial in educational practice and provision for children with dyslexia (Reid, 2000).

There are a number of key issues referred to in this book, such as early identification and early intervention, both of which can prevent a negative spiral of failure. We must however question what is meant by early identification—it is not synonymous with premature labelling or even labelling at all. Essentially, it means identifying the barriers to full and successful inclusion as early as possible. These barriers may be represented by the curriculum or the learning environment as well as any cognitive difficulty the child may display.

Teaching approaches need to be developed to incorporate the learning styles and learning preferences of students with dyslexia. An understanding of metacognition and metacognitive approaches to assessment, learning and teaching that acknowledges the learner's self-understanding and the processes of learning is essential. It is essential in fact to consider all factors—cultural and curriculum—that can affect learning.

Chapter 14, 'Perspectives', highlights a number of areas of significant importance, such as the increased interest in overlapping specific learning difficulties and the implications of this for the classroom teacher; the accompanying interest in alternative interventions and the need for clarification and co-operation in the roles of all involved; the need to acknowledge the crucial role parents play in the education of their children and how we each can learn from the experiences of others, whether at a local level or an international level. The section in Chapter 15 on international aspects, and the examples of this covered in other chapters, attempts to provide a flavour of international initiatives in dyslexia and how in the field of dyslexia there are no international frontiers. Many research studies incorporate authors from many countries, and this shared expertise is one of the important recent developments in the area of dyslexia. Indeed, this book is being used as the core text in a transnational, European-wide course in dyslexia for teachers (Comenius Action Programme, 2003).

It has been heartening to witness the recent developments in initial and postgraduate teacher-training programmes and developments in assessment, teaching and learning, all of which ultimately benefit children with dyslexia. There have been almost countless examples of good practice and significant understanding among those in close contact with children and adults with dyslexia in education and the workplace. The charitable work of celebrities who are dyslexic, inspiring others by their words and actions, are well known. But others who are less well known—classroom teachers, dyslexia advisers at college and university and employers—do this daily without national recognition and they, by doing this, provide and strengthen the fragile link of hope and support for those with dyslexia. It was inspiring to read in a popular magazine the following comment, which preceded an article written by one of the magazine staff:

> the astute amongst you may have noticed that this article appears to contain a large number of spelling mistakes, this is because Tracy suffers from dyslexia. We, the editorial staff, spent quite some time deciding what to do about this. After much deliberation and with Tracy's consent we opted to publish the article in its original unedited format. A large number of people suffer from dyslexia and this article is not meant as an offence to anyone but in support of Tracy's battle with it (Real Lancashire Magazine, summer–autumn, 2002, p. 41).

This provides a good example of enlightened colleagues who have shown a real understanding and appreciation of the feelings that can be experienced by those with dyslexia. It is essential to incorporate a broad and enlightened view of how the difficulties the child or adult may experience can be met within the education, community and work context. An enlightening account of this has been provided by Stephen Summerfield (pers. commun.), who in an autobiographical account describes the hurdles he had to deal with—social, emotional and educational—because of his dyslexia. He now has a PhD in Chemistry. In his autobiographical account he states, '. . . in the workplace many are frightened of what is different. This prejudice against those that are, and think differently has caused many problems in employment. You always think that bullying stops when you leave school. Alas this is not so . . . it is paradoxical that I have a reputation as being able to explain complex ideas with clarity but (other) explanations are incomprehensible. . . . I have been described as a "complex perceptive problem solver" . . . a former employer described me as a maverick problem solver . . . he meant independent rather than irresponsible. Being a visual spatial thinker and not so constrained by rules, I can see many ways to solve a problem.'

Stephen recounts many of the challenges throughout his education and life, particularly relating to reading, spelling, sequencing, grammar, short-term memory, handwriting, co-ordination, left–right confusion, examinations and filling in job application forms! Like many people with dyslexia, Stephen has formulated his own coping strategies. He says, 'the advent of visual signs for lavatories, telephones, etc. have been a great help. . . . When reading print, I remember where things are in a book by the visual appearance of the page . . . my lectures are given without notes using only visual clues on my overheads. . . . I have little understanding of what it is to be called "normal". I am different from most, and being diagnosed dyslexic has at least given me a reason why. My mind is too active for my body . . . and I am rightly accused of being a workaholic. I still have much to learn in the art of communication of both the written and spoken word. People remind me that I rarely start with the subject of the sentence and easily wander onto other subjects when the new idea materialises in my mind. The clutter of my workbench or desk is a good expression of my state of mind . . . whenever I am talking, my hands frame the idea that is drawn pictorially in my mind . . . it has been known for the listener to ask 20 questions in order to find the word that I was stumbling over. Self-belief was so hard for me to nurture because of all the knocks during my early years . . . instilling belief in oneself is still hard. Intelligence in this modern society is measured by the person's ability to perform with language, primarily the written word . . . the statement that "thought it possible without words" may sound rather strange but this is a constant thread through my life and others with dyslexia. The picture and image are formed before the words are put to them.' Gardner's multiple intelligence model (see p. 199) has offered Stephen an explanation, and inspiration, to utilise his talents. In Figure 16.1, the talents of well-known and successful people in their field has been plotted against the multiple intelligence model. This makes for interesting reading for, as Stephen suggests in his account, 'these people achieved greatness in their fields not in spite of, but because of their disabilities.'

Dyslexia therefore is not solely a school issue but is also a political and social concern and a community responsibility. It is a local, national and international issue and calls for understanding and co-operation between educators, parents, employers and politicians. Only with this co-operation and understanding of the real issues that daily affect children, adults and their families will the outlook for all those with dyslexia be positive. It is my sincere hope that this book will help to achieve this through greater teacher awareness and as a source of information and advice for all involved in dyslexia.

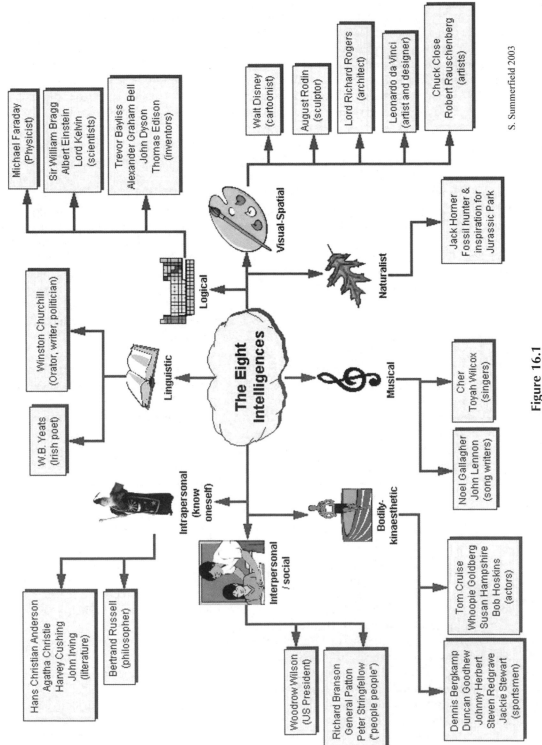

Figure 16.1

The Eight Intelligences

Visual-Spatial
- Walt Disney (cartoonist)
- August Rodin (sculptor)
- Lord Richard Rogers (architect)
- Leonardo da Vinci (artist and designer)
- Chuck Close, Robert Rauschenberg (artists)

S. Summerfield 2003

Logical
- Michael Faraday (Physicist)
- Sir William Bragg, Albert Einstein, Lord Kelvin (scientists)
- Trevor Bayliss, Alexander Graham Bell, John Dyson, Thomas Edison (inventors)

Linguistic
- Winston Churchill (Orator, writer, politician)
- W.B. Yeats (Irish poet)

Naturalist
- Jack Horner, Fossil hunter & inspiration for Jurassic Park

Musical
- Cher, Toyah Wilcox (singers)
- Noel Gallagher, John Lennon (song writers)

Intrapersonal (know oneself)
- Hans Christian Anderson, Agatha Christie, Harvey Cushing, John Irving (literature)
- Bertrand Russell (philosopher)

Interpersonal / social
- Woodrow Wilson (US President)
- Richard Branson, General Patton, Peter Stringfellow ("people people")

Bodily-kinaesthetic
- Tom Cruise, Whoopie Goldberg, Susan Hampshire, Bob Hoskins (actors)
- Dennis Bergkamp, Duncan Goodhew, Johnny Herbert, Steven Redgrave, Jackie Stewart (sportsmen)

Appendix

Further Reading and Resources

FURTHER READING

A considerable amount of information is discussed in some detail in different chapters of this book: particularly in Chapter 5, 'Assessment: Practice', Chapter 7, 'Teaching Approaches', and Chapter 12, 'Inclusion: Further and Higher Education'. To avoid repetition, this information will not be referred to here. This chapter, therefore, should be consulted alongside the respective chapters in this book. So, the books and materials referred to in this chapter is not intended to be an exhaustive list of all relevant materials. A list of the principal publishers, who usually have a detailed and informative catalogue of materials, and the main stockists of books on dyslexia, who also provide some comment on each of the publications, are provided at the end of this chapter in Resources.

STAFF DEVELOPMENT AND GENERAL TEXTS

Annals of Dyslexia
An interdisciplinary journal of the International Dyslexia Association (formerly the Orton Dyslexia Association)

This comprehensive journal is published annually by the International Dyslexia Association (IDA), Baltimore. It represents the most current issues, debates and practices from researchers, clinicians and teachers involved in the field of dyslexia.

Cognitive Styles and Learning Strategies
Richard Riding and Stephen Rayner (1998) (David Fulton Publishers, London)

This book discusses both research and practice in cognitive styles and learning strategies, provides key concepts and theoretical explanations in the above and gives evaluative comment on the research and future research directions. There are detailed chapters on cognitive style and learning styles that assess and describe a range of methodologies, and a section of the book relates cognitive style to learning and behaviour in general and behavioural difficulties.

Dyslexia, Theory and Good Practice
Angela Fawcett (ed.) (2001) (Whurr, London)

This book represents some of the papers presented at the British Dyslexia Association's (BDA) 5th International Conference in York in April 2001. There are chapters from all the keynote presenters including the conference chair Prof. Rod Nicolson. Nicolson's chapter sets the scene for the book and, indeed, reflects on the progress made in the field of dyslexia over the last 10 years. He discusses the theoretical positions, diagnostic screening and the advances in support for children and adults with dyslexia. He also provides a reflective account of the situation in 2000 from the theoretical perspective, such as lack of data on co-morbidity and lack of links with mainstream, developmental cognitive neuroscience. In terms of assessment and support, Nicolson points out that there is still a lack of positive indices of dyslexia, particularly regarding diagnosis in multilingual children, and there is still a need to clarify the principles of multi-sensory teaching and to harness new technology to benefit students with dyslexia. Nicolson presents 10 research questions for the future and suggests that there is still a need for 'consensus, for foresight, for an attitude for partnership, for inclusion ... above all, we need to be able to respect and motivate the individual, as well as analysing the group' (pp. 32–33). This book also contains chapters by Angela Fawcett and Rod Nicolson on the role of the cerebellum, as well as chapters on cognitive processes by Lundberg and Hoien and on the issues relating to fluency and speed of processing by Wolf and O'Brien. There is also a section on intervention that features chapters on the whole person by Priscilla Vail, the role of pre-school relating to identification and intervention, as well as other chapters on primary and secondary education and adults.

The Dyslexia Handbook
BDA (published annually)

This very informative handbook is published annually and always contains practical strategies and advice on dyslexia and other associated difficulties, such as dyspraxia and attention difficulties. The 2002 edition (edited by Mike Johnson and Lindsay Peer) contains a part on general information about dyslexia, including definitions, adult dyslexia, identifying dyslexia and a directory of addresses of relevant local and national dyslexia associations. There are also parts on managing dyslexia in children and adults that include parents' perspectives, dyslexia-friendly schools, strategies for number mathematics and on higher education. There is also a complete part devoted to multi-sensory teaching, including the bilingual child and diagnosing dyslexia in multilingual children. There is a part on legislation and on computers. The computer part contains an appraisal of the fast-forward technique developed by Paula Tallal. This relates to the speed of sound input as well as attention, sequencing and memory. The programme featured in the school in this chapter, Harlandvale School in the USA (see Johnson, 2002, pp. 269–271), lasts six weeks and is monitored by the student himself or herself using a computer with headphones. This part also mentions a kindergarten version of the same programme, which has also claimed to be successful in attainments, attention and participation in lessons. The BDA handbook also contains a list of BDA publications. The 2003 edition of *The BDA Handbook* (Johnson and Peer, 2003) contains articles on managing dyslexia in adults, including 'post-16 initiatives', 'survival techniques in employment', 'an adult dyslexia checklist', 'assessing adults', 'managing the dyslexic student's first year at college', 'working towards dyslexia-friendly colleges and universities' and 'working towards a dyslexia friendly city'. There are also articles on the 'Special Educational Needs and Disability Act' and the 'Revised Code of Practice'.

Dyslexia and Other Learning Difficulties—The Facts
Mark Selikowitz (1994) (Oxford University Press, Oxford)

This short text, which presents an Australian perspective, discusses a wide variety of aspects, such as theories of causation, reading, spelling, writing, arithmetic, language, attention difficulties, co-ordination and clumsiness, and social and emotional difficulties.

Dyslexia: A Practitioner's Handbook (2nd edn)
Gavin Reid (1998) (John Wiley & Sons, Chichester, UK)

This reference book provides an overview of dyslexia. There are chapters that focus on key issues, such as definitions, assessment approaches and the assessment process in schools, teaching and curriculum approaches and a chapter on the reading process indicating how research can be translated into practice. There is a chapter on resources and one on further and higher education. The book 'brings together current research, implications for assessment ... and practical activities ... for teachers and those on teacher training courses'.

Dyslexia in Children—Multidisciplinary Perspectives
Angela Fawcett and Rod Nicolson (eds) (1994) (Harvester Wheatsheaf)

This book, useful for those undertaking research in dyslexia or wishing to obtain a deeper understanding of the underlying causes and different facets within dyslexia, contains three distinct sections. These are phonological skills, reading and dyslexia; visual skills motor skills and speed of processing; and views on the underlying causes of dyslexia. Topics such as the phonological deficit hypothesis, automaticity, and visual and motor difficulties are dealt with in some detail.

Dyslexia
An international journal of research and practice: Angela Fawcett (ed.) (John Wiley & Sons, Chichester, UK)

This journal provides reviews and reports of research, assessment and intervention practice. It reports on theoretical and practical developments in the field of dyslexia, with contributions from many different countries. Published four times a year this official journal of the British Dyslexia Association is a referred periodical.

Dyslexia, Literacy and Psychological Assessment
Report of the Working Party of the Division of Educational and Child Psychology (DECP) of the British Psychological Society (BPS) (BPS, 1999a)

This report is the product of an investigation into the area of psychological assessment in dyslexia and literacy and considers the relevant research, surveys current practice and makes detailed recommendations for practice. There are sections on the discussion of a working definition of dyslexia and theoretical explanations. The authors use Morton and Frith's (1995) causal modelling framework as a basis for the theoretical explanations provided for dyslexia, encompassing the biological, cognitive and behavioural level. The report provides a description of 10 different, sometimes overlapping hypothesis relating to dyslexia: phonological deficit, temporal processing, skill automatisation, working memory, visual processing, syndrome hypothesis, hypotheses involving intelligence and cognitive profiles, subtype hypothesis, learning opportunities hypothesis and emotional factors hypothesis. There is an appendix containing a description of published tests that draw on the theoretical rationales of dyslexia.

Dyslexia—Successful Inclusion in the Secondary School
Lindsay Peer and Gavin Reid (eds) (2001) (David Fulton, London)

This book provides an overview of the potential impact of dyslexia in the secondary school and how subject teachers can deal with this in different subject areas. There is also a section on inclusion that sets the scene for the remainder of the book on individual subject areas and cross-curricular and professional aspects. For example, there are chapters on Modern Foreign Languages, English, History, Geography, Physics, Biology, General Science, Mathematics, Maths, Art, Drama and Music.

Dyslexia (2nd edn)
Margaret J. Snowling (2000) (Blackwell, Oxford)

This publication analyses and describes different theoretical positions in relation to dyslexia, such as the Phonological Representation Hypothesis, the Severity Hypothesis and sensory impairment, and discusses key issues, such as the roles of individual differences, the biological basis of dyslexia and compensation. There are also chapters on learning to read and spell, and definitions of dyslexia. The book draws heavily on perspectives and research from cognitive psychology and illustrates how phonological processing problems compromise the development of reading. It also discusses aspects such as the behavioural outcomes of dyslexia in relation to the cognitive strengths the child brings to the reading tasks as well as the weaknesses.

Dyslexia Matters
Gerald Hales (ed.) (1994) (Whurr, London)

This text contains 15 chapters that examine the theoretical constructs of dyslexia, the specific nature of dyslexia, the identification of dyslexia, education management of the dyslexic child and diverse routes to a wider understanding of dyslexia. The book can be a resource for the researcher. There are also three chapters on education management and a chapter on the importance of self-esteem and the emotional needs of dyslexic individuals. The contributors are all experienced practitioners and researchers from the UK and the USA, Canada and Australia.

Dyslexia—A Multidisciplinary Approach
Patience Thomson and Peter Gilchrist (eds) (1997) (Chapman and Hall, London)

This book presents multidisciplinary perspectives on dyslexia. These include views from an education psychologist, speech and language therapist, occupational therapist, orthoptist, paediatrician, school counsellor, remedial teacher and head teacher. The general perspective of the book is one that emphasises the need for a holistic approach in dealing with dyslexic children.

Dyslexia in Focus at 16 Plus: An Inclusive Teaching Approach
Jeanne Holloway (2000) (NASEN Publications, Tamworth, UK)

This book begins by discussing dyslexia and the use of the term in relation to the Code of Practice. It also describes different forms of assessment with follow-up examples in the appendix. One such example—Realistic Assessment Procedures—developed by the author includes a photocopiable record sheet. There are also sections on learning that focus on strategies for problem-solving, the use of the library, spelling workshops, information and communication technology (ICT) and setting examinations. There is also a section on self-awareness that looks at learning preferences and learning styles.

Dyslexia: A Psychosocial Perspective
Morag Hunter-Carsch (ed.) (2001) (Whurr, London)

This book contains chapters on relevant aspects related to the development of thinking and learning skills in dyslexic students of all ages. The book is divided into two parts. Part 1 focuses on central issues, such as the role of metacognition, reflections on key research issues, visual factors and the role of social interaction. Part 2 focuses on specific aspects, such as partnership with parents, multilingualism, Mathematics, ICT, counselling, adult support and specialist teacher-training. The aim of the book is to help teachers re-examine central issues that affect learning, teaching methods, provision and the role of metacognition.

Dyslexia and Literacy, Theory and Practice
Gavin Reid and Janice Wearmouth (eds) (2002) (John Wiley & Sons, Chichester, UK)

This book presents current theoretical and practical perspectives from a range of teachers, researchers and psychologists on topics relating to dyslexia and literacy, such as an overview of neurological, biological and cognitive factors and the implications of these for literacy. Frith provides a chapter on the influential Causal Modelling Framework and Hatcher and Snowling write on the role of phonological representations for literacy and dyslexia. There are also chapters on visual models by Everatt and the Balance Model of Reading by Robertson and Bakker. Ehri writes on the reading processes and implications for instruction, and Cline discusses bilingual issues. There are also chapters by Crombie and Todd on meeting the needs of children with dyslexia in the classroom. The theme of metacognition and reading is developed through three chapters written by Wray, Burden and Topping, respectively. There are also chapters on re-examining the role of reading and our understanding of reading, particularly on reading and writing for critical thinking by Hunt and Eames. This book is the set course book for a course in difficulties in literacy development jointly developed by the Open University and the University of Edinburgh.

Dyslexia in Practice: A Guide for Teachers

Janet Townend and Martin Turner (eds) (1999) (Kluwer Academic Publishers, Dordrecht, the Netherlands)

This book has been produced with contributions from experienced practitioners from the Dyslexia Institute. There are chapters on phonological awareness, spoken language, the bilingual dyslexic child, linking assessment with a teaching programme, the teaching of basic reading and spelling, developing writing skills, learning skills, Mathematics, the use of ICT, the challenges facing dyslexic adults and linking home and school.

Dimensions of Dyslexia

Vol. 1: *Assessment, Teaching and the Curriculum* and Vol. 2: *Literacy, Language and Learning*: Gavin Reid (ed.) (1996) (Moray House Publications, Edinburgh)

These texts each consist of over 30 chapters from the field of research, psychology and teaching from within the UK and the USA. In Volume 1 there are 12 chapters on assessment, which includes phonological assessment, listening comprehension, computer-assisted assessment, metacognitive and psychological assessment and a framework for assessment. The teaching part contains chapters on approaches to reading, spelling, Mathematics and Music. The curriculum part looks at differentiation, provision in mainstream schools and reading units, and whole-school approaches to meeting the needs of dyslexic learners. The concluding section is about continuing education. This part consists of chapters that look at the needs of adults and students in further and higher education.

In Volume 2 there are parts on reading and writing, speech and language, motor development, learning styles and strategies, social and emotional aspects and the final part provides perspectives on dyslexia from different perspectives. The reading and writing part deals with phonological difficulties, compensatory strategies, metacognition, paired-reading and assessing and promoting handwriting skills. The speech and language part provides explanations and implications for language difficulties, their relationship with dyslexia and specific factors affecting bilingual learners. The other parts include dyspraxic and motor problems, learning styles, attention deficit disorder, empowering students, policy issues, role of parents and models of assessment and intervention.

How to Detect and Manage Dyslexia

A reference and resource manual: Philomena Ott (1997) (Heinemann, Oxford)

This manual provides information for professionals, parents and dyslexic students and adults. It provides a historical acount that details the growing awareness and impact of dyslexia in education, legislation and society. There are chapters on early identification, reading writing, spelling and Mathematics that provide information on approaches for tackling dyslexia. This book also contains informative chapters on Music that look at the implications of dyslexia for the musician, and comprehensive chapters on the adolescent and adult dyslexic.

Making Your Secondary Classroom Dyslexia Friendly
Kate Moore (2000) (Desktop Publications, Barnetby-le-Wold, UK)

This short, A4, illustrated booklet (18 pages) provides an insight into those aspects—such as timetables, colour-coding, giving instructions and making worksheets—of a secondary classroom that can be challenging for students with dyslexic difficulties. There are also five photocopiable pages for students that deal with memory, including how to remember months of the year and days of the week.

Multilingualism, Literacy and Dyslexia: A Challenge for Educators
Lindsay Peer and Gavin Reid (eds) (2000) David Fulton, London

This book provides a collection of perspectives on the issues associated with multilingualism and dyslexia. There are contributors from 10 different countries, each relating how multilingualism and dyslexia can be assessed and supported in their country. The book contains sections on assessment, linking assessment and support, policy and interventions, dyslexia in adults and university students, and the challenges relating to English as an additional language.

Difficulties in Literacy Development—Readers
Addressing Difficulties in Literacy Development. Responses at family, school, pupil and teacher levels, Janice Wearmouth, Janet Soler and Gavin Reid (eds) (2002) (RoutledgeFalmer, London); and *Contextualising Difficulties in Literacy Development. Exploring politics, culture, ethnicity and ethics*, Janet Soler, Janice Wearmouth, and Gavin Reid (eds) (2002) (RoutledgeFalmer, London)

This series consists of a set of two edited readers and an authored companion guide. The three books are based on the materials developed by the authors for the jointly developed Difficulties in Literacy course by the Open University and the University of Edinburgh. The two readers are 'contextualising difficulties in literacy development' and 'addressing difficulties in literacy development'. The first looks at politics, culture, ethnicity and ethics and the second looks at responses at family, school and teacher levels. The authored book based on the course material examines research policy and practice, which includes a thorough consideration of dyslexia.

Meeting Difficulties in Literacy Development. Research, Policy and Practice
Janice Wearmouth, Janet Soler and Gavin Reid (2003) (RoutledgeFalmer, London)

This book explores different conceptualisations of literacy and their implications in terms of addressing the barriers to literacy acquisition. Practical strategies and programes to help reduce these barriers are discussed by the authors, as well as current curriculum policies, controversies and ethical considerations. The book also enables practitioners to reflect critically upon the choices available to them in assessing and supporting students who experience difficulties in literacy development. The book contains, among others, chapters on equity, inclusion and the

law, socio-cultural models and approaches, curricula frameworks for literacy development, supporting literacy acquisition at the family level and two chapters on
dyslexia—the concepts and the responses to dyslexia.

Policy, Practice and Provision for Children with Specific Learning Difficulties
Jill Duffield, Sheila Riddell and Sally Brown (1995) (Avebury, New York)

This text provides an analysis of a major research project funded by the Scottish
Office Education Department conducted by the University of Stirling. It deals with
the background to the research, an analysis of provision, the role of the examination
system and teacher education, the perceptions of parents, learning support and
voluntary organisations, and provision within the health service. It concludes with
a summary of the debate concerning policy, practice and provision in dyslexia,
highlights issues such as competing policies reflecting different ideological stances,
economic considerations, the nature of specific learning difficulties and the controversy concerning recognition and what constitutes effective provision.

The Gift of Dyslexia. Why Some of the Smartest People Can't Read and How They Can Learn
Ronald D. Davies with Eldon M. Braun (1994, revised 1997) (Souvenir Press,
London)

This book describes a specific approach to tackling dyslexia devised and, indeed,
experienced by the author. The author describes dyslexia as a type of disorientation,
similar to the type of disorientation one experiences sitting in a motionless car when
a car moves alongside. The author, therefore, sees dyslexia from a perceptual
perspective, and the programme described in the book emphasises the role of perception. The exercises that are part of the programme—Davis Orientation Mastery—
describe perceptual ability assessment, basic symbol mastery and symbol mastery for
words.

Tackling Dyslexia (2nd edn)
Anne Cooke (2002) (Whurr, London)

This revised and updated book describes teaching approaches for children with
dyslexia and relates these approaches to the classroom and to the revised National
Curriculum in the UK. There are also chapters dealing with early recognition, computer technology, numeracy and Mathematics, and handwriting.

Understanding Learning Difficulties: A Guide for Teachers and Parents
James Chapman (1988) (ERDC Press, Massey University, New Zealand)

This book is essentially written for teachers and parents, and its jargon-free style is
suitable for this dual readership. The book provides a broader understanding of the
problems children with learning difficulties experience in schools. The book is written
in the New Zealand context, but it can also be helpful to parents and teachers in
other countries.

Understanding Specific Learning Difficulties
Margot Prior (1996) (Psychology Press, Hove, UK)

This book presents an Australian perspective of some aspects of specific learning difficulties. It examines neuropsychology and its use in understanding learning difficulties, diagnosis and assessment, reading, spelling and mathematics, 'remedial' techniques and resources, and the relationship between behaviour problems and learning difficulties. There is a clear psychology bias throughout the book, which can be seen particularly in the assessment chapter. This chapter begins by providing the aims of clinical, psychological and educational assessment. Most of the chapters are accompanied by case studies.

READING

Beginning to Read: The New Phonics in Context
Marilyn Jager Adams (1990b) (Heinemann, Oxford)

This is a precis of the classic text on reading *Beginning to Read: Thinking and Learning about Print* (Adams, 1990a). The precis maintains the scholarly presentation of the main text, but because it is shorter and more direct it provides a ready means of acquiring information on principles and practices involved in reading and the reading debate. The book provides perspectives on reading and describes the development of reading skills in young readers. The last chapter 'Concerns and Conclusions' provides pointers in predictors of reading acquisition.

How to Teach Your Dyslexic Child to Read—A Proven Method for Parents and Teachers
Bernice A. Baumer (1996) (Orcha Books, Poole, UK)

This book describes an intensive, one-to-one teaching programme, which includes charts, graphs and lesson plans. The programme is aimed for the child from kindergarten through to third grade in a step-by-step procedure. It provides detailed instructions on teaching phonics, spelling and syllables. There are also examples of word lists and other exercises that focus on initial consonants, vowels, blends and diphthongs.

Reading Development and Dyslexia
C. Hulme and M. Snowling (eds) (1994) (Whurr, London)

The chapters in this book present a selection of papers presented to the Third International Conference of the BDA. The book is divided into three parts: the normal development of reading skills, the nature and causes of reading difficulties, and the remediation of reading difficulties. All the contributors are well known in their field and put forward an international perspective on issues relating to reading and dyslexia.

Helping Children with Reading and Spelling: A Special Needs Manual
R. Reason and R. Boote (1994) (Routledge, London)

This manual consists of teaching plans incorporating a range of strategies intended for use with children who have difficulty learning to read, write and spell. The main themes of the book are encapsulated in the model of literacy learning outlined by the authors—that is, one that incorporates and distinguishes between meaning, phonics and fluency. The authors suggest that these three areas interact with each other at all stages from beginning reading to achieving competency. Part 1 of the book develops this theme, Part 2 looks at reading, Part 3 looks at spelling and Part 4 at applications to the classroom. The reading parts look at assessment and development of reading skills through four stages, each stage incorporating aspects of meaning, phonics and fluency. There are plentiful examples with clearly presented case studies. The spelling part contains descriptions of the stages involved in learning to spell; developing strategies for spelling; a personalised spelling programme; and games and activities. The handwriting part follows the format of the spelling chapter, from the viewpoint that handwriting is a skill that closely supports the development of spelling. This chapter provides examples relating to concepts about handwriting, materials and resources, models and teaching methods. The last two chapters provide examples of how teachers have utilised the information, strategies and models described in the preceding pages.

Phonological Awareness Training: A New Approach to Phonics
Jo Wilson (1993) (Educational Psychology, London)

This is a specific programme on a particular aspect of literacy development—phonological awareness. The programme complements other types of activities, such as stories, poems and rhymes, that are beneficial to the development of phonological awareness. The essential component of phonological awareness training is the use of analogies to help children read and spell. It is suggested that research shows that familiarity with onsets and rimes is a necessary prerequisite to competence in phonics and that programmes that utilise the principle of onsets and rimes can help children learn to read. The programme consists of 25 worksheets, reading lists, dictation sheets and 'rime' display sheets. The programme can be used with an individual child or with a group and is suitable for children of seven years and upwards.

Sound Linkage. An Integrated Programme for Overcoming Reading Difficulties
Peter Hatcher (1994) (Whurr, London)

This book contains 10 sections on developing phonological awareness. Each part deals with a different aspect. For example, Part 3 deals with phoneme-blending and Part 6 with phoneme segmentation. Each part includes a series of activities relating to the skills being addressed in that particular part. The book opens with a test of phonological awareness, and the complete package is essentially a self-contained programme on phonological awareness.

Together for Reading
Dorothy Smith, John Shirley and John Visser (1996) (NASEN Publications, Tamworth, UK)

The theme of this book is teachers and parents, and the authors' views are consistently indicating that parents have an important role in helping their child develop reading skills. This short book (48 pages) contains suggestions on the importance of parental involvement, home–school communication, organising a partnership scheme and parts on staff development and examples of workshops that could be used to assist the teacher–parent partnership. There is an appendix that contains checklists for involving parents in reading, a summary of legislation and some suggested strategies for decoding unknown words.

Helping with Reading Difficulties (Key Stage 2)
Jane Calver, Sandy Ranson and Dorothy Smith (1999) (NASEN Publications, Tamworth, UK)

This book begins by setting the scene by summarising the reading debate from top-down and bottom-up perspectives. It looks at the importance of reading policies and why some pupils have difficulty with reading. Part of the book focuses on identification and assessment and discusses a range of different forms of assessment. The part on reading approaches looks at teaching reading at Key Stage 2 and provides examples of teaching and learning approaches through the use of visual strategies, auditory strategies, contextual strategies and motivational aspects. In the part on auditory strategies, there are examples showing how to develop phonological awareness skills. The final part of the book looks at classroom organisation and working with parents and adults. There is also an appendix that contains a precision-testing probe sheet, checking passages for word types, recording shared-reading and a list with examples of the 44 sounds (phonemes) of the English language.

Teaching the Literacy Hour in an Inclusive Classroom: Supporting Pupils with Learning Difficulties in a Mainstream Environment
Ann Berger and Jean Gross (eds) (1999) (David Fulton, London)

This book illustrates how the Literacy Hour can be made more effective for a range of children with special needs. It includes chapters on differentiation, structured programmes and managing behaviour difficulties. There is a part of the book on children with specific needs, such as children with speech and language difficulties, hearing loss, vision impairment and autistic spectrum disorder. There is also a chapter on the use of ICT.

Inclusive Education Practices
Teresa Grainger and Janet Tod (2000) (David Fulton, London)

Language, literacy and learning in context is the title of the opening chapter of this book and very much sets the tone for what follows. Focusing on the national literacy strategy, the book examines inclusive principles and practices from different perspectives: philosophical, political, practice-based, educational practice in literacy and institutional self-review. There is also a part on ideas for action, assessment and target-setting, speaking and listening principles, reading aloud, guided reading principles and shared-writing ideas for action.

Implementing the Literacy Hour for Pupils with Learning Difficulties
Ann Berger, Jean Henderson and Denise Morris (1999) (David Fulton, London)

This book highlights how the Literacy Hour can be made effective for all children. The opening chapter provides a background to the Literacy Hour and discusses some principles associated with literacy. There is also a part on planning the Literacy Hour and a significant section of the book on developing schemes of work. There are also examples of developing learning objectives for phonological awareness, word recognition, vocabulary and handwriting.

Literacy in New Zealand—Practices, Politics and Policy since 1900
Janet Soler and John Smith (eds) (2000) (Pearson Education, Auckland, New Zealand)

This book presents a history of literacy in New Zealand schools to the present day and provides some future pointers in relation to current needs and current research. There are sections on Maori literacy and contemporary issues in relation to the Maori language. The book dwells to a great extent on the ongoing debate between whole-language and phonics approaches and provides enlightened and clearly explained examples of both approaches. The book also focuses on the Literacy Taskforce in New Zealand and discusses relevant issues in pedagogy, resourcing, and critical appraisal of reading methodology and its implications for teachers.

Reading Schemes

Oxford Reading Tree
Oxford University Press

With an age suitability of 5–7+ this programme contains numerous extended and supplementary storybooks. Many of the activities are based on reading by analogy and progress through 11 stages of reading development.

Letterland Writing Programme
Lyn Wendon (1994)

Letterland consists of many different elements. The materials are aimed at teaching reading, spelling, writing and developing and sustaining motivation. The programmes are internationally renowned, and well over 50% of all primary schools in England and Ireland rely on them (Letterland International, 1997). The materials consist of teachers' guides, wall-charts, code cards, flashcards, word books, cassettes and songbooks, photocopiable materials, workbooks, games and resources, software, videos and materials specifically designed for use at home. The programme may also be seen as a preventative approach, since it is appropriate for early intervention and may also facilitate the reinforcement of important developmental concepts in learning such as object constancy. The Letterland system essentially grew out of close observations of failing readers, and the materials reinforce the importance of a reading-for-meaning orientation to print. The system encourages motivation and exploration of written language and results in schools. Wendon (1993) suggests that Letterland can account for a measurable decrease in the number of children in schools requiring extra help with reading and spelling.

Orton–Gillingham Approach

Orton–Gillingham lessons, according to Henry (1996) always incorporate card drills, spelling and reading and usually include activities such as:

- card drills—this involves the use of commercial- or teacher-made cards containing the common letter patterns to strengthen the visual modality; phonemes (sounds) for auditory and kinaesthetic reinforcement; and syllables and whole words to help develop blending skills;
- word lists and phrases;
- oral reading selection—this involves the teacher first reading the passage, then the student;
- spelling of phonetic and non-phonetic words;
- handwriting—with attention being placed on pencil grip, writing posture and letter formation (this would also include tracing, copying and practice, and making cursive connections, such as br, bl);
- composition—encouragement to develop writing sentences, paragraphs and short stories.

Reading Activities—Word-reading

Developing Literacy—Word Level Activities for the Literacy Hour Year 1
Ray Barker and Christine Moorcroft (1999) (A. C. Black, London)

This book consists of material that can be photocopied. The book is one of a series of books from Reception to Year 6. The series also contains similar books on developing literacy at the sentence level and text level. Each book aims to develop children's understanding of sound–spelling relationship and promotes independent work during the Literacy Hour. For example, the year looks at activities to develop vowels, onset and rime, phonemes, letter names, rhymes, double consonants and initial consonant clusters.

Story Rhyme Photocopy Masters
Clare Kirtley (1996) (Oxford University Press)

Based on the Oxford Reading Tree these photocopy masters help to increase awareness of rhymes and provide opportunities for writing rhymes and practising the analogy strategy. They contain activities about word families, listening, recognising, reading and writing.

Completely Out of Sight—Common Words for Reading and Spelling
Lynn Lettice and Melsa Nichols (1999) Easylearn, Southwell, UK

This book contains 151 worksheets providing a variety of activities that have strong themes. It takes the requirements of the National Literacy Strategy and Scottish National Guidelines for English into account. The worksheets on high frequency words and other common words use strategies including look, cover, write and check, and games activities.

Before Alpha

This is a programme of learning games that can be used with children under five. These games are in a series of structured stages, are multi-sensory and aim to foster language development and other pre-reading skills, such as visual and auditory perception and discrimination, fine-motor control, spatial relationships, knowledge of colour, number and directions.

Teaching Reading and Spelling to Dyslexic Children
Margaret Walton (1998) (David Fulton, London)

This practical A4 book begins with a description of different reading approaches and strategies that can be used for dyslexic children. The remainder of the book focuses on a teaching programme beginning with the alphabet, then sounds and blends. There are also activities that aid punctuation, spelling and finding suitable books, as well as photocopiable resources in the appendix.

Spotlight on Blends
Gillian Aitken (1997) (Robinswood Press, Stourbridge, UK)

This series contains two books. The other book *End Consonant Blends* provides systematic practice of consonant blends with varied tasks that help to promote phonological awareness by means of sound-blending. Detailed teaching notes and guidelines accompany the worksheets.

Phonic Rhyme Time
Mary Nash-Wortham (1993) (Robinswood Press, Stourbridge, UK)

The book contains a collection of phonic rhymes that the author suggests will help with speech and reading. It provides an understanding of speech sounds and their creation, helped by charts showing categories of phonic sounds and a phonic rhyme chart. After the first part the book provides a collection of rhymes and an analysis of the key phonic aspects of the rhymes.

Phonics and Phonic Resources
Mike Hinson and Pete Smith (1997) (NASEN Publications, Tamworth, UK)

This book contains a detailed list of resources for phonics. Divided into two parts, Part 1 covers phonics assessment and teaching, while Part 2 covers phonic resources. There is also a checklist of resources that includes brief descriptions of some reading programmes:

- *Breaking the Code* (Learning Materials Ltd.);
- *The Big Book of Early Phonics* (Prim-ed Publishing);
- *Active Phonics Workbooks* (Ginn and Co.);
- *Finger Phonics* (Jolly Learning Ltd.);
- *The First Phonic Blending Book* (Kickstart Publications);
- *Fuzzbuzz Workbooks* (Oxford University Press);
- *Ginn Phonic Workbooks 1–6* (Ginn and Co.);
- *Learning Phonics 1 and 2* (Hilda King Educational Services);
- *Phonic Links* (Collins);

- *The Phonics Bank* (Ginn and Co.);
- *The Phonics Handbook* (Jolly Learning Ltd.);
- *Rhyme and Analogy* (Oxford University Press);
- *Sounds Easy* (Egon Publishers);
- *Sounds, Patterns and Words* (Collins);
- *SpLD Phonic Skills Books 1 and 2* (Kickstart Publications);
- *Stile Early Phonics* (LDA);
- *Sure Fire Phonics* (Thomas Nelson);
- *Timesaver Phonic Books 1–8* (Precise Educational).

The book also contains references to reading programmes:

- *All Aboard* (Ginn and Co.);
- *Bangers and Mash* (Longman Group);
- *Cambridge Reading* (Cambridge University Press);
- *Flying Boot* (Thomas Nelson);
- *Fuzzbuzz* (Oxford University Press);
- *Letterland* (Collins Educational);
- *Longman Book Project* (Longman Group Ltd.);
- *New Reading 360* (Ginn and Co.);
- *Oxford Reading Tree* (Oxford University Press);
- *Wellington Square* (Thomas Nelson).

Acceleread, Accelewrite: A Guide to Using Talking Computers—Helping Children to Read and Spell
Vivienne Clifford and Martin Miles (1994) (iansyst, Cambridge, UK)

This guide helps the teacher access talking systems for the computer. The emphasis is on developing the practical skills, but the guide also provides a theoretical understanding of the system. The guide provides suggestions for using the applications for creative and curriculum-based work. The first two parts examine the hardware that can be utilised and the theory behind the approach. Essentially, it provides the basis for a structural approach to developing phonological skills in a multi-sensory way. Thus, the pupil reads the story, then types it into the computer, the computer then repeats each word of the sentence to the child as the space bar is pressed. The whole sentence is also spoken once the sentence has been completed. The guide emphasises self-monitoring, and auditory and visual feedback.

Spelling

Spelling World
Amanda Gray (1994) (Nash Pollock, Oxford)

This is a photocopiable spelling programme that contains a series of four books at different levels based on the look, cover, write, check principle. It covers 500 of the most commonly used words and contains a range of activities to help with spelling (with integrated handwriting activities).

Spelling and Spelling Resources
Pete Smith, Mike Hinson and Dave Smith (1998) (NASEN Publications, Tamworth, UK)

This book is divided into two areas: one on the teaching of spelling, assessment, approaches and policy; and the other on resources that can be used for spelling including an index of spelling resources, examples of software programmes and useful websites. There is also an annotated list of materials on spelling with an indication of the suitability level.

Assessment

Rate of Reading Test
The Rate of Reading Test is designed to assess the effects of coloured overlays. It is claimed this test has some advantages over conventional tests because it actually tests the linguistic and semantic aspects of reading at least as much as the visual. Additionally, with conventional tests performance is limited by a reader's vocabulary. The Rate of Reading Test therefore seeks to minimise the linguistic and semantic aspects of reading and maximises the visual difficulties.

The same 15 common words are used in each line in a different random order. The words were selected from the 110 most frequent words in a count of words in children's reading books. The text is printed in small typeface at an optimal level for visual distortion. The test is scored by noting the total number of words in the passage read correctly and calculating the average number correctly read per minute.

Wilkins et al. (1996) found the test both reliable and valid, and it successfully predicted the individuals who, when offered a coloured overlay, continued to use it. They also show that the use of the overlays had an effect on reading speed, and did so immediately. The authors also report on a study in which 93 children in primary school and 59 in the first year intake of a secondary school reported an improvement in perception (text with a particular colour), and the 22% of the sample who continued to use them for 10 months demonstrated a mean improvement of 14% in reading speed by using their overlay ($p < 0.02$). This improvement was not seen in children who had failed to persist in using the overlay.

Listening and Literacy Index (LLI)
Charles Weedon and Gavin Reid (2001) (Hodder and Stoughton, London)

The LLI is a group test for profiling literacy development and identifying specific learning difficulties. It consists of four subtests: listening and spelling; regular words; spelling; and sight words and reading comprehension. The battery offers a diagnostic comparison between listening and literacy, and standardised scores are available from 5 years 6 months to 9 years. There are also sample profiles and suggestions for follow-up.

Phonological Assessment of Specific Learning Difficulties
Norah Frederickson and Rea Reason (eds) (1995) in *Educational and Child Psychology*, **12**(1)

This issue (88 pages in length) discusses the role of phonological assessment in specific learning difficulties and explains the development of the Phonological Assessment Battery (PhAB). The issue begins with a paper by Frith that provides a theoretical model highlighting the role of phonological skills and that justifies the nature of the tests selected for the PhAB. The following papers provide some insights into the rationale and composition of the specific subtests that comprise the Assessment Battery.

Psychological Assessment of Dyslexia
Martin Turner (1997) (Whurr, London)

This book provides an analysis of psychological assessment. It contains chapters on abilities, individual variation, cognitive anomalies and structures for charting individual attainment and reporting. There is also a chapter on recommendations for specialist teaching, accompanied by an analysis of a casework sample. Tests that can be accessed by teachers are included, and there are also sections on the younger child, the adult and a discussion on some of the issues relating to resources. As the title suggests, the book is essentially concerned with psychological assessment, and the detailed analysis it provides should prove extremely beneficial to educational psychologists in particular.

Psychology in Education Portfolio
N. Frederickson and R. J. Cameron (1999) (NFER-Nelson, Windsor, UK)

This is a comprehensive assessment toolkit that contains eight individual tests covering such topics as motivation, learning styles and metacognition, memory and listening comprehension, the learning environment, self-perceptions, social skills and bullying behaviour. There is an introductory booklet that summarises the portfolio contents. The test materials are aimed for teacher use. The tests mainly utilise questionnaires and each incorporates an explanatory booklet.

Mathematics

Specific Learning Difficulties in Mathematics—A Classroom Approach
Olwen El-Naggar (1996) (NASEN Publications, Tamworth, UK)

This book examines the difficulties that can be experienced by children with specific learning difficulties in Mathematics. There are chapters on assessment, developing an individualised programme and implications for classroom teachers. The assessment chapter looks at the use of mathematical language and symbols. It also suggests that one should be looking at pupils' compensatory strategies and attention span.

Maths for the Dyslexic; A Practical Guide
Anne Henderson (1998) (David Fulton Publishers, London)

This comprehensive and accessible book is in two parts. The first is an overview of problems regarding mathematical concepts, language and methods of assessment. The second part consists of a wealth of teaching strategies in all aspects of mathematics.

What to Do When You Can't Learn the Times Tables
Steve Chinn (1996) (Marcko Mark, Somerset, UK)

This is a practical book aimed at providing strategies to help dyslexic students learn tables. It is not intended to be a quick-fix book, and each of the methods suggested requires practice and perseverance. It suggests that the use of a table square is a more efficient method than learning the tables through a linear collection of facts. The book contains ideas to minimise the memory load on the dyslexic student and to provide strategies that with practice can help the dyslexic student become a more efficient and successful learner in Mathematics.

Computer Information

Computer Booklets
BDA (1997) (British Dyslexia Association in conjunction with Dyslexia Computer Resource Centre, Reading, UK)

The BDA has produced a set of low-priced computer booklets with introductory leaflets. The introductory leaflets look at portable computers, keyboard skills and computer management, software, talking computers and information for dyslexic adults. There are also more detailed booklets on exams, Mathematics, early literacy and numeracy skills, and dyslexic adults and computers. ICT is an important area for dyslexic students, and these booklets offer a clear account of how this continually developing area can be effectively accessed by dyslexic students and teachers. Up-to-date comparisons of many computer software programs can be obtained from www.dyslexia.com *The Dyslexia Handbook*, published annually by the BDA, always contains an informative and up-to-date part on dyslexia and ICT.

Study Skills and Learning Styles

Eight Ways of Knowing—Teaching for Multiple Intelligences (3rd edn)
David Lazear (1999) (Skylight Professional Development, Arlington Heights, IL)

This book is subtitled *A Handbook of Techniques for Expanding Intelligence*. It is a follow-up to the *Seven Ways of Knowing*, also by the same author. The addition concerns the eighth intelligence in the multiple intelligence spectrum developed by Gardner (i.e., naturalist intelligence). This is directly related to recognition and appreciation of the natural world around us, and involves our abilities to discriminate different species, classify various flora and our general knowledge of the natural world. The author points out that those with a highly developed natural intelligence would feel a lift if flowers were brought into a room or would choose to relax by heading for the countryside. He suggests it is important to cultivate children's naturalist intelligence, and this can be done by visits to the zoo and getting involved in projects relating to conservation and tree-planting. The book also provides practical strategies on developing all eight intelligences and gives a clear summary of all eight intelligences.

Get Better Grades
Margie Agnew, Steve Barlow, Lee Pascal and Steve Skidmore (1995) (Piccadilly Press, London)

This short text on study skills looks at attitude, organisation, listening and note-taking, reading and writing skills, and revision for exams. The information is presented in an eye-catching manner, and the text contains study strategies that are more suitable for older children, and even some adults.

Get Ahead—Mind Map© Your Way to Success
Vanda North and Tony Buzan (2001) (Buzan Centres)

This book gives a colourful introduction to the use of Mind Maps and highlights the use of colours in learning and suggestions on how to use Mind Maps for such activities as note-taking, learning symbols, planning and speaking to groups. This is very suitable for all students, but particularly those with a dyslexic processing style who may find it very useful for prepration for examinations.

In the Mind's Eye. Visual Thinkers, Gifted People with Learning Difficulties, Computer Images and the Ironics of Creativity
Thomas G. West (1991) (Prometheus Books, Buffalo, NY)

This text highlights the positive side of dyslexia. It provides extensive profiles of such gifted people as Faraday, Einstein and da Vinci, who were all dyslexic, and examines patterns in creativity. It relates these patterns to computers and visual images and ponders the implications of these for dyslexic students and adults. There are some insights into the potential of the dyslexic learner, perhaps encapsulated in the statement: 'We ought to begin to pay less attention to getting everyone over the same hill using the same path. We may wish to encourage some to take different routes to the same end. Then we might see good reasons for paying careful attention to their descriptions of what they have found. We may wish to follow them some day.'

Learning Styles: A Guide for Teachers and Parents
Barbara Given and Gavin Reid (1999) (Red Rose Publications, St Anne's-on-Sea, UK)

This book provides a critical analysis of learning styles and insights into the five learning systems: emotional, social, cognitive, physical and reflective. The practical applications of an interactive observational checklist for identification of preliminary individual learning styles are also discussed.

Self-esteem

Quality Circle Time in the Primary Classroom
Jenny Mosley (1996) (LDA, Cambridge, UK)

This book is a guide to enhancing self-esteem, self-discipline and positive relationships. It focuses on quality circle time in the classroom. It follows on from the author's previous book *Turn Your School Around*. The book is divided into five parts: Part 1 is about establishing positive relationships in the classroom; Part 2 on creating a calm and positive classroom ethos; Part 3 on exploring the use of circle time activities; Part 4 on circle meetings; and Part 5 provides further information on circle time (e.g., how it can relate to the national curriculum). This book is a very comprehensive guide to circle time activities and explains how the activities can be integrated and utilised within the school setting. It contains ideas and suggestions for further activities related to circle time. The programmes and activities are all underpinned by a circular model developed by the author, which shows how circle time can be implemented within the school system.

Dyslexia and Stress
T. R. Niles and Ved Varma (eds) (1995) (Whurr, London)

This book describes the different types of stress experienced by dyslexic people. The importance of this area is highlighted by the range of chapters presented in this book that deal with stress: in early education; in the adolescent; at college; in the workplace; among gifted dyslexics; and within the family. There is also a chapter in which dyslexics speak for themselves, providing personal perspectives of how the disability has affected their lives. It is important in a book that looks at the psychological and emotional aspects of the dyslexic individual to include these personal perspectives. It is also important for all involved in the field of dyslexia to appreciate the emotional effect of the difficulty as experienced by the dyslexic person.

Motor Development

Praxis Makes Perfect
Dyspraxia Trust (2001) (Dyspraxia Trust, Hitchin, UK)

This publication contains nine chapters on areas concerning dyspraxia. Dyspraxia is defined an an 'impairment or immaturity in the organisation of movement which leads to associated problems with language, perception and thought.' There are, therefore, chapters on understanding dyspraxia and views from teachers, psychotherapists and occupational therapists. The book contains guidance on dealing with handwriting problems, advice on activities for dyspraxic children and general considerations at school, including social integration in the classroom.

Developmental Dyspraxia: A Practical Manual for Parents and Professionals
Madeleine Portwood (2001) (Durham County Council Educational Psychology Service, Durham, UK)

This illustrated manual is appropriate for both parents and teachers. The first two chapters provide a neurological-orientated background, but without the learning terminology that usually accompanies such explanations. These chapters are followed by a chapter entitled 'What is dyspraxia?'. This provides a summary from 6–12 months through to 7 years and describes some observable behaviours found in dyspraxic children. The definition that the author uses to describe dyspraxia is located in this chapter—'motor difficulties caused by perceptual problems, especially visual–motor and kinaesthetic–motor difficulties' (p. 15).

Dyspraxia 5–11
C. MacIntyre (2001) (David Fulton, London)

This guide takes a very practical view of dyspraxia in the primary school.

Graded Activities for Children with Motor Difficulties
J. Russell (1988) (Cambridge Educational, Cambridge, UK)

Russell (1988) has developed a set of graded activities for children with motor difficulties. This is a very teacher-friendly text that contains clearly illustrated activities. The programme consists of 14 parts including gross-motor, balancing, catching, throwing, kicking and jumping, directional orientation, visual–motor co-ordination and handwriting activities. These activities, though essentially directed at children with motor problems, can be extremely useful for a number of dyslexic children.

Parents

Living with Dyslexia
Barbara Riddock (1996) (Routledge, London)

This book provides an overview of dyslexia from a range of perspectives, including educational, emotional, social, parent, teacher and children. There is a chapter dedicated to case studies. The book is essentially the product of a research project conducted by the author, and one of its aims is to examine how information on living with dyslexia can be collected in a systematic manner and integrated with other forms of research to increase the understanding of dyslexia. Another aim of the book is to raise constructive debate on the advantages and disadvantages of using the label 'dyslexia'. Essentially, the author provides a broader perspective of dyslexia and indicates that it is more than just a reading disability. This, in fact, is borne out by children's own views, which is the focus of one of the chapters.

Dyslexie, Legasthénie, Dyslexia—Strategies for Success in Schools
Dyspel (2002) (Dyspel, Luxembourg, 21 rue de Luxembourg, L-5364 Schrassig, email: mccarth@pt.lu)

This book is an informative guide for parents and teachers, written in three languages: English, German and French. The book, which is colourfully and carefully presented to ensure maximum readability, includes chapters on identifying dyslexia, liaison with parents, school policy and exam revision. It is particularly useful for those involved with students with dyslexia in multilingual/multicultural environments.

Dyslexia—Parents in Need
Pat Heaton (1996) (Whurr, London)

This book describes some of the responses from parents in answer to research questions that affect the parents of dyslexic children. It deals with such aspects as early signs, language difficulties, parents' feelings and perceptions, practical aspects and factors influencing effective liaison with the school. Part 2 of the book devotes over 20 pages to word searches and other game-type activities for identifying vowels and consonants.

Language Shock—Dyslexia across Cultures. A Multimedia Training Pack for Learners, Parents and Teachers (3rd edn)
European Children in Crisis (ECIC) (2000) (Dyslexia International—Tools and Technologies (DITT), Brussels)

This package was created to provide a European-wide perspective of dyslexia and, particularly, to satisfy the needs of staff in European multicultural, multilingual schools. The package contains a detailed guide, a video and a website. The package was developed by European Children in Crisis (ECIC), which is a non-profit, non-governmental organisation to help promote the interests of children with learning difficulties. The guide is very informative and is divided into three sections. The first one deals with understanding dyslexia and includes chapters on coping with dyslexia and bilingualism and dyslexia. The second part is on 'Dealing with Dyslexia' and contains chapters on assessment that have been specially written for teachers and for parents. The other part provides details about further information that may be useful for parents and teachers. There is a chapter on children's rights, and resources and contacts. This contains details of European-wide organisations and a summary of the education system and educational initiatives in the 17 member states.

Dyslexia: A Parents' and Teachers' Guide
Trevor Payne and Elizabeth Turner (1998) (Multilingual Matters, Clevedon, UK)

This book provides an overview of certain areas that relate to dyslexia: reading, spelling, handwriting, writing and numeracy. There is also a chapter on provision for dyslexic children. Essentially, it is a practical book with many examples of practice based on the authors' experiences.

Breaking Down the Barriers: Aspects of the First 25 Years of SPELD in New Zealand
Peggy Buchanan (1996) (SPELD, Wellington, New Zealand)

The New Zealand Federation of Specific Learning Disabilities Associations (SPELD) celebrated its 25th anniversary with this publication. It describes how the Association began, its development through its extensive network of branches and how it works in relation to the education system. There is also a chapter on conferences and keynote speakers whom SPELD have invited to New Zealand over the last 25 years. It also provides an account of SPELD's drive for dyslexia to be recognised through legislation and initiatives in the field of teacher-training.

Lost for Words—Dyslexia at Second Level and Beyond—A Practical Guide for Parents and Teachers
Wyn McCormack (1998) (Tower Press, Dublin)

This book focuses on the Republic of Ireland education system and is written from a parent–teacher perspective. It provides a descriptive account of how dyslexic children may progress through the system, particularly in relation to how parents can help their child at second level and beyond, how to cope with administration, and career choice and accessing support services. Contextualised within the Irish Republic, it describes services offered by specific colleges and detailed aspects of school policy. There are also chapters on strategies for presenting and coping with different subject areas.

With a Little Help from My Friends—Dyslexia: An Introductory Guide for Parents

Gavin Reid (2002) (Moray House School of Education, Edinburgh)

This short publication aims to provide clear and relevant advice to parents on dyslexia. The booklet looks at key issues relating to assessment and provides advice on assessment and resources. There are also parts on 'What Is Dyslexia?', identification and assessment, and support and strategies.

Adults

Adult Dyslexia: Assessment, Counselling and Training

David McLoughlin, Gary Fitzgibbon and Vivienne Young (1994) (Whurr, London)

This book focuses on the needs of adult dyslexics. The introduction sets the tone of the book by examining some of the characteristics of dyslexia, particularly memory difficulties. This is followed by two chapters, one on screening and the other on formal assessment. The remainder of the book discusses methods of dealing with dyslexic difficulties in the workplace, through career-counselling and teaching strategies. Though a short book (100 pages), it contains some useful information in the important area of adult dyslexia, which has been somewhat neglected until recently.

Dyslexia in Adults: Education and Employment

Gavin Reid and Jane Kirk (2001) (John Wiley & Sons, Chichester, UK)

This book gives some insights into the issues relating to dyslexia in adults in study and in the workplace. It begins by discussing some of the issues that have relevance to this group, such as the use and misuse of labels, support in the workplace, assessment availability, the use of the term 'disability', the screening process, the use of technology-accessing resources and learning style. There are chapters on screening, assessment and support, training, dyslexia in the workplace and learning strategies, and chapters that focus on both the negative and positive consequences of the dyslexia experience. This is echoed in a chapter in which dyslexic adults recount their own experiences. The final chapter deals with sources of support and resources.

Dyslexia in the Workplace

Diana Bartlett and Sylvia Moody (2000) (Whurr, London)

This book covers the nature of dyslexic difficulties and their effects on adults in the workplace. The book discusses emotional and practical aspects. It also covers recent legislation and its impact on adults with dyslexia. There is also a part on further information for adults with dyslexia and employers.

The Dyslexic Adult in a Non-Dyslexic World
Ellen Morgan and Cynthia Klein (2000) (Whurr, London)

This book looks at the world of dyslexic adults from their own personal perspectives and experiences. It also examines cognitive styles and diagnosis as well as support issues, family and work, and career aspects.

Inclusion

Working towards Inclusive Education—Social Contexts
Peter Mittler (2001) (David Fulton, London)

'Inclusion is not about placing children in mainstream schools. It is about changing schools to make them more responsive to the needs of all children' (p. vii). This quote is from the author's introduction to this book and very much sets the tone on how to change schools to accommodate to the needs of an inclusive society. There are chapters on exclusion and inclusion. They discuss influences on the inclusion movement. The chapter on global dimensions discusses initiatives from around the world that have culminated in the thrust to inclusion evident in current UK legislation. The book also discusses such key issues as early years, social exclusion, prevention of learning difficulties, policies on inclusion, role of parents, and current and future tensions relating to inclusion. The book is essentially about inclusion, social equality, legislation and how these factors affect parents and, particularly, home–school relationships. Mittler suggests that the practice and policy of home–school links needs to be reconceptualised. Real partnerships need to be formed between school and parents and, although there is some evidence of this, some of the other areas discussed in this book fall short of achieving the goal of inclusion. The ideas in this book and the views of the author have implications for parents of children with dyslexia, especially as, although a legal framework exists, it is usually more effective to promote harmony and partnership at an early stage with parents than to resort to legal resolutions.

Special Educational Needs, Inclusion and Diversity, A Textbook
Norah Frederickson and Tony Cline (2002) (Open University Press, Buckingham, UK)

This comprehensive text is set out in three parts. One on principles and concepts, one on assessment in context and the other on areas of need. Each chapter is preceded by several objectives. The book provides an excellent and detailed overview of social, cultural and linguistic contexts that can determine the success or otherwise of inclusion. The concept of special educational needs is examined in detail, and this provides an evaluation and a summary of the development of special educational needs and the various ways of conceptualising them. This is a thought-provoking work, particularly the interactional analysis that suggests that special educational needs are not only a within-child factor but an interaction of a number of variables including society, the education system and the curriculum and teaching approaches. Therefore, areas such as reducing bias in assessment, curriculum-based assessment and learning environments are considered. In the part on areas of need, there are chapters on learning difficulties as well as language, literacy, Mathematics, social skills, and emotional and sensory factors. In relation to dyslexia the authors point out the need to consider sociocultural factors in any definition of dyslexia and, although they suggest that a phonologically based definition has most support, there are still problems with an exclusive phonologically based definition because it needs to consider learning opportunities that can affect phonological development. It also needs to differentiate between reading difficulties and phonological difficulties, as not all children with reading difficulties will have phonological difficulties. The book also contains some useful suggestions on promoting social skills in children, and this underlines the comprehensive nature as well as the key thrust of this text.

FURTHER RESOURCES AND INFORMATION

- Adult Dyslexia Organisation (ADO), 336 Brixton Road, London SW9 7AA (helpline: 0171 924 9559; admin.: 0171 737 7646; website: www.futurenet.co.uk)
- Ann Arbor—(fax: 01668 214484; email: enquiries@annarbor.co.uk; website: www.annarbor.co.uk)
- Barrington Stoke Ltd, 10 Belford Terrace, Edinburgh. EH4 3DQ
- Better Books, 3 Paganel Drive, Dudley, DY1 4AZ (tel.: 01384 253276; fax: 01384 253285)
- British Dyslexia Association, 98 London Road, Reading RG1 5AU (helpline: 0118 966 8217; admin.: 0118 966 2677; fax: 0118 935 1927; email: helpline@bda-dyslexia.demon.co.uk. or admin@bda-dyslexia.demon.co.uk; website: http://www.bda-dyslexia.org.uk)
- Buzan Centres Ltd, 54 Parkstone Road, Poole, Dorset, UK and PO Box 4, Palm Beach, FL 33480, USA (email: buzan@buzancentres.com; website: http://www.mind-map.com)
- Collins Educational, HarperCollins Publishers, Westerhill Road, Bishopbriggs, Glasgow G64 1BR
- Council for the Registration of Schools Teaching Dyslexic Pupils (CReSTeD), Greygarth, Littleworth, Winchcombe, Cheltenham GL54 5BT
- Creative Learning Company©, P.O. Box 106 239, Downtown, Auckland 1, New Zealand (tel.: +64.9.309 3701; fax: +64.9.309 3708; email: info@clc.co.nz; website: www.clc.co.nz)
- Crossbow Education, 41 Sawpit Lane, Brocton, Stafford ST17 0TE (www.crossboweducation.com)
- Department for Education and Employment (DfEE), Sanctuary Buildings, Great Smith Street, Westminster, London SW1P 3BT (tel.: 0171 925 5000; fax: 0171 925 6000; website: www.dfee.gov.uk)
- Dyslexia Association of Hong Kong (fax: 00 852 2872 5489; email: gadbury@iohk.com; website: www.dyslexia.org.hk
- Dyslexia Association of Ireland, Suffolk Chambers, 1 Suffolk Street, Dublin 2
- Dyslexia in Scotland, Unit 3, Stirling Business Centre, Wellgreen Place, Stirling FK8 2DZ (tel.: 01786 446 650; fax: 01786 471 235; http://www.dyslexia-in-scotland.org)
- Dyslexia Institute (DI), 133 Gresham Road, Staines, Middlesex TW18 2AJ (tel.: 01784 463 851; fax: 01784 460 747; email: dyslexia-inst@connect.bt.com; website: http://www.dyslexia-inst.org.uk)
- Dyslexia International—Tools and Technologies, rue Defacqz 1, B-1000, Brussels
- Dyspel asbl (the European one—this is different from the organisation that deals with probation service, also called Dyspel, see next entry), 21 rue de Luxembourg, L-5364, Schrassig, Luxembourg (email: mccarth@pt.lu) support group for families and professionals in Luxembourg who are concerned about dyslexia. It has a library of books, cassettes and videos and a regular newsletter. It has also produced a multilingual book in French, German and English for teachers

- Dyspel Project Office, G5 James House, 22–24 Corsham Street, London N1 6DR (tel.: 0207 2516770; website: www.dyspel.org.uk) (this project engages in activities relating to probation services, education and training services and music technology)
- Dyspraxia Trust, P.O. Box 30, Hitchin, Herts SG5 1UU
- Easylearn, Trent House, Fiskerton, Southwell, Notts
- Easy Reader Ltd, Norfolk (tel./fax: 01842 760 007; email: info@easyreader.org.uk; website: www.easyreader.org.uk)
- Egon Publishers Ltd., Royston Road, Baldock, Herts, SG7 6NW (tel.: 01462 894498)
- European Dyslexia Academy for Research and Training (E-Dart) 34 Deep Spinney, Biddenham, Bedford MK40 4QH (email: eda@kbnet.co.uk; website: www.bedford.ac.uk/eda)
- Gavin Reid, University of Edinburgh (email: gavin.reid@ed.ac.uk; website: www.gavinreid.co.uk)
- Ginn and Company, Prebendal House, Parsons Fee, Aylesbury, Bucks., HP20 2QY (tel.: 01296 88411)
- Heinemann Educational, School Orders Dept., Freepost, P.O. Box 381, Oxford OX2 8BR (tel.: 01865 314333)
- Helen Arkell Dyslexia Centre, Frensham, Farnham, Surrey GU10 3BW (tel.: 0125 792 400; fax: 01252 795 669)
- Hilda King Educational Services, Ashwells Manor Drive, Penn, Bucks., HP10 8EU (tel.: 01494 817947)
- Hodder & Stoughton—tests and assessment—(tel.: 01235 400454; email: orders@bookpoint.co.uk)
- Hodder Wayland—differentiated texts—(fax: 01235 400454)
- Hornsby International Dyslexia Centre, Wandsworth (tel.: 020 7223 1144; fax.: 020 7924 1112; email: dyslexia@hornsby.co.uk; website: www.hornsby.co.uk
- iansyst Ltd., The White House, 72 Fen Road, Cambridge CB4 1UN, UK (website: www.dyslexic.com).
- International Dyslexia Association, 8600 LaSalle Road, Chester Building, Suite 382, Baltimore, MD 21286-2044 (tel.: (410) 296 0232; fax: (410) 321 5069; email: info@interdys.org; website: http://www.interdys.org)
- Irlen Centre, 123 High Street, Chard, Somerset TA20 1QT (tel./fax: 01460 65555)
- John Wiley & Sons Ltd., The Atrium, Southern Gate, Chichester, West Sussex PO19 8SQ (tel.: 0800 243407 [UK] and +44 1243 779777 [overseas]; fax: +44 1243 843296; email cs-books@wiley.co.uk; website: www.wiley.com). Wiley also publishes the periodical *Dyslexia an International Journal of Research and Practice* (four issues per year). This journal is also online at www.interscience.wiley.com
- Jolly Phonics (comprehensive teaching materials, well presented with photocopiable masters and videos), Jolly Learning Ltd, Tailours House, High Road, Chigwell, Essex IG7 6DL (fax: 0181 500 1696)
- KCS-Tools for the Computer Enabled, Freepost, Southampton SO17 1YA (tel.: 0123 8058 4314; fax: 0123 8058 4320; email: info@keytools.com)
- Kickstart Publications Ltd., 38 Awbridge Road, Netherton, Dudley, West Midlands DY2 0JA (tel.: 01384 258535)

- Lancashire Centre for Specific Learning Difficulties/Dyslexia North West/Red Rose School, 28–30 North Promenade, St Anne's-on-Sea, Lancs. FY8 2NQ (tel./fax: 01253 720 570; website: www.dyslexiacentre.com)
- LDA—literacy resources for special needs—(fax: 0800 783 8648; website: www.LDAlearning.com)
- Learning Materials Ltd, Dixon Street, Wolverhampton WV2 2BX (tel.: 01902 54026)
- Learning Works®, 9 Barrow Close, Marlborough, Wiltshire
- London Language and Literacy Unit, South Bank University, 103 Borough Road, London SE1 0AA (tel.: 0171 928 8989)
- Longman Group Ltd, Customer Services, Freepost, Pinnacles, Harlow CM19 4BR (tel.: 01279 623921)
- Multi-Sensory Learning, Highgate House, Grooms' Lane, Creaton, Northants NN6 8NN
- National Council for Educational Technology (NCET), Milburn Hill Road, Science Park, Coventry CV4 7JJ (tel.: 01203 416 994; fax: 01203 411 418; email: enquiry_desk@ncet.org.uk)
- NFER-Nelson, Darville House, 2 Oxford Road East, Windsor, Berks SL4 1DF (tel.: 01753 858 961; fax: 01753 856 830; email: edu&hsc@nfer-nelson.co.uk; website: http://www.nfer-nelson.co.uk)
- Northern Ireland Dyslexia Association, 7 Mount Pleasant, Stranmilis Road, Belfast BT9 5DS
- Oxford University Press, Educational Division, Walton Street, Oxford OX2 6DP (tel.: 01865 56767)
- PATOSS (Professional Association of Teachers of Students with Specific Learning Difficulties) (website: http://www.patoss-dyslexia.org)
- Precise Educational Resource Centre, Dainsby House, 18 Market Place, Codnor, Derbyshire
- Prim-Ed. Publishing, P.O. Box 051, Nuneaton CV11 6ZU (tel.: 01203 352002)
- Psychological Corporation, 24–28 Oval Road, London NW1 1YA (tel.: 0171 424 4456; fax: 0171 424 4515; email: cservice@harcourtbrace.com)
- Right to Write Ltd, Head Office, 18 Wells Street, London W1T 3PG (tel.: 0207 436 9333; fax: 0207 436 8554; website: www.right2write.co.uk)
- (www.TheSchoolDaily.com) provides a wealth of useful and up-to-date information on education and dyslexia. The address of *The School Daily* is 5 Durham Street, Box 8577, Christchurch, New Zealand (fax: +64 3 366 5488)
- Scottish Council for Educational Technology (SCET), 74 Victoria Cresent Road, Glasgow G12 9JN (tel.: 0141 337 5051)
- Scottish Sensory Centre, Moray House School of Education, University of Edinburgh, Holyrood Road, Edinburgh EH8 8AQ
- SEN Marketing Dyslexia and Special Needs Bookshop, 618 Leeds Road, Outfield, Wakefield WF1 2LT (tel./fax: 01924 871697; email: sen.marketing@ukoline.co.uk)
- SNAP (Special Needs Assessment Profile), Weedon and Reid's 2003 Computer-aided Diagnostic Assessment and Profiling 5–14 (profiles 15 SPLDs) (website: http://www.snapassessment.com)
- Start to Finish Books, from Don Johnston, 18 Clarendon Court, Calver Road,

Winwick Quay, Warrington WA2 8QP (tel.: 01925 241642; fax: 01925 241745; website: www.donjohnston.com)
- Stass Publications—materials designed and written for speech and language therapists—44 North Road, Ponteland, Northumberland NE20 9UR (fax: 01661 860440; email: susan@stass.demon.co.uk)
- Study Scan, Pico Educational Systems Ltd, Lambeth (tel.: 020 8674 7786; fax: 020 8769 1150; website: www.studyscan.com)
- Text Help® New Zealand (http://www.heurisko.co.nz/texthelp)
- Texthelp Systems Ltd., Enkalon Business Centre, 25 Randalstown Road, Antrim BT41 4LJ (tel.: +44 1849 428 105; fax: +44 1849 428 574; email: info@texthelp.com; website: info@texthelp.com)
- TintaVision Ltd, Peterborough (tel.: 01778 349 233; fax: 01778 349 244; website: www.tintavision.com)
- Toe by Toe, 8 Green Road, W. Yorks BD17 5HL (tel.: 01274 598807)
- Whurr Publishers Ltd., 19b Compton Terrace, London N1 2UN (tel.: 0171 359 5979; fax: 0171 226 5290; email: info@whurr.co.uk)
- Xavier Educational Software Ltd., Psychology Department, University College of Wales, Bangor, Gwynedd LL57 2DG (tel.: 01248 382 616; fax: 01248 382 599; email: xavier@bangor.ac.uk; website: http:/wwwxavier.bangor.ac.uk)

References

Aaron, P. G. (1989) *Dyslexia and Hyperlexia*. Boston, Kluwer.

Aaron, P. G. (1994) Differential diagnosis of reading disabilities. In: G. Hales (ed.), *Dyslexia Matters*. London, Whurr.

Aaron, P. G. and Joshi, R. M. (1992) *Reading Problems Consultation and Remediation*. New York, Guilford Press.

Ackerman, T., Gillet, D., Kenward, P., Leadbetter, P., Mason, I., Mathews, C., Tweddle, D. and Winteringham, D. (1983) Daily teaching and assessment—primary aged children. In: *Post Experience Courses for Educational Psychologists* (1983–84, pp. 33–52). Birmingham, UK, University of Birmingham, Department of Educational Psychology.

Adamik-Jászò, A. (1995) Phonemic awareness and balanced reading instructions. In: P. Owen and P. Pumfrey (eds), *Emergent and Developing Reading: Messages for Teachers*. London, Falmer Press.

Adams, M. (1990a) *Beginning to Read: Thinking and Learning about Print*. Cambridge, MA, MIT Press.

Adams, M. J. (1990b) *Beginning to Read: The New Phonics in Context*. Oxford, Heinemann.

Ainscow, M. and Tweddle, D. (1984) *Preventing Classroom Failure: An Objectives Approach*. Chichester, UK, John Wiley & Sons.

Allen, J., Brown, S. and Munn, P. (1991) *Off the Record: Mainstream Provision for Non-Recorded Pupils*. Edinburgh, Scottish Centre for Research in Education.

Alston, J. (1993) *Assessing and Promoting Writing Skills*. Tamworth, UK, NASEN Publications.

Alston, J (1996) Assessing and promoting handwriting skills. In: G. Reid (ed.), *Dimensions of Dyslexia*, Vol. 2, *Literacy, Language and Learning*. Edinburgh, Moray House Publications.

Alston, J. and Taylor, J. (1992a) *Handwriting Helpline*. Manchester, Dextral Books.

Alston, J. and Taylor, J. (1992b) *Writing Lefthanded*. Manchester, Dextral Books.

Americans with Disabilities Act (1994) United States Federal Law, Washington, DC.

Ames, E. (1991) *Teach Yourself to Diagnose Reading Problems*. Basingstoke, UK, Macmillan Educational.

Anderson, B. and Holtsberg, A. (1999) *Stava Ratt* [Spell It Right] (Wordfinder Software). Malmo, Sweden, Hadar Amugruppen.

APA (2000) *Diagnostic and Statistical Manual of Mental Disorders* (DSM-IV TR, 4th edn). Washington, DC, American Psychiatric Association.

Aram, D. M. and Healy, J. M. (1988) Hyperlexia: A review of extraordinary word recognition. In: L. K. Obler and D. Fein (eds), *Exceptional Brain*. New York, Guilford Press.

Arnold H. (1984) *Making Sense of It*. London, Hodder & Stoughton.

Arnold, H. (1992) *Diagnostic Reading Record*. London, Hodder & Stoughton.

Ashton, C. (2001) Assessment and support in secondary schools—An educational psychologist's view in dyslexia. In: L. Peer and G. Reid (eds), *Successful Inclusion in the Secondary School*. London, David Fulton.

Ashton, C. J. (1997) SpLD, discrepancies and dyslexia, *Educational Psychology in Practice*, **13**(1), 9–11.

Atkinson, P., Davies, B. and Delamont, S. (eds) (1994) Discourse and reproduction: Essays in honour of Basil Bernstein. Cresskill, NJ, Hampton Press.

Au, K. H. and Raphael, T. E. (2000) Equity and literacy in the next millennium. In: J. E. Readence and D. M. Barone (eds), *Reading Research Quarterly*, **35**(1), 143–159.

Aubrey, C., Eaves, J., Hicks, C. and Newton, M. (1981) *Aston Portfolio*. Cambridge, UK, LDA.

Augur, J. (1992) *This Book Doesn't Make Sense*. Bath, UK, Educational Publishers.

Augur, J. and Briggs, S. (1992) *The Hickey Multisensory Language Course*. London, Whurr.

Ayres, A. J. (1979) *Sensory Integration and the Child*. Los Angeles, Western Psychological Services.

Ayres, D. B. (1994) Assessment of intelligence, cognition and metacognition: Reflections, issues and recommendations (Thesis presented in partial fulfilment of a Ph.D., George Mason University, VA).

Ayres, D. B. (1996) Assessment of intelligence, cognition and metacognition: Reflections, issues and recommendations. In: G. Reid (ed.), *Dimensions of Dyslexia*, Vol. 1, *Assessment, Teaching and the Curriculum*. Edinburgh, Moray House Publications.

Baddeley A. (1987) *Working Memory*. Oxford, Clarendon.

Badian, N. A. (1997) Dyslexia and the Double Deficit Hypothesis. *Annals of Dyslexia* (Vol. 47). Baltimore, MD, International Dyslexia Association.

Bakker, D. J. (1979) Hemispheric differences and reading strategies: Two dyslexias? *Bulletin of the Orton Society*, **29**, 84–100.

Bakker, D. J. (1990) *Neuropsychological Treatment of Dyslexia*. New York, Oxford University Press.

Bakker, D. J. and Van der Vlugt (1989) *Neuro-psychological Correlates and Treatment*. Amsterdam, Swets & Zeitlinger.

Bakker, D. J., Licht, R. and Kappers, E. J. (1994) Hemispheric stimulation techniques in children with dyslexia. In: M. G. Tramontana and S. R. Hooper (eds), *Advances in Child Neuropsychology* (Vol. 3). New York, Springer-Verlag.

Bandura, A. (1977) *Social Learning Theory*. Englewood Cliffs, NJ, Prentice Hall.

Banks, J. (1996) Towards a policy of allocating resources. Paper presented at *National Seminar Policy and Provision for Dyslexia, 3 December 1996*. Edinburgh, Scottish Dyslexia Forum.

Bannatyne, A. (1974) Diagnosis: A note on the re-categorisation of the WISC scaled scores. *Journal of Learning Disabilities*, **7**, 272–273.

Bar-Tal, D. (1984) The effects of teachers' behaviour on pupils' attributions: A review. In: P. Barnes, J. Oates, J. Chapman, V. Lee and P. Czerniewska (eds), *Personality, Development and Learning*. Sevenoaks, UK, Hodder & Stoughton.

Barkley, R. A. (1997) *ADHD and the Nature of Self-control*. New York, Guilford Press.

Barthorpe, T. and Visser, J. (1991) *Differentiation: Your Responsibility and In-service Training Pack for Staff Development*. Tamworth, UK, NASEN Publications.

Bartlett, D. and Moody, S. (2000) *Dyslexia in the Workplace*. London, Whurr.

Bath, J. B., Chinn, S. J. and Knox D. E. (1986) *The Test of Cognitive Style in Mathematics*. East Aurora, NY, Slosson (now out of print, see Chinn, 2000).

Baumer, B. A. (1996) *How to Teach Your Dyslexic Child to Read—A Proven Method for Parents and Teachers*. Poole, UK, Orcha Books.

BDA (1997) In: J. Jacobson (ed.), *The Dyslexia Handbook*, Reading, UK, British Dyslexia Association.

BDA/Ford Motor Company (2002) Dyslexia and employment: Making it work. Booklet presented at *Joint Conference BDA/Ford Motor company, 30 October 2002, Ford Motor Product and Development Centre, Dunton, Essex*.

Beard, R. (1990) *Developing Reading 3–13*. London, Hodder & Stoughton.

Becker, W. C. (1977) Teaching reading and language to the disadvantaged—What we have learned from field research. *Harvard Educational Review*, **47**, 518–543.

Bedford-Feull, C., Geiger, S., Moyse, S. and Turner, M. (1995) Use of listening comprehension in the identification and assessment of specific learning difficulties. *Educational Psychology in Practice*, **10**(4), 207–214.

Bell, J. (1993) *Doing Your Research Project*. Buckingham, UK, Open University Press.

Bell, N. (1991a) *Gestalt imagery: A critical factor in language comprehension* (a reprint from *Annals of Dyslexia*, **41**). Baltimore, Orton Dyslexia Society.

Bell, N. (1991b) *Visualizing and Verbalizing for Language Comprehension and Thinking*. Paso Robles, CA, Academy of Reading Publications.

Bender, M. L. (1976) *The Bender-Purdue Reflex Test*. San Rafael, CA, Academic Therapy Publication.

Bentley, D. and Reid, D. (2001) *Literacy Probe 7–9*. London, Hodder and Stoughton.

Bentote, P. (2001) SIDNEY (Screening and Intervention for Dyslexia, Notably in the Early Years). Paper presented at the *5th BDA Conference York, April*.

Bergeron, B. (1990) What does the term 'whole-language' mean? Constructing a definition from the literature. *Journal of Reading Behaviour*, **22**, 301–329.

Berry, R. (1986) *How to Write a Research Paper*. Oxford, Pergamon Press.

Biggar, S. and Barr, J. (1993) The emotional world of specific learning difficulties. In: G. Reid (ed.), *Specific Learning Difficulties (Dyslexia) Perspectives on Practice*. Edinburgh, Moray House Publications.

Biggar, S. and Barr, J. (1996) The emotional world of specific learning difficulties. In: G. Reid (ed.) *Dimensions of Dyslexia*, Vol. 2: *Literacy, Language and Learning*. Edinburgh, Moray House Publications.

Bishop, D. V. M. (1989) Unstable vergence control and dyslexia—A critique. *British Journal of Ophthalmology*, **73**, 223–245.

Blachman, B. A., Ball, E. L., Black, R. S. and Tangel, D. M. (1994) Kindergarten teachers develop phoneme awareness in low-income, inner city classrooms: Does it make a difference? *Reading and Writing*, **7**, 1–18.

Blagg, N., Ballinger, M., Gardner, R., Petty, M. and Williams, G. (1988) *Somerset Thinking Skills Course*. Oxford, Blackwell/Somerset County Council.

Blair, D., Milne, A., Fenton, M., Gibson, M., Masterton, J., Triay, I. and Morton, A. (1996) Learning support provision within a mainstream secondary school. In: G. Reid (ed.) *Dimensions of Dyslexia*, Vol. 1, *Assessment, Teaching and the Curriculum*. Edinburgh, Moray House Publications.

Blau, H. and Loveless, E. J. (1982) Specific hemispheric routing—TAKV to teach spelling to dyslexics: VAK and VAKT challenged. *Journal of Learning Disabilities*, **15**(8), 461–466.

Blight, J. (1986) *A Practical Guide to Dyslexia*. Royston, UK, Egon Publishers.

Bloom, B. S. (1976) *Human Characteristics and School Learning*. New York, McGraw-Hill.

Blythe, P. (1992) *A Physical Approach to Resolving Specific Learning Difficulties*. Chester, UK, Institute for Neuro-Physiological Psychology.

Blythe, P. and Goddard, S. (2000) *Neuro-physiological Assessment Test Battery*. Chester, UK, Institute for Neuro-Physiological Psychology.

Boder, E. and Jarrico, S. (1982) *Boder Test of Reading-Spelling Patterns*. New York, Grune & Stratton.

Bonar, B. and Lowe, D. (1995) *The Screening Initiative: A Project for Early Intervention*. Strathclyde, UK, Strathclyde Regional Council Psychological Service, Renfrew Division.

BPS (1999a) *Dyslexia, Literacy and Psychological Assessment*. Leicester, UK, British Psychological Society.

BPS (1999b) *The Directory of Chartered Psychologists*. Leicester, UK, British Psychological Society.

Bradley L. (1980) *Assessing Reading Difficulties: Diagnostic Remedial*. Windsor, UK, NFER-Nelson.

Bradley L. (1989b) Specific learning disability: Prediction-intervention-progress. Paper presented to the *Rodin Remediation Academy International Conference on Dyslexia, University College of North Wales*.

Bradley, L. (1989a) Predicting learning disabilities. In: J. J. Dumant and H. Nakken (eds), *Learning Disabilities. Cognitive, Social and Remedial Aspects* (Vol. 2). London, Academic Press.

Bradley, L. (1990) Rhyming connections in learning to read and spell. In: P. D. Pumfrey and C. D. Elliott (eds), *Children's Difficulties in Reading, Spelling and Writing*. London, Falmer Press.

Bradley, L. and Bryant, P. (1991) Phonological skills before and after learning to read. In: S. A. Brady and D. P. Shankweiler (eds), *Phonological Processes in Literacy*. London, Lawrence Erlbaum.

Bradley, L. and Huxford, L. M. (1994) Organising sound and letter patterns for spelling. In: G. D. Brown and N. C. Ellis (eds), *Handbook of Normal and Disturbed Spelling Development, Theory, Processes and Interventions*. Chichester, UK, John Wiley & Sons.

Bradshaw, J. R. (1990) A service to ourselves or our clients? *Support for Learning*, **5**(4), 205–210.

Brady, S. and Shankweiler, D. (1992) *Phonological Processes in Literacy*. Parkton, MD, York Press.

Bramley, W. (1996) *Units of Sound*. Staines, UK, The Dyslexia Institute.

Brand, V. (1985) *Remedial Spelling*. Royston, UK, Egon Publishers.

Brand, V. (1989) *Spelling Made Easy—A Multisensory Structured Spelling*. Royston, UK, Egon Publishers.

Brereton, A. and Cann, P. (eds) (1993) *Opening the Door—Guidance on Recognising and Helping the Dyslexic Child*. London, British Dyslexia Association.

Brice, M. (2001) Good practice framework of support for pupils and dyslexia in secondary schools. Paper presented at the *Fifth BDA International Conference, York, April*.

Brierley, M., Hutchinson, P., Topping, K. and Walker, C. (1989) Reciprocal peer tutored cued spelling with ten year olds. *Paired Learning*, **5**, 136–140.

Bronfenbrenner, U. (1979) *The Ecology of Human Development*. Cambridge, MA, Harvard University Press.

Brooks, G. (1998) Trends in standards in the United Kingdom, 1948–1996. *TOPIC*, **19**, Item 1.

Brooks, G., Pugh, A. K. and Schagen, I. (1996a) *Reading Performance at 9*. Slough, UK, NFER and the Open University.

Brooks, G., Cato, V., Fernandes, C. and Tregenza, A. (1996b) *The Knowsley Reading Project Using Trained Reading Helpers Effectively*. Windsor, UK, NFER-Nelson.

Brooks, P. (1990) The effects of different teaching strategies on severe dyslexics. In: G. Hales (ed.), *Meeting Points in Dyslexia*. Reading, UK, British Dyslexia Association.

Brough, M., Came, F. and Cooke, G. (2002) *Assessing SEN in the Classroom: A Handbook for Class Teachers and Assistants.* Marlborough, UK, Learning Works.

Brown, A., Armbruster, B. and Baker, L. (1986) The role of metacognition in reading and studying. In: J. Oraspinu (ed.), *Reading Comprehension from Research to Practice.* Hillsdale, NJ, Lawrence Erlbaum.

Brown, G. D. and Ellis, N. C. (1994) *Handbook of Normal and Disturbed Spelling Development: Theory, Processes and Interventions.* Chichester, UK, John Wiley & Sons.

Brown, M. (1993) Supporting learning through a whole-school approach. In: G. Reid (ed.), *Specific Learning Difficulties (Dyslexia) Perspectives on Practice.* Edinburgh, Moray House Publications.

Brown, T. and Knight, D. F. (1990) *Patterns in Spelling.* New York, New Readers Press.

Brown, T. and Knight, D. F. (1992) *Structures in Spelling.* New York, New Readers Press.

Brown, T. E. (1996) Brown Attention-Deficit Disorder scales. London, Psychological Corporation.

Bruce, I. (1999) *Genius, Criminals and Children* (Twenty, Twenty Television for Channel 4, July 1999).

Bruck, M. and Treiman, R. (1992) Learning to pronounce words: The limitations of analogies. *Reading Research Quarterly,* **24**(4), 375–387.

Bruner, J. S. (1986) *Actual Minds, Possible Worlds.* Cambridge, MA: MIT Press.

Brunswick, N., McCrory, E., Price, C. J., Frith, C. D., and Frith, U. (1999) Explicit and Implicit processing of words and pseudowords by adult developmental dyslexics: A search for Wernicke's Wortschatz? *Brain,* **122**, 1901–1917.

Bryant, P. (1994) Children's reading and writing. *The Psychologist,* **7**(2), 61.

Bryant, P. and Bradley, L. (1990) *Children's Reading Problems.* Oxford, Blackwell.

Bryant, P. E. (1990) Phonological development and reading. In: P. D. Pumfrey and C. D. Elliott (eds), *Children's Difficulties in Reading, Spelling and Writing.* London, Falmer Press.

Buchanan, P. (1996) *Breaking Down the Barriers: Aspects of the First 25 Years of SPELD in New Zealand.* Wellington, NZ, SPELD.

Burden, B. (2002) A cognitive approach to dyslexia: Learning styles and thinking skills. In: G. Reid and J. Wearmouth (eds), *Dyslexia and Literacy, Theory and Practice.* Chichester, UK, John Wiley & Sons.

Burden, R. L. and Fraser, B. J. (1993) The use of classroom environment assessments in school psychology: A British perspective. *Psychology in the Schools,* **30**, 232–240.

Burge, V. (1986) *Dyslexia Basic Numeracy.* Farnham, UK, Helen Arkell Dyslexia Centre.

Burns, R. B. (1986) *The Self-Concept in Theory, Measurement, Development and Behaviour.* London, Longman.

Burt, C. (1921) *Word Reading Test* (revised by P. E. Vernon [1938–67] as *Burt [Rearranged Word Reading Test]* and renormed by E. Shearer and R. Apps, 1975). London, Hodder & Stoughton.

Butler, K. A. (1987) *Learning and Teaching Style—In Theory and Practice.* Columbia, CT, Learners Dimension.

Buzan, T. (1984) *Use Your Memory.* London, BBC Publications.

Buzan, T. (1988) *Make the Most of Your Mind.* London, Pan Books.

Buzan, T. (1993) *The Mind Map Book—Radiant Thinking.* London, BBC Books.

Caine, R. N. and Caine, G. (1991) *Making Connections, Teaching and the Human Brain.* Alexandria, VA, Association for Supervision and Curriculum Development (ASCD).

Calder, I. (2001) Dyslexia across the curriculum. In: L. Peer and G. Reid (eds), *Dyslexia—Successful Inclusion in the Secondary School.* London, David Fulton Publishers.

Calfe, R. and Henry, M. K. (1985) Project read: An inservice model for training classroom teachers in effective reading instruction. In: J. Hoffman (ed.), *The Effective Teaching of Reading: Theory and Practice* (pp. 143–160). Newark, DE, International Reading Association.

Came, F. and Cooke, G. (2002) SENCO support—A draft policy for special educational needs (primary). Marlborough, UK, Learning Works.

Campione, J. C. and Brown, A. L. (1989) Assisted assessment: a taxonomy of approaches and an outline of strengths and weaknesses. *Journal of Learning Disabilities,* **22**(3), 151–165.

Canfield, A. A. and Lafferty, J. C. (1970) *Learning Styles Inventory.* Detroit, MI, Humanics Media (Liberty Drawer).

Capel, S. (1989) Stress and burnout in secondary school teachers: some causal factors. In: M. Cole and S. Walker (eds), *Teaching and Stress.* Buckingham, UK, Open University Press.

Carbo, M. (1987) De-programming reading failure. Giving unequal learners an equal chance. *Phi Delta Kappa,* November, 196–200.

Carbo, M., Dunn, R. and Dunn, K. (1986) *Teaching Students to Read through Their Individual Learning Styles.* Englewood Cliffs, NJ, Prentice Hall.

Carlisle, J. (1993) *Reasoning and Reading—Level 1.* Cambridge, MA, Educators.

Castles, A., Datta, H., Gayan, J. and Olson, R. K. (1999) Varieties of developmental reading disorder: Genetic and environmental influences. *Journal of Experimental Child Psychology,* **72/73**.

Cavey, D. W. (1993) *Dysgraphia: Why Johnny Can't Write. A Handbook for Teachers and Parents.* Austin, TX, Pro-Ed.

Cazden, C. B. (1999) The visible and invisable pedagogies of reading recovery. In: A. J. Watson and L. R. Giorcelli (eds), *Accepting the Literacy Challenge.* Sydney, Scholastic Publications.

Centro Servizi Amministrativi (Lucca) and Associazione Italiana Dislessia (2002) Paper presented at *Convegno Dislessia e Scuola, Villa Bottini, Lucca, Italy 3–4 May 2002.*

CERES (2000) *A Year On from the Lawrence Inquiry Report: Lessons for Scottish Education* (Conference report). Edinburgh, Centre for Education for Racial Equality in Scotland.

Chall, J. S. and Popp, H. M. (1996) *Teaching and Assessing Phonics: Why, What, When, How? A Guide for Teachers.* Cambridge, MA, Educators.

Channel 4 (1999) *Genius, Criminals and Children.* Twenty Twenty Television for Channel, 4 July.

Chapman, J. (1988) *Understanding Learning Difficulties: A Guide for Teachers and Parents,* Massey University, NZ, ERDC Press.

Chasty, H. and Friel, J. (1991) *Children with Special Needs: Assessment, Law and Practice. Caught in the Act.* London, Jessica Kingsley.

Childs, S. and Childs, R. (1992) *The Childs' Spelling System—The Rules.* Dudley, UK, Better Books.

Chinn, S. (1996) *What to Do When You Can't Learn the Times Tables.* Mark, Somerset, UK, Markco.

Chinn, S. (2001) Learning styles and Mathematics. In L. Peer and G. Reid (eds), *Dyslexia—Successful Inclusion in the Secondary School.* London, David Fulton Publishers.

Chinn, S. (2002) 'Count me in.' A comparison of the demands of numeracy and the problems dyslexic learners have with Maths. Paper presented at *North Kent Dyslexia Association 13th One Day Conference for Teachers, Greenwich, London, October.*

Chinn, S. J. (2000) *Informal Assessment of Numeracy Skills.* Mark, UK, Markco.

Chinn, S. J. and Ashcroft, J. R. (1993) *Mathematics for Dyslexics—A Teaching Handbook.* London, Whurr.

Chomsky, N. (1986) *Knowledge of Language.* New York, Praeger.

Cicci, R. (1987) *Dyslexia: Especially for Parents.* Baltimore, Orton Dyslexia Society.

Clark, D. B. (1988) *Dyslexia: Theory and Practice of Remedial Instruction.* Parkton, MD, York Press.

Clay, M. (1985) *The Early Detection of Reading Difficulties: A Diagnostic Survey with Recovery Procedures.* Auckland, Heinemann Educational.

Clay, M. (1992) *Reading: The Patterning of Complex Behaviour.* London, Heinemann.

Clay, M. (1993) *An Observational Survey of Early Literacy Achievement.* London, Heinemann Educational.

Clay, M. and Cazden, C. B. (1990) A Vygotskian interpretation of reading recovery. In: L. Moll (ed.), *Vygotsky and Education* (pp. 114–1350). New York, Cambridge University Press (reprinted in C. B. Cazden (1992) *Whole Language Plus: Essays on literacy in the United States and New Zealand.* New York, Teachers College Press).

Clifford, V. and Miles, M. (1994) *Acceleread, Accelewrite: A Guide to Using Talking Computers— Helping Children to Read and Spell.* Cambridge, iansyst.

Cline, A. and Frederickson, N. (1991) *Bilingual Pupils and the National Curriculum: Overcoming Difficulties in Teaching and Learning.* London, University College.

Cline, T. (1998) The assessment of special educational needs for bilingual children. *British Journal of Special Education,* **25**(4), 159–163.

Cline, T. and Cozens, B. (1999) The analysis of aspects of classroom texts that challenge children when learning to read in their second language: A pilot study. In: H. South (ed.), *Literacies in Community and School.* Watford, UK, National Association for Language Development in the Curriculum (NALDIC).

Cline, T. and Reason, R., (1993) Specific learning difficulties (dyslexia): Equal opportunities issues. *British Journal of Special Education,* **20**(1) (Research Section).

Cline, T. and Shamsi, T. (2000) *Language Needs or Special Needs? The Assessment of Learning Difficulties in Literacy among Children Learning English as an Additional Language: A Literature Review.* London, Department for Education and Employment.

Closs, A., Lannen, S. and Reid, G. (1996) Dyslexia in further and higher education—A framework for practice. In: G. Reid (ed.), *Dimensions of Dyslexia.* Vol. 1: *Assessment, Teaching and the Curriculum.* Edinburgh, Moray House Publications.

Coles, M. (1995) *A Student's Guide to Course Work Writing* (University Writing Series). Stirling, UK, University of Stirling.

Colquhoun, I. and Bunday, S. (1981) A lack of essential fatty acids as a possible cause of hyperactivity in children. *Medical Hypothesis,* **7**, 673–679.

Coltheart, M. (1978) Lexical access in simple reading tasks. In: G. Underwood (ed.), *Strategies of Information Processing* (pp. 151–216). London, Academic Press.

Coltheart, M., Masterson, J., Byng, S., Prior, M. and Riddock, M. J. (1983) Surface dyslexia. *Quarterly Journal of Experimental Psychology*, **35a**, 469–495.

Combley, M. (2001) *The Hickey Multisensory Language Course* (3rd edn). Whurr, London.

Comenius Action Programme (2003) *Transnational course* (part of Comenius Action Programme). Limerick, Ireland, Limerick College.

Conlan, J. and Henley, M. (1992) *Word Mastery*. Oxford, Oxford University Press.

Conner, M. (1994) Specific learning difficulties (dyslexia) and interventions. *Support for Learning*, **9**(3), 114–119.

Conners, C. K. (1996) *Conner's Rating Scales Revised*. London, Psychological Corporation.

Conway, N. F. and Gow, L. (1988) Mainstreaming special class students with mild handicaps through group instruction. In: *Remedial and Special Education*, **5**(9), 34–50.

Cooke, A. (1993) *Tackling Dyslexia: Bangor Way*. London, Whurr.

Cooke, A. (2002) *Tackling Dyslexia* (2nd edn). London, Whurr.

Cooper, C. (1995) Inside the WISC-III UK. *Educational Psychology in Practice*, **10**(4), 215–219.

Cooper, M., Parker, R., and Toombs, S. (1991) *Reading Assessment for Teachers* (RAT-pack). Trowbridge, UK, Wiltshire County Council.

Cooper, M., Toombs, S. and Parker, R. (1992) Reading assessment for teachers. The RAT pack course and materials. *Support for Learning*, **7**(2), 78–81.

Copeland, E. D. and Love, V. L. (1992) *Attention without Tension: A Teacher's Handbook on Attention Disorders*. Atlanta, GA, 3C's of Childhood.

Cornelissen, P., Bradley, L., Fowler, S. and Stein, J. (1991) What children see affects how they read. *Developmental Medicine and Child Neurology*, **33**, 755–762.

Cottrell, S. (1996) Assessing the learning needs of individual students in higher education. In: *Conference Proceedings, Dyslexic Students in Higher Education, 24 January 1996*. Huddersfield, UK, University of Huddersfield.

Cottrell, S. (1999) *The Study Skills Handbook* (Palgrave Study Guides). Basingstoke, UK, Palgrave.

Coventry, D., Pringle, M., Rifkind, H. and Weedon, C. (2001) Supporting students with dyslexia in the maths classroom. In: L. Peer and G. Reid (eds), *Dyslexia—Successful Inclusion in the Secondary School*. London, David Fulton.

Cowdery, L., Montgomery, D., Morse, P. and Prince, M. (1984–88) *Teaching Reading through Spelling*. Wrexham, Clwyd, UK, Frondeg Hall Technical.

Cowdery, L., McMahon, J., Morse, P. and Prince, M. (1987) *Teaching Reading through Spelling* (Diagnosis Book). Wrexham, Clwyd, UK, Frondeg Hall Technical.

Cowling, H. and Cowling, K. (1998) *Toe by Toe Multisensory Manual for Teachers and Parents*. Bradford, UK, Toe by Toe.

Cox, A. R. (1985) Alphabetic Phonics. An organisation and expansion of Orton–Gillingham. *Annals of Dyslexia*, **35**, 187–198.

Cox, A. R. (1992) *Foundations for Literacy. Structures and Techniques for Multisensory Teaching of Basic Written English Language Skills*. Cambridge, MA, Educators.

CRE (1996) *Special Educational Need Assessment in Strathclyde* (Report of a Formal Investigation). London, Commission for Racial Equality.

Cripps, C. (1992) *A Hand for Spelling*. Cambridge, UK, Institute of Education.

Cripps, C. and Cox, R. (1991) *Joining the ABC*. Cambridge, LDA.

Crisfield, J. (Ed.) (1996) *The Dyslexia Handbook*. Reading, UK, British Dyslexia Association.

Crisfield, J. and Smythe, I. (eds) (1993, 1994) *The Dyslexia Handbook*. Reading, UK, British Dyslexia Association.

Croft, S. and Topping, K. (1992) *Paired Science: A Resource Pack for Parents and Children. Centre for Paired Learning*. Dundee, UK, University of Dundee.

Crombie, M. (1997) *Specific Learning Difficulties (Dyslexia): A Teacher's Guide*. Belford, UK, Ann Arbor.

Crombie, M. (2002a) *Course Video, Difficulties in Literacy Development*. Buckingham, UK, Open University and Edinburgh, UK, University of Edinburgh.

Crombie, M. (2002b) Dyslexia: A new dawn (unpublished Ph.D. thesis, University of Strathclyde, Glasgow).

Crombie, M. (2002c) Dealing with diversity in the primary classroom—A challenge for the class teacher. In: G. Reid and J. Wearmouth (eds), *Dyslexia and Literacy: Theory and Practice*. Chichester, UK, John Wiley & Sons.

Crombie, M. (2002d) *Difficulties in Literacy Development* (interview in ED 801 course video). Milton Keynes, UK, Open University.

Crombie, M. (2002e) Early screening policy and practice. Paper presented at *'Practise Makes Perfect' Conference held by Dyslexia in Scotland, Edinburgh, 28 September 2002*.

Crombie, M. and McColl, H. (2001) Dyslexia and the teaching of modern foreign languages. In: L. Peer and G. Reid (eds), *Dyslexia—Successful Inclusion in the Secondary School*. London, David Fulton.

Crombie, M. and Reid G. (1994) 5–14 Programme and specific learning difficulties. In: Jordan, E. (ed.), *A Curriculum for All? 5–14 and Special Needs*. Edinburgh, Moray House Publications.

Cudd, E. T. and Roberts, L. L. (1994) A scaffolding technique to develop sentence sense and vocabulary. *The Reading Teacher*, **47**(4), 346–349.

Cuff, C. (1989) *Study Skills*. Cambridge, UK, Cambridge Educational.

Curtis, M. E. (1980) Development of components of reading skills. *Journal of Educational Psychology*, **72**(5), 656–669.

Curtis, S. (1990) *Peer Tutoring—Integrating 'Bilingual' Pupils into the Mainstream Classroom*. Northampton, UK, Northampton Support Service, Northamptonshire LEA Ethnic Minority.

Daniels, H., Creese, A., Hey, V., Leonard, D. and Smith, M. (2001) Gender and Learning: equity, equality and pedagogy. *Support for Learning*, **16**(3), August, 112–116.

Dargie, R. (1995) *Scotland in the Middle Ages*. Fenwick, UK, Pulse Publications.

Dargie, R. (2001) Dyslexia and History. In: L. Peer and G. Reid (eds), *Dyslexia—Successful Inclusion in the Secondary School*. London, David Fulton Publishers.

Das, J. P., Naglieri, J. A. and Kirby, J. R. (1994) *Assessment of Cognitive Processes. The PASS Theory of Intelligence*. Boston, Allyn & Bacon.

Davies, A. (1996) *Handwriting, Reading and Spelling System (THRASS)*. London, Collins Educational.

Davis, R. D. and Braun, E. M. (1997) *The Gift of Dyslexia. Why Some of the Smartest People Can't Read and How They Can Learn*. London, Souvenir Press.

De Bono, E. (1986) *CORT Thinking*. Oxford, Pergamon Press.

De Boo, M. (1992) *Action Rhymes and Games*. Leamington Spa, UK, Scholastic Publications.

De Fries, J. C. (1991) Genetics and dyslexia: An overview. In: M. Snowling and M. Thomson (eds), *Dyslexia Integrating Theory and Practice*. London, Whurr.

Deford, D. F., Pinnell, G. S., Lyons, C. A. and Young, P. (1987) *Reading Recovery* (Report on the follow-up studies, Vol. 6). Columbus, OH, Columbus Ohio State University.

Dellinger, S. (1989) *Psycho-Geometrics*. Englewood Cliffs, NJ, Prentice Hall.

Denckla, M. B. (1985) Motor co-ordination in dyslexic children: Theoretical and clinical imlications. In: F. H. Duffy and N. Geschwind (eds), *Dyslexia: A Neuroscientific Approach to Clinical Evaluation*. Boston, Little Brown.

Denckla, M. B. and Rudel, R. G. (1976) Rapid 'automatised' naming (RAN): Dyslexia differentiated from other learning disabilities. *Neuropsychologia*, **14**, 471–479.

Dennison, G. E. and Dennison, P. E. (1989) *Educational Kinesiology Brain Organisation Profiles*. Glendale, CA, Edu-Kinesthetics.

Dennison, G. E. and Dennison, P. E. (1997) *The Brain Gym® Handbook*. Glendale, CA, Edu-Kinesthetics.

Dennison, G. E. and Dennison, P. E. (2000) *Educational Kinesiology Brain Organisation Profiles* (Teacher's training manual, 3rd edition). Glendale, CA, Edu-Kinesthetics.

Dennison, G. E. and Dennison, P. E. (2001) *Brain Gym® Course Manual*. Glendale, CA, Edu-Kinesthetics.

Dennison, P. E. (1981) *Switching On: The Holistic Answer to Dyslexia*. Glendale, CA, Edu-Kinesthetics.

Dennison, P. E. and Hargrove, G. (1985) *Personalized Whole Brain Integration*. Glendale, CA, Edu-Kinesthetics.

Deno, S. L. (1989) Curriculum based measurement: and special education services: A fundamental and direct relationship. In: M. R. Shinn (ed.), *Curriculum-based Measurement: Assessing Special Children*. New York, Guilford Press.

Deponio, P., Landon J., and Reid, G. (2000a) Dyslexia and bilingualism—Implications for assessment, teaching and learning. In: L. Peer and G. Reid (eds), *Multilingualism, Literacy and Dyslexia. A Challenge for Educators*. London. David Fulton.

Deponio, P., Landon, J., Mullin, K. and Reid, G. (2000b) An audit of the processes involved in identifying and assessing bilingual learners suspected of being dyslexic: A Scottish study. *Dyslexia*, **6**, 29–41.

DES (1972) *Children with Specific Reading Difficulties* (Tizard Report—report of the advisory committee on handicapped children for the Department for Education and Skills). London, HMSO.

DES (1975) *A Language for Life* (Report of the Committee of Inquiry—chair: Sir Alan Bullock for the Department for Education and Skills). London, HMSO.

DES (1978) *Special Educational Needs* (The Warnock Report for the Department for Education and Skills). London, HMSO.

Deschler, D. and Schumaker, J. B. (1987) An instructional manual for teaching students how to learn. In: Graden, J. L., Zins, J. E. and Curtis, M. J. (eds), *Alternative Educational Delivery Systems:*

Enhancing Instructional Aspects for all Students. Kansas City, KS, University of Kansas, Institute for Research in Learning Difficulties.

Dewsbury, A. (1999) First steps: Making the links—Assessment, teaching and learning. In: A. J. Watson and L. R. Giorcelli (eds), *Accepting the Literacy Challenge* (pp. 133–156). Gosford, Australia, Scholastic Publications.

DfEE (1996) *The National Literacy Project.* London, Department for Education and Employment.

DfEE (1998) *Framework for Teaching,* London, Department for Education and Employment.

DfEE (2001) *Bridging the Gap.* London, Department for Education and Employment.

DfES (2001) *Special Education Needs Code of Practice.* London, Department for Education and Skills.

Dimitriadi, P. (1999) *Multimedia authoring and specific learning difficulties (dyslexia): A single case study.* Paper delivered at *CAL99, 29–31 March 1999.* London: Institute of Education.

Dimitriadi, Y. (2000) Using ICT to support bilingual dyslexic learners. In: L. Peer and G. Reid (eds), *Multilingualism, Literacy and Dyslexia. A Challenge for Educators.* London. David Fulton.

Diniz, F. A. (2001) The continuing dilemma of professional development and qualifications in SEN: A personal perspective. *Scottish Support for Learning Association Journal,* 2000/2001.

Diniz, F. A. and Reed, S. (2001) 'Inclusion': Issues. In: L. Peer and G. Reid (eds), *Dyslexia and Successful Inclusion in the Secondary School.* London, David Fulton.

Diniz, F. A. and Reid, G. (1994) Dyslexia in Scotland. Paper presented at the *21st Annual conference, New York Branch of the Orton Dyslexia Society, April 1994,* New York, Orton Dyslexia Society.

Ditchfield, D. (2001) Dyslexia and Music. In: L. Peer and G. Reid (eds), *Dyslexia—Successful Inclusion in the Secondary School.* London, David Fulton.

Dobie, S. (1993) Perceptual motor and neurodevelopmental dimensions in identifying and remediating developmental delay in children with specific learning difficulties. In: G. Reid (ed.), *Specific Learning Difficulties (Dyslexia) Perspectives on Practice.* Edinburgh, Moray House Publications.

Dobie, S. (1996) Perceptual motor and neurodevelopmental dimensions in identifying and remediating developmental delay in children with specific learning difficulties. In: G. Reid (ed.), *Dimensions of Dyslexia.* Edinburgh, Moray House Publications.

Dockrell, J. and McShane, J. (1993) *Children's Learning Difficulties—A Cognitive Approach.* Oxford, Blackwell.

Dodds, D. (1993) Curriculum differentiation in the secondary school. In: G. Reid (ed.), *Specific Learning Difficulties (Dyslexia) Perspectives on Practice.* Edinburgh, Moray House Publications.

Dodds, D. (1996) Differentiation in the secondary school. In: G. Reid (ed.), *Dimensions of Dyslexia.* Vol. 1: *Assessment, Teaching and the Curriculum.* Edinburgh, Moray House Publications.

Dodds, D. and Lumsden, D. (2001) Examining the challenge: Preparing for examinations. In: L. Peer and G. Reid (eds), *Dyslexia—Successful Inclusion in the Secondary School.* London, David Fulton.

Dombey, H. (1992) Reading recovery: A solution to all primary school reading problems? *Support for Learning,* 7(3), 111–115.

Dore, W. and Rutherford, R. (2001) Closing the gap. Paper presented at the *BDA 6th International Conference on Dyslexia, York.*

Dougan, M. and Turner, G. (1993) Information technology and specific learning difficulties. In: G. Reid (ed.), *Specific Learning Difficulties (Dyslexia) Perspectives on Practice.* Edinburgh, Moray House Publications.

Doyle, J. (1996) *Dyslexia: An Introductory Guide.* London, Whurr.

Dreary, I. (1993) Speed of information processing and verbal ability. Paper presented at the *Rodin Academy for the Study of Dyslexia Conference, London.*

Drummond, A., Godrey, L. and Sattin, R. (1990) Promoting parental involvement in reading. *Support for Learning,* 5(3), 141–145.

Duane, D. D. (1991) Neurobiological issues in dyslexia. In: M. Snowling and M. Thomson (eds), *Dyslexia: Integrating Theory and Practice.* London, Whurr.

Duane, D. D. (1993) The meaning and utility of differential diagnoses. *44th Annual Conference, Orton Dyslexia Society Commemorative Booklet.*

Duffield, J., Riddell, S. and Brown, S. (1995) *Policy, Practice and Provision for Children with Specific Learning Difficulties.* New York, Avebury.

Dunn, R. (1992) Strategies for teaching word recognition to the disabled readers. *Reading and Writing Quarterly,* 8(2), 157–177.

Dunn, R. (1993) *Teaching Students through Their Individual Learning Styles: A Practical Approach Learning Styles Training Workshop.* Jamaica, New York, Center for the Study of Learning and Teaching Styles, St John's University.

Dunn, R. and Dunn, K. (1992) *Teaching Elementary Students through Their Individual Learning Styles.* Boston, Allyn & Bacon.

Dunn, R. and Dunn, K. (1993) *Teaching Secondary Students through Their Individual Learning Styles.* Boston, Allyn & Bacon.

Dunn, R. and Griggs, S. A. (1989) Learning styles: quiet revolution in American secondary schools. *The Clearing House*, **63**(1), 40–42.

Dunn, R., Dunn, K. and Price, G. E. (1975, 1979, 1985, 1987, 1989) *Learning Styles Inventory*. Lawrence, KA, Price Systems.

Durham County Council (2002) *Specific Learning Difficulties: Dyslexia and Dyspraxia, Policy and Guidance*. Durham, UK, Durham County Council.

Dyer, C. (1988) Which support?: An examination of the term. *Support for Learning*, **3**(1), 6–11.

Dykes, B. and Thomas, C. (1989) *Spelling Made Easy*. Sydney, Hale & Iremonger.

Dyslexia in Scotland (2002) *The DDAT Centre (Dyslexia, Dyspraxia, Attention Disorder Treatment): Another Cure for Dyslexia?* Wellgreen, Stirling, UK, Dyslexia in Scotland.

Dyson, A. (1996) Research: The national perspective. Paper read at *Fife Dyslexia Conference, March, Scotland*.

Dyson, A. (2001) Special needs education as the way to equity: An alternative approach? *Support for Learning*, **16**(3), 99–104.

Dyson, A. and Skidmore, D. (1996) Contradictory models: The dilemma of specific learning difficulties. In: G. Reid (ed.), *Dimensions of Dyslexia*, Vol. 2: *Literacy, Language and Learning*. Edinburgh, Moray House Publications.

Dyspel (2002) *Dysléxie, Legasthénie, Dyslexia—Strategies for Success in Schools*. Luxembourg, Dyspel.

Dyspel Project Report (2000) Dyspel Project (Phase 2 report, June 1997–April 2000). London, Dyspel.

Dyspraxia Trust (1991) *Praxis Makes Perfect*. Hitchin, UK, Dyspraxia Trust.

Dyspraxia Trust (2001) *Praxis Makes Perfect*. Hitchin, UK, Dyspraxia Trust.

Eames, F. H. (2002) Changing definitions and concepts of literacy: Implications for pedagogy and research. In: G. Reid and J. Wearmouth (eds), *Dyslexia and Literacy: Theory and Practice*. Chichester, UK, John Wiley & Sons.

East Renfrewshire Council (1999) *Dyslexia* (Policy on Specific Learning Difficulties, July 1999), Paisley, UK, East Renfrewshire Council.

ECIC (2000) *European Children in Crisis*. Brussels, European Commission.

Eden, G. F., VanMeter, J. W., Rumsey, J. M., Maisog, J. M., Woods, R. P. and Zeffiro, T. A. (1996) Abnormal processing of visual motion in dyslexia revealed by functional brain imaging. *Nature*, **382**, 67–69.

Edinburgh City Council (2002a) *Dyslexia—'Good Practice' Conference for Parents, King's Manor Hotel, Edinburgh, 22 March 2002*.

Edwards, P. (1992) *Edwards Reading Test*. Sydney, Heinemann Educational.

Ehri, L. (1992) Reconceptualizing the development of sight word reading and its relationship to recoding. In: P. Gough, L. Ehri and R. Treiman (eds), *Reading Acquisition* (pp. 107–143). Hillsdale, NJ, Lawrence Erlbaum.

Ehri, L. (1995a) Phases of development in learning to read words by sight. *Journal of Research in Reading*, **18**, 116–125.

Ehri, L. (1995b) The emergence of word reading in beginning reading. In: P. Owen and P. Pumfrey (eds), *Emergent and Developing Reading: Messages for Teachers*. London, Falmer Press.

Ehri, L. (1999). Phases of development in learning to read words. In: J. Oakhill and R. Beard (eds), *Reading Development and the Teaching of Reading: A Psychological Perspective* (pp. 79–108). Oxford, Blackwell.

Ehri, L. and McCormick, S. (1998) Phases of word learning: Implications for instruction with delayed and disabled readers. *Reading and Writing Quarterly*, **14**, 135–163.

Ehri, L. C. (2002) Reading processes, acquisition, and instructional implications. In: G. Reid and J. Wearmouth (eds), *Dyslexia and Literacy: Theory and Practice*. Chichester, UK, John Wiley & Sons.

Ehri, L. C. and Robbins, C. (1992) Beginners need some decoding skill to read words by analogy. *Reading Research Quarterly*, **21**(1), 13–26.

Ekwall, E. and Ekwall, C. (1989) Using metacognitive techniques for the improvement of reading comprehension. *Journal of Reading Education*, **14**(3), 6–12.

El-Naggar, O. (1996) *Specific Learning Difficulties in Mathematics—A Classroom Approach*. Tamworth, UK, NASEN.

Elley, W. B. (1992) *How in the World Do Students Read?* The Hague, International Association for the Evaluation of Educational Achievement.

Elliot, C. D. and Tyler, S. (1986) British ability scales profiles of children with reading difficulties. *Educational and Child Psychology*, **3**(2), 80–89.

Elliott, C. D., Smith, P. and McCulloch, K. (1996) *British Ability Scales* (2nd edn, BAS II). Windsor, UK, NFER-Nelson.

Ellis, A. (1991) *Reading, Writing and Dyslexia: A Cognitive Analysis*. Buckingham, UK, Open University Press.

Ellis, N. C. (1990) Reading, phonological skills and short term memory: Interactive tributaries of development. *Journal of Research in Reading*, **13**(2), 107–122.

Ellis, N. C. and Large, B. (1981) The early stage of reading: A longitudinal study. *Applied Cognitive Psychology*, **2**, 47–76.

Ellis, S. and Friel, G. (1992) *Inspirations for Writing*. Leamington Spa, UK, Scholastic Publications.

Emerson, P. (1988) Parent tutored cued spelling in a primary school. *Paired Reading Bulletin*, **4**, 91–92.

Enfield, M. L. (1976) An alternative classroom approach. *Meeting Special Needs of Children with Reading Problems* (Ph.D. Dissertation, University of Minnesota, Minneapolis).

Enfield, M. L. and Greene, V. E. (1981) There is a skeleton in every closet. *Bulletin of the Orton Society*, **31**, 189–198.

Enfield, M. L. and Greene, V. E. (1985) *Project Read: Practical Spelling Guide*. Bloomington, MN, Bloomington Public Schools.

Engelmann, J. and Bruner, E. C. (1983) *Reading Mastery I and II: Distar Reading*. Chicago, Chicago Science Research Association.

Evans, A. (1984b) Paired reading: A report on two projects. (unpublished paper Division of Education, University of Sheffield).

Evans, A. (1989) Screening at 6+. *Dyslexia Contact*, **8**(1).

Evans, A. J. (1984a) *Reading and Thinking*. Wolverhampton, UK, Learning Materials.

Everatt, J. (2002) Visual processes. In: G. Reid and J. Wearmouth (eds), *Dyslexia and Literacy, Theory and Practice*. Chichester, UK, John Wiley & Sons.

Everatt, J., Adams, E. and Smythe, I. (2000) Bilingual children's profiles on dyslexia screening measures. In: L. Peer and G. Reid (eds), *Multilingualism, Literacy and Dyslexia. A Challenge for Educators*. London, David Fulton.

Farrer, M. (1993) Early identification—The role of the speech therapist. In: A. Brereton and P. Cann (eds), *Opening the Door*. Reading, UK, British Dyslexia Association.

Fawcett, A. (1989) Automaticity—A new framework for dyslexic research. Paper presented at the *1st International Conference of the British Dyslexia Association, Bath 1989*.

Fawcett, A. (2002) Dyslexia and literacy: Key issues for research. In: G. Reid and J. Wearmouth (eds), *Dyslexia and Literacy, Theory and Practice*. Chichester, UK, John Wiley & Sons.

Fawcett, A. J. and Nicolson (1992) Automatisation deficits in balance for dyslexic children. *Perceptual and Motor Skills*, **75**, 507–529.

Fawcett, A. J. and Nicolson, R. I. (eds) (1994) *Dyslexia in Children: Multidisciplinary Perspectives*. Hemel Hempstead, UK, Harvester Wheatsheaf.

Fawcett, A. J. and Nicolson, R. I. (1995) *Dyslexia in Children, Multidisciplinary Perspectives*. Hemel Hempstead, UK, Harvester Wheatsheaf.

Fawcett, A. J. and Nicolson, R. I. (1996) *The Dyslexia Screening Test*. London, The Psychological Corporation.

Fawcett, A. J. and Nicolson, R. I. (1997) *The Dyslexia Early Screening Test*. London, The Psychological Corporation.

Fawcett, A. J. and Nicolson, R. I. (1998) *Dyslexia Adult Screening Test*. London, The Psychological Corporation.

Fawcett, A. J. and Nicolson, R. I. (2001) Dyslexia: The role of the cerebellum. In: A. J. Fawcett (ed.), *Dyslexia: Theory and Good Practice*. London, Whurr.

Fawcett, A. J., Nicolson, R. I. and Dean, P. (1996) Impaired performance of children with dyslexia on a range of cerebellar tasks (reprinted from *Annals of Dyslexia*, **46**). Baltimore, Orton Dyslexia Society.

Fawcett, A., Nicolson, R. and Lee, R. (2001) *The Pre-school Screening Test (PREST)*, London, Psychological Corporation.

Feuerstein, R. (1979) *The Dynamic Assessment of Retarded Performers: The Learning Potential Assessment Device, Theory, Instruments and Techniques*. Baltimore, University Park Press.

Fife Education Authority (1996) *Partnership: Parents, Professionals and Pupils*. Fife, UK, Fife Education Authority.

Fisher, S. E., Marlow, A. J., Lamb, J., Maestrini, E., Williams, D. F., Richardson, A. J., Weeks, D. E., Stein, J. F. and Monaco, A. P. (1999a) A quantitative-trait locus on chromosome 6p influences different aspects of developemental dyslexia. *American Journal of Human Genetics*, **64**, 146–156.

Fisher, S. E., Stein, J. F. and Monaco, A. P. (1999b) A genome-wide search strategy for identifying quantitative trait loci involved in reading and spelling disability (developmental dyslexia). *Eur. Child and Adolesc. Psych.*, **8**(S3), 47–51.

Fitch, R. H., Miller, S. and Tallal, P. (1997). Neurobiology of speech perception. *Annual Review of Neuroscience*, **20**, 331–353.

Fitts, P. M. and Posner, M.I. (1967) *Human Performance*. Belmont, CA, Brooks Cole.

Flavell, J. H. (1979) Metacognition and cognitive monitoring. *American Psychologist*, October, 906–911.

Fletcher, J. M., Morris, R., Reid Lyon, G., Steubing, K. K., Shaywitz, S. E., Shankweiler, D. P., Katz, L. and Shaywitz, B. A. (1997) Subtypes of dyslexia: An old problem revisited. In: B. A. Blachman (ed.), *Foundations of Reading Acquisition and Dyslexia*, Mahwah, NJ, LEZ.

Flory, S. (2000) Identifying, assessing and helping dyspraxic children. *Dyslexia*, **6**, 202–214.

Forbes, S. and Powell, R. (2000) Bilingualism and literacy assessment. In: L. Peer and G. Reid (eds), *Multilingualism, Literacy and Dyslexia. A Challenge for Educators*. London, David Fulton.

Ford, M. and Trottman, A. (2002) *Funics—Responding to Sounds* Brocton, UK, Crossbow Education (www.crossbow.com).

Fox, A (1999) An evaluation of the contribution of a Brain Gym® intervention programme on the acquisition of literacy skills in a mainstream primary school setting (unpublished M.Ed. dissertation, University of Edinburgh, August).

France, L., Topping, F. and Revell, K. (1993) Parent tutored cued spelling. *Support for Learning*, **8**(1), 11–15.

Frankiewicz, R. G. (1985) *An Evaluation of the Alphabetic Phonics Program Offered in the One-to-One Mode*. Houston, TX, Neuhaus Education Center.

Fraser, I. (2002) *Difficulties in Literacy Development* (interview in ED 801 course video). Milton Keynes, UK, Open University.

Frederickson, N. (1999) The ACID test—or is it? *Educational Psychology in Practice*, **15**(1), 2–8.

Frederickson, N. and Cline, T. (2002) *Special Educational Needs, Inclusion and Diversity, A Textbook*. Buckingham, UK, Open University Press.

Frederickson, N. and Reason, R. (1995) Phonological assessment of specific learning difficulties. *Educational and Child Psychology*, **12**(1).

Frederickson, N. and Wilson, J. (1996) Phonological awareness training: a new approach to phonics teaching. *Dyslexia*, **2**(2), 101–120.

Frederickson, N., Frith, V. and Reason, R. (1997) *Phonological Assessment Battery*. Windsor, UK, NFER-Nelson.

Freeman, A. (1989) Coping and SEN: Challenging idealism. In: M. Cole and S. Walker (eds), *Teaching and Stress*. Buckingham, UK, Open University Press.

Frith, C. and Frith, U. (1996) A biological marker for dyslexia. *Nature*, **382**, 19–20.

Frith, U. (1980) Unexpected spelling problems. In: W. Frith (ed.), *Cognitive Processes in Spelling*. London, Academic Press.

Frith, U. (1985) Beneath the surface of developmental dyslexia. In: K. E. Patterson, J. C. Marshall and M. Coltheart (eds), *Surface Dyslexia*. London, Routledge & Kegan Paul.

Frith, U. (1995) Dyslexia: Can we have a shared theoretical framework? *Educational and Child Psychology*, **12**(1), 6–17.

Frith, U. (2002) Resolving the paradoxes of dyslexia. In: G. Reid and J. Wearmouth (eds), *Dyslexia and Literacy, Theory and Practice*. Chichester, UK, John Wiley & Sons.

Frith, U. and Snowling, M. (1983) Reading for meaning and reading for sound in autistic and dyslexic children. *British Journal of Developmental Psychology*, **1**, 329–342.

Galaburda, A. (1988) Ordinary and extraordinary brains: nature, nurture and dyslexia. Address presented at the *Annual Meeting of the Orton Dyslexia Society, Tampa, FL, November 1988*.

Galaburda, A. (1993a) Cortical and sub-cortical mechanisms in dyslexia. Paper presented at *44th Annual Conference, Orton Dyslexia Society, New Orleans*.

Galaburda, A. (ed.) (1993b) *Dyslexia and Development: Neurobiological Aspects of Extraordinary Brains*. Cambridge, MA, Harvard University Press.

Galaburda, A. M. and Rosen, G. D. (2001) Neural plasticity in dyslexia: A window to mechanisms of learning disabilities. In: J. L. McClelland and R. S. Siegler (eds), *Mechanisms of Cognitive Development: Behavioral and Neural Perspectives* (pp. 307–323). Mahwah, NJ, Lawrence Erlbaum.

Gallagher, A. and Frederickson, N. (1995) The phonological assessment battery (PhAB): An initial assessment of its theoretical and practical utility. *Educational and Child Psychology*, **1**, 12.

Gallagher, A., Frith, U. Snowling, M. (2000) Precursors of literacy—Delay among children at genetic risk of dyslexia. *Journal of Child Psychology and Psychiatry*, **41**, 203–213.

Gardner, H. (1983) *Frames of Mind. The Theory of Multiple Intelligences*. New York, Harper & Row.

Gardner, H. (1985) *Frames of Mind*. New York, Basic Books.

Gardner, H. (1999) Foreword. In: D. Lazear, *Eight Ways of Knowing Teaching for Multiple Intelligences* (3rd edn, pp. vii–viii). Arlington Heights, IL, Skylight Professional Development.

Garland, J. (1997) *Phelps v The Mayor and Burgesses of the London Borough of Hillingdon*.

Garner, P. and Sandow, S. (1995) *Advocacy, Self-advocacy and Special Needs*. London, David Fulton.

Gerber, P. J. (1997) Life after school: Challenges in the workplace. In: P. J. Gerber and D. S. Brown (eds), *Learning Disabilities and Employment*. Austin, TX, Pro-Ed.

Gersch, I. (2001), Listening to children. In: J. Wearmouth (ed.), *Special Educational Provision in the Context of Inclusion.* London, David Fulton.

Geschwind, N. and Galaburda, A. (1985) Cerebral lateralisation biological mechanisms associations and pathology: A hypothesis and a programme for research. *Archives of Neurology,* **42**, 428–459.

Gilger, J. W., Pennington, B. F. and De Fries, J. C. (1991) Risk for reading disability as a function of parental history in three family studies. *Reading and Writing,* **3**, 205–218.

Gillham, W. (2000) *Early Literacy Test.* London, Hodder & Stoughton.

Gillingham, A. and Stillman, B. (1956) *Remedial Training for Children with Specific Disability in Reading, Spelling, and Penmanship.* Cambridge, MA, Educators.

Gilroy, D. (1995a) *Applying to Higher Education for Dyslexic Students.* Bangor, UK, University College of North Wales.

Gilroy, D. (1995b) Stress factors in the college student. In: T. Miles and V. Varma (eds), *Dyslexia and Stress.* London, Whurr.

Gilroy, D. and T. Miles (1996) *Dyslexia at College.* London, Routledge.

Giorcelli, L. R. (1995) An impulse to soar: Sanitisation, silencing and special education. The Des English Memorial Lecture given at the *Australian Association of Special Education Conference, Darwin* (reproduced in *SPELD Celebration of Learning Styles Conference Proceedings, 1996*). Christchurch, New Zealand, SPELD.

Giorcelli, L. R. (1999) Inclusion and other factors affecting teachers attitudes to literacy programs for students with special needs. In: A. J. Watson and L. R. Giorcelli (eds), *Accepting the Literacy Challenge.* Gosford, Australia, Scholastic.

Given, B. (1993) Learning styles. Paper presented at the *Centre for Specific Learning Difficulties Two-day Conference, June 1993.* Edinburgh, Moray House Publications.

Given, B. K. (1996) The potential of learning styles. In: G. Reid (ed.), *Dimensions of Dyslexia,* Vol. 2: *Literacy, Language and Learning.* Edinburgh, Moray House Publications.

Given, B. K. and Reid, G. (1999) *Learning Styles: A Guide for Teachers and Parents.* St Anne's-on-Sea, UK, Red Rose Publications.

Glaser, R., Lesgold, A. and Lejoie, S. (1987) Toward a cognitive theory for the measurement of achievement. In: R. R. Ronning, J. A. Glover, J. C. Conoley and I. C. Witt (eds), *The Influence of Cognitive Psychology on Testing.* Hillsdale, NJ, Lawrence Erlbaum.

Glynn, T., Crooks, T., Bethune, N., Ballard, K. and Smith, J. (1989) *Reading Recovery in Context* (a report). Wellington, New Zealand, New Zealand Department of Education.

Goddard-Blythe, S. (1996) *Developmental Exercise Programme.* Chester, UK, Institute for Neuro-Physiological Psychology.

Goddard-Blythe, S. and Hyland, D. (1998) Screening for neurological dysfunction in the specific learning difficulties child. *British Journal of Occupational Therapy,* **61**(10), 459–464.

Gomez, C. and Reason, R. (2002) Cross-linguistic transfer of phonological skills: A Malaysian perspective. *Dyslexia,* **8**(1), January–March, 22–33.

Goodman, K. (1976) Reading—A psycholinguistic guessing game. In: H. Singer and R. B. Ruddell (eds), *Theoretical Models and Processes of Reading.* Newark, NY, International Reading Association.

Goodman, K. (1992) I didn't found whole language. *The Reading Teacher,* **46**(3), 189–199.

Gorrie, B. and Parkinson, E. (1995) *Phonological Awareness Procedure.* Ponteland, UK, Stass Publications.

Goswami, U. (1988) Children's use of analogy in learning to spell. *British Journal of Developmental Psychology,* **6**, 21–33.

Goswami, U. (1990) A special link between rhyming skills and the use of orthographic analogies by beginning readers. *Journal of Child Psychology and Psychiatry,* **31**, 301–311.

Goswami, U. (1992) *Analogical Reasoning in Children.* Hove, UK, Lawrence Erlbaum.

Goswami, U. (1993) Orthographic analogies and reading development. *The Psychologist,* **6**(7), 312–316.

Goswami, U. (1994) Reading by analogy: Theoretical and practical perspectives. In: C. Hulme and M. Snowling (eds), *Reading Development and Dyslexia.* London, Whurr.

Goswami, U. and Bryant, P. (1990) *Phonological Skills and Learning to Read.* Hove, UK, Lawrence Erlbaum.

Gough, P. B. and Tunmer, W. E. (1986) Decoding, reading and reading disability. *Remedial and Special Education,* **7**, 6–10.

Grampian Region Psychological Service (1988) *Reeling and Writhing: Children with Specific Learning Difficulties.* Aberdeen, UK, Grampian Education Authority.

Gregorc, A. F. (1982) *An Adult's Guide to Style.* Columbia, CT, Gregorc Associates, Inc.

Gregorc, A. F. (1985) *Inside Styles: Beyond the Basics.* Columbia, CT, Gregorc Association.

Griffiths, A. and Hamilton, D. (1984) *Parent, Teacher, Child.* London, Methuen.

Grinder, M. (1991) *Righting the Educational Conveyor Belt* (2nd edn). Portland, OR, Metamorphous Press.

Haddock, L. (2002) Preliminary study of Education Authority policy on dyslexia (part of an unpublished Ph.D. study, University of Edinburgh).

Hagley, F. (1987) *Suffolk Reading Scale*. Windsor, UK, NFER-Nelson.

Hagtvet, B. E. (1997) Phonological and linguistic–cognitive precursors of reading abilities. *Dyslexia*, **3**(3).

Hales, G. (1990a) *Meeting Points in Dyslexia*. Reading, UK, British Dyslexia Association.

Hales, G. (1990b) Personality aspects of dyslexia. In: G. Hales (ed.), *Meeting Points in Dyslexia. Proceedings of the 1st International Conference of the British Dyslexia Association*. Reading, UK, British Dyslexia Association.

Hales, G. (1994) *Dyslexia Matters*. London, Whurr.

Hales, G. (1995) Stress factors in the workplace. In: T. R. Miles and V. Varma (eds), *Dyslexia and Stress*. London, Whurr.

Hales, G. (2001) Self-esteem and counselling. In: L. Peer and G. Reid (eds), *Dyslexia—Successful Inclusion in the Secondary School*. London, David Fulton.

Haley, M. H. and Porter, M. H. (2000) Rethinking teacher training programs for linguistically diverse students with dyslexia. In: L. Peer and G. Reid (eds), *Multilingualism, Literacy and Dyslexia*. London, David Fulton.

Hall, D. (1995) *Assessing the Needs of Bilingual Pupils: Living in Two Languages*. London, David Fulton.

Hall, K. (1998) 'Our nets define what we shall catch': Issues in English assessment in England. *Reading Association of Ireland*, 153–167.

Hammill, D. D. (1990) On defining learning disabilities: An emerging consensus, UK. *Journal of Learning Disabilities*, **23**(2), 74–84.

Hammond, J. and Hercules, F. (2000) *Understanding Dyslexia, An Introduction for Dyslexic Students in Higher Education*. Glasgow, Glasgow College of Art.

Hannaford, C. (1995) *Smart Moves. Why Learning Is Not All in Your Head*. Arlington, VA, Great Ocean.

Hannaford, C. (1997) *The Dominance Factor. How Knowing Your Dominant Eye, Ear, Brain, Hand and Foot Can Improve Your Learning*. Arlington, VA, Great Ocean.

Harris, C. (1993) *Fuzzbuzz Books/Spell/Words/Letters*. Oxford, Oxford University Press.

Harrison, C. (1994) *Literature Review: Methods of Teaching Reading*. Edinburgh, Scottish Office Education Department.

Harrison, P. and Harrison, S. (1989) *Writing for Different Purposes*. Dunstable, UK, Folens.

Harrison, R. (1989) Cued spelling in adult literacy in Kirklees. *Paired Learning*, **5**, 141.

Hatcher, J. and Snowling, M. J. (2002) The phonological representations hypothesis of dyslexia: From theory to practice. In: G. Reid and J. Wearmouth (eds), *Dyslexia and Literacy, Theory and Practice*. Chichester, UK, John Wiley & Sons.

Hatcher, P. (1994) *Sound Linkage. An Integrated Programme for Overcoming Reading Difficulties*. London, Whurr.

Hatcher, P. J., Hulme, C. and Ellis, A. W. (1994) Ameliorating early reading failure by integrating the teaching of reading and phonological skills: The phonological linkage hypothesis. *Child Development*, **65**, 41–57.

Healy, J. (1982) The enigma of hyperlexia. *Reading Research Quarterly*, **17**, 319–338.

Healy, J. M. (1991) *Endangered Minds*. Touchstone, NJ, Simon & Schuster.

Healy, J. M. (1994) *Your Child's Growing Mind*. New York, Doubleday Dell.

Heaton, P. (1996) *Dyslexia—Parents in Need*. London, Whurr.

Heaton, P. and Mitchell, G. (1987) *Learning to Learn—A Study Skills Course Book*. Dudley, UK, Better Books.

Heaton, P. and Mitchell, G (2001) *Dyslexia, Students in Need*. London, Whurr.

Heaton, P. and Winterson, P. (1986) *Dealing with Dyslexia*. Dudley, UK, Better Books.

Henderson, A. (1989) *Maths and Dyslexics*. Llandudno, UK, St David's College.

Henderson, A. (1998) *Maths for the Dyslexic* (a practical guide). London, David Fulton.

Henry, M. (1996) The Orton–Gillingham approach. In: G. Reid (ed.), *Dimensions of Dyslexia*, Vol. 1: *Assessment, Teaching and the Curriculum*. Edinburgh, Moray House Publications.

Henry, M. K. (1993) *Words—Integrated Decoding and Spelling Instruction Based on Word Origin and Word Structure*. Los Gatos, CA, Lex Press.

Henry, M. K. and Redding, N. C. (1990) *Tutor 1—Structured, Sequential, Multisensory Lessons Based on the Orton–Gillingham Approach*. Los Gatos, CA, USA, Lex Press.

Henry, M. K. and Redding, N. C. (1993) *Word Lists: Structured, Sequential, Multisensory*. Los Gatos, CA, Lex Press.

Herrington, M. (1996) Examination arrangements in higher education for dyslexic students. *Conference Proceedings; Dyslexic Students in Higher Education, University of Huddersfield, 24 January 1996*.

Hill, J. E. (1964) *Cognitive Style Interest Inventory*. Oakland, MI, Oakland Community College.

Hinson, M. and Smith, P. (eds) (1993) *Phonics and Phonic Resources*. Tamworth, UK, NASEN Publications.

Hinton, J. W. (1990) Stress model development and testing. In: C. D. Spielberger (ed.), *Stress and Anxiety* (Vol. 14).

Hinton, J. W. (1991) Stress model development and testing by group psychometrics and one-subject psychophysiology. In: C. D. Spielberger, I. G. Sarason, J. Strelaw and J. M. T. Brebner (eds), *Stress and Anxiety* (Vol. 13, pp. 53–70). New York, Hemisphere.

HMG (1981) *Education Act 1981*. London, Her Majesty's Stationery Office.

HMG (1995) *Disability Discrimination Act*. London, Her Majesty's Stationery Office.

Holligan, C. and Johnston, R. S. (1988) The use of phonological information by good and poor readers in memory and reading tasks. *Memory and Cognition*, **16**, 522–532.

Holloway, J. (2000) *Dyslexia in Focus at 16 Plus: An Inclusive Teaching Approach*. Tamworth, UK, NASEN Publications.

Holmes, P. (2001) Dyslexia and physics. In: L. Peer and G. Reid (eds), *Dyslexia—Successful Inclusion in the Secondary School*. London, David Fulton.

Holt, J. (1964) *How Children Fail*. New York, Dell.

Hornsby, B. (1992) *Overcoming Dyslexia*. London, McDonald Optima.

Hornsby, B. (1996) *Before Alpha: Learning Games for the Under Fives*. London, Souvenir Press.

Hornsby, B. and Farmer, M. (1990 and 1993) Some effects of a dyslexia centred teaching programme. In: P. D. Pumfrey and C. D. Elliott (eds), *Children's Difficulties in Reading, Spelling and Writing*. London, Falmer Press.

Hornsby, B. and Miles, T. R. (1980) The effects of a dyslexic-centred teaching programme. *British Journal of Educational Psychology*, **50**(3), 236–242.

Hornsby, B. and Pool, J. (1989) *Alpha to Omega: Activity Packs Stage 1, 2 and 3*. London, Heinemann Educational.

Hornsby, B. and Shear, F. (1980) *Alpha to Omega: The A–Z of Teaching Reading, Writing and Spelling*. London, Heinemann Educational.

Howlett, C. A. (2001) Dyslexia and biology. In: L. Peer and G. Reid (eds), *Dyslexia—Successful Inclusion in the Secondary School*. London, David Fulton.

Hubicki, M. and Miles, T. R. (1991) Musical notation and multi-sensory learning in child language. *Teaching and Therapy*, **10**(1).

Hulme, C. (1993) Short term memory, speech rate, phonological ability and reading. Paper presented at the *Rodin Academy for the Study of Dyslexia Conference, October 1993, London*.

Hulme, C. and Snowling, M. (1994) *Reading Development and Dyslexia*. London, Whurr.

Hunt, G. (2002) Critical literacy and access to the lexicon. In: G. Reid and J. Wearmouth (eds), *Dyslexia and Literacy: Theory and Practice*. Chichester, UK, John Wiley & Sons.

Hunt, M. (1996) Newcastle literacy collaborative. Paper presented at *Sunderland City Challenge Reading Conference, 29 November 1996*.

Hunt, R. and Franks, T. (1993) *Oxford Reading Tree Pack*. Oxford, Oxford University Press.

Hunter, J., Connolly, V., Baillie, L. and Thomson, S. (1996) *Phonological Awareness Programme for Primary One Classes*. Edinburgh, PADG, Bonnington Primary School.

Hunter, V. (2001) Dyslexia and general science. In L. Peer and G. Reid (eds), *Dyslexia—Successful Inclusion in the Secondary School*. London, David Fulton.

Hunter-Carsch, M. (ed.) (1989) *The Art of Reading*. Oxford, Blackwell Education.

Hynd, G. S., Marshall, R. and Gonzalez, J. (1991) Learning disabilities and presumed central nervous system dysfunction. *Learning Disability Quarterly*, **14**, 283–296.

Imich, A. J. and Kerfoots, R. (1993) Educational psychology meeting the challenge of change. *Proceedings of the Annual Conference of the British Psychological Society, April 1993, Blackpool*.

Irlen, H. L. (1983) Successful treatment of learning. Paper presented at the *91st Annual Convention of the American Psychological Association, Anaheim, CA*.

Irlen, H. L. (1989) *Scotopic Sensitivity Syndrome Screening Manual* (3rd edn). Long Beach, CA, Irlen Institution.

Irlen, H. L. (1991) *Reading by the Colors: Overcoming Dyslexia and Other Reading Disabilities through the Irlen Method*. New York, Avebury.

Ivanic, R. (1998). *Writing and Identity*. Amsterdam, John Benjamin.

Iversen, S. and Tunmer, W. E. (1993) Phonological skills and the reading recovery programme. *Journal of Educational Psychology*, **85**, 112–126.

Jackson, P. and Reid, G. (1997) The assessment process (unpublished paper). Edinburgh, Centre for Specific Learning Difficulties, Moray House Institute.

Jacobson, J. (1997) *The Dyslexia Handbook*. Reading, UK, British Dyslexia Association.

Jameson, M. (1999) Setting up support groups. Workshop presented at *Dyslexia into the Year 2000 Conference, 12 June, Dundee, Scotland.*

Javorsky, J. (1993) *Alphabet Soup—A Recipe for Understanding and Treating Attention Deficit Hyperactivity Disorder.* Clarkston, MI, Minerva Press.

Johanson, K. (1997) Left hemisphere stimulation with music and sounds in dyslexia remediation. Paper presented at the *48th Annual Conference of the International Dyslexia Association* (formerly the Orton Dyslexia Association). Baltimore, MD, International Dyslexia Association.

Johanson, K. V. (1992) *Sensory Deprivation—A Possible Cause of Dyslexia* (Dyslexia Research Lab, BGC). Oslo, Scandinavian University Press.

Johnson, M. (2001) Inclusion: The challenges. In: L. Peer and G. Reid (eds), *Dyslexia—Successful Inclusion in the Secondary School.* London, David Fulton.

Johnson, M. (2002) Dyslexia and ICT: Three contrasting perspectives. In: M. Johnson and L. Peer (eds), *The Dyslexia Handbook.* Reading, UK, British Dyslexia Association.

Johnson, M. and Peer, L. (eds) (2003) *The Dyslexia Handbook 2003.* Reading, UK, British Dyslexia Association.

Johnson, M., Philips, S. and Peer, L. (1999) *Multisensory Teaching System for Reading.* Didsbury, UK, Special Educational Needs Centre, Didsbury School of Education, Manchester Metropolitan University.

Johnston, R. S. (1992) Methods of teaching reading: The debate continues. *Support for Learning,* **7**(3), 99–102.

Johnston, R. S., Anderson, M., Perrett, D. I. and Holligan, C. (1990) Perceptual dysfunction in poor readers: Evidence for visual and auditory segmentation problems in a sub-group of poor readers. *British Journal of Educational Psychology,* **60**, 212–219.

Johnston, R., Connelly, V. D. and Watson, J. (1995) Some effects of phonics teaching on early reading development. In P. Owen and P. Pumfrey (eds), *Emergent and Developing Reading: Messages for Teachers.* London, Falmer Press.

Jones, E. R. (1989) *The Cloze Line.* Belford, UK, Ann Arbor.

Jordan, E. (2001) Interrupted learning: The traveller paradigm. *Support for Learning,* **16**(3), 128–134.

Jung, C. G. (1923) *Psychological Types.* London, Pantheon Books.

Kaplan, B. J., Dewey, D. M., Crawford, S. G. and Wilson, B. N. (2001) The term comorbidity is of questionable value in reference to developmental disorders: Data and theory. *Journal of Learning Disabilities,* **34**(6), November–December, 555–565.

Kaufman, A. A. (1994) *Intelligent Testing with WISC-R.* New York, John Wiley & Sons.

Keefe, J. W. (1987) *Learning Style—Theory and Practice.* Reston, VA, National Association of Secondary School Principals.

Keefe, J. W. (1991) *Learning Style: Cognitive and Thinking Skills.* Reston, VA, National Association of Secondary School Principals.

Keefe, J. W. (1993) *Learning Style: Theory: Practice: Cognitive Skills.* Reston, VA, National Association of Secondary School Principals.

Keefe, J. W., Monk, J. S., Languis, M., Letteri, C. P. and Dunn, R. (1986) *Learning Style Profile.* Reston, VA, National Association of Secondary School Principals.

Kelly, K. (2002) Paper presented at *Multilingual Conference, IDA, Washington, DC, June 2002.*

Kettles, G., Laws, K. and Reid, G. (1996) Specific learning difficulties: A framework for assessment. In G. Reid (ed.), *Dimensions of Dyslexia,* Vol. 1: *Assessment, Teaching and the Curriculum.* Edinburgh, Moray House Publications.

Key 4 Learning (2002) *The Dyslexia and Dyspraxia Toolkit.* Chedworth, UK, Key 4 Learning Ltd.

Kiely, M. (1996) Handwriting—Skills, strategies and success. In: G. Reid (ed.), *Dimensions of Dyslexia,* Vol. 2: *Literacy, Language and Learning,* Edinburgh, Moray House Publications.

Kimmell, G. M. (1989) *Sound Out.* New York, Academic Therapy.

Kirk, J. (2001) Cross-curricular approaches to staff development in secondary schools. In: L. Peer and G. Reid (eds), *Dyslexia—Successful Inclusion in the Secondary School.* London, David Fulton.

Kirk, J. (2002) *Guidelines on Dyslexia.* Edinburgh, University of Edinburgh.

Kirk, J. and Reid, G. (2001) An examination of the relationship between dyslexia and offending in young people and the implications for the training system. *Dyslexia,* **7**(2), 77–84.

Kirk, J. and Reid, G. (2003) Adult dyslexia checklist—Criteria and considerations. *BDA Handbook.* Reading, UK, British Dyslexia Association.

Kirkcaldy, B. (1997) Contemporary tasks for psychological services in Scotland. *Educational Psychology in Scotland,* Spring–Summer, **5**, 6–16.

Kispal, A., Tate, A., Groman, T. and Whetton, C. (1989) *Test of Initial Literacy (TOIL).* Windsor, UK, NFER-Nelson.

Klein, C. (1993) *Diagnosing Dyslexia—A Guide to the Assessment of Adults with Specific Learning Difficulties.* London, Adult Literacy and Basic Skills Unit.

Klein, C. and Miller, R. R. (1990) *Unscrambling Spelling*. London, Hodder & Stoughton.

Knight, D. F. and Hynd, G. W. (2002) The neurobiology of dyslexia. In: G. Reid and J. Wearmouth (eds), *Dyslexia and Literacy, Theory and Practice*. Chichester, UK, John Wiley & Sons.

Knivsberg, A.-M., Reichelt, K.-L. and Nodland, M. (1999) Comorbidity or coexistence between dyslexia and attention deficit hyperactivity disorder. *British Journal of Special Education*, **26**(1), March, 42–47.

Kohl, M. and Tunmer, W. (1988) Phonemic segmentation skill and spelling acquisition. *Applied Psycholinguistics*, **9**, 335–356.

Kolb, D. A. (1984) *Learning Styles Inventory Technical Manual*. Boston, McBer.

Kratoville, B.L. (1989) *Word Tracking: Proverbs: High Frequency Words*. Belford, UK, Ann Arbor.

Kyd, L., Sutherland, G. and McGettrick, P. (1992) A preliminary appraisal of the Irlen screening process for scotopic sensitivity syndrome and the effect of Irlen coloured overlays on reading. *British Orthothalmic Journal*, **49**, 25–30.

Kyriacou, C. (1989) The nature and prevalence of teacher stress. In: M. Cole and S. Walker (eds), *Teaching and Stress*. Buckingham, UK, Open University Press.

Landon, J. (1999) Early intervention with bilingual learners: Towards a research agenda. In: H. South (ed.), *Literacies in Community and School* (pp. 84–96). Watford, UK, National Association for Language Development in the Curriculum (NALDIC).

Landon, J. (2001) Inclusion and dyslexia—The exclusion of bilingual learners? In: L. Peer and G. Reid (eds), *Dyslexia and Successful Inclusion in the Secondary School*. London, David Fulton.

Lane, K. A. (1991) *Developing Your Child for Success*. Louisville, TX, JWC.

Lannen, C., Lannen, S. and Reid, G. (1997) *Specific Learning Difficulties (Dyslexia): A Resource Book for Parents and Teachers*. St Annes-on-Sea, UK, Red Rose Publications.

Lannen, S. (2002a) Personal communication. Also quoted in website www.gavinreid.co.uk (Red Rose School) and www.dyslexiacentre.com.

Lannen, S. (2002b) *Difficulties in Literacy Development* (Course video). Buckingham, UK, Open University and Edinburgh, University of Edinburgh.

Lannen, S. and Reid, G. (1993) Psychological dimensions and the role of the educational psychologist in assessment. In: G. Reid (ed.), *Specific Learning Difficulties (Dyslexia) Perspectives on Practice*, Edinburgh, Moray House Publications.

Lannen, S. and Reid, G. (2002) Dyslexia and learning in Kairaranga. *The Journal of New Zealand RTLB*, **3**(2), 13–15.

Lannen, S. and Reid, G. (2003) Learning styles: Lights, sound, action. *BDA Handbook 2003*. Reading, UK, British Dyslexia Association.

Lawrence, D. (1985) Improving self-esteem and reading. *Educational Research*, **27**(3), 194–200.

Lawrence, D. (1987) *Enhancing Self-Esteem in the Classroom*. London, Paul Chapman.

Lawrence, G. (1993) *People Types and Tiger Stripes* (3rd edn). Gainsville, FL, Center for Applications of Psychological Type, Inc.

Lawson, J. S. and Inglis, J. (1984) The psychometric assessment of children with learning disabilities: An index derived from a principal component's analysis of the WISC-R. *Journal of Learning Disabilities*, **17**, 517–522.

Lawson, J. S. and Inglis, J. (1985) Learning disabilities and intelligence test results: A model based on a principal components analysis of the WISC-R. *British Journal of Psychology*, **76**, 35–48.

Lazear, D. (1994) *Multiple Intelligence Approaches to Assessment* Tucson, AZ, Zephyr Press.

Lazear, D. (1999) *Eight Ways of Knowing Teaching for Multiple Intelligences* (3rd edn). Arlington Heights, IL, Skylight Professional Development.

Lea, M. and Street, B. (2000) Student writing and staff feedback in higher education: An academic literacies approach. In: M. Lea and B. Stierer (eds), *Student Writing in Higher Education*. Buckingham, UK, Open University Press.

Leather, C. and McLoughlin, D. (2001) Developing task specific metacognitive skills in literate dyslexic adults. Paper presented at the *Fifth International Conference BDA, York, April*.

Lees, E. A. (1986) A cognitive developmental analysis of reading skills in good and poor readers. Paper presented at *Annual Conference of Developmental Psychology Section, September 1986*. Leicester, UK, British Psychological Society.

Leker, R.R. and Biran, I. (1999) Unidirectional dyslexia in a polygot. *Journal of Neurology, Neurosurgery and Psychiatry*, **66**, 517–519.

Leppanen, P. H., Pihko, E., Eklund, K. M. and Lyytinen, H. (1999) Cortical responses of infants with and without a genetic risk for dyslexia. II: Group effects. *Neuroreport*, **10**, 969–973.

Letterland International (1997) *About Letterland '97*. Cambridge, UK, Letterland International.

Levine, M. D. (1992) *Keeping A Head in School*. Cambridge, MA, Educators.

Levine, M. D. (1993) *All Kinds of Minds*. Cambridge, MA, Educators.

Lewin, K. (1936) *Principles of Topological Psychology*. New York, McGraw-Hill.

Lewis, A. and Norwich, B. (1999) Mapping a pedagogy for special educational needs. *Research and Intelligence*, **69**, 6–8.

Lewis, I. and Munn, P. (1993) *So You Want to Do Research*. Edinburgh, Scottish Council of Research in Education.

Lewkowicz, N. K. (1980) Phonemic awareness training: What to teach and how to teach it. *Journal of Educational Psychology*, **72**, 686–700.

Liberman, A. (1992). The relation of speech to reading and writing. In: R. Frost and L. Katz (eds), *Orthography, Phonology, Morphology, and Meaning* (pp. 167–177). North Holland, Elsevier.

Liberman, I. Y. and Liberman, A. M. (1992) Whole language versus code emphasis: Underlying assumptions and their implications for reading instruction. In: P. B. Gough, L. C. Ehri and R. Trieman (eds), *Reading Acquisition*. London, Lawrence Erlbaum.

Liberman, I. Y. and Shankweiler, D. P. (1985) Phonology and the problems of learning to read and write. *Remedial and Special Education*, **6**(6), 8–17.

Lidz, C. S. (1991) *Practitioners Guide to Dynamic Assessment*. New York, Guilford Press.

Lindamood, C. H. and Lindamood, P. C. (1979) *The LAC Test: Lindamood Auditory Conceptualisation Test*. Allen, TX, DLM Teaching Resources.

Lloyd, G. (1996) Introduction. In G. Lloyd (ed.), *Knitting Progress Unsatisfactory* (Gender and special issues in education). Edinburgh, Moray House Publications.

Lloyd, G. and Norris, C. (1999) Including ADHD? *Disability and Society*, **14**(4), 505–517.

Locke, A. and Beech, M. (1991) *Teaching Talking—Teaching Resources Handbook*. Windsor, UK, NFER-Nelson.

Longdon, W. (2001) Brain Gym® training in news and views. *Scottish Dyslexia Trust Newsletter*, Spring 2001.

Lovegrove, W. (1993) Visual timing and dyslexia. Paper presented at *Rodin Academy for the Study of Dyslexia Conference, October 1993, London*.

Lovegrove, W. (1996) Dyslexia and a transient/magnocellular pathway deficit: The current situation and future directions. *Australian Journal of Psychology*, **48**.

Luecking, R. G. (1997) Persuading employers to hire people with disabilities. In: P. J. Gerber and D. S. Brown (eds), *Learning Disabilities and Employment* (pp. 215–234). Austin, TX, Pro-Ed.

Luke, A., O'Brian, J. and Comber, B. (2001) Making community texts objects of study. In: H. Fehring and P. Green (eds), *Critical Literacy*. Newark, DE, International Reading Association.

Lundberg, I. (2002) The child's route into reading and what can go wrong. *Dyslexia*, **8**(1), January–March, 1–13.

Lunzer, E. and Gardner, K. (1984) *Learning from the Written Word*. London, Oliver & Boyd.

Macintyre, C. (1993) *Let's Find Why*. Edinburgh, Moray House Publications.

MacKay, N. (2001) Dyslexia-friendly schools. In: L. Peer and G. Reid (eds), *Dyslexia—Successful Inclusion in the Secondary School*. London, David Fulton.

MacPherson of Cluny, Sir William (1999) *The Stephen Lawrence Inquiry* (The MacPherson Report). London, Her Majesty's Stationery Office.

Mager, J. (1996) Local authority perspectives. Paper presented at *National Seminar Policy and Provision for Dyslexia, 3 December 1996*. Edinburgh, Scottish Dyslexia Forum.

Mailley, S. (1997) The classroom implications of visual perceptual difficulties: An exploratory study including Scotopic Sensitivity Syndrome or Irlen Syndrome (unpublished MA dissertation, University of Leicester).

Mailley, S. (2001) Visual difficulties with print. In: M. Hunter-Carsch (ed.), *Dyslexia, A Psychosocial Perspective*. London, Whurr.

Margulies, N. (1991) *Mapping Inner Space—Learning and Teaching Mind Mapping*. Tucson, AZ, Zephyr Press.

Marsh, G., Friedman, M., Welch, V. and Desberg, P. (1980) The development of strategies in spelling. In: U. Frith (ed.), *Cognitive Processes in Spelling* (pp. 339–354). London, Academic Press.

Mathews, M. (1993) Can children be helped by applied kinesiology. Paper presented at *5th European Conference in Neuro-Developmental Delay in Children with Specific Learning Difficulties, Chester*.

Mathews, M. and Thomas, E. (1993) A pilot study on the value of Applied Kinesiology in helping children with learning difficulties. Paper presented at *5th European Conference in Neuro-Developmental Delay in Children with Specific Learning Difficulties, Chester*.

McCarthy, B. (1987) *The 4-Mat System*. Barrington, IL, Excel Incorporated.

McClelland, J. L. (1988) Connectionist models and psychological evidence. *Journal of Memory and Language*, **27**, 107–123.

McCleod, J. (1994) *GAP Reading Comprehension Test*. London, Heinemann Educational.

McCormick, M. (2000) Dyslexia and developmental of verbal dyspraxia. *Dyslexia*, **6**, 202–214.

McCulloch, C. (1985) The Slingerland approach: Is it effective in a specific language disability classroom? (MA Thesis, Seattle, Seattle Pacific University).

Mcfarlane, A. & Glynn, T. (1998) Mana Maori in the professional development programme for resource teachers: Learning and behaviour. Paper presented at the *NZARE 20th Annual Conference, Dunedin, 3–6 December, 1998.* Hamilton, NZ, University of Waikato.

Mcfarlane, A., Glynn, T., Presland, I. and Greening, S. (2000) Maori culture and literacy learning: Bicultural approaches. In: L. Peer and G. Reid (eds), *Multilingualism, Literacy and Dyslexia. A Challenge for Educators.* London, David Fulton.

McGuinness, D. (1998) *Why Children Can't Read.* London, Penguin.

McIntyre, C. (2000) *Dyspraxia in the Early Years, Identifying and Supporting Children with Movement Difficulties.* London, David Fulton.

McIntyre, C. (2001) *Dyspraxia 5-11* (a practical guide). London, David Fulton.

McIntyre, C. (2002) *Early Intervention in Movement.* London, David Fulton.

McKeown, S. (ed.), (1992) *IT Support for Specific Learning Difficulties.* Coventry, UK, NCET.

McLean, B. (1993) Style counsel—Neurolinguistic programming. *Special Children,* April, 9–11.

McLoughlin, D., Fitzgibbon, G. and Young, V. (1994) *Adult Dyslexia: Assessment, Counselling and Training.* London, Whurr.

McLoughlin, D., Leather, C., and Stringer, P. (2002) *The Adult Dyslexic Interventions and Outcomes.* London, Whurr.

McNaughton, S. (1995) *Patterns of Emerging Literacy: Processes of Development and Transition.* Auckland, Oxford University Press.

McNicholas, J. and McEntree, J. (1991) *Games to Develop and Improve Reading Levels.* Tamworth, UK, NASEN Publications.

McPhillips, M., Hepper, P. G. and Mulhern, G. (2000) Effects of replicating primary-reflex movements on specific reading difficulties in children: A randomised double-blind, controlled trial. *The Lancet,* **355,** 537–541.

Meek, M. (1985) *Learning to Read.* London, Bodley Head.

Meyer, L. P. (1984) Long term academic effects of the direct instruction project. Follow through. *Elementary School Journal,* **84,** 380–394.

Miles, E. (1989) *Bangor Dyslexia Teaching System.* London, Whurr.

Miles, T. and Gilroy, D. (1986) *Dyslexia at College.* London, Methuen.

Miles, T. R. (1983a) *Bangor Dyslexia Test.* Cambridge, Learning Development Aids.

Miles, T. R. (1983b) *Dyslexia: The Pattern of Difficulties.* London, Collins Educational.

Miles, T. R. (1996) Do dyslexic children have IQs? *Dyslexia,* **2**(3), 175–178.

Miles, T. R. and Miles, E. (1991) *Dyslexia: A Hundred Years On.* Buckingham, UK, Open University Press.

Miles, T. R. and Miles, E. (eds) (1992) *Dyslexia and Mathematics.* London, Routledge.

Miles, T. R. and Varma, V. (eds) (1995) *Dyslexia and Stress.* London, Whurr.

Miller, R. and Klein, C. (1986) *Making Sense of Spelling.* London, DCLD.

Miller-Guron, L. (1999) *Wordchains.* Windsor, UK, NFER-Nelson.

Mitchell, S. (1985) An investigation into the presence or absence of postural reflex abnormalities in children with speech problems (unpublished pilot study, City of Birmingham Polytechnic).

Mittler, P. (2001) *Working towards Inclusive Education—Social Contexts.* London, David Fulton.

Mommers, M. J. C. (1987) An investigation into the relationship between word recognition, reading comprehension and spelling skills in the first two years of primary school. *Journal of Research in Reading,* **2**(10), 122–143.

Monteiro, W. (1992) Neuro-linguistic processing. Paper presented at the *Helen Arkell Dyslexic Conference, Cambridge, April 1992.*

Moody, S. (1999) *Arranging a Dyslexia Assessment: A Guide for Adults.* London, Dyslexia Assessment Service.

Moore, P. J. (1988) Reciprocal teaching and reading comprehension: A review. *Journal of Research in Reading,* **11**(1), 3–14.

Morgan, E. and C. Klein (2000). *The Dyslexic Adult in a Non-dyslexic World.* London, Whurr.

Morgan, R. T. T. (1976) Paired reading tuition: A preliminary report on a technique for cases of reading deficit. In: *Child Care, Health and Development,* **2,** 13–28.

Morgan, W. (1996) London offender study: Creating criminals—Why are so many criminals dyslexic? Unpublished dissertation, University of London.

Morrow, L. M., Tracey, D. H., Woo, D. G. and Pressley, M. (1999) Characteristics of exemplary first-grade literacy instruction. *Reading Teacher Journal,* **52**(5), 462–476.

Mortimer, T. (2000) Learning styles and dyslexia. In: I. Smythe (ed.), *The Dyslexia Handbook 2000.* Reading, UK, British Dyslexia Association.

Morton, J. and Frith, U. (1995) Causal modelling: A structural approach to developmental psychopathology. In: D. Cicchetti and D. J. Cohen (eds), *Manual of Developmental Psychopathology* (pp. 357–390). New York, Psychological Assessment of Dyslexia and John Wiley & Sons.

Moseley, D. (1989) How lack of confidence in spelling affects children's written expression. *Educational Psychology in Practice*, **5**(1), 42–46.

Moseley, D. and Nicol, C. (1995) *ACE (Actually Coded English) Spelling Dictionary*. Cambridge, LDA.

Moseley, D. V. (1988) New approaches to helping children with spelling difficulties. *Educational and Child Psychology*, **5**(4), 54–58.

Moser, C. (2000) *Better Basic Skills—Improving Adult Literacy and Numeracy*. London, Department for Education and Employment.

Mosley, J. (1996) *Quality Circle Time in the Primary Classroom*. Cambridge, LDA.

Moss, H. (2000), Using literacy development programmes. In: J. Townend and M. Turner (eds), *Dyslexia in Practice—A Guide for Teachers*. Dordrecht, Kluwer Academic.

Munn, P. and Drever, E. (1990) *Using Questionnaires in Small-scale Research. A Teacher's Guide*. Edinburgh, Scottish Council for Research in Education (SCRE).

Muskat, L. R. (1996) Empowering students with special needs: Assessment and classification revisited. In: G. Reid (ed.), *Dimensions of Dyslexia*, Vol. 2, *Literacy, Language and Learning*. Edinburgh, Moray House Publications.

Muter, V., Hulme, C. and Snowling, M. (1997) *Phonological Abilities Test*. London, Psychological Corporation.

Myers, I. and Myers, R. (1980) *Gifts Differing*. Palo Alto, CA, Consulting Psychologists Press.

Naidoo, S. (ed.) (1988) *Assessment and Teaching of Dyslexic Children*. London, ICAN.

Nash-Wortham, M. and Hunt, J. (1993) *Take Time*. Stourbridge, UK, Robinswood Press.

Nation, K. and Snowling, M. J. (1998) Individual differences in contextual facilitation: Evidence from dyslexia and poor reading comprehension. *Child Development*, **69**, 996–1011.

NCCA (1999) *Curriculum for Primary Schools: English Language*. Dublin, National Council for Curriculum and Assessment.

NCDA (2002) *The NCDA Dyslexia Awareness Campaign, Nicosia, N. Cyprus, 14–16 October 2002*. Nicosia, North Cyprus Dyslexia Association.

Neale, M. (1989) *Neale Analysis*. Windsor, UK, NFER-Nelson.

Neville, M. H. (1975) Effectiveness of rate of aural message on reading and listening. *Educational Research*, **1**(18), 37–43.

Newby, M., Aldridge, J., Sasse, B. M., Harrison, S. and Coker, J. (1995). The dyslexics speak for themselves. In: T. R. Miles and V. Varma (eds), *Dyslexia and Stress*. London, Whurr.

Newton, M. and Thomson, M. (1982) *Aston Index*. Cambridge, LDA.

Nicolson, R. I. (1996) Development dyslexia: Past, present and future. *Dyslexia*, **2**(3).

Nicolson, R. I. (2001) Developmental dyslexia: Into the future. In: A. Fawcett (ed.), *Dyslexia, Theory and Good Practice*. London, Whurr.

Nicolson, R. I. and Fawcett, A. J. (1990) Automaticity: A new framework for dyslexia research? *Cognition*, **35**, 159–182.

Nicolson, R. I. and Fawcett, A. J. (1993) Early diagnosis of dyslexia: An historic opportunity? Keynote address presented at *BDA Early Diagnosis Conference, London, June 1993*.

Nicolson, R. I. and Fawcett, A. J. (1994) Speed of processing, motor skill, automaticity and dyslexia. In: A. Fawcett and R. Nicolson (eds), *Dyslexia in Children, Multidisciplinary Perspectives*. Hemel Hempstead, UK, Harvester Wheatsheaf.

Nicolson, R. I. and Fawcett, A. J. (1996) *The Dyslexia Early Screening Test*. London, The Psychological Corporation.

Nicolson, R. I. and Fawcett, A. J. (1999). Developmental dyslexia: The role of the cerebellum. *Dyslexia: An International Journal of Research and Practice*, **5**, 155–177.

Nicolson, R. I. and Fawcett, A. J. (2000) Long-term learning in dyslexic children. *European Journal of Cognitive Psychology*, **12**, 357–393.

Nicolson, R. I., Fawcett, A. J. and Miles, T. R. (1993) *Feasibility Study for the Development of a Computerised Screening Test for Dyslexia in Adults* (Report OL176). Sheffield, Department of Employment.

Nicolson, R. I., Fawcett, A. J. and Dean, P. (2001) Developmental dyslexia. The cerebellar deficit hypothesis. *Trends in Neurosciences*, **24**(9), 508–511.

Niklasson, M. (1993) Adding meaning to life: A matter of experience. Paper presented at the *5th European Conference of Neuro-Developmental Delay in Children with Specific Learning Difficulties, Chester*.

Nisbet, J. and Shucksmith, J. (1986) *Learning Strategies*. London, Routledge.

Norwich, B. and Lewis, A. (2001) Mapping a pedagogy for special educational needs. *British Educational Research Journal*, **27**(3), 313–331.

NZ Department of Education (2001) *Let's All Read* (Education and Science Committee on the inquiry into teaching of reading in New Zealand). Wellington, New Zealand Department of Education.

O'Hagen, F. J. and Swanson, W. I. (1981) Teachers' views regarding the role of the educational psychologist in school. *Research in Education*, **29**, 29–40.

O'Hagen, F. J. and Swanson, W. I. (1983) Teachers and psychologists: A comparison of views. *Research in Education*, **36**.

OECD (2000) *Measuring Students' Knowledge and Skills* (The PISA 2000 assessment of reading, mathematical and scientific literacy). Paris: Organisation for Economic Co-operation and Development.

OECD (2001) *Knowledge and Skills for Life* (International report on the PISA 2000 assessment). Paris: Organisation for Economic Co-operation and Development.

Office of Her Majesty's Chief Inspector of Schools, New Zealand (1993) *Reading Recovery in New Zealand* (A report from the Office of Her Majesty's Chief Inspector of Schools). London, Her Majesty's Stationery Office.

Olson, R. K., Forsberg, H., Wise, B. and Rack, J. (1994) Measurement of word recognition, orthographic and phonological. In: G. R. Lyon (ed.), *Frames of Reference for the Assessment of Learning Disabilities: New Views on Measurement Issues* (pp. 243–277). Baltimore, MD, Paul, H. Brookes.

Orton Dyslexia Society (1991) *All Language and the Creation of Literacy*. Baltimore, Orton Dyslexia Society.

Osmond, J. (1993) *The Reality of Dyslexia*. London, Cassell.

Ostler, C. (1991) *Dyslexia—A Parents Survival Guide*. Godalming, UK, Ammonite Books.

Ott, P. (1997) *How to Detect and Manage Dyslexia—A Reference and Resource Manual*. Oxford, Heinemann.

OU (1991) *A Guide for First-time Researchers in Education and Social Science*. Milton Keynes, UK, Open University Press.

OU (2002) *'Philip'—Student art the Red Rose School*. (E 801 course audio tape). Milton Keynes, UK, Open University Press.

OU (2002) *Difficulties in Literacy Development* (E 801 course audio tape and study guide). Milton Keynes, UK, Open University Press.

Overy, C. S. R. (2002) Dyslexia and Music: From timing deficits to music intervention. Unpublished Ph.D., University of Sheffield, UK.

Oxley, L. and Topping, K. (1990) Peer tutored cued spelling with seven to nine year olds. *British Education Research Journal*, **16**, 63–79.

Padget, S. Y., Knight, D. F. and Sawyer, D. J. (1996) *Tennessee Meets the Challenge of Dyslexia* (reprinted from *Annals of Dyslexia*, **46**, 51–72). Baltimore, Orton Dyslexia Society.

Palincsar, A. and Brown, A. (1984) Reciprocal teaching of comprehension fostering and comprehension monitoring activities. *Cognition and Instruction*, **1**(2), 117–175.

Palincsar, A. and Klenk, L. (1992) Fostering literacy learning in supportive contexts. *Journal of Learning Disabilities*, **25**, 211–225.

Palmer, C. (2001) Good practice in learning support: The Somerset Learning Support Services. Paper presented at *Fifth BDA International Conference, York, April*.

Palmer, J., McLeod, C., Hunt, E. and Davidson, J. (1985) Information processing correlates of reading. *Journal of Memory and Language*, **24**, 59–88.

Paulesu, E., De-monet, J. F., Fazio, F., McCrory, E., Chanoine, V., Brunswick, N., Cappa, S. F., Cossu, G., Habib, M., Frith, C. D. and Frith U. (2001) Dyslexia: Cultural diversity and biological unity. *Science*, **291**, 16 March (www.sciencemag.org).

Paulesu, E., Frith, U., Snowling, M., Gallagher, A., Morton, J., Frackowiak, F. S. J. and Frith, C. D. (1996). Is developmental dyslexia a disconnection syndrome? Evidence from PET scanning. *Brain*, **119**, 143–157.

Pavlidis, G. Th. (1990a) *Perspectives on Dyslexia: Neurology, Neuropsychology and Genetics* (Vol. 1). Chichester, UK, John Wiley & Sons.

Pavlidis, G. Th. (1990b) *Perspectives on Dyslexia: Cognition, Language and Treatment* (Vol. 2). Chichester, UK, John Wiley & Sons.

Payne, N. (1997) Job accommodations: What works and why. In: P. J. Gerber and D. S. Brown (eds), *Learning Disabilities and Employment* (pp. 255–276). Austin, TX, Pro-Ed.

Payne, T. (1991) It's cold in the other room. *Support for Learning*, **6**(2), 61–65.

Peacey, N. (2001) Inclusion and the Revised National Curriculum. In L. Peer and G. Reid (eds.), *Dyslexia—Successful Inclusion in the Secondary School*. London, David Fulton.

Pearson, L. E. A. and Quinn, J. (1986) *Bury Infant Check*. Windsor, UK, NFER-Nelson.

Peck, A. (1993) *The Use of Colour in Visual Reading Difficulties* (Project Information No. 2, Summer 1993). Edinburgh, Centre for Specific Learning Difficulties, Moray House.

Peck, A., Wilkins, A. and Jordan, E. (1991) Visual discomfort in the classroom. *Child Language, Teaching and Therapy*, **7**(2), 326–340.

Peelo, M. (1994) *Helping Students with Study Problems*. Buckingham, UK, Open University Press.

Peer, L. (2001) Dyslexia and its manifestations in the secondary school. In: L. Peer and G. Reid (eds), *Dyslexia—Successful Inclusion in the Secondary School*. London, David Fulton.

Peer, L. and Reid, G. (2002) *Dyslexia and Literacy: Challenges in the Secondary School*. In: G. Reid and J. Wearmouth (eds), *Dyslexia and Literacy, Theory and Practice*. Chichester, UK, John Wiley & Sons.

Peer, L. and Reid, G. (eds) (2000) *Multilingualism, Literacy and Dyslexia: A Challenge for Educators*. London, David Fulton.

Peer, L. and Reid, G. (eds) (2001) *Dyslexia—Successful Inclusion in the Secondary School*. London, David Fulton.

Peer, L. and Reid, G. (2003) *Introduction to Dyslexia*. London, David Fulton.

Pennington, B. F. (1990) The genetics of dyslexia. *Journal of Child Psychology and Psychiatry*, **31**, 193 201.

Pennington, B. F. (1991) *Diagnosing Learning Disorders: A Neurological Framework*. New York, Guilford Press.

Pennington, B. F. (1996) The development of dyslexia: Genotype and phenotype analyses. Paper read at *47th Annual Conference, November*. Boston, Orton Dyslexia Society.

Perfetti, C. (1992) The representation problem in reading acquisition. In: P. Gough, L. Ehri and R. Treiman (eds), *Reading Acquisition* (pp. 107–143). Hillsdale, NJ, Erlbaum.

Perrin, J. (1981) *Learning Style Inventory: Primary Version*. New York, St John's University.

Perrin, J. (1983) *Learning Style Inventory: Primary Manual for Administration, Interpretation and Teaching Suggestions*. Jamaica, NY, Learning Styles Network, St John's University, Center for the Study of Learning and Teaching Styles.

Peters, M. L. (1970) *Success in Spelling* (Cambridge Monographs on Education No. 4). Cambridge, Cambridge Institute of Education.

Peters, M. L. (1975) *Diagnostic and Remedial Spelling Manual*. London, Macmillan Education.

Peters, M. L. (1985) *Spelling: Caught or Taught—A New Look*. London, Routledge.

Peters, M. L. and Smith, B. (1993) *Spelling in Context—Strategies for Teachers and Learners*. Windsor, UK, NFER-Nelson.

Philips, S. (1999) *Management Skills for SEN Co-ordinators in the Primary School*. London, Falmer.

Pinnell, G. S., Deford, D. and Lyons, C. A. (1988a) *Reading Recovery: Early Intervention for At-Risk First Graders* (ERS Monograph). Arlington, VA, Educational Research Service.

Pinnell, G. S., Lyons, C. A. and Deford, D. E. (1988b) *Reading Recovery* (Sopris West Educational Programmes that Work, 14th edn). Denver, CO, Sopris West in co-operation with the National Dissemination Study Group.

Pinnell, G. S., Lyons, C. A., Deford, D., Bryk, A. S. and Seltzer, M. (1991) *Studying the Effectiveness of Early Intervention Approaches for First Grade Children Having Difficulty in Reading* (Education Report No. 16). Columbus, OH, Martha L. King Language and Literacy Center, Ohio State University.

Pinsent, P. (ed.) (1990) *Children with Literacy Difficulties*. Roehampton, UK, David Fulton.

Plaut, D. C., McClelland, J. L., Seidenberg, M. S. and Patterson, K. (1996) Understanding normal and impaired word reading: Computational principles in quasi-regular domains. *Psychological Review*, **103**, 56–115.

Pollak, D. (2001a) Access to higher education for the mature dyslexic student: A question of identity and a new perspective. Paper presented at the *5th BDA Conference, York, April*.

Pollak, D. (2001b) Learning life histories of higher education students who are dyslexic (Thesis presented in 2001 at Leicester's De Montfort University).

Pollock, J. (1990) *Signposts to Spelling*. London, Heinemann Educational.

Portwood, M. (1994) *Developmental Dyspraxia: A Practical Manual for Parents and Professionals*. Durham, UK, Durham County Council.

Portwood, M. (1999) *Developmental Dyspraxia: Identification and Intervention, A Manual for Parents and Professionals*. London, David Fulton.

Portwood, M. (2000) *Understanding Developmental Dyspraxia. A Textbook for Students and Professionals*. London, David Fulton.

Portwood, M. (2001) *Developmental Dyspraxia: A Practical Manual for Parents and Professionals*. Durham, UK, Durham County Council Educational Psychology Service.

Portwood, M. (2002) School based trials of fatty acid supplements. Paper presented at *Education Conference Durham County Council, June 2002*.

Pottage, T. (1994) *Using Computers with Dyslexics*. Hull, UK, University of Hull, Dyslexia Computer Resource Centre.

Prashnig, B. (1994) Don't teach me—let me learn! The Learning Styles of dropouts and at-risk students. *Education Today*, March.

Pratley, R. (1988) *Spelling it Out*. London, BBC Books.

Prifitera, A. and Dersch, J. (1993) Base rates of WISC diagnostic subtest patterns among normal learning disabled and ADHD samples. *Journal of Pyschoeducational Assessment*, WISC-III Monograph, 43–55.

Pringle-Morgan, W. P. (1896) A case of congenital word-blindness. *British Medical Journal*, **2**, 1378.

Prior, M. (1996) *Understanding Specific Learning Difficulties*. Hove, UK, Psychology Press.

Pumfrey, P. (2001) Specific developmental dyslexia: 'Basics to back' in 2000 and beyond? In: M. Hunter-Carsch (ed.), *Dyslexia, A Psychosocial Perspective*. London, Whurr.

Pumfrey, P. (2002) Specific developmental dyslexia: 'Basics to back' in 2000 and beyond? In J. Wearmouth, J. Soler and G. Reid (eds), *Addressing Difficulties in Literacy Development, Responses at Family, School, Pupil and Teacher Levels*. London, Routledge Falmer.

Pumfrey, P. D. (1990) Integrating the testing and teaching of reading. *Support for Learning*, **5**(3), 146–152.

Pumfrey, P. D. (1995) The management of specific learning difficulties (dyslexia): Challenges and responses. In: I. Lunt, B. Norwich and V. Varma (eds). *Psychology and Education for Special Needs: Recent Developments and Future Directions* (pp. 45–70). London, Ashgate.

Pumfrey, P. D. (1996) *Specific Developmental Dyslexia: Basics to Back* (the 15th Vernon-Wall Lecture). Leicester, UK, British Psychological Society.

Pumfrey, P. D. and Reason, R. (1991) *Specific Learning Difficulties (Dyslexia) Challenges and Responses*. Windsor, UK, NFER-Nelson.

QCA (2000) *General Statement on Inclusion, Curriculum 2000*. London: Qualifications and Curriculum Authority.

Rack, J. (1994) Dyslexia: The phonological deficit hypothesis. In: R. I. Nicolson and A. J. Fawcett (eds), *Dyslexia in Children: Multidisciplinary Perspectives*. Hemel Hempstead, UK, Harvester Wheatsheaf.

Rack, J. and Walker, J. (1994) *Does Dyslexia Institute Teaching Work?* (reprinted from *Dyslexia Review*, **6**(2), Autumn). Staines, UK, The Dyslexia Institute.

Rack, J. P., Snowling, M. J. and Olson, R. K. (1992). The non-word reading deficit in dyslexia: A review. *Reading Research Quarterly*, **27**, 29–53.

Ramsden, M. (1992) *Putting Pen to Paper—A New Approach to Handwriting*. Devon, UK, Southgate.

Raven, J. C. (1988) *Mill Hill Manual and Vocabulary Scale*. Windsor, UK, NFER-Nelson.

Raven, J. C. (1992, 1993) *Standard Progressive Matrices*. Oxford, Oxford Psychologists Press.

Rawson, M. B. (1988) *The Many Faces of Dyslexia*. Baltimore, Orton Dyslexia Society.

Ray, B. J. (1986) A cooperative teacher education and language retraining programme for dyslexics in West Texas. Paper presented at the *Action in Research V Conference, Lubbock, TX*.

Rayner, S. and Riding, R. (1997) Towards a categorisation of cognitive styles and learning styles. *Educational Psychology*, **17**, 5–28.

Read, C. (1971) Pre-school children's knowledge of English phonology. *Harvard Educational Review*, **41**, 1–34.

Reading in Partnership Project (1992) *Sunderland City Challenge, Reading in Partnership Project*. Sunderland, UK, Sunderland Learning Support Service.

Real Lancashire Magazine (2002) Houghton Towers, summer/autumn, p. 41. St. Anne's-on-Sea, UK.

Reason, R. (2002) From assessment to intervention: The educational psychology perspective. In: G. Reid and J. Wearmouth (eds), *Dyslexia and Literacy: Theory and Practice*. Chichester, UK, John Wiley & Sons.

Reason, R. and Boote, R. (1986) *Learning Difficulties in Reading and Writing: A Teachers' Manual*. Windsor, UK, NFER-Nelson.

Reason, R. and Boote, R. (1994) *Helping Children with Reading and Spelling: A Special Needs Manual*. London, Routledge.

Reason, R. and Frederickson, N. (1996) Discrepancy definitions or phonological assessment. In: G. Reid (ed.), *Dimensions of Dyslexia: Assessment, Teaching and the Curriculum* (Vol. 1). Edinburgh, Moray House Publications.

Reason, R., Brown, P., Cole, M. and Gregory, M. (1988) Does the 'specific' in specific learning difficulties make a difference to the way we teach? *Support for Learning*, **3**(4), 230–236.

Reddington, R. M. and Wheeldon, A. (2002) Involving parents in baseline assessment: Employing developmental psychopathology in the early identification process. *Dyslexia*, **8**(2), April–June, 119–122.

Reed, T (2000) The literacy acquisition of Black and Asian 'English-as-an Additional Language' learners. In: L. Peer and G. Reid (eds), *Multilingualism, Literacy and Dyslexia*. London, David Fulton.

Reid, G. (1986) An examination of pupil stress before and after transfer from primary to secondary school (unpublished MEd thesis, University of Aberdeen).

Reid, G. (1987) The perceptions and attitudes of learning support teachers to specific learning difficulties and dyslexia. *Year Book of the Scottish Learning Difficulties Association*. Paisley, UK, Scottish Learning Difficulties Association.

Reid, G. (1988) Dyslexia: A case for training. *Times Educational Supplement*, 26 February.

Reid, G. (1989) *The Role of the Educational Psychologist in the Identification and Assessment of Specific Learning Difficulties* (Feedback paper). Fife, Fife Regional Council, Psychological Service.

Reid, G. (1990) Specific learning difficulties: Attitudes towards assessment and teaching. In: G. Hales (ed.), *Meeting Points*. Reading, UK, British Dyslexia Association.

Reid, G. (1991a) Stress factors in teaching children with specific learning difficulties. Paper presented at the *2nd International Conference: Meeting the Challenge. British Dyslexia Association, April 1991, Oxford*. Reading, UK, British Dyslexia Association.

Reid, G. (1991b) Supporting the support teacher. Stress factors in teaching children with specific learning difficulties. *Links*, **16**(3), 18–20.

Reid, G. (1992) Learning difficulties and learning styles—Observational criteria. Paper presented at *South East Learning Styles Conference, George Mason University, VA*.

Reid, G. (1993a) Dyslexia: Observation and metacognitive assessment. Paper presented at *44th Annual Conference, Orton Dyslexia Society, New Orleans, LA*. Baltimore, Orton Dyslexia Society.

Reid, G. (ed.) (1993b) *Specific Learning Difficulties (Dyslexia) Perspectives on Practice*. Edinburgh, Moray House Publications.

Reid, G. (1993c) Perspectives on reading. In: G. Reid (ed.), *Specific Learning Difficulties (Dyslexia) Perspectives on Practice*. Edinburgh, Moray House Publications.

Reid, G. (1993d) What is reading? (unpublished study, Centre for Specific Learning Difficulties (Dyslexia). Edinburgh, Moray House Institute).

Reid, G. (1994a) Metacognitive assessment and dyslexia. Paper presented at *3rd International Conference of the British Dyslexia Association, April 1994, Manchester*.

Reid, G. (1994b) *Specific Learning Difficulties (Dyslexia). A Handbook for Study and Practice*. Edinburgh, Moray House Publications.

Reid, G. (1996) *Dimensions of Dyslexia*, Vol. 1: *Assessment, Teaching and the Curriculum*; Vol. 2: *Literacy, Language and Learning*. Edinburgh: Moray House Publications.

Reid, G. (2000) Dyslexia: Evolution, revolution and devolution. *Journal of the Scottish Support for Learning Association (SSLA)*, 40–45.

Reid, G. (2001a) Specialist teacher training in the UK Issues, considerations and future directions. In: M. Hunter-Carsch (ed.), *Dyslexia, A Psychosocial Perspective*. London, Whurr.

Reid, G. (2001b) Dyslexia, metacognition and learning styles. In: G. Shiel and U. Ni Dhalaigh (eds), *Reading Matters: A Fresh Start*. Dublin, Reading Association of Ireland/National Reading Initiative.

Reid, G. (2002) Dyslexia: Research and implications for practice. Paper presented at the *RTLB national conference, Learning to Motivate, Motivate to Learn, Dunedin, New Zealand, 18 September*.

Reid, G. and Given, B. (2000) Learning styles. *BDA Handbook 2000*. Reading, UK, British Dyslexia Association.

Reid, G. and Given, B. K. (1998) The Interactive Observation Style Identification. In: B. K. Given and G. Reid (eds), *Learning Styles—A Guide for Teachers and Parents*. St. Anne's-on-Sea, UK, Red Rose Publications.

Reid, G. and Kirk, J. (2001) *Dyslexia in Adults: Education and Employment*. Chichester, UK, John Wiley & Sons.

Reid, G. and Weedon, C. (1997) *Insights Gained from Developing an Instrument to Profile the Emerging Literacy Skills of Six Year Olds*. Edinburgh, Moray House Centre for the Study of Dyslexia.

Reid, G., Carson, E. and Brydon, P. (1989) *A Pilot Study Investigating the Merits of Segregated Provision for Primary Pupils with Severely Delayed Attainments in Reading and Spelling*. Fife, UK, Fife Region Psychological Service.

Reid, G. Kirk, J., Hui, D. and Mullin, K. (1999) *Adult Dyslexia for Employment, Practice and Training* (a report on best practice in dyslexia assessment, support and training in the employment service). Sheffield, UK, Employment Service.

Reid-Lyon, G. (1994) *Toward a Definition of Dyslexia* (reprinted from *Annals of Dyslexia*, **45**, 3–27). Baltimore, Orton Dyslexia Society.

Reid-Lyon, G. (1995) *Toward a Definition of Dyslexia* (reprinted from *Annals of Dyslexia*, **45**). Baltimore, Orton Dyslexia Society.

Retief, L. (1990) A psychophysiological approach to panic disorder (doctoral thesis).

Reynolds, D., Hambly, H. and Nicolson, R. (in press) The cerebellum and dyslexia: Preliminary evaluation of an exercise-based treatment.

Reynolds, D., Nicolson, R. I. and Hambly, H. (2002) An experimental evaluation of an exercise-based treatment for children with reading difficulties. Online at www.ddat.org

Reynolds, D., Nicolson, R. I. and Hambly, H. (2003) Evaluation of an exercise-based treatment for children with reading difficulties. *Dyslexia*, **9**(1), 48–71.

Richards, R. G. (1993) *Learn Playful Techniques to Accelerate Learning*. Tucson, AZ, Zephyr Press.

Richardson, A. (1988) The effects of a specific red filter on dyslexia. *British Psychological Society Abstracts*, **56**.

Richardson, A. J. (2001) Dyslexia, dyspraxia and ADHD—Can nutrition help? Paper presented at *4th Cambridge Conference, Helen Arkell Dyslexia Association, March 2001, Cambridge*.

Richardson, A. J. (2002) Dyslexia, dyspraxia and ADHD—Can nutrition help? Paper presented at *Education Conference Durham County Council, June 2002*.

Richardson, A. J. and Puri, B. K. (2000) The potential role of fatty acids in Attention Deficit/Hyperactivity Disorder (ADHD). *Prostaglandins Leukotr. Essent Fatty Acids*, **63**, 79–87.

Riddell, S., Duffield, J., Brown, S. and Ogilvy, C. (1992) *Specific Learning Difficulties: Policy, Practice and Provision*. Stirling, UK, Department of Education, University of Stirling.

Riddick, B. (1995a) Dyslexia and development: An interview study. *Dyslexia: An International Journal of Research and Practice*, **1**(2).

Riddick, B. (1995b) Dyslexia: Dispelling the myths. *Disability and Society*, **10**(4), 457–473.

Riddick, B. (1996) *Living with Dyslexia*. London, Routledge.

Riddick, B. (2001) The experiences of teachers and trainee teachers who have dyslexia. Paper presented at the *Fifth International Conference, BDA, York, April*.

Riddick, B. (2002) Researching the social and emotional consequences of dyslexia. In: J. Soler, J. Wearmouth and G. Reid (eds), *Contextualising Difficulties in Literacy Development—Exploring Politics, Culture, Ethnicity and Ethics*. London, RoutledgeFalmer.

Riddick, B., Farmer, M. and Sterling, C. (1997) *Students and Dyslexia: Growing Up with a Specific Learning Difficulty*. London, Whurr.

Riddick, B., Sterling, C., Farmer, M. and Morgan, S. (1999) Self-esteem and anxiety in the educational histories of adult dyslexic students. *Dyslexia*, **5**(4), December.

Riding, R. and Cheema, I. (1991) Cognitive style: An overview and integration. *Educational Psychology*, **11**, 193–215.

Riding, R. and Rayner, S. (1998) *Cognitive Styles and Learning Strategies; Understanding Style Differences in Learning and Behaviour*. London, David Fulton.

Ringard, J-C. (2000) *Concerning the Dysphasic and the Dyslexic Child*. Paris, Ministry of National Education.

Robertson, A. H., Henderson, A., Robertson, A., Fisher, J. and Gibson, M. (1995) *Quest Screening, Diagnostic and Support Kit*. Windsor, UK, NFER-Nelson.

Robertson, J. (2000). *Dyslexia and Reading: A Neuropsychological Approach*. London, Whurr.

Robertson, J. and Bakker, D. J. (2002) The Balance Model of Reading and Dyslexia. In: G. Reid and J. Wearmouth (eds), *Dyslexia and Literacy: Theory and Practice*. Chichester, UK, John Wiley & Sons.

Rohl, M. and Tunmer, W. (1988) Phonemic segmentation skills and spelling acquisition. *Applied Psycholinguistics*, **9**, 335–350.

Romani, C., Ward, J., and Olson, A. (1999) Developmental Surface Dysgraphia: What is the underlying cognitive impairment? *Quarterly Journal of Experimental Psychology*, section A, **52**, 97–128.

Ronka, R. (2000) Louisiana literacy profile to identify reading difficulties. Paper presented at the *51st Annual Conference IDA, Washington, DC, November 2000*.

Rosner, J. and Rosner, J. (1987) The Irlen treatment: A review of the literature. *Optician*, 25 September, 26–33.

Rowe, H. (1988) Metacognitive skills: Promises and problems. *Australian Journal of Reading*, **11**(4), 227–237.

Roxburgh, I. (1995) *Report on Scottish Parents' Perceptions of Current Educational Provision for Dyslexic Pupils*. Scottish Dyslexia Association (now Dyslexia in Scotland), Stirling, UK.

Rudginsky, L. T. and Haskell, E. C. (1990) *How to Spell*. Cambridge, MA, Educators.

Rule, J. M. (1984) *The Structure of Words*. Cambridge, MA, Educators.

Russell, J. (1988) *Graded Activities for Children with Motor Difficulties*. Cambridge, UK, Cambridge Educational.

Russell, P. (1979) *The Brain Book*. London, Routledge.

Russell, S. (1992, revised 2000) *Phonic Code Cracker*. Glasgow, Jordanhill College Publications.

Russell, S. (1993) Access to the curriculum. In: G. Reid (ed.), *Specific Learning Difficulties (Dyslexia) Perspectives on Practice*. Edinburgh, Moray House Publications.

Rutter, M. (1995) Relationships between mental disorders in childhood and adulthood. *Acta Psychiatrica Scandinavica*, **91**, 73–85.

Scoble, J. (1988) Cued spelling in adult literacy: A case study. *Paired Reading Bulletin*, **4**, 93–96.

Scoble, J. (1989) Cued spelling and paired reading in adult basic education in Rydale. *Paired Learning*, **5**, 57–62.

Scottish Dyslexia Forum (2002) Dyslexia—Research and its implications for policy and practice. Paper presented at *Conference, University of Stirling, 13 May 2002*.

Scottish Education Department (1978) *The Education of Pupils with Learning Difficulties in Primary and Secondary Schools in Scotland* (progress report for the Scottish Education Department). Edinburgh, Her Majesty's Stationery Office.

Scottish Education Department (1987) *A Policy for the 90s: Concern over Falling Standards*. Edinburgh, Her Majesty's Stationery Office.

Scottish Education Department (1989) *A Policy for the 90s: Learning and Teaching*. Edinburgh, Her Majesty's Stationery Office.

Scottish Education Department (1990) *5-14 Development Programme* (a handbook for headteachers—curriculum and assessment in Scotland). Edinburgh, Her Majesty's Stationery Office.

Scottish Executive (2002) *Education (Disability) Strategies and Pupils' Educational Records (Scotland) Act 2002*. Edinburgh, Scottish Parliament.

Scottish Executive (2003) *Education for Excellence* (the Executive's response to the national debate). Edinburgh, Scottish Parliament.

Scottish Parliament (2001) *Report on Inquiry into Special Educational Needs: Education, Culture and Sports Committee* (3rd report). Edinburgh, Her Majesty's Stationery Office.

Seidenberg, M. S. and McClelland, J. (1989) A distributed, developmental model of word recognition. *Psychological Review*, **96**, 523–568.

Selikowitz, M. (1994) *Dyslexia and Other Learning Difficulties*. Oxford, Oxford University Press.

Selman, M. R. (1989) *Infant Teacher's Handbook*. London, Oliver & Boyd.

Selmes, I. (1987) *Improving Study Skills*. London, Hodder & Stoughton.

Seymour, P. H. K. (1986) *Cognitive Analysis of Dyslexia*. London, Routledge & Kegan Paul.

Seymour, P. H. K. (1987) Individual cognitive analysis of competent and impaired reading. *British Journal of Psychology*, **78**, 483–506.

Seymour, P. H. K. (1993) Individual variation and reaction times in dyslexia. Paper presented at *Rodin Academy for the Study of Dyslexia, October 1993 Conference, London*.

Seymour, P. H. K. and McGregor, C. J. (1984) Developmental dyslexia; Experimental analysis of phonological, morphemic and visual impairments. *Cognitive Neuropsychology*, **1**, 43–82.

Sharon, H. (1987) *Changing Children's Minds*. London, Condor Press.

SHEFC (2001) *Understanding Dyslexia*. Glasgow, Scottish Higher Education Funding Council.

Sherman, G. F. (1993) Biological research in dyslexia: Implications for differential diagnosis. Paper presented at *44th Annual Conference, Orton Dyslexia Society, New Orleans, LA*. Baltimore, Orton Dyslexia Society.

Shiel, G (2002) Literacy standards and factors affecting literacy: What national and international assessments tell us. In: G. Reid and J. Wearmouth (eds), *Dyslexia and Literacy: Theory and Practice*. Chichester, UK, John Wiley & Sons.

Shiel, G., Cosgrove, J., Sofroniou, N. and Kelly, A. (2001) *Ready for life?* (the literacy achievements of Irish 15-year-olds with comparative international data, the PISA 2000 study). Dublin, Educational Research Centre.

Siegal, L. S. (1989) IQ is irrelevant to the definition of learning disabilities. *Journal of Learning Disabilities*, **22**, 469–478.

Siegal, L. S. (1992) An evaluation of the discrepancy definition of dyslexia. *Journal of Learning Disabilities*, **25**, 618–629.

Silberberg, N. and Silberberg, M. C. (1967) Hyperlexia: Specific word recognition skills in young children. *Exceptional Children*, **34**, 41–42.

Sillars, S. (1992) *Spelling Rules OK!* Milton Keynes, UK, Chalkface Project.

Silver, L. (2001) *Controversial Therapies* (reprinted from *Perspectives*, **27**(3), p. 1–4). Baltimore, The International Dyslexia Association.

Silveri, M. C. and Misciagna, S. (2000) Language, memory, and the cerebellum. *Journal of Neurolinguistics*, **13**(2–3), 129–143.

Singleton, C. (2002) Dyslexia: Cognitive factors and implications for literacy. In: G. Reid and J. Wearmouth (eds), *Dyslexia and Literacy; Theory and Practice*. Chichester, UK, John Wiley and Sons.

Singleton, C. H. (1988) The early diagnosis of developmental dyslexia. *Support for Learning*, **3**(2), 108–121.

Singleton, C. H. (ed.) (1991) *Computers and Literacy Skills*. Hull, UK, British Dyslexia Association Computer Resource Centre, University of Hull.

Singleton, C. H. (ed.) (1994) *Computers and Dyslexia—Educational Applications of New Technology*. Hull, UK, University of Hull.

Singleton, C. H. (1996a) *COPS 1 Cognitive Profiling System*. Nottingham, UK, Chameleon Educational.

Singleton, C. H. (1996b) Computerised screening for dyslexia. In: G. Reid (ed.), *Dimensions of Dyslexia*, Vol. 1: *Assessment, Teaching and the Curriculum*. Edinburgh, Moray House Publications.

Singleton, C H. (1996c) Dyslexia in higher education. Issues for policy and practice. *Conference Proceedings: Dyslexic Students in Higher Education*. University of Huddersfield, 24 January 1996.

Singleton, C. H. (chair) (1999a) *Dyslexia in Higher Education: Policy, Provision and Practice* (report of the National Working Party on Dyslexia in Higher Education). Hull, UK, University of Hull.

Singleton, C. H. (1999b) *Computerised cognitive profiling and the development of reading and spelling skills*. Paper presented at the *11th European Conference on Reading, Stavanger, Norway, August 1999*.

Singleton, C. H. (2001) Computer-based assessment in education. *Education and Child Psychology*, **18**, 58–74.

Singleton, C. H., Horne, J. K. and Thomas, K. V. (2002) *Lucid Adult Dyslexia Screening (LADS)*. Beverley, UK, Lucid Creative Limited.

Slingerland, B. H. (1971) *A Multisensory Approach to Language Arts for Specific Language Disability Children* (a guide for primary teachers, Books 1–3). Cambridge, MA, Educators.

Slingerland, B. H. (1976) *Basics in Scope and Sequence of a Multisensory Approach to Language Arts for Specific Learning Difficulties Children*. Cambridge, MA, Educators.

Slingerland, B. H. (1985) *Screening Tests for Identifying Children with Specific Learning Disabilities*. Cambridge, MA, Educators.

Slingerland, B. H. (1993) *Specific Language Disability Children*. Cambridge, MA, Educators.

Smith, B. (1994) *Teaching Spelling*, Royston, UK, United Kingdom Reading Association (UKRA).

Smith, C. (1993) Problems with reading. *Support for Learning*, **8**(4), 139–145.

Smith, D. (1995) *Spelling Games and Activities*. Tamworth, UK, NASEN Publications.

Smith, F. (1971) *Understanding Reading*. London, Holt, Rhinehart & Winston.

Smith, F. (1973) *Psycholinguistics and Reading*. New York, Holt, Rinehart & Winston.

Smith, F. (1985) *Reading*. Cambridge, Cambridge University Press.

Smith, F. (1988) *Understanding Reading. A Psycholinguistic Analysis of Reading and Learning to Read* (4th edn). Hillsdale, NJ, Lawrence Erlbaum.

Smith, J. and Bloom, M. (1985) *Simple Phonetics for Teachers*. London, Methuen.

Smith, P., Hinson, M. and Smith, D. (1998) *Spelling and Spelling Resources*. Tamworth, UK, NASEN Publications.

Smith, S. D., Kimberling, W. J., Pennington, B. F. and Lubs, H. A. (1983) Specific reading disability. Identification of an inherited form through linkage analysis. *Science*, **219**, 1345–1347.

Smyth, G. (2000) 'I feel this challenge and I don't have the background': Teachers' beliefs about teaching bilingual pupils. Paper presented at the *Conference of the Association of Teacher Education in Europe (ATEE), Barcelona, 28 August–2 September*.

Smythe, I. (2002) Cognitive factors underlying reading and spelling difficulties: A cross linguistic study (unpublished Ph.D. dissertation, University of Surrey, UK).

Smythe, I. and Everatt, J. (2000) Dyslexia diagnosis in different languages. In: L. Peer and G. Reid (eds), *Multilingualism, Literacy and Dyslexia. A Challenge for Educators*. London, David Fulton.

Smythe, I. and Everatt, J. (2001) Adult dyslexia checklist. *BDA Handbook*. Reading, British Dyslexia Association.

Snowling, M. (1987) *Dyslexia: A Cognitive Developmental Perspective*. Oxford, Blackwell.

Snowling, M. (1990a) *Dyslexia: A Cognitive Developmental Perspective*. Oxford, Blackwell.

Snowling, M. (1990b) Dyslexia in childhood: A cognitive–developmental perspective. In: P. D. Pumfrey and C. D. Elliott (eds), *Children's Difficulties in Reading, Spelling and Writing*. London, Falmer Press.

Snowling, M. (1991) *Children's Written Language Difficulties*. Windsor, UK, NFER-Nelson.

Snowling, M. (1993a) Specific learning difficulties: A cognitive developmental perspective. Paper presented at the *Two-day Conference, Edinburgh, Centre for Specific Learning Difficulties, Moray House*.

Snowling, M. (1993b) What causes variation in dyslexic reading. Paper presented at the *Rodin Academy for the Study of Dyslexia, October 1993, Conference, London*.

Snowling, M. and Thomson, M. (eds) (1991) *Dyslexia—Integrating Theory and Practice*. London, Whurr.

Snowling, M. J. (1994) Towards a model of spelling acquisition: The development of some component skills. In: G. D. A. Brown and N. C. Ellis (eds), *Handbook of Spelling: Theory, Process and Intervention* (pp. 111–128). Chichester, UK, John Wiley & Sons.

Snowling, M. J. (1995) Phonological processing and developmental dyslexia. *Journal of Research in Reading*, **18**, 132–138.

Snowling, M. J. (2000) *Dyslexia* (2nd edn). Oxford, Blackwell.

Snowling, M. J. (2002) Individual differences in children's reading development: Sound to meaning in learning to read. Paper given at *21st Vernon-Wall Lecture for the Annual Meeting of the Education*

Section of the British Psychological Society, Saturday, 3 November 2001. Leicester, UK, British Psychological Society.

Snowling, M. J. and Hulme, C. (1994). The development of phonological skills. *Philosophical Transactions of the Royal Society B*, **346**, 21–28.

Snowling, M. J. and Nation, K. A. (1997) Language, phonology and learning to read. In: C. Hulme and M. J. Snowling (eds), *Dyslexia, Biology Cognition and Intervention*. London, Whurr.

Snowling, M. J., Hulme, C., Wells, B. and Goulandris, N. (1992) Continuities between speech and spelling in a case of developmental dyslexia. *Reading and Writing*, **4**, 19–31.

Snowling, M., Stothard, S. and McLean, J. (1996) *Graded non-word Reading Test*. Bury St Edmonds, UK, Thames Valley Test Company.

SOEID (1999) *The Manual of Good Practice in Special Educational Needs*. Edinburgh, Scottish Office Education and Industry Department.

Soler, J. (2002) Policy contexts and debates over how to teach literacy. In: J. Soler, J. Wearmouth and G. Reid (eds), *Contextualising Difficulties in Literacy Development, Exploring Politics, Culture and Ethics*. London, Routledge Falmer.

Sordy, B. J. (1995) Benefit of docosahexaenoic acid supplements to dark adaptation in dyslexia. *Lancet*, **346**, 385.

Sordy, B. J. (1997) Dyslexia, attention deficit hyperactivity disorder, dyspraxia—Do fatty acids help? *Dyslexia Review*, **9**(2).

South Lanarkshire (2002) *Pre-school to Primary 1 Transition Record*. Hamilton, UK, South Lanarkshire Council.

Spadafore, G. J. (1983) *Spadafore Diagnostic Reading Test*. Novato, CA, Academic Therapy Publications.

Spreen, O. (1988). Prognosis of learning disability. *Journal of Consulting and Clinical Psychology*, **56**, 836–842.

Springer, S. P. (1989) *Left Brain, Right Brain*. San Francisco, Freeman.

Stacey, G. (2001) Advanced reading skills for dyslexic adults. Paper presented at the *5th International Conference, BDA, York, April*.

Stainthorp, R. (1995) Some effects of context on reading. In: P. Owen and P. Pumfrey (eds), *Emergent and Developing Reading: Messages for Teachers*. London, Falmer Press.

Stamboltzis, A. and Pumfrey, P. D. (2000) Text genre, miscue analysis, bilingualism and dyslexia: Teaching strategies with junior school pupils. In: L. Peer and G. Reid (eds), *Multilingualism, Literacy and Dyslexia. A Challenge for Educators*. London, David Fulton.

Stanovich, K. and Stanovich, P. (1995) How research might inform the debate about early reading acquisition. *Journal of Research in Reading*, **18**(2), 87–105.

Stanovich, K. E. (1980) Towards an interactive–compensatory model of individual differences in the development of reading fluency. *Reading Research Quarterly*, **16**, 32–71.

Stanovich, K. E. (1986) Matthew effects in reading: Some consequences of individual differences in the acquisition of literacy. *Reading Research Quarterly*, **21**, 360–407.

Stanovich, K. E. (1988) Explaining the difference between the dyslexic and the garden-variety poor readers: The phonological core model. *Journal of Learning Disabilities*, **21**(10), 590–604.

Stanovich, K. E. (1991) Discrepancy definitions of reading disability: Has intelligence led us astray? *Reading Research Quarterly*, **26**(1), 7–29.

Stanovich, K. E. (1992) Speculations on the causes and consequences of individual differences in early reading acquisition. In: P. B. Gouch, L. C. Ehri and R. Treiman (eds), *Reading Acquisition* (pp. 65–106). Hillsdale, NJ, Lawrence Erlbaum.

Stanovich, K. E. (1996) Towards a more inclusive definition of dyslexia. *Dyslexia*, **2**(3), 154–166.

Stanovich, K. E. (1998) Refining the phonological core deficit model. *Child Psychology and Psychiatry Review*, **3**(1), 17–21.

Stanovich, K. E., Siegel, L. S. and Gottardo, A. (1997) Progress in the search for dyslexia subtypes. In: C. Hulme and M. J. Snowling (eds), *Dyslexia, Biology Cognition and Intervention*. London, Whurr.

Steffensen, M. S., Joag-dev, C. and Anderson, R. C. (1979) A cross-cultural perspective on reading comprehension. *Reading Research Quarterly*, **15**(1), 10–29.

Stein, J. (2002) The sensorimotor basis of learning disabilities. Paper presented at *New Developments in Research and Practice Conference, County Hall, Durham, 14 June 2002*.

Stein, J. and Walsh, V. (1997) To see but not to read: The magnocellular theory of dyslexia. *Trends in neuroscience*, **20**, 147–152.

Stein, J. F. (1991) Vision and language. In: M. Snowling and M. Thomson (eds), *Integrating Theory and Practice*. London, Whurr.

Stein, J. F. (1994) A visual defect in dyslexics? In: R. I. Nicolson and A. J. Fawcett (eds), *Dyslexia in Children: Multidisciplinary Perspectives*. Hemel Hempstead, UK, Harvester Wheatsheaf.

Stein, J. F. and Fowler, M. S. (1993) Unstable binocular control in dyslexic children. *Journal of Research in Reading*, **16**(1), 30–45.

Stein, J., Talcott, J. and Witton, C. (2001) The sensorimotor basis of developmental dyslexia. In: A. Fawcett (ed.), *Dyslexia; Theory and Good Practice*. London, Whurr.

Stephenson, E. (1986) *Children with Motor/Learning Difficulties. A Guide for Parents and Teachers*. Aberdeen, UK, Occupational Therapy Department, Royal Aberdeen Children's Hospital.

Stevens, L. J., Zentall, S. S., Abate, M. L., Kuczek, T. and Burgess, J. R. (1996) Omega-3 fatty acids in boys with behaviour, learning and health problems. *Physiol. Behav.*, **59**, 915–920

Stevens, M. (1992) *Into Print*. Edinburgh, Scottish Consultative Council on the Curriculum.

Stewart, J. (2002) Talk presented at *Policy and Practice Conference, Scottish Dyslexia Forum, Stirling, May 2002*.

Stirling, E. G. (1990) *Which is Witch. Checklist of Homophones*. Llandudno, UK, St David's College.

Stirling, E. G. (1991) *Help for the Dyslexic Adolescent*. Dudley, UK, Better Books.

Stoel, Van der, S. (ed.) (1990) *Parents on Dyslexia*. Clevedon, UK, Multilingual Matters.

Stracher, D. A. (2000) Dysgraphia. *The International Dyslexia Association, Houston Branch Resource Directory* (pp. 20–21). Houston, TX, International Dyslexia Association.

Sullivan, M. (1993) A meta-analysis of experimental research studies based on the Dunn and Dunn leaking styles model (doctoral dissertation, St John's University, New York).

Sunderland, H., Klein, C., Savinson, R. and Partridge, T. (1999) *Dyslexia and the Bilingual Learner: Assessing and Teaching Young People Who Speak English as an Additional Language*. London, Borough of Southwark: Language and Literacy Unit.

Sutherland, M. J. and Smith, C. D. (1997) The benefits and difficulties of using portable word processors with older dyslexics. *Dyslexia*, **3**(1), 15–26.

Sutton, R. (1992) *Assessment—A Framework for Teachers*. London, Routledge.

Tannock, R. (1976) Doman–Delacato method for treating brain injured children. *Physiotherapy*, **28**(4).

Task Force on Dyslexia (2001). *Report*. Dublin: Government Publications. Available online at http://www.irlgov.ie/educ/pub.htm

Taylor, M. F. (1998) An evaluation of the effects of educational kinesiology (Brain Gym©) on children manifesting ADHD in a South African context (unpublished M.Phil. dissertation, University of Exeter, UK).

Taylor, M. F. (2002) Stress-induced atypical brain lateralization in boys with attention-deficit/hyperactivity disorder. Implications for scholastic performance (unpublished Ph.D. thesis, University of Western Australia, Perth, Australia).

Tennessee Center for the Study of Treatment of Dyslexia (1996) *Tennessee Meets the Challenge of Dyslexia. The First Three Years—A Report of Accomplishments*. Murfreesboro, TN, Middle Tennessee State University.

Thomson, G. (1990) On leaving school, who tells? In G. Hales (ed.), *Meeting points in Dyslexia. Proceedings of the 1st International Conference of the British Dyslexia Association*. Reading, British Dyslexic Association.

Thomson, M. (2002) Access across the curriculum in secondary school. Paper presented at *Dyslexia in Scotland Annual Conference, 28 September 2002, Edinburgh*.

Thomson, M. and Chinn, S. (2001) Good practice in the secondary school. In: A. Fawcett (ed.), *Dyslexia: Theory and Good Practice*. London, Whurr.

Thomson, M. and Watkins W. (1990) *Dyslexia: A Teaching Handbook*. London, Whurr.

Thomson, M. E. (1984) *Developmental Dyslexia*. London, Edward Arnold.

Thomson, M. E. (1988) *Developmental Dyslexia: Its Nature, Assessment and Remediation* (2nd edn). London, Whurr.

Thomson, M. E. (1989) *Developmental Dyslexia* (3rd edn). London, Whurr.

Thomson, M. E. (1990) Evaluating teaching programmes for children with specific learning difficulties. In: P. D. Pumfrey and C. D. Elliot (eds), *Children's Difficulties in Reading, Spelling and Writing*. London, Falmer Press.

Thomson, P. and Gilchrist, P. (1997) *Dyslexia—A Multidisciplinary Approach*. London, Chapman & Hall.

Tod, J. (2002) Individual education plans and dyslexia: Some principles. In: G. Reid and J. Wearmouth (eds), *Dyslexia and Literacy, Theory and Practice*. Chichester, UK, John Wiley & Sons.

Tod, J. and Fairman, A. (2001) Individualised learning in a group setting. In: L. Peer and G. Reid (eds), *Dyslexia—Successful Inclusion in the Secondary School*. London, David Fulton.

Topping, K. (2001) Peer and parent assisted learning. In: G. Shiel and U. Ni Dhalaigh (eds), *Reading Matters: A Fresh Start*. St Patrick's College, Dublin, Reading Association of Ireland/National Reading Initiative, Education Research Centre.

Topping, K. J. (1986) *Paired Reading Training Pack*. Dundee, UK, University of Dundee.

Topping, K. and Bamford, J. (1998) *The Paired Maths Handbook: Parental Involvement and Peer Tutoring in Mathematics*. London, David Fulton.

Topping, K. J. (1987) Peer tutored paired reading: Outcome data from ten projects. *Educational Psychology*, **7**(2), 133–145.

Topping, K. J. (1992a) *Promoting Cooperative Learning*. London, Kirklees Metropolitan Council.

Topping, K. J. (1992b) *Paired Writing Information*. London, Kirklees Metropolitan Council.

Topping, K. J. (1992c) Short and long term follow-up of parental involvement in reading projects. *British Educational Research Journal*, **18**(4) 369–379.

Topping, K. J. (1992d) *Cued Spelling Training Tape*. London, Kirklees Metropolitan Council.

Topping, K. J. (1996) Parents and peers as tutors for dyslexic children. In: G. Reid (ed.), *Dimensions of Dyslexia*, Vol. 2: *Literacy, Language and Learning*. Edinburgh, Moray House Publications.

Topping, K. J. (2001) *Peer Assisted Learning, A Practical Guide for Teachers* (www.dundee.ac.uk/psychology/kjtopping/plearning.html). Cambridge, MA, Brookline Books.

Topping, K. J. (2002) Paired Thinking, developing thinking skills through structured interaction with peers, parents and volunteers. In: G. Reid and J. Wearmouth (eds), *Dyslexia and Literacy: Theory and Practice*. Chichester, UK, John Wiley & Sons.

Topping, K. J. and Bryce, A. (2002) Cross-age Peer Tutoring of reading and thinking in the primary school: A controlled study of influence on thinking skills (paper submitted for publication).

Topping, K. J. and Hogan, J. (1999) *Read On: Paired Reading and Thinking* (video resource pack, 2nd edition 2002). London, BP Educational Services (www.bpes.com).

Topping, K. J. and Lindsey, G. A. (1992) The structure and development of the paired reading technique. *Journal of Research in Reading*, **15**(2), 120–136.

Topping, K. J. and Watt, J. M. (1992) Cued spelling: A comparative study of parent and peer tutoring (paper submitted for publication, University of Dundee).

Topping, K. J. and Wolfendale, S. (eds) (1985) *Parental Involvement in Childrens' Reading*. London, Croom Helm.

Townend, J. (2000) Phonological awareness and other foundation skills of literacy. In: J. Townend and M. Turner (eds), *Dyslexia in Practice—A Guide for Teachers*. Dordreeht, Kluwer Academic.

Traub, N. and Bloom, F. (1993) *Recipe for Reading*. Cambridge, MA, Educators.

Tregaskes, M. and Daines, D. (1989) Effects of metacognition on reading comprehension. *Reading Research and Instruction*, **29**(1), 52–60.

Treiman, R. (1993) *Beginning to Spell: A Study of First Grade Children*. New York, Oxford University Press.

TTA (1999) *National Special Educational Needs Specialist Standards*. London, Teacher Training Agency.

TTA (2000) *Using the National Standards. For Special Education Needs Coordinators*. London, Teacher Training Agency.

Tunmer, W. and Chapman, J. (1998). Language, prediction skill, phonological recording ability, and beginning reading. In: C. Hulme and R. Joshi (eds), *Reading and Spelling: Development and Disorders* (pp. 33–68). Mahwah, NJ: Lawrence Erlbaum.

Tunmer, W. E. (1994) Phonological processing skills and reading remediation. In: C. Hulme and M. Snowling (eds), *Reading Development and Dyslexia*. London, Whurr.

Tunmer, W. E. and Chapman, J. (1996) A developmental model of dyslexia. Can the construct be saved? *Dyslexia*, **2**(3), 179–89.

Tunmer, W. E., Herriman, M. L. and Nesdale, A. R. (1988) Metalinguistic abilities and beginning reading. *Reading Research Quarterly*, **23**, 134–158.

Turner, E. (2001) Dyslexia and English. In: L. Peer and G. Reid (eds), *Dyslexia—Successful Inclusion in the Secondary School*. London, David Fulton.

Turner, E. (2002a) Multisensory teaching and tutoring. *The Dyslexia Handbook 2002*. Reading, UK, British Dyslexia Association.

Turner, E. (2002b) Dyslexia and English. In L. Peer and G. Reid (eds), *Dyslexia—Successful Inclusion in the Secondary School*. London, David Fulton.

Turner, M. (1991) Finding out. *Support for Learning*, **6**(3), 99–102.

Turner, M. (1993a) Testing times. *Special Children*, **65**, 12–16.

Turner, M. (1993b) More testing times. *Special Children*, **66**, 12–14.

Turner, M. (1995) Children learn to read by being taught. In: P. Owen and P. Pumfrey (eds), *Emergent and Developing Reading: Messages for Teachers*. London, Falmer Press.

Turner, M. (1997) *Psychological Assessment of Dyslexia*. London, Whurr.

Tyler, S. (1980) *Keele Pre-school Assessment Guide*. Windsor, UK, NFER-Nelson.

Ulmer, C. and Timothy, M., (2001) How does alternative assessment affect teachers' practice? Two years later. Paper presented at the *12th European Conference on Reading, Dublin, Ireland, 1–4 July 2001*.

University of Edinburgh (2002a) *Moray House Tests*. London, Hodder & Stoughton.

University of Edinburgh (2002b) *Edinburgh Reading Tests*. London, Hodder & Stoughton.

Usmani, K. (1999) The influence of racism and cultural bias in the assessment of bilingual children. *Educational and Child Psychology*, **16**(3), 44–54.

Vail, P. L. (1990) *About Dyslexia—Unravelling the Myth*. Rosemont, NJ, Modern Learning Press.

Vail, P. L. (1992) *Learning Styles*. Rosemont, NJ, Modern Learning Press.

Vail, P. L. (1993) Reading comprehension: Reading for reason, the reason for reading. Paper presented at the *44th Annual Conference of the Orton Dyslexia Society, New Orleans, LA*.

Vellutino, F. R. and Scanlon, D. M. (1986) Experimental evidence for the effects of instructional bias on word identification. *Exceptional Children*, **53**(2), 145–155.

Venezky, R. (1970) *The Structure of English Orthography*. The Hague, Mouton.

Venezky, R. (1999) *The American Way of Spelling: The Structure and Origins of American English Orthography*. New York, Guilford Press.

Vernon, P. E. (1977) *Graded Word Spelling Test*. Sevenoaks, UK, Hodder & Stoughton.

Vernon, P. E. (1979) *Intelligence: Heredity and Environment*. San Francisco, Freeman.

Viall, J. T. (2000) *High Stakes Assessment in Perspectives* (Summer 2000 issue, Vol. 26, No. 3, p. 3). Baltimore, International Dyslexia Association.

Vincent, D. and Claydon, J. (1982) *Diagnostic Spelling Test*. Windsor, UK, NFER-Nelson.

Vincent, D. and Crumpler, M. (2001) *Numeracy Progress Tests*. London, Hodder & Stoughton.

Vincent, D. and De La Mare, M. (1987) *New Macmillan Reading Analysis*. London, Macmillan Educational.

Visser, J. (1993) *Differentiation: Making It Work*. Tamworth, UK, NASEN Publications.

Vitale, B. M. (1982) *Unicorns Are Real (A Right-Brained Approach to Learning)*. Rolling Hill Estates, CA, Jalmar Press.

Vitale, B. M. and Bullock, W. B. (1989) *Learning Inventory Manual—Tests and Remediation*. Belford, UK, Ann Arbor Publishers.

Vogel, S. A. (2001) IALS1—An overview of the International Adult Literacy Survey. Paper presented at the *5th International Dyslexia Conference, BDA, York, April*.

Vogel, S. A. and Reder, S. (2001) International perspectives on dyslexia. In: A. Fawcett (ed.), *Dyslexia, Theory and Good Practice*. London, Whurr.

Vygotsky, L. (1986) *Thought and Language*. Cambridge. MA, MIT Press.

Vygotsky, L. S. (1978) *Mind in Society: The Development of Higher Psychological Processes*. Cambridge, MA, Harvard University Press.

Wade, B. and Moore, M. (1994) *The Promise of Reading Recovery* (Educational Review Publications—Headline Series No. 1). Birmingham, University of Birmingham.

Wagner, R. K. and Torgesen, J. K. (1987) The nature of phonological processing and its causal role in the acquisition of reading skills. *Psychological Bulletin*, **101**, 192–212.

Walker, J. (2000) Teaching basic reading and spelling. In: J. Townend and M. Turner (eds), *Dyslexia in Practice—A Guide for Teachers*. New York, Kluwer Academic.

Walmsley, S. A. and Allington, R. L. (1995) Refining and reforming instructional support programs for at-risk students. In: R. L. Allington and S. A. Walmsley (eds), *No Quick Fix: Rethinking Literacy Programs in America's Elementary Schools*. Newark, DE, International Reading Association.

Walton, D. and Brooks, P. (1995) The Spoonerism Test. In: N. Frederickson and R. Reason (eds), *Phonological Assessment of Specific Learning Difficulties. Educational Child Psychology*, **12**, 50–52.

Ward, C. and Daley, J. (1993) *Learning to Learn Strategies for Accelerating Learning and Boosting Performance*. Christchurch, New Zealand, Ward and Daley.

Ward, S. B., Ward, T. J., Hatt, C. V., Young, D. L. and Molner, N. R. (1995) The incidence and utility of the ACID, ACIDS, and SCAD profiles in a referred population. *Psychology in the Schools*, **32**(4), 309–319.

Waterfield, J. (1996) Provision for dyslexic students in higher education: A whole institution approach. *Conference Proceedings: Dyslexic Students in Higher Education, University of Huddersfield, 24 January 1996*.

Waterland, L. (1986) *Read with Me: An Apprenticeship Approach to Reading*. Stroud, UK, Thimble Press.

Watkins, M. W., Kush, J. C. and Glutting, J. J. (1997) Discriminant and predictive validity of the WISC III ACID profile among children with learning disabilities. *Psychology in the Schools*, **34**(4), 309–319.

Wearmouth, J. (2001) Inclusion—Changing the variables. In: L. Peer and G. Reid (eds), *Dyslexia—Successful Inclusion in the Secondary School*. London, David Fulton.

Wearmouth, J. and Reid, G. (2002) Issues for assessment and planning of teaching and learning. In G. Reid and J. Wearmouth (eds), *Dyslexia and Literacy, Theory and Practice*. Chichester, UK, John Wiley & Sons.

Wearmouth, J. and Soler, J. (2002) How inclusive is the literacy hour? In: J. Soler, J. Wearmouth and G. Reid (eds), *Contextualising Difficulties in Literacy Development—Exploring Politics, Culture, Ethnicity and Ethics*. London, RoutledgeFalmer.

Wearmouth, J., Soler, J. and Reid, G. (2003) *Meeting Difficulties in Literacy Development, Research, Policy and Practice*. London, RoutledgeFalmer.

Wearmouth, J., Soler, J. and Reid, G. (2002) *Addressing Difficulties in Literacy Development—Responses at Family, School, Pupil and Teacher Levels*. London, Routledge Falmer.

Webster, A. and McConnell, C. (1987) *Children with Speech and Language Difficulties*. London, Cassell.

Wechsler, D. (1981) *Wechsler Adult Intelligence Scale—Revised*. San Antonio, TX, The Psychological Corporation.

Wechsler, D. (1992a) *Wechsler Intelligence Scale for Children* (3rd edn, WISC III). New York: Harcourt Brace Jovanovitch/Psychological Corporation.

Wechsler, D. (1992b) *Wechsler Individual Achievement Test (WIAT)*. San Antonio, TX, Psychological Corporation.

Wechsler, D. (1996) *The Wechsler Dimensions. The Fundamental Test between Achievement and Ability*. San Antonio, TX, The Psychological Corporation.

Wechsler, D. (1999a) *Wechsler Adult Intelligence Test (WAIS 111)*. San Antonio, TX, The Psychological Corporation.

Wechsler, D. (1999b) *Wechsler Memory Scale (WMS 111)*. San Antonio, TX, The Psychological Corporation.

Weedon, C. (1992) *Specific Learning Difficulties and Mathematics*. Stirling, UK, University of Stirling and Tayside Region.

Weedon, C. and Reid, G. (1998) The learning of able dyslexics within the normal curriculum. *Education Today*, **48**(4), 31–38.

Weedon, C. and Reid, G. (2001) *Listening and Literacy Index*. London, Hodder & Stoughton.

Weedon, C. and Reid, G. (2002) *Special Needs Assessment Portfolio* (pilot version). Edinburgh, George Watson's College.

Weedon, C. and Reid, G. (2003) *Special Needs Assessment Portfolio*. London, Hodder and Stoughton.

Weedon, C., Ferguson, B., Snell, P., Smith, E. and Reid, G. (1996) *A Diagnostic Profile of Literacy Development in Early Primary School*. Edinburgh, George Watson's College.

Welch, A. R. (1991) Education and legitimation in comparitive education. *Comparative Education Review*, **34**, 3.

Welch, A. R. and Freebody, P. (2002) Explanations of the current international 'literacy crises'. In: J. Soler, J. Wearmouth and G. Reid (eds), *Contextualising Difficulties in Literacy Development—Exploring Politics, Culture, Ethnicity and Ethics*. London, RoutledgeFalmer.

Wendon, L. (1985 and 1987) *Letterland Teaching Programme 1 and 2*. Cambridge, Letterland.

Wendon, L. (1993) Literacy for early childhood: Learning from the learners. *Early Child Development and Care*, **86**, 11–12.

Wertheim, C., Vogel, S. and Brulle, A. (1998) Students with learning disabilities in teacher education programmes. *Annals of Dyslexia*, **48**, 293–309.

West, T. G. (1997) *In the Mind's Eye. Visual Thinkers, Gifted People with Learning Difficulties, Computer Images and the Ironies of Creativity* (2nd edn). Buffalo, NY, Prometheus Books.

White, M. (1991) *Self-esteem—Its Meaning and Value in Schools*. Cambridge, Daniels.

Whittaker, E. M. (1992) Specific learning difficulty (dyslexia) and neurological research. An educational psychologist's evaluation. *Educational Psychology in Practice*, **8**(3), 139–144.

Wilkins, A. (1990) *Visual Discomfort and Reading*. Cambridge, MRC.APU.

Wilkins, A. J. (1993) *Intuitive Overlays*. London, IOO Marketing.

Wilkins, A. J. (1995) *Visual Stress*. Oxford, Oxford University Press.

Wilkins, A., Milroy, R., Nimmo-Smith, I., Wright, A., Tyrill, K., Holland, K. and Martin, J. (1992) Preliminary observations concerning treatment of visual discomfort and associated perceptual distortion. *Ophthalmology, Physiology, Optics*, **12**, 257–263.

Wilkins, A. J., Jeanes, J. R., Pumfrey, P. D. and Laskier, M. (1996) *Rate of Reading Test R: Its Reliability and Its validity in the Assessment of the Effects of Coloured Overlays*. Cambridge, MRC Applied Psychology Unit.

Wilkinson, A. C. (1980) Children's understanding in reading and listening. *Journal of Educational Psychology*, **72**(4), 561–574.

Wilkinson, G. S. (1993) *Wide Range Achievement Test (WRAT™)*, San Antonio, TX, The Psychological Corporation.

Wilkinson, M. (2002) *Guide to Dyslexia*. Edinburgh, Queen Margaret University College.

Willcutt, E. G. and Pennington, B. F. (2000) Comorbidity of reading disabilty and Attention-Deficit/Hyperactivity Disorder: Differences by gender and subtype. *Journal of Learning Disabilities*, **33**(2), March–April, 179–191.

Williams, F. and Lewis, J. (2001) Dyslexia and Geography. In: L. Peer and G. Reid (eds), *Dyslexia—Successful Inclusion in the Secondary School*. London, David Fulton.

Williams, L. V. (1983) *Teaching for the Two-Sided Mind*. New York, Simon & Schuster.

Wilsher, C. R. (2002) A miracle cure? *Tonight with Trevor McDonald*, ITV, 21 January 2002 (reproduced in *Dyslexia*, **8**(2), April–June, 116–117).

Wilson, J. (1993) *Phonological Awareness Training: A New Approach to Phonics*. London, Educational Psychology.

Wilson, J. and Frederickson, N. (1995) Phonological awareness training: An evaluation. *Educational and Child Psychology*, **12**(1), 68–79.

Wimmer, H. (1993) Characteristics of developmental dyslexia in a regular writing system. *Applied Psycholinguistics*, **14**(1), 1–33.

Wimmer, H. (1996) The early manifestation of developmental dyslexia: Evidence from German children. *Reading and Writing*, **8**, 171–188.

Wimmer, H. and Goswami, U. (1994) The influence of orthographic consistency on reading development: Word recognition in English and German children. *Cognition*, **51**, 91–103.

Wise, B. W., Ring, J. and Olson, R. (1999) Training phonological awareness with and without explicit attention to articulation. *Journal of Experimental Child Psychology*, **72**, 271–304.

Witkin, H. and Goodenough, D. (1981) *Cognitive Styles: Essence and Origins* (Psychological Issues Monograph No. 51). New York, International Universities Press.

Wolf, B. J. (1985) The effect of Slingerland instruction on the reading and language of second grade children (Ph.D dissertation, Seattle Pacific University, Seattle, WA).

Wolf, M. (1991) Naming speed and reading: The contribution of the cognitive neurosciences. *Reading Research Quarterly*, **26**, 123–141.

Wolf, M. (1996) The double-deficit hypothesis for the developmental dyslexics. Paper read at the *47th Annual Conference of the Orton Dyslexia Society, November 1996, Boston*.

Wolf, M. and O'Brien, B. (2001) On issues of time, fluency and intervention. In: A. Fawcett (ed.), *Dyslexia, Theory and Good Practice*. London, Whurr.

Wolfendale, S. (1989) *Parental Involvement: Developing Networks between School, Home and Community*. London, Cassell.

Wolfendale, S. and Bryans, T. (1990) *Word Play*. Stafford, UK, NARE Publications.

Wood, F. B. (2000) Surprises ahead: The new decade of dyslexia, neurogenetics and education. Keynote lecture at the *51st Annual Conference of the International Dyslexia Association, Washington, DC, 8–11 November 2001*.

Wray, D. (1991) A chapter of errors: A response to Martin Turner. *Support for Learning*, **6**(4), 145–149.

Wray, D. (1994) *Literacy and Awareness*. London, Hodder & Stoughton.

Wray, D. (2002) Metacognition and literacy. In: G. Reid and J. Wearmouth (eds), *Dyslexia and Literacy: Theory and Practice*. Chichester, UK, John Wiley & Sons.

Wright, A. (1992) Evaluation of the first British reading recovery programme. *British Educational Research Journal*, **18**(4), 351–368.

Wright, A. (1993) Irlen—The never ending story. Paper presented at the *5th European Conference of Neuro-developmental Delay in Children with Specific Learning Difficulties, Chester*.

Wright, A. and Prance, L. J. (1992) The reading recovery programme in Surrey Education Authority. *Support for Learning*, **7**(3), 103–110.

Wyatt, S. (2002) *Difficulties in Literacy Development* (interview in ED 801 course video). Milton Keynes, UK, Open University.

Wydell, T. N. and Butterworth, B. (1999) An English–Japanese bilingual with monolingual dyslexia. *Cognition*, **70**, 273–305.

Young, D. (1989) *Non-Reading Intelligence Tests*. London, Hodder & Stoughton.

Young, G. (2001) Seven critical needs for successful programs for adults with dyslexia/LD. Paper presented at the *5th International Conference, BDA, York, April*.

Young, P. and Tyre, C. (1990) *Dyslexia or Illiteracy: Realising the Right to Read*. Buckingham, UK, Open University Press.

Zdienski, D. (1997) *StudyScan*. Limerick, Republic of Ireland, ISL.

Zeffiro, T. and Eden, G. (2000) The neural basis of developmental dyslexia. *Annals of Dyslexia*, **50**, 3–30.

Index

SHREWSBURY COLLEGE
LONDON RD LRC

Dyslexia

A Practitioner's Handbook

Third Edition

SHREWSBURY COLLEGE LIBRARY

INV. No. L640987   11.4.03

C'T No. 14830   18.303

041456

371.9144 REI

20.39   CHECKED